Theory and Practice of Couns

Theory and Practice
of
Counselling & Therapy

3rd EDITION

Richard Nelson-Jones

CONTINUUM
London and New York

Continuum

The Tower Building	370 Lexington Avenue
11 York Road	New York
London SE1 7NX	NY 10017-6503

First edition published by Holt, Rinehart and Winston Ltd.
Second edition published by Cassell.
Third edition published 2001 by Continuum.

British Library Cataloguing-in-Publication Data
A catalogue record for this book is available from the British Library.

ISBN   0-8264-5193-4

Designed and typeset by Kenneth Burnley, Wirral, Cheshire
Printed and bound in Great Britain by TJ International Ltd, Padstow, Cornwall

Contents

Preface

Welcome to the third edition of *Theory and Practice of Counselling & Therapy*. In this book I aim to provide you with clear, concise and easily accessible presentations of the major concepts and practices of many of the main therapeutic approaches used in the helping professions. The focus of this book is on individual therapy. Its purpose is to help you become more aware of both *how* you might counsel or conduct therapy and also of the underlying reasons *why* you might choose to work that way. Furthermore, the relevance of the theoretical positions extends beyond assisting clients in therapy to become happier and more fulfilled, to the personal agenda of helping you too.

INTENDED READERSHIP

This is a basic textbook for undergraduate and postgraduate counselling and psychotherapy courses in counsellor education, psychology, social work, nursing, personnel and human resources management, career development, pastoral care, welfare, teacher training and other areas of helping-professions education. Another important readership consists of participants in counselling and therapy courses run by voluntary agencies. In addition, this book can be used as a user-friendly introduction to the theory and practice of counselling and therapy for undergraduate students in the behavioural and social sciences.

CONTENTS

The first chapter discusses the structure and functions of theoretical statements, explores the creation of therapeutic approaches, and then looks at how you can develop your own ideas. In the following chapters I review therapeutic approaches selected from each of the three main schools influencing contemporary therapy practice. From the psychodynamic school, I present Freud's psychoanalysis and Jung's analytical therapy. From the humanistic–existential school, I present person-centred therapy, gestalt therapy, transactional analysis, reality therapy, existential therapy and logotherapy. From the cognitive–behavioural school, I present behaviour therapy, rational emotive behaviour therapy, cognitive therapy, multimodal therapy and cognitive–humanistic therapy.

The next two chapters on cultural perspectives and gender perspectives cover topics relevant to all therapeutic approaches. In the book's final chapter I review issues in assessing the quality of the different therapeutic approaches as well as the important issue of originating and developing new therapeutic approaches. In addition, the book contains a glossary and appendices on training information and journal information.

For those of you familiar with the second edition of this text, the main changes in this expanded third edition are: a revision and update of all existing chapters; four new chapters – Jung's analytical therapy, cultural issues, gender issues, evaluating counselling and therapy approaches; and the glossary and appendices on training and journal information.

FEATURES

I draw your attention to the following features of the book, which I hope will make it attractive for you.

- *Authoritative.* This book, which is written from primary sources, provides up-to-date and accurate presentations of each counselling and therapy approach. For instance, when preparing the book, I contacted living theorists for their most recent material. In addition, I gave either the theorists themselves or prominent adherents of the approach the opportunity to preview chapters and to suggest alterations.
- *Thorough and clear presentation.* Each of the therapeutic approaches is in a standard chapter format that helps to ensure that the approach is thoroughly and clearly presented. Though you may not understand the meaning some of the following headings now, once you start working with the book you should experience no difficulty in so doing.

> Introduction
> > Originator's biography
> Theory
> > Basic concepts
> > Acquisition
> > Maintenance
> Therapy
> > Therapeutic goals
> > Process of therapy
> > The therapeutic relationship
> > Therapeutic interventions
> > Case material
> > Further developments
> Annotated bibliography
> References and further reading

- *Focus on fundamentals.* The chapters emphasize presenting the theory and practice of the originator of each approach. Some contributions by other adherents of the approach are mentioned in the 'Further developments' section of each chapter. However, the chapters present the basic or classical version of each approach. Getting down to basics is important, since introducing developments from the original approach too soon can be confusing. In all of the chapters I review the originator's case material and in most chapters I give directions about accessing audio-visual resources. If available and where budgets permit, I encourage lecturers to use audio-cassettes and videotapes of the originators engaging in therapy as an accompaniment to using this book.

- *Personal focus.* Originating counselling and therapy approaches is a personal journey. A distinctive feature of this book is the degree to which the lives of the originators are seen as important in understanding the development of their therapeutic approaches. Learning about counselling and therapy approaches is also a personal journey. Each chapter ends not only with review questions, but also with personal questions that encourage you to relate the material to your own life.
- *Aids to comprehension and revision.* Boxes are used throughout the book to highlight concepts and provide examples of specific interventions. Towards the end of each chapter, I provide a summary and review questions designed to help you learn and revise material for assignments and course requirements.
- *Help with further reading.* I encourage you to use the chapters in this book as stepping stones to reading primary sources. Each chapter ends with an annotated bibliography and with a listing of references.
- *Simple English.* I have tried to use simple, accessible English, while remaining sensitive to the distinctive therapeutic languages used by the different theorists.

ACKNOWLEDGEMENTS

I acknowledge with gratitude the distinctive contributions of all the originators of counselling and therapy approaches presented in this book. While accepting full responsibility for any shortcomings, I am extremely grateful to the following people for contributing to the preparation of and for previewing chapters: Dr Judith Beck, John Brickell, Ann Casement, , Andrea Chester, Professor Petruska Clarkson, Dr Albert Ellis, Dr Arnold Lazarus, Dr Ian Stewart, Professor Brian Thorne, Professor Franz Vesely, Professor Danny Wedding, Professor Robert Wubbolding, and Dr Irvin Yalom.

I also thank the numerous individuals who provided information for the 'Training information' and 'Journal information' appendices of this book and helped me in other ways. Furthermore, a special word of appreciation for Professor Danny Wedding, co-editor of the best-selling American textbook *Current Psychotherapies*, who gave me pre-publication access to all the relevant chapters in the sixth edition of that book. In addition, I thank Philip Sturrock, Janet Joyce and Karen Haynes at Continuum, who were involved in the decision to commission this book. Last but not least, I thank the production staff at Continuum for their work in copy-editing and bringing this book to life.

*   *   *

Since each of the approaches is presented as a self-contained unit, you can choose which parts to study in the order that best suits your purposes. I hope that you enjoy reading and interacting with this book and share my enthusiasm for studying and learning more about counselling and therapy approaches.

I welcome feedback on this book. If you have any comments you would like to share with me you can either send them or e-mail them to me at the following address:

Richard Nelson-Jones
Cognitive–Humanistic Institute
Suite 715, Supakit Condominium
90/1 Moo 8, Soi Suthep 4
Suthep Road
Chiang Mai
Thailand 50200.
e-mail: rnjchi@loxinfo.co.th

Creating Counselling and Therapy Approaches

It may be that each person who develops his own system of psychotherapy writes, in the final analysis, his own case history.

Viktor Frankl

Studying theories of counselling and therapy is both an intellectual undertaking and a personal journey. All people develop a set of ideas, albeit not fully articulated, about how people become the way they are, how they stay the way they are – often at great personal cost – and how they can change. As a counselling and therapy student you are challenged to develop a more thorough and accurate theory of human behaviour so that you can help clients more. However, when reviewing these theoretical approaches you will find yourself applying the concepts to yourself and testing whether they have validity for helping you to become happier and more fulfilled. Thus, the fruits of your studying counselling and therapy approaches will become manifest in how you influence both clients' biographies and your own autobiography.

As this chapter attempts to show, theoretical approaches to counselling and therapy did not spring fully formed out of the heads of their originators. Rather, their creation was a process in which many personal, academic and professional factors interacted. Furthermore, the theorists covered in this book tended to refine and rework their ideas. Thus theory creation and development was an intensely human and ongoing process combining both subjective experiencing and objective information.

As a counselling and therapy student, you too are engaging in a process of trying to make sense of numerous personal, academic and professional factors to create and develop a way of seeing the therapeutic world that has validity for you and gets results for your clients. Even though you may be on a course built round a central or core model of therapy, you can expand your horizons by becoming familiar with other theoretical positions. Later on, as you practise counselling and therapy, you will see a range of clients and get further experience to confirm or negate the adequacy of your theory-building to date. In addition, as you get older you may see the problems of the afternoon of clients' lives as being rather different from those of life's morning. Just like the major theorists, you are likely to find yourself continually refining and reworking your ideas. Working with a theoretical approaches text, such as this one, is an early step in an exciting and lifelong endeavour of creating, developing and refining your theory and practice.

COUNSELLING AND PSYCHOTHERAPY

The word 'therapy' is derived from the Greek word *therapeia* meaning 'healing'. Literally, psychotherapy means healing the mind or the soul. Nowadays, most commonly the meaning of psychotherapy is broadened to become healing the mind by psychological methods which are applied by suitably trained and qualified practitioners. However, as illustrated in this book, there are different approaches to therapy and, consequently, it is more accurate to speak of the psychotherapies than of a uniform method of psychotherapy. Moreover, there are different goals for therapy, including dealing with severe mental disorder, addressing specific anxieties and phobias, and helping people find meaning and purpose in their lives. Each of the different therapeutic approaches may be more suitable for attaining some goals than others.

Does counselling differ from psychotherapy? The British Association for Counselling's *Code of Ethics & Practice for Counsellors* states that 'Counselling may be concerned with developmental issues, addressing and resolving specific problems, making decisions, coping with crisis, developing personal insight and knowledge, working through feelings of inner conflict or improving relationships with others' (BAC, 1998, p. 1). Attempts to differentiate between counselling and psychotherapy are never wholly successful. Both counselling and psychotherapy represent diverse rather than uniform knowledge and activities and both use the same theoretical models.

Nevertheless, some people try to distinguish counselling from psychotherapy. For instance, psychotherapists may be more thoroughly trained; psychotherapy may focus more deeply on uncovering unconscious influences and be longer term; and psychotherapy may be more a medical term that characterizes the work of psychiatrists and clinical psychiatrists, whereas counselling relates more to activities in non-medical settings: for example, college counselling centres. All of these distinctions can be refuted: for example, there are psychodynamic counsellors; both counselling and therapy can be either brief, medium-term or long-term; and much counselling is performed both by medically and non-medically qualified people inside and outside of medical settings.

Though some perceive different shadings of meaning between counselling and psychotherapy, when it comes to the offering of professional as contrasted with voluntary services, similarities outweigh differences. Frequently the terms are used interchangeably and most theorists view their work as applicable to both counselling and psychotherapy, Carl Rogers and Albert Ellis being prime examples. In this book, I use the terms counselling and therapy interchangeably.

DEFINING TERMS

Throughout this book, for the sake of consistency, for the most part I use the terms 'therapy', 'therapist' and 'client'. Therapy refers both to the theoretical approach and to the process of helping clients. It is notable that the originators of most therapeutic approaches included the word 'therapy' in their approach's title: for instance, person-centred therapy, gestalt therapy, rational emotive and cognitive therapy. 'Therapist' refers to the providers of therapy services to clients, be they psychoanalysts, psychiatrists, clinical psychologists, counselling psychologists, counsellors, social workers or other suitably trained and qualified persons. 'Client' refers to the recipient of therapeutic services whether inside or outside of medical settings.

OVERVIEW OF COUNSELLING AND THERAPY APPROACHES

A useful distinction exists between *schools* of counselling and therapy and *theoretical approaches* to counselling and therapy. A theoretical approach presents a single position regarding the theory and practice of counselling and therapy. A school of counselling and therapy is a grouping of different theoretical approaches which are similar to one another in terms of certain important characteristics that distinguish them from theoretical approaches in other counselling and therapy schools

Probably the three main schools that influence contemporary individual counselling and psychotherapy practice are the psychodynamic school, the humanistic school, and the cognitive–behavioural school. Sometimes the humanistic school incorporates existential therapeutic approaches and then gets the broader title of being the humanistic–existential school. Be careful not to exaggerate the differences between counselling and therapy schools, since there are similarities as well differences among them. Box 1.1 briefly

---

BOX 1.1

Three counselling and therapy schools

The psychodynamic school
The term 'psychodynamic' refers to the transfer of *psychic or mental energy* between the different structures and levels of consciousness within people's minds. Psychodynamic approaches emphasize the importance of *unconscious influences* on how people function. Therapy aims to increase clients' abilities to exercise *greater conscious control* over their lives. *Analysis or interpretation of dreams* can be a central part of therapy.

The humanistic–existential school
The humanistic school is based on humanism, a system of values and beliefs that emphasizes the better qualities of humankind and people's abilities to develop their *human potential.* Humanistic therapists emphasize enhancing clients' abilities to *experience their feelings* and think and act in harmony with their underlying tendencies to *actualize themselves* as unique individuals. Existential approaches to therapy stress people's capacity to *choose* how they create their existences.

The cognitive–behavioural school
Traditional behaviour therapy focuses mainly on changing *observable behaviours* by means of providing different or rewarding consequences. The cognitive–behavioural school broadens behaviour therapy to incorporate the contribution of *how people think* to creating, sustaining and changing their problems. In cognitive–behavioural approaches, therapists *assess* clients and then *intervene* to help them to *change specific ways of thinking and behaving* that sustain their problems.

describes some distinguishing features of the psychodynamic, humanistic–existential and cognitive–behavioural schools.

Box 1.2 introduces the theoretical approaches, grouped as closely as feasible according to the counselling and therapy school, selected for inclusion in this book. So that readers can obtain a sense of the history of the development of ideas within counselling and therapy, I have included the dates of the originators of each approach. Those of you wishing further brief introductions to the different approaches are referred to the summaries provided at the end of each chapter. The descriptions provided in Box 1.2 reflect the position of the originators of the different positions, rather than developments within a theoretical approach stimulated by others. With some humility, I include my cognitive–humanistic therapy in Box 1.2. However, I stress this position is work in progress, currently not widely adopted, and I lack the eminence of the other theorists.

BOX 1.2
Overview of counselling and therapy approaches

Psychodynamic school

Classical psychoanalysis   *Originator: Sigmund Freud (1856–1939)*
Pays great attention to unconscious factors related to infantile sexuality in the development of neurosis. Psychoanalysis, which may last for many years, emphasizes working through the transference, in which clients perceive their therapists as reincarnations of important figures from their childhoods, and the interpretation of dreams.

Analytical therapy   *Originator: Carl Jung (1875–1961)*
Divides the unconscious into the personal unconscious and the collective unconscious, the latter being a storehouse of universal archetypes and primordial images. Therapy includes analysis of the transference, active imagination and dream analysis. Jung was particularly interested in working with clients in the second half of life.

Humanistic–existential school

Person-centred therapy   *Originator: Carl Rogers (1902–1987)*
Lays great stress on the primacy of subjective experience and how clients can become out of touch with their actualizing tendency through introjecting others' evaluations and treating them as if their own. Therapy emphasizes a relationship characterized by accurate empathy, respect and non-possessive warmth.

Gestalt therapy   *Originator: Fritz Perls (1893–1970)*
Individuals become neurotic by losing touch with their senses and interfering with their capacity to make strong contact with their environments. Therapy emphasizes increasing clients' awareness and vitality through awareness techniques, experiments, sympathy and frustration, and dream work.

Transactional analysis   *Originator: Eric Berne (1910–1970)*
Transactions between people take place between their Parent, Adult and Child ego states. Therapy includes structural analysis of ego states, analysis of specific transactions, analysis of games – a series of transactions having ulterior motivations, and analysis of clients' life scripts.

Reality therapy   *Originator: William Glasser (1925–)*
Clients choose to maintain their misery through choosing inappropriate ways to control the world to satisfy their needs. Therapy includes identifying clients' wants and needs, teaching choice theory, planning and, where appropriate, training clients in behaviours they need to succeed.

Existential therapy   *Originators: Irvin Yalom (1931–) and Rollo May (1909–1994)*
Draws on the work of existential philosophers and focuses on helping clients deal with anxieties connected with four main ultimate concerns of human existence: death, freedom, isolation and meaninglessness. Therapy focuses on clients' current situations, with different interventions used according to the nature of clients' enveloping fears.

Logotherapy   *Originator: Viktor Frankl (1905–1997)*
Clients can become neurotic because they face an existential vacuum in which they are unable to find meaning in their lives. Logotherapists use methods such as teaching the importance of assuming responsibility for finding meaning, Socratic questioning, offering meanings and analysing dreams.

Cognitive–behavioural school

Behaviour therapy   *Important figures: theory, Ivan Pavlov (1849–1936) and B. F. Skinner (1904–1990); practice, Joseph Wolpe (1915–1997)*
Emphasizes the learning of behaviour through classical conditioning, operant conditioning and modelling. Therapy consists of learning adaptive behaviours by methods such as systematic desensitization, reinforcement programmes and behaviour rehearsal.

Rational emotive behaviour therapy   *Originator: Albert Ellis (1913–)*
Emphasizes clients reindoctrinating themselves with irrational beliefs that lead to unwanted feelings and self-defeating actions. Therapy involves disputing clients' irrational beliefs and replacing them with more rational beliefs. Elegant or profound therapy entails changing clients' philosophies of life.

Cognitive therapy   *Originator: Aaron Beck (1921–)*
Clients become distressed because they are faulty processors of information with a tendency to jump to unwarranted conclusions. Therapy consists of educating clients in how to test the reality of their thinking by interventions such as Socratic questioning and conducting real-life experiments.

Multimodal therapy   *Originator: Arnold Lazarus (1932–)*
Clients respond to situations according to their predominant modalities: behaviour,

affect, sensation, imagery, cognition, interpersonal and drugs/biology. Based on a multi-modal assessment, therapists are technically eclectic, using a range of techniques selected on the basis of empirical evidence and client need.

Cognitive–humanistic therapy   *Originator: Richard Nelson-Jones (1936–)*
Consists of two interrelated components – lifeskills therapy for everyday adaptation and mental discipline therapy for supra-normal functioning. Lifeskills therapy uses a range of interventions focused on thinking, communication and actions, and feelings. Mental discipline therapy focuses on developing the mind to awaken and strengthen the heart and incorporates mind training and human sympathy activities.

So far, I have presented the different schools and theoretical approaches as though they are separate. In reality, many counsellors and therapists regard themselves as working in either eclectic or integrative ways. A detailed discussion of eclecticism and integration is beyond the scope of this book. Suffice to say that eclecticism is the practice of drawing from different counselling and therapy schools in formulating client problems and implementing treatment interventions. Integration refers to attempting to blend together theoretical concepts and/or practical interventions drawn from different counselling and therapy approaches into coherent and integrated wholes.

WHAT IS A COUNSELLING AND THERAPY THEORY?

A theory is a system of suppositions or ideas explaining something. Hall and Lindzey write: 'A theory is an unsubstantiated hypothesis or speculation concerning reality which is not yet definitely known to be so. When the theory is confirmed it becomes a fact' (1970, p. 10). These authors make the division between theory and fact too rigid. Rather, a theory is a formulation of the underlying principles of certain observed phenomena which have been verified to some extent. A criterion of the power of a theory is the extent to which it generates predictions which are confirmed when relevant empirical data are collected. The more a theory receives confirmation or verification, the more accurate it is. Facts strengthen rather than replace theories.

Functions of counselling and therapy theories

What do counselling and therapy theories do? Why are they useful? Therapists cannot avoid being counselling and therapy theorists. All make assumptions about how clients become and stay the way they are and about change. Three of the main functions of counselling and therapy theories are: providing conceptual frameworks, providing languages, and generating research.

Theories as conceptual frameworks

Therapists are decision-makers. They continually make choices about how to think about clients' behaviour, how to treat them, and how to respond on a moment-by-moment basis during therapy sessions. Theories provide therapists with concepts that allow them to think systematically about human development and the therapeutic process.

Counselling and therapy theoretical approaches may be viewed as possessing four main dimensions if they are to be stated adequately:

1. a statement of the *basic concepts* or assumptions underlying the theory;
2. an explanation of the *acquisition* of helpful and unhelpful behaviour;
3. an explanation of the *maintenance* of helpful and unhelpful behaviour; and
4. an explanation of how to help clients *change* their behaviour and *consolidate* their gains when therapy ends.

In this context behaviour incorporates both observable behaviour and internal behaviour or thinking. Box 1.3 shows how counselling and therapy theoretical approaches can be viewed as containing a model of human development and a model of therapy.

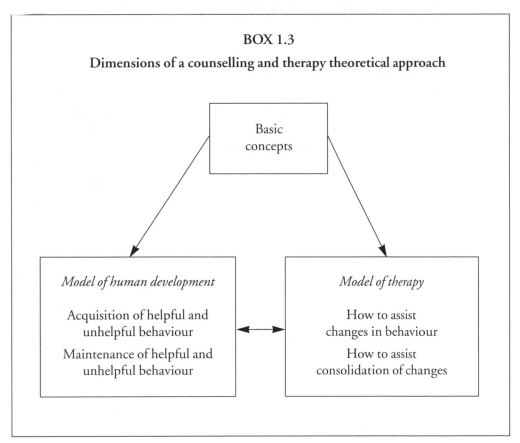

BOX 1.3

Dimensions of a counselling and therapy theoretical approach

When reading about the different counselling and therapy approaches, you may observe that many, if not most, have significant gaps in their conceptual frameworks. They are partial rather than complete or comprehensive theoretical statements. Arguably, some of the missing concepts in the theories are implicit rather than explicit. Also, theorists select for more thorough treatment those dimensions of a theory that they consider important. For instance, Ellis's rational emotive behaviour theory has a wider variety of explanatory concepts concerning how behaviour is maintained than how it is initially acquired.

Theories as languages

Swiss psychiatrist Carl Jung used to stress that, since all clients are different individuals, therapists require a different language for each client (Jung, 1961). Another function of theories is similar to that provided by languages. Languages are vocabularies and linguistic symbols that allow communication about phenomena. Like the major spoken languages of English, French, Spanish and Mandarin Chinese, the different theorists develop languages for the phenomena they wish to describe: for instance, cognitive, psychoanalytic or person-centred languages. Language can both unite and divide. It can encourage communication between people who speak they same language, but discourage communication if they do not. Each theoretical position has concepts described in unique language. However, the uniqueness of the language may mask common elements among theories: for example, the meaning of conditions of worth in person-centred therapy overlaps with that of super-ego in Freud's psychoanalytic therapy, though you would not know this from the language!

The therapy process is a series of conversations requiring languages. In any therapeutic relationship there are at least four kinds of conversations going on: therapist and client inner and outer speech. All therapists who operate out of explicit theoretical frameworks are likely to talk to themselves about clients in the language of that framework. In varying degrees their therapeutic practice will match their language. Therapists do not always act according to how they think. Also, in varying degrees therapists share their theoretical language with clients. For example, unlike in rational emotive behaviour therapy, the language in which person-centred theory is expressed tends not to be shared with clients. Instead, person-centred therapists try to reflect and match clients' outer speech.

Clients are also theorists, though usually without the sophistication of their therapists. Approaches like rational emotive behaviour therapy and cognitive therapy actively try to influence the language in which clients talk to themselves so that it becomes helpful rather than harmful. These approaches educate clients to converse with themselves. In a sense the therapist's language is being exported to and imported by clients so that they can better assist themselves once therapy ends.

Theories as sets of research hypotheses

The social psychologist Kurt Lewin is reported to have said that 'Nothing is more practical than a good theory.' Paraphrasing him, perhaps 'Nothing is more scientific than a good theory.' Theories can be both based on research and stimulate research. For example, cognitive–behavioural therapy is based on research into how people think and into how both people and animals behave. Furthermore, cognitive–behavioural approaches, such as rational emotive behaviour therapy and cognitive therapy, have stimulated research into their processes and outcomes.

Theories also provide therapists with frameworks within which to make predictive hypotheses during their practice of therapy. Whether acknowledging it or not, all therapists are practitioner-researchers. Therapists make hypotheses every time they decide how to work with specific clients and how to respond to single or series of client utterances.

Clients are also practitioner-researchers who make predictions about how best to lead their lives. If valid theories of counselling and therapy are transmitted to clients, they may increase the accuracy with which clients can predict the consequences of their behaviours and, hence, gain more control over their lives.

Limitations of counselling and therapy theories

All counselling and therapy theories should carry the psychological equivalent of health warnings. They can be used for ill as well as for good. Following are some potential disadvantages of theories.

Restriction of focus

A criticism of many theories is that they present partial truths as whole truths. Rogers may be viewed as an example of this tendency to overgeneralize. He posits a unitary diagnosis of all clients' problems, namely that they are out of touch with their actualizing tendencies, and sees the helping relationship as necessary and sufficient in all instances (Rogers, 1957). Ellis focuses on irrational beliefs at the risk of paying insufficient attention to other aspects of thinking, for instance perceiving accurately or using coping self-talk. Freud emphasizes uncovering unconscious material through the analysis of dreams, but says little about developing specific effective behaviours to deal with everyday problems. The trend to eclecticism among many therapists, who draw upon aspects from different theories, attests to this negative aspect of the major theories.

Therapist rigidity

A function of theory can be that it meets insecure therapists' need for certainty. Instead of acting as effective practitioner-researchers who test their theoretical hypotheses, such therapists allow theory to interfere with the accuracy with which they assess and treat clients. However, a beneficial side-effect of theoretical faith may be that it provides therapists with confidence that then gets transmitted to clients. Unfortunately, such confidence can be misplaced

Tendencies to theoretical rigidity are heightened by the institutionalizing of theoretical approaches, with prescribed training routes. On the positive side, the institutionalizing of theoretical approaches can foster useful research and training. On the negative side, organizations and associations representing theoretical approaches can turn into self-congratulatory status systems that reinforce rigidity. Preferment goes to those that toe the line rather than those too interested in theoretical breadth.

The different languages of theoretical approaches can disguise similarities between them. Theoretical rigidity is fostered when language differences lead therapists only to talk with those speaking the same language rather than to a broader sharing of knowledge and experience.

Depowering clients

Some theories may lead to pathologizing clients by focusing more on what is wrong rather than on what is right. In addition, theories can make clients' problems out to be more severe than they are. For instance, psychoanalysts can view learned ineffective behaviour as symptomatic of deeper underlying conflicts. In addition, if clients give negative feedback to analysts, they can be labelled as resisting and acting out their negative transferences rather than having their feedback taken seriously.

The language of theories can create a power imbalance between therapists and clients. Therapists who think in a special theoretical language that they do not share can put themselves in superior–inferior relationships with clients. Furthermore, the language of some theories does little to empower clients once they end therapy. Ideally, the language of therapy is that of self-helping. Clients unable to articulate what to think and do when faced with problems after therapy are less likely to maintain gains than clients who can instruct themselves appropriately.

Supporting the *status quo*

Counselling and therapy theories can contain many assumptions about how people should behave and about the causes of their behaviour. For example, possibly all theories in this book insufficiently take into account cultural differences. Instead, theorists present their ideas as more culture-universal and less culture-specific than they really are. In addition, theories of counselling and therapy, by focusing on individuals, couples and families, can either ignore or underestimate how much socio-environmental conditions like poverty, poor housing and racial discrimination may contribute to explaining ineffective behaviour. Though feminist and gender-aware theorizing is attempting to redress the balance, most theories insufficiently take into account the influence of sex-role conditioning. In addition, theories tend to assume heterosexuality and insufficiently take into account the needs of gay, lesbian and bisexual clients.

ORIGINS OF COUNSELLING AND THERAPY APPROACHES

Only the wounded physician heals.
Carl Gustav Jung

Theoretical approaches to counselling and therapy are created by human beings. To a large extent these theories reflect the historical context and personal and intellectual life histories of their founders. All the theorists were influenced by their families of origin and by previous writers and thinkers. The following section suggests some important factors that have influenced the creation and development of counselling and therapy theory and practice (Nelson-Jones, 2000).

Historical and cultural contexts

Theoretical approaches do not incubate and emerge in vacuums. Theorists are influenced by the historical and cultural contexts in which they live. For example, the prevalence of sexual repression in turn-of-the-century Austria influenced Freud to develop a theoretical position in which unacknowledged sexuality plays a large part. Another example is that, during the first half of the twentieth century, parents tended to dominate their families more than they do now. Carl Rogers was brought up in the first quarter of the century. His person-centred counselling reflects the need for individuals to have nurturing and accepting relationships within which to work through the effects of judgemental family upbringings so that they can 'become persons' (Rogers, 1961, 1980). Whereas Rogers reacted against certainty, the popularity of existential counselling in the latter part of this century partly represents a reaction to the structurelessness of much of modern society (Yalom, 1980). Old certainties provided by institutions like family and church no longer exist to the same extent and many people are faced with a more obvious need to create their own meaning.

Culture also influences how theoretical approaches develop. For example, ideas of desirable behaviour differ greatly between Western and Eastern cultures. Western therapies place a high value on individualism that people from Eastern cultures, with their greater emphasis on group harmony, may find uncongenial (Ho, 1985; Laungani, 1999). The topic of cultural considerations in therapy theory and practice is developed in greater detail later in this book.

Wounded theorists

The origins of behaviour therapy lie more in the animal laboratory than in the personal experiences of behavioural theorists. However, without exception, all the other theorists whose work is described in this book encountered periods of significant psychological suffering in their lives. Box 1.4 illustrates this point. Jung's observation 'Only the wounded physician heals' might be amended to become 'Only the wounded healer creates a counselling and therapy approach.'

BOX 1.4
Wounded theorists

Sigmund Freud *(Psychoanalysis)* suffered for many years from periodic depressions, mood variations and anxiety attacks. Freud also had occasional attacks of dread of dying, some psychologically-induced fainting spells, and became very frightened about train travel.

Carl Jung *(Analytical therapy)* was a solitary child who, at one stage, used fainting spells to get out of going to secondary school. In his late 30s and early 40s Jung experienced schizophrenic-like symptoms.

Carl Rogers *(Person-centred therapy)* was an extremely shy and solitary child who grew up in a home where he considered his parents as masters of subtle emotional manipulation. Rogers felt it unsafe to share much of his personal feelings at home for fear of being judged negatively.

Fritz Perls *(Gestalt therapy)* grew up in a distressed family where his parents had many bitter verbal and physical fights. Perls' mother beat him with carpet-beating rods. He hated his father's pompous righteousness.

Eric Berne *(Transactional analysis)*, when 11, experienced the death from tuberculosis of his beloved physician father, leaving his mother to support him and his sister.

William Glasser *(Reality therapy)* by age 4 realized his parents were highly incompatible. His father was gentle and non-possessive. If there was an Olympic event in being controlling, his energetic mother could have gone for the gold medal. Glasser was very shy when an undergraduate and, probably, at an earlier age too.

Irvin Yalom and Rollo May *(Existential therapy)* Yalom grew up spending many hours hating his mother's vicious tongue. May grew up in a discordant and unhappy family atmosphere. He described his mother as a 'bitch-kitty on wheels'.

Viktor Frankl *(Logotherapy)* as a young man went through a period of hellish despair about the total meaninglessness of life. Later Frankl suffered the horrors of Nazi concentration camps and the extermination of family members.

Albert Ellis *(Rational emotive behaviour therapy)* was a sickly child who was unusually shy and introverted during his childhood and adolescence. Ellis's mother was self-involved and neglectful while, much of the time, his father was physically absent. At 12, Ellis discovered his parents had divorced.

Aaron Beck's *(Cognitive therapy)* mother periodically was deeply depressed. She could also be moody, inconsistent and excitable. While growing up, Beck developed many anxieties, including fears related to abandonment, surgery, suffocation, public speaking and heights.

Arnold Lazarus *(Multimodal therapy)* was the youngest of four children and grew up feeling ignored and unimportant at home, which contributed to his feeling shy, inadequate and hypersensitive. Lazarus was also a skinny kid who was bullied a lot.

If one accepts that many originators of counselling and therapy theories experienced more than their share of psychological suffering, the question still remains how this affected their theorizing. For some leading theorists, shyness with people may have stimulated a desire to communicate through words. In addition, early feelings of inferiority may have fuelled their ambition to make their mark. Furthermore, having suffered themselves, theorists may be motivated to develop theories that can alleviate the suffering of others.

Some theorists seem to have been motivated to develop theoretical positions that would help not just clients, but themselves. Freud's self-analysis helped him address his personal suffering at the same time as providing important insights for his main work, *The Interpretation of Dreams* (Freud, 1976; Jones, 1963). Jung's confrontation with his own unconscious archetypes and primordial images provided a rich source of ideas for helping both himself and others (Jung, 1961). Frankl's logotherapy stems from his youthful despair over the apparent meaninglessness of life (Frankl, 1988). Rogers' person-centred therapist has the attributes of empathy, respect and non-possessive warmth that Rogers found missing in his parents and required for his own growth.

Albert Ellis, in his late teens, regularly went to the Bronx Botanic Gardens in New York and forced himself to sit next to women on park benches and strike up conversations with them so that he could learn to control his shyness and build his relating skills. Here, early in life, Ellis was trying to think and behave more rationally in one of his problem areas.

Interest in writing and communicating ideas

As well as a talent for theorizing, theorists need the ability to write passably well in order to get published. When researching the biographical sketches for this book, I was struck by how many of the theorists early in their lives showed an interest in writing. Furthermore, some theorists, for instance Jung and Yalom, were avid readers right from their early years.

In his teens, Lazarus helped edit a body-building magazine and then entered university with a view to becoming a journalist and a writer. Beck was editor of his high school newspaper and an undergraduate English major. Skinner majored in English and planned to become a writer. Ellis too envisaged a writing career and wrote reams in his quest to become the Great American Novelist. May's main interest at college was English literature. Berne studied English along with psychology and pre-medicine as an undergraduate and his mother was a journalist. Later in their lives at least two theorists, Skinner and Yalom, branched out to write novels (for example, Skinner, 1948; Yalom, 1992, 1996).

An ambition to communicate distinctive ideas, become known and, possibly, reap the financial rewards of successful authorship may also fuel theorists' productivity. However, readers should be circumspect about attributing commercial motives to theorists. For example, for over 30 years, Ellis has donated all his royalty, client and workshop income to the Institute for Rational Emotive Behavior Therapy. Furthermore, when theorists start writing books they have no guarantee that their time and effort will be remunerative.

All theorists think they have something of value to offer and want to share it. For instance, throughout his professional life Rogers was very concerned with making an impact on others. Though motivation is complex, probably altruism, social interest and enjoyment are primary factors shaping theorists' willingness to generate and share ideas.

Professional experiences and frustrations

Though behaviour therapy owes much to experimental psychology, for the most part major counselling and therapy theories emanate from people who were practitioners as well as scholars. Frustration, creative insights, clinical experimentation and careful observation can each contribute to developing a theory. Beck, Berne, Ellis, and Perls were trained in psychoanalysis. Their negative experiences practising psychoanalysis challenged them to develop their own positions. Each used their work with clients to develop and experiment with different ways of helping them. In addition, Glasser's reality therapy stems from his disillusionment with the psychoanalytic psychology to which he was exposed during his training and from observing many analytic teachers not practising what they taught. Lying can take place behind, as well as on, the couch.

Lazarus was stimulated to develop his multimodal therapy approach as a reaction to the restrictiveness of traditional behaviour therapy. Rogers developed his person-centred approach from discovering the limitations of existing ways of working. He recalls that, when in the 1930s he worked at the Rochester Child Study Department (later renamed the Child Guidance Center), he obtained far better results with clients from listening to them than from diagnostic understanding and advice (Rogers, 1980).

Research findings

Research can influence both the initial development of theory and test its usefulness. Behaviour therapy theory is based on the findings of experimental research: for instance, Pavlov's classical conditioning is based on experiments with dogs; Skinner's operant conditioning on experiments with pigeons and rats; and Wolpe's counter-conditioning by reciprocal inhibition on experiments with cats.

Theory can also be developed and validated from researching the processes and outcomes of psychotherapy. Theorists are practitioner-researchers generating and testing hypotheses in their therapy practice. Thus, professional experience can act as informal psychotherapy process and outcome research. Theorists and their adherents differ in the extent to which they either engage in or generate more formal therapy research. On the one hand, the processes and outcomes of approaches like cognitive therapy, rational emotive behaviour therapy, person-centred therapy and behaviour therapy are heavily researched. On the other hand, there is a paucity of research into approaches like transactional analysis, gestalt therapy, existential therapy and reality therapy.

Professional affiliation

Most theorists whose work is presented in this book were or are psychiatrists: for example, Freud, Jung, Perls, Berne, Glasser, Yalom, Frankl, and Beck. The remainder trained as clinical psychologists: for instance, May, Rogers, Ellis, and Lazarus. None of the major theorists are counselling psychologists, counsellors or social workers. Of the clinical psychologists, only Lazarus was primarily affiliated with an academic psychology department. Thus, psychology may be 'punching below its weight' when it comes to creating counselling and therapy approaches. Possibly this scarcity of original output is because of the rigid conventions of contemporary academic psychology. On the other hand, psychiatry appears to allow for more individuality and creativity.

Access to money

Creating a counselling and therapy approach and getting it published takes time and money. A possible reason why more psychiatrists than psychologists have developed original theories is that they generally get paid more too. Hence psychiatrists, who are budding theorists, can afford to schedule more writing time than psychologists. Jung, especially, also married into considerable wealth. In academic life, despite creativity being the seed corn of important research, grants are more likely to be awarded for researching existing approaches to counselling and therapy than for creating new ones. In addition, appointments, promotions and higher salaries go to those with strong research records.

Sex and sexual orientation

Probably most readers have noticed that all of the major theorists presented in this book are men. However, women have been prominent in psychodynamic approaches to therapy: for instance, Melanie Klein, Karen Horney, and Anna Freud. In addition, Perls' wife Laura is considered by some to be the co-founder of gestalt therapy (Yontef and Jacobs, 2000). Furthermore, women have contributed to the development of other approaches presented in this book, as well as being the driving force behind feminist therapy. All the major theorists appear to have been heterosexual, at least as far as their public personas.

Country of origin and race

The countries of birth of the theorists are as follows: America – Glasser, May, Yalom, Beck, Rogers, and Ellis; Austria – Freud, and Frankl; South Africa – Wolpe, and Lazarus; Switzerland – Jung; Germany – Perls; Canada – Berne. Of the non-American born theorists, Wolpe, Lazarus, Perls, and Berne have spent the bulk of their professional lives in the United States. A high proportion of the theorists in this book were or are Jewish: for example, Freud, Frankl, Yalom, Beck, Perls, and Berne. In addition, Ellis had a Jewish mother.

Longevity

If you are going to be a major counselling theorist, it helps to have good genes. Longevity helps major theorists to develop, refine, proselytize and defend their work. Freud, Jung, Rogers, and May lived into their 80s, and Perls lived to over 75. Berne's premature death at aged 60 probably robbed transactional analysis of many useful developments and insights. Of the living theorists Ellis (b. 1913) is now over 85, Beck (b. 1921) is approaching 80, Glasser (b. 1925) is well over 70, and Yalom (b. 1931) and Lazarus (b. 1932) are over 65. Another aspect of longevity is that many, if not most, major theorists did not publish original work until they were over 40. Dying young may not be a good career move for the budding theorist.

Recency of theory creation

One of the most worrying aspects of analysing the creation of counselling and therapy theories is that so little original work of high quality appears to be of recent origin. None of the major theorists selected for this book were born in the second half of the twentieth century!

CREATING YOUR OWN THEORETICAL APPROACH

There is no psychology; there is only biography and autobiography.
Thomas Szasz

As a reader of this book, you are engaging in the process of creating your own theoretical approach. Theory creation is both a subjective process of making sense of material as well as an external process of reading, learning, researching and practising therapeutic skills. How can you make yourself a better theorist and hence a more effective therapist? Here are some suggestions.

Work with this book

Though based on the writings of the original theorists, this book is a secondary source. Nevertheless, it should provide you with a faithful overview of some of the main counselling and therapy theories. To understand any theory you need to master its basic concepts. It is insufficient just to read about them. You will need actively to work on understanding and memorizing them. At the end of each theory chapter, I provide review questions that test your knowledge of basic concepts.

Get personal

Jung observed: 'My life is a story of the realisation of the unconscious' (Jung, 1961, p. 17). What about your life's story and what are you trying to realize through your interest in counselling and therapy? Applying the different theories to your own life is one way to make learning more personal, involving and interesting. What do the theories say that seems applicable to you, and why? Another way to understand the theories is to think about how applicable they are to past, present or future clients. What in different theories might prove useful in your practical work, and why? Also, you can compare and contrast different theories in an attempt to critically evaluate their strengths and weaknesses for you as a person and as a therapist. At the end of each chapter I provide personal questions so that you may apply your learnings and insights to yourself.

Still a further way to learn about the theories is to try to develop a theoretical approach of your own. For over twenty years I asked counselling and counselling psychology students taking my theories classes to write a paper presenting their current theoretical approach.

Read primary sources

Primary sources are books and articles written by the theorists themselves. Ultimately, there is no substitute for reading primary sources. You will get a much broader and deeper impression of the different theories if you read widely the works of their originators. You can also learn about how the originators applied their counselling and therapy theories by reading case studies of their work. I include a section on case material toward the end of each chapter on the different therapies. In addition, after describing the work of each theorist, I provide a brief annotated bibliography plus other primary source references.

Read secondary sources

You can read secondary sources other than this book. Some secondary sources are counselling and therapy textbooks and here you should always look out for the most recent editions. *Current Psychotherapies* is a widely respected edited therapy textbook containing a mixture of primary and secondary sources (Corsini and Wedding, 2000). All major therapy approaches beget many secondary source books: for instance, Mearns and Thorne's (1999) *Person-Centred Counselling in Action.*

A warning about reading secondary sources: choose carefully, because some secondary source writers do not really understand the theoretical positions they present. Following are three more traps into which secondary source textbook writers can fall. One trap is to mix the writings of the original theorist together with recent developments in theory, so the student has difficulty in knowing which is which. A second trap is to merge the writings of different theorists into the same chapter: for example, to have a chapter combining either psychodynamic theories or humanistic theories. A problem with this approach is that no theory gets presented thoroughly. If you doubt this point, look at the next two chapters on Freudian Psychoanalysis and Jung's Analytical Therapy and see how well-nigh impossible it would be to combine them so that readers obtain a good introduction to both Freudian and Jungian theory and practice. A third trap is for the secondary source writer only to present case examples of their own work. A risk here is that this secondary source case material does not truly reflect how the originator practised or practises therapy.

Watch and listen to audio-visual material

You can obtain a further insight into the different theorists by watching films and video-tapes and listening to audio cassettes of them discussing their theories and working with clients. For instance, audio-visual material is available for theorists like Rogers, Perls, Ellis, and Beck.

Attend training courses and workshops

You may expand your knowledge and skills in the different theories by attending training courses and workshops run by competent adherents of the different approaches. Introductory theories of counselling and therapy courses are likely to be limited in presenting different approaches both by time constraints and by lecturer preferences. You may get a much more thorough introduction to any single approach if you attend workshops and courses run by specialists in it. However, when considering training courses and workshops, be careful about spreading yourself too thin.

Undergo supervision

A good way to learn about the theory and practice of a counselling approach is to be supervised by a practitioner skilled in it. For instance, you can learn the theory and practice of one therapeutic approach more thoroughly by being supervised by someone knowledgeable and competent in that approach. Then you can broaden how you work by obtaining supervision from practitioners of one or more different approaches.

Undergo personal therapy

If a counselling and therapy approach particularly appeals to you, one way to learn about its theory and practice is to become a client of a skilled practitioner in the approach. For some approaches, e.g. psychoanalysis and analytical therapy, a training analysis is an integral part of learning the approach.

Evaluate theoretical approaches

In creating your own theoretical approach you will undoubtedly undergo a process of evaluating the existing theoretical approaches. Many considerations go into evaluating theoretical approaches: for instance, how well you understand the theoretical approaches you are trying to evaluate, how thoroughly each approach is researched, and how their goals differ. I leave a more detailed discussion about evaluating counselling and therapy approaches to this book's final chapter.

SUMMARY

- *Therapy is derived from the Greek word for healing. Though there may be differences of emphasis between counselling and therapy, there are more similarities than differences.*
- *A theoretical approach represents a single position regarding the theory and practice of counselling and therapy.*
- *A school of counselling and therapy is a grouping of different theoretical approaches which are similar to one another in terms of certain important characteristics that distinguish them from approaches in other counselling and therapy schools.*
- *Probably the three main schools that influence contemporary individual counselling and therapy theory and practice are the psychodynamic school, the humanistic–existential school, and the cognitive–behavioural school.*
- *A theory is the formulation of the underlying principles of certain observed phenomena which have been verified to some extent. Three of the main functions of counselling and therapy theories are: providing conceptual frameworks, providing languages, and generating research.*
- *Counselling and therapy theories can be for good or ill. Potential limitations of therapy theories include: restriction of focus, therapist rigidity, depowering clients, and supporting the status quo.*
- *The origins of counselling and therapy theories include: historical and cultural contexts; and theorists' personal histories, suffering, interest in writing and communicating ideas, and professional experiences and frustrations.*
- *The creation of counselling and therapy theory is also influenced by research findings, professional affiliation, access to money, sex of theorists, country of origin, race and longevity. There is a notable dearth of theorists born in the second half of the twentieth century.*
- *In addition to working with this book, you can create your own theoretical position by: applying the theories to yourself; reading primary sources, secondary sources and case studies; watching and listening to audio-visual material; attending training courses and workshops; and undergoing supervision and personal therapy by skilled practitioners.*

REVIEW AND PERSONAL QUESTIONS

REVIEW QUESTIONS

1. How would you define the terms 'counselling' and 'therapy'?
2. To what extent do you consider the terms 'counselling' and 'therapy' describe different activities, and why?
3. What is a theory?
4. What are the functions of counselling and therapy theories?
5. What are some potential limitations or disadvantages of counselling and therapy theories?
6. What factors are influential in creating counselling and therapy theoretical approaches?

PERSONAL QUESTIONS

1. Do you consider yourself a prospective counsellor and/or a prospective therapist, and why?
2. Describe your present preferences regarding counselling and therapy theoretical approaches.
3. How can you best learn about counselling and therapy approaches?
4. How can you best develop a theoretical position to guide your counselling and therapy practice?

ANNOTATED BIBLIOGRAPHY

Corsini, R. J. and Wedding, D. (eds) (2000). *Current Psychotherapies* (6th edition). Itasca, IL: Peacock.

> This book is a mixture of primary and secondary sources. Chapters on cognitive, existential, multimodal, person-centred, and rational–emotive therapies are written by their originators, sometimes with co-authors. Secondary source chapters review psychoanalytic, Adlerian, gestalt, behaviour, and family therapy. There is also a strong chapter on Asian psycho-therapies.

REFERENCES AND FURTHER READING

British Association for Counselling (1998). *Code of Ethics & Practice for Counsellors.* Rugby: Author.

Corsini, R. J. and Wedding, D. (eds) (2000). *Current Psychotherapies* (6th edition). Itasca, IL: Peacock.

Frankl, V. E. (1988). *The Will to Meaning: Foundations and Applications of Logotherapy.* New York: Meridian.

Freud, S. (1976). *The Interpretation of Dreams.* Harmondsworth, Middlesex: Penguin Books. Original edition, 1900.

Hall, C. S. and Lindzey, G. (1970). *Theories of Personality.* New York: John Wiley.

Ho, D. Y. F. (1985). Cultural values and professional issues in clinical psychology: Implications from the Hong Kong experience. *American Psychologist, 40,* 1212–18.

Jones, E. (1963). *The Life and Work of Sigmund Freud.* New York: Anchor Books.

Jung, C. G. (1961). *Memories, Dreams, Reflections.* London: Fontana Press.

Laungani, P. (1999). Culture and identity: Implications for counselling. In S. Palmer and P. Laungani (eds), *Counselling in a Multicultural Society* (35–70). London: Sage.

Mearns, D. and Thorne, B. (1999). *Person-Centred Counselling in Action* (2nd edition). London: Sage.

Nelson-Jones, R. (2000). Creating counselling and therapy theories. *Counselling, 11,* 10–13.

Rogers, C. R. (1957). The necessary and sufficient conditions of therapeutic personality change. *Journal of Consulting Psychology, 21,* 95–104.

Rogers, C. R. (1961). *On Becoming a Person.* Boston, MA: Houghton Mifflin.

Rogers, C. R. (1980). *A Way of Being.* Boston, MA: Houghton Mifflin.

Skinner, B. F. (1948). *Walden Two.* New York: MacMillan.

Yalom, I. D. (1980). *Existential Psychotherapy.* New York: Basic Books.

Yalom, I. D. (1992). *When Nietzsche Wept*. New York: Basic Books.
Yalom, I. D. (1996). *Lying on the Couch*. New York: HarperPerennial.
Yontef, G. and Jacobs, L. (2000). Gestalt therapy. In R. J. Corsini and D. Wedding (eds). *Current Psychotherapies* (6th edition, 303–39). Itasca, IL: Peacock.

2

Freud's Psychoanalysis

We believe that civilisation has been built up, under the pressure of the struggle for existence, by sacrifices in the gratification of primitive instincts.

Sigmund Freud

INTRODUCTION

A woman who is very anxious to bear children always reads 'storks' instead of 'stocks'. The notion of Freudian slips, or people inadvertently betraying their underlying thoughts, has become part of Western culture. Furthermore, humour about Freudian psychoanalysis is common, with Woody Allen being a prime example. For example, when asked 'How long have you been in psychoanalysis?', he replied 'Twenty-one years.' When further asked 'How is it going?', he answered 'Slowly.' In the film *Annie Hall*, the character played by Woody Allen observes: 'I was depressed . . . I was suicidal; as a matter of fact I would have killed myself but I was in analysis with a strict Freudian and if you kill yourself they make you pay for the sessions you miss.'

Sigmund Freud, the originator of psychoanalysis, is easily the best known of the theorists whose work is described in this book. Freud, an Austrian, lived the first 44 years of his life in the second half of the nineteenth century. This was a period of intellectual ferment with a crucial issue being the challenges posed by Darwin's ideas on the evolution of the species. Around this time, psychology was gradually starting to separate itself from philosophy. Freud, like William James in the United States, was interested in both areas. Along with the intellectual challenges, the old ways of life were also being challenged by the Industrial Revolution and technological inventions like the discovery of electricity and the motor car.

Freud also lived in a time of conflict, a major theme of his work. One area of conflict was that between the strait-laced 'Victorian' public morality of late-nineteenth-century Austria and human sexuality. To a large extent public acknowledgement of sexuality was frowned upon, an attitude which fostered widespread ignorance of healthy sexual functioning. Another area of conflict was that caused by human aggression. The nineteenth century had started with the Napoleonic wars, in the second half of the century the Franco–Prussian war took place, and in the second decade of the twentieth century matters were to get worse with the horrors of the First World War. Though Freud died within a month of the start of the Second World War, he was very conscious of the factors leading up to it, not least because throughout his professional life, as a Jew he had been acutely aware of the anti-Semitism in his homeland, and he was to die in exile in Britain, a refugee from Nazism.

SIGMUND FREUD (1856–1939)

Sigmund Freud was born at Freiberg, a small town in what is now Czechoslovakia. He was the eldest son of his father's second wife, who subsequently bore five daughters and two other sons. Jones (1963) writes of Freud's mother's pride in and love for her first-born and also mentions that between the ages of 2 and 2½ Freud's libido had been aroused towards his mother on seeing her naked. Freud writes: 'My parents were Jews, and I have remained a Jew myself' (Freud, 1935, p. 12). His father, Jakob, was a wool merchant who, when Freud was 4, moved his family to Vienna. Freud's early years in Vienna were hard and, throughout his upbringing, his family appears to have been short of money.

When he was 9 Freud went to high school (Sperl Gymnasium), where he was at the top of his class for seven years, enjoyed special privileges, and was required to pass few examinations. Freud was a hard worker who enjoyed reading and studying. On leaving school with distinction at 17 he faced the choice of a career, which for a Viennese Jew had to be in industry, business, law or medicine. He recalls not feeling any particular predilection for medicine, since his interests were directed more towards human concerns than natural objects. Freud writes: '. . . and it was hearing Goethe's beautiful essay on Nature read aloud by Professor Carl Bruhl just before I left school that decided me to become a medical student' (Freud, 1935, p. 14).

In 1873 Freud enrolled at the University of Vienna to study medicine, though when he was there his academic interests were more wide-ranging. In 1876 he began the first of his researches, a study of the gonadic structure of eels. Soon afterwards he entered Ernst Brücke's physiological laboratory, where he worked, with short interruptions, from 1876 to 1882. During this period Freud focused chiefly on work connected with the histology of nerve cells. He found 'rest and satisfaction' in Brücke's laboratory as well as scientists 'whom I could respect and take as my models' (Freud, 1935, p. 15). He thought especially highly of Brücke himself. Freud recalls being decidedly negligent in pursuing his medical studies. Nevertheless, in 1881 he passed his final examinations to become a Doctor of Medicine with the grade of 'excellent'.

In 1882 Freud left Brücke's laboratory, where the year before he had been appointed a demonstrator. For financial reasons, probably influenced by falling in love, Freud decided to earn his living as a physician. He entered the General Hospital of Vienna, where he gained experience in various departments and became an active researcher in the Institute of Cerebral Anatomy. During this period 'with an eye to material considerations, I began to study nervous diseases' (Freud, 1935, p. 18). Because of inadequate opportunities for learning this subject, Freud was forced to be his own teacher. He published a number of clinical observations on organic diseases of the nervous system and, in 1885, was appointed lecturer in neuropathology. Around this period Freud both took cocaine and conducted research into its use. Jones (1963) observes: 'For many years he suffered from periodic depressions and fatigue or apathy, neurotic symptoms which later took the form of anxiety attacks before being dispelled by his own analysis' (pp. 54–5). Cocaine apparently calmed the agitation and eased the depression. Jones also mentions that all his life Freud was subject to severe bouts of migraine which were refractory to any treatment.

On the award of a travelling fellowship Freud went to Paris where, from October 1885 to February 1886, he studied at the Sâlpetrière (hospital for nervous diseases) under Charcot. He was very impressed with Charcot's investigations into hysteria, confirming the genuineness of hysterical phenomena, including hysterical paralyses and contractures by hypnotic suggestion. In 1886 Freud returned to Vienna to marry Martha Bernays and to set up a private practice as a specialist in nervous diseases. His 'therapeutic arsenal contained only two weapons, electrotherapy and hypnotism . . .' (Freud, 1935, p. 26). He soon dropped electrotherapy and increasingly realized the limitations of hypnotic suggestion. During the period 1886 to 1891 he did little scientific work, though in 1891 he jointly published the first of his studies on the cerebral paralyses of children.

In the early 1880s Freud had developed a close friendship with Joseph Breuer, a prominent Viennese physician, who told him how, between 1880 and 1882, he had successfully treated a young girl with hysterical symptoms. His method was to hypnotize her deeply and then encourage her to express in words her memories of earlier emotional situations which were oppressing her. In the late 1880s Freud began repeating Breuer's technique with his own patients, being aware 'of the possibility that there could be powerful mental processes which nevertheless remained hidden from the consciousness of man' (Freud, 1935, p. 29). In 1893 Freud and Breuer wrote a preliminary paper on the cathartic method and, in 1895, published their book *Studies on Hysteria*.

During the 1890s the transition from catharsis to psychoanalysis proper took place. Jones (1963) writes: 'there is ample evidence that for ten years or so – roughly comprising the nineties – he suffered from a very considerable psychoneurosis . . . yet it was just in the years when the neurosis was at its height, 1897–1900, that Freud did his most original work' (p. 194). Although he showed no conversion symptoms, he had extreme alterations of mood between elation and self-confidence, and depression and inhibition. In the latter moods Freud could neither write nor concentrate, apart from his professional work. Additionally, he had occasional attacks of dread of dying and also became very anxious about travelling by rail.

During the period 1887 to 1900 Freud had an intense friendship with Wilhelm Fleiss, a nose and throat specialist two years younger than him. Fleiss saw sexual problems as central to his own work, encouraged Freud and gave him permission to develop his theories. Jones notes Freud's dependency on Fleiss's good opinion and calls him Freud's 'sole public' during this period. Jones rated Fleiss as intellectually far inferior to Freud.

Against this background, Freud started developing his ideas on the sexual bases of neuroses, abandoned hypnotism yet retained his practice of requiring the patient to lie on a sofa while he sat behind. During 1897 to 1899, he wrote his major work, *The Interpretation of Dreams*. In the summer of 1897 Freud undertook a psychoanalysis of his own unconscious, and this self-analysis generated material for the book. Freud discovered his childhood passion for his mother and jealousy for his father, which he considered a pervasive human characteristic; he termed it the Oedipus complex. It took eight years to sell the first edition of 600 copies of *The Interpretation of Dreams*. Jones (1963) observes of Freud's self-analysis: 'The end of all that labor and suffering was the last and final phase in the evolution of Freud's personality. There emerged the serene and benign Freud, henceforth free to pursue his work in imperturbable composure' (p. 205). Fromm's (1959) biography is less kind, suggesting that Freud continued to exhibit some insecurity and egotism in areas of both his professional and his personal life. In 1905 Freud published what is perhaps his other major work, *Three Contributions to the Theory of Sex*, which traces the development of sexuality from its earliest childhood beginnings.

In his autobiographical study Freud observed that, after the preliminary cathartic period, the history of psychoanalysis falls into two phases. From 1895–6 until 1906 or 1907 he worked in isolation, but thereafter the contributions of his pupils and collaborators increasingly grew in importance. The historical development of Freud's ideas will be left at this stage. Suffice it to say that for the remainder of his life he published numerous books and articles not only on psychoanalysis as a method of treating the disturbed, but also on the relevance of his theories to everyday life. In 1910, at a congress held at Nuremberg, the analysts formed themselves into an International Psychoanalytical Association divided into a number of local societies, but under a common president. By 1935 the number of the Association's supporters had increased considerably. The growth of psychoanalysis, however, was not smooth, and it aroused considerable antipathy.

Freud was in the habit of smoking an average of twenty cigars a day and, in 1923, learned that he had cancer of the jaw. He lived the last sixteen years of his life in pain which was often extreme, and a total of 33 operations were performed on his jaw. In 1938 Nazism caused Freud to leave Austria with his family and settle in his admired England, which he had first visited when he was 19. He died in London a year later.

Freud had observed that he was by temperament a conquistador or adventurer, with the accompanying traits of curiosity, boldness and tenacity. A modern term for Freud might be an 'ideas person'.

THEORY

Where id was, there shall ego be.
Sigmund Freud

BASIC CONCEPTS

Although many of Freud's basic concepts are to be found in *The Interpretation of Dreams*, he was developing and refining his ideas continuously. Thus the same concept may appear in different sources, only some of which will be mentioned here. In general, this chapter represents Freud's later presentation of his work.

The pleasure principle

Originally presented as the unpleasure principle, the pleasure principle follows from the constancy hypothesis that 'the mental apparatus endeavours to keep the quantity of excitation in it as low as possible or at least to keep it constant' (Freud, 1961, p. 3). Thus everything which increases the quantity of excitation will be felt as unpleasurable and anything which diminishes it will be experienced as pleasurable. Freud qualified the idea of the dominance of the pleasure principle by observing that, although in the mind there exists a strong tendency towards the pleasure principle, there are also other forces opposing it, with the final outcome not always fulfilling the tendency towards pleasure.

The instincts

Instincts represent somatic or biological demands upon the mind. While acknowledging the possibility of distinguishing many instincts, Freud assumed that these could be grouped into two basic instincts, *Eros* and the *destructive instinct*. The erotic instincts 'seek to combine more and more living substance into even greater unities', while the death instincts 'oppose this effort and lead what is living back to an inorganic state' (Freud, 1973, p. 140). Eros includes the instincts of self-preservation, the preservation of the species, ego-love and object-love, and its energy is called *libido*. Throughout life the basic instincts may either work together (for instance the sexual act is also an act of aggression) or oppose each other.

Freud saw instincts as historically acquired and conservative, and stated: 'It seems, then, that an instinct is an urge inherent in life to restore an earlier state of things' (Freud, 1961, p. 30). Given the assumption that living things appeared later than inanimate ones and arose out of them, the death instinct may be viewed as a compulsion to repeat this earlier inorganic state. Consequently, the aim of all life is death. Eros, however, does not follow the same formula. Freud considered that sexual instincts were the single exception among the instincts in not seeking to restore an earlier state of things.

Freud viewed the inclination to aggression as an original instinctual disposition in humans. He quoted Plautus: '*Homo homini lupus*', a translation of which is 'Man is a wolf to man'. The aggressive instinct is the derivative and main representative of the death instinct. The evolution of civilization represents the struggle between the life and death instincts in the human species. The fateful question that Freud posed at the end of *Civilization and its Discontents* was whether Eros would assert itself, 'But who can foresee with what success and what results?' (Freud, 1962c, p. 92).

The unconscious and consciousness

Heavily influenced by his study of dreams, Freud made a distinction between the unconscious and consciousness. From the very beginning, he stated that there were two kinds of unconscious. Hence, Freud asserted that there were three levels of consciousness.

The unconscious

The unconscious (Ucs), or unconscious proper, is material that is inadmissible to consciousness through repression. In other words, with the unconscious the censorship on material coming into awareness is very strong indeed. The object of psychoanalysis is to help make some of this material accessible to awareness, though during the process strong resistances may be aroused, not least because of the forbidden sexual connotations of much of what is being repressed.

The preconscious

The preconscious (Pcs) consists of everything that can easily exchange the unconscious state for the conscious one. Thus the preconscious is latent and capable of becoming conscious, while the unconscious is repressed and is unlikely to become conscious without great difficulty. Material may remain in the preconscious, though usually it finds its way into consciousness without any need for psychoanalytic intervention. The preconscious may be viewed as a screen between the unconscious and consciousness, with, as in the case of dreams, modifications being made in unconscious material through censorship.

Consciousness

Consciousness (Cs or Pcpt Cs) has the function of a sense organ for the perception of psychical qualities. Unlike the two kinds of unconscious, consciousness has no memory and a state of consciousness is usually very transitory. Material becomes conscious, or flows into the consciousness sense-organ, from two directions: the external world and inner excitations. Furthermore, the function of speech enables internal events such as sequences of ideas and intellectual processes to become conscious.

Structure of the mental apparatus

Freud structured the mental apparatus into three systems or agencies: the id, the ego and the super-ego. Psychological well-being depends on whether these three systems are interrelating effectively. Box 2.1 shows Freud's own sketch of the structural relations of the mental apparatus, though he acknowledges that the space occupied by the unconscious id ought to have been much greater (Freud, 1973, p. 111).

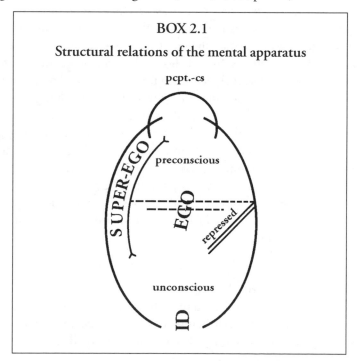

BOX 2.1

Structural relations of the mental apparatus

pcpt.-cs

SUPER-EGO

preconscious

EGO

repressed

unconscious

ID

The id

The id or 'it' is the oldest of these systems and contains everything that is inherited and fixed in the constitution. The instincts, which originate in the somatic organization, find their mental expression in the id. The id, filled with energy from the instincts, strives to bring about the satisfaction of instinctual needs on the basis of the pleasure principle. Thus the activity of the id is directed towards securing the free discharge of quantities of excitation. The psychical processes of the id are known as primary processes because they are present in the mental apparatus from the first. Furthermore, no alteration in the id's mental processes is produced by the passage of time. Freud viewed the id as 'a chaos, a cauldron full of seething emotions', which 'knows no judgements of values: no good and evil, no morality' (Freud, 1973, pp. 106–7). The id consists of wishful impulses. It is not governed by logic, and this applies especially to the law of contradiction, since it contains contrary impulses side by side. In short, the id is the individual's primary subjective reality at the unconscious level.

The ego

The ego or 'I' is first and foremost a bodily ego ultimately derived from bodily sensations, in particular those coming from its surface. The ego is a portion of the id which has undergone a special development or modification through the influence of the external world. The ego acts as an intermediary between the id and the external world and ideally represents reason and common sense, whereas the id contains instinctual passions and would destroy itself without the intervention of the ego. The ego strives to bring the reality principle to bear upon the id in substitution for the pleasure principle. The processes of the ego, which include perception, problem solving and repression, are later developments or secondary processes, in contrast to the original or primary processes of the id. Nevertheless, the ego seeks pleasure and the avoidance of unpleasure, differing from the id only in the means of attaining common ends. A foreseen increase in unpleasure is met by a signal of anxiety. As Box 2.1 shows, the perceptual-conscious system is the outer layer of the ego, which also includes much preconscious and unconscious material.

The ego is in control of voluntary movement, but interposes thought between experiencing a need and acting on it. The ego deals with external events through perception, memory, avoiding excessive stimuli, adapting to moderate stimuli, and engaging in activities designed to modify the external world to its advantage. Regarding internal events in relation to the id, the ego attempts to control instinctual demands by deciding the timing and manner of their gratification or by suppressing their excitations. Freud makes the analogy of the id being the horse, while the ego is the rider. He observes that often, however, the ego is weak in relation to the id and so is in the habit of transforming the id's will into action as if it were its own.

The super-ego

The super-ego is a residue formed within the ego in which parental influence is prolonged. Parental influence may be defined broadly as including cultural, racial and family influences. As the person grows up, the nature of the 'parental' influence may vary, partly because parents may behave differently. Also, teachers, admired figures in public life and many others may contribute to the development of an individual's super-ego, which normally departs more and more from original parental influences.

The function of the super-ego, which engages in self-observation, is to contain the demands of the id through moral influence on the ego. Originally the child engages in instinctual renunciation through fear of loss of love or through fear of aggression from an *external* or parental authority. Subsequently a secondary situation develops in which the external restraint is internalized and thus instinctual renunciation comes about through fear of an *internal* authority, or super-ego.

A characteristic of the super-ego is the ego-ideal, based on the admiration which the child felt for the perfection it saw in its parents and which it strives to emulate. In fact the terms 'super-ego' and 'ego-ideal' are virtually synonymous. The ego-ideal consists of both precepts – 'You ought to be like this' – and prohibitions – 'You ought not to be like that.' These precepts and prohibitions are based in part on the identifications and repressions resulting from the resolution of the Oedipus complex. They represent the individual's conscience, transgressions of which are likely to result in a sense of inferiority and guilt and also possibly in a need for punishment. Freud observed: 'The super-ego is the representative for us of every moral restriction, the advocate of a striving towards perfection – it is, in short, as much as we have been able to grasp psychologically of what is described as the higher side of human life' (Freud, 1973, p. 98).

In addition to the demands of the instincts and of the external world, the ego has to take into account the demands of the super-ego. Individuals vary in the severity of their super-egos, which may be benign or punitively harsh and restricting. Conflicts can arise between ego and super-ego, with large portions of both agencies remaining unconscious.

Anxiety

Freud defined anxiety as a specific state of unpleasure accompanied by motor discharge along definite pathways. He saw anxiety as the universal reaction to the situation of danger and the ego as the sole seat of anxiety. In later life, a source of anxiety which is involuntary occurs whenever a dangerous situation arises. Another source is anxiety generated by the ego when danger is merely threatened and the ego feels weak in relation to it. Hence there are three kinds of anxiety, one for each of the ego's three 'taskmasters':

1. *realistic* anxiety regarding the dangers of the external world;
2. *moral* anxiety regarding conflict with the super-ego; and
3. *neurotic* anxiety regarding conflict with the strength of the id's instinctual impulses.

Thus anxiety is either a reaction to actual danger or a signal involving the perception of impending danger.

Psychical energy, cathexis and anti-cathexis

Psychoanalysis is often referred to as having a dynamic view of psychology. What this means is that the concept of psychical or mental energy and its distribution among the id, ego and super-ego is central to psychoanalysis. The id is the source of this somatically based psychical energy, being filled with energy reaching it from the instincts. Sexual excitation is an example of instinctual psychical energy. As the ego and the super-ego are formed they also become charged with energy.

The words 'cathexis' and to 'cathect' describe the idea of psychical energy being drawn to mental agencies and processes, somewhat analogous to an electric charge. Cathexes are the charges of instinctual energy seeking discharge, whereas anti-cathexes are charges of energy which block and inhibit such discharge. The id has only primary-process instinctual cathexes seeking discharge. However, the ego and the super-ego have both urging cathexes and restraining anti-cathexes. Throughout life the ego is the avenue by which libidinal cathexes are transferred to objects and into which they may also be withdrawn again. Two characteristics of libidinal cathexes are mobility, the ease with which they pass from one object to another, and, in contrast, fixation, or being bound to particular objects.

Bisexuality

Freud observed that it was a long-known anatomical fact that in every normally formed male or female there are traces of the apparatus of the other sex, though in atrophied form. Anatomically there may have been an original predisposition to bisexuality, which in the course of the development of the human species has largely been altered to monosexuality.

Psychologically Freud considered that the sexual impulse is probably entirely independent of its object and therefore is not originated by chemical attraction. Another way of stating this is that there is only one libido and it cannot be assigned a sex. Therefore the direction of both heterosexual and homosexual object selection requires further explanation. By studying covert sexual excitations, psychoanalytic research discovered that all men were capable of homosexual object selection and actually accomplish this in the unconscious. Furthermore, homosexual libidinous feelings 'play no small role as factors in normal psychic life' and an even greater role as 'causative factors of disease' (Freud, 1962a, p. 10).

Freud considered that the same free attachment to male and female objects as observed in childhood and primitive and prehistoric states forms the basis on which both normal and homosexual or inverted sexual development takes place. A degree of homosexuality is congenital in everyone, with the final determination of sexual behaviour being the result of the intensity of constitutional predisposition as well as of life experiences and restrictions in one or the other direction. Both the woman and the man develop out of a child with a bisexual disposition.

ACQUISITION
Infantile sexuality and amnesia

Freud distinguished between the sexual impulse, the sexual object, and the sexual aim. The sexual impulse is the sexual aspect of libido, the sexual object is the person in whom sexual attraction is lodged, and the sexual aim refers to the action, such as touch or intercourse, towards which the sexual impulse strives. Freud further made a sharp distinction between 'sexual' and 'genital', considering that sexual life consists of gaining pleasure from erotogenic zones of the body and that this is not necessarily in the service of reproduction. Additionally, sexual life includes affectionate and friendly impulses often called 'love'. In a sense, all adult sexual behaviour whose goal is not reproduction, a heterosexual object and intercourse may be considered perverse. Adult sexual behaviour does not suddenly emerge at puberty but has developed out of prior sexual dispositions and experiences.

Sexual life starts soon after birth. Infantile sexuality, in the absence of genital maturation and of ego and super-ego development, lacks a central co-ordinating focus. Instead the component sexual instincts seek their own pleasure. Infantile sexuality is fundamentally auto-erotic in that the infant finds its pleasure in the object of its own body. Freud considered that the infantile sexual disposition contained great tendencies to perversion and that normal sexual behaviour develops partly in response to organic changes and partly as a result of psychic inhibitions and repressions.

The years of childhood are when the individual is most impressionable. Nevertheless, people are largely unaware of the beginnings of their sexual life and tend to view their childhood as if it were a prehistoric time. However, infantile and childhood sexual experiences leave deep traces in the individual's psychical life, acting as significant determinants for future development. Freud used the term 'infantile amnesia' to refer to the phenomenon by which a veil is drawn over early sexual experiences.

Sexual development

The onset of sexual life is diphasic. The first or pre-genital stage of sexual development is a steady process that reaches a climax towards the end of a child's fifth year. After this there is a lull or period of latency. The second or genital stage starts with the re-emergence of the sexual impulse at menarche or puberty. The pre-genital and genital stages of sexual organization are distinguished by whether or not the genital zones have assumed a dominating role.

The pre-genital stage (birth to about age 6)

The pre-genital stage itself consists of three separate phases of sexual organization through which individuals normally pass smoothly, though fixations or arrested development may occur at each phase. Both sexes seem to pass through the early stages of sexual development in the same manner.

Oral phase (first eighteen months)

The first organ to be an erotogenic zone is the mouth, and hence sexual development starts with the *oral* phase. The infant's act of sucking goes beyond that needed for the taking of nourishment to what may be viewed as the seeking of sexual organ-pleasure independent of nourishment. The oral phase can be further subdivided. The first sub-stage is where there is a focus only on oral incorporation, whereas the second sub-stage is 'oral-sadistic', with the emergence of biting activity. These two sub-stages of the oral phase are the first manifestation of the phenomenon of ambivalence.

Anal phase (eighteen months to 3 years of age)
The second organ to become an erotogenic zone is the anus, and normal sexual development proceeds from the oral to the *sadistic-anal* phase. The active aspect of this phase is the impulse for mastery (sadism), with the strengthening of the musculature of the body and control of sphincter functions. The erotogenic mucous membrane of the anus also manifests itself as an organ with a passive sexual aim. Character traits associated with this phase are orderliness, parsimony and obstinacy, which together define the so-called 'anal character'.

Phallic phase (from about age 3 to 5 or 6)
The third organ to become an erotogenic zone is the genital apparatus. The period of sexual development in which the male sexual organ (the phallus) and the female clitoris become important is known as the *phallic* phase, which starts in about the child's third year. Here pleasure is obtained from masturbation. During the phallic phase the sexuality of early childhood reaches its greatest intensity and it is during this phase that male and female sexual development become differentiated. The *Oedipus* phase is part of the phallic phase for both sexes (see Box 2.2).

The latency period (about age 6 to 12)
The period from around the beginning of the child's sixth year, probably later for girls, to menarche and puberty constitutes the sexual latency period. Latency may be total or partial and, during this period, sexual inhibitions develop. One of the mechanisms by which sexual energy is diverted is called sublimation or the displacement of libido to new aims and cultural pursuits. Furthermore, as the individual develops, libidinous impulses may call forth contrary anti-cathexes or reactions (reaction formations) such as disgust, shame and morality.

The genital stage (age about 12 and then onwards)
The *genital* stage, which starts at menarche or puberty, involves the subordination of all sources of sexual feeling to the primacy of the genital zones. Earlier libidinal cathexes may be retained, included in sexual activity or preliminary or auxiliary acts, or in some way repressed or diverted. Puberty brings a greater increase of libido in boys, but in girls there is an increase in repression, especially regarding clitoral sexuality. Also at menarche and puberty, along with the overcoming of incestuous object-choices, comes the breaking away from parental authority. Given a reasonably adequate prior sexual development, the individual is now ready to engage in a heterosexual genital relationship.

Identification

Identification is an important concept for understanding ego and super-ego development. Identification may be viewed in three ways:

BOX 2.2

The Oedipus complex

For boys

At an early age the little boy develops an object-cathexis for his mother and identifies with his father. During the phallic phase the body's libidinal object-cathexis of his mother intensifies and he wishes to get rid of his father and to take his father's place with his mother. The threat of castration causes the boy to abandon and repress his incestuous wishes. The resolution of the boy's Oedipus complex involves renouncing his object-cathexis of his mother, which may lead to an identification with his mother or, more normally, to an intensification of his identification with his father, consolidating the masculinity in his character. The Oedipus situation is often more complex because of the child's bisexual disposition. Thus, instead of affection for his mother and ambivalence towards his father, he may have a mixture of affection for and ambivalence towards each parent. Freud observes that 'in both sexes the relative strength of the masculine and feminine sexual dispositions is what determines whether the outcome of the Oedipus situation shall be an identification with the father or with the mother' (Freud, 1962b, p. 23). Perhaps it is more accurate to consider the outcome as a predominant rather than an exclusive identification with one or the other parent. Freud further asserts that, especially with neurotics, a bisexual Oedipus complex should be assumed.

For girls

As with the boy, the girl's mother is the first object of her love. During the phallic phase the clitoris is her predominant erotogenic zone. Freud considered that during the girl's development to femininity she should change both her predominant erotogenic zone (to the vagina) and also the sex of her love object. The powerful attachment of the girl to her mother is ended when the girl, discovering the inferiority of her clitoris and the fact that she does not have a penis, holds her mother responsible. Penis envy or the wish for a penis is a very important feminine trait. The wish for a penis-baby from the father replaces the wish for a penis, and it is at this stage that the girl has entered her Oedipus situation, desiring her father and wishing to be rid of her mother. Again the situation may be complicated by her bisexual disposition. Girls remain in their Oedipus situation for an indeterminate length of time and resolve it late and often incompletely. Whereas the boy is encouraged to surmount the Oedipus complex through fear of castration, the girl has no such motivation. As time goes by the female Oedipus complex weakens, partly as a result of inevitable disappointments from her father.

1. as the original form of emotional tie with an object;
2. as a regressive substitute for a libidinal object-tie by means of introjection of the object with the ego, so that the ego assumes the characteristics of the object (e.g. a female patient imitating her father's cough); and
3. as a feeling generated by the perception of a common quality with another person who is not libidinally cathected.

The development of the super-ego may be seen in terms of identification with the parental agency, by which young people, wishing to be like their parents, mould their egos after the fashion of those taken as their models. Identification is part of the normal process of development. However, the ego may be restricted, as well as enhanced, depending on the nature of the identification.

Defence mechanisms

During the child's early years its ego is relatively feeble, yet it has to deal with strong instinctual sexual impulses. At this stage anxiety may be generated by loss of an object or loss of love, which may persist into later life. Later sources of anxiety include fear of castration during the phallic phase, and fear of the super-ego during and after the latency period.

In order to cope with the sources of anxiety the ego utilizes defence mechanisms. Freud doubted that the ego could do without them during normal development. In many instances, however, the ego pays a high price for the use of the mechanisms, since they restrict its functioning, also using in their anti-cathexes psychical energy which might better be expended elsewhere. Defence mechanisms are infantilisms which operate unconsciously and may impede realistic behaviour long after they have outlived their usefulness. Individuals do not make use of all the possible mechanisms of defence, but select some, which become fixated in their egos. The establishment of defensive mechanisms is largely a feature of the child's struggle against its sexuality during the first five years of life. Box 2.3 describes the five main defensive ways in which the ego strives to contain the threatening instinctual cathexis when the ego observes that an emerging instinctual demand may place it in danger.

Normal development

To summarize, the Freudian view of the normal development of personality may be seen in terms of three interrelated strands.

1. The individual's libidinal development, which starts with a mixture of constitutional and infantile predispositions which mature into genital sexuality in successive but overlapping phases, interrupted by the latency period.
2. The development of both the ego, as it gains in ability to mediate between instinctual demands and the reality of the external world, and the super-ego, based on identifications with parental influences.

BOX 2.3

The ego's main mechanisms of defence

Repression   Purposely forgetting something and remaining unaware of having done this. The process of repression is of two kinds:

1. material which is in the preconscious and hence admissible to consciousness is pushed back into the unconscious; and
2. unconscious material may be forbidden by censorship to enter the preconscious and hence has to remain unconscious.

For example, either kind of repression might apply to an individual's latent sexually perverted impulses. Repression is the central underlying defensive mechanism of the ego, the basis of all other defences.

Reaction-formation   Adopting thoughts, feelings and behaviours that are the opposite to one's true thoughts and feelings. The ego acknowledges impulses contrary to the ones by which it is threatened. For instance, sexual impulses may be warded off by excessive shame, disgust and loathing of sexuality.

Projection   The ego deals with the threat of an unacceptable instinctual impulse by externalizing it. Thus individuals, instead of acknowledging the extent of their own libidinal and aggressive impulses, may become very aware of such characteristics in others and actually attribute them incorrectly.

Fixation   Where people get highly anxious about moving on to the next phase of their sexual development, they may lag behind or become fixated in varying degrees to an earlier stage in terms of satisfaction of their instincts. For instance, children may cling dependently to their mothers' love rather than make new object-cathexes.

Regression   Resuming behaviours appropriate to an earlier stage of sexual development. Under threat, an individual returns to an earlier phase at which he or she may previously have been fixated. In fact, regressions may be of two kinds: a return to the incestuous objects first cathected by the libido, and a return of the sexual organization as a whole to an earlier phase.

---

3. The establishment of favoured defensive mechanisms on the part of the ego to ward off the anxiety caused by the strength and persistence of the id's libidinal impulses.

Thus normal development may be viewed as passing through successive stages of sexual maturation without major fixations and regressions, developing an ego which copes reasonably effectively with the external world, developing a super-ego based on identifications which are constructive and not punitively moralistic, and evolving defensive mechanisms which drain off some of the energy of the id without serious restriction of ego functioning. Normal development is a dynamic process entailing a continuing distribution and redistribution of psychical energy among id, ego and super-ego, the three systems of the mental apparatus.

Development and activation of neurosis

Freud saw biological, phylogenetic and psychological factors as each contributing to neurosis.

The *biological* factor is that the human animal is born relatively unfinished and thus has to undergo a protracted period of helplessness and dependence. This helplessness creates the initial situation of danger regarding fear of object loss, which in turn creates the human's need to be loved, which it never renounces.

The *phylogenetic* factor is inferred from the interruption in human sexual development of the latency period, whereas the sexual maturation of related animals proceeds uninterrupted. Freud believed that something momentous must have taken place in the history of the human species to bring about this situation and that its pathogenic importance is that most of the instinctual demands of infantile sexuality are treated as dangers to be guarded against by the ego. Furthermore, there is the danger that the sexual impulses of puberty will follow their infantile prototypes into repression.

The *psychological* factor involves three elements which together make for a pathogenic neurotic conflict.

1. *Frustration of sexual impulses* or the damming up of the sexual instinct by the ego. Repressions are especially likely to take place in infancy and early childhood, when the ego is underdeveloped and feeble in relation to the strength of the sexual impulses. Freud observed: 'We recognise the essential precondition of neuroses in this lagging of ego development behind libidinal development' (Freud, 1949, p. 113). The process of repression takes place under the influence of anxiety, in that the ego anticipates that satisfaction of the emerging sexual cathexis will lead to danger. In fact the ego allows an initial reproduction of the feared unpleasure. This feeling of anxiety brings the unpleasure–pleasure mechanism into operation and so causes the ego to repress the dangerous instinctual impulse. By the act of repression, however, the ego has renounced a portion of its organization and the repressed instinctual impulse remains inaccessible to its influence.
2. *Transformation of frustrated sexual impulses into neurotic symptoms.* Frustrated sexual impulses may not disappear, instead getting transformed into neurotic symptoms. Freud saw symptoms such as hysterical or conversion symptoms as the substitute satisfactions for the frustrated sexual instincts. Repression, however, does not always result in symptom formation. For instance, in a successful dissolution of the Oedipus complex the repressed sexual impulses may be destroyed, with their libido being put permanently to other uses.
3. *Inadequacy of previously used repressions.* While repressions may be effective during early childhood and the latency period, they may turn out to be inadequate with the

reawakening and intensification of the sexual instincts at menarche and puberty. When this occurs the individual may experience an intense neurotic conflict with all its suffering. Without assistance in undoing its repressions, the ego will have little or no influence over the transformed instincts of the repressed id. Furthermore, the conflict is often heightened through an alliance of the id and super-ego against the ego.

BOX 2.4

Examples of normal and neurotic development

Freud (1973) gives as an example of normal and neurotic development the story of the caretaker's and the landlord's little daughters. When young, the two girls played games which took on a sexual character, including exciting each other's genitals. These experiences awakened sexual impulses which afterwards found expression in masturbation.

Normal development   The caretaker's daughter, unscarred by her early sexual activity, which she regarded as natural and harmless, took a lover and became a mother.

Neurotic development   While still a child the landlord's daughter, as a result of education, got the idea that she had done something wrong. She turned into an intelligent and high-minded girl who renounced her sexuality and whose subsequent neurosis precluded her from marrying. While consciously unaware of her sexual impulses, unconsciously these impulses were still attached to her experiences with the caretaker's daughter. Freud observes that, owing to the higher moral and intellectual development of her ego, she came into conflict with the demands of her sexuality.

MAINTENANCE

Freud considered that neuroses are acquired only during early childhood, up to the age of 6, even though the symptoms of the neurotic conflict may not appear until much later. He acknowledged the truth of the common assertion that the child is psychologically father of the man or woman. Neurotic people, despite their suffering, are unable to heal their disordered egos and thus their misery is maintained. The reason for this is that, by definition, the significant repressions made by their weak childhood egos are unconscious. Thus their egos pay the price of their defensive operations by not having conscious access to the material through which the neurotic conflict might be resolved. Neurotic people's egos are weakened by their repressions and their personality functioning is impaired by psychical energy being utilized in harmful defensive anti-cathexes. Also, as long as the repressions continue, so do the conditions for the formation of neurotic symptoms through the rechannelling of frustrated libidinous impulses.

In a broader sense, maintenance of neurosis results from the unsatisfactory way in which society tries to regulate sexual matters. Freud considered that what is described as morality, or the group super-ego, requires a bigger sacrifice of libidinal impulses than is necessary or desirable. He found it impossible to side with conventional sexual morality and considered that anyone with real self-knowledge would be protected against the dangers of morality, while possibly adopting a lifestyle different from the conventions of their society.

THERAPY

The interpretation of dreams is the royal road to a knowledge of the unconscious activities of the mind.

Sigmund Freud

THERAPEUTIC GOALS

The goals of psychoanalysis are threefold:

1. *a less constricted id* – the freeing of impulse;
2. *a stronger ego* – the strengthening of reality-based ego functioning, including widening its perceptions so that it appropriates more of the id; and
3. *a more humane super-ego* – the alteration of the contents of the super-ego so that it represents humane rather than punitive moral standards.

A definition of a neurotic is someone who is incapable of enjoyment and efficiency. To be capable of enjoyment neurotics require the ability to deploy their libido onto real objects instead of transforming it into symptoms. To live efficiently the ego needs to have the energy of the libido at its disposal rather than wasting energy in warding off libidinous impulses through repression. Furthermore, people's super-egos need to be such as to allow them libidinal expression and the efficient use of their egos.

Freud considered psychoanalytic treatment effective for a number of nervous diseases, such as hysteria, anxiety states and obsessional neurosis. Since the alliance between the analyst and the client's ego is a mutual one, the client's ego needs to have retained a minimum degree of coherence or reality orientation. This is not to be expected with psychotics, with whom, therefore, psychoanalysis is contra-indicated.

PROCESS OF THERAPY

Freud saw the practice of psychoanalysis as having three main parts:

1. inducing clients' weakened egos to participate in the intellectual work of interpretation to fill in the gaps of their mental resources and transfer to their analysts the authority of their super-egos;
2. stimulating clients' egos to struggle against each of the id's demands and to defeat the resistances arising in connection with them; and
3. restoring order to clients' egos 'by detecting material and impulses which have forced their way in from the unconscious' (Freud, 1949, p. 77). Such material is both traced back to its origin and exposed to criticism.

Psychoanalysis is a process of re-educating the ego. Repressions were instituted when clients' egos were weak. However, now not only have clients' egos grown stronger, but they possess allies in analysts. Methods by which analysts help weakened egos to lift their repressions, gain insight and make realistic decisions are discussed below. The pathogenic conflicts of neurotics are different from normal mental conflicts because of the ego's weakness relative to the other mental agencies.

Classical psychoanalytic therapy often involves at least four sessions a week with each session lasting for a minimum of 45 minutes. A course of psychoanalytic therapy may last for several years (Arlow, 2000). Freud considered ultimately the success of psycho-analysis depended upon the quantitative relationship between the amount of energy analysts can mobilize in clients to their advantage in comparison with the amount of energy of the forces working against them.

THE THERAPEUTIC RELATIONSHIP

As I write this section, I am looking at pictures of Freud's consulting rooms in Vienna and Hampstead. In each, there is a couch which has no back, but one end is raised so that the client's head may comfortably rest there. Cushions are placed at back of the couch against the wall. A Middle-Eastern rug hangs on the wall just above the couch, which itself has a thick Middle-Eastern cover. Freud's tub chair facing into the room is placed against the wall behind the raised part of the couch. The nature and positioning of the furniture in psychoanalysis indicates that this is going to be a relationship far removed from normal social interaction: for example, the client cannot see the therapist who, in turn, cannot directly see the client's face.

Seated behind the couch and thus physically keeping out of the way, the analyst encourages the client to say whatever comes into her or his mind without censorship. A major feature of the therapeutic relationship is the development of transference, which is discussed below.

As well as the positioning of client and therapist, a number of other features of the therapist–client relationship aim to encourage clients to reveal the intimate secrets of their minds. Therapists remain anonymous in terms of their own personal life and views. Furthermore, any form of immature personal gratification from the therapeutic relation-ship is forbidden: for instance, meeting the therapist's own needs for friendship and affection. In addition, confidentiality is strictly observed.

Analysts keep their relationships with clients formal. At the same time they are intensely involved with helping clients gain insight, compassionate, yet emotionally detached. Much power resides with analysts who, like Freud, decide which interpreta-tions are valid and when and how their clients are resisting the therapeutic process.

The practical aspects of the therapeutic contract are strictly regulated. For example, clients are expected to adhere to a fixed schedule of appointments and fees. However, even Freud had problems with bad debts, one of which contributed to the following slip of the tongue and possibly reveals the unconscious fulfilment of a wish. Freud reported repeatedly addressing a patient, Mrs James, who was refusing to pay for her treatment, as Mrs Smith, who paid her fees promptly (Freud, 1960).

THERAPEUTIC INTERVENTIONS

Free Association

A basic pact lies at the heart of analytic relationships. Freud (1949) stated: 'The patient's sick ego promises us the most complete candor, . . . we, on the other hand, assure him of the strictest discretion and put at his service our experience in interpreting material that has been influenced by the unconscious' (p. 63). The fundamental rule for clients is that of free association. Clients must tell their analysts everything that occurs to them, even if it is disagreeable and even if it seems meaningless. As far as possible, clients are encouraged to put their self-criticism out of action and share all their thoughts, feelings, ideas, memories and their associations. The object of free association is to help lift repressions by making unconscious material conscious.

Transference

From early in his career Freud attached great importance to his relationships with clients. He discovered that clients perceive their analysts as reincarnations of important figures from their childhoods and transfer onto them moderate to intense feelings and emotions appropriate to these earlier models. Freud speaks of transference-love and observes that this love is ambivalent, being a mixture of affection with a reverse side of hostility, exclusiveness and jealousy. The transference represents a development of the original neurosis into a transference neurosis in relation to the analyst.

The transference has at least three advantages.

1. It may start by being positive, which helps analysts, since their clients work to please them. The weak ego can become stronger and the client achieve gains out of love for the analyst.
2. When clients place analysts in the places of their fathers or mothers, they give them access to the power their super-egos have over their egos. Analysts as new super-egos can use their power for 'a sort of *after-education* of the neurotic' (Freud, 1949, p. 67). They can remedy earlier errors in parental education. However, analysts need always respect their clients' need for independence.
3. In the transference clients reproduce, rather than just remember, important parts of their life history. They act out in front of their analysts mental attitudes and defensive reactions connected with their neuroses.

Almost invariably the transference becomes negative and hostile, thus turning into a resistance. The onset of the negative transference is connected with analysts frustrating their clients by being unwilling to satisfy their erotic demands towards them. The revival of pathogenic conflicts gives analysts access to much-repressed material, insight into which helps to strengthen their clients' egos.

Handling the transference is a critical skill of analysts, who must again and again show clients the prototype of their feelings in their childhoods. Analysts need take care that transferences do not get out of hand. They can forewarn clients of this possibility and be alert to early signs of this happening. Also, they can encourage clients not to act out their transferences outside of the analytic setting.

Resistance

Free association is not really free, in that clients associate within the context of the analytic situation. Thus everything that occurs to them has some reference to that situation and they are likely to resist reproducing the repressed material. At its simplest level, resistance involves intentionally not adhering to the fundamental rule. Even if this level of resistance is overcome, resistance will find less obvious means of expression. The client's ego is fearful of potential unpleasure caused by exploring material that it has repressed in the unconscious. The ego protects itself from the repressed id by means of anti-cathexes. The more threatening the repressed material is, the more tenaciously the ego clings to its anti-cathexes and the more remote are clients' associations from the unconscious material that their analysts seek.

Freud described all the forces that oppose the work of recovery as clients' resistances. He outlined five kinds of resistance:

1. The repression resistance described above.
2. The transference resistance mentioned earlier.
3. The resistance to forgoing the gain from illness.
4. The resistance of the id, which may resist a change in the direction of its satisfaction and need to 'work through' to a new mode of satisfaction.
5. The resistance, emanating from the super-ego, of the unconscious sense of guilt or need for punishment which resists any success through analysis. Clients must remain ill for they deserve no better. This is the most powerful kind of resistance and the one analysts most dread.

The struggle to overcome resistances is the main work of psychoanalysis and this part of analytic treatment cannot easily be hurried. Forces helping analysts to overcome resistances are clients' needs for recovery, any intellectual interest they may have in the analytic process and, most important, their positive transferences with their analysts.

Interpretation

Interpretations are constructions or explanations. They can focus both on what has happened to clients and been forgotten, and on what is now happening to clients without their understanding it. Interpretation is the means by which material that is repressed and unconscious is transformed into preconscious material and consciousness.

Analysts employ interpretation not only to understand the impulses of the id, but also to help clients to gain insight into the defensive mechanisms and resistances that their egos use both to cope with the repressed material and to thwart the analytic endeavour. Part of the work of interpretation consists of filling in memory gaps. Analysts interpret the impulses that have become subject to repression and the objects to which they have become attached with the aim of helping clients to replace these repressions by acts of judgement appropriate to their present-day rather than to their childhood situations. The analyst works with the client's ego, encouraging it to overcome resistances and to take control of her hitherto repressed libidinal energy. Unconscious impulses are exposed to criticism by being traced back to their origin.

The material for interpretation is obtained from a number of sources. These include the clients' free associations, parapraxes or slips of the tongue, dreams, and their transference relationships with their analysts. Analysts need to clearly distinguish between their own and their clients' knowledge. Appropriate timing of interpretations is very important, since if attempted at the wrong time, they meet with resistance. Therefore clients need to be very near to the moment of insight before analysts make interpretations. Also, the closer interpretations are to the details of what has been forgotten, the easier it is for clients to accept them. The later stages of psychoanalysis involve a working through by repeated interpretations, and this is often the most difficult and frequently an incomplete part of analysis.

Interpretation of dreams

Interpreting dreams represents an important – sometimes the most important – part of the analyst's work. When Freud's clients were told to communicate to him every idea or thought that occurred in relation to a particular topic, among other things they told him their dreams. This taught Freud that 'a dream can be inserted into the psychical chain that has to be traced backwards in the memory from a pathological idea' (Freud, 1976, p. 175). During sleep the ego reduces its repression and thus unconscious material becomes conscious in the shape of dreams. Freud saw dreams as wish-fulfilments, being the disguised fulfilment of repressed wishes. However, even in sleep the ego still retains some censorship over repressed material and the latent dream thoughts are distorted so as to make the manifest dream content less threatening. Dreams, in fact, are compromises between repressed id impulses and the defensive operation of the ego.

The interpretation of a dream involves understanding the latent dream thoughts which are disguised by the process of dream work. Elements of dream work involve condensing the latent dream thoughts into a much smaller dream content, displacing the psychical intensity between elements, and using symbolism. Frequently, symbols in dreams represent sexual material. For instance, all elongated objects, such as sticks, tree trunks, knives, daggers and umbrellas may stand for the penis. The opening of an umbrella may symbolize an erection. Boxes, cases, chests, cupboards and ovens represent the uterus. A dream of going through a suite of rooms is a brothel or harem dream. Not all dream symbols are sexual: for instance, emperors or empresses may represent parents.

Freud prepared clients in two ways for working with their dreams. First, he asked them to increase the attention that they paid to their psychical perceptions. To enhance this, it was advantageous that they 'lie in a restful attitude' (Freud, 1976, p. 175). However, he soon abandoned stressing that they need shut their eyes. Second, he explicitly insisted that clients abandon all criticism of the thoughts that they perceived (a feature of free association). Clients differed in the ease with which they could adopt the required mental attitude and abandon their critical functions.

Box 2.5 provides a brief illustration, taken from *The Interpretation of Dreams*, of Freud interpreting one of his own dreams (Freud, 1976, pp. 180–99). Dream interpretation can be a complex, multi-layered and lengthy process. For example, Freud took about twenty pages to describe the interpretation of the dream illustrated in Box 2.5. Also, in his famous study of Dora, a case of hysteria, Freud's descriptions of his interpretations of her first and second dreams take up about thirty and twenty pages respectively (Freud, 1963).

BOX 2.5

An example of dream interpretation

The context   Freud had been giving psychoanalytic treatment to Irma, a good friend of his and his family's. The treatment was partially successful in that Irma was relieved of her hysterical anxiety, but without losing all somatic symptoms. One day Freud received a visit from a junior colleague called Otto, who had been staying with Irma and her family at a country resort. Otto answered Freud's enquiry about Irma with: 'She's better, but not quite well.' Freud was annoyed with Otto's words, detecting reproof in them. That evening he wrote out Irma's case history with the idea of giving it to Dr M, a common friend.

The dream   The following night or morning, Freud had a dream, which he noted down as soon as he awoke. The dream involved Irma, Otto, Dr M, and a friend called Leopold. Without going into great detail, in the dream Otto was implicated in infecting Irma by giving her an injection with a syringe that was probably unclean.

The interpretation of the dream   The conclusion of Freud's interpretation of his dream was that, in it, he was not responsible for the persistence of Irma's present pains, rather Otto was. Freud observed of his dream: '*Thus its content was the fulfilment of a wish and its motive was a wish*' (Freud, 1976, p. 196).

CASE MATERIAL

Accounts of analyses by other therapists lose the flavour of how Freud actually worked. Freud published few case studies, possibly because he feared breaking confidentiality. Those wishing to become familiar with how Freud worked are encouraged to read one or more of the following case studies.

Dora was an 18-year-old young woman. Freud's analysis revealed her hysterical symptoms as manifestations of repressed sexual impulses that included her homosexual love for an older admirer's wife (Freud, 1963).

Little Hans, 5 years old, feared a horse would bite him if he went out into the street. Freud helped Hans' doctor father treat him and his analysis demonstrated that Hans' fear expressed phallic phase dynamics, including the Oedipus complex and castration anxiety (Freud, 1955a).

Schreber was an appeals court judge who wrote an account of his illness, diagnosed as paranoia. Based only on Schreber's written account, Freud's analysis demonstrated how Schreber's paranoid delusions were related to his latent homosexuality (Freud, 1958).

Wolf Man, in his twenties, had contracted gonorrhoea, which in turn triggered castration anxiety. Freud's analysis established the relationship between the castration anxiety and a frightening childhood dream involving wolves that followed real or imagined observation of parental sexual intercourse (Freud, 1955b).

FURTHER DEVELOPMENTS

Psychoanalytic theory possesses a unique historical interest, not only in terms of its being an early major psychological theory, but also because of its influence on other theorists. Other analysts influenced by Freud include Jung, Adler, Horney, Sullivan and Fromm, the last four of whom are sometimes termed the 'neo-Freudians'. In addition, under the leadership of Melanie Klein a British school of psychoanalysis emerged, emphasizing the importance of primitive fantasies of loss (the depressive position) and persecution (the paranoid position) in the pathogenesis of mental illness. Winnicott and Bowlby were other prominent British analysts whose work was influenced by Freud.

In varying degrees Freud has influenced humanistic and existential psychologists and psychiatrists. For example, points of contact with transactional analysis include the tripartite structure of personality and the importance of early experience. Furthermore, Rogers' concept of levels of awareness resembles Freud's idea of levels of consciousness. In addition, May and Yalom's version of existential dynamics, motivated by underlying death anxiety, also has its origins in psychoanalysis.

Classical psychoanalysis, based on the Freudian model, continues to develop and evolve. One stimulus for change is that problems tend to alter with the times: for instance, hysteria and conversion symptoms are less frequent now, but there is an increase in clients suffering from masochistic character disorders and from narcissistic neuroses (Arlow, 2000). Often clients complain of inner emptiness, lack of goals, and of inability to make lasting love relationships.

In addition, some analysts have developed forms of brief psychoanalytic therapy. Reasons for brief psychoanalysis include hoped-for cost-effectiveness; the fact that governments, health insurers and most private individuals cannot afford long-term therapy; and to meet the pressing need to treat more people.

SUMMARY

- *Psychoanalytic theory groups human instincts into two broad categories: the erotic or life instincts and the death or destructive instincts. The energy of the life instincts is termed 'libido'. To a large extent people are motivated by the pleasure principle. Mental life takes place on conscious, preconscious and unconscious levels.*

- *The mental apparatus consists of three agencies: the id, which is constantly striving for instinctual satisfaction; the super-ego, which represents parental and moral influence; and the ego, which aims to meet the instinctual demands of the id on the basis of the reality principle.*

- *The ego has three task-masters – the external world, the id and the super-ego – and each may cause it anxiety. Psychical energy is distributed among the three mental agencies, which may be in harmony or in conflict with each other.*

- *People are sexual from infancy, though they tend to be subject to amnesia about this. Humans are constitutionally bisexual and infantile sexuality contains great tendencies to perversion.*

- *Sexual development takes place in two phases: a pre-genital phase up to the end of the fifth year and a genital phase starting at menarche and puberty. The period in between is the latency period. There are some differences in sexual development between the sexes, including development during the Oedipus situation.*

- *While the child's ego is relatively weak, it develops defensive mechanisms to ward off the strong sexual impulses emanating from the id. Thus much of its early sexual life becomes repressed or is not allowed access to consciousness. Excessive repression may lead to the development of neurosis. Since the ego is weakened by having to maintain the repression, it does not have access to the repressed material, and the repressed impulses become transformed into neurotic symptoms.*

- *The goals of psychoanalysis include the freeing of impulse, the strengthening of reality-based ego functioning, and humanizing the super-ego's standards.*

- *While clients reclined, Freud would sit in a tub chair out of sight at the head of the client's couch. He encouraged clients to free associate or tell the analyst everything, however disagreeable it may be.*

- *Transference occurs when clients perceive their analysts as reincarnations of important figures from their childhoods and transfer onto them moderate to intense feelings and emotions appropriate to these earlier people. Analysts require great skill in showing clients the prototypes of their feelings in their childhoods.*

- *Resistances are all the forces that oppose the work of a client's recovery. The struggle to overcome resistances is the main work of psychoanalysis and cannot easily be hurried.*

- *Interpretation is the means by which analysts transform material which is repressed and unconscious into preconscious material and consciousness. Material for interpretations comes from clients' free associations, slips of the tongue, dreams and transference relationships with their analysts.*

- *The interpretation of a dream involves understanding the latent dream thoughts which are disguised by the process of dream work.*

- *Freudian psychoanalysis has been the precursor of many other analytic schools, including the object-relations approach of Melanie Klein, the British psychotherapist. Classical psychoanalysis, based on the Freudian model, continues to develop and evolve.*

REVIEW AND PERSONAL QUESTIONS

REVIEW QUESTIONS

1. How did Freud view the instincts?
2. Describe each of Freud's three levels of consciousness.
3. How did Freud describe the id, the ego and the super-ego and their functions?
4. Why is psychoanalysis often referred to as presenting a dynamic view of psychology?
5. Describe each stage and phase of a person's sexual development.
6. What is the function of defence mechanisms? Illustrate with specific examples.
7. Describe Freud's views on the development and maintenance of neurosis.
8. In psychoanalysis, what is meant by the term 'transference' and why is it so important?
9. In psychoanalysis, what is meant by the term 'resistance' and why is it so important?
10. Describe as best you can how Freud approached the interpretation of a dream.

PERSONAL QUESTIONS

1. Can you think of material or events in your life which you might view as evidence for unconscious mental processes? If so, provide examples (e.g. dreams).
2. What are some of the significant influences which contributed to the formation of your super-ego? With what moral guidelines, if any, do you consider that your super-ego restricts you from the realistic pursuit of pleasure?
3. Are you aware that your ego uses defence mechanisms to ward off anxiety? If so, what are they? Do you consider that your use of defence mechanisms is normal or neurotic?
4. What do you consider the relevance of Freud's ideas on the interpretation of dreams to interpreting your own dreams?
5. What is the relevance of Freud's work to understanding your life?
6. How has Freud influenced the way you think about and practise counselling and therapy?

ANNOTATED BIBLIOGRAPHY

Freud, S. (1976). *The Interpretation of Dreams.* Harmondsworth, Middlesex: Penguin Books. Original edition 1900.

> This book is Freud's major work. In it he reviews the scientific literature about dreams, demonstrates his method of interpreting dreams, and discusses dreams as fulfilments of wishes, distortion in dreams, the material and sources of dreams, dream work, and the psychology of the dream process. The present translation is based on the reprint of the eighth edition (1930), the last published during Freud's life. This volume is part of The Pelican Freud Library, which is intended to contain all Freud's major writings.

Freud, S. (1962a). *Three Contributions to the Theory of Sex.* New York: E. P. Dutton. Original edition 1905.

> This book is Freud's major statement on the nature and development of human sexuality. The three contributions are entitled: the sexual aberrations, infantile sexuality, and the transformations of puberty. Apart from *The Interpretation of Dreams*, this was the only other book that Freud kept more or less systematically up to date.

Freud, S. (1949). *An Outline of Psychoanalysis.* New York: W. W. Norton. Originally published posthumously in 1940.

> Written just before Freud's death, this book provides an excellent concise introduction to psychoanalysis. The book consists of three parts: the mind and its workings, the practical task, and the theoretical yield.

Jones, E. (1963). *The Life and Work of Sigmund Freud.* Edited and abridged in one volume by Lionel Trilling and Steven Marcus. New York: Anchor Books. Also available in a Penguin edition.

> Written in three volumes by a close associate, this book is the definitive biography of Freud. It records the main facts of Freud's life and relates his personality and life experiences to the development of his ideas. In addition, the book traces the history of the psychoanalytic movement during Freud's lifetime.

Hall, C. S. (1954). *A Primer of Freudian Psychology.* New York: Mentor Books.

> This concise but comprehensive book presents Freud's ideas on the organization, dynamics, and development of stabilized personality. It is a highly recommended secondary source.

REFERENCES AND FURTHER READING

All Freud's writings can be found in the 24 volumes of:

Freud, S. (1953–73). *Standard Edition of the Complete Works of Sigmund Freud.* London: Hogarth Press.

Arlow, J. A. (2000). Psychoanalysis. In R. J. Corsini and D. Wedding (eds). *Current Psychotherapies* (6th edition). Itasca, IL: Peacock, 16–53.

Bowlby, J. (1958). The nature of the child's ties to the mother. *International Journal of Psychoanalysis*, *52*, 137–44.

Brenner, C. (1973). *An Elementary Textbook of Psychoanalysis.* New York: International Universities Press.

Freud, S. (1935). *An Autobiographical Study.* London: Hogarth Press.

Freud, S. (1936). *The Problem of Anxiety.* New York: W. W. Norton. Originally published in 1926 under the title *Inhibitions, Symptoms and Anxiety.*

Freud, S. (1949). *An Outline of Psychoanalysis.* New York: W. W. Norton. Originally published posthumously in 1940.

Freud, S. (1950). Analysis terminable and interminable. In S. Freud, *Collected Papers (Vol. 5).* London: Hogarth Press. Originally published in 1937.

Freud, S. (1955a). Analysis of a phobia in a five-year-old boy. In S. Freud, *Standard Edition (Vol. 10).* London: Hogarth Press. Original edition 1909.

Freud, S. (1955b). From the history of an infantile neurosis. In S. Freud, *Standard Edition (Vol. 17).* London: Hogarth Press. Original edition 1918.

Freud, S. (1958). Psycho-analytic notes on an autobiographical account of a case of paranoia (Dementia Paranoides). In S. Freud, *Standard Edition (Vol. 12)*. London: Hogarth Press. Original edition 1911.

Freud, S. (1959). *Group Psychology and the Analysis of the Ego.* London: Hogarth Press. Original edition 1921.

Freud, S. (1960). *Psychopathology of Everyday Life.* London: Hogarth Press. Original edition 1901.

Freud, S. (1961). *Beyond the Pleasure Principle.* London: Hogarth Press. Original Edition 1920.

Freud, S. (1962a). *Three Contributions to the Theory of Sex.* New York: E. P. Dutton. Original edition 1905.

Freud, S. (1962b). *The Ego and the Id.* London: Hogarth Press. Original edition 1923.

Freud, S. (1962c). *Civilization and its Discontents.* New York: W. W. Norton. Original edition 1930.

Freud, S. (1963). *Dora: An Analysis of a Case of Hysteria.* New York: Collier Books. Original edition 1905.

Freud, S. (1964). *The Question of Lay Analysis.* New York: Anchor Books. Original edition 1926.

Freud, S. (1973). *New Introductory Lectures on Psychoanalysis.* Harmondsworth, Middlesex: Penguin Books. Original edition 1933 (1932).

Freud, S. (1976). *The Interpretation of Dreams.* Harmondsworth, Middlesex: Penguin Books. Original edition 1900.

Freud, S. and Breuer, J. (1956). *Studies on Hysteria.* London: Hogarth Press. Original edition 1895.

Fromm, E. (1959). *Sigmund Freud's Mission.* London: George Allen and Unwin.

Hall, C. S. (1954). *A Primer of Freudian Psychology.* New York: Mentor Books.

Jones, E. (1963). *The Life and Work of Sigmund Freud.* (Edited and abridged in one volume by Lionel Trilling and Steven Marcus). New York: Anchor Books. Also available in a Penguin edition.

Klein, M. (1932). *The Psychoanalysis of Children.* London: Hogarth Press.

Winnicott, D. W. (1953). Transitional objects and transitional phenomena: A study of the first not-me possession. *International Journal of Psychoanalysis, 34*, 89–97.

3

Jung's Analytical Therapy

*Although we human beings have our own personal life, we are yet in large measure
the representatives, the victims and the promoters of a collective spirit whose years
are counted in centuries.*

Carl Jung

INTRODUCTION

Do you ever think of yourself or other people as being predominantly introverted or
extroverted? How do you feel about your persona or social mask? What about your
shadow, the aspects of yourself with which you experience difficulty or refuse to acknowledge? If a woman, are you aware that you have an animus, the masculine nature of your
unconscious, or if a man, that you have an anima, the female nature of your unconscious? Furthermore, are you aware that underneath, all humans share the same
collective unconscious?

The two most significant theorists of the unconscious are Sigmund Freud and Carl
Jung. Freud's and Jung's lives overlapped, for a time they were close associates, and what
Jung called his 'analytical psychology' has some of its roots in Freudian psychoanalysis.
Nevertheless, as you can sense from the first paragraph to this chapter, Jung was to
develop a very different psychodynamic theory and practice to that of Freud. In particular, Jung and Freud diverged in their views of the unconscious. Whereas Freud
emphasized sexual repression, Jung considered that, at its deepest level, the unconscious
consisted of archetypes, or inborn possibilities for psychological apprehension and representation, which may then be expressed in universal myths and symbols.

In 1906, Jung and Freud became friends and intellectual companions. Freud admired
Jung's brilliance and regarded him as his crown prince and heir apparent. In addition,
Freud thought that, by having Jung prominent in the movement, he might avoid the risk
of psychoanalysis being viewed as a mainly Jewish activity. Jung had gone through a
troubled relationship with his own father and was fiercely intellectually independent. It
was an error of judgement on both men's part to think that any 'father–son' relationship
could be maintained. In 1913, Jung and Freud split bitterly never to meet again in the
remaining 26 years of Freud's life.

CARL GUSTAV JUNG (1875–1961)

In July 1875, Carl Gustav Jung was born in Kesswil, a small village by Lake Constance in north-eastern Switzerland, the only surviving son of his parents who had lost two previous boys in infancy. Jung was named after his paternal grandfather who, in 1822, had moved from Germany to become Professor of Surgery at the University of Basel. Jung's father was a Swiss Reform Church pastor and his mother was the daughter of a well-established Basel family. When Jung was 9, the family was completed by the birth of his sister.

Jung was an introverted, sensitive, solitary and lonely child. His parents, Paul and Emilie, had a troubled marriage and, in 1878, his parents separated temporarily and his mother spent some time in a mental hospital. During his childhood Jung suffered from his mother's depressive invalidism and critical tongue. However, Jung admired his mother and could enjoy her companionship and cooking. Jung also had to contend with his father's irritability, partly connected with his agonizing over his religious faith. Nevertheless, in the autobiography compiled at the end of his life, Jung refers to his 'dear and generous father', who never tyrannized over him (Jung, 1961).

The earliest dream Jung remembers was when he was between 3 and 4. Jung had a rich inner life of dreams, fantasies and thoughts about the world. When he was 10, Jung carved, at the end of a ruler, a manikin about two inches long with frock coat, top hat, and shiny black boots. He placed the manikin and an oblong blackish stone from the Rhine in a case and took it to the attic. Whenever Jung felt hurt or stressed he would think of the manikin and, from time to time, visit it in the forbidden attic. Jung regarded this manikin episode, which lasted about a year, as the conclusion of his childhood.

In 1879, the Jungs had moved to Klein Hünigen, near Basel. At 6, Jung went to the local school and, at 11, he was uprooted from his rustic schoolmates and sent to the Gymnasium at Basel. Jung hated mathematics, was exempted from drawing on the grounds of incapacity, and also loathed gymnastics. Regarding mathematics he writes: 'But my fear of failure and sense of smallness in face of the vast world around me created in me not only a dislike, but a kind of silent despair which completely ruined school for me' (Jung, 1961, p. 45). For a time Jung suffered from fainting spells connected with school. He also saw himself as being two persons: a schoolboy who was less intelligent, hard-working and decent than many other boys, and an old man mistrustful of humans but close to nature, to dreams and to whatever God worked through him.

In reality, Jung was a highly intelligent student who, in 1895, passed his final examinations at the Gymnasium and entered the University of Basel Medical School. During medical school Jung suffered from financial worries, partly stemming from the death of his father in 1896. In 1900, Jung graduated equal first in his medical school class. His medical school thesis was on the psychological foundations of the occult. Jung chose to specialize in psychiatry, which provided a bridge between his scientific, humanities and psychological interests. Shortly after graduation he accepted a post at the Burghölzli Mental Hospital in Zurich.

At the Burgholzli, the director was Eugen Bleuler, an expert on schizophrenia, whose influence Jung valued. In 1902, Jung spent several months studying at the Sâlpetrière

Hospital in Paris with the famous psychiatrist Pierre Janet. In 1905, Jung became Lecturer in Psychiatry at the University of Zurich and senior physician at the psychiatric clinic. He also had a private practice which became so successful that, in 1909, he resigned from the Burghölzli. However, he continued to lecture at the University of Zurich until 1913. At the Burghölzli, as well as working with patients, Jung conducted research on word associations and the underlying psychological complexes indicated by how people responded. As mentioned, Jung also developed a relationship with Freud and became prominent in the psychoanalytic movement.

After his break with Freud, Jung went through a profound mid-life crisis which lasted from 1913 to 1918, and which took him to the edge of insanity. During this period of inner uncertainty and disorientation, much of the time Jung continued seeing patients. Jung developed his ideas of the collective unconscious during this period of confrontation with his own unconscious. He writes:

> *The years when I was pursuing my inner images were the most important in my life – in them everything essential was decided. It all began then; the later details are only supplements and clarifications of the material that burst forth from the unconscious, and at first swamped me. It was the* prima materia *for a lifetime's work.* (Jung, 1961, p. 225)

Jung was fond of women, who played a crucial role throughout his life. In 1903 he had married the extremely wealthy Emma Rauschenbach. Under Swiss law at the time Jung married Emma, husbands had complete access to their wife's money and could spend it as they wished without consent. In short, though Jung was always a hard worker, he was financially set up for life independent of his own endeavours.

Despite his wife's disapproval of his behaviour and his growing family, Jung was sexually attracted to other women, allegedly extending to intimate relationships with one or more of his patients, for example Sabina Spielrein. An ex-patient, Toni Wolff, was able to be of special comfort to him during his near psychotic period – so much so that, in 1916, Jung persuaded Emma to accept her as part of a permanent domestic threesome. Probably Jung abandoned his philandering at this stage. He encouraged Emma to become a Jungian therapist and, eventually, Toni became one too.

After Jung returned to feeling more normal, there were a number of ongoing and interweaving strands in his life. At his beautiful home by Lake Zurich, though not the warmest and most present of fathers, Jung engaged in family activities with his wife, four daughters and a son. In 1922, Jung bought some land at Bollingen, at the upper end of Lake Zurich and, over the next thirty or so years, developed the 'Tower', a house he built for himself as a retreat from his family. Whereas the family home was the territory of his wife, the only person Jung allowed to stay at Bollingen was Toni Wolff and, in later years, a companion-housekeeper.

Jung continued his large private practice, which he regarded as a valuable source of information for understanding the psyche. Most of Jung's clients were women, almost all were reasonably well off, and a minority were fabulously wealthy Americans, for instance one of John D. Rockefeller's daughters and a member of the Mellon banking family.

Jung also continued his own inner journey, analysing his dreams, fantasies and visions.

Jung engaged in wide-ranging scholarly activities. In 1921, he published a large work on psychological types. As well as reading widely in philosophy, world literature, mythology and astrology Jung became increasingly interested in alchemy. He also conducted what might be called field work, by visiting North Africa, Kenya and Uganda, the Pueblo Indians in North America, and India. Jung was immensely interested in the presence and universality of myths and symbols across cultures and in primitive as well as civilized cultures. Based on his scholarly researches, field trips, wide reading and professional and personal experiences, right up to his death Jung was a prolific author across a range of subjects including psychiatry and psychology, parapsychology, alchemy, and religion.

Jung lectured extensively not only in the Germanic, but in the English-speaking world. In 1909, he had gone with Freud to Clark University in Massachusetts, where both men received honorary doctorates, and he was to return to America repeatedly in the following 30 years. Jung was also an Anglophile and visited England many times, for example giving a notable series of lectures at the Tavistock Clinic in 1935. His honorary doctorates included those from Harvard and Oxford Universities. In addition, from the early 1930s, Jung regularly attended the annual Eranos conferences on Jungian studies. At these conferences, held at the northern end of Lake Maggiore on the estate of a wealthy woman who had built a conference hall specially for them, Jung tended to be lionized by the mostly female participants.

Intimations of Jung's mortality included a severe heart attack in 1944, the death of Toni Wolff in 1953, and his wife's death in 1955. Jung's companion-housekeeper during his final years was Ruth Bailey, an Englishwoman. On 6 June 1961, Jung died after a brief illness.

It is tempting when looking at pictures of Jung to view him as a gentle, spiritual, scholarly sage full of the milk of human kindness. Undoubtedly, Jung had many attractive features as well as a charismatic personality, especially for women. However, Jung was not without his shadow aspects. He held extreme right-wing Social Darwinist political views and strongly believed that different rules applied to 'beasts' and 'supermen' (McLynn, 1996). For various reasons, he strongly favoured the death penalty. Though probably not anti-Semitic, Jung has been criticized for not speaking out loudly enough against the rise of Nazism. He could be domineering and hectoring at professional meetings and a domestic tyrant at home. Jung could also be a bile-laden person and his relationship with Freud became particularly bitter. In addition, Jung had been a philandering husband, conceivably including some clients among his lovers, though there is no real proof of this.

Like Freud, Jung was an ideas man with an amazing breadth of vision. Some of his ideas have stood the test of time in terms of becoming part of Western psychological consciousness, for example the concepts of the collective unconscious and extraversion/introversion. In addition, Jung was the founder of an analytical approach to therapy that still claims many adherents.

THEORY

The primordial images and the nature of the archetype took a central place in my researches and it became clear to me that without history there can be no psychology, and certainly no psychology of the unconscious.

Carl Jung

BASIC CONCEPTS

Psychology is first the science of consciousness and then the science of the products of the unconscious psyche. Jung used the term 'psyche' to refer to the mind or soul. He distinguished between three psychic levels of consciousness. In addition, his was a dynamic psychology that paid attention to the distribution of psychic energy between the different psychic levels. Furthermore, Jung presented a typology of different personality types.

Structure of the psyche

Jung goes beyond distinguishing consciousness from unconsciousness to divide the latter into its personal and collective elements. Thus, the psyche's three levels are consciousness, the personal unconscious, and the collective unconscious. Though Jung did not wish to push the analogy too far, he saw consciousness like an island arising out of a vast sea of unconsciousness.

Consciousness

Jung observes: '. . . the child develops out of an originally unconscious, animal condition into consciousness, primitive at first, and then slowly becoming more civilised' (Jung, 1981, p. 53). Consciousness is an intermittent phenomenon since people enter the unconscious every time they go to sleep. The conscious mind is narrow since it can only hold a few simultaneous contents at a given moment. Furthermore, consciousness is transitory and people can only get an awareness of the external world through a succession of conscious moments.

The *ego* is the indispensable centre of a person's consciousness. Sometimes Jung refers to it as the ego-complex. The ego gives a person a sense of identity and continuity. The ego has both external and internal tasks. Its external task is to provide a system of relationship between consciousness and the facts and data coming from the environment. Sensation, thinking, feeling and intuition are four functions by means of which it performs its ectopsychic task. The ego's internal task is to provide a system of relationship between the contents of consciousness and the processes of the unconscious. Jung (1968) states: 'The ego is only a bit of consciousness that floats on an ocean of dark things. The dark things are the inner things' (p. 21).

The personal unconscious

The contents of the personal unconscious are definitely of a personal origin. These contents fall into two main categories: first, material that lost its intensity either because it was forgotten or repressed; second, material which never possessed sufficient intensity to reach consciousness but has somehow entered the psyche: for instance, some sense-impressions. There is nothing peculiar about the contents of the personal unconscious, and its contents might just as well be conscious. People differ in regard to the contents of their personal unconscious: some people are conscious of things which other people are not.

Complexes are an important feature of the personal unconscious. Jung discovered the complex through his research on word associations, finding that complexes disturbed memory and produced blockages in the flow of associations. Complexes are accumulations of associations, sometimes of a traumatic nature, that possess strong emotional content. They possess a tendency to develop a life of their own apart from a person's intentions. A saying of Jung's was: 'A person does not have a complex; the complex has him.'

The mother complex is an example of a complex. Jung considered that 'the mother always plays an active part in the origin of the disturbance, especially in infantile neuroses or in neuroses whose aetiology undoubtedly dates back to early childhood' (Jung, 1982, p. 113). Typical effects of the mother complex on the son are homosexuality, Don Juanism and, sometimes, impotence. In daughters the mother complex can lead to an exaggeration of the feminine side of personality or its neglect. Other examples of complexes include those connected with inferiority, sex, aesthetic beauty and money.

The collective unconscious

Unlike Freud, who saw the unconscious as a receptacle for things which were repressed, Jung considered that the deeper layers of the unconscious lose their uniqueness as they retreat further and further from consciousness. At its deepest levels the unconscious is a vast collective and universal historical storehouse whose contents belong to mankind in general. Whereas the contents of the personal unconscious owe their existence to personal experience, the contents of the collective unconscious have never been in consciousness, but owe their existence to heredity.

Archetypes are inborn possibilities or patterns for representation. Jung borrowed the term 'archetype' from St Augustine. He observes: 'Whereas the personal unconscious consists for the most part of *complexes*, the content of the collective unconscious is made up essentially of *archetypes*' (Jung, 1976a, p. 60). Similar to instinctive patterns for action, archetypes provide instinctive patterns for mental activity. Archetypes are 'primordial images' and 'primordial thoughts' rather than the representations of the images or thoughts themselves. For example, well-known motifs appear in myths, fairy tales, legends and folklore across a range of cultures and historical periods. Such motifs include the hero, the redeemer, the dragon, the mother, the wise old man and the descent into the cave. Archetypes are evolutionary predispositions or potentials for such motifs, rather than the forms in which the contents become expressed.

Symbols are the images by means of which archetypes are expressed. Jung distinguished between a sign and a symbol. If the image denotes a known thing it is a sign. Symbolic images express the best possible formulation of a relatively unknown thing, which for that reason cannot be more clearly or characteristically represented. For example, a triangle with a bare eye enclosed in it is so meaningless that it conjures up a symbolic interpretation.

Archetypes important in shaping the development of personality include the persona, the anima and animus, the shadow and the self.

The persona

The persona is a concept derived from the mask worn by actors in antiquity. At one level, the persona is the individual's system of adaptation or way of coping with the world. At a different level, the persona is not just an individual mask, but a mask of the collective psyche, 'a mask that *feigns individuality*, making others and oneself believe that one is an individual, whereas one is simply acting out a role through which the collective psyche speaks '(Jung, 1976b, p. 105).

The persona exists for reasons of personal convenience, but should not be confused with genuine individuality. The persona is exclusively concerned with relation to outer objects, an outer attitude. This outer attitude must be distinguished from an inner attitude, which is the relation to the subject or 'inner object' which is the unconscious.

In reality, individuals may have more than one persona, for example wearing different masks at work and home. Furthermore, each profession has its own characteristic persona. However, there is a danger that people become identified with their personas, for instance the professor with his textbook. Too rigid adherence to a persona can lead people to become alienated from the 'subject', the stirrings, feelings, thoughts and sensations that well up from their unconscious. Identifications with social roles are often fruitful sources of neuroses. Jung regarded it as essential for individuals to be able to distinguish themselves from their personas.

The anima and the animus

People are psychologically bisexual. The larger number of male or female genes is the decisive factor in the determination of biological sex. However, the smaller number of opposite sex genes appears to produce a corresponding opposite sex character, which usually remains unconscious. The anima is the personification of the feminine nature in a man's unconscious, whereas the animus is the personification of the masculine nature in a woman's unconscious. Every man or woman carries within themselves an imprint or archetype of all the ancestral experiences of the opposite sex.

Jung thought that in its primary form the animus is composed of spontaneous, unpremeditated opinions that exercise a powerful influence on the woman's emotional life. Similarly, the anima is composed of feelings which thereafter distort and influence a man's understanding. He wrote: 'as the anima produces *moods*, so the animus produces *opinions*; and as the moods of a man issue from a shadowy background, so the opinions of a woman rest on equally unconscious prior assumptions' (Jung, 1982, pp. 95–6). Jung stressed the importance of people acknowledging their distinction, not only from their persona but from their anima or animus as well. The animus and anima should function as a bridge leading to the images of the collective unconscious. Both men and women should learn to acknowledge and appropriately express the opposite sex characteristics of their personalities and avoid falsely projecting them onto others.

The shadow

The shadow archetype reflects the realm of humans' animal ancestors and, as such, comprises the whole historical aspect of the unconscious. For the most part, the shadow consists of inferior traits of personality that individuals refuse to acknowledge. Though Jung emphasized the darker aspects of the shadow, he acknowledged that it also displayed some good qualities, such as normal instincts, appropriate reactions, realistic insights and creative impulses. The shadow is compensatory to consciousness and its effects can be positive as well as negative.

In general people do not like looking at the shadow-side of themselves. However, with insight and goodwill, much of the shadow can be assimilated into the conscious personality without too much difficulty. Nevertheless, there are some unconscious projections from the shadow whose recognition meets the most obstinate resistance and thus prove almost impossible to influence.

The self

The self is the central archetype, the archetype of order. The self, which expresses the unity of personality as a whole, encompasses both conscious and unconscious components. The self is a superordinate construct to the ego which is restricted to being the focal point of the conscious mind. The ego is related to the self like a part to the whole. Jung considered that there was little hope of ever being able to reach even approximate consciousness of the self given the huge and indeterminate amount of unconscious material that belongs to it.

The main symbol for the unity of the self archetype is the mandala. The word 'mandala' (Sanskrit for 'circle') is a circular form that often contains a quaternity, symmetrical arrangements of the number 4 and its multiples. The self also appears in dreams, myths and fairytales in the figure of a superordinate personality, such as a king, hero, prophet or saviour.

Dynamics of the psyche

Psychodynamics refers to the activity and interrelation of the various parts of an individual's personality or psyche. More specifically, psychodynamics entails the generation and transfer of energy within the structure of the psyche. Jung's ideas on psychodynamics were influenced by his interest in and knowledge of physics, the branch of science dealing with the properties and interactions of matter and energy.

Psychic energy

Jung emphasized the concept of psychic energy, sometimes referred to as libido, as the psychic analogue of physical energy. All the instincts, including hunger, sex and aggression, are expressions of psychic energy. In physics there are different manifestations of energy, such as electricity, heat and light. The same situation occurs in psychology where energy can appear in various guises. Psychic energy is also provided from the external environment by way of one's senses and feelings. The psyche is a relatively closed energy system. Psychic energy derived from both internal and external sources is continually being shifted and redistributed among the structures of the psyche.

A psychic value is the amount of energy invested in a particular psychic element. When a person places a high value on something, such as an idea or feeling, this means that the idea or feeling exerts a particularly strong influence on them. Complexes, which by definition are strongly emotionally toned, are examples of mental elements with high psychic value.

Opposition

Jung (1961) observed: 'Among other things, the psyche appears as a dynamic process which rests on a foundation of antithesis, on a flow of energy between two poles' (p. 383). Just as in physics all energy proceeds from opposition, so the psyche possesses an inner polarity which is an essential prerequisite for its aliveness. Tension and conflict arising from the clash of opposites are central to Jungian personality dynamics. Consciousness opposes unconsciousness, feminine opposes masculine, ego opposes shadow, and positive aspects of archetypal images oppose their negative elements.

Compensation

The function of compensation is to balance or adjust the energy distributed throughout the psyche. Compensation, for the most part, is an unconscious process that entails an inherent self-regulation of the psychic apparatus. The activity of the unconscious balances the one-sidedness produced by consciousness. Consciousness, because of its selectiveness and need for focus, is bound to become one-sided. As consciousness becomes more and more one-sided, the more antagonistic are the contents arising from the unconscious, so that there is a real opposition between the two. For the most part, unconscious compensation balances rather than opposes consciousness. For example, in dreams the unconscious supplies 'all those contents that are constellated by conscious situation but are inhibited by conscious selection, although a knowledge of them would be indispensable for complete adaptation' (Jung, 1971, p. 420).

Breakthrough of unconscious content

The energy of all unconscious contents, once they are activated, is normally insufficient to propel their content into consciousness. A lowering of energy in the conscious mind that allows unconscious material to break through into consciousness may come about in two ways. First, there may be a malfunctioning of the conscious mind. Just as primitive people can suffer from 'loss of soul', so can civilized people suffer from loss of initiative for no apparent reason. Carelessness, neglected duties, wilful outbursts of defiance can dam up energy so that certain quanta of it, no longer finding a conscious outlet, stream off into the unconscious. Here they activate other compensating contents, which can in turn start exerting a compulsive influence on the conscious mind. Jung (1966) illustrates this point with the common example of extreme neglect of duty combined with a compulsion neurosis.

The second way in which a loss of energy to the conscious mind may come about is through a 'spontaneous' activation of unconscious contents, which then react upon consciousness. During the incubation period of changes in personality, the new development draws off the energy it needs from consciousness. For example, lowering of energy from the conscious mind takes place before the onset of psychosis, and a fallow and quiet period precedes creative work. Jung (1966) observed: 'The remarkable potency of unconscious contents, therefore, always indicates a corresponding weakness in the conscious mind and its functions' (p. 181). In the near psychotic period of his life, Jung himself had to struggle with the heightened energy of his unconscious contents in relation to his conscious ego.

The transcendent function

The transcendent function is a psychological function similar to a mathematical function of the same name, which is a function of real and imaginary numbers. In face of the disturbing energy of the unconscious, Jung postulates a synthesizing process, the transcendent function, which can get rid of some of the separation between consciousness and unconsciousness.

The transcendent function is both a process and a method. Jung postulated that there are certain spontaneous *processes* in the unconscious which, by virtue of their symbolism, can compensate the defects in the conscious mind. In turn these reactions, usually manifested in dreams, are brought to conscious realization through the analytical *method* (Jung, 1971).

The confrontation of two opposed positions can generate a tension charged with energy which creates a living, third thing. Jung (1976c) talked about the transcendent function manifesting itself as 'a movement out of the suspension between opposites, a living birth that leads to a new level of being, a new situation. The transcendent function manifests itself as a quality of conjoined opposites' (p. 298). By means of the transcendent function, consciousness is widened through the confrontation with previously unconscious contents.

The transcendent function is the means by which progress is made toward realizing the unfolding of the individual's original potential for wholeness. However, attaining integration at a new level of consciousness by means of the transcendent function does not always take place. Apart from insufficient skills on the part of therapists, there are many reasons why the synthesizing of opposites to create a new way of being may not take place. These reasons include people having insufficient intelligence to understand the procedure, lacking self-confidence, and being mentally and morally too lazy.

Psychological types

In 1921, Jung published his famous work entitled *Psychological Types*. Here Jung distinguished between attitude-types, based on the habitual direction of an individual's interests, and function-types, based on the individual's most differentiated function of psychological adaptation. For simplicity, here these are called attitudes and functions.

Attitudes: Introversion and extraversion

The *introvert's* predominant, but not exclusive, conscious attitude is one in which the main interest is the withdrawal of psychic energy from the object as though to prevent the object from gaining power over her or him. The introvert thinks, feels and acts as though the subjective is what is most important and the object is of secondary importance. The introverted attitude type is characterized by an orientation in life that particularly values subjective psychic contents. Introverts tend to be reserved, inscrutable and rather shy people.

The *extravert's* predominant, but not exclusive, conscious attitude is characterized by concentration of interest on the external object. The extravert thinks, feels and acts as though the object were of most importance. This is done so directly and clearly that no doubt can remain about his or her dependence on the object. Extraverts tend to be open, friendly and sociable or they may quarrel with everybody. Nevertheless extraverts always relate to people in some way and in turn are affected by them.

In sum, introversion is characterized by interest in one's internal world and extraversion is characterized by interest in the external world. However, matters are not that simple, since a conscious extraverted attitude is compensated by an unconscious introverted attitude, and a conscious introverted attitude is compensated by an extraverted unconscious attitude.

Functions: Thinking, feeling, sensation and intuition

The four psychological functions are thinking, feeling, sensation and intuition. As a rule one function predominates.

The *thinking* individual is mainly governed by reflective thinking so that important actions proceed, or are intended to proceed, from intellectually considered motives. The *feeling* individual is mainly governed by values placed on things arising from feelings. Here Jung is regarding feeling as an evaluative function. Thinking and feeling individuals are *rational* types because they are characterized by the primacy of the reasoning and judging functions.

The *sensation* individual is mainly governed by their awareness of external facts provided through the function of the senses: seeing, hearing, touching, tasting and smelling. The *intuition* individual is mainly governed by hunches and insights. Intuition is a predominantly unconscious process. The conscious aspect of intuition is to transmit images or perceptions of relations between things, that could not be transmitted by the other functions. Sensation and intuition individuals are *irrational* types because their actions are based on the sheer intensity of perception rather than on any rational judgement.

Combining attitudes and functions to form psychological types

Jung combined attitudes and functions to provide eight main psychological types (see Box 3.1). Though one main attitude and one main function combine in each individual, people categorized within the eight psychological types vary. Furthermore, the other attitude and functions are always part of someone's personality.

ACQUISITION

Jung never developed a rigorous elaboration of the development of the psyche and of human behaviour. A possible reason for this is that he was more interested in researching

BOX 3.1

Jung's psychological types

Following are brief descriptions of each of the eight main psychological types.

Extraverted-thinking type
This type makes all activities dependent on intellectual functioning oriented to objective data in the form of external facts or generally accepted ideas. Jung cites the scientist Charles Darwin as an example.

Introverted-thinking type
This type makes all activities dependent on intellectual functioning oriented to subjective data. Jung cites the philosopher Immanuel Kant as an example.

Extraverted-feeling type
This type consists almost exclusively of women who are guided by feelings that appear adjusted to harmonize with objective situations and general values: for instance, the love choice of a 'suitable' man.

Introverted-feeling type
This type is predominantly guided by subjective feelings, and their true motives generally remain hidden. This type mainly consists of women of whom it may be said 'still waters run deep'.

Extraverted-sensation type
This type consists mainly of men for whom anything new that comes within their range of interest is acquired by way of sensations received from the outside. Guided by the intensity of objective influences, this type encompasses the grossly sensual and those whose sensations are aesthetically highly developed.

Introverted-sensation type
This type is guided by the intensity of the subjective sensation. No proportional relationship exists between object and sensation, but one that is unpredictable and arbitrary.

Extraverted-intuition type
For this type intuition as the function of unconscious perception is directed wholly to external objects. This type uses intuition to apprehend the widest range of possibilities in objective situations and to discover what they hold in store.

Introverted-intuition type
The peculiar intuition of this type produces mystical dreamers, seers, artists and cranks. The intensification of intuition may lead this type to be out of touch with tangible reality and to experience difficulty in communicating to others.

and understanding the collective unconscious, which he perceived as the inherited foundation of psychological life.

Stages of life

To Jung the arc of life has four stages: childhood, youth, middle age, and extreme old age (Jung, 1989). He was particularly interested in the problems of middle age.

Childhood (birth to puberty)

Jung likened children, during the first two or three years of life when they are unconscious of themselves, to being in an animal state. In early infancy the psyche is to a large extent the maternal psyche and soon comprises the paternal psyche as well. Gradually the ego develops as the organizing centre for the child's psychic processes, and only when children begin to say 'I' is there any perceptible continuity of consciousness. The conscious mind progressively arises out of the unconscious as fragments of the unconscious are added to consciousness and separated from their previous source in the unconscious (Jung, 1981).

Jung saw the origins of childhood neuroses mainly as symptoms of the mental conditions of parents. He wrote: 'The child is hopelessly exposed to the psychic influence of the parents and is bound to copy their self-deception, their insincerity, their hypocrisy, cowardice, self-righteousness, and selfish regard for their own comfort, just as wax takes up the imprint of the seal' (Jung, 1981, p. 79). Jung did not expect parents to commit no faults, but to recognize them for what they were, thus creating a more honest psychological atmosphere for their children.

Youth (puberty to 35–40 years)

The human mind's growth keeps pace with a widening range of consciousness and each step forward can be an extremely painful and laborious achievement. During youth the demands of life put an end to childhood, for example the transitions to marriage and a career. In addition, young people may experience inner psychic difficulties concerned with the sexual instinct or feelings of inferiority. The essential feature of the problems of youth is a clinging to the childhood level of consciousness. Achievement, usefulness and getting established are ways of proceeding out from the problems of the period of youth. People can adapt what they have been given from the past to the possibilities and demands of the future.

Middle age (35–40 to extreme old age)

Jung used the analogy of the sun which rises to a peak in the first part of the day and then descends and in the process illuminates itself. Likewise human life does not inexorably expand, but there is an inexorable and deep-seated shift in the psyche towards contraction with the possibility of self-illumination. While the tasks of the first half of life concern the individual's development and entrenchment in the outer world, the tasks of the second half of life are for people to devote serious attention to understanding and developing themselves more fully. Just as neurotic problems in youth sprang from people not escaping from their childhood, so neurotic problems in middle age can spring from people not escaping from their youth. Jung did not regard this psychological shrinking from approaching old age to be caused by fear of death, rather than from a basic change in the human psyche taking place around that time. Middle age is a time for contemplation, self-realization and learning to live more in harmony with primordial images and symbols.

Extreme old age

Though childhood and extreme old age are utterly different, Jung regarded them as having one thing in common: submersion into unconscious psychic happenings. The child's mind and ego grow out of unconsciousness. The very old person sinks again into unconsciousness and progressively vanishes within it. Jung viewed childhood and extreme old age as being stages of life without any conscious problems and, hence, they were not his major focus.

Progression and regression

Life requires an ongoing process of psychological adaptation to the reality of the environment. Progression and regression are two important uses of psychic energy. *Progression* is 'the daily advance of the process of psychological adaptation . . . a continual satisfaction of the demands of environmental conditions' (Jung, 1983, p. 59). In progression, the psychic values of conscious and unconscious opposites become balanced through regular interaction and mutual influence.

Regression is the backward movement of psychic energy when a frustrating situation dams the energy of the libido: for instance, a thinking-attitude may attempt to deal with a situation that can only be solved by feeling. Regression confronts the individual with the problem of the inner psyche as contrasted with outward adaptation to reality. The struggle between opposites would persist, but for regression which raises the psychic value of material of which the individual was only dimly conscious or totally unconscious. Regression can be positive as well as negative with its unconscious contents containing not only psychological slime, but the seeds of new possibilities. For example, if thinking fails as the adopted function, the unconscious material activated by regression will contain the missing feeling function, although still in embryonic, archaic and undeveloped form. Regression occurs regularly in dreams which can reveal important unconscious material.

Individuation

The central concept of Jung's psychology is the process of individuation. Individuation is the process by which the person becomes differentiated as a separate psychological individual, a separate whole as distinct from the collective psychology. However, the process of individuation also raises a person's consciousness of the human community since it makes people aware of the unconscious, which unites all mankind.

The goal of psychic development is the self which, as shown previously, differs from the ego. Individuation may be viewed as coming to self-hood or self-realization. The transcendent function is the means by which individuals are able to bridge some of the gap between consciousness and unconsciousness and live more in harmony with their unconscious processes.

Individuation involves a process of assimilating unconscious content into consciousness. There is a shift of the centre of personality from the ego, which is the centre of consciousness, to the self which moves from being located in the centre of unconsciousness to being at the central point between consciousness and unconsciousness. Creating this new balance between consciousness and unconsciousness allows the personality to rest on a new and more solid foundation.

Although the self-archetype is present from birth, its influence does not become significant until middle age. Individuation proceeds in life's morning though education and appropriate life experiences. However, a major emphasis on realizing the self through the process of individuation might be viewed more as a task of the afternoon of human life.

MAINTENANCE

Jung never systematically identified the factors that contribute to individuals maintaining lower levels of psychic development and individuation than desirable. He differentiated between the tasks of the first part of life, which entailed practical adaptations concerning such matters as relationships and occupation, and the second part of life, which concerned realizing the underlying self. The concept of maintenance should ideally take into account the different factors contributing to problems connected to addressing the tasks of each life stage. To avoid repetition and for the sake of simplicity, the following discussion is restricted to some central, sometimes overlapping, factors.

- *Rigid persona.* People who develop rigid personas develop in a very one-sided fashion and become out of touch with the subjective and unconscious side of themselves. This one-sidedness seeks social adaptation at the expense of inner alienation.
- *Mass collective consciousness.* The collective consciousness in a group, for instance the Swiss nation, may be one that encourages people to avoid examining themselves and dealing more deeply with problems in life. Allied to this, the collective consciousness may be conducive to people reinforcing one another's rigid personas.
- *Complexes.* Complexes, such as the mother complex, form part of the personal unconscious. Individuals who remain unaware of their complexes are likely to maintain them.
- *Fear of the shadow.* Individuals tend not to like examining what they perceive as undesirable and inferior traits in themselves. People who possess rigid personas may be particularly prone to avoid looking at their shadow sides.
- *Fear of the contents of the unconscious.* Fear of the shadow is just one aspect of fear of the unconscious. At varying levels of awareness, individuals may fear that their conscious functioning may be overwhelmed by the strength of their unconscious, with its archetypes and symbolic messages. People may possess insufficient courage to face their inner selves. For example, men and women may be reluctant to admit and explore the feminine (anima) and masculine (animus) aspects of themselves, respectively.

- *Projection.* Projection means the expulsion of a subjective content into an object. By means of projections, which are unintentional and purely automatic occurrences, individuals get rid of incompatible aspects of themselves by projecting them onto others. Most often these subjective contents are painful, for instance aspects of one's shadow. However, sometimes projections are positive, but for reasons of self-depreciation are inaccessible to individuals.

- *Regression.* Earlier, it was mentioned that regression involves the backward flow of psychic energy. Regression only becomes negative when the individual becomes stuck in the unconscious activity and material generated by it, rather than being able to use it for regeneration.

- *Inability to understand the language of dreams.* The issue of understanding dreams is covered in the following section on therapy. Suffice it to say that inability to attend to dreams and understand their language and meaning is likely to contribute to maintaining pathology. The corollary of this is that heeding and understanding the language of dreams can foster the process of individuation.

- *Problems using the transcendent function.* The transcendent function is the synthesizing or integrating process whereby unconscious material opposes conscious material to provide a third living thing resembling the conjunction of opposites. Reasons why this synthesizing of opposites to create something new may not take place include ignorance, laziness, and insufficient intelligence and courage.

THERAPY

As far as we can discern, the sole purpose of human existence is to kindle a light in the darkness of mere being.

Carl Jung

THERAPEUTIC GOALS

In his paper entitled 'The aims of psychotherapy', Jung (1966) talks about the psychology of life's morning and the psychology of its afternoon. The main therapeutic goal for youth is normal adaptation to overcome neuroses connected with shrinking back from the concrete life tasks. Therapy is mainly focused on attaining specific goals, dealing with complexes, and strengthening consciousness and ego functioning. Jung emphasized the importance for young people, who were still unadapted and yet to achieve anything, to educate their conscious will.

People in the second half of life no longer need to educate their conscious will, but to understand their own inner being and the meaning of their lives. Fully two-thirds of Jung's clients were in the second half of life and about one-third of his clients were not suffering from any clinically definable neuroses, but from the senselessness and aimlessness of their lives. Most of these patients were socially well-adapted individuals to whom normalization meant nothing. For such people, the major therapeutic goal was self-realization involving a deeper comprehension of their psyche and incorporating more unconscious material so that a new balance was created between consciousness and unconsciousness.

Jung did not believe in the concept of cure, rather in being better able to engage in the processes of attaining life's tasks and of synthesizing conscious and unconscious material. Until his death, Jung continued his quest for individuation and self-realization by understanding the meaning of the dreams and symbols from his own unconscious.

PROCESS OF THERAPY

Jungian analysis definitely does not follow the medical model of diagnosis, prognosis and treatment. Jung thought that clinical diagnosis was all but meaningless and that the true nature of a neurosis only reveals itself during the course of therapy.

Jung postulated four stages in analytic psychotherapy: confession, elucidation, education, and transformation (see Box 3.2). Though each of the stages has a curious sense of finality about it, normal adaptation will usually only be achieved by proceeding through

---

BOX 3.2

The four stages of analytical therapy

Stage one: Confession
The prototype of analytical therapy is confession. The first step in the therapeutic process is to share secrets and reveal inhibited emotions. Cathartic confession restores to the ego contents which should normally be part of it and which are capable of becoming conscious. However, confession should not be regarded as a panacea.

Stage two: Elucidation
Elucidation is a process of throwing light upon and clearing up the contents elicited by the transference. Partly by analysing clients' dreams, therapists interpret and explain what clients project on to them. The effects of elucidation are that clients gain insight into their personal unconscious and the infantile origins of their projections and, thus, become more accepting of their shortcomings.

Stage three: Education
Elucidation can leave clients intelligent, but still incapable children. Education entails helping clients draw out of themselves new and adaptive habits to replace the self-defeating habits of their neurosis. In this stage, therapy moves beyond insight to training clients in responsible actions.

Stage four: Transformation
For many people completion of the first three stages may be sufficient. However, some people wish to move beyond being normal and adapted persons because their deepest needs are to be healthy in leading 'abnormal' lives. In the transformation stage with such clients, the therapist as well as the client is 'in the analysis'. In the personal relationship between them there are imponderable factors which bring about a mutual transformation, with the stronger and more stable personality deciding the final issue. The personality of the therapist is the curative or harmful factor and the educator must now become the self-educator going through the stages of confession, elucidation and education so that his or her personality does not react unfavourably on the client.

the first three stages. The fourth stage, transformation, fulfils a further need beyond the scope of the other stages, but is not a final truth.

Jungian analysis is very much tailored to each individual. The process of therapy varies depending on such factors as: the client's stage of life, their personality characteristics, and the nature of their problems. The four stages of therapy are indicative rather than prescriptive. For instance, clients vary in how much work is required in dealing with the transference and its projections. Furthermore, the fourth stage of transformation is more appropriate to those facing problems of self-realization in the afternoon of their lives.

With difficult cases, Jung would start with three or four sessions a week. He would commence seeing most clients twice weekly, but once analytic therapy was under way, sessions would be reduced to once a week. Under his direction, Jung would also encourage clients to perform between-session activities, for instance recording dreams and painting, which would enable them to make a contribution to their common work. Approximately once every ten weeks Jung would break off treatment both to stop clients from becoming too dependent and to allow time to be a healing factor. A thorough course of analytic therapy could last for some years. Jung thought that, in most instances, very frequent sessions did not shorten the length of treatment. With clients of limited means, Jung would space sessions out and get clients to work on their own in the interim.

THE THERAPEUTIC RELATIONSHIP

Jung (1961) wrote: 'Analysis is a dialogue involving two partners. Analyst and patient sit facing one another, eye to eye; the doctor has something to say, but so does the patient' (p. 153). Therapy is different in every case, with each client requiring individual understanding. Furthermore, clients needed to reach their own view of things without therapist compulsion or attempts at conversion.

Jung was very aware that within and between therapists and clients, relationships take place on conscious and unconscious levels. Since treatment is a dialectical process in which the therapist participates just as much as the client, the personalities of therapists and clients may be more important to treatment outcomes than what the therapist says or does. Therapists should not hide behind professional façades, but be human enough to allow themselves to be influenced by their clients. Jung (1961) observed: 'Only the wounded physician heals' (p. 156). Nevertheless, boundaries must be observed, including therapists monitoring themselves and questioning how their unconscious experiences situations.

As an example of unconscious contamination, the transference can evoke a counter-transference. Just as patients project unconscious material onto therapists, the reverse might be the case to the detriment of therapeutic outcomes. Jung strongly favoured training analyses so that therapists would be better able to protect clients from their own infections as well as to resist being infected by their clients' problems. Furthermore, Jung favoured ongoing contact with a third person who could monitor the therapist's functioning, observing that even the Pope had a confessor.

The relationship in analytic therapy differs according to the stage of therapy. For example, the relationship established during the confession stage can lay the foundation for the development of a transference relationship. Furthermore, the deeper levels of therapists' personalities are likely to be more involved in the transformation stage than in the earlier stages, which is why Jung stressed the self-education aspects of this stage.

The therapeutic relationship takes place not only face to face, but also in both therapist and client dreams and fantasies. Therapists need be sensitive to the meaning of any dreams involving their clients. Once when analysing his dreams, Jung understood the message that he was putting a woman, whom he recognized to be a patient, so high that his neck hurt to see her, as a compensation for the fact that he was looking down on her in therapy. After disclosing the dream and sharing his analysis of it with her, treatment proceeded much better (Jung, 1968).

Jung could also confront clients if he thought it necessary. When one imperious aristocratic lady client threatened to slap him after he had to say something unpleasant to her, Jung jumped up and said to her: 'Very well, you are the lady. You hit first – ladies first! But then I hit back!' (Jung, 1961, p. 165). The client then slumped back into her chair, observed that no one had ever talked to her like that before, and proceeded to work better in therapy.

THERAPEUTIC INTERVENTIONS

Jung advocated flexibility in adapting the therapy to the client. With people in the morning of life, Jung (1966) generally went along with Freudian and Adlerian approaches since these seemed to bring clients to appropriate levels of adaptation without leaving disturbing after-effects. He also observed: 'We need a different language for every patient. In one analysis I can be heard talking the Adlerian dialect, in another the Freudian' (Jung, 1961, p. 153). Jungian language and dialect appears most appropriate for those in the second half of life.

Analysis of the transference

Transferences are emotionally toned unconscious projections that occur from client to therapist. Projections take place because an activated unconscious content seeks expression. The intensity of the transference is related to the importance of the emotional content to the client. Because they are emotionally toned, transference projections arouse emotions in therapists. Counter-transference takes place when the unconscious contents of a client's projections are identical with the therapist's own unconscious processes. If therapist and client are bound together by mutual unconsciousness, the result can be highly counterproductive for analytical therapy.

Any highly emotional contents of the unconscious can be a matter for projection, including erotic material and activated archetypes. Thus transference projections can come from the personal and the collective unconscious. Though transference can be a spontaneous reaction, usually it occurs during analysis. Very often transference is a compensation for lack of genuine rapport between therapist and client. Therapists should not actively seek to promote transference projections. Transferences are not necessary for effective analysis, because therapists can obtain all the material they need from dreams anyway.

Transferences take up clients' psychic energy. Once the transference projections are extracted and consciously understood, a corresponding amount of energy will fall back into the client's possession, instead of being wasted.

Jung (1968) described four stages of analysis or therapy of the transference. However, it is possible to condense these four stages into two main stages: handling transference projections from the personal unconscious, and handling transference projections from the collective unconscious.

The main first stage involves working through transference projections that are repetitions based on clients' former personal experiences with authority figures. There are basically two tasks. The first task is for clients to realize that they are projecting past negative and positive experiences, with their associated emotions, onto their therapists. The second task is for clients to withdraw the projections from their therapists and assimilate them into their own personalities. Clients need to learn how to assume responsibility for being whole persons, including their good and bad sides. For example, clients who project negative qualities can realize that these qualities represent their shadow side which they find difficulty in acknowledging because they would rather possess a more positive image of themselves. Clients who project positive qualities can realize that perhaps they should develop these qualities in themselves.

The second main stage of transference analysis comes after the projection of personal images has been worked through and dissolved through conscious realization. A transference may still remain based on impersonal and collective rather than on personal unconscious contents. Clients need to learn to discriminate between the personal and the impersonal contents that they project onto their therapists. Jung advocated great sensitivity in handling impersonal projections and taking them seriously rather than trying to dissolve their contents. He provides the example of it being a great mistake to say to a client: 'You see, you simply project the saviour image into me. What nonsense to expect a saviour and to make me responsible' (Jung 1968, pp. 180–1). The saviour archetypal image is everywhere and clients need to keep in touch with their impersonal images.

As part of the second stage of transference analysis, clients can learn to differentiate their personal relationship to the therapist from impersonal archetypal images. Clients can have normal human reactions to their therapists for helping them, but such reactions are human and decent only when not sullied by impersonal factors. Clients need also to realize the importance of their archetypal images, many of which have a religious nature. For some clients, the recognition of impersonal values may mean that they join a church or religious creed.

Therapy of the transference is complete when clients learn to objectify their impersonal images. Detaching consciousness from the object, a major aim of Eastern religious practices, is an essential part of the process of individuation. Clients learn to assume responsibility for their lives and no longer place the guarantees of their happiness on factors outside of themselves. They attain a condition of detachment in which their centre of gravity becomes themselves rather than external objects on which they depend.

Active imagination

Active imagination is a technique devised by Jung to help people get in touch with unconscious material. Clients begin by concentrating on a starting point. Then they allow their unconscious to produce a series of images, which may make a complete story. Box 3.3 provides two examples of active imagination, the second in abbreviated form (Jung, 1968, pp. 190–3).

BOX 3.3

Examples of active imagination

Example 1: Jung as a child
As a little boy, Jung would go to a spinster aunt's house. The house was full of beautiful, old, coloured engravings. One of these was a picture of his grandfather on his mother's side, a sort of bishop represented as coming out of the house and standing at the top of a little terrace. There were some stairs coming down from the terrace and a footpath leading to the cathedral. Jung would kneel and look at the picture until he 'actively imagined' his grandfather coming down the steps.

Example 2: The young artist
A young artist client of Jung's looked at a railway station poster about a place in the Bernese Alps and imagined himself in the poster. He walked up the hill and among the cows depicted in the poster and then imagined himself coming to the top and looking down the other side. He walked down the meadow on the other side, over a stile, and then down a footpath that ran round a ravine, and a rock, and then he came to a small chapel with the door ajar. He pushed open the door and saw an altar with flowers and a wooden Mother of God. At the exact moment he looked up at her face, something with pointed ears disappeared behind the altar.

Though not the only starting point, clients can use a dream as a stimulus for active imagination. If clients do not allow conscious reason to interfere, the images can have a life of their own, which is the origin of the term 'active imagination'. After the active imagination process stops, some clients proceed to develop their unconscious images through painting, drawing, sculpting, weaving, dancing or writing.

Jung stressed that active imagination is not a panacea and that he only used it with some clients. He advised against forcing active imagination upon clients. Sometimes Jung found using active imagination particularly valuable in the later stages of therapy.

Dream analysis

Dreams are utterances or statements from the unconscious. They are the doors to the innermost secrets of the psyche. Jung thought that the idea that dreams were merely wish fulfilments was hopelessly out of date. As well as wishes and fears, dreams 'may contain ineluctable truths, philosophical pronouncements, illusions, wild fantasies, memories, plans, anticipations, irrational experiences, even telepathic visions, and heaven knows what else besides' (Jung, 1968, p. 147). Dreams may also point to solutions to issues and problems and be prescient about future events.

Jung regarded dreams as containing their whole meaning and not having false fronts. Dreams are comparable to texts that appear unintelligible, but the therapist has to discover how to read them. Dreams do not conceal, rather therapists need to discover their language. An understanding of myths and symbols is central to being able to read the language of dreams.

Jung distinguished between various kinds of dreams. Initial dreams are those that occur at the start of analysis and may deal with the client's attitude towards the therapist. For instance, a client predicted a brief and unsuccessful therapeutic contact with the dream 'I have to cross the frontier into another country, but cannot find the frontier and nobody can tell me where it is' (Jung, 1968, p. 144). Another distinction is between little dreams which are concerned with relatively unimportant matters, and 'big' dreams. Big dreams are numinous, a favourite Jung term for inexpressible, mysterious, terrifying and intensely mysterious experiences. Big dreams are of particular importance. Another distinction is that between single dreams and a series of dreams, with Jung's strong preference being to work with series of dreams.

Tasks of dream analysis

The first task in analysing a dream is to establish its context. Here, Jung used a technique he called amplification. Amplification involves the elaboration and clarification of dream images by way of directed association. Rather than encourage free association, therapists must encourage clients' associations that stick as close as possible to the dream images. For example, the dream image of a simple peasant's house may mean different things to different clients. To establish the context of the simple peasant's house, Jung would ask: 'So how does that appear to you?' or 'What are your associations to a simple peasant's house?' In this instance, the client replied: 'It is the lazar-house of St Jacob near Basel' (Jung, 1968, p. 97). From this association, Jung was able to make many connections: for example, the client feeling himself an outcast and being in great danger.

Another example of clarifying context is that of a client, whose writing desk is different, dreaming of a 'deal table'. Jung would keep returning to the image and say: 'Suppose I had no idea what the words "deal table" mean, describe this object and give me its history in such a way that I cannot fail to understand what sort of thing it is' (Jung, 1966, pp. 149–50). Therapist and client need to work on establishing the context for all the images in the dream.

Interpretation is the second task of dream analysis. Since basic ideas and themes can be much more clearly recognized in dream series than in single dreams, clients should keep a careful record of their dreams and of the interpretations made. Jung would also train clients in how to work on their dreams between sessions so that they could come prepared to the next consultation with the dream and its context written out. When interpreting dreams, a basic question for the therapist to address is: 'What conscious attitude does it compensate?'

Related to the interpretation of dreams is the third task of dream analysis, assimilation. Jung valued unconscious contents and sought to bring about change in and through the unconscious as well. Assimilation 'means mutual penetration of conscious and unconscious, and not – as is commonly thought and practised – a one-sided evaluation, interpretation, and deformation of unconscious contents by the conscious mind' (Jung, 1966, p. 152). Unconscious contents lose their danger the moment clients begin to assimilate contents that were previously repressed.

Assimilation requires the assent of the client to the therapist's interpretations. The values of the client's conscious personality must be respected and left intact, because unconscious compensation requires co-operation with an 'integral consciousness'. Box 3.4 provides an abbreviated version of Jung's analysis of a young man's dream (Jung, 1966, pp. 154–5).

BOX 3.4

Example of dream analysis

The young man's dream
My father is driving away from the house in his new car. He drives very clumsily, and I get very annoyed over his apparent stupidity. He goes this way and that, forwards and backwards, and manoeuvres the car into a dangerous position. Finally he runs into a wall and damages the car badly. I shout out at him in a perfect fury that he ought to behave himself. My father only laughs and then I see that he is dead drunk.

Context of the dream
The young man has a genuinely positive and admiring relationship with an unusually successful father. There was nothing neurotically ambivalent about the relationship.

Jung's interpretation of the dream
The client's relationship to his father is too good and his father is still doing too much for him, so that the client's unconscious is compensating by trying to take the father down a peg. The son's danger is that he cannot see his own reality. The dream forces the son to contrast himself with his father so that he can become conscious of himself.

The client's assimilation of the dream
Jung's interpretation struck home with the client and received his immediate assent. Jung points out that the interpretation damaged no real conscious values for either father or son.

Dream symbols are expressions of content not yet consciously recognized or consciously formulated. Symbols can be relatively fixed, but interpretation of their content in the last resort is not definite. Box 3.5 illustrates Jung's interpretation of the symbolism in one of the dreams of a 17-year-old female client (Jung, 1966, pp. 158–60).

The dream illustrated in Box 3.5 was taken from long-term analytical therapy where the goal is the client's progressive individuation. In such therapy, over a period of months and years there are successive assimilations of unconscious dream material. This process realizes more of the client's self in the interests of becoming a whole human being.

BOX 3.5

Example of interpreting a dream symbol

The young woman's dream
I was coming home at night. Everything is quiet as death. The door to the living room is half open, and I see my mother hanging from the chandelier, swinging to and fro in the cold wing that blows through the open windows.

Part of the dream's context
Jung was called in after two specialists had made contrary diagnoses of this 17-year-old young woman. One specialist thought she might be in the first stages of progressive muscular atrophy. The other specialist thought that she was a case of hysteria.

Jung's interpretation of the dream
The mother symbol refers to the archetype of the place of origin, to nature. The symbol also stands for the instinctive and unconscious life and the body. Jung's interpretation was that the unconscious life is destroying itself or that the dream pointed to a grave organic disease that would have a fatal outcome. This prognosis was soon confirmed.

CASE MATERIAL

Perhaps some indication of Jung's attitude to case material can be gleaned from the following quotation: 'Each individual analysis by itself shows only one part of one aspect of the deeper process, and for this reason nothing but hopeless confusion can result from comparative case histories' (Jung, 1966, p. 161). Case material that illustrates analytic therapy comes from both primary and secondary sources. In his autobiographical *Memories, Dreams, Reflections*, Jung (1961) provides case material, including many dreams, from his own explorations and confrontations with his unconscious. In his 1935 Tavistock Lectures, published as *Analytical Psychology* (1968), Jung provides case examples illustrating active imagination and dream analysis. Numerous further examples of how Jung worked are to be found in the various papers that comprise *The Practice of*

Psychotherapy (Jung, 1966). In addition, *Symbols of Transformation* (Jung, 1967) provides lengthy analyses of symbolic material contained in the fantasies of a young American lady, Miss Miller.

Jung was a very original and individualistic therapist with a vast range of scholarship to draw upon. Secondary source case material, such as that provided by Douglas (2000) and Casement (1996) can only go part way to catching the real essence of how Jung himself worked.

FURTHER DEVELOPMENTS

Samuels (1985) divided the development of analytical psychology into three schools: classical, developmental and archetypal. The classical school is that most closely based on Jung's original theory and practice, the topic of this chapter. The developmental school incorporates psychoanalytic ways of thinking and working. The archetypal school focuses on the development of symbols and images in the psyche. Douglas (2000) talks of developments in Jung's work extending to many different areas, including child analysis, group work, art therapy and a hybrid of Jungian psychology and Melanie Klein's object-relations theory. The rise of feminism is also leading to a reappraisal of Jung's ideas about masculine and feminine characteristics.

In 1922 a Jung club was established in London and, in 1946, a Society of Analytical Psychology (SAP) was founded in Britain. There is an International Association of Analytical Psychology which, as of 1 December 1999, had 2,305 members. Particularly in the Western world, interest in Jungian psychology remains strong. Jung has been called a 'homo religiosus' (Casement, 1996) or 'theologian manqué' (McLynn, 1996). His work has continuing appeal to many of those who are dissatisfied with the narrowness of scientific psychology and who seek to understand human beings in their wholeness.

SUMMARY

- *The psyche's three levels are: consciousness, the personal unconscious, and the collective unconscious.*
- *Consciousness or awareness is transitory. The centre of consciousness is the ego. The ego has the external task of providing a system of relationship between consciousness and input from the environment and the internal task of providing a system of relationship between consciousness and unconscious processes.*
- *The contents of the personal unconscious are personal to the individual. Complexes, such as the mother complex, are accumulations of associations, sometimes of a traumatic nature, that possess strong emotional content. Complexes are an important feature of the personal unconscious.*
- *The contents of the collective unconscious are a universal historical storehouse made up essentially of archetypes. Archetypes are primordial images or primordial thoughts that appear in myths, for example the hero or the redeemer, and are represented by symbols, such as the mandala.*
- *Important archetypes include: the persona, anima and animus, shadow, and self. The*

persona, or mask, is the individual's system of adaptation or way of coping with the world. The persona can also be a mask of a collective psyche. The anima is the personification of the feminine nature in a man's unconscious, whereas the animus is the personification of the masculine nature in a woman's unconscious.

- *For the most part, the shadow represents inferior traits of personality that individuals are reluctant to acknowledge. The self, which is a superordinate construct to the ego, expresses the unity of the personality as a whole and encompasses both conscious and unconscious components.*

- *Psychic energy is the psychic analogue of physical energy. Two important aspects of Jungian psychodynamics are opposition, the flow of energy between two poles, and compensation, a largely unconscious process that for the most part balances rather than opposes consciousness.*

- *The transcendent function is a synthesizing process whereby the tension between consciousness and unconsciousness creates a third thing that allows for a new level of consciousness.*

- *The introverted attitude is characterized by an orientation in life that particularly values subjective psychic contents, whereas the extraverted attitude reflects a focus on the external object or world. Thinking and feeling are rational functions, whereas sensing and intuiting are irrational functions. Jung combined attitudes and functions to provide eight main psychological types.*

- *There are four stages of life: childhood, youth, middle age, and extreme old age, with the inner challenges of middle age being of particular interest to Jung.*

- *Progression is the forward movement of psychic energy to advance the process of psychological adaptation, whereas regression is the backward movement of psychic energy.*

- *Individuation is the process by which the person becomes differentiated as a separate psychological individual and learns to live more in harmony with unconscious content.*

- *Ways in which individuals maintain levels of adaptation that may be lower than desirable include: rigid personas, complexes, fears of the contents of the unconscious, projection, and regression.*

- *Therapeutic goals differ according to the individual's stage of life and particular circumstances. Therapy for people in life's morning focuses more on attaining specific goals of adaptation, whereas goals for life's afternoon focus more on realizing the self.*

- *Though not intended as a strait-jacket, there are four stages of analytic therapy: confession, elucidation, education, and transformation.*

- *The relationship between therapist and client involves a human dialogue, with each client requiring individual understanding. Therapists and clients relate to each other on both conscious and unconscious levels. The nature of the relationship varies according to the stage of therapy.*

- *Analysis of the transference involves first handling projections from the personal unconscious and then those from the collective unconscious. Counter-transference takes place when the client's unconscious contents activate material in the therapist's unconscious.*

- *Active imagination entails clients concentrating on a starting point or stimulus and then actively imagining themselves participating in a flow of images which take on a life of their own.*

- *Therapists need to learn the language of their clients' dreams. Three tasks of dream analysis are: establishing the context of the dream, interpreting it, and the client being able to assimilate the interpretation. In long-term therapy clients successively assimilate interpretations of unconscious dream material as part of the process of individuation.*
- *The theory and practice of analytic therapy continue to develop. In addition to members of professional societies affiliated to the International Association of Analytical Psychology, numerous other people, both professional and lay, are interested in analytic therapy and its focus on the development of the whole person.*

REVIEW AND PERSONAL QUESTIONS

REVIEW QUESTIONS

1. Describe consciousness and the ego.
2. Describe the personal unconscious and its complexes.
3. Describe the collective unconscious and its archetypes.
4. What are Jungian psychodynamics and how do they differ from Freudian psychodynamics?
5. What are Jung's views on psychological types?
6. What are the four stages of life and how do the tasks of life's morning and afternoon differ?
7. How do people maintain levels of adaptation lower than desirable?
8. Describe the goals and process of analytic therapy.
9. Describe Jung's ideas on the analysis of the transference.
10. Describe as best you can how Jung approached the task of dream analysis.

PERSONAL QUESTIONS

1. Do Jung's ideas of the personal unconscious and the collective unconscious resonate in terms of your own life? If so, please elaborate.
2. Me and my shadow. What are some aspects of your shadow and what do you intend doing about them?
3. What do you consider is your personality type, and why?
4. Try using Jung's method of active imagination.
5. Take one of your dreams and, to the best of your ability, apply Jung's methods of dream analysis to it.
6. What goals would you set for yourself if you were to be a client in Jungian therapy?

ANNOTATED BIBLIOGRAPHY

Jung, C. G. (1968). *Analytical Psychology: Its Theory and Practice.* New York: Vintage Books.
This book presents the five lectures, plus discussion, that Jung gave at the Tavistock Clinic in London in 1935. Topics covered include the structure of the mind, word association and psychological types, and the methods of active imagination, dream analysis and the analysis of

the transference. This book provides an excellent concise introduction to analytical psychology.

Jung , C. G. (1966). *The Practice of Psychotherapy* (2nd edition). London: Routledge (Volume 16 in *The Collected Works of C. G. Jung*).

This book is divided into two parts. Part one, entitled 'General problems of psychotherapy', contains nine papers, including one on the aims of psychotherapy. Part two, entitled 'Specific problems of psychotherapy', contains Jung's ideas on the therapeutic value of abreaction, the practical use of dream analysis, and the psychology of the transference. Some useful case study material is included in an appendix, entitled 'The realities of practical psychotherapy'.

Jung , C. G. (1961). *Memories, Dreams, Reflections.* London: Fontana Press.

Jung regarded his life as a story of the realization of the unconscious. In this book, compiled at the end of his life, Jung tells his personal myth, an inner journey structured around the following chapter headings: first years, school years, student years, psychiatric activities, Sigmund Freud, confrontation with the unconscious, the work, the tower, travels, visions, on life after death, and late thoughts. Some controversy exists over the extent of Jung's secretary's contribution to this book rather than its being a solely primary source.

Jung , C. G. (1971). *Psychological Types.* London: Routledge.

This book, Volume 6 in the *Collected Works*, was originally published in 1921 after Jung's fallow period. It starts with a scholarly discussion of the notion of psychological types drawing on material from literature, aesthetics, religion and philosophy as well as from psychology. Jung then presents his ideas on attitudes, functions and psychological types. The book ends with an appendix containing four papers on psychological typology.

Hall, C. S. and Nordby, B. J. (1973). *A Primer of Jungian Psychology.* New York: New American Library.

A valuable and relatively short secondary source book about Jungian theory. However, there is little mention of the practice of analytical therapy. Good coverage of the structure, dynamics and development of personality, the psychological types and of symbols and dreams.

REFERENCES AND FURTHER READING

All of Jung's writings can be found in the eighteen volumes of *The Collected Works of C. G. Jung*, published in Britain by Routledge, London, and in America by Princeton University Press, Princeton, NJ.

Casement, A. (1996). Psychodynamic therapy: The Jungian approach. In W. Dryden (ed.). *Handbook of Individual Therapy.* London: Sage, 77–102.

Douglas, C. (2000). Analytical psychotherapy. In R. Corsini and D. Wedding (eds). *Current Psychotherapies* (6th edition). Itasca, IL: Peacock, pp. 99–132.

Hall, C. S. and Nordby, B. J. (1973). *A Primer of Jungian Psychology.* New York: New American Library.

Jung, C. G. (1961). *Memories, Dreams, Reflections.* London: Fontana Press.

Jung, C. G. (1966). *The Practice of Psychotherapy* (2nd edition). London: Routledge (Volume 16 in the *Collected Works*).

Jung, C. G. (1967). *Symbols of Transformation* (2nd edition). Princeton, NJ: Princeton University Press. (Volume 5 in the *Collected Works*).

Jung, C. G. (1968). *Analytical Psychology: Its Theory and Practice.* New York: Vintage Books.

Jung, C. G. (1971). *Psychological Types.* London: Routledge.

Jung, C. G. (1976a). The concept of the collective unconscious. In J. Campbell (ed.). *The Portable Jung.* London: Penguin Books, 59–70.

Jung, C. G. (1976b). The relations between the ego and the unconscious. In J. Campbell (ed.). *The Portable Jung.* London: Penguin Books, 70–138.

Jung, C. G. (1976c). The transcendent function. In J. Campbell (ed.). *The Portable Jung.* London: Penguin Books, 273–300.

Jung, C. G. (1981). *The Development of Personality: Papers on Child Psychology, Education and Related Subjects.* London: Routledge.

Jung, C. G. (1982). *Aspects of the Feminine.* London: Ark Paperbacks.

Jung, C. G. (1983). Fundamental concepts of libido theory. In A. Storr (ed.). *The Essential Jung.* Princeton, NJ: Princeton University Press, 59–64.

Jung, C. G. (1989). *Aspects of the Masculine.* Princeton, NJ: Princeton University Press.

McLynn, F. (1996). *Carl Gustav Jung: A Biography.* London: Bantam Press.

Samuels, A. (1985). *Jung and the Post-Jungians.* London: Routledge and Kegan Paul.

4

Person-centred Therapy

It seems to me that at bottom each person is asking, 'Who am I really? How can I get in touch with this real self, underlying all my surface behaviour? How can I become myself?'

Carl Rogers

INTRODUCTION

Have you ever felt that you would like to find yourself and be more truly your own person? Are you able to experience your feelings and act autonomously, or are you still mainly a creation of your parents and of the influence of significant others in your background? Carl Rogers was the originator of an approach to counselling and therapy that aimed to help clients fulfil their unique potential and become their own persons. His approach was partly an attempt to get away from the interpretive psychodynamic therapies described in the previous two chapters. In addition, Rogers was trying to emancipate people from the overbearing influence that parents of his time often had on the thoughts, feelings and actions of their offspring. In the early part of the twentieth century, when Rogers was growing up, parents exercised much more power in the home than they do now at the start of the twenty-first century. Rogers' person-centred therapy challenged authoritarian tendencies in both therapy and parenting and championed the rights of clients to discover their own directions.

On 11 December 1940, Rogers gave a presentation at the University of Minnesota entitled 'Some newer concepts in psychotherapy' which is the single event most often identified with the birth of client-centered therapy (Raskin and Rogers, 2000). In 1974, Rogers and his colleagues changed the name from 'client-centred' to 'person-centred'. They believed that the new name would more adequately describe the human values and the mutuality underlying their approach and would apply to contexts other than counselling and psychotherapy. However, Thorne observes: 'Rogers never completely jettisoned the term "client-centred therapy". He uses client-centred and person-centred interchangeably when talking about counselling and psychotherapy but *always* employs the term "the person-centred approach" when referring to activities outside the one-to-one therapy situation' (B. Thorne, personal communication, 15 March 1994).

Rogers regarded himself as having one seminal idea. The central hypothesis of the person-centred approach is that every person has within himself or herself 'vast resources for self-understanding, for altering his or her self-concept, attitudes, and self-directed behaviour – and that these resources can be tapped only if a definable climate of facilitative psychological attitudes can be provided' (Rogers, 1986a, p. 197). Empathy, congruence and unconditional positive regard are the three therapist-offered faciliative conditions that Rogers regarded as necessary and sufficient for therapeutic change (Rogers, 1957).

This chapter is drawn mainly from Rogers' writings. However, he encouraged colleagues and associates to develop it and, consequently, regarded his theory as a group enterprise (Rogers, 1959). In addition, Rogers was influenced by psychologists like Combs, Snygg and Maslow. I incorporate the ideas of Rogers' collaborators when it adds to or clarifies his position.

CARL ROGERS (1902–87)

Carl Ransom Rogers was born in Illinois, America, the fourth of six children. His father was a civil engineer and contractor who had a successful construction business. A rather sickly boy, Rogers lived his childhood in a close-knit family in which hard work and a highly conservative, almost fundamentalist Protestant Christianity were almost equally revered. Rogers was a shy boy who was teased a lot at home. Included among reasons for the teasing were that he was rather a bookworm and extremely absent-minded; in fact, his family called him 'Professor Moony' after a famous comic-strip character (Cohen, 1997).

When Rogers was 12 his parents bought a farm and this became the family home. Rogers regarded his parents as masters of the art of subtle, loving control. He shared little of his private thoughts and feelings with them because he knew these would have been judged and found wanting. Until Rogers went to college he was a loner who read incessantly and who adopted his parents' attitude toward the outside world, summed up in the statement: 'Other persons behave in dubious ways which we do not approve in our family' (Rogers, 1980, p. 28). Such dubious ways included playing cards, going to the cinema, smoking, dancing, drinking and engaging in other even less mentionable activities. He was socially incompetent in other than superficial contacts and, while at high school, had only two dates with girls. He relates that his fantasies during this period were bizarre and would probably have been classified as schizoid by a psychological diagnostician.

Rogers entered the University of Wisconsin to study agriculture, but later changed to history, feeling that this would be a better preparation for his emerging professional goal of becoming a minister of religion. His first real experience of fellowship was in a group there who met in a YMCA class. When he was 20, Rogers went to China for an international World Student Christian Federation Conference and, for the first time, emancipated himself from the religious thinking of his parents, a fundamental step towards becoming an independent person. Also, at about this time Rogers fell in love, and, on completing college, married Helen Elliott, who was an artist. This marriage lasted until she died in 1979.

In 1924, Rogers went to Union Theological Seminary, but after two years moved to Teachers College, Columbia University, where he was exposed to the instrumentalist philosophy of John Dewey, the highly statistical and Thorndikean behavioural approaches of Teachers College, and the Freudian orientation of the Institute for Child Guidance where he had an internship. Along with his formal learning, he was starting to understand relationships with others better, and was beginning to realize that, in close relationships, the elements that 'cannot' be shared are those that are the most important and rewarding to share.

Rogers received his MA from Columbia University in 1928 and then spent twelve years in a community child guidance clinic in Rochester, New York. In 1931, he received his PhD from Columbia University and in 1939 published his first book, entitled *The Clinical Treatment of the Problem Child*. During this period Rogers felt that he was becoming more competent as a therapist, not least because his experience with clients was providing him with valuable learning and insights which contributed to a shift from diagnosis to listening. Furthermore, such a relationship approach met his own needs, since, stemming from his early loneliness, the therapy interview was a socially approved way of getting really close to people without the pains and longer time-span of the friendship process outside therapy.

In 1940, Rogers accepted a position as a Professor of Psychology at Ohio State University and two years later published *Counseling and Psychotherapy*, the contents of which were derived primarily from his work as a counsellor rather than as an academic psychologist. After initial poor sales, the book became well known because it offered a way to work with veterans returning from the Second World War. From 1942, Rogers had undertaken consultancies relating to the war effort, including training counsellors. After leaving Ohio State University, Rogers spent a very brief spell as director of counselling for the United Services Organisation, a servicemen's welfare organization. From 1945 to 1957 Rogers was Professor of Psychology and executive secretary of the university counselling centre at the University of Chicago, where non-directive, or client-centred therapy as it came to be called, was further developed and researched. In 1951, Rogers published *Client-Centered Therapy*, which contained a theoretical statement as well as a series of chapters related to client-centred practice.

In 1957, Rogers was appointed Professor of Psychology and Psychiatry at the University of Wisconsin, where he examined the impact of the client-centred approach on hospitalized schizophrenics. In 1959, Rogers published by far the most thorough statement of his theoretical position (Rogers, 1959), and in 1961 *On Becoming a Person*, one of his most commercially successful books, came out. From 1962 to 1963 Rogers was a fellow at the Center for Advanced Study in the Behavioral Sciences at Stanford University. In 1964 he went to the Western Behavioral Sciences Institute at La Jolla, California, as a resident fellow. Then, in 1968, with some colleagues, Rogers formed the Center for Studies of the Person at La Jolla, where he was a resident fellow until his death. During the latter part of his career Rogers developed a great interest in the application of person-centred ideas to group work, community change, and preventing 'nuclear, planetary suicide' and ran many large-scale workshops around the world (Kirschenbaum and Henderson, 1990). In addition, as Rogers grew older, having earlier firmly rejected his Christian past, he realized he had underestimated the mystical or spiritual dimension in life.

From the age of 13 Rogers had viewed himself as a scientist. He was a committed researcher and pioneered the use of tape recorders to study counselling and therapy processes. In 1956 he received the American Psychological Association's Award for Distinguished Scientific Contributions. Rogers was also an author with a deep commitment to clear and cogent communication. When he was 75, he observed: 'Yet there is, I believe, a much more important reason for my writing. It seems to me that I am still – inside – the shy boy who found communication very difficult in interpersonal situations . . .' (Rogers, 1980, p. 80). As well as those already mentioned, his books include: *Freedom to Learn*; *Encounter Groups*; *Becoming Partners*; *Carl Rogers on Personal Power*; and *A Way of Being*. A chronological bibliography of Rogers' books and articles published in the period 1930 to 1980 is printed at the end of *A Way of Being*.

Although the years since 1940 were very successful for Rogers and his ideas, they also contained professional and personal struggles. Two professional struggles were those with psychiatry and with behavioural psychology. Rogers fought for psychologists, as contrasted with psychiatrists, to be allowed to practise psychotherapy and to have administrative responsibility over 'mental health' work. Also, he constantly highlighted the philosophical and practical issues involved in a humanistic or person-centred as against a behavioural view of human beings.

On a more personal level, Rogers continued striving to become a more real, open and growing person. He struggled, with varying degrees of success, with some personal crises and difficulties. During his Chicago period, with counselling help, he worked through a crisis arising from a 'badly bungled therapeutic relationship' (Rogers, 1980, p. 39) with 'a particularly demanding and highly disturbed female client' (Thorne, 1992). In the 1970s, Rogers faced the strains of his wife's long illness – from 1972 she was intermittently in a wheelchair and in 1979 she died. In the last years of her life, there was much pain in his relationship with Helen. Nevertheless Rogers movingly talks of how he was able to express his appreciation and love for her two days before she died (Rogers, 1980).

Toward the end his life Rogers was increasingly aware of his 'capacity for love, my sensuality, my sexuality' (Rogers, 1980, p. 96) and wished to have loving relationships outside of marriage. In August 1975, Rogers met and fell in love with a much younger divorcee called Bernice Todres, but the relationship was never sexually consummated. In December 1979 this only intermittently satisfactory and episodic relationship finally ended. In the 1970s Rogers was drinking heavily, consuming over 12 oz of vodka a day, which contributed to his putting on weight. At one stage, his daughter Natalie was so worried about his drinking that she is said to have suggested he book himself into a detox clinic (Cohen, 1997).

Rogers was a complex mixture of high intelligence, high energy, ambition, competitiveness, Protestant work ethic, strength, vulnerability, charisma, idealism, altruism, self-centredness, caring, shyness, sensitivity, warmth, and ability to touch others deeply. Arguably, as his career developed, Rogers allowed the need to become and maintain the professional persona of Carl Rogers to get in the way of his becoming a more highly developed person. Clearly very conscious of his place in the history of American counselling and therapy, Rogers left the United States Library of Congress 140 boxes of his papers, as well as tapes and films of his work.

Even as an old man, Rogers was still prone to blame his parents for making him feel that he did not deserve to be loved (Cohen, 1997). A wounded theorist, he was influenced by his own early emotional deprivations to design a counselling approach to overcome their effects and hence to meet his own companionship and growth needs. Other sources of learning included his clients and the stimulus provided by younger colleagues. Rogers claimed that serendipity or 'the faculty of making fortunate and unexpected discoveries by accident' had also been important (Rogers, 1980, p. 64). Rogers enjoyed gardening and finding the right conditions for plants to grow. As with plants, so with people. While regarding the following saying from Lao-Tse as an oversimplification, Rogers considers that it sums up many of his deeper beliefs about human growth.

> *If I keep from meddling with people, they take care of themselves,*
> *If I keep from commanding people, they behave themselves,*
> *If I keep from preaching at people, they improve themselves,*
> *If I keep from imposing on people, they become themselves.*

THEORY

I have formed some philosophical impressions of the life and goal toward which the individual moves when he is free.

Carl Rogers

BASIC CONCEPTS

In 1951 Rogers presented his theory of personality and behaviour as the final chapter of *Client-Centred Therapy*. Eight years later, in an edited publication entitled *Psychology: A Study of Science*, he presented an updated version which he regarded as his major and most rigorous theoretical statement and 'the most thoroughly ignored of anything I have written' (Rogers, 1980, p. 60). Later, with collaborators, Rogers restated his theory, but did not alter it (for instance, Raskin and Rogers, 2000). Rogers thought that this and any theory should be a stimulus for further creative thinking rather than a dogma of truth.

Perceptual or subjective frame of reference

Combs and Snygg (1959) state that, broadly speaking, behaviour may be observed from either the point of view of outsiders or the point of view of the behavers themselves. It is sometimes stated that the former is viewing behaviour from the external frame of reference while the latter is viewing behaviour from the internal, subjective or perceptual frame of reference. Rogers writes of his fundamental belief in the subjective, observing that 'Man lives essentially in his own personal and subjective world, and even his most objective functioning, in science, mathematics, and the like, is the result of subjective purpose and subjective choice' (Rogers, 1959, p. 191). It is this emphasis on the subjective, perceptual view of clients which has led to the term 'client-centred'. The perceptions of clients are viewed as their versions of reality.

Later, Rogers was again to stress that the only reality people can possibly know is the world which they individually perceive and experience at this moment. The notion that there is a 'real world', the definition of which can be agreed upon by everyone, is a luxury that the human race cannot afford, since it leads to false beliefs, like faith in technology, which have brought our species to the brink of annihilation. His alternative hypothesis is that there are as many realities as there are people. Furthermore, people are increasingly 'inwardly and organismically rejecting the view of one single, culture-approved reality' (Rogers, 1980, p. 26).

Actualizing tendency

The actualizing tendency is the single basic motivating drive. It is an active process representing the inherent tendency of the organism to develop its capacities in the direction of maintaining, enhancing and reproducing itself. The actualizing tendency is operative at all times in all organisms and is the distinguishing feature of whether a given organism is alive or dead. The organism is always up to something. In addition, the actualizing tendency involves a development toward the differentiation of organs and functions.

Rogers observes, from his experiences with individual and group counselling and from his attempts to provide students in classes with 'freedom to learn', that 'the most impressive fact about the individual human being seems to be the directional tendency toward wholeness, toward actualisation of potentialities' (Rogers, 1977, p. 240). Furthermore, he cited support for the actualizing tendency both in his observations of the natural world, for instance the behaviour of seaweed and of children learning to walk, and in empirical research, be it on sea urchins, rats, human infants and brain-damaged war veterans. The cornerstone of both Rogers' therapeutic and his political thinking was that, because of their actualizing tendency, people move towards self-regulation and their own enhancement and away from control by external forces.

The actualizing tendency is basically positive. It represents Rogers' trust in the wisdom of the organism and its constructive directional flow toward the realization of each individual's full potential. People have the capacity to guide, regulate and control themselves, provided certain definable conditions exist. The person-centred approach posits a unitary diagnosis that all psychological difficulties are caused by blockages to this actualizing tendency and, consequently, the task of therapy is to release further this fundamentally good motivating drive. Maslow (1970) reiterates this assessment of people's basic nature when he writes that the human being does seem to have instinct remnants and that clinical and other evidence suggests that those weak instinctoid tendencies are good, desirable and worth saving.

Often, however, people appear to have two motivational systems, their organismic actualizing tendency and their conscious self. Maslow (1962) writes of the basic conflict in humans between defensive forces and growth trends and observes that the actualizing tendency may involve both deficiency and growth motivations. However, given a certain emotional environment, growth motivations will become increasingly strong.

Organismic valuing process

The concept of an organismic valuing process is central to the idea of a real or true and unique self. A person's organismic valuing process relates to the continuous weighing of experience and the placing of values on that experience in terms of its ability to satisfy the actualizing tendency. For instance, the behaviour of infants indicates that they prefer those experiences, such as curiosity and security, which maintain and enhance their organism, and reject those, such as pain and hunger, which do not. This weighing of experience is an organismic rather than a conscious symbolic process. The source of the valuing process or values placed on the various experiences seems clearly to be in the infants, who react to their own sensory and visceral evidence. As people grow older, their valuing process is effective in helping them to achieve self-actualizing to the degree that they are able to be aware of and perceive the experiencing which is going on within themselves.

Experience and experiencing

Rogers uses the term 'sensory and visceral experience' in a psychological rather than a physiological sense. Perhaps another way of stating sensory and visceral experience is the undergoing of facts and events, which are potentially available to conscious awareness, by the organism's sensory and visceral equipment. People may be unaware of much of their experiencing. For instance, when sitting, you may not be aware of the sensation on your buttocks until your attention is drawn to it. Another example is that you may not be aware of the physiological aspects of hunger because you are so fascinated by work or play. However, this experience is potentially available to conscious awareness. The total range of experience at any given moment may be called the 'experiential', 'perceptual' or 'phenomenal' field. Rogers stressed that physiological events such as neuron discharges or changes in blood sugar are not included in his psychological definition of experience.

The verb 'experiencing' means that the organism is receiving the impact of any sensory or visceral experiences that happen at the moment. Experiencing a feeling includes receiving both the emotional content and the personal meaning or cognitive content 'as they are experienced inseparably in the moment' (Rogers, 1959, p. 198). Experiencing a feeling fully means that experiencing, awareness and expression of the feeling are all congruent.

Perception and awareness

Perception and awareness are virtually synonymous in person-centred theory. When an experience is perceived, this means that it is in conscious awareness, however dimly, though it need not be expressed in verbal symbols. Another way of stating this is that 'perceiving' is 'becoming aware of stimuli or experiences'. Rogers viewed all perception and awareness as transactional in nature, being a construction from past experience and a hypothesis or prediction of the future. Perception or awareness may or may not correspond with experience or 'reality'. When an experience is symbolized accurately in awareness, this means that the hypothesis implicit in the awareness will be borne out if tested by acting on it. Many experiences may not be symbolized accurately in awareness because of defensive denials and distortions. Other experiences, such as buttocks sitting on a chair, may not be perceived, since they may be unimportant to the actualizing tendency.

Awareness, or conscious attention, is one of the latest evolutionary developments of the human species. One way in which Rogers regarded it was as 'a tiny peak of awareness, of symbolizing capacity, topping a vast pyramid of non-conscious organismic functioning' (Rogers, 1977, p. 244). Box 4.1 attempts to illustrate this. When a person is functioning well, awareness is a reflection of part of the flow of the organism at that moment. However, all too often people are not functioning well, and organismically they are moving in one direction while their aware or conscious lives are struggling in another.

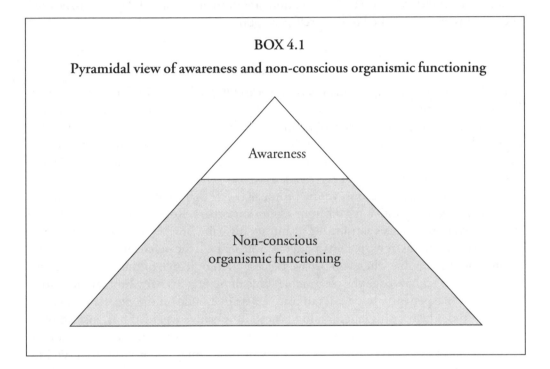

BOX 4.1

Pyramidal view of awareness and non-conscious organismic functioning

Awareness

Non-conscious
organismic functioning

ACQUISITION

Person-centred theory may become clearer to the reader by maintaining a distinction between self and self-concept. The self may be viewed as the real, underlying, organismic self expressed in popular sayings such as 'To thine own self be true' and 'To be that self which one truly is'. People's self-concepts are their perceptions of themselves, which do not always correspond with their own experiencing or organismic selves. Thus, ideally the actualizing tendency refers to self-actualizing where aspects of self and of self-concept are synonymous or congruent. However, where self and self-concept are incongruent, the desire to actualize the self-concept may work against the deeper need to actualize the organismic self. In Rogers' writings, the above distinction is always implicit, if not always explicit.

Early development of self-concept

The self-concept is the self as perceived and the values attached to these perceptions, or what a person refers to as 'I' or 'me'. Initially, the self-concept may be made up largely of self-experiences, events in the phenomenal field discriminated by the individual as 'I', 'me', or 'self', even though in a pre-verbal way. For instance, infants who discover their toes may incorporate the fact that they have toes into their self-concept. Also, infants who are hungry may incorporate into their self-concepts the fact that they negatively value hunger. As young people interact with the environment, more and more experience may become symbolized in awareness as self-experience. Not least through interaction with significant others who treat them as a separate self, they develop a self-concept which includes both their perceptions about themselves and the varying positive and negative values attached to these self-perceptions.

Conditions of worth

A need for positive regard from others is a learned need developed in early infancy. Positive regard means here the perception of experiencing oneself as making a positive difference in the experiential field of another. It is likely that on many occasions young people's behaviour and experiencing of their behaviour will coincide with positive regard from others and hence meet their need for positive regard. For instance, smiling at parents may reflect a pleasurable experience as well as generating positive regard.

However, on other occasions, young people may feel that their experiencing conflicts with their need for positive regard from significant others. Rogers gives the example of the child who experiences satisfaction at hitting his baby brother, but who experiences the words and actions of his parents as saying 'You are bad, the behaviour is bad, and you are not loved or lovable when you behave this way.' An outcome of this may be that the child does not acknowledge the pleasurable value of hitting his baby brother emanating from his own experience, but comes to place a negative value on the experience because of the attitudes held by his parents and his need for positive regard. Thus, instead of an accurate symbolization of the experience, such as 'While I experience the behaviour as satisfying, my parents experience it as unsatisfying', there may come a distorted symbolization, such as 'I perceive this behaviour as unsatisfying' (Rogers, 1951, p. 500). Such values, which are based on others' evaluations rather than on the individual's own organismic valuing process, are called conditions of worth. Conditions of worth are prevalent because all too often 'individuals are culturally conditioned, rewarded, reinforced, for behaviors that are in fact perversions of the natural directions of the unitary actualizing tendency' (Rogers, 1977, p. 247).

The concept of conditions of worth is important because it means that people develop a second valuing process. The first is the organismic valuing process which truly reflects the actualizing tendency. The second is a conditions of worth process, based on the internalization or 'introjection' of others' evaluations, which does not truly reflect the actualizing tendency but may serve to impede it. However, people possess a false awareness in regard to this second valuing process, since they feel that decisions based on it are in fact based on their organismic valuing process. Thus experiences may be sought or avoided to meet false rather than real needs.

Self-actualizing, when it takes the form of self-concept actualizing based on conditions of worth, is by no means always a good thing. Rogers advocated self-actualizing based on an individual's organismic valuing process that genuinely reflects their unique actualizing tendency. This distinction can be an area of great confusion for students.

Family life

The adequacy of the self-concepts of parents affects the ways in which they relate to their children. Thomas Gordon, a contributor to Rogers' 1951 book *Client-Centered Therapy*, has emphasized that the level of self-acceptance or self-regard of parents may be related to their degree of acceptance of the behaviour of their children, though this is not something which is static. Box 4.2 is a representation, albeit oversimplified, of the possible effects of parents on their children. Rogers observed that parents are able to feel unconditional positive regard for a child only to the extent that they experience unconditional

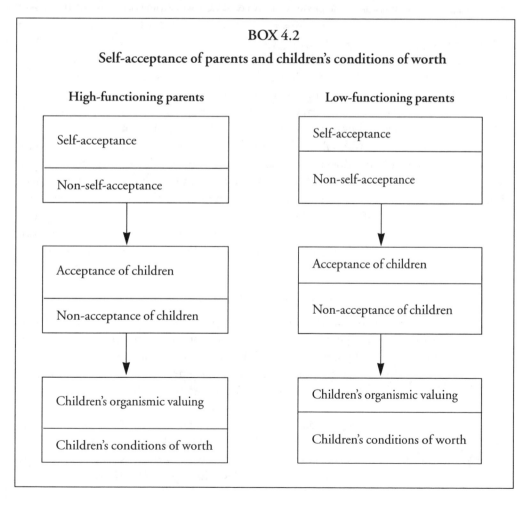

BOX 4.2

Self-acceptance of parents and children's conditions of worth self-regard. By 'unconditional positive regard' Rogers meant prizing a child even though the parent may not value equally all of his or her behaviours. The greater the degree of unconditional positive regard that parents experience toward the child, the fewer the conditions of worth in the child and the higher the level of its psychological adjustment. Put simply, high functioning parents create the conditions for the development of high-functioning children. In 1970, Gordon published *Parent Effectiveness Training* based on person-centred principles. This book attempts to teach parents how to listen to and talk with their children, thus helping the attitude of prizing to be communicated to them.

Effect of conditions of worth on self-concept

People differ in the degree to which they internalize conditions of worth depending not only on the degree of unconditional positive regard they are offered by significant others, but also on the degree of empathic understanding and congruence shown to them. In addition, the extent of their need for positive regard influences their vulnerability to introjecting conditions of worth. For some, their self-concepts will develop so as to allow much of their experience to be accurately perceived. However, even the most fortunate are likely to internalize some conditions of worth, and the less fortunate are fated to internalize many.

Some common examples of conditions of worth are: 'Achievement is very important and I am less of a person if I do not achieve', 'Making money is very important and, if I do not make much money, then I am a failure', and 'Sexual fantasies and behaviours are mostly bad and I should not like myself for having them.' Thus, conditions of worth entail not only internalized evaluations of how people should be, but also internalized evaluations about how they should feel about themselves if they perceive that they are not the way they should be. Rogers believed that it is common for most people to have their values largely introjected, held as fixed concepts and rarely examined or tested. Thus, not only are they estranged from their experiencing, but their level of self-regard is lowered and they are unable to prize themselves fully. Furthermore, by internalizing conditions of worth, they have internalized a process by which they come to be the agents of lowering their own level of self-regard or, more colloquially, of 'self-oppression'.

Marriage and education

The person-centred view is that the conditions for the development of adequate self-concepts and those for remedying inadequate self-concepts are essentially the same. Both contain the characteristics of good and loving interpersonal relationships. Implicit in this is the notion that significant experiences for the development of adequate and, regrettably, also of inadequate self-concepts are neither restricted to childhood and adolescence nor to family life.

Rogers saw contributions to the development of adequate self-concepts as potentially available in many other human situations. Most people are less self-actualizing than desirable because they are cluttered up with conditions of worth. Rogers increasingly turned his attentions to the problems of the less disturbed. Relationships between partners, whether marital or otherwise, can have growth-inducing properties in which conditions of worth dissolve and the level of self-regard increases. In *Becoming Partners*, Rogers (1973) gave a moving case study involving Joe's steady and healing concern for and trust in Irene's potential, despite her initial self-conception that 'I don't let you see this little, black, rotten, ugly ball I have buried down inside that's really me, that's unlovable and unacceptable' (Rogers, 1973, p. 100).

Rogers also turned his attention to the under-realized potential of educational institutions for creating emotional climates for the development of healthy self-concepts. He particularly favoured significant experiential learning which was self-initiated and reflected the concerns of students rather than those of teachers or administrators (Rogers, 1969). In addition, he focused on the politics of interpersonal and intergroup relationships and saw his faith in the actualizing tendency as indicating a more democratic sharing of power and control (Rogers, 1977).

MAINTENANCE

For practising counsellors and therapists the question is not so much how clients become the way they are, as what currently causes them to maintain behaviour which does not meet their real needs. The concept of maintenance, or of how maladjusted behaviour and perceptions are perpetuated, often in the face of conflicting evidence, is critical to a full understanding of person-centred theory and practice. Person-centred theory may be viewed as a theory of human information processing or of the processing of experiences into perceptions. This is a process in which, especially for those who are disturbed, conditions of worth play a large part.

Processing of experience

Rogers observed that when experiences occur in people's lives there are four possible outcomes. First, like the sensation of sitting, they may be ignored. Second, they may be accurately perceived and organized into some relationship with the self-concept either because they meet a need of the self or because they are consistent with the self-concept and thus reinforce it. Third, their perception may be distorted in such a way as to resolve the conflict between self-concept and experiencing. For instance, students with low academic self-concepts may receive some positive feedback about their essays and perceive 'The teacher did not read it properly', or 'The teacher must have low standards.' Fourth, the experiences may be denied or not perceived at all. For example, people may have had their self-concepts deeply influenced by strict moral upbringings and thus be unable to perceive their cravings for sexual satisfaction.

Box 4.3 represents the processing of experience by low-functioning and high-functioning people. Previously I mentioned that people have two valuing processes, their own organismic valuing process and an internalized process based on conditions of worth. Low-functioning people are out of touch with their own valuing process for large areas of their experiencing. In these areas their self-concepts are based on conditions of worth which cause them to distort and deny much of their experiencing. On the other hand,

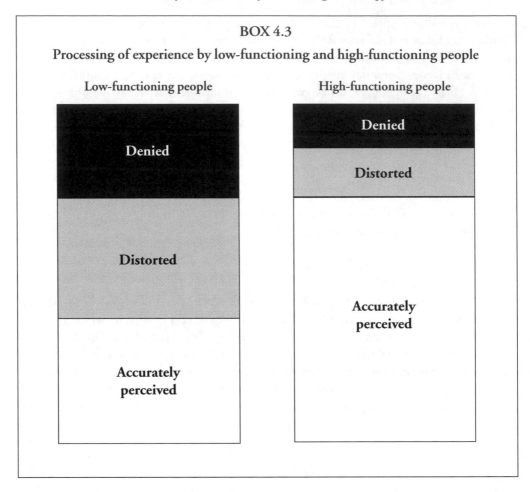

BOX 4.3

Processing of experience by low-functioning and high-functioning people

Low-functioning people   High-functioning people

high-functioning people have fewer conditions of worth and thus are able to perceive most of their experiences accurately.

Both high-functioning and low-functioning people are motivated by the actualizing tendency. In addition, they possess a general tendency toward self-actualization, or actualization of that portion of the organism's experience symbolized in the self. The self-concepts of high-functioning people allow them to perceive most significant sensory and visceral experiences and thus their self-actualizing entails no significant blockages to their actualizing tendency. However, with low-functioning people a split occurs and 'the general tendency to actualize the organism may work at cross purposes with the sub-system of that motive, the tendency to actualize the self' (Rogers, 1959, p. 197). Low-functioning people engage in a process of self-actualizing insufficiently based on their organism's own valuing process. Consequently, while high-functioning people are able to interact with others and their environments on the basis of largely realistic information, low-functioning people do not have that capacity to any great extent.

Incongruence between self-concept and experience

When experiences are accurately symbolized and included in the self-concept, there is a state of congruence between self-concept and experience or, stated another way, between the self-concept and the organismic valuing process. When, however, experience is denied and distorted, there exists a state of incongruence between self-concept and experience. This state of incongruence may exist where experiences are positive as well as where they are negative. Counselling and therapy clients tend to have low self-concepts and frequently deny and distort positive feedback from outside as well as inhibit positive feelings from within.

Threat, anxiety and subception

Rogers uses the concept of subception or pre-perception to explain the mechanism by which sensory and visceral experiences relevant to the actualizing tendency may be denied or inaccurately perceived. He quotes McCleary and Lazarus' finding that 'Even when a subject is unable to report a visual discrimination he is still able to make a stimulus discrimination at some level below that required for conscious recognition' (1949, p. 178). Subception involves a filtering of experience in such a way that experiences contradictory and threatening to the self-concept may be excluded or altered. Thus the organism may discriminate the meaning of an experience without using the higher nerve centres involved in conscious awareness or perception. The process of subception is the mechanism of defence of the self-concept in response to threats to its current structure or set of self-conceptions.

Anxiety is a state of uneasiness or tension which is the response of the organism to the 'subception' that a discrepancy or incongruence between self-concept and experience may enter perception or awareness, thus forcing a change in the currently prevailing self-concept. The term 'intensionality' is used to describe characteristics of the individual who is in a defensive state. Intensional reactions include seeing experience in absolute and rigid terms, overgeneralization, confusing facts and evaluation, and relying on abstractions rather than on reality testing.

Breakdown and disorganization

This section relates to serious disturbance. The self-concepts of very low-functioning people block their accurate perception of large areas of their significant sensory and visceral experience. If, however, a situation develops in which a significant experience occurs suddenly, or very obviously, in an area of high incongruence, the process of defence may be unable to operate successfully. Thus, not only may anxiety be experienced to the extent to which the self-concept is threatened, but, with the process of defence being unsuccessful, the experience may be accurately symbolized in awareness. People are brought face-to-face with more of their denied experiences than they can handle, with an ensuing state of disorganization and the possibility of a psychotic breakdown. Rogers mentioned that he had known psychotic breakdowns to occur when people sought 'therapy' from many different sources simultaneously and also when clients were prematurely faced with material revealed under the influence of sodium pentathol. Once acute psychotic behaviours have been exhibited, the defensive processes may work to protect people against the pain and anxiety generated by the perception of the incongruence.

Importance of self-concept

A person's self-concept, especially certain self-perceptions which are viewed as central, has been demonstrated to be fundamental to understanding how psychological maladjustment is maintained. The self-concept is so important to people because it is the constellation of their perceptions about themselves and, as such, the means by which they interact with life in such a way as to meet their needs. Effective self-concepts allow people to perceive their experiences realistically, whether they originate within their organisms or in their environments; in other words, such self-concepts allow them open access to their experiences.

Ineffective self-concepts may be maintained tenaciously for a number of reasons. First, as with the effective self-concepts, ineffective self-concepts are perceived as the means of need gratification and the source of personal adequacy. Second, ineffective self-concepts contain within them many conditions of worth which may have been functional at one stage of people's lives, but which have outgrown any usefulness they once possessed. Nevertheless, because they originate from people's need for positive regard, they may be deeply embedded in the structure of their self-concepts as a kind of 'emotional baggage'. Third, the more deeply embedded such conditions of worth have become, the more tenaciously they are maintained, since to alter them would involve the anxiety of perceiving the incongruence between these self-perceptions and experiencing. Fourth, the conditions of worth have the effect of lowering people's sense of worth and thus making it less likely that they will have the confidence to acknowledge and face their areas of incongruence. There is a threshold area for both high-functioning and low-functioning people in which they may be able to assimilate incongruent perceptions into their self-concepts. This threshold area appears to be narrower and more tightly defined for low-functioning people.

Characteristics of self-concept

Since the idea of self-concept, sometimes expressed as 'self-structure', 'perceived self', 'phenomenal self', or just 'self', is so fundamental to person-centred theory, I briefly review some of its characteristics.

Content areas

People's self-concepts are unique complexes of many different self-conceptions which constitute their way of describing and distinguishing themselves. Some content areas of peoples self-concepts include: bodily, social, sexual, feelings and emotions, tastes and preferences, work, recreation, intellectual activity, and philosophy and values. People vary in the importance they attach to these various areas and also in the kinds of self-conceptions they have in them. For instance, the shape of their nose may be felt as important by one person, while another may be scarcely aware of it. The self-concept may be described in self-referent statements such as 'I am a good carpenter', 'I like ice-cream' and 'Meeting new people makes me nervous.'

Structure or process

The self-concept may be viewed as a structure made up of different self-conceptions related to each other in various ways. Also, the self-concept is the means or process by which people interact with the environment and by which they ignore, deny, distort or accurately perceive experience.

Central–peripheral

Combs and Snygg (1959) distinguish between the phenomenal self, the organization or pattern of all those aspects which people refer to as 'I' or 'me', and the self-concept, those perceptions about self which are most vital to people themselves and which may be regarded as their very essence. For all people, some self-conceptions are much more central than others, and everyone has their unique way of ordering self-conceptions as central or peripheral, even though this is often more implicit than explicit.

Congruence–incongruence

Many self-conceptions may match the reality of people's experiencing, in which case there is congruence between self-conception and experience. Other self-conceptions may be different in varying degrees from the reality of their experiencing, in which case a state of incongruence exists.

Conditions of worth

Incongruence implies that a self-conception is based on a condition of worth rather than on the organism's own valuing process. For example, an incongruent self-conception for a person may be 'I want to be a doctor', whereas a congruent self-conception may be 'I want to be an artist.' Being a doctor may be based on values internalized from parents, whereas being an artist represents the organism's own valuing process.

Subception and defence

This is an area of self-concept as a process. Experiences may be denied or distorted by the process of subception. This process defends existing self-conceptions by preventing the person from perceiving incongruence and hence possibly changing both self-conceptions and behaviour.

Intensionality–extensionality

Intensionality describes characteristics of a self-concept in a defensive state, for example rigidity and absence of adequate reality testing. Extensionality describes characteristics of a mature self-concept, such as seeing experience in limited, differentiated terms and testing inferences and abstractions against reality.

Level of self-regard

Another way of expressing 'level of self-regard' is 'the degree to which individuals prize themselves'. Rogers stated that when people's self-concepts were such that no self-experience could be discriminated as more or less worthy of positive regard than any other, then they were experiencing unconditional positive self-regard. 'Level of self-acceptance' is another way of stating 'level of self-regard'.

Real–ideal

Whereas real self-conceptions represent my perceptions of how I am, ideal self-conceptions represent my conceptions of how I would most like to be. Both real and ideal self-conceptions form parts of people's self-concept complex.

THERAPY

The person-centred approach, then, is primarily a way of being that finds its expression in attitudes and behaviours that promote a growth-promoting climate. It is a basic philosophy rather than simply a technique or method.

Carl Rogers

THERAPEUTIC GOALS

The question of goals in person-centred therapy can be addressed in two ways: first, the goals of individual clients in therapy and, second, overall goals reflecting the human potential for growth. Clients in person-centred therapy are responsible for having their own purposes and goals. Therapists do not tell clients where they should be going or how to get there. At the start of therapy there is no process of assessment and goal-setting. Rather, clients may come with some goals and then, within the context of a safe therapeutic relationship, may choose to reveal further goals and, as therapy progresses, still different goals may emerge. Much of person-centred therapy focuses on helping clients become more in touch with their feelings and organismic valuing process. During this process, clients may evolve a greater sense of what truly are their goals. For some clients, working through to what are personal goals, as contrasted with goals that are 'hand-me-downs' from significant others, may take many therapy sessions.

Much of the time Rogers saw overall goals in terms of characteristics of the fully functioning person (Rogers, 1959, 1961). However, Rogers also wrote a later statement on the qualities of the person of tomorrow who can live in a vastly changed world (Rogers, 1980). He considered that a paradigm shift was taking place from old to new ways of conceptualizing the person. Box 4.4 presents characteristics, albeit overlapping, of the fully functioning person and the person of tomorrow.

Here I identify six main dimensions or themes concerning goals in Rogers' writings, including the scale he developed with some colleagues to measure process changes in psychotherapy (Walker, Rablen and Rogers, 1960). Clients might come into therapy at differing levels on these dimensions and then, during the course of successful therapy, move forward to higher levels of functioning.

BOX 4.4

Characteristics of the fully functioning person and the person of tomorrow

The fully functioning person	The person of tomorrow
Open to experience and able to perceive realistically	Openness to the world, both inner and outer
Rational and not defensive	Desire for authenticity
Engaged in existential process of living	Scepticism regarding science and technology
Trusts in organismic valuing process	Desire for wholeness as a human being
Construes experience in extensional manner	The wish for intimacy
Accepts responsibility for being different	Process persons
Accepts responsibility for own behaviour	Caring for others
Relates creatively to the environment	Attitude of closeness toward nature
Accepts others as unique individuals	Anti-institutional
Prizes himself or herself	Trusts the authority within
Prizes others	Material things unimportant
Relates openly and freely on the basis of immediate experiencing	A yearning for the spiritual
Communicates rich self-awareness when desired	

Openness to experience

A self-concept which allows all significant sensory and visceral experiences to be perceived is the basis for effective functioning. Rogers frequently used the term 'openness to experience' to describe the capacity for realistic perception and observed that 'There is no need for the mechanism of "subception" whereby the organism is forewarned of experiences threatening to the self' (Rogers, 1959, p. 206). Openness to experience makes for more efficient behaviour in that people have a wider perceptual field and are able to behave more often from choice than from necessity. Openness to experience may also increase the possibility of spontaneity and creativity, since people are less bound by the strait-jacket of conditions of worth. In other words, openness to experience enables people to engage in an existential process of living where they are alive, able to handle change, and alert to the range of their choices for creating their lives.

Rationality

A feature of openness to experience is that it allows for rationality. When people are in touch with their actualizing tendency their behaviour is likely to be rational in terms of maintaining and enhancing their organism. Rogers thought it tragic that most people's defences kept them out touch with how rational they could be. What was earlier described as extensionality rather than intensionality is a characteristic of this rationality.

Personal responsibility

The term 'personal responsibility' refers to people's taking responsibility *for* their self-actualizing and not just feeling responsible to others. This covers Rogers' ideas of individuals' trust in their organismic valuing process, trust of the authority within, acceptance of responsibility for their own behaviour, and also acceptance of responsibility for being different from others. Personally responsible people, within the existential parameters of death and destiny, are capable of taking control of their lives and of self-actualizing. The person-centred philosophy in many aspects is one of self-control, self-help and personal power, hopefully within the context of caring relationships. Acknowledgement of personal responsibility is a central part of the self-concepts of effective people.

Self-regard

Self-regard is another important part of the self-concepts of effective people. One way of expressing this is that a person possesses a high degree of unconditional self-regard, or self-acceptance. It is a self-regard based on their organismic valuing process rather than on the praise and needs of others. People with a high degree of unconditional self-regard will prize themselves, even though they may not prize all their behaviours and attributes.

Capacity for good personal relationships

Self-acceptance means that people are less likely to be defensive and hence more likely to accept others. The capacity for good personal relationships incorporates Rogers' notions of accepting others as unique individuals, prizing others, relating openly and freely to them on the basis of immediate experiencing, and having the capacity, when appropriate, to communicate a rich self-awareness. These relationships are characterized by mutual concern for both persons' self-actualizing. Rogers considered congruence, genuineness, or 'realness' to be probably the most important element in the ordinary interactions of life, while empathy has the highest priority where the other person is anxious and vulnerable.

Ethical living

Person-centred theory is based on a view that people, at their core, are trustworthy organisms. This shows itself in the social relations of self-actualizing people in at least two ways. First, they are capable of a wide identification with other human beings, so they are likely to seek others' self-actualizing along with their own. Consequently, they are careful not to infringe on the rights of others while pursuing their own ends. Second, they appear to be able to distinguish sharply between ends and means and between good and evil. Qualities which are likely to contribute to such people's ethical living are: trust in internal rather than in external authority; an indifference to material things, such as money and status symbols; an attitude of closeness to and reverence for nature; and a yearning and seeking for spiritual values that are greater than the individual.

PROCESS OF THERAPY

The process of person-centred therapy is built on a basic trust of the client's ability, within a growth promoting climate, to actualize her or his human potential. Right from the beginning Rogers would encourage clients to assume responsibility for the contents of the therapy sessions. Therapy starts with an invitation indicating that the therapist will be an interested listener to whatever the clients want to share. Following is Rogers' opening statement from a demonstration interview conducted in his later years (Raskin and Rogers, 2000).

> *I don't know what you might want to talk about, but I'm very ready to hear. We have half an hour, and I hope that in that half an hour we can get to know each other as deeply as possible, but we don't need to strive for anything, I guess that's my feeling. Do you want to tell me whatever is on your mind?*

There is no formal assessment in person-centred therapy, since all clients are viewed as being out of touch with their actualizing tendency on account of their conditions of worth. If therapists were, from their own external frames of reference, to assess clients, they would risk replicating the circumstances that had led clients to acquire and maintain their conditions of worth. In addition, therapists avoid any interpretations or placing external constructions on what the client reveals. Rather, they act as companions as clients share whatever seems important at the time. In particular, Rogers would assist clients to express, experience and explore feelings, be they positive, negative, ambivalent or confused, at a rate comfortable for them.

Rogers would define his and the client's role not only by his opening remarks but also by how he listened carefully to what clients communicated without trying to judge or influence their stream of talk in any direction other than their own. Furthermore, Rogers would refuse to allow clients to place him in roles that allowed him to assume responsibility for directing and leading them. For example, if a client said: 'What do you think I should do?' Rogers would show acceptance and understanding of the client's feeling of really wanting an answer about what to do without usurping the client's authority and supplying the answer. In such situations, Rogers might indicate that, without having the answers himself, he hoped he could assist the client to find an answer than was right for him or her. The initial session would end without any attempt to summarize the session or tie up loose ends before closing. Therapist and client would respectfully take their leave of one another.

Person-centred therapy is a process which goes on between, as well as within, sessions. Though no formal homework is set, most often clients continue the process of therapy by means of their thoughts, feelings and actions between sessions. Subsequent sessions start with clients being allowed to assume responsibility about where to begin: for instance, with an opening remark such as 'Where would you like to start today?' Again, Rogers would attempt to provide a growth-promoting climate as clients attempted to get in touch with and experience their own feelings, explore the circumstances of their lives, and settle upon goals and directions that seemed appropriate for them. The same growth-promoting climate allows clients, when ready, to address the issue of terminating therapy and how best to lead their lives afterwards.

A more poetic impression of the process of person-centred therapy can be gathered from one of Rogers' favourite sayings from Lao-Tse:

> *It is as though he listened*
> *and such listening as his enfolds us in a silence*
> *in which at last we begin to hear*
> *what we are meant to be.*

THE THERAPEUTIC RELATIONSHIP

The therapist in the relationship

How is a growth-promoting relationship achieved? Person-centred therapy does not rely on techniques or on doing things to clients. Rogers believed that in therapy 'it is the *quality* of the interpersonal encounter with the client which is the most significant element in determining effectiveness' (Rogers, 1962, p. 416). Person-centred therapy is a process that can intensely involve the thoughts and feelings of both clients and their therapists. There is a coherence between how person-centred therapists see the origins of clients' self-alienation and inner schisms, and how they can assist them to grow and become healed. Person-centred therapists try to provide the attitudinal conditions that are the antidote to the emotional deprivations that their clients have experienced.

What are the conditions for client growth and reintegration? In 1957, Rogers presented his six necessary and sufficient conditions for therapeutic personality change. He stated that the following conditions had to exist and continue over a period of time for constructive personality change to occur. Also, that 'No other conditions are necessary' (Rogers, 1957, p. 96). First, two people need to be in psychological contact. Second, the client is in a state of incongruence and is vulnerable or anxious. Third, the therapist 'is congruent or integrated in the relationship'. Fourth and fifth, the therapist experiences 'unconditional positive regard for the client', and 'an empathic understanding of the client's internal frame of reference and endeavours to communicate this to the client' (p. 96). Sixth, the therapist is minimally successful in communicating empathic understanding and unconditional positive regard to the client. Rogers regarded congruence, unconditional positive regard and empathy as 'the attitudinal conditions that foster therapeutic growth . . .' (Rogers and Sanford, 1985, p. 1,379). He stressed that they were not all or none conditions, but exist on continua.

Congruence

Other words for congruence are 'genuineness', 'realness', 'openness', 'transparency' and 'presence'. Congruence is the most basic of the attitudinal conditions. Therapists need to be in touch with the feelings that they experience, have them available to awareness, and 'to live these feelings, be them in the relationship, and . . . communicate them if appropriate' (Rogers, 1962, p. 417). Therapists should encounter their clients in direct person-to-person contact. They should avoid an intellectual approach in which clients get treated as objects. Congruent therapists are not playing roles, being polite, and putting on professional façades.

Rogers acknowledged that no one fully achieves congruence all the time. Imperfect human beings can be of assistance to clients. It is enough for therapists, in particular moments in immediate relationships with specific persons, to be completely and fully themselves with their experiences accurately symbolized into their self-concepts.

Congruence does not mean that therapists 'blurt out impulsively every passing feeling . . .' (Rogers, 1962, p. 418). Nor does it mean that they allow their sessions to become therapist-centred rather than client-centred. However, it can mean that they take the risk of sharing a feeling or giving feedback that might improve the relationship because it is expressed genuinely. An example is that of therapists sharing their experience of fatigue rather than trying to cover it up. Such openness may restore the therapist's energy level and allow the client to see that they are dealing with a real person. Another example is that Rogers thought that, if he felt persistently bored with a client, he owed it to the client and their relationship to share the feeling. He would own the bored feeling as located in himself rather than make it into an accusatory statement. Also, he would share his discomfort at sharing the feeling and communicate that he would like to be more in touch with the client. Rogers strove to overcome the barrier between them by being real, imperfect and sharing his genuine feeling. He would hope that the client could use this as a stepping-stone to speak more genuinely.

Another insight into congruence may be obtained from what Rogers says about the concept of presence. In therapy, both therapists and clients can attain altered states of consciousness in which they feel they are in touch with and grasp the meaning of the underlying evolutionary flow (Rogers, 1980, 1986a). There can be a mystical and spiritual dimension in counselling and therapy. Rogers considered he was at his best as a therapist when he was closest to his inner intuitive self and 'when perhaps I am in a slightly altered state of consciousness. Then simply my *presence* is releasing and helpful to the other' (Rogers, 1980, p. 129). In such a state, behaviours which may be strange, impulsive, and hard to justify rationally turn out to be right. Rogers wrote: 'it seems that my inner spirit has reached out and touched the inner spirit of the other. Our relationship transcends itself and becomes a part of something larger. Profound growth and healing and energy are present' (Rogers, 1980, p. 129).

Unconditional positive regard

Other terms used to describe this condition include 'non-possessive warmth', 'caring', 'prizing', 'acceptance' and 'respect'. Unconditional positive regard relates to Rogers' deep trust in his clients' capacity for constructive change if provided with the right nurturing conditions. Rogers stressed the importance of the therapist's attitude toward the worth and significance of each person. The therapist's own struggles for personal integration are relevant to unconditional positive regard since they can be only respectful of clients' capacities to achieve constructive self-direction as that respect is an integral part of their own personality make-ups.

Unconditional positive regard involves the therapist's willingness for clients 'to *be* whatever immediate feeling is going on – confusion, resentment, fear, anger, courage, love, or pride . . .' (Rogers, 1986a, p. 198). This respect is equivalent to the love expressed by the Christian concept of 'agape', without any romantic or possessive connotations. Rogers makes the analogy between the kind of love parents can feel for their children, prizing them as people regardless of their particular behaviours at any moment. Therapists do not show positive regard for their clients – *if. If* they are smarter, less defensive, less vulnerable and so on. Person-centred theory explains the need for clients to seek therapy because in their pasts they were shown positive regard – *if.*

There are boundaries to showing unconditional positive regard, for instance if a client were to physically threaten a therapist. Also, unconditional positive regard does not mean that therapists need, from their frames of reference, to approve of all their clients' behaviours. Rather, unconditional positive regard is an attitude and philosophical orientation, reflected in therapist behaviour, that clients are more likely to move forward if they feel prized for their humanity and they experience an emotional climate of safety and freedom in which, without losing their therapist's acceptance, they can show feelings and relate events.

Empathy

Other terms for empathy include 'accurate empathy', 'empathic understanding', 'empathic responsiveness', 'an empathic way of being', 'an empathic stance', and 'an empathic attitude'. Rogers (1957) wrote: 'To sense the client's private world as if it were your own, but without ever losing the "as if" quality – this is empathy . . .' (p. 99). There are various facets to an empathic way of being with clients. Therapists need to 'get into the shoes of' and 'get under the skin' of their clients to understand their private subjective worlds. They need to be sensitive to the moment-by-moment flow of experiencing that goes on both in clients and in themselves. They need the capacity to pick up nuances and sense meanings of which clients are scarcely aware. With tact, sensitivity and awareness of what clients can handle, they need to communicate their understandings of their sensings of clients' worlds and personal meanings.

Therapists should communicate their commitment to understanding their clients' worlds by frequently checking the accuracy of their understandings and showing their willingness to be corrected. Empathy is an active process in which therapists desire to know and reach out to receive clients' communications and meanings (Barrett-Lennard, 1998). An empathic attitude creates an emotional climate in which clients can assist their therapists to understand them more accurately.

Responding to individual client statements is a process of listening and observing, resonating, discriminating, communicating and checking your understanding. Needless to say, the final dimension is that the client has, to some extent, perceived the therapist's empathy. Even better is that the therapist's empathy has enabled the client to get more in touch with the flow of her or his experiencing. Box 4.5, taken from a demonstration film with Rogers as the therapist (Rogers, 1965), illustrates this process. The client, Gloria, is talking about how her father could never show he cared for her the way she would have liked.

BOX 4.5

Dimensions of the empathy process

Gloria's statement
'I don't know what it is. You know when I talk about it feels more flip. If I just sit still a minute, it feels like a great big hurt down there. Instead, I feel cheated.'

Rogers' responding processes

Observing and listening:	Observes and listens to the client's verbal, vocal and bodily communication.
Resonating:	Feels some of the emotion the client experiences.
Discriminating:	Discriminates what is really important to the client and formulates this into a response.
Communicating:	'It's much easier to be a little flip because then you don't feel that big lump inside of hurt.'
	Communicates a response that attempts to show understanding of the client's thoughts, feelings and personal meanings. Accompanies verbal with good vocal and bodily communication.
Checking:	In this instance, Gloria quickly made her next statement which followed the train of her experiencing and thought. However, Rogers could either have waited and allowed Gloria space to respond or could have inquired if his response was accurate.

Gloria's perception of Rogers' responding
How Gloria reacted indicated she perceived that Rogers showed excellent empathy and that she was able to continue getting more in touch with her experiencing.

Though the next example of empathy comes from an encounter group (Rogers, 1975, p. 3), the empathic process it demonstrates holds true for working with individual clients. A man has been making vaguely negative statements about his father. First, the facilitator enquires whether he might be angry with his father. When the man says he doesn't think so, the facilitator says 'Possibly dissatisfied with him?', to which the man rather doubtfully responds 'Well, yes, perhaps.' Then the facilitator enquires whether the man is disappointed in his father, to which he quickly responds 'That's it! I *am* disappointed that he's not a strong person. I think I've always been disappointed in him ever since I was a boy.'

In the above example, the facilitator is not interpreting the client, nor would Rogers. Rather the facilitator progressively checks out his understanding to grasp exactly what the man wishes to say. Gendlin (1988) mentions how Rogers would take in each correction until the client indicated 'Yes, that's how it is. That's what I feel' (p. 127). Characteristically this statement would be followed by a silence in which the client fully received the empathic understanding. Very often during these silences, clients would get in touch with something deeper.

A word now about what empathy is not. True empathy does not have any judgemental or diagnostic quality about it. Also, empathy is most definitely not a 'wooden technique of pseudo-understanding in which the counselor "reflects back what the client has just said"' (Rogers, 1962, p. 420). In his 1975 article on empathy, Rogers observed how at first he found it helpful to think that the best response was to 'reflect' feelings back to clients, but that later on in his career the word 'reflect' made him cringe. Still unhappy with the term 'reflection of feelings', Rogers later suggested that therapists' mirroring responses be better labelled as 'testing understanding' or 'checking perceptions' (Rogers, 1986b). To Rogers, empathy was an attitude, a very special form of companionship, a gentle and sensitive way of being with clients. However well intended, mechanical reflections form no part of offering empathy.

The client in the relationship

Here, I draw parallels between how presence of the three therapist attitudinal conditions of congruence, unconditional positive regard, and empathy can promote the growth of client congruence, unconditional positive regard, and empathy.

Congruence

Given the right growth-promoting emotional climate, clients will feel less need to be defensive and to look for external regard. Though painful at times, they may progressively take more risks in disclosing themselves to their therapists. Therapists who accept clients and prize their rights to be their true selves allow them to share parts of themselves that they may find embarrassing, abnormal or frightening. Also, they give clients the opportunity to share parts of themselves that they like, without being negatively judged for such disclosures. As the therapy relationship develops, a mutuality of congruence can develop between therapist and client, with each making it easier for the other to be real in the relationship. For some clients, the relationship can transcend itself into becoming a profound spiritual experience in which they, like their therapists, attain an altered state of consciousness. Also, an outcome of successful person-centred therapy is that clients become more congruent in their outside relationships.

Unconditional positive regard

Here I refer to clients' regard for themselves rather than for their therapists. Most often clients lack self-esteem. Rogers (1975) suggested a number of ways in which an empathic attitude may raise clients' level of regard. First, having the hidden and unacceptable parts of themselves understood and accepted dissolves clients' alienation and helps connect them to the human race. Second, being cared for and valued for their true selves allows clients to think 'this other individual trusts me, thinks I'm worthwhile. Perhaps I *am* worth something. Perhaps *I* could *value* myself. Perhaps I could care for myself' (p. 7). Third, not being judged by their therapists may lead clients to judge themselves less harshly, thus gradually increasing the possibility of self-acceptance. Also, as clients gain in self-esteem, they are likely to shift their locus-of-evaluation from other people's standards and beliefs to their own. Thus, they become less vulnerable to the damaging effects of conditions of worth.

Empathy

The three therapist attitudinal conditions make it easier for clients to be empathic to themselves both inside and outside of therapy. At varying rates, clients' self-concepts can allow more of their experiencing into awareness. Having their feelings sensitively listened to provides clients with the opportunity to experience and explore these feelings and so understand themselves better. Furthermore, clients learn the importance of listening on their own to their feelings as a guide to their actions and future directions. Also, the more empathic clients are able to be to themselves, the more likely they are to experience and show empathy to their therapists and other people, thus improving the quality of their relationships with them.

THERAPEUTIC INTERVENTIONS

Person-centred therapy is unique among the therapies covered in this book in that Rogers considered a growth-promoting relationship characterized by the attitudinal conditions necessary and sufficient for client change to occur. The same attitudinal conditions are relevant when dealing with clients' feelings towards therapists. Rogers considered that some client feelings towards their therapists were understandable responses to therapist behaviour, whereas other feelings were projections 'transferred' from previous relationships. Even in dealing with clients' transference feelings, there was no call for special interventions, such as interpreting the transference. Rogers observed, whether the feelings be therapist-caused or transference reactions, 'If the therapist is sensitively understanding and genuinely acceptant and non-judgemental, then therapy will move forward through these feelings' (Rogers, 1990, p. 130).

CASE MATERIAL

Rogers was very diligent in providing case material and researching the processes and outcomes of person-centred therapy. Readers are encouraged to explore primary sources to get a feel of how Rogers worked. Following are some suggestions about where to look. In *Counseling and Psychotherapy*, Rogers provides a transcript plus some commentary for each of his eight sessions with Herbert Bryan, a young man in his late 20s whom he regarded as definitely neurotic (Rogers, 1942). In *On Becoming a Person*, Rogers provides two excerpts from the case of Mrs Oak, a housewife in her late 30s who was experiencing difficulties in marital and family relationships (Rogers, 1961). Rogers' work with Gloria is both on film (Rogers, 1965) and written up as a case example (Raskin and Rogers, 2000). Raskin and Rogers (2000) also provided an example of the first and final thirds of a demonstration interview conducted by Rogers in 1983 illustrating the process of therapy, followed by a brief commentary. Elsewhere Rogers presented excerpts and commentary from another demonstration interview, with a woman called Jan, conducted before a workshop of 600 participants in Johannesburg, South Africa (Rogers, 1986a).

FURTHER DEVELOPMENTS

Person-centred therapy has been presented here in relation to individual work. However, Rogers' interests and influence were much more extensive. Rogers championed the use of person-centred principles in encounter groups, classroom teaching, management, and peace and conflict resolution.

Rogers has also influenced other people to develop his ideas. For example, in Britain Dave Mearns has been addressing the concept of *relational depth* between therapists and clients and how best to train for it (Mearns, 1997). The Canadian psychologist David Rennie has developed what he terms an *experiential approach* to person-centred therapy (Rennie, 1998). Rennie's approach revolves around clients' and therapists' *reflexivity*, which he defines as self-awareness and agency within that self-awareness. Rennie's approach goes beyond empathic responding to focus on both client and therapist processes. Two elements of process work are process *identification*, 'I notice that you seem to have come to a halt'; and process *direction*, 'I don't know if it would be useful or not, but one thing you could try would be to see if you can make contact with the feeling of *being* stuck' (Rennie, 1998, p. 119).

Rogers' influence pervades the work of therapists of other theoretical orientations: for example, now all competent cognitive and cognitive–behavioural therapists heavily emphasize the quality of the relationship when assessing clients and delivering interventions. Rogers has also influenced many therapists who describe themselves as eclectic. For example, some eclectic therapists might use a person-centred approach as the treatment of choice for some clients either at the start of therapy or throughout therapy. Furthermore, eclectic therapists can also integrate a more client-focused approach into how they apply interventions derived from many other theoretical positions. However, for many person-centred therapists such eclecticism or integration of person-centred ideas and practices constitutes a violation of the person-centred approach as a coherent functional philosophy.

The development of person-centred therapy and therapists proceeds by means of journals and training centres. Journals devoted to Rogers' approach include *The Person-Centered Journal* and *Person-Centred Practice*. Training opportunities for developing person-centred counselling and therapy skills are provided in numerous countries throughout the world (Barrett-Lennard, 1998).

SUMMARY

- *Person-centred or client-centred theory emphasizes the importance of people's subjective self-concept, which consists of the ways in which they perceive and define themselves.*
- *The actualizing tendency inherent in the organism to maintain and enhance itself is people's single motivating drive.*
- *Very early on in life humans start developing a self-concept. Many of the self-conceptions which form the self-concept are likely to be based on the organism's own valuing process. However, other self-conceptions reflect internalized conditions of worth or the values of others treated as if they were based on the organism's own valuing process. Thus a conflict arises between the actualizing tendency and the self-concept, which is a subsystem of the*

actualizing tendency, in that conditions of worth impede accurate perception of both inner and outer experiences

- *Subception is the mechanism by which the organism discriminates experience at variance with the self-concept. Depending on the degree of threat inherent in the experience, the organism may defend its self-concept by denying the experience or distorting its perception. People are psychologically well to the extent that their self-concepts allow them to perceive all their significant sensory and visceral experiences.*

- *Six key characteristics of the self-concepts of fully functioning or self-actualizing persons are: openness to experience, rationality, personal responsibility, self-regard, capacity for good personal relations, and ethical living.*

- *Clients in person-centred therapy are responsible for finding and formulating their own goals and directions. Such goals may emerge and become clearer during therapy.*

- *The process of person-centred therapy emphasizes clients taking responsibility for the contents of therapy sessions and working on material that has personal meaning for them.*

- *The central assumption of person-centred therapy is that if therapists provide clients with certain growth-promoting attitudinal conditions then constructive personality change will occur.*

- *The person-centred therapist provides to all clients the same attitudinal conditions of congruence, unconditional positive regard and empathy.*

- *The impact of these attitudinal conditions on clients leads them to possess more congruence, self-regard and empathy. In short, clients are in the process of becoming persons and regulating their own lives.*

- *Further developments in person-centred therapy include elaborating the concept of relational depth and focusing on process identification and direction.*

REVIEW AND PERSONAL QUESTIONS

REVIEW QUESTIONS

1. Critically review Rogers' concept of the actualizing tendency. What evidence might support or negate Rogers' views about the concept?
2. What does Rogers mean by organismic valuing process?
3. What does Rogers mean by the terms 'experience', 'experiencing' and 'awareness'?
4. What are conditions of worth, and how do they develop?
5. Specify how low-functioning people process their experiences differently from high-functioning people?
6. With reference to a person's self-concept and experience, what does Rogers mean by the term 'incongruence'? Provide an example.
7. Why does Rogers present how to conduct therapy in terms of growth-promoting attitudinal conditions rather than techniques?
8. Describe each of the three therapist-offered growth-promoting attitudinal conditions.
9. In what ways do clients change both during and at the end of successful person-centred therapy?

10. What do you consider the strengths and weaknesses of Rogers' model of the person?
11. What do you consider the strengths and weaknesses of Rogers' model of therapy?

PERSONAL QUESTIONS

1. Are you aware of any of your conditions of worth? If so, what are they and how did you acquire each of them?
2. Examine a past or current relationship which you think has helped or is helping you to attain a more adequate self-concept. What characteristics of the other person were or are helpful?
3. Examine a past or current relationship which you think has hindered or is hindering you from attaining a more adequate self-concept. What characteristics of the other person were or are harmful?
4. Assess yourself on each of the following attributes of fully functioning or self-actualizing people: openness to experience, rationality, personal responsibility, self-regard, capacity for good personal relationships, and ethical living.
5. If you conduct therapy, how congruent are you and how do you know?
6. If you conduct therapy, how well do you offer unconditional positive regard, and how do you know?
7. If you conduct therapy, how empathic are you, and how do you know?
8. What relevance, if any, has the theory and practice of person-centred therapy for how you conduct therapy?
9. What relevance, if any, has the theory and practice of person-centred therapy for how you live?

ANNOTATED BIBLIOGRAPHY

Rogers, C. R. (1959). A theory of therapy, personality, and interpersonal relationships, as developed in the client-centred framework. In S. Koch (ed.). *Psychology: A Study of Science* (Study 1, Volume 3, pp. 184–256). New York: McGraw-Hill.

    Rogers regarded this chapter as one of his most significant publications. He worked for three or four years on it and was proud of its thoroughness and rigour. He endeavoured to make every major statement in it something that could be tested by research. This chapter is the major reference for readers wishing to understand Rogerian theory.

Rogers, C. R. (1951). *Client-Centered Therapy*. Boston: Houghton Mifflin.

    This book describes the attitudinal orientation of the counsellor, the therapeutic relationship experienced by the client, the process of counselling and various issues and applications of the client-centred approach. The book concludes with an important nineteen-proposition statement of Rogers' theory of personality and behaviour.

Rogers, C. R. (1957). The necessary and sufficient conditions of therapeutic personality change. *Journal of Consulting Psychology, 21*, 95–103.

    Also regarded by Rogers as one of his most significant publications, this article presents and discusses six conditions for effective counselling practice. The paper elaborates the counsellor conditions of congruence, unconditional positive regard and empathic understanding.

Rogers, C. R. (1961). *On Becoming a Person.* Boston: Houghton Mifflin.

Another publication regarded by Rogers as one of his most significant. Rogers acknowledged the book as certainly his most popular, and thought it had spoken to people all over the world. The book comprises seven parts: speaking personally; how can I be of help?; the process of becoming a person; a philosophy of persons; the place of research in psychotherapy; what are the implications for living?; and the behavioural sciences and the person.

Rogers, C. R. (1975). Empathic: An unappreciated way of being. *The Counseling Psychologist*, 5, 2–10.

This paper, reprinted in *A Way of Being*, is Rogers' re-evaluation of the attitudinal condition of empathy. It is his major statement on the subject.

Rogers, C. R. (1980). *A Way of Being.* Boston: Houghton Mifflin.

A collection of fifteen papers written between 1960 and 1980, this book is divided into four parts: personal experiences and perspectives; aspects of a person-centred approach; the process of education – and its future; and looking ahead – a person-centred scenario. This book is written in the same reader-friendly style as *On Becoming a Person*.

Kirschenbaum, H. and Henderson, V. L. (eds) (1990). *The Carl Rogers Reader.* London: Constable.

The portable Rogers. Rogers had begun to work on a selection of his writings before his death in 1987. This book contains 33 selections from Rogers' life-work of books and articles divided into nine sections: speaking personally; the therapeutic relationship; the person in process; theory and research; a human science; education; the helping professions; a philosophy of persons; and a more human world.

Raskin, N. J. and Rogers, C. R. (2000). Person-centered therapy. In R. J. Corsini and D. Wedding (eds). *Current Psychotherapies* (6th edition). Itasca, IL: Peacock, 133–67.

An authoritative overview of the theory and practice of person-centred therapy based on a chapter originally written by Rogers.

Mearns, D. and Thorne, B. (1999). *Person-Centred Counselling in Action* (2nd edition). London: Sage.

Engagingly written, this best-selling text introduces person-centred theory and practice in a way that clearly and sensitively brings to life the processes going on within and between counsellors and clients. The book's eight chapters are: the person-centred approach; the counsellor's use of the self; empathy; unconditonal positive regard; congruence; 'beginnings'; 'middles'; and 'endings'.

REFERENCES AND FURTHER READING

Barrett-Lennard, G. T. (1998). *Carl Rogers' Helping System: Journey and Substance.* London: Sage.
Cohen, D. (1997). *Carl Rogers: A Critical Biography.* London: Constable.
Combs, A. W. and Snygg, D. (1959). *Individual Behavior* (Revised edition). New York: Harper and Row.
Gendlin, E. T. (1988). Carl Rogers (1902–1987). *American Psychologist*, 43, 127–8.
Gordon, T. (1970). *Parent Effectiveness Training: The Tested New Way to Raise Responsible Children.* New York: Wyden.

Kirschenbaum, H. and Henderson, V. L. (eds) (1990). *The Carl Rogers Reader.* London: Constable.

Maslow, A. H. (1962). *Toward a Psychology of Being.* Princeton, NJ: Van Nostrand.

Maslow, A. H. (1970). *Motivation and Personality* (2nd edition). New York: Harper and Row.

McCleary, R. A. and Lazarus, R. S. (1949). Autonomic discrimination without awareness. *Journal of Personality, 18,* 171–9.

Mearns, D. (1997). *Person-Centred Counselling Training.* London: Sage.

Mearns, D. and Thorne, B. (1999). *Person-Centred Counselling in Action* (2nd edition). London: Sage.

Raskin, N. J. and Rogers, C. R. (2000). Person-centered therapy. In R. J. Corsini and D. Wedding (eds). *Current Psychotherapies* (6th edition). Itasca, IL: Peacock, 133–67.

Rennie, D. L. (1998). *Person-Centred Counselling: An Experiential Approach.* London: Sage.

Rogers, C. R. (1939). *The Clinical Treatment of the Problem Child.* Boston: Houghton Mifflin.

Rogers, C. R. (1942). *Counseling and Psychotherapy.* Boston: Houghton Mifflin.

Rogers, C. R. (1951). *Client-Centered Therapy.* Boston: Houghton Mifflin.

Rogers, C. R. (1957). The necessary and sufficient conditions of therapeutic personality change. *Journal of Consulting Psychology, 21,* 95–103.

Rogers, C. R. (1959). A theory of therapy, personality, and interpersonal relationships, as developed in the client-centred framework. In S. Koch (ed.). *Psychology: A Study of Science* (Study 1, Volume 3, 184–256). New York: McGraw-Hill.

Rogers C. R. (1961). *On Becoming a Person.* Boston: Houghton Mifflin.

Rogers, C. R. (1962). The interpersonal relationship: The core of guidance. *Harvard Educational Review, 32,* 416–29.

Rogers, C. R. (1969). *Freedom to Learn.* Columbus, Ohio: Charles E. Merrill.

Rogers, C. R. (1970). *Encounter Groups.* London: Penguin.

Rogers, C. R. (1973). *Becoming Partners: Marriage and its Alternatives.* London: Constable.

Rogers, C. R. (1974). In retrospect: Forty-six years. *American Psychologist, 29,* 115–23.

Rogers C. R. (1975). Empathic: An unappreciated way of being. *The Counseling Psychologist, 5,* 2–10.

Rogers, C. R. (1977). *Carl Rogers on Personal Power.* London: Constable.

Rogers, C. R. (1980). *A Way of Being.* Boston: Houghton Mifflin.

Rogers, C. R. (1986a). A client-centered/person-centered approach to therapy. In I. Kutash and A. Wolf (eds). *Psychotherapist's Casebook: Theory and Technique in the Practice of Modern Therapies* (197–208). San Fransisco: Jossey Bass. Reproduced in Kirschenbaum and Henderson (eds). *The Carl Rogers Reader,* 135–52.

Rogers, C. R. (1986b). Reflection of feelings. *Person-Centred Review, 1,* 375–7.

Rogers, C. R. (1990). Reflection of feelings and transference. In H. Kirschenbaum and V. Henderson (eds). *The Carl Rogers Reader.* London: Constable, 127–34.

Rogers, C. R. and Sanford, R. A. (1985). Client-centered psychotherapy. In H. I. Kaplan, B. J. Sadock and A. M. Friedman (eds). *Comprehensive Textbook of Psychiatry* (4th edition, 1,374–88). Baltimore, MA: William & Wilkins.

Thorne, B. (1992). *Carl Rogers.* London: Sage.

Walker, A. M., Rablen, R. A. and Rogers, C. R. (1960). Development of a scale to measure process changes in psychotherapy. *Journal of Clinical Psychology, 16,* 79–85.

Rogers on film

Rogers, C. R. (1965). Client-centred therapy. In E. Shostrom (ed.). *Three Approaches to Psychotherapy.* Santa Ana, CA: Psychological Films.

5

Gestalt Therapy

Every individual, every plant, every animal has only one inborn goal – to actualise itself as it is.

Fritz Perls

INTRODUCTION

Gestalt therapy, according to Perls, its main originator, is an existential approach 'not just occupied with dealing with symptoms or character structure, but with the total existence of a person' (Perls, 1969a, p. 71). Toward the end of his life Perls (1969a) wrote that he considered gestalt therapy one of the three then-existing types of existential therapy: the two others being Frankl's logotherapy and Binswanger's daseins therapy. Clients who come for gestalt therapy are in states of existential crisis and need to learn to take responsibility for their existences. Perls considered all other existential philosophies borrowed concepts from other sources: for example, Binswanger from psychoanalysis, Tillich from Protestantism, and Sartre from Communism. Gestalt therapy is the only existential approach which has support in its own formation since gestalt formation, the emergence of needs, is a primary biological phenomenon. He observed: 'Gestalt therapy is a philosophy that tries to be in harmony, in alignment with everything else, with medicine, with science, with the universe, with what *is*' (Perls, 1969a, p. 17).

FRITZ PERLS (1893–1970)

Friederich (Frederick or Fritz) Soloman Perls was born in Berlin, the son of a Jewish travelling salesman of Palestinian wines. He grew up with his two sisters in a disturbed family in which his parents had many bitter fights, both verbal and physical. Perls' mother used carpet-beating rods on him but he claims she did not break his spirit; rather, he broke the carpet-beaters. He saw his father as a hypocrite who preached one thing and lived another and who progressively isolated himself from his family. Perls wrote: 'Basically I hated him and his pompous righteousness, but he could also be loving and warm. How much my attitude was influenced by my mother's hatred of him, how much she poisoned us children with it, I could not say' (Perls, 1969b, pp. 250–1). During his puberty years, a period during which he was initiated into both sex and acting, Perls was the black sheep of his family. Throughout his life Perls was a rebel rather than a complier, a man with a very quick eye for others' phoniness and pseudo-authenticity, and somewhat of an exhibitionist himself. His early experiences of rejection and insecurity may have deeply influenced his later life.

Perls' ideas were largely formed in the Austro-Germanic world. On leaving high school, he enrolled as a medical student at Berlin University. At the start of the First World War, Perls had been declared physically unfit for active service. However, by 1916 fitness requirements were much lower and Perls interrupted his medical studies to serve as a medical officer, including a spell in the trenches from 1916 to 1917. In 1918 Perls returned to being a student at the universities of Freiburg and Berlin, and in 1920 he received his MD from the latter institution.

In 1926 Perls moved to Frankfurt where he accepted a post as assistant to the gestalt psychologist Kurt Goldstein at the Frankfurt Neurological Institute. Also in 1926, Perls met Laura Posner, whom he was to marry in 1929. Together they shared a strong interest in gestalt psychology. Perls considered he had a peculiar relationship with the gestalt psychologists, admiring much of their work, but unable to go along with them when they became logical positivists. He did not read any of their textbooks, but had read some papers by Lewin, Wertheimer and Köhler. He observed : 'Most important for me was the idea of the unfinished situation, the incomplete gestalt' (Perls, 1969b, p. 62). The academic gestaltists never accepted Perls and he did not regard himself as a pure gestaltist.

For some years, Perls had been undergoing training as a Freudian psychoanalyst. He moved to Vienna in 1927 and a year later completed his analytical training. On returning to Germany, from 1928 to 1933 Perls worked as a certified Freudian psychoanalyst, mainly in Berlin.

In addition to gestalt psychology and Freudian psychoanalysis there were numerous other influences on Perls. Perls had a love of acting and, early in his life, studied under Max Reinhardt, the noted director of the Deutsche Theater. Reinhardt insisted that his students observe very closely how people express emotions through their voice and gestures (Clarkson and MacKewn, 1993). Perls was also interested in Reich's idea of character armour, whereby repressions and resistances became total organismic functions. Later influences were to include Moreno, with his ideas on therapy by means of psychodrama, American humanistic psychology and Eastern religion, especially Zen Buddhism.

In 1933, with the rise of Hitler, Perls fled from Germany to Holland. Apart from being a Jew, Fritz and Laura Perls had to leave Germany quickly to avoid being rounded up by the Nazis because of their left-wing political activism. At the time of his departure his analyst was Wilhelm Reich and his supervisors were Otto Fenichel and Karen Horney. Perls wrote: 'From Fenichel I got confusion; from Reich, brazenness; from Horney, human involvement without terminology' (Perls, 1969b, p. 39). In 1934, on the recommendation of Ernest Jones, Freud's friend and biographer, accompanied by wife and young daughter, Renate, Perls moved to Johannesburg as a training analyst. In 1935, despite Perls wanting her to abort her pregnancy, Laura give birth to their son Stephen, who came to regard Fritz as a distant and disengaged father very much wrapped up in his own world (Perls, 1993).

Fritz and Laura Perls soon had successful private practices and, in 1935, they established the South African Institute for Psychoanalysis. From 1942 to 1945, Perls worked as a South African army medical officer and psychiatrist near Pretoria in the war against the Nazis. During his South African years Perls was influenced by the holism of Jan Smuts, the South African general, prime minister and philosopher. Smuts wrote about the way individuals and the universe are actively 'whole-making' and introduced the idea from physics that everything has a field and that things and organisms must be considered in relation to their fields (Smuts, 1987). In 1942 Perls' first book *Ego, Hunger and Aggression* was published in South Africa, with the British edition being published in 1947, with the sub-title *A Revision of Freud's Theory and Method*. Several chapters in this book were written by Perls' wife Laura, an important collaborator in the founding of gestalt therapy (Yontef and Jacobs, 2000).

In 1946 Perls emigrated to the United States and established a private practice in New York City. Laura and their two children joined him in the autumn of 1947. In 1951 Perls published *Gestalt Therapy: Excitement and Growth in the Human Personality*, a book co-authored by Ralph Hefferline, Professor of Psychology at Columbia University, and Paul Goodman, a social philosopher and writer. Some view Goodman, an uninhibited radical bisexual, as the third co-founder of gestalt therapy (Clarkson and Mackewn, 1993).

In 1952 Perls established the New York Institute of Gestalt Therapy and, in 1954, the Cleveland Institute for Gestalt Psychotherapy. Between 1952 and 1956, Perls had increasing differences of opinion with Laura Perls and Paul Goodman about directions for gestalt therapy. In 1957, partly for health reasons due to a recently diagnosed heart condition, Perls moved to the milder climate of Miami and was never again to live with Laura for any length of time. In Miami, Perls became friends and lovers with Marty Fromm, even as she continued to be in therapy with him (Clarkson and Mackewn, 1993).

In 1960 Perls moved to the West Coast of the United States and, in 1964, joined the staff of the Esalen Institute at Big Sur, California, as resident associate psychiatrist. During this period, Perls began doing gestalt demonstrations on stage in front of increasingly large groups, including illustrating his hot-seat technique. However, Perls realized that large group gestalt demonstrations were not gestalt therapy proper. In May 1969, Perls moved to Cowichan on Vancouver Island in British Columbia where he was establishing a gestalt community. Here he was very happy and finally at peace with the world. In December 1969 Perls left Cowichan for what was to be the last time, went to Europe, but was clearly unwell on his return. After a brief illness Perls died in a Chicago hospital of a heart attack on 14 March 1970, at the age of 76. During his last illness, Laura had flown to join him, only to find Perls sometimes confiding in her and sometimes shouting at and ignoring her.

In 1969, Perls had published *Gestalt Therapy Verbatim* and the autobiographical potpourri of prose, poetry and psychology entitled *In and Out of the Garbage Pail*. At the time of his death Perls was working on two books, *The Gestalt Approach* and *Eyewitness to Therapy*, and these were published posthumously in 1973 as a single book entitled *The Gestalt Approach & Eyewitness to Therapy*.

Perls had extensive experience of personal relations, including many affairs. In his autobiographical book *In and Out of the Garbage Pail*, Perls admits to many compulsions including smoking and leching. He also wrote poems, and painted. While Perls may have not always possessed the amount of responsibility (response-ability or freedom of choice) for which his therapeutic approach strives, he appears to have been a tremendously vital and charismatic person. The gestalt prayer of this restless gypsy was:

> *I do my thing, and you do your thing*
> *I am not in this world to live up to your expectations*
> *And you are not in this world to live up to mine.*
> *You are you, and I am I,*
> *And if by chance, we find each other, it's beautiful.*
> *If not, it can't be helped*
> 　　　　　　　(Perls, 1969a, inside front cover page).

THEORY

The basic premise of Gestalt psychology is that human nature is organised into patterns or wholes, that it is experienced by the individual in these terms, and that it can only be understood as a function of the patterns or wholes of which it is made.

　　　　　　　　　　　　　　　　　　　　　　　　　　Fritz Perls

BASIC CONCEPTS

Perls (1973) wrote in his introduction to *The Gestalt Approach & Eyewitness to Therapy* that gestalt theory was grounded in experience and observation, had changed with years of practice and application, and was still growing. The following presentation is almost exclusively based on Perls' own writings, some in conjunction with collaborators. Though others have developed gestalt therapy after Perls' death, no other really major figure has emerged since then.

Gestalt

The German noun *gestalt* means form or shape and among the meanings of the verb *gestalten* are to shape, to form, to fashion, to organize and to structure. Other terms for gestalt are pattern, configuration or organized whole. The major thrust of the experimental work of the gestalt psychologists was to show that humans do not perceive things in isolation but organize them through their perceptual processes into meaningful wholes (for example, a row of dots may be perceived as a straight line).

People's visual fields are structured in terms of 'figure' and 'background' or 'ground'. Whereas 'figure' is the focus of interest (an object or pattern, etc.), 'ground' is the setting or context. Perls and his colleagues (Perls, Hefferline and Goodman, 1951) noted that the interplay between figure and ground was dynamic. For instance, the same ground may, with differing interests and shifts of attention, give rise to different figures. Also, a given figure may itself become ground in the event that some detail of its own becomes figure.

The holistic doctrine

The human organism is a unified whole. In particular, Perls objected to the old mind–body split. The emergence of psychosomatic medicine made the close relationship of mental and physical activity increasingly apparent. In fact, mental activity seemed to be an activity of the whole person carried out at a lower energy level than those activities called physical. Human beings are wholes engaging in fantasizing, play-acting and doing. For instance, people's actions provide clues as to their thoughts and their thoughts, provide clues concerning what they would like to do. In short, people do not have organisms but *are* organisms engaged in activities of the same order which are often wrongly dichotomized into mental and physical activities.

Another erroneous dichotomy is that between self and external world. Individuals are not self-sufficient but can only exist in an environmental field. Environments do not create individuals, neither do individuals create environments. Rather, each is what it is because of its relationship to the other and the whole. For instance, in the example of a person seeing a tree, there is no sight without something to be seen, neither is anything seen if there is no eye to see it.

There are numerous other false dichotomies such as those between emotional (subjective) and real (objective); infantile and mature; biological and cultural; love and aggression; and conscious and unconscious. For instance, regarding the split between infantile and mature, it is often lack of certain childhood traits which devitalizes adults, while other traits called infantile may be the introjections of adult neuroses. A consistent theme of the gestalt approach is to search for the overall pattern rather than for false dichotomies.

Contact boundary and contact

Earlier I mentioned that Perls disdained the split between self and the external world, considering that the organism and the environment stood in a relationship of mutuality to one another. The contact boundary is the boundary between organism and environment and it is at this boundary that psychological events take place. Perls and his colleagues (1951) considered that 'psychology studies the operation of the contact boundary in the organism/environment field' (p. 229). Such 'contact' or 'being in touch with' involves both sensory awareness and motor behaviour. The organism's sensory system provides it with a means of orientation, with the motor system providing a means of manipulation. Both orientation and manipulation take place at the contact boundary. In healthy functioning, once the system of orientation has performed its function, the organism manipulates itself and the environment in such a way that organismic balance is restored and the gestalt is closed.

All thoughts, feelings and actions take place at the contact boundary. In healthy functioning, people have an effective contact–withdrawal rhythm or means of meeting psychological events at the contact boundary. Contacting the environment represents forming a gestalt, whereas withdrawal is either closing a gestalt completely or mobilizing resources to make closure possible. More simply, contact and withdrawal may respectively be viewed as acceptance and rejection of the environment. The components of contact and withdrawal are almost invariably present, but the neurotic person has a reduced capacity to discriminate between the appropriateness of these dialectical elements, and consequently behaves with reduced effectiveness, as will be seen in the later section on interruptions of contact.

Homeostasis and balance

The basic tendency of every organism is to strive for balance. The organism is continuously faced with imbalance that is disturbing through either external (demands from the environment) or internal (needs) factors. Life is characterized by a continuous interplay of balance and imbalance in the organism. Homeostasis or organismic self-regulation is the process by which the organism satisfies its needs by restoring balance when faced with a demand or need which upsets its equilibrium. Health constitutes the appropriate operation of the homeostatic process, whereas sickness means that for too long the organism has remained in a state of disequilibrium, of being unable to satisfy its needs. Death constitutes a total breakdown of the homeostatic process.

Though psychological and physiological are interrelated, the organism may be perceived as having psychological as well as physiological contact needs. A simple example of a physiological need is that, for the organism to be in good health, the water content of the blood must be kept at a certain level, neither too low nor excessive. If, for instance, the water content of the blood falls too low the individual feels thirst, with its symptoms of dry mouth and restlessness and the wish to restore the imbalance by drinking. A possible example of a more psychological need is that of mothers to keep their children happy and contented. Consequently, even when sleeping, they may be very sensitive to the cries and whimpers of their offspring.

The homeostatic process also operates where several needs are experienced simultaneously. However, here a selective process takes place based on the organism's need for survival and for self-actualization; with the simultaneous experiencing of many needs, the individual attends to the dominant survival and self-actualization need before attending to the others. Put another way, the dominant need or the need which presses most sharply for satisfaction becomes the foreground figure while the other needs recede, at least momentarily, into the background. Perls (1969a) wrote about doing away with the whole of instinct theory and simply considering the organism as a system that needs balance if it is to function properly. Though practically people have hundreds of unfinished situations in them, the most urgent situation always emerges. Individuals, to be able to satisfy their needs (to complete or to close incomplete *gestalten*) must be able both to sense what they need and also to manipulate themselves and their environments to obtain what is necessary.

Life is basically an infinite number of unfinished situations or incomplete gestalts, with no sooner than one gestalt being completed than another comes up. The homeostatic process is the means by which the organism maintains itself 'and the only law which is constant is the forming of gestalts – wholes, completeness. A gestalt is an organic function. A gestalt is an ultimate experiential unit' (Perls, 1969a, p. 16). With the introduction of the concept of the homeostatic process, it was possible to see gestalt formation as a primary biological drive, with the gestalt being the basic experiential unit having such properties as figure and ground and completeness or incompleteness.

The self and self-actualization

The self is the system of contacts at the contact boundary at any moment. The self exists where there are boundaries of contact, and its activity is that of forming figures and grounds. The self always integrates the senses, motor co-ordination and organic needs. It is the integrator or artist of life and though it 'is only a small factor in the total organism/environment interaction . . . it plays the crucial role of finding and making the meanings that we grow by' (Perls *et al.*, 1951, p. 235).

The self consists of the identifications and alienations at the contact boundary. For instance, individuals may identify with their families, but feel alien to people from different countries. Inside the boundary tends to be perceived as good, and outside as bad. Self-actualization may be viewed as the expression of appropriate identifications and alienations. Healthy functioning involves identifying with one's forming organismic self, not inhibiting one's creative excitement, yet alienating what is not organismically one's own. Sickness involves restricting one's areas of contact through alienating parts of one's forming organismic self by means of false identifications.

Perhaps a more accessible way of stating this is to make a distinction between self-actualizing based on the existential principle that 'a rose is a rose is a rose' and self-image actualizing in which people live for their image of how they should be rather than how they are. Perls (1969a) considered: 'Every external control, even *internalised* external control – "you should" – interferes with the healthy working of the organism. There is only one thing that should control: the *situation*' (p. 20). If people understand the situations which they are in, and let these situations control their actions, then they learn how to cope with life. An even more simple view of Perls' ideas on self-actualization may be gained from his dictum: 'So lose your mind and come to your senses' (Perls, 1970a, p. 38).

Excitement

Humans secure their energy from the food and air they take in. Perls emphasized vitality and the need to integrate the social being and the animal being. Perls used the word 'excitement' to describe the energy we create, because it coincides with the physiological function of excitation. This life force or *élan vital* is at the heart of the gestalt approach. Perls observed: 'Now normally the *élan vital*, the life force, energizes by sensing, by listening, by scouting, by describing the world – how is the world there. Now this life force first mobilizes the center – *if* you have a center. And the center of the personality is what used to be called the soul: the emotions, the feelings, the spirit' (Perls, 1969a, p. 68).

Excitement varies according to the task on the basis of hormonal differentiation: for instance, it gets tinged with some other substance, for example adrenalin for anger, or sexual hormones for erotic contact. Much of our excitement goes into energizing the motor system because the muscles link people with the environment. Even for most emotional events, emotion is transferred into movement. However, some excitement goes into energizing the senses. Healthy people allow their excitement to get to their senses and muscles, but unfortunately many people allow much of their excitement to be drained off into their fantasy life, into their computer (unproductive thinking), and into self-image actualization. Perls (1969a) considered modern humans live in a state of low-grade vitality in which the average person at most lives only 5 to 15 per cent of their potential, and the person who has even 25 per cent of their potential available is considered a genius.

Emotion

Emotion, which is the organism's direct evaluative experience of the organism/environment field, is immediate rather than being regulated by thoughts and verbal judgements. Emotion is a continuous process since all instances in people's lives carry some feeling tone of pleasantness or unpleasantness. Excitement is modified into specific emotions according to the situation that has to be met, and the emotions mobilize the sensory and motor system so that needs may be satisfied. Gestalt therapy attaches great importance to the emotions, which are not only essential as energy or excitement regulators but are also 'unique deliveries of experience which have no substitute – they are the way we become aware of our concerns, and, therefore, of what we are and what the world is' (Perls *et al.*, 1951, p. 96).

ACQUISITION

Aggression, assimilation and introjection

An aggressive attitude toward experience is necessary if it is really to be assimilated or made the organism's own. An analogy may be made between the aggression required for eating and that required for assimilating experience. Food needs to be destroyed or de-structured before what is valuable to the organism can be retained and undesirable substances can be eliminated. Undesirable substance which is not eliminated may be poisonous and detrimental to the organism. Every organism in an environmental field grows by incorporating, digesting or destructuring, and assimilating or absorbing selectively new matter, whether it be food, lectures or parental influence. Loving parents are likely to provide their children with experiences which they will assimilate since they are relevant to their own needs as they grow from environmental support to self-support.

Not all experience, however, goes through the destructuring and assimilation process required for healthy functioning. Introjections are experiences which are swallowed as a whole rather than being properly digested. The outcome of introjection is that undesirable as well as desirable substances have been retained, thus weakening the organism. Hateful parents are likely to provide their children with experiences which have to be introjected or taken in whole even though they are contrary to the needs of the organism.

Frustration and manipulation

The young baby is virtually totally dependent on its mother, but as time goes by the child learns to communicate, to crawl and walk, to bite and chew, and to accept and reject. In short, the child learns to realize some part of its potential for existence. Growth comes about through learning to overcome frustrations by mobilizing one's innate resources to manipulate the environment to satisfy needs. The term 'manipulation' refers to a person's ways of mobilizing and using the environment to satisfy needs. Both healthy and unhealthy organisms manipulate the environment, with healthy organisms manipulating it on an underlying basis of self-support, whereas unhealthy organisms are seeking environmental rather than self-support.

Perls wrote: 'Without frustration there is no need, no reason to mobilise your resources, to discover that you might be able to do something on your own, and in order not to be frustrated, which is a pretty painful experience, the child learns to manipulate the environment' (Perls, 1969a, p. 35). Perhaps it would be more accurate to say that with the right kind of frustrations the child learns to manipulate the environment in such a way as to meet its needs and restore effective organismic balance. However, with lack of frustration (the spoiled child) or with frustrations which block or are beyond the child's coping capacity, the outcome is likely to be that the child starts to mobilize the environment by playing phoney roles and games: for instance playing stupid, playing helpless, playing weak and flattering. These false manipulations cause individuals to alienate parts of themselves, be it their eyes, ears or genitals.

Interruptions of contact

Humans are forced to learn much more through education than by using their biologically based instincts. Consequently much of the animal's intuition as to what is the 'right' procedure is either missing or blocked. Instead there is a whole range of composite fantasies, handed down and modified through the generations, as to what constitutes the 'right' procedures. These procedures perform mostly support functions for social contacts (*viz.* manners and ethics) and have the disadvantage of not necessarily being biologically based. Consequently there are frequently interruptions in the contact provided by ongoing organismic processes which, if left alone, would be conducive to self-support. Examples of such interruptions are 'Don't touch that' or 'Don't do this.' Even withdrawals may be interrupted, as in the example 'You stay here now, keep your mind on your homework and don't dream.' People often incorporate their parents' interruptions as introjections in their own lives, for example 'Grown men don't cry.' Unhealthy organisms or neurotics are self-interrupters who need to become aware both of the fact that they are interrupting themselves and also of what they are interrupting.

Suppression of emotion

Suppression of emotion is a major way in which adults interrupt the contact of their children. Such adults, who frequently have been brought up in environments in which 'the authorities' were afraid of emotion, tend to squelch the emotions of their children and thus prevent their emotions from undergoing natural development and differentiation. This is mainly achieved through an overemphasis of the 'external world' and the demands of 'reality' and a belittling of organismic needs and emotions. The outcome of this is that children 'adjust' to such unremitting pressure by dulling their body-sense and losing some of their vitality. However, because emotions are inherent to the organism, this suppression of emotions does not eliminate 'undesirable' emotions; rather, it disturbs 'the intricate organism/environment field by setting up a great number of situations which, *unless avoided, are immensely emotion-arousing*!' (Perls *et al.*, 1951, p. 97).

MAINTENANCE

Though Perls often used the terms 'neurosis' and 'neurotic', he considered that problems of poor gestalt formation and closure were extremely widespread. In this section I examine the gestalt view of how people maintain their contact deficiencies. Needless to say, an individual's difficulties are compounded by living in a culture or environment where self-image actualizing rather than self-actualizing is common.

Zones of awareness

There are three zones or layers of awareness: outer, self and intermediate (see Box 5.1). Perls sometimes used the Indian word *maya* to describe the intermediate zone or DMZ. *Maya* means illusion or fantasy and is a kind of dream or trance. More colloquial and crude is Perl's use of the term 'mind-f**king' to describe the activity of the DMZ which hinders people from coming to their senses.

BOX 5.1

The three zones of awareness

The outer zone (OZ)
This zone consists of awareness of the world, of those things, facts and processes that are available to everyone.

The self zone (SZ)
This zone is the place within the skin, our authentic organismic selves.

The intermediate zone (DMZ)
This zone, which is located within the self zone, is often called 'mind' or consciousness and prevents people from good contact or being 'in touch' with themselves or the world. The DMZ is a zone of fantasy activity which consumes excitement and leaves little energy over for being in touch with reality.

Anxiety and stage fright

Gestalt theory has both a physiological and psychological definition of anxiety. The physiological definition is: 'Anxiety is the experience of breathing difficulty during any blocked excitement' (Perls *et al.*, 1951, p. 128). The idea underlying this definition is that heightened energy mobilization, with the need for more air (an increase in the rate and amplitude of breathing), occurs whenever there is strong concern and contact. As such it is a healthy way of being in erotic, aggressive, creative and other sorts of exciting or energy-mobilizing situations. A less healthy response is to control, interfere with and interrupt the excitement by trying to continue breathing at the rate that was adequate prior to it. This leads to a narrowing of the chest to force exhalation in order to create a vacuum into which fresh air can rush. Anxiety, derived from the Latin word 'angustia' meaning narrowness, is the product of an emergency measure caused by the conflict between excitement and control.

The psychological definition of anxiety is that it is 'the gap between the now and the later' or 'stage fright' (Perls, 1969a, pp. 32–3). As such it is the result of the fantasy activity of the DMZ. This fantasy activity is rehearsing for a future that people do not really want to have because they are afraid of it. Perls wrote: 'We fill in the gap where there should be a future with insurance policies, status quo, sameness, *anything* so as not to experience the possibility of openness towards the future' (Perls, 1969a, pp. 48–9). People who are in the now and have access to their senses are unlikely to be anxious because their excitement can flow immediately into the kind of spontaneous, creative and inventive activity which achieves solutions to unfinished situations. They are not blocked from good contact with themselves and the environment by *maya* or fantasies, prejudices, apprehensions and so on. They are prepared to take reasonable risks in living. Perls distinguished between catastrophic fantasies, which entail too much precaution, and anastrophic fantasies, which entail too little. He thought some people managed a balance between catastrophic and anastrophic fantasies, thus having both perspective and rational daring.

Neurosis

Neurotic individuals allow society to impinge too heavily on them. They cannot clearly distinguish their own needs and see society as larger than life and themselves as smaller. Society can consist of any one of a number of groups: for example, the family, the state, the social circle and co-workers. When the neurotic and one or more of these groups simultaneously experience different needs, the neurotic is incapable of distinguishing which need is dominant and thus can make neither a good contact nor a good withdrawal. Consequently one or more of the contact boundary disturbances of neurosis seem the most effective way to maintain balance and a sense of self-regulation in situations where the odds appear to be overwhelmingly adverse.

Perls distinguished between health, psychosis and neurosis. In health, people are in touch with the realities both of themselves and the world. In psychosis, people are out of touch with reality and in touch with *maya*, especially fantasies about megalomania and worthlessness. In neurosis a continual fight is taking place between *maya* and reality.

Contact boundary disturbances

The neuroses, which entail significant contact boundary disturbances, operate primarily through four mechanisms, albeit interrelated. These neurotic boundary disturbances are 'nagging, chronic, daily interferences with the processes of growth and self-recognition' (Perls, 1973, p. 32). However, not all disturbances in the organism/environment search for balance are evidence of or produce neurosis. Introjection, projection, confluence and retroflection are the four mechanisms of contact boundary disturbance.

Introjection

I have already mentioned *introjection* as the process by which material from outside is swallowed whole rather than digested properly with the valuable elements being assimilated and the undesirable or toxic elements discarded. Introjects, or undigested thoughts, feelings and behaviour, are the results of the process of introjection. Introjection may be viewed as the tendency to 'own' as part of the self what actually is part of the environment. Two outcomes of introjection are: first, that the introjects prevent individuals from getting in touch with their own reality because all the time they are having to contend with these foreign bodies; and, second, that the introjects may be incompatible with one another and thus contribute to personality disintegration.

Projection

Projection is the reverse of introjection in that it is the tendency to 'own' as part of the environment what actually is part of the self. Projection can take place on two levels: in relation to the outer environment and in relation to the self. Perhaps most commonly, projection involves shifting those parts of ourselves that we dislike and devalue onto others rather than recognizing and dealing with the tendencies in ourselves. Projections are associated with introjects because people usually devalue themselves in relation to introjected self-standards, whose unacceptable derivatives in terms of self-evaluations are then projected onto the environment.

Projection in relation to the self takes place when people disown as part of themselves certain impulses that arise. For instance, people may say of their anger 'It took control of me' whereby the anger is given an objective existence outside of themselves so that they can make it responsible for their troubles and avoid full recognition of the fact that *it* is part of *him* or *her.*

Confluence

With *confluence*, the individual lacks any distinction or experiences no boundary at all between self and environment. People who are unaware of the contact boundaries between themselves and others are neither able to make good contact with them nor, where appropriate, to withdraw. A feature of confluence is demanding likeness and refusal to tolerate differences. Two examples of confluence are marital partners and parents who, respectively, refuse to see their spouses and children as different from themselves.

Retroflection

In *retroflection*, the individual fails to discriminate self and others accurately by treating themselves the way they originally wanted to treat other people or objects. For instance, the harassed mother at the end of a long day in which everything has gone wrong may turn her destructive impulses against herself. Retroflection means literally 'to turn sharply back against'. When people retroflect they redirect their activity inward and substitute themselves instead of the environment as the targets of their behaviour. Retroflection is not necessarily neurotic. In certain situations it may be to the individual's advantage to suppress particular responses. However, retroflection is pathological when it is chronic, habitual and out of control.

Perls was sensitive to the use of language both in representing and helping to sustain contact boundary disturbances. For example: in introjection the personal pronoun 'I' is used when the real meaning is 'they'; in projection the pronouns 'they' or 'it' are used when the real meaning is 'I'; in confluence the pronoun 'we' is used when there may really be differentness; and retroflection uses the reflexive 'myself' as in the statement 'I am ashamed of myself.'

The following is Perl's (1973) succinct summary of the lacks of discrimination, interferences and interruptions entailed in the four main contact boundary disturbances:

> *The introjector does as others would like him to do, the projector does unto others what he accuses them of doing to him, the man in pathological confluence doesn't know who is doing what to whom, and the retroflector does to himself what he would like to do to others.* (p. 40)

Layers of neurosis

Perls (1969a, 1970a) came to see the structure of neurosis as consisting of five layers, each of which is described in Box 5.2. A major feature in the maintenance of neuroses is that people are not willing to undergo the pain of the impasse, the feeling of being stuck and lost. An example involving the later layers of neurosis is that of a young woman who had recently lost her child and who needed to be able to face her nothingness and her grief to be able to came back to life and make real contact with the world.

BOX 5.2

The five layers of neurosis

The cliché layer
For example, the meaningless tokens of meeting such as a handshake or 'Good morning'.

The Eric Berne or Sigmund Freud layer
The layer where people engage in the counter-productive manipulations of phoney roles

and games (e.g. the bully, the very important person, the cry-baby, the nice little girl, the good boy).

The impasse
When the role-playing layer is worked through, then therapist and client come to the third layer called the impasse or sometimes the sick-point. This layer is characterized by a phobic attitude manifested in avoidance and flight from authentic living. In particular, suffering is avoided, especially the suffering of frustration.

The death or implosive layer
Behind the impasse is the death or implosive layer, which appears either as fear of death or a feeling of not being alive. Here people implode by contracting and compressing themselves.

The explosion
The explosion is the final neurotic layer. There are four basic kinds of explosions from the death layer: into grief, if a person works through a loss which has not been assimilated; into orgasm for sexually blocked people; into anger; and into joy. The explosions, which may be mild depending on the amount of energy invested in the implosive layer, connect with the authentic, organismic person.

THERAPY

From the point of view of psychotherapy, when there is good contact – e.g., a clear bright figure freely energized from an empty background – then there are not peculiar problems concerning the relations of 'mind' and 'body' or 'self' and 'external world'.

Fritz Perls

THERAPEUTIC GOALS

Clients come to gestalt therapy because they are in existential crises. Perls had a rather cynical view of their motivation, stating: 'Anybody who goes to a therapist has something up his sleeve. I would say roughly 90% don't go to a therapist to be cured, but to be more adequate in their neuroses' (Perls, 1969a, p. 79). Gestalt therapy goals revolve around the client's movement from environmental support to self-support. Beginning clients are mainly concerned with solving problems. Gestalt therapists assist clients to support themselves, not only in solving current problems, but in living more authentically. In order to be self-supporting, clients need to be in touch with their organismic existential centres (I am what I am). People who are in touch with their organismic selves or with their senses are self-actualizing or self-supporting.

The process of self-actualizing involves an effective balance of contact and withdrawal at the contact boundary and the ability to use energy or excitement to meet real rather than phoney needs. Furthermore, self-actualizing involves being able to withstand frustration until a solution emerges. Self-supporting people take responsibility for their existences and possess *response-ability* or freedom of choice. They are able appropriately to use aggression to assimilate their experiences and they are largely free from the neurotic contact boundary disturbances of introjection, projection, retroflection and confluence. Also, they possess relatively little self-destructive unfinished business since they are good at forming and closing strong gestalts.

Yontef and Jacobs (2000) observe that the only goal of gestalt therapy is awareness. Clients require awareness both in particular areas, awareness of content, and also of the processes or automatic habits by which they block awareness, awareness of process. This latter self-reflective kind of awareness, sometimes called 'awareness of awareness', enables clients to use their skills in awareness to rectify disturbances in the awareness process.

PROCESS OF THERAPY

It is important to distinguish how Perls worked towards the end of his life and the practice of ongoing individual gestalt therapy. Perls was a showman who conducted gestalt therapy in workshops which included, as an adjunct at Esalen, communal baths. He required six elements for his performance: '1) My skill 2) Kleenex 3) The hot seat 4) The empty chair 5) Cigarettes 6) An ashtray' (Perls, 1969b, p. 227). Perls viewed all therapy interviews as experimental. Therapists need to try things out to help clients become aware of how they are now functioning as persons and organisms. Sometimes he would do mass experiments or exercises, but mostly he worked with a series of single people, or sometimes couples, in front of the group.

In ongoing individual gestalt therapy, assessment is done as part of the therapeutic process rather than as an initial diagnostic procedure. Clients need to be willing to work within the gestalt therapy framework and feel that their therapist is someone whom they can trust. In the initial session therapists are likely to discuss details of fees, cancellation of sessions policy and other pertinent practical matters.

Gestalt therapists' offices are designed to be friendly and comfortable and avoid having desks or tables between therapists and clients. Where possible, space is available for movement and experimentation. In addition, every effort is made to ensure privacy in terms of both soundproofing and safeguarding of records.

Sessions are usually once weekly, which gives clients time to digest what happened in the previous session. Though more frequent sessions are possible, gestalt therapists take care to encourage self-support rather than dependency by not becoming too available. Often individual therapy is combined with group therapy, couples therapy, family therapy, workshops and with meditation or biofeedback training.

Evaluation of therapeutic process and outcomes occurs as part of therapy and both therapists and clients participate. Beginning clients may be most concerned with solving problems and relief of psychological discomfort. Therapists encourage their clients to assume responsibility for self-support in addressing their problems and resultant discomfort. Initially clients may talk about problems but show little insight into the 'how' of their behaviour. As therapy progresses, clients become more aware both of how they behave and of how unaware they have hitherto been. As therapy continues, client and therapist may pay more attention to general personality issues and the general patterns and conditions which contribute to clients' insufficient awareness. The idea is that increasingly clients carry their higher levels of awareness into their everyday lives and maintain and build upon them after therapy ends.

THE THERAPEUTIC RELATIONSHIP

There are at least two ways of looking at the therapist–client relationship in gestalt therapy: that of Perls in his demonstrations and workshops and that of other important practitioners, for instance Laura Perls, Gary Yontef and James Simkin. The relationship and style of Perls' Esalen workshops is often called 'Perlsism' or 'Perlsian Gestalt' to differentiate it from the relationship and style of therapy practised by those other leading gestalt therapists.

Perls was a charismatic and dominating personality who, once he became well known, may have attracted clients who felt they might benefit from his confronting approach. Though ostensibly he advocated a democratic dialogue between therapist and client, the reality was that much of the time he was controlling the therapeutic process. Perls' son Stephen was to observe that his father did not know how to relate to another person on an equal basis (Perls, 1993). Fritz Perls' relationships with clients contained the paradox of advocating personal responsibility at the same time as assuming the major responsibility for the therapeutic process himself.

At his best Perls was so concerned with helping clients that he would not allow them to sabotage their growth by being phoney, an important word in his vocabulary. A contemporary phrase for Perls' relationships with clients is 'tough love'. Other leading practitioners have conducted gestalt therapy within the context of more equal or horizontal therapist–client relationships.

All gestalt therapists regard the therapeutic relationship as a 'working' rather than a 'talking' relationship. Yontef and Simkin observe: 'When one moves from talking about a problem or being with someone in a general way to studying what one is doing, especially being aware of how one is aware, one is working' (1989, p. 341). In this working relationship, both therapists and clients are self-responsible: therapists for the quality of their presence and self-awareness, their knowledge and skills in relating to the client, and for maintaining an open and non-defensive stance; and clients for their commitment to working to become more in charge of their lives through developing greater self-awareness. Furthermore, therapists are responsible for not colluding in clients' manipulations to get them to do what clients fear they cannot do for themselves. Instead, therapists should relate to clients in a warm, respectful, direct and honest manner.

THERAPEUTIC INTERVENTIONS

The use of gestalt therapy interventions 'hinges on questions of *when*, *with whom*, and *in what* situation' (Shepherd, 1970, p. 324). In 'Perlsian' therapy, he would be likely to intervene without much, if any, consultation. With most gestalt therapists, appropriate interventions are decided upon in an ongoing dialogue between therapist and client. Such interventions are considered as experiments. A major purpose of encouraging clients to experiment with different ways of thinking and acting is to collect information to achieve genuine understanding rather than mere changes in behaviour. Repeatedly clients are encouraged to 'Try this and see what you experience' (Yontef and Jacobs, 2000). Creativity from therapists and clients in setting up and carrying out appropriate experiments is highly valued.

Awareness technique

Gestalt therapy is an experiential rather than a verbal or interpretive approach. Assessment data about how clients interrupt their contact with life are collected as therapists and clients work together. Gestalt therapy demands that clients experience themselves as fully as possible in the here and now, both to understand their present manipulations and contact boundary disturbances, and also to re-experience the unfinished business of past problems and traumas.

Perls (1973) regarded the simple phrase 'Now I am aware' as the foundation of the gestalt approach. The 'now' because it keeps therapists and clients in the present and reinforces the fact that experience can only take place in the present. The 'aware' because it gives both therapists and clients the best picture of clients' present resources. Awareness always takes place in the present and opens up possibilities for action.

Clients are asked to become aware of their body language, their breathing, their voice quality and their emotions as much as of any pressing thoughts. Below are some examples of Perls directing the attention of Gloria, the client, to her non-verbal behaviour taken from the *Three Approaches to Psychotherapy* film series (Dolliver, 1991, p. 299; Perls, 1965).

> *'What are you doing with your feet now?'*
> *'Are you aware of your smile?'*
> *'You didn't squirm for the last minute.'*
> *'Are you aware that your eyes are moist?'*
> *'Are you aware of your facial expression?'*

One way of following up a client's awareness report is for the therapist to say 'Stay with it' or 'Feel it out.' Such instructions can encourage clients to more fully experience and work through feelings to completion. For example, staying with moist eyes may lead to further experiencing and then identifying the reasons for feeling sad and to crying.

Exaggeration, which may focus on either movement and gesture or on verbal statements, is another way of heightening clients' awareness of how they communicate. In each instance, clients are asked progressively and repeatedly to exaggerate the behaviour. Examples of exaggeration requests from Perls' interview with Gloria are as follows (Dolliver, 1991, p. 300; Perls, 1965).

'Can you develop this movement?'
'Develop it as if you were dancing.'
'Now exaggerate this.'
'What you just said, talk to me like this.'
'Do this more.'

Yet another way of heightening clients' awareness of their here and now communication is to ask them to use the phrase 'I take responsibility for it.' For instance, 'I am aware that I am moving my leg and I take responsibility for it.'

When using awareness techniques, therapists may self-disclose and provide here-and-now feedback about how they see the client communicating. Furthermore, therapists can judiciously share how they are affected by the client communicating that way.

Since clients are self-interrupters they often find it difficult to remain in the here and now. The awareness technique is really a concentration technique, sometimes called focal awareness, by which clients learn to experience each now and each need and also how their feelings and behaviour in one area are related to feelings and behaviour in other areas. Thus they come to an awareness, not only of the fact that they are interrupting their contact with themselves and the world, but also of what they are interrupting and how they are doing it through the neurotic mechanisms of introjection, projection, etc. Clients are also asked to do some homework which consists of reviewing the session in terms of a systematic application of the awareness technique.

Sympathy and frustration

Empathizing with clients is insufficient since the therapists are then withholding themselves and at worst allowing confluence. Sympathy alone spoils clients. What is needed is a combination of sympathy and of frustration. Clients must be frustrated in their efforts to control the therapist by neurotic manipulations and instead learn to use their powers of manipulation to meet their real needs. The therapist focuses on getting clients to become more aware and not to become phobic when they start feeling uncomfortable.

Perls provided situations in which his clients experienced being stuck in frustration and then frustrated their avoidances still further until they were willing to mobilize their *own* resources. He repeatedly frustrated clients until they were face to face with their blocks, inhibitions, and ways of avoiding having eyes, ears, muscles, authority, and security in themselves. Frustration often leads to the discovery that the phobic impasse does not exist in reality but in fantasy, in that clients have been preventing themselves from using their own available resources through catastrophic expectations. Furthermore frustration helps clients to express their needs and requests directly rather than to cover them over with neurotic manipulations. The imperative is the primary form of communication, and clients who can actually state what they need and mean what they state have made the most important step in their therapy.

Eliciting fantasies

A limitation of the awareness technique is its slowness. In order to speed up therapy, Perls made considerable use of fantasizing, be it verbal, written down or acted out as a drama. Below is an example taken from the *Three Approaches to Psychotherapy* film series in which Perls encourages Gloria to describe a fantasy (Dolliver, 1991, p. 300; Perls, 1965).

> *'Can you describe the corner you'd like to go to?'*
> *'Imagine you are in this corner and you are perfectly safe. Now what would you do in that corner?'*
> *'What should I do when you are in that corner?'*

During the interview, Perls also asked Gloria to describe her fantasies about him (Dolliver, 1991, p. 301).

> *'Now what can I do to you?'*
> *'How old must I be?' (for Gloria to scold him)*
> *'How should I be? Give me a fantasy. How could I show my concern for you?'*
> *'What would I do? How would I conceal my feelings?'*

Dolliver observes that whenever Gloria offered Perls feedback about her experience of him, Perls always regarded it as a transference fantasy representing her projected attributes.

Drama techniques

'Monotherapy', perhaps better termed 'monodrama', is a form of psychodrama with a difference. In monotherapy, instead of having other people as well as the client involved in the drama, the client creates his own stage and plays all the roles under his own direction and expression.

In the *shuttle* technique clients are asked to shuttle their attention from one area to another. For instance, a client can shuttle between the visualization of a memory and the organismic reliving of it in the here and now. Another example involves getting clients to shuttle between their feelings in and about an incident and their projections in the incident. For example, a client who feels angry with a colleague for 'apple-polishing' his boss may shuttle to experiencing his own needs and desires for approval from the boss. A further example is that of getting clients to shuttle between talking and listening to themselves. After each sentence, clients are asked: 'Are you aware of this sentence?' The purpose here is to help clients stop compulsive talking which interrupts their experiencing of themselves and listening to others.

Drama and fantasy work can involve both the *hot seat* and the *empty chair*. The hot seat is occupied by the individual with whom at any time the counsellor is working in front of the group. The empty chair is a second chair which is a 'projection-identification gimmick . . . waiting to be filled with fantasised people and things' (Perls, 1969b, p. 224). Essentially it is a method of highlighting the shuttling process by getting clients to change chairs as they shuttle between parts of themselves or between different people in a drama.

Topdog–underdog dialogues are one of the main examples of the use of the shuttle technique involving both fantasy work and the empty chair. Perls considered that in their fantasies many people played self-torture games in which they were fragmented into an inner conflict between controller (topdog) and controlled (underdog). The topdog (or super-ego) is righteous, authoritarian, full of 'shoulds' and 'should nots', perfectionistic and manipulates with threats of catastrophe if his demands are not carried out. The underdog (or intra-ego) is cunning and manipulates with being wheedling, defensive, apologetic, playing the cry-baby and so on. Typical underdog statements are 'Mañana', 'I try my best' and 'I have such good intentions.' Through shuttling between these polarities, clients are helped to understand the structure of their behaviour and also to bring about a reconciliation between these two fighting clowns by becoming more in touch with their organismic selves.

Dreamwork

Perls (1970b) regarded dreams as the royal road to integration. Dreams are existential messages, not just unfinished situations, current problems or symptoms. Especially if the dreams are repetitive, a very important existential issue for the client is likely to be involved. There are four stages to dreamwork (see Box 5.3).

BOX 5.3

The four stages of dreamwork

Stage 1: Sharing the dream
The client relates the dream.

Stage 2: Retelling the dream in the present tense
The client retells the dream or a section of it as a drama by changing the past tense into the present tense, for example 'I was climbing a mountain' becomes 'I am climbing a mountain.' Perls would ask clients to say their dreams, or parts of their dreams, again 'in the *present tense*: as if you were dreaming it *now*?' (Perls, 1970b, p. 205).

Stage 3: Talking to the different actors in the dream
The client becomes the stage director and sets the scene and talks to the different actors in the dream or section of it. For example, when working with Mary Anne's dream, Perls introduced the action element with the statement: 'Now let's start acting it out. Tell this to the man. Talk to the man – express your resentment' (Perls, 1970b, p. 206). The client is encouraged to become the different actors, the props and all that is there. Clients do not have to work with a whole dream for, even if they re-identify with just one or a few items in the dream, the exercise is valuable.

Stage 4: Conducting a dialogue between different elements in the dream
The fourth stage of dreamwork may be facilitated by the empty chair technique to allow for dialogues between the different people, objects or parts of the self that are encountering each other. These dreamwork encounters provide opportunity for two things: the integration of conflicts and re-identification with those parts of the self that are alienated, especially the assimilation of projections. Dreamwork is an excellent way of finding the holes in a client's personality. These tend to be manifested as voids and blank spaces which are accompanied by nervousness and confusion.

Responsibility language

Perls was interested in semantics and he was conscious of how clients could interfere with self-support through poor use of language (Levitsky and Perls, 1970; Perls, 1970a). Using verbs that acknowledge choice and personal agency is one example of using responsibility language: for example, rephrasing 'I can't do that' to 'I *won't* do that.' In addition, clients can be alerted to use the personal pronoun 'I' rather than 'it' or 'they' and send messages directly to their therapists and to others. Furthermore, if clients ask the kind of questions which manipulate the environment for support, therapists can encourage them to change those passive questions into more active and self-supporting statements.

CASE MATERIAL

Perls' book *Gestalt Therapy Verbatim* (1969a) is primarily made up of verbatim transcripts from his large-scale weekend dreamwork seminars between 1966 and 1968 and from an intensive four-week Gestalt Therapy workshop in 1968, all of which were held at Esalen. Perls presents his work with a number of different clients from the seminars and the workshop. In addition, the *Eyewitness* part of *The Gestalt Approach & Eyewitness to Therapy* (1973) contains transcripts, that Perls considered had great teaching potential, taken from his conducting therapy films. In the 'Gestalt therapy' film in the earlier *Three Approaches to Psychotherapy* series, Perls introduces his approach, conducts a brief interview with Gloria and then summarizes his impressions of the session (Perls, 1965).

Another example of gestalt therapy is that of Laura Perls working first with a 25-year-old black woman and then with a 47-year-old Central European Jewish refugee (Perls, 1968). Joen Fagan (1974) presents transcripts with commentary for three sessions with Iris, who had agreed to be videotaped and had no previous experience with gestalt therapy. Simkin presents a case example with a transcript excerpted from a demonstration film with Peg who had originally been seen in a gestalt training workshop, where she worked on the grief and anger she felt towards her husband who had committed suicide (Yontef and Simkin, 1989). In the same chapter, Simkin presents selected excerpts from a condensed transcript of a gestalt therapy workshop with six volunteers in which he illustrates some gestalt techniques.

Clarkson (1999) illustrates the various stages of long-term gestalt therapy with a progressive case example where the client is Gary, a university lecturer. At the start of therapy, Gary had been in an unsatisfactory relationship with Jessica for the previous two of the six years they had lived together. Yontef and Jacobs (2000) present a case example in the form of an excerpt taken from the fourth year of therapy with Miriam, whose world was characterized by extreme isolation.

FURTHER DEVELOPMENTS

Already I have mentioned that many other leading gestalt therapists developed more horizontal relationships with clients than did Perls. Since Perls' death, the practice of gestalt therapy has altered in many other ways and continues to develop (Clarkson, 1999; Mackewn, 1994; Parlett and Hemming, 1996; Yontef and Jacobs, 2000). Contemporary gestalt therapists are more supportive, compassionate and kind. There is less emphasis on frustration and abrasively confronting clients perceived as manipulative. When using confrontation, gestalt therapists take great care not to humiliate or re-traumatize clients by triggering unnecessary shame in them.

Therapists are less likely to pose as experts and more likely to reveal their humanity, including their fears, defensiveness and confusions. Gestalt therapists are encouraged to make 'I' statements to enhance their contact with clients and clients' focusing. In describing how she works, Laura Perls (1970c) provides examples of disclosing her awareness and feelings, sharing personal problems and life experiences, and using physical contact. Her guiding principle is to use such disclosures only if they might help clients take their next steps.

Many contemporary gestalt therapists attempt to exemplify Buber's concept of the 'I–Thou' relationship in which two unique people encounter and openly respect one another's essential humanity (Buber, 1958). 'I–Thou' relationships are here-and-now, person-to-person existential encounters in therapist and client are open to being changed by the other (Clarkson, 1997). Such relationships may be contrasted with 'I–It' relationships in which others are treated as objects to be used and manipulated.

Contemporary gestalt therapy tends to be highly individual, with a different therapy being tailor made for each client. Therapists and clients creatively generate and carry out appropriate experiments as therapy progresses. Clarkson (1999) provides a good example of how one leading gestalt therapist works. She presents a seven-stage cycle of gestalt formation and production: sensation, awareness, mobilization, action, final contact, satisfaction, and withdrawal. The cycle's last six stages are then used as a framework for illustrating the gestalt therapy process. Clarkson suggests some appropriate experiments for each stage.

Another development is that, drawing on gestalt therapy's empty chair technique, Greenberg and his colleagues have devised an empty chair dialogue intervention geared to the resolution of 'unfinished business' with significant others (Greenberg, Rice and Elliott, 1993). Such unresolved negative feelings can contribute to anxiety and depression as well as be transferred into other relationships where they are inappropriate. This intervention 'in which the client engages in an imaginary dialogue with the significant other, is designed to access restricted feelings allowing them to run their course and be restructured in the safety of the therapy environment' (Pavio and Greenberg, 1995, p. 419).

Some gestalt therapists may openly use psychoanalytic formulations to describe character structure (Yontef, 1988). Also, when conducting groups, though some gestalt therapists still use Perls' working with individuals in front of the group style, the trend is for gestalt therapists to make greater use of the interactions between and contributions from group members than Perls did. A further development is that gestalt therapy techniques have been integrated into other approaches. For example, gestalt techniques and experiments are commonly used in conjunction with transactional analysis (Dusay and Dusay, 1989; James and Jongeward, 1971).

Gestalt therapy has training institutes in every major city of the United States and in most countries of Europe and South America as well as in Australia. Training standards for gestalt therapists in Britain are among the most stringent in the United Kingdom Council for Psychotherapy (Parlett and Hemming, 1996). In Britain there are several hundred psychotherapists who primarily identify themselves as gestalt therapists (Clarkson, 1999). There are national gestalt therapy associations in many countries and the International Gestalt Therapy Association is a new group attempting to form a more international governing structure.

SUMMARY

- *Fritz Perls, its main originator, regarded gestalt therapy as an existential approach. Gestalt means form, shape, pattern or configuration. The human organism is a unified whole which can only exist in an environmental field. Consequently mind–body and person–environment splits are erroneous.*
- *The contact boundary is the boundary between organism and environment and it is here that psychological events take place.*
- *Life is characterized by a continuous process of balance and imbalance in the organism, with homeostasis being the process whereby the organism satisfies its needs by restoring balance. No sooner is one gestalt completed than another comes up.*
- *Perls emphasized vitality and the need to integrate the social being and the animal being. The word 'excitement' describes the energy people create. This life force or* élan vital *is at the heart of the gestalt approach.*
- *Healthy functioning involves identifying with one's forming organismic self and keeping in touch with one's senses. An aggressive attitude toward experience is necessary if it is to be destructured and then assimilated as one's own.*
- *People need frustrations in order to learn to mobilize their own resources to manipulate the environment. However, children often experience interruptions from significant others which interfere with their capacity for self-support and cause them to suppress their emotions.*
- *Between the self zone and the outer zone is an intermediate zone consisting of* maya *or of fantasy activity. Anxiety or stage fright is the result of this fantasy activity. In neurosis there is a continuous fight between reality and* maya.
- *The four main neurotic mechanisms or contact boundary disturbances are introjection, projection, confluence, and retroflection. The structure of neurosis consists of five layers: the cliché layer; the Eric Berne or Sigmund Freud layer of manipulative roles and games;*

the impasse; the death or implosive layer; and the explosion.

- *Goals for therapy include heightened awareness, self-support rather than environmental support, being in touch with one's senses and existential centre, response-ability or freedom of choice, and the ability to form and close strong gestalts.*
- *Towards the end of his life Perls worked primarily in groups, and a distinction can be made between 'Perlsian' therapy in a workshop format and ongoing individual gestalt therapy.*
- *The relationship in gestalt therapy is an active working rather than a passive talking relationship. Other leading gestalt therapy practitioners conduct therapy within the context of a more horizontal relationship than appears to have been the case with Perls.*
- *Change involves focusing on the 'how' of clients' contact boundary disturbances in the now. Experientially engaging clients so that they can become more aware of how they communicate and interfere with their communication in the here-and-now is central to the practice of gestalt therapy.*
- *Perls would frustrate clients so that they experienced being stuck in their frustration and then he frustrated their avoidances still further until they were willing to mobilize their own resources.*
- *Drama and fantasy work in gestalt therapy can involve the shuttle technique, where clients shuttle between different aspects of themselves and their situations, and the hot seat and empty chair.*
- *The four stages of gestalt dreamwork are: sharing the dream, retelling the dream in the present tense, talking to the different actors in the dream, and conducting a dialogue between different elements in the dream.*
- *Clients are encouraged to use personal responsibility language: for example, using verbs that acknowledge choice, the personal pronoun 'I', and making statements rather than asking questions.*
- *Gestalt therapy developments include a more horizontal therapist–client relationship, less emphasis on frustrating clients, more therapist self-disclosure, more emphasis on forming authentic 'I–Thou' therapeutic relationships, creative use of experiments to individualize and enhance the therapeutic process, development of the empty chair technique to resolve unfinished business with significant others, use of psychoanalytic formulations to describe character structure, and integrating gestalt techniques with those from other approaches, such as transactional analysis.*
- *Gestalt therapy continues to develop its national and international governing structures and training programmes.*

REVIEW AND PERSONAL QUESTIONS

REVIEW QUESTIONS

1. What did Perls mean by gestalt formation?
2. Why did Perls consider it important for people to take an aggressive attitude to experience?

3. In growing up, what is the role of frustration?
4. Describe each of Perls' three layers of awareness.
5. Describe each of the following mechanisms of contact boundary disturbance: introjection, projection, confluence, and retroflection.
6 What are the goals of gestalt therapy?
7. How and why do gestalt therapists use awareness techniques?
8. How and why do gestalt therapists use sympathy and frustration?
9. How and why do gestalt therapists use drama techniques?
10. What is the purpose of dreamwork and what are its four stages?
11. What is 'Perlsian' gestalt therapy and how does it differ from the way some of Perls' collaborators and many contemporary therapists practise gestalt therapy?

PERSONAL QUESTIONS

1. What specific events in your life may have influenced you to come to your mind and lose your senses?
2. Assess how you relate to your environment in terms of each of Perl's mechanisms of contact boundary disturbance: introjection, projection, confluence and retroflection.
3. What are the phoney roles and games that you use to obtain environmental support rather than rely on self-support?
4. Sit in a comfortable chair and, for the next three minutes, say to yourself 'Now I am aware . . .' each time you become aware of your body language, your breathing, your emotions, and any pressing thoughts. For example, 'Now I am aware I'm uncrossing my legs.'
5. Spend the next three minutes focusing on your response-ability for your life by staying in the now and saying to yourself about all your current behaviour '. . . and I take responsibility for it.'
6. Use the shuttle technique and change chairs as you shuttle between different parts of yourself or between yourself and another person.
7. What is your fantasy of how it would be like for you to be in the hot seat being in therapy with a gestalt therapist like Fritz Perls?
8. What relevance, if any, has the theory and practice of gestalt therapy for how you conduct therapy?
9. What relevance, if any, has the theory and practice of gestalt therapy for how you live?

ANNOTATED BIBLIOGRAPHY

Perls, F. S., Hefferline, R. F. and Goodman, P. (1951). *Gestalt Therapy: Excitement and Growth in the Human Personality.* London: Souvenir Press.
This book contains an introduction and two volumes. Volume 1 is a series of eighteen experiments: experiments 1 to 11 focus on contacting the environment, technique of awareness, and directed awareness; experiments 12 to 18 focus on retroflection, introjection, and projections. Volume 2 is a major statement of gestalt theory consisting of three parts: introduction;

reality, human nature, and society; and theory of the self. This detailed book is for serious students and therapists.

Perls, F. S. (1969a). *Gestalt Therapy Verbatim*. New York: Bantam Books.
This book consists of three parts: talk, dreamwork seminar, and intensive workshop. The talk and dreamwork seminar parts are selected and edited material from audio tapes made at weekend dreamwork seminars conducted by Perls at the Esalen Institute, Big Sur, California between 1966 and 1968. The intensive workshop part is taken from audio tapes of a four-week intensive workshop conducted in 1968. The talk part of the book provides an easily readable introduction to gestalt theory.

Perls, F. S. (1969b). *In and Out of the Garbage Pail*. New York: Bantam Books.
As the book's cover says, 'Joy. Sorrow. Chaos. Wisdom. The free-floating autobiography of the man who developed Gestalt Therapy.' A pot-pourri of self-disclosure by means of prose and poetry. This book is a good way to meet Perls, the man.

Perls, F. S. (1973). *The Gestalt Approach & Eyewitness to Therapy*. New York: Bantam Books.
This book is a combination of two projects that Perls was working on at the time of his death. *The Gestalt Approach* is Perls' final statement of his theory and was written because he regarded his two previous theoretical works *Ego, Hunger and Aggression* and *Gestalt Therapy* as too outdated and difficult to read. *Eyewitness to Therapy* provides descriptions of gestalt therapy in action.

Clarkson, P. (1999). *Gestalt Counselling in Action* (2nd edition). London: Sage.
This book starts by introducing gestalt theory and the fundamentals of gestalt practice. A seven-stage cycle of gestalt formation and production is presented and, using the cycle as a framework, the practice of gestalt counselling is reviewed. This engaging and well-written book is a rich source of ideas about how to integrate experiments into gestalt practice.

Yontef, G. and Jacobs, L. (2000). Gestalt therapy. In R. J. Corsini and D. Wedding (eds). *Current Psychotherapies* (6th edition). Itasca, IL: Peacock, 303–39.
This chapter provides a good overview of contemporary gestalt therapy. However, the annotated bibliography at the end of the chapter does not contain a single book written by Perls.

REFERENCES AND FURTHER READING

Buber, M. (1958). *I and Thou* (2nd edition). Edinburgh: T and T Clark. First published in 1937.
Clarkson, P. (1997). Variations on I and thou. *Gestalt Review*, *1* (1), 56–70.
Clarkson, P. (1999). *Gestalt Counselling in Action* (2nd edition). London: Sage.
Clarkson, P. and Mackewn, J. (1993). *Fritz Perls*. London: Sage.
Dolliver, R. H. (1991). Perls with Gloria re-viewed: Gestalt techniques and Perls' practices. *Journal of Counseling and Development*, *69*, 299–304.
Dusay, J. M. and Dusay, K. M. (1989). Transactional analysis. In R. J. Corsini and D. Wedding (eds). *Current Psychotherapies* (4th edition, 405–53). Itasca, IL: Peacock.
Fagan, J. (1974). Three sessions with Iris. *The Counseling Psychologist*, *4* (4), 42–60.
Fagan, J. and Shepherd, I. L. (eds) (1970). *Gestalt Therapy Now: Theory, Techniques, Applications*. Palo Alto, CA: Science and Behavior Books.

Greenberg, L. S., Rice, L. N. and Elliott, R. (1993). *Facilitating Emotional Change: The Moment by Moment Process.* New York: Guilford Press.

James, M. and Jongeward, D. (1971). *Born to Win: Transactional Analysis with Gestalt Experiments.* Reading, MA: Addison-Wesley.

Levitsky, A. and Perls, F. S. (1970). The rules and games of gestalt therapy. In J. Fagan and I. L. Shepherd (eds). *Gestalt Therapy Now: Theory, Techniques, Applications* (140–9). Palo Alto, CA: Science and Behavior Books.

Mackewn, J. (1994). Modern Gestalt – An integrative and ethical approach to counselling and psychotherapy. *Counselling, 5* (2), 105–8.

Parlett, M. and Hemming, J. (1996). Developments in Gestalt Therapy. In W. Dryden (ed.). *Developments in Psychotherapy: Historical Perspectives.* London: Sage, 91–110.

Pavio, S. C. and Greenberg, L. S. (1995). Resolving 'unfinished business': Efficacy of experimental therapy using empty-chair dialogue. *Journal of Consulting and Clinical Psychology, 63,* 419–25.

Perls, F. S. (1947). *Ego, Hunger and Aggression: A Revision of Freud's Theory and Method.* London: Allen and Unwin.

Perls, F. S. (1969a). *Gestalt Therapy Verbatim.* New York: Bantam Books.

Perls, F. S. (1969b). *In and Out of the Garbage Pail.* New York: Bantam Books.

Perls, F. S. (1970a). Four lectures. In J. Fagan and I. L. Shepherd (eds). *Gestalt Therapy Now: Theory, Techniques, Applications* (14–38). Palo Alto, CA: Science and Behavior Books.

Perls, F. S. (1970b). Dream seminars. In J. Fagan and I. L. Shepherd (eds). *Gestalt Therapy Now: Theory, Techniques and Applications* (204–33). Palo Alto, CA: Science and Behavior Books.

Perls, F. S. (1973). *The Gestalt Approach & Eyewitness to Therapy.* New York: Bantam Books.

Perls, F. S., Hefferline, R. F. and Goodman, P. (1951). *Gestalt Therapy: Excitement and Growth in the Human Personality.* London: Souvenir Press.

Perls, L. P. (1968). Two instances of Gestalt therapy. In P. D. Pursglove (ed.). *Recognition in Gestalt Therapy* (42–68). New York: Funk and Wagnalls.

Perls, L. P. (1970c). One gestalt therapist's approach. In J. Fagan and I. L. Shepherd (eds). *Gestalt Therapy Now: Theory, Techniques, Applications* (125–9). Palo Alto, CA: Science and Behavior Books.

Perls, S. (1993). Frederick Perls: A son's reflections. Talk given by Stephen Perls on 23 April at the Fifteenth Annual Conference on the Theory and Practice of Gestalt Therapy, Hotel du Parc, Montreal, Canada (the text of this talk is available on www.gestalt.org).

Shepard, I. L. (1970). Limitations and cautions in the Gestalt approach. In J. Fagan and I. L. Shepherd (eds). *Gestalt Therapy Now: Theory, Techniques, Applications* (234–8). Palo Alto, CA: Science and Behavior Books.

Smuts, J. (1987). *Holism and Evolution.* Cape Town, SA: N and S Press. First published in 1926.

Yontef, G. M. (1988). Assimilating diagnostic and psychoanalytic perspectives into Gestalt therapy. *Gestalt Journal, 11* (1), 5–32.

Yontef, G. M., and Simkin, J. S. (1989). Gestalt therapy. In R. J. Corsini and D. Wedding (eds). *Current Psychotherapies* (4th edition, 323–61). Itasca, IL: Peacock.

Yontef, G. and Jacobs, L. (2000). Gestalt therapy. In R. J. Corsini and D. Wedding (eds). *Current Psychotherapies* (6th edition). Itasca, IL: Peacock, 303–39.

Perls on film, videotape and cassette

Perls, F. (1965). Gestalt therapy. In E. Shostrom (ed.). *Three Approaches to Psychotherapy.* Santa Ana, CA: Psychological Films.

The Gestalt Journal Press lists a comprehensive bibliography of gestalt books, articles, videotapes and cassettes. (The Gestalt Journal Press, PO Box 990, Highland, NY 12528-0990 USA. Website: www.gestalt.org)

6

Transactional Analysis

The basic interest of transactional analysis is the study of ego states, which are coherent systems of thought and feeling manifested by corresponding patterns of behaviour.

Eric Berne

INTRODUCTION

Eric Berne, the originator of transactional analysis (TA), stated that the criterion distinguishing his approach from other approaches was that it was based on the personality theory of Child, Parent and Adult ego states. Throughout this chapter Parent, Adult and Child start with a capital letter when describing ego states. The dividing line between what was and what was not transactional analysis rested on whether or not human behaviour was explained in terms of such ego states. Although Berne was strongly influenced by Freud, the theory and practice of transactional analysis are very different from those of psychoanalysis. Berne saw an element of his approach, called script analysis, as being 'para-Freudian' rather than anti-Freudian (Berne, 1970, p. 400), and conceivably the same might be said for the whole of transactional analysis.

Berne differed from other humanistic theorists and from Freud in his greater emphasis on social psychiatry, which he defined as 'the study of the psychiatric aspects of specific transactions or sets of transactions which take place between two or more particular individuals at a given time and place' (Berne, 1961, p. 12). Berne analysed what was going on in people's internal worlds when they came into contact with, influenced and were influenced by others in their external worlds.

In Chapter 1, I mentioned that one of the functions of counselling and therapy theories was to provide languages for conducting the therapeutic conversation. Berne was a leader in realizing the importance of therapists and clients using the same language. Transactional analysis provides an easily understood language that therapists and clients can use together to analyse and work on problems and transactions in the interests of clients achieving greater autonomy and intimacy. This chapter mainly focuses on traditional or classical Bernian transactional analysis. However, towards the chapter's end, I overview some more recent TA developments.

ERIC BERNE (1910–70)

In 1910, Eric Berne was born Eric Lennard Bernstein in Montreal, Canada, and grew up in a poor Jewish section of the city. His father appears to have been a dedicated general practitioner who often took Berne on his rounds. His mother, Sara, was a professional writer and editor who, after her husband died in 1921, supported Berne and his sister by her writing. Berne dedicated his first book to his mother, who was probably influential in developing his writing interest and skills.

Berne's interest in medicine stemmed more from his father's example. James (1977) considers that the little child in Berne was traumatized by his father's death. Certainly his father appears to have had a strong influence on Berne, whose goal was always to cure patients. This influence is reflected in the Latin dedication in Berne's seminal book *Transactional Analysis in Psychotherapy*, a translation of which is 'In Memory of My Father David, Doctor of Medicine, Master of Surgery, and Doctor to the Poor' (Berne, 1961).

Berne studied English, psychology and pre-medicine at McGill University in Montreal and received his BA in 1931. In 1935 he obtained his MD and Master of Surgery degree from the same institution. Berne then went to the United States, where he became an American citizen. After an internship at Englewood Hospital in New Jersey, he became a psychiatric resident at Yale University School of Medicine. Reacting to the anti-Semitism of this period, he changed his name to Berne and began a private psychiatric practice in Norwalk, Connecticut. He also contracted the first of three marriages, each of which ended in divorce. Berne became Clinical Assistant at Mt Zion Hospital in New York and, in 1941, began training at the New York Psychoanalytic Institute, being analysed by Paul Federn, a former colleague of Freud.

In 1943 Berne entered the Army Medical Corps as a psychiatrist and it was during the war period that he started working with groups. On his discharge in 1946 he moved to Carmel, California, and finished *The Mind in Action*, since extensively revised and now published as *A Layman's Guide to Psychiatry and Psychoanalysis*. He also resumed his psychoanalytic education at the San Francisco Psychoanalytic Institute and underwent a training analysis with Erik Erikson. In 1950 he took a position at Mt Zion Hospital, San Francisco, and restarted private practice. For the remainder of his life he worked both in San Francisco and in Carmel, 125 miles away.

From his days in the army, Berne developed a research interest in intuition and developed the concept of ego image, which is a therapist's intuitive image of a person which in some ways describes his ego. Ego images are largely based on observation and listening to what patients say about themselves. During the period 1954 to 1958 Berne developed his ideas on: the diagnosis of ego states or structural analysis; the analysis of individual transactions; the analysis of a series of transactions with covert as well as overt content, otherwise known as game analysis; and the longitudinal view of a patient's whole life from which it was possible to extrapolate her or his future, now called script analysis. In September 1954 Berne started his first transactional analysis group. His ideas were developed further in a series of regular seminars in Carmel which, in 1958, were succeeded by the San Francisco Social Psychiatry Seminars, later called the Eric Berne Seminars.

Berne was moving away from orthodox psychoanalysis and, in 1956, his application for membership of the Psychoanalytic Institute of San Francisco was rejected for the third time. Of this event he comments: '. . . after fifteen years the psychoanalytic movement and the writer officially parted company (on the most friendly terms) . . .' (Berne, 1961, p. 13). When, some years later, the Psychoanalytic Institute offered him membership, he declined with thanks. Berne had increasingly felt that the effective therapist had to be more active than was allowed in orthodox psychoanalysis and had to practise transactionally rather than from the head of a couch.

At the November 1957 Western Regional Meeting of the American Group Psychotherapy Association in Los Angeles, Berne presented a paper entitled 'Transactional analysis: a new and effective method of group therapy', which was published in 1958. During three successive summers he broadened his experience by going to the South Pacific to study socialization and mental illness in various island cultures. By 1961 he had visited mental hospitals in about 30 different countries in Europe, Asia, Africa and the islands of the Atlantic and Pacific to test his ideas in various racial and cultural settings.

In 1961 Berne's most systematic statement, *Transactional Analysis in Psychotherapy*, was published. In 1963 he published a discussion of the application of transactional analysis to groups in *The Structure and Dynamics of Organizations and Groups*. In 1964 his ideas on analysing psychological games were publicly presented in *Games People Play: The Psychology of Human Relationships*, though these ideas had appeared three years earlier in a private edition of the book. The principles of transactional analysis for therapists were explained in his 1966 book *Principles of Group Treatment*, and his ideas on script analysis were developed in *What Do You Say After You Say Hello?*, published posthumously in 1972. Berne also wrote *The Happy Valley* for children and *Sex in Human Loving* for both non-professionals and professionals

During the 1960s, along with his writing and private practice, Berne held a number of appointments. These included Consultant in Psychiatry to the Surgeon General, US Army; Attending Psychiatrist to the Veterans Administration Mental Hygiene Clinic; Lecturer in Group Therapy, Langley-Porter Neuropsychiatric Clinic; Visiting Lecturer in Group Therapy, Stanford Psychiatric Clinic; and Adjunct Psychiatrist, Mt Zion Hospital, San Francisco. Early in 1970 Berne and his third wife were divorced. He died of a heart attack on 15 July the same year. Berne's work was continued by a number of his colleagues who attended the San Francisco seminars, including Claude Steiner, who developed script analysis.

It is interesting to speculate on Berne's own life script. The son of a doctor and a writer, he spent his life curing and writing about curing people. Some idea of his professional ideals may be gleaned from the introduction to his *Principles of Group Treatment*, which is written for those who wish to become 'real doctors' as contrasted with the 'non-real' or 'unreal' variety. A 'real doctor':

> *(a) has the overriding consideration throughout his practice of curing his patients;*
> *(b) plans his treatment so that at each phase he knows what he is doing and why he is doing it;*

(c) *clearly distinguishes research and experimentation from good medical or surgical care, the former always being subsidiary to the latter; and*

(d) *takes complete responsibility for the welfare of his patients.* (Berne, 1966, p. xvii)

The development of transactional analysis represents Berne's own commitment to being a 'real doctor'.

THEORY

Transactional analysis, because of its clear-cut statements rooted in easily accessible material, because of its operational nature, and because of the small size of its specialized vocabulary (consisting in practice of only five words: Parent, Adult, Child, game, and script), offers an easily learned framework for clarification.

Eric Berne

BASIC CONCEPTS

Berne saw transactional analysis both as a theory of personality and social interaction and as a method of therapy. Some of his assumptions and basic concepts are presented below.

The fundamental OK position

Berne had a positive view of human nature which is stated in the transactional-analytic position 'I am OK; you are OK.' Another way he expressed this is by his statement 'Every human being is born a prince or a princess; early experiences convince some that they are frogs, and the rest of the pathological development follows from this' (Berne, 1966, pp. 289–90).

Related to the basic assumption of human OK-ness are two further assumptions. First, Berne regarded practically every human being as possessing the complete neurological apparatus for adequate reality-oriented or Adult functioning. The only exceptions were those with the most severe type of organic brain injuries. Thus the therapeutic task is that of how to strengthen this already existing apparatus so that it may take its normal place in the client's psychic organization. Second, Berne believed that people have a built-in drive to both mental and physical health. The transactional analyst's job is to help nature by removing obstructions to patients' emotional and mental development, so letting them grow in their own directions.

Ego states

The fundamental building block of transactional analysis is the concept of ego states. Berne (1961) wrote: 'An ego state may be described phenomenologically as a coherent system of feelings related to a given subject, and operationally as a set of coherent behaviour patterns; or pragmatically as a system of feelings which motivates a related set of behaviour patterns' (p. 17). Though not always emphasized by Berne, ego states involve thinking as well as feeling and behaviour.

Each human being exhibits three kinds of ego states: Parent, Adult, and Child. At any given moment any individual in a social grouping will predominantly exhibit one or another of these states. The three ego states, depicted in Box 6.1, are described as follows.

Parent

The Parent or exteropsychic ego state is a set of feelings, thoughts, attitudes, and behaviours which resemble those of parental figures. It is both an accumulation of data and a way of relating to people. The Parent ego state may be seen behaviourally in one of two forms. The *controlling* or prejudicial Parent is manifested as a set of seemingly arbitrary and rigid rules, usually prohibitive, which may either agree or disagree with the rules of a person's culture. The *nurturing* Parent is manifested as sympathy and care for another individual or for oneself. Thus the Parent can be over-controlling and inhibiting or supportive and growth-enhancing. The Parent ego state may also influence a person's Adult or Child ego states. The function of the Parent is to conserve energy and to diminish anxiety by making certain decisions automatic.

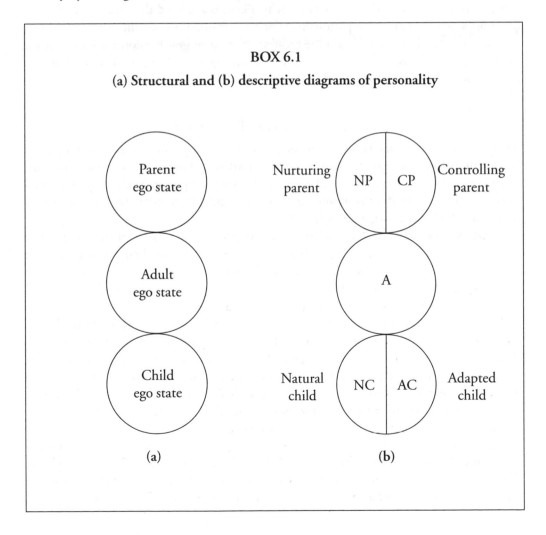

BOX 6.1

(a) Structural and (b) descriptive diagrams of personality

Adult

In the Adult or neopsychic ego state the person autonomously and objectively appraises reality and makes judgements. Berne likened the neopsyche to a partially self-programming probability computer and stressed that the criterion of its adequacy was the use made of data available to a given individual. Characteristics by which an Adult ego state may be recognized include organization, adaptability and intelligence.

Child

The Child or archaeopsychic ego state is a set of feelings, thoughts, attitudes and behaviour patterns which are archaic relics of an individual's childhood. Berne considered that we all carry within ourselves a little boy or girl who feels, thinks, acts and responds just as we did when we were children of a certain age. The Child ego state is exhibited behaviourally in two major forms. The *adapted* Child is manifested by feelings and behaviour which inferentially are under parental influence, such as sulking, compliance, rebelliousness, withdrawal, and inhibition. The *natural* Child is manifested by spontaneous expression such as self-indulgence or creativity. Berne considered the natural Child to be the most valuable part of the personality. The proper function of a 'healthy' Child is to motivate the Adult so as to obtain the greatest amount of gratification for itself. This it does by letting the Adult know what it wants and by consulting the Parent about its appropriateness.

Structural analysis of ego states

Structural analysis consists of diagnosing and separating one feeling-thinking-and-behaviour pattern or ego state from another. Further analysis of ego states does not provide new ego states, but rather subdivisions of the existing ones. Such analysis is called second-order structural analysis and can get very detailed. In particular, it focuses on further analysis of the Parent and Child.

In Box 6.2 the Parent is divided into two components, one derived from the father and one derived from the mother. Children incorporate some characteristics of each parent into their Parent ego state, including the ways in which their parents exhibited thinking and feeling when expressing values. Consequently, second-order structural analysis includes the Parent, Adult and Child ego states of both parents.

Within the Child ego state, Parent, Adult and Child ego states, which were already there when the child made its basic decision concerning its life script, can be observed. Berne (1972) sometimes called the Parent in the Child the 'electrode', and Steiner (1974) described it as the 'Pig Parent'. Berne called the Parent in the Child the electrode because when it 'pushes the button', the person automatically does something negative. Examples of such negative behaviour include excessive alcohol consumption, reckless gambling, and getting sexually turned off if coming on too strong.

Berne saw the Adult in the Child as a keen and perceptive student of human nature, which he called the Professor (Berne, 1961). Steiner calls the Adult in the Child the Little Professor and observes that it is the ego state which Berne himself used in his studies on intuition, when he would guess the occupations of people using his own intuition

BOX 6.2
Second-order structural diagram of personality

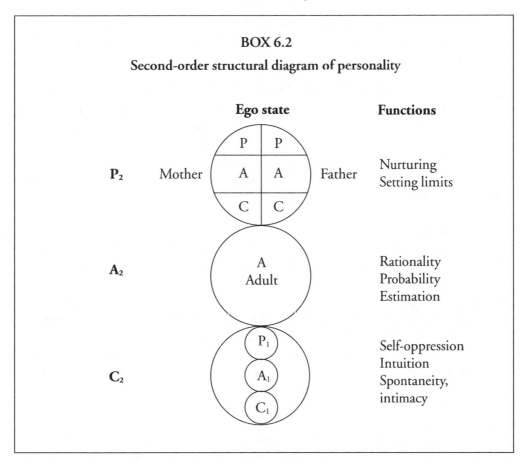

	Ego state		Functions

(Steiner, 1974). The Adult in the Child is the source both of intuitive and creative thinking and of delusion, since it may not always be right. The Child in the Child ego state is the source of innate wants and feelings. Spontaneity is a central characteristic of the Child in the Child, but sometimes this spontaneity can be self-destructive.

Psychic energy and cathexis

Transactional analysis is a dynamic theory of personality in that it uses the concepts of psychic energy and of cathexis or distribution of energy. At a given moment the ego state which is most strongly cathected will have executive power. Berne wrote of the flow of cathexis which gives rise to shifts in ego states. He considered that the most convenient way of acknowledging the differentiation of ego states was to view each state as having a boundary which separates it from other ego states. Under most conditions ego-state boundaries are semi-permeable. Shifts in ego state depend on three factors:

1. the forces acting on each state;
2. the permeability of the boundaries between ego states; and
3. the cathectic capacity of each ego state.

Berne (1961) observed that it is the quantitative balance between these three factors which determines the clinical condition of the client and thus indicates the counselling procedures.

Stimulus, recognition and structure hunger

The psychobiological basis of social psychiatry is that the ability of human beings to maintain coherent ego states depends on a changing flow of sensory stimuli. Berne cited Spitz's work (Spitz, 1945), which demonstrated that sensory deprivation in infants resulted not only in psychological changes, but also in organic deterioration. Berne posited that there were three principal forms of drive, hunger or motivation: stimulus, recognition, and structure hunger.

Stimulus hunger

The most favoured forms of stimuli are those offered by physical intimacy. Berne acknowledged the dangers of over-stimulation as well as of under-stimulation.

Recognition hunger

Recognition hunger may be viewed as a partial transformation of infantile stimulus hunger. Berne used the term 'stroking' to denote any act implying recognition of another's presence. There are numerous rituals, such as saying 'Hello!', which imply recognition and give gratification. Biologically, even negative recognition has an advantage over no recognition at all. Put colloquially, 'Folks need strokes!'

Structure hunger

Structure hunger addresses the everyday problem of how to structure one's waking hours. Such time structuring is concerned only with social time or the time people spend with others.

Time structuring

Berne observed that if two or more people were in a room together they had six possible kinds of social behaviour or time structuring from which to choose. These are discussed below.

1. *Withdrawal.* Here two people do not overtly communicate with one another, for example if they are on a bus or are withdrawn schizophrenics. In withdrawal, people remain wrapped up in their own thoughts.
2. *Rituals.* Rituals are stylized signs of mutual recognition dictated by tradition and social custom. At the simplest level, two people saying 'Good morning' engage in a ritual.
3. *Activities.* Activities, more commonly called work, are not just concerned with dealing with the material means of survival. They also have a social significance in that they offer a framework for various kinds of recognition and satisfactions. Berne considered that work transactions were typically Adult-to-Adult, oriented mainly towards external reality.

4. *Pastimes.* Pastimes are semi-ritualistic, topical conversations which last longer than rituals but are still mainly socially programmed. Pastimes might include 'Ain't it Awful' and 'Motor Cars'. The focus of pastimes tends to be external to the participants rather than directly self-referent.

5. *Games.* Games, in contrast to pastimes, are sequences of transactions which are based more on individual than on social programming. A psychological game is a set of covert or ulterior as well as overt transactions which lead to a predictable outcome or payoff. Frequently these payoffs involve negative feelings or 'rackets' such as anger and depression. Collecting racket feelings is known as collecting 'trading stamps', which may some day be cashed in for behaviours such as a good cry or going out and buying some new clothes. More drastically, 'trading stamps' may be cashed in for divorce or attempted suicide. Each game has a motto by which it can be recognized, for example 'Why don't you? – Yes but' and 'If it weren't for you' (Berne, 1964).

6. *Intimacy.* Berne defined bilateral intimacy as 'a candid, game-free relationship, with mutual free giving and receiving and without exploitation' (Berne, 1972, p. 25). Intimacy represents individual and instinctual programming in which social programming and ulterior motivations are largely, if not totally, suspended. Intimacy is the most satisfying solution to stimulus, recognition, and structure hunger, but unfortunately it is not very common for people to live as 'princes' and 'princesses'. Berne's idea of intimacy included, but was not restricted to, sexual intimacy.

Types of transactions

In transactional analysis a stroke or unit of recognition is viewed as the fundamental unit of social interaction. An exchange of strokes constitutes a transaction. Thus rituals, activities, pastimes, games, and intimacy may all be viewed as involving transactions. During transactions, at any given time each person is likely to have one of their three ego states predominantly energized or cathected. Thus transactions take place between ego states and, at its simplest level, transactional analysis involves diagnosing the ego states involved in a stimulus and response exchange. In other words, the transactional stimulus may come from the Parent, Adult or Child of one person and the transactional response from the Parent, Adult or Child of the other person.

There are three main types of transactions: complementary, crossed and ulterior.

Complementary transactions
Complementary transactions are ones in which the directions of the stimulus-response transactions are consistent, such as discussing the ills of the world (Parent–Parent), talking about work (Adult–Adult), or having fun together (Child–Child). Another way of stating this is that complementary transactions are ones in which people receive a response from the ego state that they have addressed. An example of a complementary transaction is given in Box 6.3. There are nine possible types of complementary transactions (PP, PA, PC, AP, AA, AC, CP, CA, CC). Berne's first rule of communication was that communication will proceed smoothly as long as transactions are complementary. In the example in Box 6.3 Mike responds (a) from the ego state addressed by Bill and (b) to the ego state from which Bill addressed him.

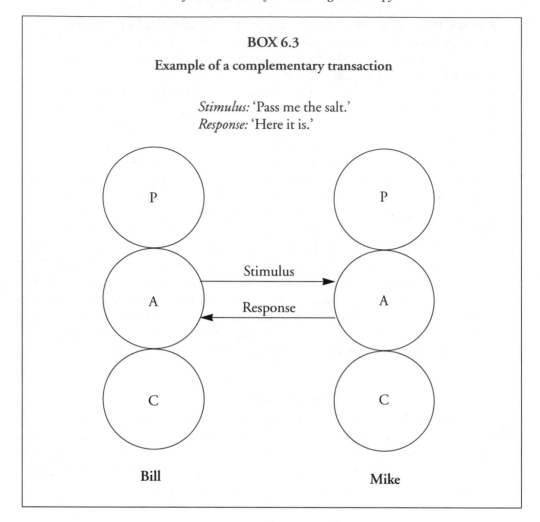

BOX 6.3

Example of a complementary transaction

Stimulus: 'Pass me the salt.'
Response: 'Here it is.'

Bill

Mike

Crossed transactions

In a crossed transaction the transactional response (a) comes from an ego state different from the one addressed, and/or (b) may go to an ego state which did not send the original stimulus. Berne's second or converse rule of communication was that communication is broken off when a crossed transaction occurs. In fact, the break may be only slight and momentary. However, at the other extreme, communication may be broken off completely. Box 6.4 is an example of a crossed transaction. There are 72 possible types of crossed transactions, but only a few occur frequently.

Ulterior transactions

An ulterior communication is where, under the guise of an overt and socially more acceptable communication, an individual engages in an underlying and socially more risky communication. Another way of viewing this is that in much human interaction

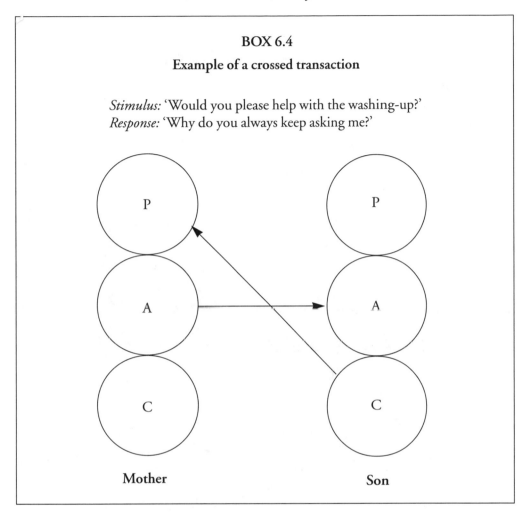

BOX 6.4

Example of a crossed transaction

Stimulus: 'Would you please help with the washing-up?'
Response: 'Why do you always keep asking me?'

there is an underlying psychological as well as an overt social agenda. Psychological games, by definition, involve ulterior transactions.

Ulterior transactions may occur in everyday situations such as when a salesman says to a customer, 'Perhaps you shouldn't buy that beautiful and expensive coat', when his psychological message is 'Come on, I want you to buy it.' Potential sexual situations are other everyday situations in which ulterior transactions may occur. Box 6.5 illustrates such an ulterior transaction.

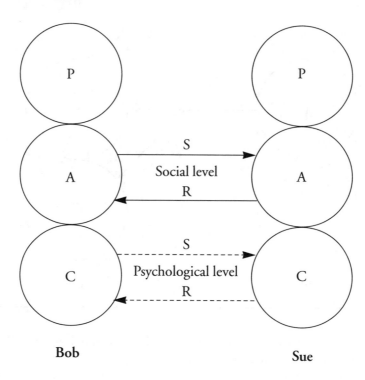

BOX 6.5

Example of an ulterior transaction

Social level
Bob: 'That was a great film. How about coming back to my place for a drink?'
Sue: 'Yes, I'd like that.'

Psychological level
Bob: 'Let's have some fun together.'
Sue: 'I'm available.'

ACQUISITION

The script

Berne defined a script as: 'A life plan based on a decision made in childhood, reinforced by the parents, justified by subsequent events, and culminating in a chosen alternative' (1972, p. 445). He regarded scripts as preconscious life plans by which people structure their time. Scripts determine people's destinies, including their approach to relationships and to tasks. He considered that scripts are usually based on childlike illusions which may persist throughout a whole lifetime. People's scripts are the product of parental programming plus the decisions they made in response to parental programming. Children seek out parental programming for three reasons:

1. to give a purpose in life which otherwise might be wanting;
2. to provide a way of structuring their time acceptable to their parents; and
3. since people have to be told how to do things (Berne, 1972).

Scripts lead people to have an illusion of personal autonomy when in fact they are carrying out, often unthinkingly, the directives of their scripts. At times, however, some people may question their scripts and this may cause identity crises which may or may not be resolved satisfactorily by removal of some of the blockages to genuine autonomy and a well-functioning Adult. Berne's view of human life, as contrasted with human nature, was pessimistic, as he tended to see humans as driven by script directives which led to ways of time structuring seriously detrimental to attaining autonomy and creative activity.

The script matrix

The script matrix is a diagram used to help understand the development of people's scripts. It is helpful to an understanding of the transmission of scripts if the matrix depicts a second-order structural breakdown of the Child. Box 6.6 depicts such a script matrix for a hypothetical person, Mary. The diagram aims to show how script directives are transmitted to her. Although, during her upbringing, it is desirable for Mary to experience much of the nurturing Parent ego state of her parents and also their reasoning Adult and spontaneous Child, she may also be experiencing negative directives from the Parent in the Child ego state of one or both of her parents. As depicted in Box 6.6, the directives to Mary may be contradictory.

Although a chapter in Berne's 1961 book *Transactional Analysis in Psychotherapy* is devoted to analysis of scripts, he acknowledged the valuable work of Steiner in devising the script matrix and in helping to develop script theory. Berne proposed that it was the parent of the opposite sex who usually tells the child what to do and the parent of the same sex who usually demonstrates how to do it. Steiner (1974) added that it was the Child in the Parent who gives the restrictive directives or injunctions and the Adult in the Parent who gives the child the pattern or programme of behaviour.

Injunctions, attributions and discounts

Although directives from parents can be nurturing and conducive to the child's emotional development, they can also be restrictive, reflecting the fears and insecurities of the Child in the Parent.

Injunctions

Injunctions are expressed as messages beginning with 'Don't.' They can be relatively mild or highly restrictive. Steiner (1974) gives the following as injunctions by which people learn to block intimacy:

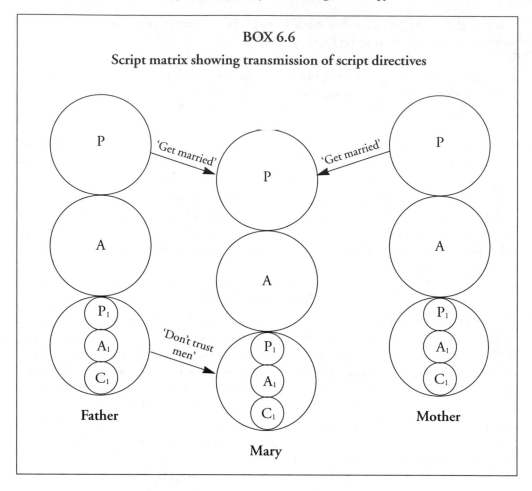

BOX 6.6

Script matrix showing transmission of script directives

(a) do not give strokes if you have them to give;
(b) do not ask for strokes when you need them;
(c) do not accept strokes if you want them;
(d) do not reject strokes when you do not want them; and
(e) do not give yourself strokes.

He considers that the above injunctions are the basis of depression. Other injunctions may stop people from thinking, especially perhaps if they are female. Still others may interfere with the capacity to experience feelings, especially perhaps for males.

Box 6.7 presents twelve injunctions that Mary and Robert Goulding have repeatedly found when analysing scripts (Goulding and Goulding, 1979, pp. 34–9; Stewart, 1996a).

Attributions

Steiner states that children are also strongly influenced by attributions, or being told what they are and what they must do, and how they are feeling. Family reinforcement

---

BOX 6.7

List of common script injunctions

- 'Don't exist.'
- 'Don't be you' (sometimes, 'Don't be the sex you are').
- 'Don't be a child' (or 'Don't enjoy').
- 'Don't grow up' (or 'Don't leave me').
- 'Don't make it' ('Don't succeed').
- 'Don't' (i.e. 'Don't do anything').
- 'Don't be important'.
- 'Don't belong'.
- 'Don't be close'.
- 'Don't be well' (or 'Don't be sane').
- 'Don't think'.
- 'Don't feel'.

---

schedules tend to reward children who follow attributions and punish children who disobey injunctions.

Discounts

Children are also liable to receive discounts from their parents. Steiner regards a discount as a crossed transaction in which a person says something from an Adult ego state to another person's Adult and the other person responds from his or her Parent or Child. For instance, children's inquisitiveness may be discounted by parental rebuffs. More generally, a discount in TA is the minimization of some aspect of oneself, another person, or a situation.

Decisions

On the basis of early transactions related to feeding, toilet training, weaning and family relationships, the young person starts developing a view of the world. Where children are given unconditional protection they are less likely to develop restrictive scripts. However, when parents make their nurturing conditional on their child's submission to their injunctions and attributions, the child may make a conscious decision to adhere to parental wishes even though this means the sacrifice of autonomy. These decisions tend to be made in the pre-school years and are as realistic as the capacity of the Adult in the Child or Little Professor at the time of the decision. As a result of this decision, however, the child tends to take a different and more negative position and also develops a script. Berne acknowledged that some scripts could be winners' scripts.

Life positions

The fundamental assumption of transactional analysis is that of human OK-ness as expressed in the statement or life position 'I'm OK – You're OK.' By making a decision children move out of this position. Instead, they adopt one of three other life positions, namely: 'I'm not-OK – You're OK'; 'I'm OK – You're not-OK'; and 'I'm not-OK – You're not-OK.' Each of these three 'not-OK' positions reflects and sustains impaired ego state development. Also, 'not-OK' positions militate against the development of intimacy and are the bases on which individuals play out their games. Just as stimulus, recognition and structure hunger can be viewed as motivators, it is also possible to view the need to justify a basic life position as a motivator. Perhaps, though, it is more accurate to consider position hunger as a refinement of the other motivators, indicating how their fulfilment is to be attained. Box 6.8 is an example of a decision leading to a life position in the case of Rita (Berne, 1966).

BOX 6.8

Rita: An example of a decision leading to a life position

Rita, when little, used to run to greet her father when he came home from work. As time went on her father's behaviour became erratic because of his drinking and he would push Rita away. One day her father had a particularly bad row with her mother. Rita, who was 6 years, 2 months and 23 days, was bewildered and frightened and at 5 p.m. that afternoon she made a decision that she would never again love a man. In order to maintain her decision, Rita took a position regarding her father that, even when amiable and sober, he was fundamentally bad. Over time she generalized her position to most other men, the not-OK-ness of whom she epitomized in the slogan 'All men are beasts.' Her position also became the basis of a game in which her seductive behaviour provoked 'decent' men to make advances, which she then rejected. Berne observed that Rita's seductive manoeuvres were an attempt to establish an intimate relationship which she was unable to carry through.

Development of games

During children's upbringing they are taught the rituals, activities and pastimes appropriate to their situations in life. They also learn games through significant experiences in their family life from their earliest months. Berne (1964) gave an example of how a game might be learned the case of 3-year-old Mike who, when his 7-year-old brother was allowed to leave the dinner table and lie down because of a stomach-ache, said 'I have a stomach-ache too', as though he wanted the same consideration. Mike's parents, however, did not co-operate and thus may have saved him from the game of pleading illness (social transaction) in order to gain some privilege for himself (ulterior or psychological transaction). Berne considered that games are imitative in nature, and also that they are deliberately initiated by the neopsychic Adult or Little Professor in the Child, frequently between the ages of 2 and 8. As illustrated by Rita, games are often formulated to help justify a life position.

The counterscript

In the development of a script, the person is given not only script injunctions and attributions from their parents' Parent in the Child, but also counterscript messages from their parents' Parent. Berne (1972) used the word 'prescription' for counterscript messages and observed that prescriptions were usually transmitted from grandparents. Examples of prescriptions are 'Be a good boy (or girl)!' and 'Work hard.' Script injunctions and counterscript prescriptions are sometimes contradictory, and life may involve an alternation between compliance first to one and then to the other. The counterscript may lead to a period of time in which an unhappy life plan gives way to a happier period. However, in the end the script injunctions always prevail, though again the possibility of winners' scripts should be acknowledged.

Steiner (1974) indicates that an alcoholic's Parent may give the counterscript 'Be sober' while the Parent in the Child is giving the injunction 'Don't think! Drink.' In Box 6.6 Mary's parents' Parent counterscript prescription was 'Get married' while her father's Parent in the Child injunction was 'Don't trust men.' Frequently injunctions are transmitted non-verbally by approval or disapproval of certain kinds of behaviour, and this may make them harder to bring into awareness than when they are transmitted more openly.

MAINTENANCE

In the preceding section the ways in which people acquire scripts and games were described. The question to be answered in this section is why people persist in acting out scripts and playing games rather than enjoying autonomy and intimacy, or, in other words, why people stay frogs when it might seem more rewarding to revert to being princes or princesses. Part of the answer is that both scripts and games have their rewards or payoffs.

Script payoffs

Berne (1972) defined the script payoff as the ultimate destiny or final display that marks the end of a life plan. He considered that there were four main payoffs in clinical practice: be a loner, be a bum, go crazy or drop dead. While these ultimate destinies are one way of viewing the concept of script payoff, another way is to look at it in terms of current as contrasted with ultimate rewards. Steiner (1974) observes that when people enter their counterscript phase, despite a superficial sense of well-being, they experience a deep visceral discomfort. However, people experience visceral comfort when reverting to script behaviour. This is because adherence to script injunctions represents acquiescence to parental wishes, albeit the parental Parent in the Child, and thus is associated with the well-being and comfort of parental protection. Steiner notes that an alcoholic, even in the pain of a hangover, is receiving approval for acquiescing to the parental Child's injunction 'Don't think! Drink.' Steiner is perhaps more pessimistic about scripts than many other TA therapists.

Game payoffs

Games too have their payoffs, which are related to the life positions adopted in their players' scripts. For instance, the payoff in Rita's script was manipulating men to boorish behaviour which confirmed her position that men are not-OK. Berne (1964) observed that, beyond their social function of time structuring, games are urgently needed by some for the maintenance of their health. Their life positions are so tenaciously maintained that to interfere with or deprive them of the payoffs from their games may cause disturbance, or even psychosis. Thus game analysis must be approached cautiously.

An example of a game with a payoff is 'If it weren't for you.' A person can complain endlessly that if it were not for a husband, wife, child, boss or some other person, they could engage in an activity from which at present they feel restricted. Sometimes, however, these other people are being used to defend the person against the realization that, if it were not for them, he or she might be unable to perform a difficult or anxiety-evoking task. Also, if the task were performed, it would no longer be possible to cause the other person discomfort by saying 'If it weren't for you.' This game validates the life position that others are not-OK.

The illusion of autonomy

Berne (1972) considered that only the strongest can live without illusions and that one of the illusions which is hardest to relinquish is that of autonomy or self-determination. An autonomous person knows what is practical and Adult, what he accepts that comes from others, and what he does that is determined by early impulses. The illusion of autonomy is where a person does not acknowledge feelings and behaviours coming from his Child and Parent ego states, but instead believes that they come from the Adult ego state.

Berne distinguished between delusions and illusions, both of which are contaminations of the Adult ego state and, as such, prevent it from effectively dealing with here-and-now situations. Delusions are the prejudices and directives from parents which a person treats as though they were his own ideas. Illusions are those wishful ideas, impulses and early tastes coming from the Child which are accepted as Adult and rational. The significance of the illusion of autonomy is that an individual, being unaware of the delusions and illusions which are causing 'frog-like' behaviour, lacks the necessary insight and motivation for change. Thus destructive ways of time structuring are sustained rather than ameliorated. What is needed is a re-alignment and strengthening of the Adult ego-boundary to allow accurate processing of all relevant information.

Contamination and exclusion

With a truly autonomous person the ego-boundaries are strong, yet appropriately permeable to allow psychic energy to move between Parent, Adult and Child ego states. The illusion of autonomy indicates a structure where ego-boundaries are insufficiently well defined and the Adult ego state is being contaminated by the Parent and/or Child ego states. Exclusion, on the other hand, occurs in situations where psychic energy becomes exclusively cathected in a constant Parent, a constant Adult, or a constant Child (Berne, 1961). Thus one ego state is strongly cathected while the other two are decommissioned.

Berne considered that the excluding Parent is to be found in 'compensated' schizophrenics, where exclusion is the principal defence against confused Child or archaeopsychic activity. He gave as an example of an excluding Adult, Dr Quint, who had a sincere commitment to data processing as a way of life, yet possessed no healthy Child or Parent characteristics. Narcissistic impulsive personalities exhibit the excluding Child, where both rational and nurturing and limit-setting ego states are avoided. The excluding Parent, Adult or Child may defend itself: for instance, by the use of intellectualization in the case of the excluding Adult.

Inadequate information

The last point to be made regarding the maintenance of maladaptive behaviour is that the effectiveness of the Adult is dependent on the adequacy of the information available to it. Furthermore, the Adult may need to develop some skills of effective Adult functioning, including the ability to collect and adequately assess relevant information. James and Jongeward (1971) state that the computer phrase 'Garbage in, garbage out' applies to the Adult or, for that matter, to any other ego state.

THERAPY

Transactional analysis does not try to 'make' the patient better, but to bring him into a position where he can exercise an Adult option to get better.

Eric Berne

THERAPEUTIC GOALS

Four categories of goals

Transactional analysis seeks to help clients obtain an 'I am OK, you are OK' life position. For clients who have been turned by their life's experiences from princes and princesses into frogs, Berne saw four possible goals (Berne 1961, 1972). Stewart views these goals as progressive stages in the direction of cure (Stewart, 1996a).

1. *Symptomatic control.* Though still feeling distress, clients can control their symptoms in their interactions with others.
2. *Symptomatic relief.* Getting better, or 'progress', which Berne regarded as making clients into more comfortable frogs.
3. *Transference cure.* Here clients can stay out of their scripts so long as they can keep their therapists either literally or mentally around.
4. *Autonomy.* Casting 'off the frog skin and taking up once more the interrupted development of the prince or princess' (Berne, 1966, p. 290). The client's Adult takes over the role of the therapist as the client attains autonomy. Autonomy refers to the

capacity for 'non-script' behaviour 'with no particular time schedule, developed later in life, and not under parental influence' (Berne, 1972, p. 418).

Autonomous behaviour is the opposite of script behaviour. It involves the total or partial overthrow of: (a) the weight of a whole tribal or family historical tradition; (b) the influence of the individual's parental, social and cultural backgrounds; and (c) seeking ulterior payoffs from games. Furthermore, autonomy consists of the active development of personal and social control so that significant behaviour becomes a matter of free choice. Berne summarized the process of the attainment of autonomy as 'obtaining a friendly divorce from one's parents (and from other Parental influences) so that they may be agreeably visited on occasion, but are no longer dominant' (Berne, 1964, p. 183).

The attainment of autonomy involves the person's regaining three basic capacities of the fundamental OK position: awareness, spontaneity and intimacy.

- *Awareness.* Awareness means the capacity to see and hear directly and not in the way in which one was brought up. It means living in the here-and-now, open to the sensations coming from the environment in the way a painter, poet or musician might be.
- *Spontaneity.* Spontaneity means the capacity to feel directly and to express feelings directly and not in the way in which one was brought up. The spontaneous person can choose feelings, be they Parent, Adult or Child feelings.
- *Intimacy.* Intimacy means the capacity to relate to another person or persons in an aware, spontaneous, loving and game-free way. Berne regarded intimacy as essentially a function of the natural, uncorrupted Child.

Contractual therapy goals

Transactional analysis takes a contractual approach to therapy. A key question in such an approach is 'How will both you and I know when you get what you came for?' (Dusay and Dusay, 1989, p. 427). Therapist and client negotiate a contract that defines both treatment goals and mutual responsibilities in achieving the goals. Contract goals can focus on outcomes and actions. Outcome goals include: physiological changes, for instance lowering of diastolic blood pressure; and relief of psychological symptoms, such as impotence or a specific phobia. Action goals specify behaviour changes, for instance not hitting children, refraining from alcohol or drugs, or holding a job for a specified time period. Stewart (1996a, p. 68) suggests the following principles for establishing contracts:

1. *Contracts in TA may be either for outcomes or for actions.*
2. *However, any contract for an outcome must be supported by at least one contract for a related action.*

Contracts are open to amendment as therapy proceeds. Updates and changes of goals are frequent. Furthermore, the therapist's or client's ultimate goal may differ from the set of operational criteria for improvement stated as initial goals. During therapy, transactional analysts always observe determinants underlying symptoms and responses. Berne (1966) gave the example of the therapist, who wished to investigate a client's archaic attitudes towards parental figures, stating goals in terms of alleviation of symptoms first and later proposing an amendment to the contract that focused on the goal of altering attitudes toward parent figures.

PROCESS OF THERAPY

Settings for transactional analysis range from homelike surroundings to more business-like offices. Since body language clues are important in conducting transactional analysis, in most therapists' offices there are no tables or chairs that block therapist and client views of one another. The majority of TA settings include whiteboards, blackboards or giant paper pads that both therapists and clients can use to illustrate transactions and games and other relevant matters. Some therapists employ audiovisual aids to provide feedback and heighten clients' awareness.

In the initial session or sessions, therapists work in a number of ways. Therapists introduce and use a simple common vocabulary. During therapy there is no gossiping or small talk. Ground rules for the therapeutic contact are agreed, such as no violence or threats of violence, and no use of alcohol or mind-altering drugs. Furthermore, an initial fee-for-service business contract may be established. Therapists conduct an initial assessment of clients and work with them to establish contract goals, including a time frame for ending therapy.

THE THERAPEUTIC RELATIONSHIP

Transactional analysts provide supportive and nurturing relationships conducive to clients assuming greater personal responsibility for their lives. Within the framework of a common and easily understandable language, therapists provide permission for clients to play an active role in therapy. Therapists support clients as they reveal and analyse themselves more fully and try out more Adult patterns of feeling, thinking and behaving.

Transactional analysis, as originally formulated by Berne, is largely an educational process and thus the therapist–client relationship resembles a democratic teacher–learner relationship. Early on in therapy, therapist and clients establish ground rules and define the elements of their working or learning contract. Therapists train clients in the skills of analysing ego states, transactions, games and scripts. Furthermore therapists encourage and assist clients to identify Adult options for dealing with people, problems and situations in their lives. As indicated earlier, more often than not therapists' offices contain educational aids like whiteboards and large writing pads.

Therapists are sensitive to clues regarding clients' inauthentic ways of relating to others, including their therapists. Where there are problems in the therapeutic relationship, such as non-payment of fees or missing appointments, therapists view these transactions as psychological games and provide therapy accordingly (Dusay and Dusay, 1989).

THERAPEUTIC INTERVENTIONS

Berne regarded transactional analysis as an umbrella term for four different, but inter-related, approaches to treatment. These approaches are structural analysis, transactional analysis, game analysis, and script analysis. Berne (1961) saw a progression from structural analysis, through transactional and game analysis, to script analysis, though he realized that the script analysis state was not always attained.

Structural analysis

As mentioned earlier, structural analysis consists of diagnosing and separating one feeling-thinking-and-behaviour pattern or ego state from another. Structural analysis helps clients to identify and become aware of both the existence and the contents of their ego states. Its aim is to free people to have appropriate access to all their ego states without debilitating exclusions and contaminations. A related aim is to help the Adult to remain in control of the personality in stressful situations.

Transactional analysis

Berne (1961) saw one aim of transactional analysis as social control or the ability of the Adult to decide when to release the Parent or Child and when to resume the executive. If a person does not have social control, others can consciously or unconsciously activate that person's Parent or Child ego states in ways which may not be helpful. Transactional analysis proper, as Berne (1972) called it, is the analysis of single transactions by means of transactional diagrams. Clients are helped to understand the ego state transactions involved in situations and relationships in which they are experiencing difficulty as a means towards greater competence in handling them.

Game analysis

Game analysis is another way of attaining social control. Just as an understanding of structural analysis is a prerequisite of transactional analysis, so an understanding of analysis of single transactions is a prerequisite of understanding the more complex series of transactions called games. In game analysis the client is encouraged to learn more satisfying ways of structuring time and acquiring strokes. The methods of game analysis include helping a client to see what game he or she is playing, what the moves are, what the racket or bad feeling payoffs are, and how the games justify a life position. It is also important to help the client to express constructively the natural Child need or feeling which he or she has been discounting.

Script analysis

The script analyst must take care not to behave in ways which promote a client's script. The purpose of script analysis is to help clients to get out of their script and thus to behave autonomously. The therapist needs to listen carefully to and observe the client's verbal and non-verbal behaviour for script signs or signals. Additionally, script analysis may involve the use of a script checklist to help both analyst and client to know the client's script (Berne, 1972). Script analysis aims to help clients to abandon their early decisions, *previously* made in different circumstances and with an incomplete neopsychic or Adult apparatus, by *now* making and enacting re-decisions for change.

A script antithesis is a therapeutic intervention which directly contradicts a parental injunction and thus brings temporary or permanent release from a script. Berne (1972) considered that the final common pathway of a patient's behaviour is the preconscious dialogue between Parent, Adult and Child, or voices in the head, which can easily be brought into consciousness. Re-decision can be helped by getting into the client's head another voice, that of the therapist. This process involves the three 'Ps' of script antithesis: potency, permission, and protection.

Potency is defined by whether the therapist's voice in the client's head has been powerful enough to prevail over the voices or injunctions of the client's Parents in the Child. Permissions can be positive or negative. Positive permissions or licences involve the therapist saying 'Let him/her do it!', whereas with negative permissions or releases the therapist is saying 'Stop pushing him/her into it!' When clients follow a script antithesis and go against a parental injunction, their Child may get very anxious. Protection means that during the period of change the client can call upon their therapists to exercise their potency again in time of need.

Basic interventions and interpositions

Berne originally designed transactional analysis as a group therapy adjunct to psychoanalysis. Berne (1966, pp. 233–47) identified eight categories of basic therapeutic techniques which have relevance for individual, couples and family work as well as for groups of seven to eight clients. He divided these basic techniques into interventions and interpositions. Dusay and Dusay (1989) observe that interpositions go beyond interventions by being 'an attempt by the therapist to interpose something between the patient's Adult and other ego states to stabilize the Adult and make it more difficult to slide into Parent or Child activity' (p. 441). Berne specified as interventions: interrogation, specification, confrontation, and explanation. He regarded as interpositions: illustration, confirmation, interpretation, and crystallization.

1. *Interrogation.* Therapists use interrogation primarily to clarify, pin down and document specific points that might be clinically useful in future. Examples of interrogation are 'Did you actually steal the money?' and 'Did you really hit her?' Therapists who ask too many questions may find clients happy to play 'Psychiatric history'.
2. *Specification.* Specification is intended to fix something in both the therapist's and the client's minds so that it can be referred to later in therapy. Examples are: 'So you always wanted to buy more expensive things' and 'I'm hearing that you felt angry.'
3. *Confrontation.* In confrontation therapists use information previously elicited and

specified in order to point out an inconsistency and, thereby, to disconcert a client's Parent, Child or contaminated Adult. Therapists should not use confrontation when genuinely convinced that clients are incapable of seeing the inconsistency.

4. *Explanation* Therapists use explanation to strengthen, decontaminate or reorient the client's Adult. An example is: 'So you see the Child in you was threatening to become active, and when that happens your Adult fades out and your Parent takes over and that's when you shout at the children.'

5. *Illustration.* Illustrations are anecdotes, similes or comparisons that follow a successful confrontation for the purpose of reinforcing it and softening any undesirable after-effects. Illustrations are attempts by therapists to interpose something between the client's Adult and the other ego states to make it more difficult for her/him to slide into Parent or Child activity.

6. *Confirmation.* When clients provide confirmatory evidence after confrontations, therapists can use confirmation to stabilize the client's Adult. For example, if a client were to say 'I just can't do this – Oops, I mean I won't do it' the therapist will immediately confirm the client's greater self-awareness (Dusay and Dusay, 1989, p. 441).

7. *Interpretation.* Therapists use the preceding interventions and interpositions with the primary object of cathecting and decontaminating the Adult. Interpretations are not always necessary for treatment to be successful. However, in some cases the therapist may choose to postpone moving on to crystallization until the Child has been deconfused by psychodynamic interpretation. Alternatively, therapists may first use crystallization to establish Adult control and then undertake the analytic deconfusion of the Child.

8. *Crystallization.* Transactional analysis aims to bring clients to the point where crystallizing statements from therapists are effective. A crystallization is a statement of a client's position from the therapist's Adult to the client's Adult. An example of a crystallization is: 'So you are now in a position to stop playing that game if you want to.'

Berne (1966) stressed that therapists using interventions and interpositions should:

1. never get ahead of the clinical material offered by clients;
2. never miss a legitimate opportunity to forge ahead; and
3. never push against resistance except for testing purposes based on well-thought-out concrete hypotheses.

CASE MATERIAL

As an appendix to *Transactional Analysis in Psychotherapy*, Berne (1961) presents 'A terminated case with follow-up'. The client, a 34-year-old woman called Mrs Enatosky, had complained initially of depression, though Berne stated the formal diagnosis was best stated as schizo-hysteria. The client showed a special aptitude for structural and transactional analysis and soon began to exert social control for the games that went on between her, her husband and her 13-year-old son. In *Games People Play*, Berne (1964) illustrated the characteristics of games in general by choosing the most common game between spouses, colloquially called 'If It Weren't for You' (IWFY). Towards the end of *What Do Say After You Say Hello?* Berne (1972) presented three brief case histories that illustrate working with scripts.

Case material has also been presented by those who have developed Berne's work. Dusay's (1978) book *Egograms* illustrates the functional aspects of ego states and presents many examples of how energy imbalance in clients is treated by re-decision and exercises. The case of Judd, who had been diagnosed as a hypochondriac by many physicians, illustrates the use of egograms in TA group work (Dusay and Dusay, 1989). In another example drawn from group therapy, the Gouldings (1978) present the case of Tim, which demonstrates in detail combining transactional analysis and gestalt, a fairly common practice.

FURTHER DEVELOPMENTS

Dusay and Dusay state that, to date, there have been four transactional analysis phases: the ego state phase (1955–62); the transactions and games phase (1962–66); the script analysis phase (1966–70); and a fourth post-Berne phase 'stimulated by the action techniques of the human-potential movement, Gestalt, psychodrama, encounter, and many of the other explosive, energy-liberating systems' (Dusay and Dusay, 1989, p. 448). Stewart (1996b) observes that in the 1970s three main schools emerged in TA: the classical (Bernian) school; the re-decision school; and the cathexis (Schiffian) school. Since then further developments have included both a focus on the Process Model and personality and also a renewed interest in the psychodynamic ideas that provided the original base for transactional analysis. Below I selectively overview some developments that have taken place after Berne's untimely early death.

The use of egograms

Ego states may be viewed not only in terms of their content, but also in terms of the degree to which they are cathected both before and after treatment. Dusay (1972; Dusay and Dusay, 1989) devised a diagram called the egogram which graphs the extent to which each of a person's ego states are cathected. An egogram shows in bar-graph form how much of a person's energy exists in the five functional ego states: Critical Parent (CP); Nurturing Parent (NP); Adult (A); Free Child (FC); and Adapted Child (AC). A bar graph profile identifies what may be the client's probable types of problems and where their strengths and weaknesses lie. Box 6.9 is an example of an egogram.

Dusay (1972) suggested a constancy hypothesis: namely, that the amount of psychic energy within a person is constant and that if energy is taken away from one ego state more will be available for other ego states. Thus, as treatment progresses, the AC ego state may be less strongly cathected, while the A and FC ego states may attain stronger cathexes. In terms of the Box 6.9 egogram, the height of AC would become lower, with the amount taken away distributed between raising the heights of A and FC.

Dusay and Dusay (1989) observe that each person has different ego-state imbalances. They use a variety of techniques and exercises for people needing to raise or lower the energy cathected in specific ego states: for example, assertiveness techniques for those low

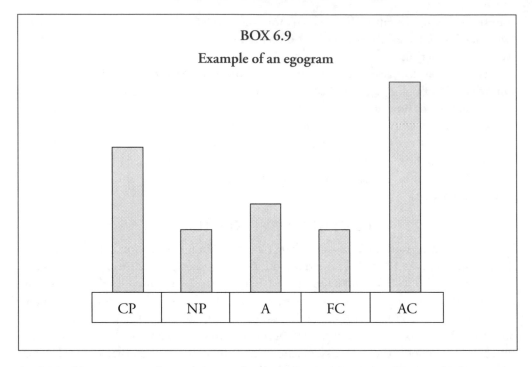

BOX 6.9

Example of an egogram

| CP | NP | A | FC | AC |

in Critical Parent; empathy techniques for those low in Nurturing Parent; thinking exercises for those low in Adult; creative and intuitive activities for those low in Free Child; and compromise and getting-along-with-others exercises for those low in Adapted Child.

The cathexis school and reparenting

Stewart and Joines (1987) identified a cathexis school of transactional analysis based on the Schiffs' reparenting work with schizophrenics (Schiff, 1969, 1970, 1975). Performed in residential treatment centres, severely disturbed clients with a tendency to regress and relive early childhood experiences are 'reparented' by positive parents. This level of intense and continuing therapeutic involvement is not appropriate for non-psychotic clients. Nevertheless, therapists may act as 'replacement parents' for less disturbed clients giving them positive messages and permissions to replace restrictive injunctions received from their natural parents.

The re-decision school and incorporation of gestalt methods

Gestalt and psychodrama methods may be used in conjunction with transactional analysis. The Gouldings (Goulding, 1974; Goulding and Goulding, 1976, 1979) have developed an approach called *re-decision therapy* that combines TA and gestalt theory and practice. They consider that early decisions are made from a feeling rather than a thinking position. Therefore, to get out of script decisions, people must get in touch with their original feelings at the time of the decisions, deal with unfinished emotional business, and make more appropriate *re-decisions* (Stewart and Joines, 1987). The

Gouldings see impasses as developing between ego states. They use the gestalt empty-chair technique to enable clients to have dialogues between ego states. During this process, clients may connect with and reveal strong feelings suppressed since childhood.

Another example of the incorporation into TA of gestalt techniques are the exercises and experiments in James and Jongeward's (1971) book *Born to Win*. For instance, as part of an exercise on the Adapted Child, readers are asked 'Can you admit to any top-dog and/or under-dog positions with yourself?' and 'Can you relate these to your Parent and Child ego states?' (p. 155).

The Process Model and personality adaptations

The Process Model developed by Kahler (1979) rests upon Berne's idea that people might enact their scripts within extremely short time periods. By focusing on the process rather than the content of clients' communication, therapists can identify driver behaviours. In the TA tradition, Kahler has given his five drivers colloquial names: 'Be Perfect', 'Be Strong', 'Try Hard', 'Please You' and 'Hurry Up'. Driver behaviours are so called because they have a 'driven' quality about them. While over time everyone shows all five driver behaviours, most people have a primary driver that they show most often and first in any interaction. Stewart (1996a) regards driver behaviours as the 'gateway to the script'. Drivers are external indicators or early warning signals that the person may be replaying a specific script belief internally. Clients always enact driver behaviours just before they move into their scripts.

Ware (1983) presents six personality adaptations: obsessive-compulsive, paranoid, schizoid, passive-aggressive, hysteric, and antisocial. Since each adaptation contains a specific set of script beliefs about the world, correct identification of a client's adaptation assists the therapist to plan the most appropriate treatment. Being able to spot a client's primary driver helps therapists reliably diagnose her or his main personality adaptation. With each of the adaptations, often primary drivers are accompanied by secondary drivers. For example, clients whose primary driver is 'Try Hard' will have the passive–aggressive personality adaptation. Clients who have the driver behaviours 'Be Perfect' and 'Be Strong' shown with approximately equal intensity will have the paranoid adaptation (Stewart, 1996b). Combining the Process Model with personality adaptations provides a powerful means of analysing and treating scripts.

Journal and training

The *Transactional Analysis Bulletin* started in 1962 with Berne as editor. This journal has now become a quarterly *Transactional Analysis Journal*. In 1964 the International Transactional Analysis Association (ITAA) was formed as a training and accreditation body for transactional analysis. Now the European Association for Transactional Analysis also performs training and accreditation functions.

SUMMARY

- *Transactional analysis was originated by Eric Berne and comprises a theory of personality, a theory of social interaction, and an analytic tool for therapy.*
- *Humans start from a fundamentally OK life position, which early experiences often cause them to lose.*
- *Ego states are patterns of feeling, thinking and behaviour. Each person has three classes of ego state: Parent, Adult and Child, representing influences copied from parent figures, age-appropriate reality appraisal, and relics of the individual's childhood, respectively.*
- *Further analyses of ego states tend to focus on elaborating the Parent and Child. At any time the ego state which is most cathected with psychic energy will have executive power.*
- *People are motivated principally by stimulus, recognition, and structure hungers. Six ways of structuring social time are: withdrawal, rituals, activities, pastimes, games and intimacy.*
- *Transactions involve the exchange of strokes, or units of recognition, between the ego states of those involved in a social interaction. Transactions between ego states can be complementary, crossed or ulterior.*
- *Scripts are preconscious life plans by which people structure their time and have their destinies determined. They are based on early decisions when the young person moves into one of the not-OK life positions and relinquishes some autonomy in order to acquiesce with parental injunctions.*
- *The script matrix is a way of conceptualizing directives given from the ego states of parents to those of any particular child. Ways in which parents hamper the ego-state development of their children include injunctions, attributions and discounts.*
- *Games, which involve ulterior transactions and a payoff, are developed on the basis of a script decision and justify a life position. Ways in which maladaptive behaviour is maintained include: script payoffs, game payoffs, the illusion of autonomy involving ego-state contamination, ego-state exclusion, and inadequate information.*
- *The goals of transactional analysis focus on autonomy. Awareness, spontaneity and intimacy are three features of autonomous people. Therapists and clients negotiate contracts specifying treatment goals.*
- *Structural analysis of ego states, transactional analysis, game analysis and script analysis are approaches to transactional analysis practice.*
- *Berne identified four basic interventions – interrogation, specification, confrontation, and explanation; and four basic interpositions – illustration, confirmation, interpretation and crystallization – for use by TA therapists.*
- *Some more recent developments in transactional analysis include: the use of egograms, the cathexis school and reparenting, the re-decision school and the incorporation of gestalt methods, and the Process Model and personality adaptations.*

REVIEW AND PERSONAL QUESTIONS

REVIEW QUESTIONS

1. Describe each of the following ego states: Parent; Adult; Child.
2. Why is transactional analysis a dynamic theory of personality?
3. What are stimulus, recognition and structure hungers?
4. What did Berne mean by time structuring and what are the ways in which people can structure time?
5. Provide an example of and draw a diagram for each of the following types of transactions: complementary; crossed; and ulterior.
6. What did Berne mean by a script?
7. What are games and how do people develop them?
8. What are script payoffs and game payoffs?
9. What are the goals of transactional analysis?
10. Describe briefly each of the following: structural analysis; transactional analysis; game analysis; and script analysis.

PERSONAL QUESTIONS

1. Do a first-order PAC structural analysis on yourself (Box 6.1 (a)) indicating thoughts, feelings and behaviours belonging to your: Parent ego state; Adult ego state; and Child ego state.
2. Assume that you have 100 units of energy to divide among your Critical Parent, Nurturing Parent, Adult, Free Child, and Adapted Child ego states. In terms of the way you usually feel and behave, draw an egogram distributing the 100 units of energy among the five ego states.
3. Provide an example from your own life of each of the following types of transactions: complementary; crossed; and ulterior.
4. Take a relationship with a significant other in your life (parent, spouse, child, colleague, etc.) and analyse one or more of the transactions in it in terms of the Parent, Adult and Child ego state, or states, cathected in each person.
5. Identify some of the games you play, including the moves involved and their negative feeling payoff or your racket. Suggest an easily remembered name for each of your games.
6. Draw a script matrix for yourself as in Box 6.6 and indicate some of the main script injunctions and counterscript prescriptions you received from your parents.
7. Identify any early decisions you made which are no longer appropriate. Formulate appropriate statements of re-decision which will allow you to change the ways in which you are currently scripted to feel and behave.
8. What relevance, if any, has the theory and practice of transactional analysis for how you conduct therapy?
9. What relevance, if any, has the theory and practice of transactional analysis for how you live?

ANNOTATED BIBLIOGRAPHY

Berne, E. (1961). *Transactional Analysis in Psychotherapy.* New York: Grove Press.
    This book is Berne's major statement of structural analysis and transactional analysis. It consists of four parts: psychiatry of the individual and structural analysis; social psychiatry and transactional analysis; psychotherapy; and frontiers of transactional analysis. A case study is provided as an appendix.

Berne, E. (1964). *Games People Play: The Psychology of Human Relationship.* New York: Grove Press.
    This book is Berne's international best-seller. It consists of three parts: analysis of games; a thesaurus of games; and beyond games. The chapters in the thesaurus of games cover: life, marital, party, sexual, underworld, consulting room, and good games. Berne gave each game a catchy title.

Berne, E. (1966). *Principles of Group Treatment.* New York: Oxford University Press.
    This book is a systematic treatise on the use of transactional analysis in groups. The book's first part describes the basic principles of group treatment. The focus of the book's second part is transactional analysis, its general principles and basic techniques, and the handling of the more common games that occur in the course of group treatment.

Berne, E. (1972). *What Do You Say After You Say Hello?* London: Corgi Books.
    Published posthumously, this book elaborates Berne's ideas on scripts. The book is divided into five parts: general considerations; parental programming; the script in action; the script in clinical practice; and scientific approaches to script theory.

Steiner, C. M. (1974). *Scripts People Live.* New York: Bantam Books.
    A comprehensive discussion of script theory by the creator of the script matrix. There is a special focus on political and social institutions.

Stewart, I. and Joines, V. (1987). *TA Today: A New Introduction to Transactional Analysis.* Nottingham: Lifespace Publishing.
    This is a systematic textbook, aimed at the general reader, which explains TA ideas from basic principles upwards. The book's presentation is structured around the syllabus of the internationally-recognized basic TA training course and includes numerous examples and exercises.

Stewart, I. (2000). *Transactional Analysis Counselling in Action* (2nd edition). London: Sage.
    This book introduces the core concepts and basic techniques of TA. The systematic process of TA is illustrated by a case study from the client's first contact and intake, through diagnosis and treatment planning, to contract-making and the implementation of the planned treatment sequence. Self-assessment questions are incorporated to build readers' TA skills.

REFERENCES AND FURTHER READING

Berne, E. (1958). Transactional analysis: A new and effective method of group therapy. *American Journal of Psychotherapy, 12*, 735–43.

Berne, E. (1961). *Transactional Analysis in Psychotherapy.* New York: Grove Press.

Berne, E. (1963). *The Structure and Dynamics of Organizations and Groups.* Philadelphia: J. B. Lippincott Co.

Berne, E. (1964). *Games People Play: The Psychology of Human Relationships.* New York: Grove Press.

Berne, E. (1966). *Principles of Group Treatment.* New York: Oxford University Press.

Berne, E. (1968). *A Layman's Guide to Psychiatry and Psychoanalysis.* Harmondsworth: Penguin Books. First published in 1947 as *The Mind in Action.*

Berne, E. (1968). *The Happy Valley.* New York: Grove Press.

Berne, E. (1970). *Sex in Human Loving.* Harmondsworth: Penguin Books.

Berne, E. (1972). *What Do You Say After You Say Hello?* London: Corgi Books.

Dusay, J. M. (1972). Egograms and the 'constancy hypothesis'. *Transactional Analysis Journal, 2*, 27–41.

Dusay, J. M. (1978). *Egograms.* New York: Harper and Row.

Dusay, J. M. and Dusay, K. M. (1989). Transactional analysis. In R. J. Corsini and D. Wedding (eds). *Current Psychotherapies* (4th edition, 405–53). Itasca, IL: Peacock.

Goulding, M. and Goulding, R. E. (1979). *Changing Lives Through Redecision Therapy.* New York: Brunner Mazel.

Goulding, R. E. (1974). Thinking and feeling in psychotherapy (three impasses). *Voices, 10*, 11–13.

Goulding, R. E. and Goulding, M. (1976). Injunctions, decisions and redecisions. *Transactional Analysis Journal, 6*, 41–8.

Goulding, R. E. and Goulding, M. (1978). The case of Tim. *The Power is in the Patient: A Transactional Analysis/Gestalt Approach to Psychotherapy* (43–55). San Franscisco: TA Press.

James, M. and Contributors (1977). *Techniques in Transactional Analysis: For Psychotherapists and Counselors.* Reading, MA: Addison-Wesley.

James, M. and Jongeward, D. (1971). *Born to Win.* Reading, MA: Addison-Wesley.

Kahler, T. (1979). *Process Therapy in Brief.* Little Rock, AR: Human Development Publications.

Schiff, J. (1969). Reparenting schizophrenics. *Transactional Analysis Bulletin, 8*, 158–64.

Schiff, J. (1970). *All My Children.* New York: Evans.

Schiff, J. (1975). *The Cathexis Reader.* New York: Harper and Row.

Spitz, R. (1945). Hospitalism, genesis of psychiatric conditions in early childhood. *Psychoanalytic Study of the Child, 1*, 53–74.

Steiner, C. M. (1974). *Scripts People Live.* New York: Bantam Books.

Stewart, I. (1996a). *Developing Transactional Analysis Counselling.* London: Sage.

Stewart, I. (1996b). Developments in transactional analysis. In W. Dryden (ed.). *Developments in Psychotherapy: Historical Perspectives* (62–90). London: Sage.

Stewart, I. (2000). *Transactional Analysis Counselling in Action* (2nd edition). London: Sage Publications.

Stewart, I. and Joines, V. (1987). *TA Today: A New Introduction to Transactional Analysis.* Nottingham: Lifespace Publishing.

Ware, P. (1983). Personality adaptations. *Transactional Analysis Journal, 13* (1), 11–19.

7

Reality Therapy

Choice theory is about making better choices, but we have to understand the reason for bad choices before we can make good ones.

William Glasser

INTRODUCTION

Reality therapy is an approach developed in the 1950s and 1960s by William Glasser, a Californian-based psychiatrist. Glasser (1984a) admits that originally the approach had no systematic theory, but rested on the assumption that people are responsible for what they do. In the early 1980s, Glasser (1981, 1984b) added control theory as a theoretical base for the practice of reality therapy. Glasser (1989) wrote: 'Control theory contends that *our behavior is always our best attempt to control the world and ourselves as part of that world so that we can best satisfy our needs*' (p. 5).

In 1996, Glasser changed the name of the theory underlying reality therapy from control theory to choice theory (Glasser, 1999). Glasser strongly emphasizes the distinction between relationship-destroying external control psychology, based on the ancient 'I know what is right for you' tradition, and choice theory, which gives people the freedom to sustain healthy relationships and lead productive lives.

WILLIAM GLASSER (1925–)

William Glasser grew up in Cleveland, Ohio. By the time he was about 4, he realized that his parents were almost totally incompatible. Glasser's parents were living illustrations of the difference between choice theory and external control psychology. His father was a gentle man, with his own business, who gave him the freedom to develop on his own terms. His mother presented much more a challenge. Glasser writes: 'If the Olympics had an event in controlling, my mother could have gone for the gold medal. My father was totally choice theory. Never in the more than 60 years that I knew him did I ever see him try to control another person except when he was goaded by my mother. And even then his heart was not in it' (Glasser, 1999, p. 90). Had she been born 50 years later, Glasser thinks his mother could have used her brains and tremendous energy in a job.

Glasser studied chemical engineering at Case Institute of Technology in Cleveland. At 19 Glasser was extremely shy, though this did not prevent him from marrying his first wife Naomi during his undergraduate years. For three years Glasser studied for a PhD in clinical psychology at Western Reserve University, but did not complete the degree, switching to medicine instead. In 1953, Glasser obtained his MD from Western Reserve University. He then commenced psychiatric training at the Veterans Administration Brentwood Hospital and, in 1957, completed his final year at the University of California at Los Angeles.

Reality therapy stems from Glasser's dissatisfaction with psychoanalytic psychiatry as taught during his training. He thought that there was too much emphasis on clients' feelings and past history and insufficient emphasis on what clients were doing and on 'What are you doing about what you are doing?' (Evans, 1982, p. 460). Also he noticed that many of his teachers did not practise what they taught and that what seemed to work was not what they said worked.

In 1956, after an attempt at private practice which was hampered by a shortage of referrals, Glasser accepted a position with the California Youth Authority as head psychiatrist at the Ventura School for Girls. Glasser (1984a) observes that reality therapy evolved in its initial phase from his work with delinquent teenage girls (1956–67), with private outpatients with a variety of problems (1956–82), and with physically injured clients in a rehabilitation centre (1957–66). A further influence was the work of his former residency consultant and mentor G. L. Harrington with severely psychotic patients at a Veterans Administration Hospital (1955–62). In 1961, Glasser's first book, *Mental Health or Mental Illness?* was published, followed in 1965 by *Reality Therapy: A New Approach to Psychiatry.*

In 1965, Glasser began consulting in the California school system, spending much time in elementary schools in the deprived Watts area of Los Angeles. This work led to his focus on applying his ideas to education and institutional change and not just to individuals. In 1968, Glasser opened the Institute for Reality Therapy in Brentwood, a suburb of Los Angeles. Also that year he created the Educator Training Center to research and develop programmes for the prevention of school failure. In 1969, Glasser's *Schools Without Failure* was published. In this book he advocated that education was causing students to fail because of non-involvement, non-relevance, and limited emphasis on thinking, and that schools needed to move towards the opposite philosophy of involvement, relevance, and thinking. By 1974, Glasser was saying 'I've all but given up my private practice' (Barr, 1974, p. 67).

Glasser's interest in control theory was stimulated after his 1976 book *Positive Addiction* in which he discussed how addictions like running and meditation are extremely strengthening. While reading widely on how the brain functions during meditation, he discovered William Power's 1973 book *Behavior: The Control of Perception.* Power's theory of how the brain functions as a control system provided a theoretical base both for positive addiction and reality therapy. Glasser writes: 'As Powers defines it, a control system acts upon the outside world, or upon itself as a part of the outside world to fulfill some purpose intrinsic to the system' (Glasser, 1984a, p. 321). People with psychological disorders fail in their attempts to control the world to satisfy what they need right now. Glasser's 1981 book *Stations of the Mind* related control theory to the practice of reality therapy.

In 1982, Glasser began teaching control theory to the general public. His 1984 book

Control Theory: A New Explanation of How We Control Our Lives both describes the theory and then shows how people can apply it to gain greater control over their lives. Glasser's books *The Quality School* (1990, 1992) and *The Quality School Teacher* (1993) apply control theory ideas to school management and teaching, respectively. Though much of the content remains the same, Glasser now uses the term 'choice theory' instead of 'control theory'. In addition to *Choice Theory: A New Psychology of Personal Freedom* (Glasser, 1999), he has collaborated with his second wife Carleen Glasser to produce a short book called *The Language of Choice Theory* (Glasser and Glasser, 1999).

In 1946, Glasser married Naomi Glasser, and together they raised three children. In December 1992, after a brief illness, Naomi died of cancer. Naomi had been very supportive of Glasser's work and edited two books of case studies, *What Are You Doing?: How People are Helped Through Reality Therapy* (1980) and *Control Theory in the Practice of Reality Therapy* (1989). Shortly before her death, Naomi said to Glasser: 'You won't do well by yourself; I hope you can find someone with whom you can be happy.' Glasser did not see himself as a good bachelor and his difficult search for a new mate culminated in his meeting, marrying and finding happiness again with his second wife, Carleen (Glasser, 1995). Carleen Glasser is a senior instructor at the William Glasser Institute

Glasser continues training and certifying reality therapists through the William Glasser Institute, over which he presides. He remains positively addicted to promoting, both in the United States and overseas, his choice theory, reality therapy, quality school and institutional change ideas.

THEORY

Choice theory explains that, for all practical purposes, we choose everything we do, including the misery we feel.

William Glasser

BASIC CONCEPTS

Choice theory versus external control psychology

Glasser encourages people to replace external control psychology with choice theory or internal control psychology (Glasser, 1999). In the twentieth century, the huge strides in technical progress have not been accompanied by human progress as represented by better relationships. The main reason for this is that many people are still trying to control others and allowing themselves to be controlled by others. External control is doubly dangerous because people's belief in it both creates the problems they are trying to solve and is also used to deal with the problems. For example, when punishment does not work, invariably people punish harder.

To create and maintain the high quality of relationships that people need, they must move from *external control psychology* – choosing to coerce, force, compel, punish, reward, boss, manipulate, motivate, criticize, blame, complain, nag, badger, rank, rate, and withdraw, to *choice theory or internal control psychology* – choosing to care, listen, support, negotiate, encourage, love, befriend, trust, accept, welcome, and esteem.

Reality therapy is based on choice theory. Box 7.1 presents an abridged version of the ten axioms of choice theory (Glasser, 1999, pp. 332–6).

BOX 7.1

The ten axioms of choice theory

1. The only person whose behaviour we can control is our own.
2. All we can give or get from other people is information.
3. All long-lasting psychological problems are relationship problems.
4. The problem relationship is always part of our present lives.
5. Revisiting the painful past can contribute little or nothing to what we need to do now to improve an important, present relationship.
6. We are driven by five genetic needs: survival, love and belonging, power, freedom, and fun.
7. We can satisfy these needs only by satisfying a picture or pictures in our quality worlds.
8. All behaviour is total behaviour and is made up of four inseparable components: acting, thinking, feeling, and physiology.
9. All total behaviour is designated by verbs named by the component that is most recognizable: for example, 'I am choosing to depress' or 'I am depressing.'
10. All total behaviour is chosen, but we have direct control only over the acting and thinking components – we can control our feelings and physiology indirectly through how we choose to act and think.

Basic needs and feelings

Choice theory sees humans as driven by basic needs that are genetic in origin. All human behaviour represents an attempt to control the world to best satisfy these needs. People have no rest from their needs. Once aware of a need they have no choice but to attempt to satisfy the need and, when satisfied, other needs emerge. Human life is a constant struggle to satisfy these different needs and to solve the ever-present conflicts between them. The five basic needs are survival, love and belonging, power, freedom and fun (Glasser 1995, 1999).

Glasser distinguishes between the old brain and cerebral cortex or 'new brain' that evolved much later than the old brain. There is much communication between the small unconscious old brain and the huge conscious new brain, which is the source of awareness and of voluntary behaviour. For most people, the old brain with the assistance of the new brain satisfies the survival need reasonably well. However, much of life is concerned with satisfying the more complex and often conflicting needs that arise in the conscious new brain. Glasser (1984b) calls these 'psychological needs' because people have to satisfy their genetic instructions psychologically rather than physically. He stresses that their source is still biologic and their genetic instructions no less urgent than the genetic instructions for the physical need to survive and reproduce. Following are the five needs, one physical and the remaining four psychological.

1. *Survival.* This physical need is located in the old brain which is located in a small group of structures clustered at the top of the spinal chord. People's genes instruct their old brain to carry out all the survival activities that promote health and reproduction.

2. *Love, loving sex and belonging.* People's love and belonging needs demand that they keep love going throughout their lives. This need for love and belonging may be satisfied by marital partners, family, friends, groups, classes and even pets. Love and friendship are two-way streets. Probably failure to meet love and belonging needs is the prime cause of human misery.

3. *Power.* The power need may be satisfied by status, recognition and getting others to obey us. Most people's power needs are satisfied if they are listened to and respected. It is also possible to gain power by working for the common good. Power is ultimately a sense of self-worth and can be met by valuing oneself independently of external recognition. Good marriages and friendships are based on equal power

   The need for power is often in competition with the need to belong. The need to belong propels people into relationships that can then turn into power struggles. In an external control world, the need for power is often at someone else's expense.

4. *Freedom.* People need freedom to choose how they live their lives or at least some aspects of their lives. They need to move around as they like, express themselves freely and associate with whom they choose. The need for freedom can conflict with other needs, for instance the need to belong as either a spouse or parent. Furthermore, it is fundamental that chosen need satisfying behaviours should not prevent others engaging in need satisfying behaviours.

5. *Fun.* The need for fun or enjoyment is as fundamental a need as the other needs. Fun is a basic genetic instruction for all higher animals because that is how they learn. Fun removes the drudgery from learning and enhances motivation. Even in old age, learning without play is difficult. Sharing a strong need for fun supports all human relationships and is a vital ingredient in successful marriages. When asked how he knows he is having fun, Glasser says he finds himself laughing a lot. The need for fun and enjoyment also includes being interested and having interests.

It is possible to rate each of the needs on a five-point scale: 1 = very weak; 2 = below average; 3 = average; 4 = above average; and 5 = very strong. By putting their individual need assessments together, people can create a need-strength profile. For example, Glasser rates himself as follows: survival – 3, average; love and belonging – 4, above average; power – 4, above average; freedom – 5, very strong; and fun – 5, very strong. It is also possible to compare people's need-strength profiles and assess their compatibility (Glasser, 1995).

The quality world

Throughout their lives, people develop personal picture albums consisting of detailed pictures of what they want to satisfy their needs. Glasser (1984b) gives the example of the baby who was screaming and then given a chocolate-chip biscuit which was much liked. Immediately the baby took a picture of the biscuit and stored it away as something to look for when hungry again. Human senses combine into a sensory camera that, among others, can take visual, gustatory, and tactile pictures. Glasser prefers the word 'pictures' to 'perceptions' both because it is easier to understand and because about 80 per cent of perceptions stored in personal albums are visual.

Personal picture albums are a small and selective part of total memory. The personal picture album is a special world that Glasser now calls the quality world. It is more than an ideal world of 'What I would like to be' since it contains very specific pictures of what will satisfy my needs for love, worth, success, freedom and fun right now. The pictures in people's quality worlds fall into three categories:

1. the *people* they most want to be with;
2. the *things* they most want to own or experience; and
3. the *ideas or systems of belief* that govern much of their behaviour.

Glasser observes: 'Anytime we feel good, we are choosing to behave so that someone, something, or some belief in the real world has come close to matching a person, thing, or belief in our quality worlds' (Glasser, 1999, p. 45).

All pictures are need-fulfilling. People must have at least one picture in their quality worlds for every need. It is virtually impossible to have a need without quickly finding a picture to satisfy it. However, people commonly have pictures in their albums that cannot be satisfied in the real world. Furthermore, the pictures in their quality worlds may be neither rational or compatible with each other. In addition, some pictures can be blurred and ill-defined, though individuals may define them more sharply later (Wubbolding, 1985).

People can add pictures to their quality worlds or remove them if they do not satisfy needs. When people change important pictures, they change their lives. The only way pictures can be taken out of quality worlds is to replace them with something that fits the same basic need reasonably well. For example, the picture of a loved one is usually replaceable with someone else. Sometimes people choose a lifetime of misery because they cannot replace pictures: for example battered wives who stay with husbands because they remain the only 'possible' pictures of loving persons.

Changing our own pictures is difficult. Changing other people's pictures is even more difficult and can only be achieved through negotiation and compromise. It is the pictures in each person's quality world, and nobody else's, that causes them to do what they do. Box 7.2 illustrates the importance of understanding the individual nature of people's quality worlds (Glasser, 1999).

The pictures in people's quality worlds are central to understanding the choice theory view of motivation. Behaviour always starts with the pictures in people's quality worlds.

BOX 7.2

Example of harmful and helpful quality worlds in a school

Students' harmful quality worlds

In an inner-city middle school in which he and Carleen Glasser worked, the students did not have teachers, each other or schoolwork in their quality worlds. However, in their quality worlds they did have drugs, violent clowning around and non-loving sex. The more teachers used punishment and threats, the more the students resisted and focused on what was in their own and not their teachers' quality worlds. The students had no idea that it was possible to be happy at school.

Students' helpful quality worlds

Using choice theory, the Glassers began to build relationships with the students and through these relationships helped them so that they began to picture themselves satisfying their needs in school. As the students began to put the staff and each other into their quality worlds, they also became happier.

Behaviour is generated by the difference between the pictures in people's quality worlds, what they want, and what is going on in the real world, what they have. When a difference exists, people behave to reduce this difference. It is a biological fact that people must choose to do something to reduce the difference. However, what they do is almost invariably their choice.

Total behaviour

In choice theory, behaviour is how people choose to attempt to control the world to satisfy needs rather than a response to stimulation. Behaviour is more than conduct or action. Glasser uses the term 'total behaviour' to describe his expanded concept of behaviour. Total behaviour, the whole, is always the sum of the following four components:

1. *Acting*. The acting component consists of active behaviours like walking or running which involve voluntarily moving some part of the body. However, some involuntary actions accompany routine activities, for instance swallowing when eating.
2. *Thinking*. The thinking component consists of voluntarily generating thoughts as well as involuntarily generating them, for instance in dreams.
3. *Feeling*. The feeling component consists of a wide variety of pleasurable and painful feelings that people generate and choose.
4. *Physiology*. The physiological component, for instance sweating, encompasses the voluntary and involuntary body mechanisms that people generate and choose involved in the doing, thinking and feeling components of total behaviour.

Glasser (1989) uses the analogy of total behaviour as a four-wheel-drive car, with each component as one wheel of the car. The front wheels are the acting and thinking components and the rear wheels are the feeling and physiology components. The needs are the engine and the driver steers in the direction closest to the picture most wanted from his or her quality world album. As in a car, the person has total voluntary control of where to steer the front wheels of his or her 'car'. Whatever clients' problems are they can choose to steer their life 'cars' in better directions than they do now. However, clients have nowhere near the degree of voluntary control over the rear wheels of feeling and physiology that they have over the front wheels of acting and thinking. Consequently, reality therapy focuses on helping clients change their actions and thoughts (the front wheels) much more than their feelings and physiology (the rear wheels).

While doing and thinking are always expressed as verbs, such as running and meditating, feelings are usually expressed as adjectives, for instance depressed, or nouns, for instance depression. However, people not only choose how they think and act, they choose how they feel. A feeling like depression does not happen to people, they choose to depress. Consequently, Glasser uses verbs rather than nouns and adjectives to refer to feelings. Examples of the use of verbs to denote feelings are depressing for depression, anxietying for anxiety, headaching for headache, angering for anger, and phobicking for phobia. Active language attempts to describe the behaviour that people generate and choose in their attempts to control the world to satisfy their needs.

Glasser (1989) provides the example of a client who admits to being depressed. From the viewpoint of choice theory, this client is depressing or choosing to depress. The four components of this depressing total behaviour are as follows. The acting component may be sitting round lethargically. The feeling component is pain and misery. The thinking component may be thoughts like 'What's the use? There is nothing I can do.' The physiology component may be stomach-ache and trouble sleeping. The more this depressed client can both realize that the feeling component is just one of the four components of a total behaviour and use a verb like depressing to describe the behaviour, the more the client will be in control of his or her life. The client who admits to depressing or choosing to depress then has three choices: (1) change what s/he wants, (2) change what s/he is doing, or (3) change both.

People as control systems

As control systems, people, like all living organisms, are always attempting to control the world for the purpose of fulfilling basic needs genetically built into their systems. People as control systems act upon the world and themselves as part of the world to attempt to get the picture in their quality worlds that they want. All living organisms have two fundamental ways to control the world. First, they need to perceive what in the world can possibly get them the picture they see as satisfying their need. This is the input dimension of controlling the world. Second, they need to act upon or control what they see as satisfying their need, the output dimension. For instance, thirsty people first have to perceive what thirst is and how it can be satisfied by water. Second, to satisfy their thirst they must act upon or control the world by looking for water and, if this is unobtainable, for some other fluid.

People as control systems choose all their behaviour to satisfy one or more basic needs.

Neurotic, psychotic, psychosomatic and addictive behaviours are ineffective choices that people generate to control the world to satisfy their needs. Most ineffective behaviours, for instance angering, are consciously chosen. Other behaviours that people generate, for instance psychosomatic behaviours like arthritis or heart disease, may be less consciously chosen and blocked from awareness because people find it too painful to realize that they choose their misery. Regarding stress, Glasser (1984a) considers that there are few, if any, genuinely stressful situations in the outside world. People use the term 'stress' to describe situations that they cannot control satisfactorily with the behaviours that they choose.

Though control systems like to be in control, no control system likes to be controlled. If others attempt to control people or if people attempt to control themselves in ways that frustrate their needs, they will always choose to rebel. Sometimes the rebellion is direct. Most often the rebellion is in indirect ways like choosing to depress, migraine or be ill. No one can control another person, unless that person is persuaded that it satisfies some picture in their quality world.

ACQUISITION

Learning about needs

At birth, people do not know what their needs are or how to satisfy them. However, babies do know how they feel. They also know that when their needs are not satisfied they do not feel good. This knowledge enables them to gain some idea of what their needs are. For instance, babies do not have concepts of food, eating or survival. However, they know when they hurt and, when fed, they usually feel better. As this occurs, babies first begin to know about food and then later about eating and about their survival need. People can also learn about their psychological needs for power, belonging, freedom and fun in that they know that, when these needs are satisfied, they feel better. Even if never clear what their needs are, through their efforts to feel good people will still try to satisfy these needs.

Acquisition of quality worlds

Already, the example has been given of the baby who was given a chocolate-chip biscuit when screaming, took a picture of it, and stored it in their quality world as something to look for when hungry. As people go through life, they store in their quality worlds anything that they believe will satisfy one or more of their basic needs. Glasser (1984b) considers it likely that people have hundreds and even thousands of pictures that will satisfy each need. People may acquire pictures in their quality worlds that put them at risk. For example, anorexic people have pictures about the desirability of being excessively thin. Alcoholics have pictures about satisfying their needs through alcohol. Abused and rejected people who have given up on being happy in relationships may replace people pictures in their quality worlds with non-people pictures of violence, drugs and unloving sex.

Acquisition of total behaviours

Babies know that to survive they must do all that they can to control the world around them to meet their needs. For the sake of their survival, babies are born with the total behaviour of angering. Angering is the baby's way of signalling to the world that he or she has unmet needs. In order to encourage independence, shortly after birth most mothers stop allowing their babies totally to control them with angering. When babies scream and nothing happens they quickly learn to look for different behaviours, for instance smiling, with which to control their worlds. Humans are creative and, aided by imitating, quickly learn other total behaviours. Children's most effective teachers are people they care for and respect. Other ways of learning new behaviours to control the world include going to school, reading books and watching television.

Glasser (1989) considers that, usually early in life, everyone learns to add misery, craziness, sickness, and dysfunctional angering behaviours like fighting to their existing repertoires of total behaviours. It is common for children to pout and depress to control adults or to fight to control other children. Thus children add miserabling or angering as ways to control themselves and others to meet their needs. In these examples, children learn to choose behaviours that may have short-term payoffs. However, as time goes by, the same choices are likely to lessen people's control over their lives because they are more likely to produce negative than positive consequences for self and others.

Raising children

Glasser (1984b) advises: 'Try as hard as possible to teach, show and help your children to gain effective control over their lives' (p. 198). Children are going to live according to their own and not their parents' quality worlds. Too often parents try to mould their children to their quality worlds and, by doing so, create power struggles. It is important that parents keep their children's pictures of them as loving people. Around 2 years old, babies start checking out the extent of their power to control their parents. Then, if parents allow it, children can begin to take advantage of their parents' love to control them. Good parents who make clear what they and others will do and what children have to do for themselves can help the children create sensible quality worlds.

Children are born without knowing how to fulfil their needs. Glasser (1984b) distinguishes between doing things *for*, *to* and *with* children and leaving them alone. Many parents do too much for their children in ways that assist them to have less control over their lives later. Also, parents do far too much to their children, for instance yelling at them and punishing them when they do not do as parents want. Most parents do too little with their children, for example playing with them or discussing mutual interests. Also, at all ages, parents do not leave children alone enough, for instance letting them cry out temper tantrums or make their own entertainment on rainy days. Allowing children space to achieve goals on their own can lead to feelings of success that satisfies their power needs. In short, children learn most about how to have healthy quality worlds and be in control of their lives from adults who do things with them and encourage them to do things for themselves.

Inevitably children will break rules and challenge parents. Since both parents and children have strong needs for power, negotiation and compromise are the only ways that they can get along with each other. Choice theory distinguishes between discipline and punishment. Discipline always starts with trying to teach children to follow reasonable rules through negotiation. Parents attempt to assist children to see that there are better pictures for their quality worlds and behaviours that would be within the rules. Punishment starts and finishes with trying to force children to follow rules, whether reasonable or not, by trying to inflict pain if they refuse. Parents make no attempt to give them the opportunity to negotiate and review other pictures for their quality worlds and behaviours that fall within the rules. Punished children feel deep losses of power and control.

When negotiating plans with children, parents should try to do as much with and as little to or for them as possible. Where children do not want to change or negotiate, parents can impose sanctions appropriate to the child's age until the problem is worked through: for instance, going to one's room for ten minutes might be a maximum sanction for a 5-year old and an evening without television appropriate for a 10-year-old. Sanctions should not be so great that children lose their willingness to try to correct the situation. Furthermore, it is preferable that parents not impose sanctions unless they have previously discussed with the child the consequences of not complying. Always parents should explain to children their element of personal choice regarding the sanction, that they can either choose to comply or choose to accept the consequences of not complying.

MAINTENANCE

Glasser (1989, 1999) sees all clients at the start of therapy as choosing some form of self-destructive behaviour that represents their misguided attempts to regain control over their poorly controlled and frustrating lives. People who are depressing, guilting, angering, and headaching insufficiently realize both what their needs are and that they can make better choices about satisfying them than they currently do.

Reasons for choosing misery

There are three main reasons that people choose the suffering, pain and misery in their lives.

1. *Restraining anger.* By about 2 years old, most children realize that angering will not get them what they want and look for alternatives. Children unable to go for walks when everyone else is busy may choose to keep angering under control. Instead, they may choose depressing out of their behavioural systems. Depressing, despite its pain, may be a safer and more effective way for children to take control over others. By the time people become adults, they have created and learned from others a wide variety of painful feeling behaviours that they substitute for displaying anger, for instance depressing, anxietying, guilting or headaching.
2. *Attracting help.* Depressing is a very powerful way of getting help without begging

and risking damaging one's need for power. Many people are vulnerable to being controlled by being the targets of depressing behaviour.

3. *Avoidance.* Pain, misery and depressing are commonly used as excuses for either doing nothing, or being frightened of doing something, or a mixture of the two. The choice to stay miserable, despite the pain, protects people from becoming aware of the need to work on problems. Furthermore, depressing can hide their fears of failure which might make their lives even harder to control than they are now. However, depressing can also help people 'buy time' and allow them to recoup before taking more positive action.

Reasons for remaining unaware of choosing misery

A major reason that people maintain their choosing to stay miserable behaviour is that they remain unaware that they are doing so. They do not want to take the responsibility of doing something about it as soon as they accept that their misery is a choice. Following are three important reasons blocking people from becoming aware that negative feelings involve choices.

1. *Mistaking short-term pure feelings for long-term feeling behaviours.* What people feel is divided into two stages. First, there is the immediate experiencing of a feeling, which Glasser (1984b) calls 'pure feeling'. These pure feelings are derived from the early evolutionary need to be aware of threats to survival and tell people whether or not they are in control. Such feelings are not chosen and begin to diminish as soon as they occur. Second, people choose a long-term feeling behaviour, for instance depressing or loving, to prolong either the pain or the pleasure initiated by the pure unchosen feeling.

   Glasser (1984b) gives the example of Tom who had the pure feeling of a sharp pang of disappointment when he opened his pay packet and saw a dismissal slip. This pain alerted him that he had lost control of an important part of his life. Then Tom chose the long-term pain of depressing that quickly superseded the pure pain of the initial disappointment. However, since it is difficult to tell when the switch occurs, people tend to confuse the pure brief unchosen pain with the chronic chosen pain.

2. *Most painful choices become automatic.* Frustrated children often consciously choose whether to sulk or to anger. However, for adults who have been making such choices over a period of years, the choice process has become automatic and below awareness. Distinctly painful behaviours, such as headaching, are limited to about twenty and most people use only four or five that 'work well' for them. People are more likely to acknowledge in awareness their responsibility for choosing pleasurable total behaviours than for choosing painful ones.

3. *Not wanting to lose self-esteem.* People's need for power and self-esteem is so strong that, if they were to acknowledge that they choose painful feelings, this knowledge might cause them to experience some loss of control. Consequently, to maintain control of themselves as well as of others, people repress from awareness that they are

choosing much of the misery they feel. However, to regain control people need to acknowledge that they choose their misery and can choose other behaviours and, if necessary, change the pictures in their quality worlds to satisfy their needs.

Staying controlled by others' misery

Glasser stated that one of the most important guidelines of control theory was 'Never let anyone control you with the pain and misery he or she chooses' (Glasser, 1984b, p. 202). The same guideline holds true for choice theory. People can give up their freedom of choice about how they lead their lives to others who have their own control agendas. Box 7.3 provides an example of someone choosing to stay controlled by another's misery (Glasser, 1984b).

BOX 7.3

Example of choosing to stay controlled by another's misery

Physically healthy Carol chooses to depress for the purpose of controlling her middle-aged daughter Phyllis. Phyllis in turn creates her own misery and guilting by allowing her mother to control her with misery. Carol is not going to change of her own accord since choosing misery is her way of keeping control of her life. Phyllis needs to realize that Carol is choosing all the misery about which she complains. Then she needs to regain control by separating herself from her mother's control, for instance, by choosing to set regular times to visit and not going over for 'emergencies'. In addition, she needs to stop choosing to set herself up for letting her mother take control of her by keeping asking 'How do you feel, Mum?'

THERAPY

The therapy or counselling I practice is called reality therapy. It is based on choice theory and focuses on improving present relationships, almost always disregards past relationships, and depends for its success on creating a good relationship between the client and the counsellor.

William Glasser

THERAPEUTIC GOALS

The main goal of reality therapy is to assist clients to replace external control psychology with choice theory so that they may have healthy, life-enhancing relationships. More specifically, reality therapy has the following goals. First, reality therapists try to impart to clients the choice theory framework for understanding their behaviour. Second, the approach aims to raise clients' awareness of their choosing behaviours and how they try to control their worlds through them. Third, reality therapy increases clients' sense of their responsibility for making choices that work for them. Clients are taught that they need no longer be victims of self-defeating past and current choices. Fourth, clients are assisted to identify and understand their basic needs for survival, belonging, power, freedom and fun. Fifth, reality therapy assists clients to have realistic pictures in their quality worlds to satisfy their basic needs. Sixth, reality therapy teaches clients to evaluate the effectiveness of their total behaviour in light of what they want and choose different behaviours as needed. Seventh, reality therapists assist clients to develop and implement specific behaviours that will help them meet their present and future needs without infringing others' needs. Eighth, reality therapy teaches clients how to avoid allowing themselves to be controlled by others' negative controlling behaviour.

Glasser (1989) writes 'what we really do is help clients to help themselves' (p. 14). Clients are better prepared not only to deal with current problems, but to prevent or solve future problems.

PROCESS OF THERAPY

Most clients who enter reality therapy voluntarily are seen in individual therapy (Glasser and Wubbolding, 1995). The reality therapist discusses professional details which may encompass the therapist's credentials, informed consent and confidentiality, and its limitations. The therapist also briefly explains the reality therapy approach including the rights and responsibilities of therapist and client. Then the therapist invites clients to tell their stories.

The therapist attempts to use good active listening skills, such as reflection and clarification, to create a safe emotional climate in which clients can share their inner worlds. As clients talk, the therapist listens carefully for the extent to which clients engage in external control rather than choice theory psychology and how much responsibility they have taken for past behaviour and how much responsibility they can be expected to take for immediate future choices. Having gained a sense of their perceived locus of control by patiently listening to clients' perception of their problems, the therapist helps them to set therapeutic goals by asking what they want to get from therapy. In particular, therapists encourage clients to focus on what they want to get out of this session. As part of this process, reality therapists offer encouragement to clients for coming to therapy and being willing to work on their problems. Clients are helped to see such behaviours as strengths.

Glasser (1999) saves time in therapy in three main ways. First, he does not probe at length for the problem, since it is always an unsatisfying present relationship. Second, since the problem is in the present, there is no need to make a long investigation into clients' pasts. Third, he focuses on what clients are choosing to do now since the only persons clients can control are themselves.

Wubbolding (Glasser and Wubbolding, 1995) has formulated the process of reality therapy into the following WDEP system, with each letter representing a cluster of skills and techniques for assisting clients to make better choices in their lives.

W   Ask clients what they want.
D   Ask clients what they are doing and their overall direction.
E   Ask clients to conduct a searching self-evaluation.
P   Ask clients to make plans to fulfil their needs more effectively.

W: 'What do you want?'

Therapists attempt to discover what in their quality worlds clients want or are 'controlling for' by their current behaviour. When therapists ask clients 'What do you want?', they are asking 'What do you really want right now?' Therapists try to find out how much clients are in touch with what they really want. The less in touch they are, the more difficult it can be to work with them. Clients may answer that they want to obtain another job, have a better relationship with someone, or find someone to love. Then therapists try to get them to describe in some detail the pictures in their quality world of what they want right now. Reality therapists introduce clients to the choice theory concept of basic needs. Then they can assist the client to explore which of their basic needs they want to satisfy. Brierly (1989) mentions the 'needs tray' technique whereby clients are asked 'If I had a tray and you could have one or more of these needs today before you leave, which would you choose: love, personal power, fun or freedom?' (p. 174). Clients' answers can illuminate where therapy might focus. Clients are in a better position to generate and evaluate pictures in their quality worlds for satisfying needs when clear about the needs they wish to satisfy.

The W refers to perceptions as well as to wants. Therapists discuss with clients their perceived source or locus of control over events in their lives. Reality therapists consider that there is a high correlation between perceived external locus of control and ineffective behaviours. Where clients focus on wanting to change someone else, they are refocused on how they can change themselves, since their behavioural systems cannot control others. Reality therapists help clients to focus on what it is possible for them to achieve and on assuming personal responsibility for achieving their goals.

D: 'What are you doing and in what direction are you going?'

When clients identify what they want and need, the next step is to ask clients 'What are you doing now?' or 'What behaviours are you choosing now?' Frequently clients talk as though they are passive victims of circumstances or of other people. Clients who sit at home depressed and yet say they want love choose the action behaviour of sitting at home, the feeling behaviour of depressing, the thinking behaviour that 'I'm too depressed to do anything', and any accompanying physiological symptoms or behaviours, for instance disturbed sleep.

Often reality therapists ask significant others whom clients are trying to control or feel controlled by to join the client in a session. The purpose of this is to help both clients and therapists understand the client's behaviour better. Sometimes these ancillary people benefit too from the session.

In particular, reality therapists focus on the action and thinking components of total behaviour because they are the components most amenable to change. Also, therapists look for effective behaviours that clients have in their repertoires and may enquire about times in the past when clients functioned effectively. Therapists look for strengths both to help clients understand their assets and also because often it is easier to develop behaviours that are already in clients' repertoires than those which are not.

Reality therapists also ask clients questions about overall direction, such as:

- 'Where are your current choices taking you?'
- 'Are you headed in a direction where you want to be in a month, a year, two years from now?'
- 'Will you describe the direction you are going without making a judgement about it?'

Such global questions increase clients' awareness of how helpful or harmful are their current choices 'from a distance'. This can have the effect of loosening up clients so that they are more ready to evaluate and change their thinking and behaviour (Wubbolding and Glasser, 1995).

E: 'Conduct a thorough self-evaluation'

Reality therapy emphasizes client inner self-evaluation as a central and necessary step in the process of change. Furthermore, assisting clients to self-evaluate speeds the change process. Wubbolding writes: 'In the counselling technique of self evaluation, the helper holds a metaphorical mirror before clients' eyes and asks them to evaluate themselves, to examine the effectiveness of their lives. This is done in an explicit and precise manner' (Wubbolding, 1998, p. 196). Because they have not conducted a thorough self-evaluation, many people seeking change do not realize how and why their behaviour is ineffective.

Reality therapists assist clients to judge their behaviour in light of their wants and needs. As well as 'Is your behaviour getting you what you want?', other questions that reality therapists use to get clients to evaluate their behaviour include: 'Is what you're doing getting you what you want?', 'How is your behaviour helping you?', and 'Is this what is best for you?' The purpose of such questions is to encourage clients to realize that the behaviours they are choosing are not getting them what they claim they need. For instance, the client who wants love and sits at home and depresses is forced to face that by this behaviour he is choosing not to obtain love. The middle-aged client Phyllis, who wants more independence yet keeps going over whenever her mother Carol complains, is led to realize that her behaviour is not getting her what she wants. Evaluating behaviour questions encourage clients to acknowledge that their current choices are not giving them effective control over their lives.

Box 7.4 provides a range of illustrative questions that reality therapists might ask to help clients to evaluate themselves (Wubbolding, 1998). Such questions would be adapted to the specific situation, age and degree of insight of clients.

BOX 7.4

Some illustrative questions that help clients to evaluate themselves

1. 'Is the overall direction of your life a plus or a minus?'
2. 'Are your specific actions effective in getting what you want?'
3. 'Did such and such a behaviour violate the rules?'
4. 'Is what you are doing in line with or against any unwritten rules?'
5. 'Is what you want from others, from yourself, from school, from work, and from society realistically attainable?'
6. 'Is what you want genuinely good for you?'
7. 'Does it help you to view the world – parents, students, friends, employees, etc. – in the manner you have chosen?'
8. 'Are the plans you have made for change genuinely satisfying to you, and are they helpful in attaining your wants (goals that have been evaluated previously)?'

P: 'What is your plan?'

Planning and changing total behaviour involves the following components: searching for alternative behaviours, negotiating plans, getting commitment to plans, developing relevant behaviours, and evaluating progress in implementing plans.

If your current behaviour is not getting you what you want, then what do think might be better?

Once clients realize that their current behaviour is not giving them effective control over their lives, they are ready to look at alternative ways of regaining control. Reality therapists realize that clients are sensitive to being told what to do, so they ask questions that encourage clients to come up with their own better behaviour. Such questions include: 'If your current behaviour is not getting you what you want, then what do you think might be better?', 'What are better choices than those you are currently making?', and 'What can you do to regain more control over your life?'

Tell me your plan

Plans are ways in which clients can satisfy important pictures in their quality worlds outside of therapy. Reality therapists lead clients to develop their own plans rather than do it for them. This involves therapists working closely with clients, yet encouraging their self-reliance. Plans focus particularly on the doing and thinking components of total behaviour, since, to use the earlier analogy, these are the front wheels of the car. Plans can include finding new quality world pictures that are satisfying. Plans should be feasible in terms of clients' abilities and motivation. They should not attempt too much too soon since clients seeking to regain control may need small successes to build up confidence for more difficult tasks. Glasser and Wubbolding summarize what makes for an effective plan when they write: 'The plan should have SAMIC characteristics – i.e., it should be Simple, Attainable, Measurable, Immediate, and Committed to' (1995, p. 306). Frequently, simple planning sheets are used to help clients make plans that fulfil these characteristics.

When planning, reality therapists often ask questions that pin clients down to clarifying the specific details of their plans. For instance, when a teenage girl who has never looked for a job says she is going to do so, the therapist might ask: what time and day she is going to start, what she plans to wear, and how she is going to look up what jobs to apply for. In addition, the therapist might pin down the client regarding what she would do if her first three or four attempts at going for a job interview were unsuccessful. In general, the more reality therapists pin down clients with respect to the details of their behaviour change plans, the more chance clients have of successfully implementing them. Box 7.5 presents an example of developing and implementing a plan (Glasser, 1984b).

BOX 7.5

Example of developing and implementing a plan

The client
Randy was a business school graduate student who was phobicking about going to class because, if he finished business school, he might not obtain the high-level job that he pictured in his quality world.

The plan
Together Glasser and Randy developed a plan focusing on the action component of total behaviour and having implications for the thinking component. Randy was to disclose his phobia to his instructors and ask them if he could sit at the back of the class near the open door, leave quietly if it became too difficult to stay, pull himself together in the empty hall, and then return to class.

The outcome
By implementing his plan Randy was able to regain some control in a previously out-of-control situation. Partly because his instructors did not reject him when he disclosed his phobia, Randy also altered the self-defeating perfectionist pictures in his quality world. He obtained more realistic pictures both of job requirements and of his resources as a potential employee. Randy implemented his plan with the feelings behaviour outcome so that he stopped phobicking almost entirely.

Do you commit yourself to making an effort to follow your plan through?
It is one thing to make a plan and another to have the commitment to implementing it. Reality therapists seek commitments from clients to implementing plans. If therapists have established themselves as need-fulfilling people in clients' quality worlds, clients will take their commitments to them seriously. In addition, clients are making commitments

to themselves. Strong commitments enhance the likelihood of strong follow-through. A key to feelings of control is the ability to make and follow through on plans.

Developing relevant behaviours

Where necessary, reality therapists work with clients to develop specific behaviours required to implement plans. For instance, in the above case of the teenage girl who has never looked for a job, a reality therapist might develop her skills by role-playing an employer interviewing her. Brierly (1989) gives the example of practising conversational skills in her office with Susan, a shy, quiet spoken girl of 20, to build her skill level to where she could succeed when trying out her new behaviours.

Evaluating progress: No excuses and no punishment

Clients are asked to implement plans as homework. Within the context of firm but always friendly relationships, reality therapists check progress by helping clients to self-evaluate their own progress. They assume that commitments to reasonable plans can always be fulfilled. In accepting no excuses therapists might say 'I'm not interested in why you can't do it. I'm interested in when you can do it and how you can do it' (Glasser, 1984a, p. 336). Reality therapists assist clients to keep focusing on what they can do now rather than lose control by looking for reasons to be miserable and ineffective. Frequently reality therapists use confrontations: for instance, 'You said you will do it, when will you do it?' Less frequently, they use even stronger confrontations like firmly saying 'Wake up, you can't control me with your usual behaviour.' However, in instances where plans genuinely turn out to be unreasonable, therapists and clients work together to remake better ones.

Therapists praise clients who succeed in carrying out plans. Any kind of negative statement by therapists is viewed as punishment. Punishment weakens clients' involvement with their therapists and reinforces their failure identities. The negative consequences stemming from not carrying out plans are viewed as quite different from punishment.

In private therapy, termination decisions are made by both therapists and clients on the basis of whether clients have learned to use choice theory sufficiently well to adopt more effective need-fulfilling behaviours in their relationships and lives.

THE THERAPEUTIC RELATIONSHIP

The therapeutic relationship is very important. Glasser and Wubbolding (1995) write: 'The atmosphere in the counseling relationship is one of firmness and friendliness. The ideal relationship is a partnership in which both client and therapist struggle to find more effective behavioral patterns for the client' (p. 304). A first step in reality therapy is to 'make friends' with clients. Most clients who come for therapy are lonely. Therapists should be caring and involved human beings to whom clients can relate and by whom they can feel supported. However, being involved also means being honest about the limits of involvement, such as length of sessions and rules about between-session contact. Compassion, acceptance and patience are further desirable therapist attributes. In addition, without trivializing their work together, both therapists and clients are encouraged to use humour.

In reality therapy a tension exists between showing acceptance and communicating to clients that their needs must be met and their problems solved in the present. Reality therapists try to avoid allowing clients to control them with the same inadequate behaviours that they use to control others, such as angering, depressing and anxietying. Usually reality therapists, while showing sympathy for what clients have experienced, do not allow them to dwell on past hurts and sufferings. However, on occasion, clients may be allowed to dwell on their pasts and talk about their feelings to strengthen the relationship for subsequent work on the role of their present choices in sustaining problems.

Reality therapists are strongly committed to their clients. Glasser (1984a) advises them 'Never give up' (p. 337). Frequently, reality therapists tell clients 'Don't give up so easily.' Therapists persevere with clients to the point where clients realize that therapists will neither allow themselves to be controlled nor give up. Good friends do not give up easily.

THERAPEUTIC INTERVENTIONS

Following are two broad categories of interventions – teaching choice theory and questioning within the WDEP system – that characterize all stages of reality therapy. Applying the interventions depends on such factors as the nature of the client, including his or her culture, and how the therapist likes to work.

Teaching choice theory

Reality therapists make an active effort to teach choice theory to any client whom they believe may be receptive to these ideas. Rather than focus on the past, Glasser helps clients make better choices now in their lives. He writes: 'To do so, I begin to teach the clients choice theory, which they can then use to make better choices and learn to handle many problems that might have lengthened therapy. It's a kind of therapeutic stitch in time that saves nine' (Glasser, 1999, p. 117). Reality therapists approach teaching choice theory in a number of ways.

Initial structuring
Reality therapists try to instil hope in clients early on by letting them know that, during therapy, they will learn to make better choices and, in doing so, gain better control over their lives. Clients are also informed that they will have to work hard to achieve and maintain this control.

Using choice theory concepts
Reality therapists teach choice theory concepts by getting clients to rework their problems within them. For instance, clients learn to use concepts like basic needs, quality world and total behaviour. In addition, they learn the basic assumption of choice theory that their behaviour is always their best attempt at controlling the world and themselves so that they can best satisfy their basic needs for survival, belonging, power, freedom and

fun. Furthermore, therapists work with clients on the assumption that the only person whose behaviour they can control is their own.

Bibliotherapy

Assuming they are receptive and capable of understanding the ideas, reality therapists can ask clients to read Glasser's book *Choice Theory: A New Psychology of Personal Freedom* (1999) and together they can discuss its contents. Then therapists and clients can analyse the client's problems according to choice theory. Though not necessary to therapy, much time may be saved by clients reading and using this book. In addition, clients can be helped to become creative in how they use choice theory language, as contrasted with external control language, by reading all or some of the examples in Glasser's and his wife Carleen Glasser's book *The Language of Choice Theory* (1999). Box 7.6 shows two examples in the area of love and marriage from this book (pp. 48–51).

BOX 7.6

Examples of the language of choice theory

Example 1
External control
'Why are you so afraid of making a commitment? Our relationship is going nowhere! I'm tired of waiting for you to make up your mind. Marry me or I'm leaving.'

Choice theory alternative
'Since we're spending the weekend together, I want to have a really good time. I've decided not to talk about our future. In fact, I'm not ever going to talk about it again. Ever! It's up to you. And I'm not going to nag or criticize you. I've just given up begging you to marry me. I haven't given up on getting married.

Example 2
External control
'You said you'd call last night, but you didn't. You'd better have a damn good reason why.'

Choice theory alternative
'It's good to hear from you. What's happening? Any news about that contract you've been working on so hard?

Questioning within the WDEP system

Reality therapists need to develop and use good questioning skills within the WDEP system. Skilled questioning can accelerate the therapy process more than if the therapist had taken a more passive stance. Purposes of questioning include: entering clients' inner worlds, gathering information, giving information, enabling clients to mentally 'stand back' and evaluate their situations or lives with greater perspective, and helping clients take more effective control of their lives by making better choices (Brickell and Wubbolding, 1996; Wubbolding, 1988).

The ability of therapists to ask skilled questions within the WDEP system is not an end in itself. The ultimate purpose of reality therapist questioning is to help clients develop self-questioning and self-evaluation skills for when they are no longer in therapy. Reality therapy is an educational process in which therapists heighten clients' awareness of themselves as persons who can make good or poor choices. Therapists also train clients to engage in a process of questioning the wisdom of their choices. An example is that of a therapist assisting a client to relate better by developing the habit of asking her/himself before raising sensitive issues with a partner: 'How might I phrase that in choice theory rather than in external control language?'

CASE MATERIAL

In *Choice Theory*, Glasser presents excerpts from a number of different cases illustrating his use the choice theory framework in reality therapy. He conducts and comments on an imaginary initial interview with Franscesca, the leading female character from James Waller's *The Bridges of Madison County*. A brief extramarital romantic interlude has left Franscesca feeling that she is dead inside, stuck in the confines of her current rural life and marriage. Glasser shows how he instils hope in her that she can start rebuilding her life. Another case excerpt shows Glasser helping Tina move from external control psychology to choice theory in her relationship with Kevin, whom she had been dating for two years and wanted to marry.

A further case example is that of using reality therapy with Terri, who came to see Glasser because she was unable to have satisfying emotional and sexual relationships in that, as soon as she would get close to a man, she chose to behave in ways that destroyed the relationship. Other case material in *Choice Theory* includes Glasser's work with Linda, a divorced woman suffering from tension headaches and a troubled relationship with her 16-year-old daughter Samantha, and Glasser conducting structured marital therapy with Ed and Karen whose quality world pictures of each other as husband and wife were very shaky, but still intact.

In 1996, Glasser replaced control theory with choice theory, so case material before then must be viewed with that change in mind. Glasser and Wubbolding (1995) present a typical first session with Louis, unemployed for eight months and unsuccessfully looking for a job at middle management level. Louis also had long-standing tensions with his wife Sally. In the same chapter, Glasser and Wubbolding present the case example of Fay who, when men got too close, turned away from them. Wubbolding (1988) illustrates the use of reality therapy in two cases: Jane, a divorced mother of two, who came to see him having previously been diagnosed as manic-depressive; and Helen and Stephen, who had considerable strengths, yet a number of serious areas of conflict in their marriage. Another source of reality therapy case material is the book of thirteen case studies, each written by a different certified reality therapist, edited by Naomi Glasser (1989), Glasser's first wife.

FURTHER DEVELOPMENTS

Reality therapy based on the choice theory framework is used in marital therapy. Early on it is important to clarify whether the partners want to evaluate the advantages and disadvantages of continuing the marriage or whether they have made a definite decision to try to preserve the marriage. Marital therapy focuses on how couples can live together within a choice theory framework without attempting to control one another in ways in which they do not want to be controlled.

Reality therapists also work in groups, often as joint leaders. Group members can help each other to evaluate the adequacy of current behaviours in satisfying needs and quality world pictures, planning alternative behaviours, and making commitments. For example, a member's plan can be written down and a public commitment made by having each member of the group read and sign it.

Reality therapy and choice theory principles are widely used in educational settings. Many of Glasser's books (Glasser, 1990, 1992, 1993) have been focused on improving the skills of administrators and teachers in creating environments in which students can learn to take effective control of their lives. Glasser's book *Choice Theory* includes chapters on the application of choice theory in quality schools. Regarding the workplace, Glasser has written about the difference between boss management, based on external control psychology, and lead management, based on choice theory (for example, Glasser, 1999).

Reality therapy as a system is being developed not only by Glasser, but by prominent adherents such as Robert Wubbolding in the United States and John Brickell in Britain (Wubbolding, 2000; Wubbolding and Brickell, 1999). In 1981, the *Journal of Reality Therapy* was launched, edited by Lawrence Litvak. This journal is now called the *International Journal of Reality Therapy*. By 1999, over 5,000 people had completed the reality therapy certification process worldwide (Glasser, 1999). In addition to the United States, training opportunities in reality therapy exist in Britain and Australia as well as many other countries.

SUMMARY

- *Reality therapy is based on choice theory. Choice theory's fundamental assumption is that people's behaviour always represents their best attempt at choosing how to control the world to satisfy their needs.*
- *People's basic needs comprise the physical need for survival and the psychological needs for belonging, power, freedom and fun.*
- *People develop personal quality worlds consisting of pictures of how to satisfy their needs.*
- *Total behaviour is the sum of the four components of acting, thinking, feeling and physiology.*
- *People as control systems behave to get the quality world pictures they want.*
- *Children develop their quality worlds through experiences of getting their needs satisfied. They learn total behaviours by creatively choosing different ways to control the world and by imitation.*

- *Reasons that people choose to maintain their misery are: to keep angering under control, to attract help, and to avoid attempting more effective action.*

- *Reasons that most people remain unaware that they choose misery are: mistaking short-term pure feelings for long-term feeling behaviours, most of their painful choices becoming automatic, and not wanting to lose self-esteem. People can also choose to stay controlled by others' misery.*

- *Reality therapists always require a clear choice theory reason for anything they do. The main goal of reality therapy is to help clients make better choices so that they can take effective control of their lives.*

- *After initial introductions and dealing with professional issues, the process of reality therapy can be viewed within the WDEP system: W, ask clients what they want; D, ask clients what they are doing and their overall direction; E, ask clients to conduct a searching self-evaluation; and P, ask clients to make plans to fulfil their needs more effectively.*

- *The therapeutic relationship is characterized by involvement, compassion, caring, honesty, and not giving up on clients.*

- *Reality therapists teach choice theory through their initial structuring, using choice theory concepts, and by bibliotherapy.*

- *Reality therapy relies heavily on skilful questioning to help clients share their inner worlds, to get and give information, to encourage self-evaluation, and to help clients to make better choices. Clients are encouraged to develop skills of self-questioning and self-evaluation independent of their therapists.*

- *Applications of reality therapy and choice theory include marriage therapy, group therapy, working with school administrators and teachers to develop quality schools, and training managers in lead management.*

- *Reality therapy has its own journal and a reality therapist certification programme exists with over 5,000 successful graduates to date.*

REVIEW AND PERSONAL QUESTIONS

REVIEW QUESTIONS

1. What are the main differences between external control psychology and choice theory?
2. List and define the five basic needs.
3. Define and identify the content of the quality world.
4. What is total behaviour? Provide an example illustrating each element of total behaviour.
5. Why do people choose their misery and how do people remain unaware that they are choosing misery?
6. What are the goals of reality therapy?
7. Define the content of and therapist skills required for each element of the WDEP system outlining the process of reality therapy:

- • What do you want?
- • What are you doing and what is your overall direction?
- • Conduct thorough self-evaluation.
- • What is your plan?

8. In reality therapy, what is the nature of the therapeutic relationship?
9. How might reality therapists teach choice theory to clients?
10. Why is it important for reality therapists to become skilled questioners and for clients to become skilled at questioning and evaluating themselves?

PERSONAL QUESTIONS

1. Do you think Glasser's view of basic needs is accurate in reflecting your basic needs?
2. To what extent do you consider the pictures in your quality world are helpful or harmful to fulfilling your basic needs?
3. In an area where your current total behaviour in a relationship is not getting you what you want, apply the WDEP system to yourself so that you can make better choices in future.
4. What relevance, if any, has reality therapy and its choice theory framework for how you conduct therapy?
5. What relevance, if any, has choice theory for how you live?

ANNOTATED BIBLIOGRAPHY

Glasser, W. (1999). *Choice Theory: A New Psychology of Personal Freedom.* New York: HarperPerennial.

   Glasser makes a passionate plea for a shift from relationship-destroying external control psychology to relationship-enhancing choice theory psychology. There are chapters on the main concepts of choice theory as well as on the practice of reality therapy within a choice theory framework in marital therapy, families, schooling and the workplace. In addition, Glasser presents his ideas on the quality community and on how to redefine your personal freedom.

Glasser, W. and Glasser, C. (1999). *The Language of Choice Theory.* New York: HarperPerennial.

   This small companion volume to *Choice Theory* contains a brief introduction highlighting the difference between traditional external control language and creative choice theory language. The remainder of the book comprises a series of examples contrasting external control language with its choice theory alternative in four areas: parent to child, love and marriage, teacher to student, and manager to employee.

Glasser, W. (1984b). *Control Theory: A New Explanation of How We Control our Lives.* New York: Harper and Row.

   This book starts with presenting the major concepts of control theory such as the basic needs, pictures in our heads, total behaviour, and people as control systems. The middle part of the book includes chapters on psychosomatic illness and addictive drugs. The contents of the final part of the book have a self-help emphasis on taking control of your life and health, controlling others or ourselves with pain and misery, and how to start using control theory. The book does not focus on the use of control theory in therapy.

Glasser, W. and Wubbolding, R. (1995). Reality therapy. In R. J. Corsini and D. Wedding (eds). *Current Psychotherapies* (5th edition, 293–321). Itasca, IL: Peacock.
   This is an authoritative account of the theory and practice of reality therapy just prior to the change from a control theory to a choice theory framework.

Glasser, W. (1965). *Reality Therapy: A New Approach to Psychiatry.* New York: Harper and Row.
   This book represents an evolutionary stage in the development of reality therapy. Part one, entitled 'Theory', covers basic concepts of reality therapy and the differences between reality therapy and conventional therapy. Part two, entitled 'Practice', contains chapters on the use of reality therapy with seriously delinquent adolescent girls, hospitalized psychotic patients and in private practice. The final chapter discusses the application of reality therapy to the public schools.

Wubbolding, R. and Brickell, J. (1999). *Counselling with Reality Therapy.* Bicester, Oxon: Winslow Press Ltd.
   This first British published book on reality therapy provides an introduction to choice theory concepts, creating the counselling environment and the 'Cycle of Counselling' procedures that can be applied to virtually any setting, including coaching and managing. Applications to specific areas include: one-to-one counselling, working with groups, relationship counselling, and working in schools.

Wubbolding, R. (2000). *Reality Therapy for the 21st Century.* Bristol, PA: Accelerated Development.
   Reality therapy is extended with an emphasis on self-evaluation. Special attention is given to cross-cultural applications. The book includes an interview with William Glasser and a chapter summarizing the research that validates using the reality therapy system.

REFERENCES AND FURTHER READING

Barr, N. I. (1974). The responsible world of reality therapy. *Psychology Today*, *7* (9), 64–8.

Brickell, J. and Wubbolding, R. (1996). Understanding reality therapy. *CMS News*, *47*, 5–7. (CMS stands for the Counselling in Medical Settings Division of the British Association for Counselling.)

Brierly, S. A. (1989). Breaking away from the family mold and developing a strong comfortable identity. In N. Glasser (ed.). *Control Theory in the Practice of Reality Therapy: Case Studies* (163–80). New York: Harper and Row.

Evans, D. B. (1982). What are you doing? An interview with William Glasser. *Personnel and Guidance Journal*, *60*, 460–5.

Glasser, N. (ed.) (1980). *What Are You Doing? How People Are Helped Through Reality Therapy.* New York: Harper and Row.

Glasser, N. (ed.) (1989). *Control Theory in the Practice of Reality Therapy: Case Studies.* New York: Harper and Row.

Glasser, W. (1961). *Mental Health or Mental Illness.* New York: Harper and Row.

Glasser, W. (1965). *Reality Therapy: A New Approach to Psychiatry.* New York: Harper and Row.

Glasser, W. (1976). *Positive Addiction.* New York: Harper and Row.

Glasser, W. (1981). *Stations of the Mind.* New York: Harper and Row.

Glasser, W. (1984a). Reality therapy. In R. J. Corsini (ed.). *Current Psychotherapies* (3rd edition, 32–53). Itasca, IL: Peacock.

Glasser, W. (1984b). *Control Theory: A New Explanation of How we Control our Lives.* New York: Harper and Row.

Glasser, W. (1989). Control theory. In N. Glasser (ed.) *Control Theory in the Practice of Reality Therapy: Case Studies* (1–15). New York: Harper and Row.

Glasser, W. (1990). *The Quality School: Managing Students Without Coercion.* New York: Harper and Row.

Glasser, W. (1992). *The Quality School: Managing Students Without Coercion* (2nd edition). New York: Harper and Row.

Glasser, W. (1993). *The Quality School Teacher.* New York: Harper and Row.

Glasser, W. (1995). *Staying Together: A Control Theory Guide to a Lasting Marriage.* New York: HarperCollins.

Glasser, W. (1999). *Choice Theory: A New Psychology of Personal Freedom.* New York: HarperPerennial.

Glasser, W. and Glasser, C. (1999). *The Language of Choice Theory.* New York: HarperPerennial.

Glasser, W. and Wubbolding, R. (1995). Reality therapy. In R. J. Corsini and D. Wedding (eds). *Current Psychotherapies* (5th edition, 293–321). Itasca, IL: Peacock.

Powers, W. T. (1973). *Behavior: The Control of Perception.* Chicago: Aldine.

Waller, J. (1992). *The Bridges of Madison County.* Secacus, NJ: Warner Books.

Wubbolding, R. (1985). Characteristics of the inner picture album. *Journal of Reality Therapy,* 5 (1), 28–30.

Wubbolding, R. (1988). *Using Reality Therapy.* New York: Harper and Row.

Wubbolding, R. (1998). Client inner self-evaluation: A necessary prelude to change. In H. Rosenthal (ed.). *Favorite Counseling and Therapy Techniques* (196–7). Washington, DC: Accelerated Development.

Wubbolding, R. and Brickell, J. (1999). *Counselling with Reality Therapy.* Bicester, Oxon: Winslow Press Ltd.

Wubbolding, R. (2000). *Reality Therapy for the 21st Century.* Bristol, PA: Accelerated Development.

Two useful American reality therapy addresses are:

The William Glasser Institute, 22024 Lassen Street, Suite 118, Chatsworth, CA 91311-360, USA. Tel: (818) 700-8000. Fax: (818) 700-0555. e-mail: wginst@earthlink.com Website: hhtp://www.wglasserinst.com

Dr Robert Wubbolding, Director, Center for Reality Therapy, 7672 Montgomery Street, Cincinnati, Ohio 45236, USA. Tel: (513) 561-1911. Fax: (513) 561-3568. e-mail: wubsrt@fuse.net

8

Existential Therapy

Existential psychotherapy is a dynamic approach to therapy which focuses on concerns that are rooted in the individual's existence.

Irvin Yalom

INTRODUCTION

The word 'existence' is derived from the Latin word *existere*, literally meaning 'to stand out, to emerge'. Existence is not a static process, but entails the process of coming into being or becoming. Existential approaches to therapy are concerned with the science and processes of being. The science of being is known as *ontology*, from *ontos*, the Greek word for 'being'. Existential therapists assist clients to stand out or to affirm their existences, despite and within the constraints involved in existence.

The existential approaches to therapy are rooted in existential philosophy. Prominent existential philosophers include Kierkegaard, Nietzsche, Heidegger and Sartre. Kierkegaard's existentialism was within a Christian framework and he described the dread, anxiety and despair – 'the sickness unto death' – of humans estranged from their essential nature (Kierkegaard, 1954). Nietzsche was an atheist existentialist who presented a nihilistic picture of the world in which 'God is dead' as the background for human self-affirmation (Tillich, 1952). Heidegger's (1962) *Being and Time* focused on the quest for being and analysed the concept of *Dasein*, being there or existence. Sartre, a Marxist, echoed Nietzsche's thoughts about a godless world. He emphasized humans' inescapable need, in their struggle against despair and non-being, to make the choices that make the essence of their existences (Sartre, 1956). So long as they are alive, humans have no exit from the need to define themselves.

Existential approaches to therapy have also been influenced by religious philosophers, such as Buber, the Jewish theologian, and Tillich, the Protestant Christian theologian. Buber (1965, 1970) thought that humans were not separate entities, but existed as creatures of the in-between. The two special types of in-between relationships were 'I–It' relationships, involving functional relationships in which others were objects, and 'I–Thou' relationships, involving mutual influence and a full experiencing of another. Tillich's (1952) book *The Courage to Be* examines human existence within a religious framework. For Tillich the courage to be is 'the ethical act in which man affirms his own being in spite of those elements which conflict with his essential self-affirmation' (p. 3).

Existential psychotherapeutic approaches go beyond dealing with surface problems to assist clients to confront the basic issues of their existence: anxiety, despair, death, loneliness, alienation, and meaninglessness. All the preceding issues have the potential to generate 'existence pain' (Yalom, 1989). Existential approaches to therapy are also concerned with questions of freedom, responsibility, love, and creativity.

Yalom (1980) observes that therapeutic approaches 'reflect, and are shaped by, the pathology that they must treat' (p. 223). He distinguishes between the therapy needs of restrictive and sexually repressed end-of-the-nineteenth-century Viennese people and the therapy needs of the compulsively permissive end-of-the-twentieth-century American culture. In former times, much of people's existences were defined for them, whereas now people face far more of a challenge to create and define their own existences.

There are many existential approaches to therapy. Yalom and May's existential therapy and Frankl's logotherapy are two such approaches that widely influence contemporary counselling and psychotherapy. This chapter describes the theory and practice of Yalom and May's existential therapy, and the next chapter reviews Frankl's logotherapy.

IRVIN YALOM AND ROLLO MAY

Irvin Yalom (1931–)

In 1931, Irvin Yalom was born in Washington DC, the son of Russian immigrant parents who, in the 1920s, had arrived penniless in the United States. His parents had virtually no formal education, never read books and struggled to survive economically by running a grocery store. The family lived in a cockroach-infested apartment above the store, in a poor, black neighbourhood of Washington. Though he admired his father, Yalom 'spent too many hours in my childhood silently hating my mother's vicious tongue' (Yalom, 1989, p. 147). For instance, when Yalom was 13, his father suffered a serious coronary in the early hours of the morning. As mother, father and son waited for the family physician to arrive: '"It's all your fault," she shouted, "you did this – all the aggravation, all the grief you gave him – you did this to him. You. You"' (Yalom, 1998, p. 437). Yalom grew up facing two additional existential perils because 'In the streets, the black attacked me for my whiteness, and in school, the white attacked me for my Jewishness' (Yalom, 1989, p. 88). However, reading – especially reading fiction – provided a refuge from the external harshness and, early in life, Yalom developed the notion that novel-writing was the finest thing a person could do (Yalom, 2000).

Facing a choice between medical school and going into business with his father, Yalom opted for the former. In 1952, he received a BA degree from George Washington University and, in 1956, obtained a MD from Boston University. During the next six years, Yalom served as an intern at New York's Mt Sinai Hospital, a psychiatric resident at Baltimore's Johns Hopkins Hospital, a consultant at the Patuxent Institution in Maryland, and a US Army Captain in Honolulu. In 1962, Yalom was appointed an instructor in psychiatry at Stanford University School of Medicine, followed by becoming an assistant professor, associate professor and professor in 1963, 1968 and 1973 respectively.

In 1993, Yalom retired from Stanford and now devotes his time to writing psychotherapy novels and stories. In 1963 Yalom married his wife Marilyn, who received a PhD in

Comparative Literature from Johns Hopkins and went on to become a university professor. The Yaloms have four grown-up children and an increasing number of grandchildren.

Yalom has published numerous scientific papers. In addition, his professional writing includes: *The Theory and Practice of Group Psychotherapy, Existential Psychotherapy, Inpatient Group Psychotherapy*, and co-authorship of *Encounter Groups: First Facts, Everyday Gets a Little Closer*, and *Concise Guide to Group Psychotherapy*. Furthermore, Yalom has collaborated with his former therapist, Rollo May, to write and keep updating a chapter about existential therapy for a current psychotherapies textbook (May and Yalom, 2000).

Yalom's psychological novels and non-fiction stories include: *Love's Executioner and Other Tales of Psychotherapy, When Nietzsche Wept* – which won the Commonwealth Club's Gold Medal for Fiction for the Best Novel of 1992, *Lying on the Couch* and *Momma and the Meaning of Life*. Yalom intends these best-selling books both as entertainment and as pedagogical works representing a new genre of teaching psychotherapy novels and stories. A Yalom compilation, entitled *The Yalom Reader*, combines material illustrating his three major interests: group psychotherapy, existential psychotherapy, and writing.

Rollo May (1909–94)

In 1909, Rollo May was born in Ohio. One of seven children, his father was a YMCA secretary who moved his family quite often. May's parents' relationship was discordant and his family life unhappy, a stimulus for his later interest in therapy. May describes his mother as a 'bitch-kitty on wheels' (Rabinowitz, Good and Cozad, 1989, p. 437). His only sister, who was older than him, was psychotic and spent some time in a mental hospital. May obtained relief from family misery by sitting and playing on the shores of the St Clair river.

A rebel during high school, May studied liberal arts at Oberlin College, obtaining his BA in 1930. May then went to Greece for three years where he taught boys aged 12–18 in a gymnasium and studied ancient Greek civilization. In addition, one summer vacation he went to Vienna where he studied individual psychology with Alfred Adler. In 1938, May received his BD from Union Theological Seminary, where he met and developed an ongoing friendship with Paul Tillich, who had recently been expelled from Nazi Germany, and who was a major influence on his thinking. In 1949 May obtained his PhD in clinical psychology from Teachers College of Columbia University.

While pursuing his doctoral degree, May came down with tuberculosis. His recovery involved spending nearly two years bed-ridden in an upstate New York sanatorium where he spend much time reading and thinking about the nature of anxiety. Ultimately, this work led to his writing *The Meaning of Anxiety*. During his New York City years, May conducted a private practice, authored books and articles, was an adjunct professor at the New School of Social Research and New York University, and served as a training analyst and supervisor at the William Alanson White Institute. May then lived in San Franscisco where he wrote, taught and saw clients. May was divorced twice and, in 1989, confided 'I've always had good friends and lovers, but I'm scared to death of marriage' (Rabinowitz, Good and Cozad, 1989, p. 437). He died on 22 October 1994, at the age of 84.

Reflecting his early interest in English literature, May has been a prolific author of books and articles. Over a long period he has been at the forefront of applying existential and humanistic ideas to counselling. May's books include *The Art of Counseling*, *The Meaning of Anxiety*, his edited book *Existential Psychology* (which includes two important chapters by him), *Psychology and the Human Dilemma*, *Love and Will*, *Power and Innocence: A Search for Sources of Violence*, *The Courage to Create*, *Freedom and Destiny*, and *My Quest for Beauty*. Though he enjoyed his twilight years, towards the end of his life May observed: 'I wouldn't want to go through this life again. I mean, one time is enough. I don't know that I'd do anything differently, but it would be too boring' (Rabinowitz, Good and Cozad, 1989, p. 439).

THEORY

The reality of death is important in psychotherapy in two distinct ways: death awareness may act as a 'boundary situation' and instigate a radical shift in life perspective; and death is a primary source of anxiety.

Irvin Yalom

BASIC CONCEPTS

Being and non-being

May (May, Angel and Ellenberger, 1958) observes that 'being' is a participle of a verb and implies that someone is in the process of becoming something. He states that, when used as a noun, 'being' means *potentia*, the source of potential. An analogy is that the acorn has the potential to become an oak. This analogy is only partially accurate for humans since they have the capacity for self-consciousness. Humans can choose their own being. The choices that they make about being are not just concerned with whether or not to commit suicide, but are relevant to every instant of their lives.

Because of widespread collectivist and conformist trends in society, modern humans have repressed their sense of being. People's sense of being refers to their whole experience of existence, both conscious and unconscious. They need to experience themselves as beings in the world and have a basic 'I-Am' experience, expressed by one of May's clients as 'Since, I Am, I have the right to be' (May *et al.*, 1958, p. 43). The 'I-Am' experience is not the solution, but rather the precondition for the solution to clients' problems.

The opposite of being is non-being or nothingness. Existence implies the possibility of not existing. Death is the most obvious form of non-being. However, there are numerous other threats to being in the form of loss of potentiality through anxiety and conformity, and through lack of clear self-awareness. In addition, destructive hostility and physical sickness can pose threats to being. However, people who are able to confront non-being can emerge with a heightened sense of being, including a greater awareness not only of themselves, but of others and the world around them.

The three forms of being-in-the-world

Existential therapy distinguishes three modes of world that characterize people's existence as being-in-the-world. First, there is the *Umwelt*, the 'world around'. The *Umwelt* represents the natural world, the laws of nature and the environment. For animals and human beings alike, the *Umwelt* includes biological needs, drives, instincts. Also, it includes each organism's daily and life cycles. The natural world is accepted as real.

Second, there is the *Mitwelt*, the 'with-world'. This is the social world of relating to fellow humans singly and in groups. Both in personal and group relationships people influence each other and the structure of meaning that develops. May writes: 'The essence of relationship is that in the encounter both persons are changed' (May *et al.*, 1958, p. 63). How people relate in intimate relationships, for instance their degree of commitment, influences the meaning of the relationships for them. Similarly, how much of themselves people put into groups influences the meaning of the groups for them.

Third, there is the *Eigenwelt*, or 'own world'. The *Eigenwelt* is uniquely present in humans and entails self-consciousness and self-awareness. Also, the *Eigenwelt* entails grasping the personal meaning of a thing or person. Individuals need to own their relationships to things and people: for instance, 'This flower is beautiful' means 'For me, this flower is beautiful.'

The three modes of being are interrelated. For instance, love entails more than the biological drives of the *Umwelt*. Furthermore, it entails more than the social or interpersonal relationship of the *Mitwelt*. In addition, love requires the *Eigenwelt*, in that, when relating to another, people need to be sufficient to themselves.

Normal and neurotic anxiety

To be human is to be anxious. Anxiety is an unavoidable part of human life. May (1950) distinguishes between normal and neurotic anxiety. He defines anxiety as 'the threat to our existence or to values we identify with our existence' (May, 1977, p. 205). In the course of normal development everyone experiences various threats to their existence. One source of normal anxiety is humans' existential vulnerability to nature, sickness and death. Another source is the need to progressively become independent from parents with the tensions and crises that this process can create. However, people can use such threats constructively as learning experiences and continue to develop.

The reaction of normal anxiety has three characteristics. First, it is proportionate to the objective threat in the situation being confronted. Second, it does not involve repression. Third, it can be used creatively to identify and confront the conditions bringing it about. Existential therapists view their main function as helping clients come to terms with the normal anxieties that are part of human existence.

Neurotic anxiety possesses the opposite characteristics to normal anxiety. Neurotic anxiety is a disproportionate reaction to an objective threat, involves repression, and is destructive rather than constructive. Another way of viewing neurotic anxiety is that people subjectively react to objective threats in terms of their inner psychological patterns and conflicts. The repression and blocking of awareness involved in neurotic anxiety leave people more vulnerable to threats since they lose access to important information with which to distinguish and deal with the threats.

Normal, neurotic and existential guilt

Like anxiety, guilt is part of human existence. A distinction may be drawn between normal and neurotic guilt. Neurotic guilt derives from *imagined* transgressions against others, parental injunctions, and societal conventions. Normal guilt is a call to conscience and sensitizes people to the ethical aspects of their behaviour.

Existential or ontological guilt represents another form of guilt. May distinguishes between three forms of existential guilt. The first form, which corresponds to *Eigenwelt*, is failure to live up to potential. As such, people can be guilty of transgressions against themselves. The second form, which corresponds to *Mitwelt*, relates to distorting the reality of one's fellow humans. The third form of existential guilt, which involves *Umwelt* as well as the other two modes-of-being, is 'separation guilt' in relation to nature as a whole.

Existential guilt is universal. It is rooted in self-awareness. Existential guilt does not arise from violation of parental injunctions, 'but arises from the fact that I can see myself as the one who can choose or fail to choose' (May *et al.*, 1958, p. 55). Thus existential guilt is inexorably linked with the notion of personal responsibility. Existential guilt is not in itself a form of neurotic guilt, though it possesses the potential to turn into neurotic guilt. However, if correctly addressed, existential guilt can have constructive outcomes both in terms of greater humility and sensitivity to others and in increased creativity.

Transcendence

The unique capacity of humans to think and talk in symbols allows them the possibility of transcending time and space. Humans can project themselves into the past and into the future. In addition humans can transcend themselves in their social relations and see themselves as others see them and give appropriate weight to others' perceptions. The capacity to transcend immediate concrete situations provides humans with the basis of both their freedom and their responsibility.

'Transcendence' is derived from the Latin word *transcendere*, meaning 'to climb over and beyond'. The ability to transcend immediate situations is part of the ontological nature of human beings. Existing involves humans in a continuous process of emerging in which they transcend their pasts and presents to create their futures. Unless seriously ill or blocked by anxiety or despair, all humans engage in this process.

Existential ultimate concerns

Yalom (1980) has identified four existential ultimate concerns – death, freedom, isolation, and meaninglessness – with considerable relevance for counselling and therapy. Each concern begets a different existential conflict.

Death

Life and death, being and non-being, are interdependent rather than concurrent. Death is the fundamental source of anxiety, whether it be neurotic, normal or existential. Perhaps the term 'death terror' denotes the force of death concern better than 'death anxiety'. Death anxiety, the fear of ceasing to be, can be both conscious and unconscious. From early in their lives children are extremely preoccupied with death. Strong death anxiety is likely to be repressed. To cope with the terror of potential non-being, people erect denial-based defences against death anxiety. To a large extent psychopathology has its origins in failed attempts to transcend death.

The first existential conflict is that between awareness of the inevitability of death and the wish to continue to live: the conflict between fear of non-being and wishing to be.

Freedom

Humans are 'condemned to freedom' (Sartre, 1956, p. 631). Humans do not live in a well-ordered and structured universe. There is no secure ground undergirding existence. Rather there is lack of structure and groundlessness which generates both anxiety and dread. Because of their freedom, humans are also condemned to responsibility. They are not only responsible for imbuing the world with significance, but entirely responsible for their lives, for their actions and their failures to act.

The second existential conflict is that between people's confrontation with ground-lessness and freedom, and their wish for ground and structure.

Isolation

There are three forms of isolation:

1. *Interpersonal isolation*, often experienced as loneliness, means that people are in varying degrees cut off from others. This may be through deficient social skills, psychopathology or by choice and of necessity.
2. *Intrapersonal isolation* means that people are blocked from awareness of or dissoci-ated from parts of themselves. Whereas interpersonal isolation may not contain pathology, intrapersonal isolation does so by definition.
3. *Existential isolation* is rooted in the human condition in that each person enters, lives in, and leaves the world alone. Ultimately there is an unbridgeable gap between self and others. Yalom (1980) observes that existential isolation refers to an even more fundamental form of isolation, namely 'Separation from the world' (p. 355).

The third existential conflict is that between people's awareness of their fundamental isolation and their wish for contact, protection and to be a part of a larger whole.

Meaninglessness

What is the meaning of life? Humans require coherence, purpose and significance. They organize random stimuli into figure and ground. They are neuropsychologically orga-nized to seek patterns and meaning. However, the human paradox is that of existence in an indifferent universe with no predetermined meaning. A distinction may be made between cosmic meaning, whether human life fits into some overall cosmic pattern, and terrestrial meaning, the meaning of my life. With the decline in religious beliefs, modern humans are faced with the need to discover secular personal meaning in the absence of cosmic meaning.

The fourth existential conflict is that of humans confronting their need for meaning in an indifferent world that has no meaning.

Existential psychodynamics

In personality theory, the term 'dynamics' relates to the concept of energy or force. The notion of psychodynamic conflict relates to the clash between opposing forces. The Freudian model of dynamic conflict was that of the clash between ego and instinctual sexual and aggressive drives. To Freud, the deeper conflicts were associated with the earliest psychosexual conflicts.

Existential psychodynamics differs in two important ways from Freudian psychodynamics. First, existential conflicts and existential anxiety flow from people's inescapable confrontations with the givens of existence: death, freedom, isolation and meaninglessness. Second, existential psychodynamics does not assume a developmental or archaeological model where first is synonymous with deep. When existential therapists and clients explore deeply, they do so not by focusing on everyday concerns, but thinking deeply about existential ultimate concerns.

ACQUISITION

Despite existential anxieties and conflicts being inescapable parts of life, the question still remains of how people develop different modes of dealing with the ultimate concerns of existence.

Death

Young children, even though not intellectually equipped to understand what death means, grasp its essence. Yalom (1980) believes that children then deny their first knowledge of death. Mechanisms of denial include such beliefs as death is temporary, children do not die, I will not die because I am special, and there is an ultimate rescuer. Coming to terms with the concept of death is a major developmental task which some children handle better than others.

Exposure to death can be for good or ill. Factors likely to be helpful include the presence of already existing ego resources, good genes, and supportive adults able to deal with their own death anxieties. However, exposure to death can be traumatic when these factors are insufficiently present. Deaths of siblings and of parents can be especially frightening and exceed children's coping resources. Research indicates that both neurotic and psychotic psychiatric patients have lost a parent more frequently than the general population. The degree of cultural acceptance of death also influences how much anxiety death will generate in both adults and children.

The quality of death education that parents offer to their children affects their awareness and acceptance of death. Children are often shielded from death by misinformation, denial, fairy tales, euphemisms, and assurances that children do not die. As with sex, children do not ignore the issue, but turn to other sources of information of varying degrees of reliability. Western cultures offer no real guidelines about how parents should educate their children about death and this is not helped by many adults seeking comfort in childlike beliefs.

Freedom

The modern-day emphasis on freedom and responsibility as existential concerns derives from the breaking down of traditional belief systems, religions, rituals and rules. In the twentieth century, there was a rapid disintegration of structures and values. Permissive parenting has now left many young people with the need to choose but without clear guidelines as to how or what to choose. Numerous people are unprepared for the freedom they now have. Frequently, when confronted with the existential fact of their responsibility for their lives, they experience difficulty in handling this realization. Now people are less faced with what they *must* do, instead the emphasis is on what they *want* to do. In what may be a transitional period between old and new ways of being-in-the-world, many people have failed to learn adequately how to wish, how to will and how to decide and stay committed to their decisions.

Isolation

- *Interpersonal isolation.* Cultural and technological change plays a large part in the creation of this form of isolation. In the United States and other Western cultures there has been a decline in community links – churches, local shops, neighbours who know each other and have local roots, family doctors and so on.
- *Intrapersonal isolation* stems from obstructions and frustrations that occur early in life and threaten some vital aspect of the individual's nascent sense of self.
- *Existential isolation* is closely interwoven with interpersonal isolation. Many people fail to develop the inner strength, confidence and sense of identity that enables them to face existential isolation. Never having received genuine growth-inducing love, they do not know how to offer it to others. If committed and authentic therapist–client relationships can help clients confront and come to terms with their existential isolation, it can safely be inferred that clients have insufficiently experienced such relationships in their pasts.

Meaninglessness

Many factors in contemporary culture contribute to people having a diminished sense of life's meaning compared to their forebears in the pre-industrial agricultural world. First, instead of meaning being supplied by religion, now most people neither believe in religion nor go to church. Second, the spread of urbanization and industrialization has contributed to people losing a sense of meaning through their contact with nature. No longer are most people closely connected with the cycles of the land and of farm animals.

Third, most contemporary humans no longer belong to and have roles in rural communities, but instead often live in relatively impersonal urban communities. Fourth, many contemporary humans are alienated from their work and think that they engage in mechanical and routine tasks of little intrinsic interest. Fifth, contemporary humans are less beset with basic survival needs, such as food, shelter, and water. Their greater security and leisure confronts them much more with the abyss of meaninglessness. Time on their hands means time to be haunted by issues of meaning. In addition, in economic recessions, many people are confronted by unemployment with the loss of and need for meaning. Sixth, contemporary humans face the possibility of nuclear annihilation and global environmental destruction. If the world is not going to last, why bother?

MAINTENANCE

Existential model of defence mechanisms

How do people maintain insufficient awareness and psychopathological behaviour within the existential framework? They evolve both conscious and unconscious psychological operations to deal with the anxiety generated by existential ultimate concerns. These psychological operations or *defence mechanisms* are of two types. First, there are conventional defence mechanisms, such as projection, which defend people against anxiety regardless of its source. Second, there are specific defences for each of the four ultimate concerns which defend people against these fundamental fears. These defence mechanisms may not only be relevant to individual clients, but they may be reinforced by whole cultures colluding in them.

Box 8.1 depicts the existential model of defence mechanisms in reaction to awareness at some level of an inner conflict raised by an ultimate concern. Such defence mechanisms provide a modicum of psychological safety at the expense of restricting people's potential for growth and of generating existential guilt.

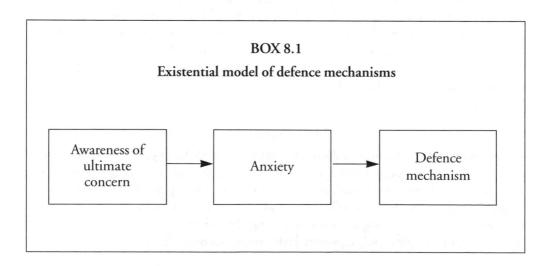

BOX 8.1

Existential model of defence mechanisms

Awareness of ultimate concern → Anxiety → Defence mechanism

Death anxiety defences

Though the specific defences for each ultimate concern are mentioned separately, they may overlap. Furthermore, they require recombining or merging into an overall existential model of psychopathology. Children's modes of coping with death awareness and death terror involve denial. For children and adults alike, Yalom (1980) has identified two major death anxiety defence mechanisms.

1. *Specialness.* While at the conscious level most people accept their lives as finite, deep down they can develop irrational beliefs about their own immortality and inviolability. Where this defence is weak or absent, then people may develop one of a number of clinical syndromes, including: compulsive heroism, being a 'workaholic' and turning a deaf ear to time's message, narcissism, and the drive for power and control. Frequently, such people seek therapy when they no longer can ward off their death anxiety through these pretences.
2. *Belief in an ultimate rescuer.* This defence represents the belief that, however bad things may get, the individual is not alone in an indifferent universe and some omnipresent servant will come to the rescue. People using the defence of the ultimate rescuer may restrict their lives by locating and serving a 'dominant other'. Most people do not acknowledge their belief system until it fails to serve its purpose: for instance, if they acquire a fatal illness or their 'dominant other' dies or psychologically withdraws.

Freedom anxiety defences

Freedom anxiety defences protect individuals from awareness of their responsibility for the authorship of their lives. Awareness of responsibility entails being 'aware of creating one's own self, destiny, life predicament, feelings and, if such be the case, one's own suffering' (Yalom, 1980, p. 218). Compulsivity is one defence against responsibility awareness. Yalom gives the example of Bernard, a 25-year-old salesman who was compulsively driven in his sex, work, and leisure lives. His compulsivity obliterated choice, yet Bernard was responsible for creating as well as maintaining his compulsivity. Other defences against freedom anxiety include: displacing responsibility onto others, including therapists; denying responsibility by posing as the innocent victim or losing control; avoidance of autonomous behaviour; and pathology in wishing, willing and deciding.

Isolation anxiety defences

In isolation anxiety defences people do not relate to others in their own right, but use them for defensive functions. One defence against ultimate aloneness is to exist and seek affirmation in others' eyes. Such people exist so far as they are part of others' consciousness and receive approval from them. Frequently, under the guise of loving, they can hide their inability to love. However, ultimately others are likely to get fed up with meeting their needs for affirmation. Fusion with an individual or group is another isolation anxiety defence. Rather than confront and come to terms with their fundamental isolation, people feel and think they are not alone because they are part of others. In addition, compulsive sexuality is a defence against isolation anxiety. Sexually compulsive people treat their partners as objects rather than persons. They do not take the time to know and be known. Instead, their serial relationships are caricatures of the real thing.

Meaninglessness anxiety defences

People handle meaninglessness anxiety in different ways. Compulsive activity is one way of avoiding a confrontation with meaninglessness. Individuals compulsively engage in any of a range of activities as a reaction to an underlying deep sense of purposelessness. Sooner or later many individuals who have compulsively sought money, pleasure, power, recognition and status start questioning their values. Crusadism is a form of compulsive activity where people seek out issues that they can make into time- and energy-consuming crusades. Nihilism is another defence against meaninglessness anxiety. Here people avoid confronting meaninglessness by disparaging all sources of meaning that others find in their lives, for instance love or service.

THERAPY

Most people's problems are now loneliness, isolation, and alienation.
Rollo May and Irvin Yalom

THERAPEUTIC GOALS

Existential therapy is more a mode of viewing human beings than a rigorous system. In the final analysis, existential therapists view clienthood as ubiquitous. However, generally clients are more troubled than their therapists.

The overriding goal of existential therapy is that clients experience their existence as real. The underlying assumption is that the fundamental neurotic process is the repression of the ontological sense, thus involving the loss of a sense of being and the truncation of awareness and potential. Since therapy is primarily concerned with helping clients experience their existence, any symptomatic 'cure' is a by-product or secondary goal. Existential therapists attempt to avoid a technical, mechanical approach to clients that can lead to clients obtaining a symptomatic 'cure' at the expense of constricting their existence. Great stress is placed in viewing clients in human rather than behavioural terms and on authentic therapist–client relationships.

More specifically, existential therapy entails assisting clients to embark on a journey of self-investigation, whose goals are:

* to understand the unconscious conflict;
* to identify the maladaptive defence mechanisms;
* to discover their destructive influence;

- to diminish secondary anxiety by correcting restrictive modes of dealing with self and others; and
- to develop other ways of coping with primary anxiety (May and Yalom, 2000).

PROCESS OF THERAPY

Existential therapists respect the individuality of each client and approach each client with the aim of sharing the story they have to tell. Yalom observes:

> . . . *the therapy process I ultimately developed is closely linked to the creative process, to the reading and writing of fiction:* reading *in that I always listen for the unique fascinating story of each patient's life;* writing *in that I believe, with Jung, that therapy is a creative act and the effective therapist must invent a new therapy for each patient.* (Yalom, 1998, p. 307)

Clear instances of when to use the existential approach to therapy are when clients face boundary situations associated with ultimate concerns. Such existential crises include death, personal and work transitions, irreversible decisions, and becoming unexpectedly isolated among others. The decision to work on existential conflicts should be a joint therapist–client decision.

Existential therapists seek to assist clients to understand their inner conflicts in relation to the ultimate existential concerns of death, freedom, isolation and meaning-lessness. They continually focus on how clients avoid assuming personal responsibility for their distress. They attempt to identify clients' maladaptive defence mechanisms and help raise awareness of their negative consequences. As well as assisting clients to develop other ways of coping with primary or existential anxiety, existential therapists work to lessen secondary anxiety by helping clients alter limiting ways of relating to self and others. For this purpose therapists may use a variety of interventions employed by other therapeutic approaches so long as they are consistent with a basic existential framework.

Long-term therapy is most appropriate for thoroughly addressing existential issues which affect deeper layers of the individual's mode of being-in-the-world. However, aspects of an existential approach, for instance an emphasis on responsibility and authen-ticity, can still be incorporated into briefer therapy.

THE THERAPEUTIC RELATIONSHIP

The quality of the therapist–client relationship is central to existential therapy. The therapy relationship is not viewed in terms of transference and little time is spent trying to dig up clients' pasts. Since existential therapists emphasize the depth of confrontations with ultimate concerns at the given moment, they try to understand their clients' *current* situations and enveloping fears.

Presence, authenticity and commitment are words that describe the quality of rela-tionship that existential therapists strive to offer. Existential therapy conducted on an individual basis takes place between two real people. The existential therapist is not a shadowy reflector, but a live human who tries to understand and experience the client's being. May considers that any therapist is existential who, despite technical knowledge, can still relate to clients 'as "one existence communicating with another", to use Binswanger's phrase' (May *et al.*, 1958, p. 81).

Therapists who are present to clients do not impose their own thoughts and feelings on them. Nor do they transfer to clients thoughts and feelings coming from previous relationships, what is sometimes called *countertransference*. Yalom (1989) recalls that he had always been repelled by fat women and had to work through these feelings to be fully present to a grossly overweight client who entered his office. Furthermore, existential therapists are conscious that clients have many ways of inviting involvement with their therapists in order to avoid focusing on personal problems.

Yalom (1980) talks about surreptitious 'throw-ins' making all the difference in therapy. He cites a number of critical incidents in therapy in which therapists showed their commitment and engaged their clients in human rather than stereotyped encounters. An example is that of a therapist seeing an acutely ill client for a long emergency session on a Saturday afternoon. In Yalom's case study *Every Day Gets a Little Closer* (Yalom and Elkins, 1974), written from both therapist's and client's perspectives, he was struck by the importance his client attached to small personal touches, such as warm looks and compliments about the way she looked. In addition to presence, characteristics of good therapist–client relationships include caring, extending oneself, touching clients at a profound level and wisdom (Yalom, 1980). Therapists help clients 'by being lovingly present with that person; by being trustworthy, interested; and by believing that their joint activity will ultimately be redemptive and healing' (Yalom, 1989, p. 227).

Self-disclosure

Therapist self-disclosure is an important issue in existential therapy. The overriding goal is that of an authentic relationship in the client's best interests. Existential therapists can use two kinds of self-disclosure. First, they can disclose about their own struggles to come to terms with existential ultimate concerns and be human. Yalom (1989) regards himself as having erred on the side of too little self-disclosure and writes that 'whenever I have shared a great deal of myself, patients have invariably profited . . .' (p. 164).

Second, existential therapists can have a process as contrasted with a content focus. They can use their thoughts and feelings about what is going on in the here-and-now to try to improve the therapeutic relationship. For instance, Yalom (1989) felt bored with his fat lady client, Betty. Initially he tried to sort out how much of his boredom was countertransference. However, he pinpointed two reasons for his boredom: that Betty was always revealing something that occurred elsewhere and that she hid behind a mask of false gaiety. He tactfully confronted Betty by pointing out he thought she masked her pain by staying jolly and asking her permission to interrupt and point out when she was entertaining him the moment it occurred. This self-disclosure acted as a springboard for deepening their relationship.

THERAPEUTIC INTERVENTIONS

Each of the ultimate concerns has implications for which therapeutic interventions may be appropriate.

Therapy and death

Increased awareness of death can lead to heightened appreciation of life. Terminally ill cancer patients react to the diagnosis in varying ways. Many patients do not fully hear what their doctors say. Some are flooded with existential terror. Others acknowledge the news briefly, regroup their defences, engage in internal processing, and then are ready for more information. Many cancer patients are able to use their illness as an opportunity for personal growth. They reassess priorities, choose not to do the trivial, gain an enhanced sense of living in the present, become more in touch with nature, communicate more deeply with loved ones, and have fewer interpersonal fears about rejection and taking risks. Mechanisms for change in cancer patients include the beliefs that existence cannot be postponed and in the wisdom of counting one's blessings. Increased death awareness can also bring about a radical shift in perspective in clients who are not terminally ill.

Yalom states that a good working rule for clinicians is 'death anxiety is inversely proportional to life satisfaction' (Yalom, 1980, p. 207). Interventions for increasing death awareness may increase clients' anxiety in the short term. The objective is not to anaesthetize the anxiety, but to help clients come to terms with it and use it constructively. Following are some methods that existential therapists use to increase clients' death awareness.

Giving permission

Existential therapists can cue clients that discussion of issues concerning death is valued in therapy. Some of this cueing may be by encouraging and showing interest in clients' disclosures in the area. Another part of giving permission is that of avoiding colluding in clients' denial of death. Therapists can play active roles in keeping therapy superficial. They require the ability to tolerate their own death anxiety to follow adequately clients' leads. Some therapists may require further personal therapy until they work through personally and professionally debilitating death anxiety blockages.

Identifying defence mechanisms

Two of the main defence mechanisms against death anxiety are the belief in specialness and the belief in the existence of an ultimate rescuer. Existential therapists collaborate with clients to identify such maladaptive defence mechanisms and their negative consequences. Clients are assisted to acknowledge the reality of their finiteness rather than deny it. Existential therapists require tact, persistence and good timing to help clients to identify and relinquish childlike ways of viewing death.

Working with dreams

Existential therapists encourage clients to share their dreams. In dreams and nightmares unconscious themes can appear without being repressed or heavily edited. Death themes are common in dreams and nightmares. Discussion and analysis of dreams relates to clients' current existential conflicts. However, clients are not always ready to deal with the material revealed in their dreams. Box 8.2 illustrates a nightmare of Marvin, a 64-year-old client of Yalom's, Yalom's private reflections about it, and what happened afterwards (Yalom, 1989, pp. 242–6).

BOX 8.2

Example of working with a dream

Marvin's nightmare
The two men are tall, pale and very gaunt. In a dark meadow they glide along in silence. They are dressed entirely in black. With tall black stovepipe hats, long-tailed coats, black spats and shoes, they resemble Victorian undertakers or temperance workers. Suddenly they come upon a carriage, ebony black, cradling a baby girl swaddled in black gauze. Wordlessly, one of the men begins to push the carriage. After a short distance he stops, walks around to the front, and, with his black cane, which now has a glowing white tip, he leans over, parts the gauze, and methodically inserts the white tip into the baby's vagina.

Yalom's private reflections about the meaning of Marvin's nightmare
I am old. I am at the end of my life's work. I have no children, and I approach death full of dread. I am choking on darkness. I am choking on the silence of death. I think I know a way. I try to pierce the blackness with my sexual talisman. But it is not enough.

What happened afterwards
Afterwards, when Yalom asked Marvin to associate to his dream he said nothing. When Marvin was then asked what he made of all the death imagery, he preferred to discuss the dream from the perspective of sex rather than of death.

Working with reminders of finiteness

Therapists can assist clients to identify and constructively deal with their death anxiety by being 'tuned into' the signs of mortality that are parts of normal life. The death of loved ones can be powerful reminders of personal mortality. The death of parents means that ours is the next generation to die. The death of children can invoke a sense of power-lessness in relation to cosmic indifference. Also, where it is an only child who dies, parents realize that they will not be immortal through passing on their seed. In addition, severe illness can confront clients with their finiteness and vulnerability.

Transitions remind clients of their mortality. Such transitions include the passage from adolescence to adulthood, commitment to a permanent relationship, children leaving home, and marital separation and divorce. In middle age many clients become more aware of death, realizing that they are no longer growing up, but instead growing old. In addition, retirement or unexpected career threats can powerfully increase death awareness.

In daily life, reminders of the passage of time are ever present. Physical signs of ageing – for instance greying, wrinkling, skin plaques, stiffening of the joints, loss of stamina, poorer eyesight – shatter the illusion of permanent youthfulness. Going to reunions shows that everyone else is ageing. Frequently, since they are milestones of the ageing process, birthdays and anniversaries can generate existence pain as well as or instead of joy.

Aids to increasing death awareness

While many existential therapists would not use artificial aids to increase clients' death awareness, some therapists use them. Clients can be asked to write their own obituaries or fill out death anxiety questionnaires. In addition they can be taken on guided fantasies regarding their deaths, imagining 'where', 'when', 'how', and the funeral. Yalom (1980) describes two different ways of getting clients to interact with the dying: observing a group of terminally ill people and introducing a person with terminal cancer into an everyday therapy group.

Desensitizing clients to death

Therapists can assist clients to deal with death terror by exposing them over and over to the fear in lessened doses. Yalom (1980) cites that in working with groups of cancer patients, he has seen many times their dread gradually diminish through sheer familiarity.

Understanding anxieties associated with death

Therapists may break down and identify the anxieties associated with death. A distinction needs be made between the true helplessness arising from the fundamental existential fact of death and the ancillary feelings of helplessness. Clients can be encouraged to regain more of a sense of control over aspects of their lives they can influence. Also, clients can be helped to identify and rationally confront their ancillary fears, such as having a painful death, loneliness and concern over loved ones. In the adult's unconscious dwell childlike irrational terrors about death. Such terrors can be brought into the open and assessed realistically.

Therapy and freedom

Therapy in relation to the ultimate concern of freedom focuses on increasing clients' awareness of their responsibility for their lives and on assisting them to assume this responsibility. Yalom (1980) reports that all the research data suggest that successful therapy clients become more aware of their personal responsibility for their lives. Therapists can use a wide variety of techniques to assist responsibility awareness and assumption.

Identifying defences and methods of responsibility avoidance

Therapists can help clients to understand the functions of certain of their behaviours, for instance compulsiveness, in avoiding responsibility for choices. In addition, therapists can explore with and, if necessary, confront clients with their responsibility for their own distress. For instance, when lonely clients keep belittling others, the therapist can say 'And you are lonely.' A general guideline is that when clients complain about their situations, therapists enquire about how they created them. In addition, therapists can focus on how clients use responsibility avoidance language: for instance, saying 'I can't' instead of 'I won't.'

Identifying responsibility avoidance in the here-and-now

Clients' responsibility avoidances can manifest themselves in the therapist–client relationship. Therapists need awareness of their own feelings about clients to identify how they might elicit similar reactions from others. For instance, a woman with a history of relating to abusive men may distort her perception of her male therapist and behave towards him in ways that, in another context, might elicit the abuse she dreaded. Therapists can also confront clients with their here-and-now attempts to transfer responsibility for what happens either inside or outside of therapy onto them. If so, therapists may need to work through clients' resistances such as 'If I knew what to do, I wouldn't need to be here.'

Confronting realistic limitations

All human beings have realistic adverse circumstances with which to deal. Therapy can help clients to change their attitude to or reconstrue external circumstances that they cannot alter. In addition, therapists can assist clients in identifying areas in their lives that they can influence. For instance, therapists dealing with cancer patients can assist them to assume more responsibility for their relationships to their doctors, such as assertively requesting information about their illness.

Confronting existential guilt

Existential therapists view one of the functions of anxiety as a call to conscience. One source of anxiety is guilt about failure to actualize potential. For instance, a client who engaged in compulsive sexual behaviour also had difficulty being assertive in his business life. Identifying how he transgressed his potential as a human being through limiting his life through compulsive sex, was the springboard for his gaining the confidence to become more assertive. No longer was the client inwardly terrified about exposure of all the shameful episodes in his life. As his compulsiveness declined, his sense of being a chooser increased. A distinction exists between guilt for bad choices made in the past and refusal to make new choices. So long as clients continue to behave in the present as they did in the past, then they cannot forgive themselves for their past choices.

Freeing up wishing

Wishing precedes willing (May, 1969). However, for clients to wish, they need to be in touch with how they feel. Working with affect-blocked clients can be a slow and repetitive process. Dramatic breakthrough methods are avoided since their effects tend not to be sustained. Instead, within the context of authentic relationships, existential therapists explore the source and nature of clients' blocks and the underlying feelings they try to express. In addition, therapists repeatedly ask affect-blocked clients questions like 'What do you feel?' and 'What do you want?'

Facilitating deciding

Existential therapists encourage clients to see that every action is preceded by decision. Decisions are difficult because alternatives exclude. As such, decisions are boundary situations in which people create themselves, despite their fundamental groundlessness. Many clients paralyse their decision-making capacity through 'What-ifs': for instance, 'What if I lose my job and can't find another?' Therapists can assist clients to explore the ramifications of each 'What-if' and analyse the feelings they generate. While ensuring that responsibility for decisions remains with clients, therapists can assist them to generate and evaluate decision options. Therapists can encourage clients to make decisions actively in ways that reinforce acceptance of their power and resources.

Where necessary, existential therapists try to disencumber their clients' wills. Therapist acceptance is crucial for clients learning to trust their wills and gain the belief that they have a right to act. Following are 'insights' that existential therapists commonly offer to will-stifled clients: 'Only I can change the world I have created', 'There is no danger in change', 'To get what I really want, I must change', and 'I have the power to change.' Decisions to change may take place over a considerable period of time.

Therapy and isolation

Following are ways in which existential therapists can assist clients in confronting and dealing better with the ultimate concern of isolation.

Confronting isolation

Therapists can help clients realize that ultimately everyone is alone. Clients can learn both what they can and what they cannot obtain from relationships. Therapists can ask clients to experiment with periods of self-enforced isolation in appropriate doses. Benefits of this experiment can include increased awareness both of the terror of loneliness and of hidden resources and courage.

Identifying defence mechanisms

Clients can be helped to identify defences that they use to cope with the conflict of the need to belong and the fact of existential isolation. Becoming aware that existing in the eyes of others, fusion with others, and compulsive sexuality are defence mechanisms against existential anxiety can act as a springboard for doing something about them.

Identifying interpersonal pathology

Using the ideal of a need-free or 'I–Thou' relationship as a yardstick, clients' ways of avoiding real relationships with others can be identified. To what extent do they relate to others as objects to satisfy their wants and needs? How well can they love others? How good are they at listening and revealing themselves? What are their specific distancing operations? Therapists can instruct clients in 'the ABCs of the language of intimacy . . .' (Yalom, 1989, p. 43). Such ABCs include how to own and express feelings.

Using the therapist–client relationship to illuminate pathology

Existential therapists have reservations about seeing clients as transferring feelings and attitudes from important past relationships onto them. Instead they prefer to use the therapist–client relationship to illuminate pathology that may interfere with current and future relationships. Frequently clients distort aspects of their relationship with their therapists. Therapists can raise clients' awareness of such distortions, including their consequences for other relationships.

The healing relationship

As mentioned earlier, existential therapists strive to develop real relationships with clients. Even though therapist–client relationships are temporary, the experience of intimacy can be permanent. The relationship can be powerfully affirming for clients because someone whom they respect and who *really* knows them fully accepts them. Therapists who have deep relationships with clients can help them face their existential isolation. Also, they help clients realize that they alone are responsible for their lives.

Therapy and meaninglessness

Following are some ways in which existential therapists can work with clients complaining of lack of meaning in their lives.

Redefining the problem

When clients complain that 'life has no meaning', they appear to assume that life has a meaning that they cannot find. The existential position is that people are meaning-giving rather than meaning-getting. Existential therapists raise clients' awareness that there is no inherent meaning in life, rather they are responsible for creating their own meaning. Frequently, what is subsumed under meaninglessness is best pursued under the other ultimate concerns of death, freedom and isolation.

Identifying meaninglessness anxiety defences

Existential therapists can assist clients to become more aware of their meaninglessness anxiety defences. To what extent does their search for money, pleasure, power, recognition and status flow from their failure to confront the existential issue of meaninglessness? Clients can be helped to recognize the consequences and costs of their defences. Their defences against meaninglessness may contribute to their leading superficial lives that create the very problems that consciously or unconsciously they seek to avoid.

Assisting engagement in life

Therapists should approach the problem of meaninglessness by assisting their clients to become more engaged in the stream of life. They should assume that the desire to engage in life is always present in clients. Therapists can offer clients authentic relationships that demonstrate their own engagement in the therapeutic process. They can explore clients' long-range hopes and goals, belief systems, capacity to love and attempts to express themselves creatively. In addition, they can identify and try to remove blocks in the clients' progress toward engagement. Clients may find insufficient meaning in their relationships, work, leisure, creative pursuits and religious strivings. Each area can be analysed for obstacles that clients can then work to remove.

CASE MATERIAL

May gives an example of existential therapy with Mercedes, a black woman who moved during therapy from almost complete impotence to self-esteem and the capacity for aggression. Being black and a woman were two contributing factors in Mercedes' sense of powerlessness (May, 1973, pp. 81–9; reproduced in Wedding and Corsini, 1995). A further case example, that of David, a 50-year scientist highly anxious about confronting his wife of 27 years about his decision to separate from her, is provided toward the end of May and Yalom's summary chapter on existential psychotherapy (May and Yalom, 2000). Numerous brief case illustrations illuminate Yalom's (1980) *Existential Psychotherapy*. In addition, in *Everyday Gets a Little Closer*, Yalom as therapist and Ginny Elkins as client share their end-of-session thoughts over the course of long-term therapy (Yalom and Elkins, 1974).

Yalom's use of literature as a teaching device also sheds light on the processes of and issues in conducting existential therapy. Yalom is acutely aware that effective therapists need to be humanly involved when relating to clients, a point well illustrated in his books of therapeutic short stories *Love's Executioner* (Yalom, 1989) and *Momma and the Meaning of Life* (Yalom, 1999). In addition, in *Lying on the Couch*, he illustrates issues of therapist and client transparancy, therapeutic boundaries, and the use of dreams in existential therapy (Yalom, 1996).

FURTHER DEVELOPMENTS

Yalom (1998) writes: 'I considered revising *Existential Psychotherapy* but in the end rejected that plan – there was no tradition of an evolving literature, no research to update and review. Besides it seemed silly to update a book that purported to deal with timeless elements of the human condition' (p. 339). In addition, further developments in May and Yalom's existential therapy have been forestalled somewhat by Rollo May's death in 1994 and Irvin Yalom's journey from conducting psychotherapy to concentrating on writing psychotherapy fiction.

Though primarily an individual approach, sometimes existential therapy is conducted in groups of eight to ten members (Yalom, 1995). Therapy groups provide here-and-now information on members' ways of avoiding or assuming responsibility. Also, the interactional format of groups gives therapists and members opportunities to observe and work on interpersonal distortions and maladaptive behaviours. Existential group therapists attempt to take group members through the following sequence: learning how their behaviour (1) is viewed by others, (2) makes others feel, (3) creates the opinions others have of them, and (4) influences their opinions of themselves. In addition, groups can work on issues surrounding the ultimate concerns of death and meaninglessness. For instance, in groups of cancer patients the issue of confronting death is likely to be a major area for work.

SUMMARY

- *Yalom and May's existential therapy is a dynamic approach which focuses on clients' confrontations with universal existential concerns. Existence is an active process involving becoming something.* Umwelt, Mitwelt *and* Eigenwelt *are three forms of being-in-the-world.*

- *Anxiety can be normal or neurotic. Existential therapists focus on helping clients cope with anxieties that are inherent in human existence. Guilt can be normal, neurotic or existential, the latter being guilt over transgressing one's potential.*

- *Human life involves confronting four existential ultimate concerns: death, freedom, isolation, and meaninglessness.*

- *Young and old alike use denial as a means of coping with death anxiety. The rapid disintegration of traditional structures and pace of technological change are increasingly exposing humans to the need to confront issues of responsibility, meaning and isolation.*

- *Existential therapy offers a psychodynamic model in which the core inner conflicts centre around awareness of existential concerns leading to anxiety which in turn may be handled by defence mechanisms. Defences against the anxiety generated by death, freedom, isolation and meaninglessness are reviewed.*

- *Existential therapy's main goal is that clients experience their existences as real. Within the context of authentic relationships, existential therapists help clients confront and come to terms with their inner conflicts in relation to death, freedom, isolation and meaninglessness. The major focus is on clients' current situations and enveloping fears.*

- *Therapeutic approaches to death anxiety include giving clients permission to talk about it, identifying defence mechanisms, and working with dreams and reminders of finiteness.*

- *Therapeutic approaches to freedom and responsibility include identifying defences and avoidance strategies, freeing up wishing, and facilitating willing and deciding.*

- *Therapeutic approaches to isolation anxiety include helping clients to confront isolation, identifying defence mechanisms and interpersonal pathology, and offering healing therapist–client relationships.*

- *Therapeutic approaches to meaninglessness anxiety include re-defining the problem, identifying defences, and assisting engagement in the stream of life.*

- *Though primarily an individual approach, existential therapy can be conducted beneficially in groups.*

REVIEW AND PERSONAL QUESTIONS

REVIEW QUESTIONS

1. What does the word 'existential' mean?
2. What are the characteristics of and inner conflicts associated with each of the four existential ultimate concerns: death, freedom, isolation, and meaninglessness?
3. What is existential psychodynamics and what is the existential model of defence mechanisms?
4. What are some defences for anxiety attached to each ultimate concern?
5. What are the goals of existential therapy?
6. What are desirable characteristics in existential therapist–client relationships?
7. Describe some interventions existential therapists can use for working with clients' death anxiety.
8. Describe some interventions existential therapists can use for enhancing clients' responsibility awareness and assumption.
9. Describe some interventions existential therapists can use for working with clients' problems of existential isolation.
10. Describe some interventions existential therapists can use for working with clients' problems of meaninglessness.

PERSONAL QUESTIONS

1. To what extent do you experience your existence as real? Answer as specifically as possible.
2. To what extent and in what ways do you experience existential anxiety? What are some of your main defences against existential anxiety?
3. Assess the degree to which you currently take personal responsibility for making or creating your existence. In what ways might you engage in less responsibility avoidance and in greater responsibility assumption?
4. Do you consider that meaninglessness is a major problem for people in Western society? If so, how does this affect you personally?
5. What relevance, if any, has the theory and practice of Yalom and May's existential therapy for how you conduct therapy?
6. What relevance, if any, has the theory and practice of Yalom and May's existential therapy for how you live?

ANNOTATED BIBLIOGRAPHY

Yalom, I. D. (1980). *Existential Psychotherapy*. New York: Basic Books.
    This book is a major contribution to the counselling and therapy literature. It develops a psychodynamic theory of existential anxiety centred on humans' confrontations with the ultimate concerns of death, freedom, isolation and meaninglessness. The book suggests ways in which existential therapists can assist clients to confront and come to terms with each of

these sources of existential anxiety. Both theory and practice are illuminated by numerous vignettes and case examples.

May, R., and Yalom, I. D. (2000). Existential psychotherapy. In R. J. Corsini and D. Wedding (eds). *Current Psychotherapies* (6th edition). Itasca, IL: Peacock, 273–302.

This chapter provides an authoritative overview of the theory and practice of May and Yalom's existential therapy.

May, R., Angel, E. and Ellenberger, H. F. (eds) (1958). *Existence: A New Dimension in Psychiatry and Psychology.* New York: Basic Books.

May authored the first two of the ten chapters in this edited book. Chapter 1 is on 'The origins and significance of the existential movement in psychology'. Chapter 2 is on 'Contributions to existential psychotherapy'. Both are important contributions for the serious student of the theory and practice of existential counselling and therapy.

May, R. (1950). *The Meaning of Anxiety.* New York: Ronald Press.

In 1977, this book came out in a revised edition. This book was an early presentation of the importance of anxiety as a normal as well as neurotic condition. The book's first part, entitled 'Modern interpretations of anxiety', looks at its roots in philosophy, biology, psychology and contemporary culture. The book's second part, entitled 'Clinical analysis of anxiety', presents a series of case studies and May's conclusions about anxiety drawn from them.

Yalom, I. D. (1998). *The Yalom Reader: Selections from the Work of a Master Therapist and Story Teller.* New York: Basic Books.

This book charts Yalom's writing career as it has progressed from texts of psychotherapy to novels of psychotherapy. The material selected for the book's three parts addresses each of Yalom's major interests: 1. group therapy; 2. existential psychotherapy; and 3. writing.

Yalom, I. D. (1989). *Love's Executioner and Other Tales of Psychotherapy.* London: Bloomsbury.

The human face of existential therapy. A series of beautifully written case studies in which Yalom works with his clients. Both therapist and clients come alive as real people struggling with the concerns of existence. The book provides Yalom's insights into 'grey areas' regarding their own behaviour existential therapists are likely to face.

Yalom, I. D. (1996). *Lying on the Couch.* New York: HarperPerennial.

This psychological novel is a deliciously funny spoof on contemporary psychotherapy in which all participants interweave with their hidden agendas, duplicity, self-deceptions and potential for unexpected growth and human intimacy. On a more serious note, the book illustrates issues of therapist and client transparency, therapeutic boundaries, and working with dreams.

REFERENCES AND FURTHER READING

Buber, M. (1965). *Between Man and Man.* New York: MacMillan.
Buber, M. (1970). *I and Thou.* New York: Charles Scribner.
Heidegger, M. (1962). *Being and Time.* London: SCM Press.

Kierkegaard, S. (1954). *Fear and Trembling and the Sickness unto Death.* Garden City, NY: Doubleday.

Lieberman, M. A., Yalom, I. D. and Miles, M. B. (1973). *Encounter Groups: First Facts.* New York: Basic Books.

May, R. (1939). *The Art of Counseling.* Nashville: Cokesbury.

May, R. (1950). *The Meaning of Anxiety.* New York: Ronald Press.

May, R. (1953). *Man's Search for Himself.* New York: W. W. Norton.

May, R. (1967). *Psychology and the Human Dilemma.* Princeton, NJ: Van Nostrand.

May, R. (1969). *Love and Will.* New York: Norton.

May, R. (1973). *Power and Innocence: A Search for Sources of Violence.* New York: W. W. Norton.

May, R. (1975). *The Courage to Create.* New York: Norton.

May, R. (1977). *The Meaning of Anxiety* (revised edition). New York: Norton.

May, R. (1981). *Freedom and Destiny.* New York: Norton.

May. R. (1985). *My Quest for Beauty.* New York: Norton.

May, R., Angel, E. and Ellenberger, H. F. (eds) (1958). *Existence: A New Dimension in Psychiatry and Psychology.* New York: Basic Books.

May, R. and Yalom, I. D. (2000). Existential psychotherapy. In R. J. Corsini and D. Wedding (eds). *Current Psychotherapies* (6th edition). Itasca, IL: Peacock.

Rabinowitz, F. F., Good, G. and Cozad, L. (1989). Rollo May: A man of myth and meaning. *Journal of Counseling and Development, 67,* 436–41. (Interview with Rollo May.)

Sartre, J. P. (1956). *Being and Nothingness.* New York: Philosophical Library.

Tillich, P. (1952). *The Courage to Be.* New Haven, CT: Yale University Press.

Wedding, D. and Corsini, R. (1995). *Case Studies in Psychotherapy.* Itasca, IL: Peacock.

Yalom, I. D. (1980). *Existential Psychotherapy.* New York: Basic Books.

Yalom, I. D. (1983). *Inpatient Group Psychotherapy.* New York: Basic Books.

Yalom, I. D. (1989). *Love's Executioner and Other Tales of Psychotherapy.* London: Bloomsbury.

Yalom, I. D. (1991). *When Nietzsche Wept.* New York: Basic Books/Harper. Paperback: HarperCollins, 1992.

Yalom, I. D. (1995). *The Theory and Practice of Group Psychotherapy* (4th edition). New York: Basic Books.

Yalom, I. D. (1996). *Lying on the Couch.* New York: HarperPerennial.

Yalom, I. D. (1998). *The Yalom Reader: Selections from the Work of a Master Therapist and Story Teller.* New York: Basic Books.

Yalom. I. D. (1999) *Momma and the Meaning of Life.* New York: Basic Books.

Yalom, I. D. (2000). Autobiographical information. www.yalom.com

Yalom, I. D. and Elkins, G. (1974). *Every Day Gets a Little Closer.* New York: Basic Books.

Yalom, I. D. and Vinogradov, S. (1989). *Concise Guide to Group Psychotherapy.* Washington, DC: American Psychiatric Press.

9

Logotherapy

I have seen the meaning of my life in helping others to see in their lives a meaning.
Viktor Frankl

INTRODUCTION

Logotherapy is sometimes called the third Viennese school of psychotherapy, the other two being Freud's psychoanalysis and Adler's individual psychology. Another way of viewing logotherapy is that it is a supplement rather than a replacement for psychotherapy (Frankl, 1975a). *Logos* is a Greek word that connotes both 'meaning' and 'spirit', the latter word without any primary religious connotation. Humans are meaning-seeking beings and the search for meaning in itself is not pathological. Existence confronts people with the need to find meaning in their lives. The main purpose of logotherapy is to assist clients in their search for meaning.

VIKTOR FRANKL (1905–97)

Viktor E. Frankl, born on 26 March 1905 in Vienna, Austria, was the son of Jewish parents. His mother was descended from an old, established, patrician Prague family. His father, the son of an impecunious master bookbinder, was a public servant who became director of the Austrian government's Ministry of Social Service. One of three children, Frankl grew up in a secure environment, describing his mother as kind-hearted and deeply pious and his father as Spartan, Stoic, religious and with a strong sense of duty. Frankl saw himself as possessing a tension between the rationality of his father and the deep emotions of his mother.

Aged 3, Frankl decided to become a physician, which probably pleased his father, who had given up his medical studies for financial reasons. Frankl's own search for meaning started early in life, and during the years of his youth, as he had breakfast or coffee in bed, he would ponder for a few minutes about the meaning of life, especially about the meaning for him in the coming day (Frankl, 1997a). Frankl was an intellectually gifted and precocious schoolboy, who corresponded with Freud. In 1924, the young Frankl had his first article published at Freud's invitation in the *International Journal of Psychoanalysis*.

Frankl was both influenced by and reacted against some of the ideas of Freud and Adler. In addition, he was influenced by the existential philosophers, such as Heidegger, Jaspers and Scheler. The origins of logotherapy go back to Frankl's early struggles to find meaning in his own existence. Frankl readily confesses that when a young man '. . . I had to go through the hell of despair over the apparent meaninglessness of life, through total and ultimate nihilism, until I could develop an immunity against nihilism. I developed logotherapy' (Frankl, 1988, p. 166).

Frankl coined the term 'logotherapy' in the 1920s and in the 1930s used the word *Existenzanalyse*, existential analysis, as an alternative word for logotherapy. To avoid confusion he mostly refrains from using the term 'existential analysis' in his English-speaking publications. In 1928, Frankl founded the Youth Counselling Centres in Vienna, heading them until 1938. In 1930, he received his MD from the University of Vienna. From 1930 to 1938, he was on the staff of the Neuropsychiatric University Clinic. From 1938 to 1942 he was Specialist in Neurology and Psychiatry, and then Head of the Neurological Department, at the Jewish Hospital in Vienna. During this time he wrote the first draft of his first book.

Shortly before America entered the Second World War, Frankl was given the opportunity to emigrate to the United States. He let this opportunity pass because he chose to abide by the commandment 'Honor father and mother and you will dwell in the land' (Frankl, 1988, p. 59). He thought that, by retaining his hospital position, he might protect his parents from being sent to a concentration camp. Though unable to do so, Frankl was able to administer morphine to his beloved father as he was dying from pulmonary oedema in Theresienstadt concentration camp 'and had spared him the unnecessary agony of death' (Frankl, 1997a, p. 26). Frankl's mother, brother and first wife, Tilly, died in concentration camps, but his sister, who had emigrated to Australia, survived.

From 1942 to 1945, Frankl had the harrowing experience of being imprisoned in four Nazi concentration camps: Theresienstadt, Auschwitz, Kaufering 3, and Turkheim. On arrival at Auschwitz, Frankl was shaved of all his body hair. He was number 119,194. The manuscript of his first book was confiscated. During the next three years, he survived selections of who should live or die, forced labour, brutal Capos (guards), beatings, malnutrition, disease, the vagaries of fate and the existential challenge to find meaning in his suffering. Most of the time his work was digging and laying tracks for railway lines. Only in the last few weeks of his internment did he work as a doctor.

During this period, Frankl had the opportunity to observe human nature under extreme circumstances. Most prisoners made the choice to vegetate. However, other prisoners deepened spiritually and took the camps' difficulties as tests of their inner strength. They rose to the challenge of finding meaning in their lives. Frankl quotes Nietzsche: 'He who has a *why* to live for can bear almost any *how*' (Frankl, 1963, p. 121). Despite their adversity, these prisoners retained their freedom to choose both in their inner life and in how they behaved toward others. They turned their tragedies into triumphs. On returning to Vienna after the war, between spells of collapsing into a chair weeping, Frankl dictated the third and last draft of *The Doctor and the Soul*. Afterwards, in nine days, he dictated *Man's Search for Meaning*, at that time thinking it would be published anonymously. By 1992, the book had sold over five million copies.

In 1946, Frankl became Head of the Department of Neurology at the Poliklinik Hospital in Vienna and also met his second wife, Elly, whom he married the next year. In

1947, Frankl was appointed Assistant Professor of Psychiatry and Neurology at the University of Vienna and then, in 1955, University Professor. Frankl was a past president of the Austrian Medical Society of Psychotherapy. In addition, he had been Distinguished Professor of Logotherapy at the US International University in California and also Visiting Professor at Stanford, Harvard, and Duquesne Universities, among others. Frankl lectured widely in Europe, Australia, South America, Asia and Africa.

Frankl was a prolific author, writing over 30 books, some of which have been translated into many languages, and numerous articles. In addition to those already mentioned, his books include: *Psychotherapy and Existentialism: Selected Papers on Logotherapy*, *The Will to Meaning: Foundations and Applications of Logotherapy*, *The Unconscious God: Psychotherapy and Theology*, and *The Unheard Cry for Meaning: Psychotherapy and Humanism*.

Until his 80th birthday, mountain climbing was Frankl's most passionate hobby. Having experienced the depths of human depravity, Frankl was able to ascend the heights of human achievement by turning his personal tragedy into a triumph of the human spirit. In his autobiographical recollections, Frankl writes: 'As I have said, I know of only a few good qualities in myself, and perhaps only one: I do not forget any good deed done to me, and I carry no grudge for a bad one' (Frankl, 1997a, p. 35). Frankl died in 1997, but his work and the inspiration of his indomitable spirit live on.

THEORY

The theme runs like a radiant thread through all my work, and it concerns the border area that lies between psychotherapy and philosophy, with special attention to the problems of meanings and values in psychology.

Viktor Frankl

BASIC CONCEPTS

Freedom of will

Frankl uses the term 'existential' in three ways. First, the term refers to *existence* itself, which is a specifically human mode of being. Second, it refers to the *meaning* of existence. Third, it refers to the *striving* to find meaning in personal existence or, put another way, to the will to meaning. Life is transitory. However, this transitoriness does not make life meaningless. Rather the transitory aspects of life are potentialities. Humans need to realize the transitory possibilities. They are constantly choosing which of the mass of transitory potentialities will be actualized and which condemned to non-being.

Humans possess freedom of will. Alone among animals, they possess the capacity for self-detachment. Humans are capable of reflecting upon and judging their choices. What matters is not the features of people's character or their drives and instincts, but the stand they take towards them. People are free to shape their own characters and are responsible for what they make out of themselves. When people rise above the somatic and psychic dimensions of their existence, they enter a new dimension which is termed the 'noological' dimension. In this noological dimension are located distinctly human functions, for instance reflection, the capacity to make self into an object, humour, and conscientiousness.

Will to meaning

The will to meaning is the fundamental motivational force in humans. People are confronted with the need to detect meaning literally to their last breaths. Frankl writes 'Man's search for meaning is a primary force in his life . . . This meaning is unique and specific and can be fulfilled by him alone; only then does it achieve a significance that will satisfy his own will to meaning' (Frankl, 1963, p. 154). As Frankl observed in his concentration camp experiences, people need something to live for. Humans are beings who encounter other people and reach out for meanings to fulfil. However, meaning does not coincide with being, rather it sets the pace for being. Human existence is at risk unless people live in terms of transcendence towards something beyond themselves.

Logotherapy focuses on the will to meaning whereas psychoanalysis focuses on the will to pleasure and individual psychology focuses on the will to power. Frankl acknowledges that Freud and Adler did not use the terms 'will to pleasure' and 'will to power' as such. However, both pleasure and power are by-products or derivatives of the will to meaning. The will to meaning is not a rationalization of instinctual drives neither is it concerned with reducing tension and returning to a state of homeostasis. What people need is not a tensionless state, but rather the tension of striving for some meaning that is worthy of them.

The will to meaning also differs as a motivating force from self-actualizing. Frankl views self-actualization as only a side-effect of the will to meaning. People can only actualize themselves to the extent that they fulfil meaning.

Consciousness and the unconscious

What is the source or referent point against which people can detect meaning in their lives? The search for meaning can involve both conscious activity and getting in touch with unconscious layers of the self.

Consciousness

Humans are spiritual beings and logotherapy focuses on their spiritual existence. In this context, the word 'spirit' has no religious connotations. Spiritual phenomena in humans can be either conscious or unconscious. Consciousness implies awareness. Logotherapy aims to increase clients' consciousness of their spiritual selves. Humans need to be conscious of their responsibility for detecting and acting in terms of the unique meaning of their lives in specific situations in which they are involved.

The spiritual unconscious

Each human has an existential, personal spiritual core. Centred around their spiritual core, people are not only individualized, but integrated in their somatic, psychic and spiritual aspects. Though the border between the conscious and the unconscious is 'fluid', Frankl regards the spiritual basis of human existence as ultimately unconscious. The deep centre of each human is unconscious.

A sharp distinction exists between the instinctual unconscious and the spiritual unconscious. Freud saw the unconscious as a reservoir of repressed sexual and aggressive instincts. For Frankl depth psychology, instead of focusing on repressed instincts, needs to follow humans into the depths of their spirits. However, the self does not yield to total self-reflection and, in a sense, this makes human existence basically unreflectable. Frankl writes: 'Existence exists in action rather than reflection' (Frankl, 1975a, p. 30).

Conscience

The origins of conscience are located in the spiritual unconscious. *Logos* is deeper than logic. Existentially authentic decisions take place completely unreflectively and unconsciously. Frankl writes: 'It is the task of conscience to disclose to man the *unum necesse*, the one thing that is required' (Frankl, 1975a, p. 35). Conscience can intuitively reveal the unique possibilities for meaning to be actualized in specific situations. Conscience, or the 'ethical instinct', is highly individual in contrast to the other instincts, which work for the greatest number of the species. In addition to moral conscience, Frankl considers love and art are rooted in the emotional, intuitive, non-rational depths of the spiritual unconscious.

Freedom can be considered in terms of 'from what' and 'to what'. The 'to what' is responsibleness to conscience. Conscience has a transcendent quality. People can only be the servants of their conscience when they can have a dialogue rather than a monologue with it as something other than themselves. Through conscience a trans-human agent 'is sounding through' (Frankl, 1975a, p. 53). 'Sounding through' is *per-sonare* in Latin, which is linked to the concept of the human 'person'. Conscience has a key position in disclosing the essential transcendence of the spiritual unconscious. Conscience is the voice of transcendence and is itself transcendent.

The religious unconscious

The existential analysis of dreams makes obvious the fact of repressed and unconscious religiousness. Not only is *libido* repressed, but *religio* also. Conscience is not the last 'to what' of responsibleness. Though humans are responsible for themselves, they are not responsible before themselves. This 'to what' of responsibleness is prior to responsibleness itself. Unconscious religiousness, or the religious unconscious, exists within the spiritual unconscious. Humans have always stood in an intentional relation to transcendence, even if only on an unconscious level. This 'unconscious God' is hidden in two ways. First, the human relationship to God is hidden. Second, God is hidden. Even in highly irreligious people, religiousness is latent.

The religious unconscious is an existential agent rather than an instinctual factor. Frankl calls it 'a deciding being unconscious rather than a being driven by the unconscious' (Frankl, 1975a, p. 65). In relation to Jung, he stresses that unconscious religiousness stems from the personal centre of each individual rather than from an impersonal pool of images shared by mankind.

Repression of religiousness, as with repression of other aspects of the unconscious, leads to neurosis: '. . . once the angel in us is repressed, he turns into a demon' (Frankl, 1975a, p. 70). The existentiality of religiousness needs to be spontaneous. Genuine religiousness must unfold at its own pace. Humans commit themselves to it by choosing to be religious.

Meaning of life and death

Meaning of life

Frankl writes that 'being human means being responsible for fulfilling the meaning potential inherent in a given life situation' (Frankl, 1975a, p. 125). Being human means being at the same time different, conscious and responsible. The concept of responsibility is the foundation of human existence. Human freedom as not a 'freedom from', but rather a 'freedom to', namely the freedom to accept responsibility. Freedom is what people 'are': it is not something that they 'have' and can therefore lose. People have many potentialities within them. They are not fully conditioned or determined. Rather, moment by moment, they are free to decide what they will become in the next moment. Their decisions determine which of their potentialities gets actualized. During no stage of their lives can people 'escape the mandate to choose among possibilities' (Frankl, 1955, p. 85).

All the time people are questioned by life. The way to respond is by being responsible for their lives. Working with the matter that fate has supplied them, people are like sculptors who chisel out and hammer unshaped stone so that it takes more and more form. Though always surrounded by biological, sociological and psychological restrictions, humans can either conquer and shape them or deliberately choose to submit to them.

Meaning of death

Death does not rob life of its meaning. If people were immortal they might put off doing things indefinitely. Death belongs to life and gives it meaning. People's responsibility springs from their finiteness. Consequently, they need to realize the full gravity of the responsibility that they bear throughout every moment of their lives. Destiny, like death, is essential to the meaning of life. Destiny refers to those factors that are beyond people's power. Freedom can be viewed not only in the contexts of life and death, but also in the context of destiny. The opportunities and tribulations that come people's way are unique. Nevertheless, people still can exercise their inner freedom to take a stand against their destiny.

Self-transcendence

Self-transcendence is an essential characteristic of human existence. Humans are essentially beings who reach out beyond themselves. They become most human when they transcend the boundaries of their selves by either fulfilling a meaning or encountering another person lovingly. Frankl sees the basic human need as a search for meaning rather than a search for the self. Identity is only achievable through being responsible for the fulfilment of meaning. People can become overly focused on themselves. The self-transcendent quality of human life is most apparent when people forget themselves. Frankl regarded the main lesson he learned from Nazi concentration camps was that unless life pointed to something beyond itself, survival was pointless, meaningless and impossible.

Suffering from neurotic problems that reflect difficulties in self-transcendence is the converse of people finding meaning by transcending themselves. Hyper-reflection and hyperintention are two of the main ways in which people choose not to transcend themselves. Hyper-reflection is a tendency to overbearing self-reflection. Hyperintention is a tendency to pay excessive attention to achieving that which one desires.

Sources of meaning

Frankl suggests that self-transcendence is achievable by discovering or detecting meaning in three different ways: by doing a deed, by experiencing a value, and by suffering (Frankl, 1963). Elsewhere (Frankl, 1967, 1988), he talks of three principal ways in which people can find meaning in life:

1. by what they give to life (creative values);
2. by what they take from life (experiential values); and
3. through the stand they take towards a fate they can no longer change, for instance an inoperable cancer (attitudinal values).

In addition, past experiences and religion are two further areas in which people can discover meaning.

Meaning in work

Work is a major area in which people can reach out beyond themselves. The meaning of work goes beyond a particular occupation to include the manner in which people bring their unique human qualities to their work. For instance, a nurse may go beyond her regimented duties to say a kind word to a critically ill patient. Frankl views all work as allowing such opportunities, though acknowledges that some jobs are very routine. In such instances, much creative meaning may need to be found in leisure pursuits.

Unemployment is an example of how people can be affected by lack of creative meaning. Frankl views unemployment neurosis, characterized by apathy and depression, as an existential position. Some people respond to the existential challenge of unemployment by remaining active and involved and so stay free of unemployment neurosis. Employment can also be for good or ill. Some people run away from the emptiness of their existence by taking refuge in their work or profession. Achieving creative meaning in life is not synonymous with work satisfactions alone.

Meaning in love

Unlike in psychoanalysis, in logotherapy love is not regarded as a secondary phenomenon to sex. While sex can be an expression of mature love, it is not a form of love in itself. Love as a form of self-transcendence has various characteristics. It entails relating to another person as a spiritual being. As such, love involves understanding or grasping the inner core of the personality of another person. People are moved to the depths of their spiritual beings by their partner's spiritual core. Infatuation seldom lasts long. When gratified, the sex drive vanishes promptly. Love, however, has a quality of permanence in that the spiritual core of the other person is unique and irreplaceable. Furthermore, love can outlast death in that the essence of the unique being of the beloved is timeless and imperishable.

Another characteristic of love is that, since it is directed at what the other 'is' rather than at the other as a possession, it leads to a monogamous attitude. A further characteristic is that it involves seeing the potential in the beloved and helping him or her achieve this potential. In addition, in a real love relationship, there is no room for jealousy since the other person is not treated as a possession.

Frankl (1967) is at pains to point out that love is not the only, nor even the best, way to fill life with meaning. Furthermore, he distinguishes between neurotic failure and failure to attain love imposed by destiny.

Meaning in suffering
Human destiny has a twofold meaning: to be shaped where possible and to be endured where necessary. Attitudinal values are inherent in the stand that people take to circumstances that they cannot change, for instance an incurable illness or concentration camp internment. Through attitudinal values even the tragic aspects of human existence – the 'tragic triad' of pain, guilt and death – can be turned into something positive and creative. However, people need to be careful not to accept fate too readily. The time to enlist attitudinal values is only when they can be certain that they cannot alter their fates.

Inescapable negative situations give people the opportunity 'to actualise the highest value, to fulfil the deepest meaning, the meaning of suffering' (Frankl, 1963, p. 178). People have choices in how they respond to suffering. For instance, life can retain meaning up to the last moment for people with terminal illnesses who accept the challenge to suffer bravely. Frankl quotes Goethe: 'There is no predicament that we cannot ennoble either by doing or enduring' (Frankl, 1955, p. 115). Some people can rise to the challenge of suffering and grow richer and stronger because of it. Though people may be helpless victims of fate, they can still exercise the inner freedom to turn their predicaments into accomplishments at the human level.

Meaning from the past
Though the search for meaning is primarily oriented towards people's futures, the past can still be a source of meaning. Often people discount their past experiences as a source of meaning. In Auschwitz concentration camp, Frankl went through considerable soul searching about the meaning of suffering when the manuscript of his first book was confiscated. However, he came to realize that nothing in his past was lost, but rather it was irrevocably stored. The meaning of his life did not depend on whether a manuscript of his was printed. His experiences in the past constituted a full granary. Often in times of suffering, but not always so, the search for meaning can entail acknowledging and identifying sources of meaning in the past relevant to creating meaning in the present. Also, even short lives can still have pasts full of meaning. Furthermore, even for those who have led sterile lives, their unconditional faith in an unconditional meaning may turn their failure into a triumph (Frankl, 1988).

The supra-meaning

Humans are incapable of understanding the ultimate meaning of human suffering. However, that does not mean that suffering does not have an ultimate meaning. Frankl (1963, 1988) uses the term 'supra-meaning' to denote the ultimate meaning of suffering and life. People cannot break through the dimensional differences between the human world and the divine world. The supra-meaning can only be grasped by faith and not by intellectual means. Unlike in secular existential philosophy, the human task is not to endure life's meaninglessness. Instead, people need to bear their inability to grasp in rational terms life's ultimate meaningfulness. Trust in God precedes people's ability to have faith in life's ultimate meaning. As always, the infinite God is silent rather than dead.

The trend in modern life is not away from religion, but away from an emphasis on differences between individual denominations. Frankl (1988) does not advocate a form of universal religion. Rather, he sees a trend toward a profoundly personalized religion in which people address themselves to the ultimate being in their own individual language and words.

The existential vacuum

The existential vacuum describes a state in which people complain of an inner void. They suffer from a sense of meaninglessness, emptiness and futility. The existential vacuum is an 'abyss experience' in contrast to the peak experience described by Maslow.

Frankl suggests three causes of the existential vacuum.

1. Unlike other animals, humans are no longer programmed by drives and instincts in what to do.
2. Humans are no longer told by traditions, conventions and values what they should do. Sometimes they do not know what they wish to do and retreat into conformism, doing what others do, or into totalitarianism, doing what others wish them to do.
3. Especially in America, students are exposed to 'reductionism'. Humans are reduced to drives, instincts, creatures of conditioning, reaction formations and defence mechanisms rather than viewed as deciding agents. Frankl cites as an example of reductionism the case of a couple who were told, during their induction into the American Peace Corps, that they were helping the less privileged because of their unconscious need to prove themselves superior (Frankl, 1975a, p. 94).

Existential frustration

Existential frustration results when the will to meaning is frustrated. Apathy and boredom are the main characteristics of existential frustration. Existential frustration is not in itself pathological or pathogenic. People's concern, even their despair, over the meaning of their lives is a spiritual distress rather than a disease. Frankl regards the existential vacuum, with its attendant frustration, as 'something sociogenic and not at all a neurosis' (Frankl, 1975a, p. 139). Despair over the meaninglessness of life can be a sign of intellectual sincerity and honesty. In his later writings, Frankl (1988) stated that there was no doubt that the existential vacuum was spreading.

Noogenic neurosis

The existential vacuum can lead to neuroticism. The term 'noogenic neurosis' refers to those cases where the existential vacuum leads to clinical symptomatology. Frankl defines the noogenic neurosis as 'a neurosis which is caused by a spiritual problem, a moral or ethical conflict, as for example, a conflict between the mere superego and the true conscience . . .' (Frankl, 1988, p. 89). Existential frustration plays a large part in noogenic neuroses. Such neuroses arise from spiritual conflicts to do with people's aspirations for a meaningful existence and the frustration of their will to meaning. Doctors and therapists need to distinguish sharply between the spiritual dimension of problems as against the instinctual.

The mass neurotic triad

Frankl speaks of the neurotization of humanity because of the existential vacuum. The worldwide effects of the existential vacuum go beyond feelings of meaninglessness and noogenic neuroses. Frankl uses the term 'mass neurotic triad' (Frankl, 1975a, p. 96) for the three main effects: depression, addiction and aggression.

- Regarding *depression*, there is ample evidence that suicide rates are increasing, especially among the young. Frankl sees the cause as the spreading existential frustration.
- Regarding *addiction*, people with low purpose in life are more likely to try to find feelings of meaningfulness in drugs than those with high purpose in life. A frequently cited reason for taking drugs is the desire to find meaning in life. Also, many alcoholics suffer from a sense of meaninglessness in their lives.
- Regarding *aggression*, not only does sexual libido thrive in an existential vacuum, but also 'aggressive destrudo'. Frankl considers that statistical evidence favours his hypothesis that people are most likely to become aggressive when they are caught in feelings of emptiness and meaninglessness.

ACQUISITION

A sense of meaninglessness is not necessarily acquired through learning and indoctrination. It can be part of the human response to life and, if worked through satisfactorily as in Frankl's own case, a growth experience. However, Frankl considers that the existential vacuum and existential frustration are becoming more widespread; furthermore, that there is an increasing neurotization of humanity. If this is the case, individuals are more likely to acquire a sense of meaninglessness because they grow up in cultures and societies in which it is harder to find meaning than in the past. First, the erosion of traditional values and the tendencies to reductionism make it more difficult for many people to find meaning in their lives. Second, because there are fewer people in society who have satisfactorily found meaning, it is more difficult for young people to grow up learning from models who are successful at realizing the spiritual aspects of themselves. Put another way, young people may suffer from a lack of access to meaning educators and exemplars. Despite Frankl's belief in people's potential humanness, '*humane* humans are, and probably will always remain, a minority' (Frankl, 1975a, p. 84).

MAINTENANCE

Maintaining the existential vacuum

How do people maintain their sense of meaninglessness? Some suggestions may be drawn from Frankl's writings.

- *Repression.* Logotherapy concerns itself with the frustration and consequent repression of the will to meaning. Frankl observes: 'Not eros but logos is the victim of repression' (Frankl, 1975a, p. 131). People repress their spirituality and religiousness. Thus they remain out of touch with their spiritual centres, which are the deepest sources for a sense of meaning. Their repression of the will to meaning blocks their perception of the existence of meaning.
- *Avoiding responsibility.* Among mechanisms mentioned by Frankl for avoiding responsibility for the search for meaning are conformism, totalitarianism, and taking refuge in the neurotic triad of depression, addiction and aggression.
- *Erosion of traditions and values.* The erosion of traditions has a continuing influence on creating and maintaining the existential vacuum.
- *Reductionism.* Reductionist models of psychology and education lead people to believe, and then maintain their belief, that they are determined rather than determining.
- *Insufficient emphasis on self-transcendence.* Much of modern psychology focuses on self-actualization and on self-expression. People continue to be insufficiently helped to realize that happiness and fulfilment are by-products of self-transcendence, of forgetting oneself rather than excessively focusing on oneself.
- *Neurotization of humanity.* The fact that problems and symptoms of meaninglessness are widespread makes it harder for individuals to obtain assistance in their personal search for meaning, thus contributing to maintaining their inner void.

THERAPY

Logotherapy regards its assignment as that of assisting the patient to find meaning in his life.

Viktor Frankl

THERAPEUTIC GOALS

Frankl divides what he terms 'mental illness' into three categories: noogenic (neurosis), psychogenic (neurosis), and somatogenic (psychosis). The existential vacuum is not a neurosis. However, therapeutic goals are similar whether the existential vacuum is on its own or a part of a noogenic neurosis.

Logotherapy is the treatment of choice for dealing with the existential vacuum. The meaning of logotherapy is in helping clients find meaning in their lives. Logotherapists seek to confront and reorient clients toward their life's tasks. Logotherapy is an education for responsibility that seeks to unblock clients' will to meaning. With their will to meaning unblocked, clients are more likely to find ways of self-transcendence through creative, experiential and attitudinal values. Clients need to become aware of their existential responsibility for finding their life's meaning through their conscience. However, making the spiritual unconscious conscious is only a transitory phase in the therapy process. What therapy seeks to achieve is, first, to convert an unconscious potential into a conscious act, and then to allow it to recede back into an unconscious habit. Frankl (1975a) is at pains to stress that, while a religious therapist may bring religion into therapy, logotherapists have to refrain from setting preconceived religious goals.

The overcoming of symptoms of existential frustration, such as apathy and boredom, is a by-product of searching for and discovering meaning. Furthermore, when clients find more meaning in their lives, any symptoms they possess from the mass neurotic triad of depression, addiction and aggression, are likely to get better, if not disappear.

The psychogenic neuroses include obsessive-compulsions and phobias where the therapeutic goal is to overcome clients' tendencies to hyperintention or trying too hard. Also the psychogenic neuroses include sexual and sleep problems where the therapeutic goal is to overcome clients' tendencies to hyper-reflection or excessive self-consciousness.

With the psychoses, such as endogenous depression and schizophrenia, logotherapy may be used in conjunction with medication that addresses the somatic aspect that has become diseased. Logotherapy itself deals with the healthy part of the personality and frequently its goal is to help clients find meaning in their suffering.

A broader goal of Frankl's logotherapy is the rehumanization of psychiatry. Therapists should not view the mind as a mechanism and the treatment of mental illness merely in terms of technique. Within the limits of their environment and endowment, humans are ultimately self-determining. In the concentration camps, some chose to behave like swine and others like saints.

PROCESS OF THERAPY

In diagnosing the existential vacuum, logotherapists are alert to overt signs, for instance saying 'My life lacks meaning', and covert signs, for instance apathy and boredom, that indicate clients feel an inner void. Issues of meaning are considered legitimate areas in which clients can work, though noogenic neuroses account for 'only about 20 percent of the case material accruing to our clinics and offices' (Frankl, 1988, p. 68). Often Frankl reassures 'non patients' that their existential despair is an achievement rather than a neurosis. It is a sign of intellectual depth rather than of superficiality.

Frankl stressed that meaning is an individual matter. Logotherapists must both individualize how they work and improvise. Logotherapy is not teaching, preaching or moral exhortation. Frankl (1963) uses the analogy of the opthalmologist who enables people to see the world as it really is. Similarly, the logotherapist's role is that of widening and broadening clients' visual fields so that the whole spectrum of meaning and values becomes visible to them. For clients facing the existential vacuum, Frankl employed a range of interventions to assist them to find meaning in their lives. For clients with hyperintention or hyper-reflection, Frankl used paradoxical intention and dereflection, respectively.

THE THERAPEUTIC RELATIONSHIP

Frankl (1988) observed that therapy usually consists of both strategies and 'I–Thou' relationships. He also stressed that logotherapy cannot become too individualized. Thus, though the logotherapist is a responsibility educator, it is in the context of a committed and caring relationship which respects the uniqueness of each client. Frankl appreciated humane humans and was concerned for the rehumanization of psychiatry. His work shows much compassion and wisdom. By offering humane relationships, logotherapists provide contexts for assisting clients to find their own meanings. If necessary, Frankl assured clients that their wish to search for meaning was an accomplishment rather than a drawback. Furthermore, Frankl could be forthright in sharing his opinions about how to search for meaning.

THERAPEUTIC INTERVENTIONS

Logotherapy for the existential vacuum

How does the logotherapist deal with clients in states of existential vacuum? Though Frankl has not systematically listed his methods, below are some suggestions drawn from his writings. Box 9.1 illustrates ways in which Frankl would increase clients' existential awareness of the finiteness of life and the importance of responsibility.

BOX 9.1

Methods of increasing existential awareness

Explaining
Explaining that finiteness gives meaning to human existence rather than robs life of meaning.

Offering maxims
One of Frankl's leading maxims is: 'Live as if you were living for the second time and had acted as wrongly the first time as you are about to act now' (Frankl, 1955, p. 75).

Using similes
- Clients can imagine their lives as moving pictures that are being 'shot'. However, the irreversibility of life is brought home to them by being told that they cannot 'cut' anything and that nothing can be retrospectively changed.
- Clients can see themselves as sculptors who have a limited time span for completing their works of art, but are not informed of when the deadline will be.

Following are some methods by which Frankl focused on issues of meaning.

Teaching the importance of assuming responsibility for meaning

Frankl viewed his task as helping clients achieve the highest possible activation of their lives. He shared his view that human life never, under any circumstances, ceases to have a meaning. Clients need to learn that they are always responsible for detecting the meaning of specific situations in their unique lives. Logotherapy teaches clients to view their lives as an assignment. For religious logotherapists working with religious clients, this can go one stage further in that they assist clients to see that they are not only responsible *for* fulfilling their life's tasks but they are also responsible *to* the taskmaster.

Assisting clients to listen to their consciences

Frankl often said that meaning must be found and cannot be given. Clients are guided in their search for meaning by their consciences. Clients require alert consciences if they are 'to listen to and obey the ten thousand demands and commandments hidden in the ten thousand situations with which life is confronting him' (Frankl, 1975a, p. 120). Though therapists cannot give meanings to clients, they can provide existential examples of their commitment to the search for meaning.

Asking clients about meanings

Therapists can ask clients about creative accomplishments they might bring about, and support them as they search for answers. Clients can also be asked to explore and identify meanings in their relationships and in their suffering.

Broadening horizons about sources of meaning

Logotherapists can assist clients to obtain broader views of sources for meaning. Frankl (1955) cites a client who declared her life was meaningless and that she would only get better if she found a job that fulfilled her, such as doctor or nurse. Frankl assisted her to see that it was not only the job that she did but her attitude towards how she performed her job that might allow her a unique opportunity for fulfilment. Furthermore, in her private life outside her occupation, she could find meaning as a wife and mother.

Eliciting meaning through Socratic questioning

Frankl (1988) gives the example of the female client who expressed concern with life's transitoriness. Frankl asked her to identify a man whose accomplishments she respected, and she named her family doctor. Then by means of a series of questions he led her to acknowledge that, even though the doctor died and even though through lack of gratitude some patients might not remember what they owed him, the meaningfulness of his life remained.

Eliciting meaning through logodrama

Frankl (1963) gives an example of eliciting meaning through a 'logodrama' in a therapy group. A woman, admitted to his clinic after a suicide attempt, had lost a son who died aged 11 and was left alone with an older son who had infantile paralysis. Frankl first asked another woman in the group to imagine she was 80 and look back on a life that was childless, but full of financial success and prestige. This woman ended by saying her life had no purpose. Frankl then asked the mother of the handicapped son similarly to look back over her life. During her reply she realized her life was full of meaning because she had made a better and fuller life possible for her crippled son.

Offering meanings

Logotherapists can offer suggestions regarding the meaning of situations. Frankl provides the example of an elderly and severely depressed doctor who could not get over his grief for his beloved wife who had died two years earlier. First, Frankl asked him what would have happened if he had died first. The doctor replied that she would have suffered terribly. Whereupon Frankl replied: 'You see, Doctor, such a suffering has been spared her, and it is you who have spared her this suffering; but now, you have to pay for it by surviving and mourning her' (Frankl, 1963, pp. 178–9).

Analysing dreams

Logotherapists can work with clients' dreams to lift spiritual phenomena into consciousness. Frankl (1975a) gives the example of the woman who dreamed that, along with her dirty wash, she took a dirty cat along to the laundry. On going to pick up her wash, she found the cat dead. Her free associations indicated that 'cat' was the symbol for 'child' and 'dirty' was the 'dirty linen' of gossip surrounding her daughter's love life, about which mother had been very critical. Frankl saw the dream as expressing a warning to the mother not to keep tormenting her daughter or else she might lose her. Religious logotherapists may also analyse dreams to bring the religious unconscious into consciousness. Frankl considers that many people conceal and repress their religiousness because of 'the intimate quality inherent in genuine religiousness' (Frankl, 1975a, p. 48).

Logotherapeutic techniques for psychogenic neurosis

Paradoxical intention and dereflection are the two main logotherapeutic techniques for the psychogenic neuroses (Frankl, 1955, 1975b). Both techniques rest on the essential human qualities of self-transcendence and self-detachment.

Paradoxical intention

Paradoxical intention's use is recommended for the short-term treatment of obsessive-compulsive and phobic clients. With phobias, paradoxical intention targets anticipatory anxiety whereby clients react to events with fearful expectations of their recurrence. These fearful expectations cause excessive attention, or hyperintention, which prevents clients from accomplishing what they want. In short, anticipatory anxiety brings about the very things that clients fear.

In paradoxical intention, clients are invited to intend precisely that which they fear. Their fear is replaced by a paradoxical wish through which 'the wind is taken out of the sails of the phobia' (Frankl, 1955, p. 208). In addition, paradoxical intention enlists clients' sense of humour as a means of increasing their sense of detachment towards their neuroses by laughing at them.

While obsessive-compulsive neurotics also display fear, their fear is more fear of themselves than 'fear of fear'. They fear the potential effects of their strange thoughts. However, the more these clients fight their thoughts, the stronger their symptoms become. If therapists succeed in assisting clients through paradoxical intention to stop fighting their obsessions and compulsions, their symptoms soon diminish and may finally disappear. Box 9.2 provides examples of logotherapists helping clients to use paradoxical intention.

Dereflection

Just as paradoxical intention tries to counteract hyperintention, or excessive intention, dereflection aims to counteract hyper-reflection, or excessive attention. Frankl (1988) considers the compulsive tendency to self-observation particularly a problem in the United States. Paradoxical intention tries to assist clients to ridicule their symptoms,

---

BOX 9.2

Examples of using paradoxical intention

Example 1: Paradoxical intention for fear of perspiring
A young physician who was afraid of perspiring on meeting people. Whenever he met someone who triggered his anticipatory anxiety he was encouraged to say to himself: 'I only sweated out a litre before, but now I am going to pour out at least ten litres!' (Frankl, 1955, p. 139). After one session of paradoxical intention he freed himself of a phobia that had lasted four years.

Example 2: Paradoxical intention for fear of trembling
A medical student whose fear of trembling led her to begin trembling when the anatomy instructor entered the dissecting room. She overcame her problem by using the following paradoxical intention technique. Whenever the instructor came in she said to herself: 'Oh, here is the instructor! Now I'll show him what a good trembler I am – I'll really show him how to tremble!' (Frankl, 1955, p. 140). However, whenever she tried, she was unable to tremble.

Example 3: Paradoxical intention for counting and checking compulsions
A married woman who had been suffering for fourteen years from a counting compulsion and a compulsion to check whether or not her dresser drawers were in order and securely locked (Frankl, 1955, p. 143). Her doctor demonstrated how to practise paradoxical intention. She was shown how to throw things carelessly into her dresser and to say to herself 'These drawers should be as messy as possible!' After two days her counting compulsion disappeared, and after the fourth day she felt no need to recheck her dresser. She continued her improvement and, whenever occasionally any obsessive-compulsive ideas returned, she was able to ignore them or make them into a joke.

while dereflection assists clients to ignore them. Sexual neuroses, such as frigidity and impotence, are one area for dereflection. Clients must be dereflected from their disturbance to the task at hand. Box 9.3 provides examples of logotherapists helping clients to use dereflection.

BOX 9.3

Examples of using dereflection

Example 1
Dereflection to counter excessive self-observation regarding sexual performance
A young woman, who complained of being frigid, had been sexually abused by her father in her childhood. However, this event in itself did not cause her frigidity. Because she had read popular psychoanalytic literature, she feared all the time that her traumatic sexual abuse experiences would create sexual difficulties. As a result of excessive intention to confirm her femininity and excessive attention to herself, the orgasm was no longer an unintended effect of her commitment to her partner. When her attention was dereflected from herself and refocused toward her partner, she experienced spontaneous orgasms (Frankl, 1963).

Example 2
Dereflection to counter excessive self-observation regarding swallowing
A woman became very thin because she compulsively observed her swallowing and feared her food would go down the wrong way. The client was dereflected by the formula: 'I don't need to watch my swallowing, because I don't really need to swallow, for actually I don't swallow, but rather *it* does' (Frankl, 1955, p. 235). She learned to trust the automatically regulated functioning of her organism.

Medical ministry for somatogenic psychoses

Frankl (1988) uses the term 'medical ministry' for how the logotherapist works with somatogenic cases where the somatic cause cannot be removed. Frankl regards it as a responsibility of the medical profession to comfort and console the sick. The medical ministry is not to be confused with the pastoral ministry. Where possible, the logotherapeutic treatment of clients with endogenous depressions and psychoses is aimed at working with the non-diseased part of clients to assist them in finding meaning in the attitude that they take towards their suffering. A residue of freedom is left even to people with psychoses and their innermost core is not touched by their psychosis. It is extremely demoralizing for sick people to believe that their suffering is meaningless. Box 9.4 provides an example of Frankl medically ministering to a psychotic patient.

BOX 9.4

Example of medical ministry with a somatogenic case

A 17-year-old schizophrenic Jewish youth, who had been institutionalized in Israel for two and a half years because of the severity of his symptoms. The youth started doubting his Jewish faith and blamed God for having made him different from other people. Frankl suggested to the youth that perhaps God wanted to confront him for a specific period in his life with the task of his confinement. The youth said that is why he still believed in God and that possibly God wanted him to recover. Frankl responded that what God wanted was not only his recovery but that his spiritual level should be higher than before his illness. Afterwards the youth improved dramatically and Frankl considers that he enabled him to find meaning 'not only despite but because of psychosis' (Frankl, 1988, p. 131).

CASE MATERIAL

Three sources of case material are available concerning logotherapy.

1. *Client case material.* Case vignettes, such as the ones I have used in abbreviated form in this book, are to be found throughout Frankl's writings: for example in *The Doctor and the Soul* (1955). In addition, in *The Will to Meaning* (1988) Frankl provides transcripts of excerpts taken from logotherapy interviews with a 25-year-old man, who for several years had been suffering from states of anxiety, and with an 80-year-old woman, depressed because she was suffering from a cancer that could not be successfully treated.
2. *Concentration camp testimony.* In books such as *Man's Search for Meaning* (1963) and *Viktor Frankl Recollections* (1997a) Frankl bears witness to the effect that presence or absence of a sense of meaning or purpose in life had on concentration camp inmates.
3. *Personal example.* Frankl's own life is a testimony to the strengthening and ennobling effect that meaning can provide to individuals, however harsh and tragic their circumstances.

FURTHER DEVELOPMENTS

Frankl's legacy continues in terms of institutional structures and how many therapists work. A Viktor Frankl Institute exists in Vienna and institutes of logotherapy and existential analysis are present in various parts of the world. From 1993 to 1998 the Viktor Frankl Institute in Vienna published the *International Journal for Logotherapy and Existential Analysis.* Currently comprehensive audio-visual editions of Frankl's lectures are in preparation. Information about these editions may be obtained from the Viktor Frankl Institute, Langwiesgasse 6, A-1140 Wein, Austria, and from the Institute's website (www.logotherapy.univie.ac.at).

SUMMARY

- *Logotherapy's purpose is to assist clients in their search for meaning. The will to meaning is the primary motivational force in humans. The search for meaning involves both conscious activity and getting in touch with the spiritual unconscious.*
- *Conscience, the origins of which are located in the spiritual unconscious, can intuitively reveal an individual's unique meanings in specific situations. The religious unconscious exists within the spiritual unconscious.*
- *Human freedom is 'freedom to' accept responsibility for fulfilling meaning within the confines of death and destiny. Self-transcendence, in which people reach out for meaning beyond themselves, is an essential characteristic of human existence. Sources of meaning include: work, love, suffering, the past, and the supra-meaning.*
- *The existential vacuum is when people suffer from an inner void and lack meaning in life. Existential frustration results when the will to meaning is frustrated. The existential vacuum is not in itself neurotic, but can lead to noogenic neurosis. Humanity is becoming more neurotic and the mass neurotic triad consists of depression, addiction and aggression.*
- *Causes of the existential vacuum include the weak instinctual basis of human behaviour compared to other animals, the erosion of values and traditions, and tendencies to reductionism where humans are viewed as determined rather than determining.*
- *Ways in which people maintain the existential vacuum include repression, avoiding responsibility and insufficiently emphasizing self-transcendence.*
- *The goal of logotherapy for the existential vacuum and noogenic neuroses is to help clients find meaning in their lives. Logotherapists are responsibility educators. In addition, goals for the psychogenic neuroses and somatogenic psychoses are described.*
- *Within the context of humane relationships, logotherapy for existential concerns focuses on increasing existential awareness and on assisting clients to find meaning.*
- *Methods for focusing on meaning include teaching clients the importance of assuming responsibility for meaning, helping clients listen to their consciences, asking clients about meanings, broadening horizons about sources of meaning, eliciting meaning through Socratic questioning, using logodrama, offering meanings, and analysing dreams.*
- *Paradoxical intention and dereflection are logotherapeutic techniques for working with psychogenic neuroses.*
- *Medical ministry, in which logotherapists assist clients to find meaning in their suffering, is advocated for somatogenic psychoses.*

REVIEW AND PERSONAL QUESTIONS

REVIEW QUESTIONS

1. What is the will to meaning?
2. How does Frankl distinguish between consciousness and the unconscious? What are some important characteristics of the unconscious?
3. What does Frankl mean by self-transcendence?
4. Describe each of the following sources of meaning: meaning in work; meaning in

love; meaning in suffering; meaning from the past; and the supra-meaning.

5. What do the terms existential vacuum and existential frustration mean?
6. What do the following terms mean: noogenic neuroses; psychogenic neuroses; and somatogenic psychoses?
7. What are the goals of logotherapy? Please specify according to category of human distress.
8. Describe how a logotherapist might use each of the following methods to focus clients on finding meaning in their lives:
    • teaching the importance of assuming responsibility for meaning;
    • assisting clients to listen to their consciences;
    • asking clients about meanings;
    • broadening horizons about sources of meaning;
    • eliciting meaning through Socratic questioning;
    • eliciting meaning through logodrama;
    • offering meanings; and
    • analysing dreams.
9. Describe the technique of paradoxical intention and give an example of its use.
10. Describe the technique of dereflection and indicate its uses.
11. What does Frankl mean by medical ministry?

PERSONAL QUESTIONS

1. To what extent do you experience the existential vacuum and suffer from existential frustration?
2. Assess the extent to which you find meaning in each of the following sources: work, love, suffering, the past, and the supra-meaning.
3. If currently you have insufficient meaning in your life, how might you help yourself to find more meaning?
4. If possible, apply the technique of paradoxical intention to coping with a problem in your life.
5. If possible, apply the technique of dereflection to coping with a problem in your life.
6. What relevance, if any, has the theory and practice of logotherapy for how you conduct therapy?
7. What relevance, if any, has the theory and practice of logotherapy for how you live?

ANNOTATED BIBLIOGRAPHY

Frankl, V. E. (1963). *Man's Search for Meaning: An Introduction to Logotherapy.* New York: Washington Square Press.

Part one of this small volume, entitled 'Experiences in a concentration camp', provides a highly readable and moving account of Frankl's experiences as a concentration camp inmate. Frankl recounts instances of human brutality, weakness and nobility. He incisively describes qualities making for psychological survival and growth. The second part of the book, entitled 'Basic concepts of logotherapy', was written some years later. It provides a clearly written and concise introduction to logotherapy theory and practice. This book provides an excellent introduction to Frankl, the man and the therapist.

Frankl, V. E. (1955). *The Doctor and the Soul: From Psychotherapy to Logotherapy.* Harmondsworth, England: Penguin Books.

This book traces the development of logotherapy. Frankl next discusses the meanings of life, suffering, work and love. Then he gives his views of the psychology of anxiety neurosis, obsessional neurosis, melancholia and schizophrenia. Next come descriptions of the logotherapeutic techniques of paradoxical intention and dereflection. Frankl ends the book by presenting logotherapy as a form of medical ministry.

Frankl, V. E. (1988). *The Will to Meaning: Foundations and Applications of Logotherapy.* New York: Meridian.

This book arose from a series of lectures Frankl gave in 1966. Part one of the book, entitled 'Foundations of logotherapy', covers metaclinical implications of psychotherapy, self-transcendence as a human phenomenon, and what is meant by meaning. Part two, entitled 'Applications of logotherapy', discusses the existential vacuum, logotherapeutic techniques, and medical ministry. The book concludes with a chapter on dimensions of meaning and then has an afterword on the de-gurufication of logotherapy.

Frankl, V. E. (1975a). *The Unconscious God: Psychotherapy and Theology.* New York: Simon and Schuster (now out of print). Extended by a lecture manuscript and published in 1997 under the title *Man's Search for Ultimate Meaning.* New York: Plenum.

The first part of the 1975 book, entitled 'The unconscious god', was originally published in 1948 in Austria. Frankl asserts that there is not only an instinctual unconscious, but a spiritual unconscious as well. Within the spiritual unconscious, there exists unconscious religiousness. Frankl discusses unconscious religiousness as well as the relationship between psychotherapy and theology. The second part of the book, entitled 'Postscript 1975: New research in logotherapy', presents Frankl's ideas interspersed with references to research.

Frankl, V. E. (1967). *Psychotherapy and Existentialism: Selected Papers on Logotherapy.* Harmondsworth, England: Penguin.

This book is a compilation of many of Frankl's most important articles regarding the theory and practice of logotherapy.

Frankl, V. E. (1997a). *Viktor Frankl Recollections: An Autobiography.* New York: Insight Books.

Frankl discusses his childhood and youth, his experiences as a young doctor of neurology in pre-war Vienna, his early disagreements with Sigmund Freud and Alfred Adler, the impact of Nazism on himself and his family, the rebuilding of his life in post-war Vienna, and the development of logotherapy. The book provides numerous personal insights, such as his pleasures and hobbies, and contains some very personal and heart-rending passages.

REFERENCES AND FURTHER READING

Frankl, V. E. (1955). *The Doctor and the Soul: From Psychotherapy to Logotherapy.* Harmondsworth: Penguin Books.

Frankl, V. E. (1963). *Man's Search for Meaning: An Introduction to Logotherapy.* New York: Washington Square Press.

Frankl, V. E. (1967). *Psychotherapy and Existentialism: Selected Papers on Logotherapy.* Harmondsworth: Penguin.

Frankl, V. E. (1975a). *The Unconscious God: Psychotherapy and Theology.* New York: Simon and Schuster.

Frankl, V. E. (1975b). Paradoxical intention and dereflection. *Psychotherapy: Theory, Research and Practice, 12*, 226–37.

Frankl, V. E. (1985). *The Unheard Cry for Meaning: Psychotherapy and Humanism.* New York: Simon and Schuster.

Frankl, V. E. (1988). *The Will to Meaning: Foundations and Applications of Logotherapy.* New York: Meridian.

Frankl, V. E. (1997a). *Viktor Frankl Recollections: An Autobiography.* New York: Insight Books.

Frankl, V. E. (1997b). *Man's Search for Ultimate Meaning.* New York: Plenum.

10

Behaviour Therapy: Theory

The behaviorist asks: Why don't we make what we can observe the real field of psychology? Let us limit ourselves to what can be observed, and formulate laws concerning only those things.

John Broadus Watson

INTRODUCTION

Adherents of behaviour therapy view their practice as firmly rooted in experimentally derived principles of learning. However, behavioural theory is an overall theory as well as an experimentally based attempt to describe the specific laws or principles of human behaviour. As an overall theory the distinctive emphasis is on the overwhelming role of environmental contingencies in influencing the acquisition and maintenance of behaviour. In its most radical form the behavioural model sees human actions as derived solely from three sources: biological deprivations, such as hunger and sexual tension, the individual's learning history, and the characteristics of and contingencies provided by environmental contexts. There is no place for concepts such as mind and free will. However, a distinction has emerged in behaviour therapy between approaches based on conditioning (radical behaviour therapy) and those which emphasize cognitive mediating variables (cognitive–behaviour therapy). The latter emphasis is less deterministic than the former.

As a set of experimentally derived principles of learning, the behavioural model offers a greater degree of specificity in analysing observable, as contrasted with intrapsychic, human behaviour than that offered by the humanistic, existential or psychoanalytic models. Much of the research on the behavioural model has been performed on animals such as dogs, cats and pigeons. This raises issues of the generalizability of a model derived largely from non-human animals in laboratory settings to humans in natural settings. Nevertheless, the point remains that, at the molecular level or level of observations of specific behaviours, behavioural psychologists and researchers have made a distinctive contribution to developing a theoretical framework for psychotherapy.

This chapter differs from that of the preceding ones. It aims to introduce the reader to some key behavioural concepts through discussing selectively the ideas and experimental work of five leading theorists: Pavlov's classical conditioning, Watson's conditioned behaviourism, Skinner's operant conditioning, Wolpe's reciprocal inhibition, and Bandura's social cognitive theory. Of these theorists, only Wolpe was also a practising therapist. Both in the biographical and theory sections of this chapter, the theorists are presented in roughly historical order, though their working lives overlapped.

BIOGRAPHICAL INFORMATION

Ivan Petrovich Pavlov (1849–1936)

Pavlov was born in 1849, his father a priest in the Russian Orthodox Church known for his erudition and his mother a bright, but illiterate, priest's daughter. After the death of her third child, his mother suffered a 'nervous condition', an experience that may have contributed to Pavlov's lifelong interest in psychiatry (Windholz, 1997). In the 1860s, while studying at the Riazan Ecclesiastic Seminary, Pavlov became interested in the natural sciences and subsequently rejected a career in the Church. In 1870 Pavlov matriculated at the Faculty of Physical–Mathematical Sciences of the University of St Petersburg. In 1883, he was awarded an MD degree by the Imperial Military–Medical Academy in St Petersburg. In 1890, Pavlov was appointed a Professor of Pharmacology and then, in 1895, became a Professor of Physiology at the Imperial Military–Medical Academy.

Beginning in 1891, Pavlov made fundamental discoveries concerning the nature and physiology of digestion and, in 1904, received the Nobel Prize in physiology and medicine for this work. In 1901, Pavlov redirected his research interests from the digestive processes to the functioning of the cerebral hemispheres of dogs by means of the salivary reflex conditioning method. He spent the remainder of his life on this research, eventually with a large staff. Pavlov's books include *The Work of the Digestive Glands* and *Conditioned Reflexes: An Investigation of the Physiological Activity of the Cerebral Cortex.*

John Broadus Watson (1878–1958)

Watson, sometimes viewed as the founder of behaviourism, was born in Greenville, South Carolina, to an energetic and religious mother and a philandering father, who left home when Watson was 13 years old. He was educated at Furman University in Greenville and at the University of Chicago, where his doctoral thesis was on animal education. Watson married when he was 25. At 30, he became Professor of Psychology at Johns Hopkins University in Baltimore and, at 36, he was elected president of the American Psychological Association. During the 1910s, Watson moved his emphasis from animal to human observation and experimentation. From 1913 Watson worked hard at establishing behaviourism as a method of psychology.

In his personal life Watson had a decided tendency to respond to female stimuli, a characteristic with which his first wife was prepared to live so long as the relationships were not really serious. However, in 1919 Watson, who was then 41, met an overwhelming stimulus in the person of a 19-year-old graduate student called Rosalie Raynor. In 1920, Watson was forced to resign from Johns Hopkins University on the grounds of adultery with a student, and no other university would employ him. Divorced in late 1920, Watson married Rosalie in January 1921 and lived happily with her until her tragic death from illness in 1936.

After leaving university life Watson became a highly successful advertising executive with J. Walter Thompson's and later with Esty's agencies. In the 1920s, Watson conducted some research on children with Mary Cover Jones and also did some popular psychological writing. His two children by his second marriage, Billy and Jimmy, were brought up by behavioural methods, including an absence of overt shows of parental affection so that they would not become dependent. Billy, who became a psychiatrist interested in Freudian ideas, committed suicide a few years after Watson's death in 1958, and Jimmy underwent psychoanalysis.

Watson's books include *Animal Education, Behavior, Psychology from the Standpoint of a Behaviorist, The Psychological Care of the Infant and Child* and *Behaviorism*. A bibliography of Watson's work can be found at the end of David Cohen's biography, *J. B. Watson, the Founder of Behaviourism*.

Burrhus Frederick Skinner (1904–90)

Skinner was born in Susquehanna, Pennsylvania. In 1926 he graduated from Hamilton College where, majoring in English, he had planned to become a writer. In 1928, after an unsuccessful trial period at writing, Skinner entered Harvard University as a graduate student in psychology, obtaining his doctorate in 1931. From 1931 to 1936 he worked as a postdoctoral fellow in the laboratory of W. J. Crozier, a distinguished experimental biologist.

Skinner held early academic appointments, from 1936 to 1945 at the University of Minnesota, and from 1945 to 1948 at Indiana University. In 1948 he became Professor of Psychology at Harvard where he retired from active teaching in 1974. Throughout the remainder of his life Skinner continued writing and lecturing. Among his numerous academic awards, in 1958 Skinner received the American Psychological Association's Award for Distinguished Scientific Contributions.

Skinner's nineteen books include his seminal work *The Behavior of Organisms, Walden Two* (a novel about a behavioural utopia), *Science and Human Behavior, Verbal Behavior* (which he considered his most important book), *Schedules of Reinforcement* (co-written with C. B. Ferster), co-authorship with J. G. Holland of a programmed textbook *The Analysis of Behavior, Contingencies of Reinforcement, Beyond Freedom and Dignity, About Behaviorism* and *Particulars of My Life*. Skinner 'always viewed his own work – as he views science generally – as the product of environmental contingencies and not the result of a creative mind' (Holland, 1992, p. 667).

Joseph Wolpe (1915–97)

Wolpe was born on 20 April 1915, and educated in Johannesburg, South Africa. Trained as a doctor, during the Second World War Wolpe served in the South African Medical Corps, where the failure of conventional treatments to war neuroses stimulated his interest in psychology. From 1948 to 1956 and again from 1957 to 1959 Wolpe was a lecturer in the Department of Psychiatry at the University of Witwatersrand, Johannesburg, as well as conducting a private psychiatric practice.

In the late 1940s, as a result of laboratory experiments with cats as subjects, he developed a method based on reciprocal inhibition for de-conditioning neurotic fear responses. Wolpe then applied his experimental findings in his clinical work, with great success. From 1956 to 1957, Wolpe was a fellow at the Center for Advanced Study in the Behavioral Sciences at Stanford University in California. As the fruits of his Stanford sabbatical, in 1958 both Wolpe's experimental work and its psychotherapeutic derivatives were published in a book entitled *Psychotherapy by Reciprocal Inhibition.* This publication created a great stir and acted as a major impetus to the burgeoning development since the early 1960s of behaviour therapy.

Wolpe later returned to the United States where, from 1960 to 1965, he was Professor of Psychiatry at the University of Virginia at Charlottesville; from 1965 to 1984 at Temple University in Pennsylvania, and afterwards at the Medical College of Pennsylvania in Philadelphia. Wolpe's other books include *The Practice of Behaviour Therapy, Theme and Variations: A Behaviour Therapy Casebook*, and *Life Without Fear: Anxiety and its Cure*, which he co-authored with his son David. In 1979 Wolpe received the American Psychological Society's Distinguished Scientific Award for his pioneering research that contributed to the establishment of behaviour therapy.

Albert Bandura (1925–)

Bandura was born and raised in Mundare in northern Alberta, Canada. In 1949, Bandura graduated from the University of British Columbia with a psychology major. In 1952, he received a doctorate in clinical psychology from the University of Iowa, followed by a one-year postdoctoral internship at the Witchita Guidance Center. Afterwards he went to Stanford University in California as an instructor and, by 1964, had been appointed a full professor. In 1974, the university awarded him an endowed chair named the David Starr Jordan Professorship of Social Science in Psychology. Also, in 1974, Bandura was President of the American Psychological Association. Among his many honours and awards, in 1980 he received the American Psychological Association's Award for Distinguished Scientific Contributions.

Bandura has published numerous journal articles on his experimental work on such topics as moral development, observational learning, fear acquisition, participant modelling treatment strategies, effects of the media, and the cognitive regulation of behaviour, especially the mechanisms of human agency and people's perceptions of their efficacy to exercise influence over events which affect their lives. His books include: *Social Learning and Personality Development*, which he co-authored with Richard Walters; *Principles of Behaviour Modification*; *Aggression: A Social Learning Analysis*; *Social Learning Theory*; *Social Foundations of Thought and Action: A Social Cognitive Theory*; *Self-Efficacy in Changing Societies* (edited by him); and *Self-Efficacy: The Exercise of Control.*

PAVLOV'S CLASSICAL CONDITIONING

Pavlov considered that both instincts and reflexes were alike in being inevitable responses of the organism to internal and external stimuli. 'Reflex' was the preferred term since it had been used from the beginning with a scientific connotation. The whole nervous activity of animals is based on inborn reflexes, which may be either excitatory or inhibitory. Such reflexes 'are regular causal connections between certain definite external stimuli acting on the organism and its necessary reflex reaction' (Pavlov, 1927, p. 16). The inborn reflexes alone are inadequate to ensure the continued existence of the organism, with the more specialized interaction between the animal and the environment provided through the medium of the cerebral hemispheres. The 'most general function of the hemispheres is that of reacting to signals presented by innumerable stimuli of interchangeable signification' (Pavlov, 1927, p. 16).

In his book *Conditioned Reflexes*, subtitled 'An investigation of the physiological activity of the cerebral cortex', Pavlov describes the precautions taken to build a laboratory so as to eliminate, as far as possible, any stimuli outside his control. In order to register the intensity of the salivary reflex, all the dogs used in his experiments were subjected to a minor operation which consisted of transferring the opening of the salivary duct from the mucous membrane of the mouth to the outside skin. In the experimental laboratory a dog would be harnessed to a stand in one section of a double chamber, while the experimenter was in the other section.

In the following experiment a conditioned reflex was obtained by pairing or linking up the action of a new stimulus with an unconditioned reflex. An experimental dog was introduced to a routine in which stimulation by a metronome was linked with feeding. If the dog was then placed in the experimental condition its salivary glands remained inactive as long as no special stimulus was introduced. However, when it was allowed to hear the sounds of a beating metronome, salivary secretion began after nine seconds, and in the course of 45 seconds eleven drops were secreted. Furthermore, in this experiment the dog turned in the direction from which it had customarily received food and began to lick its lips vigorously.

In another experiment food was shown to the animal. After five seconds salivary secretion began, and in the course of fifteen seconds six drops were collected. In yet another experiment food was introduced into the dog's mouth and secretion began in one to two seconds.

Food in the dog's mouth, as contrasted with the sight of food or the association of food with the beating of a metronome, produces an inborn reflex. This reflex is brought about by the physical and chemical properties of the food acting upon the mucous membrane of the mouth and tongue. However, even salivation at the sight of food is a learned reflex, as is salivation at the beating of the metronome. Both the sight of food and the beating of the metronome are signals, and the reaction to them involves signalization through the activity of the cerebral hemispheres. Thus inborn reflexes do not involve learning or signalization, while conditioned reflexes are learned and involve signalization. The definition of reflexes as causal connections between definite external stimuli and their necessary reflex reactions still holds true when signalization is involved. The difference is that the reflex reaction to signals depends on more variables than those entailed in unconditioned reflexes.

In a further experiment on the same dog, contrary to the usual routine, stimulation by the metronome was not followed by feeding. The stimulus of the metronome was repeated for periods of 30 seconds at intervals of two minutes. Pavlov gives details indicating a lengthening of the latency period prior to secretion and a diminution of drops of saliva over successive trials. He writes that the phenomenon of the weakening of a reflex to a conditioned stimulus which is repeated a number of times without reinforcement might appropriately be termed 'extinction of conditioned reflexes'. Indeed, if the above experiment had been continued, the conditioned reflex would have disappeared entirely.

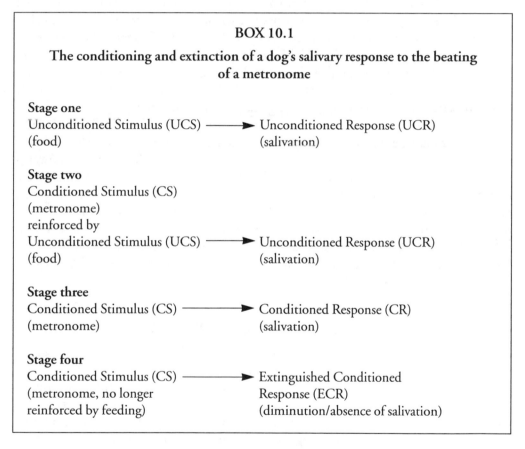

BOX 10.1

The conditioning and extinction of a dog's salivary response to the beating of a metronome

Stage one
Unconditioned Stimulus (UCS) ⟶ Unconditioned Response (UCR)
(food) (salivation)

Stage two
Conditioned Stimulus (CS)
(metronome)
reinforced by
Unconditioned Stimulus (UCS) ⟶ Unconditioned Response (UCR)
(food) (salivation)

Stage three
Conditioned Stimulus (CS) ⟶ Conditioned Response (CR)
(metronome) (salivation)

Stage four
Conditioned Stimulus (CS) ⟶ Extinguished Conditioned
(metronome, no longer Response (ECR)
reinforced by feeding) (diminution/absence of salivation)

Box 10.1 diagrammatically depicts the metronome experiments, with the term 'response' substituted for 'reflex'. Food in the mouth is an unconditioned stimulus (UCS), which automatically elicits the inborn response of salivation (UCR). Through repeated reinforcement consisting of stimulation by the metronome followed by feeding, the metronome becomes a conditioned stimulus (CS), thus becoming a signal for food and eliciting the conditioned response of salivation (CR). However, if the metronome (CS) is no longer reinforced by feeding, then the conditioned response (CR) undergoes extinction and diminishes, or even disappears (ECR).

Learning a conditioned response in the above manner has come to be termed 'classical' or 'respondent' conditioning. Pavlov and his colleagues explored many other areas, such as conditioned inhibition and the generalization of stimuli, but these researches are not described here. Pavlov's researches into the conditioned reflex were essential to the founding of behaviour therapy.

WATSON'S CONDITIONED BEHAVIOURISM

To the behaviourist 'the subject matter of human psychology is *the behaviour of the human being*' (Watson, 1931, p. 2). Furthermore, the behaviourist views psychology as a purely objective experimental branch of natural science, with its theoretical goal being the prediction and control of behaviour. In his 1913 paper 'Psychology as the behaviorist views it', Watson observed that he had devoted nearly twelve years to experimentation on animals and that it was natural that he should drift to a theoretical position in harmony with his experimental work. What is observable is the real field of psychology and what can be observed is what the organism does or says, i.e. its behaviour.

Watson considered that there were two points of view dominant in the American psychological thinking of his time: introspective or subjective psychology, which he termed the old psychology, and the new and objective psychology of behaviourism. Concepts such as consciousness and introspection, the subject matter of the old psychology, were magic. Psychology, being an objective and experimental branch of the natural sciences, needs such concepts as little as do the sciences of chemistry and physics. As the behaviour of animals can be investigated without referring to consciousness, so can the behaviour of man. In fact 'the behaviour of man and the behaviour of animals must be considered on the same plane; as being equally essential to a general understanding of behaviour' (Watson, 1913, p. 176).

Stimulus, response and conditioning

Both human and animal adjust themselves to their environments by means of hereditary and habit equipments. Through the process of evolution humans have developed sense organs, such as the eye, skin and viscera, which are most sensitive to differing kinds of stimuli. A stimulus, or thing that evokes a reaction, may come from objects in the external environment. Also, humans are affected constantly by stimuli in their internal environment arising from tissue changes in their bodies. By means of conditioning there is an ever-increasing range of stimuli to which people respond.

Stimuli evoke responses which usually involve the organism moving or altering in such a way that the stimulus no longer arouses reaction. One classification of responses is that between overt and implicit. Another general classification is that between learned and unlearned responses. Unlearned responses include all the things people do from earliest infancy, such as perspiration and breathing, prior to the processes of conditioning and habit formation which produce learned responses.

The Watsonian behaviourist sees all psychological problems and their solutions as being schematized in *stimulus* (or the more complex *situation*) and *response* terms, often abbreviated to S-R terms. In the ideal behaviourist world, given the response the stimuli can be predicted and given the stimuli the response can be predicted. Box 10.2 illustrates this view of psychological problems.

BOX 10.2

Schematization of unsolved and solved psychological problems

Unsolved

S..R

Given   ? (to be determined)

S..R

? (to be determined)   Given

Solved

S..R

has been determined   has been determined

Stimuli may be unconditioned in that from birth they call forth definite responses, such as the responses of turning the eyes away from or closing the eyes to light. On the other hand, most stimuli to which humans respond are conditioned or learned, for example all the printed words to which humans respond. Similarly, responses may be unconditioned, as in the above light example, but very frequently they are conditioned, as in the case of a 2-year-old child who has learned to substitute screaming for laughter at the sight of a dog. Watson observed that the whole body of man is built around the keynote 'rapid, and when needed, complicated reactions to simple and complex stimuli' (Watson, 1931, p. 91).

Hereditary equipment

Watson viewed humans as animals born with certain types of structure, subject to individual variations, which force them to respond to stimuli in certain ways. For instance, at birth the human responds with breathing, heartbeat, sneezing, etc. These kinds of reactions are the human's unlearned behaviour. Some unlearned behaviours, such as suckling and unlearned grasping, are short-lived. Others, such as blinking, menstruation and ejaculation, begin later in life and last much longer. Unlearned behaviours form a relatively simple list of human responses, each of which, including our respiration and circulation, becomes conditioned shortly after birth. The concept of instinct is redundant in psychology, since observation of children indicates that everything which people tend to call 'instinct' is largely the result of training or conditioning and, as such, is part of the human's learned behaviour.

Watson developed the idea of the activity stream, a 'ceaseless stream of activity beginning when the egg is fertilised and becoming more complex as age increases' (Watson, 1931, p. 139). Each human action system starts with an unlearned beginning and is then made more complex by conditioning. For instance, vocal responses constitute unlearned behaviour while talking represents a conditioned action system.

Determinism and habit formation

The Watsonian behaviourist is a strict determinist. Watson considered that, given total control over a dozen healthy infants from birth, he could take any one at random and train this person to become any type of specialist he might select, including doctor, lawyer, artist, beggar-man and thief. Inheritance of capacity, talent, temperament, mental constitution and characteristics does not really exist, since these things depend on training.

Habit formation probably starts in embryonic life and is very rapid after birth. Though very helpless at birth, greater development of three habit systems differentiates the human from other animals. These habit systems are:

1. visceral or emotional;
2. manual; and
3. laryngeal or verbal.

The development of emotional habits will be used to illustrate the importance of conditioning.

Conditioning of emotions

Watson states that there are three types of unlearned beginnings of emotional reactions, or unlearned emotional responses, to stimuli. These responses are fear, rage and love. These emotional reactions might be viewed as unconditioned reflexes or responses. For instance, a loud sound is a fundamental stimulus for eliciting the fear response.

Watson and Raynor did a series of experiments on an 11-month-old boy called Albert. (Watson and Raynor, 1920). The first experiment involved the establishment of a conditioned emotional response of fear to a white rat. This was achieved by linking on some trials the loud sound of the striking of a bar with Albert's touching the white rat. When later the white rat was presented alone, Albert exhibited fear responses of crying, falling over and crawling away.

A second experiment showed that there was a transfer of the conditioned fear response, though less strong, from the white rat to other furry animals (rabbit, dog) and objects (fur coat, cotton wool) when five days later they were presented to him. The above tests were carried out on a table covered with a mattress in a small, well-lit room.

A further experiment indicated, after 31 days, the persistence in a less intense form of both the conditioned fear response to the rat and the transferred fear responses to the fur coat and the rabbit. Watson and Raynor concluded that it was probable that many of the phobias in psychopathology are conditioned emotional reactions of either the direct or the transferred type. Emotional disturbances can be retraced to conditioned and transferred responses set up in infancy and childhood to all three of the fundamental human emotions.

Watson and Raynor did not remove Albert's conditioned emotional responses prior to his discharge from hospital, to be adopted by a family that lived outside Baltimore. However, Mary Cover Jones, an associate of Watson's, conducted an experiment in which Peter, a boy of about 3 years, was unconditioned or reconditioned of his 'home grown' fears of a rabbit, a white rat and related stimuli (Jones, 1924).

The experimenters were given permission to give Peter his lunch of crackers and a glass of milk. As he began to eat his lunch, the rabbit was displayed in a cage of wire mesh just far enough away not to disturb his eating. Gradually the rabbit was brought closer and closer and finally Peter would eat with one hand and play with the rabbit with the other. There was a transfer of unconditioning of fear responses to other furry objects, with degrees of success varying from total to greatly improved.

Watson contended that human emotional life is the result of the wear and tear of environmental forces. Through experiments such as those described above, an initial understanding was developing of how emotional reactions could be conditioned and unconditioned. Watson was excited and cautiously optimistic about the place of his natural science approach in the treatment of the emotionally disturbed.

Thinking and memory

Watson argued that 'thinking' referred to all subvocal word behaviour. In other words, thinking is the same as talking to oneself. Furthermore, language development represents the conditioning of verbal responses on unlearned vocal sounds. Sometimes the subvocal use of words has become an automatic habit. On other occasions, for example in reacting to a new situation, human thinking is similar to the trial-and-error behaviour of a rat in a maze. When subjects are asked to think aloud it is easy to see how they worked out their problem by word behaviour. New verbal creations, such as a poem, are arrived at by manipulating words and shifting them about until a new pattern is arrived at. There is no such thing as personal meaning in the behaviourist's theory.

Memory is viewed as the retention of verbal habits. If people meet a stimulus again after a period of time, they do the habitual thing they learned to do when the stimulus was first present. For instance, a person who meets a friend after an absence will say the old words and exhibit the old visceral reactions.

Watson considered there is no need to introduce the concept of mind into the so-called mental diseases. Diagnosis should involve an analysis of behaviour alone. Personality problems are behaviour disturbances and habit conflicts which need to be cured by unconditioning and conditioning.

SKINNER'S OPERANT BEHAVIOURISM

Behavior is shaped and maintained by its consequences.
B. F. Skinner

Like Watson, Skinner was dedicated to a science of behaviour which deals with facts, and searches for lawful relations among the events in nature. Skinner's distinctive contribution to psychology has been to elaborate the importance of the after-effects or consequences of behaviour. He was assiduous in conducting experiments with pigeons and rats to map out the details of this principle. He considered that he had gone beyond stimulus and response to take into account the action of the environment upon the organism *after* the response has been made.

Operant behaviour

Skinner observed that a response which has occurred cannot be predicted or controlled, but all that can be predicted is the probability of a similar response occurring in the future. The unit of a predictive science of behaviour is an operant. The term 'operant' emphasizes the fact that behaviour *operates* on the environment to generate consequences. Thus the consequences define the properties with respect to which responses are viewed as similar. Skinner used the term 'operant' both as an adjective, as in operant behaviour, and as a noun, which indicates the behaviour defined by a given consequence. He acknowledged that Pavlov called all events which strengthened behaviour in his dogs 'reinforcement' and the resulting changes in their voluntary and involuntary behaviour 'conditioning'. However, the critical difference is that in Pavlov's work the reinforcer is paired with the *stimulus*, whereas in operant behaviour it is contingent upon a *response*. Classical and operant conditioning are the only two possible kinds of conditioning.

Contingencies of reinforcement

Skinner stressed the role of the environment in shaping and maintaining behaviour. Behaviour both operates on the environment to produce consequences and also is controlled or contingent upon the consequences produced by that environment. Any adequate description of the interaction between an organism and its environment must specify three elements:

1. the occasion on which a response occurs;
2. the response itself; and
3. the reinforcing consequences.

The interrelationship of these three elements constitutes the contingencies of reinforcement. For example, in an experiment with pigeons, any stimuli deriving from the experimental space, such as sound or light, and from the operanda of the experiment, such as a translucent disc on the wall which may be pecked, and from any special stimulating devices prior to the response, are the 'occasion' of the response. The response itself might be pecking the disc, and the reinforcing consequence might be food provided at a time when the pigeon is hungry.

Positive and negative reinforcement

The probability of a response is increased after both positive and negative reinforcement. Positive reinforcements consist of presenting something, such as food, water or sexual contact, in a situation. Negative reinforcements consist of removing something, such as a bright light or an electric shock, from the situation. Thus the difference between positive and negative reinforcement hinges on whether it is the presence or absence of a given reinforcer which increases the probability of a response. The withdrawal of a positive reinforcer has the same effect as the presentation of a negative reinforcer.

Primary and conditioned reinforcers

Skinner considered that all reinforcers eventually derive their power from evolutionary selection and that it is part of 'human nature' to be reinforced in particular ways by particular things. For instance, both the positive reinforcer of food and the negative reinforcer of escape from a dangerous situation have obvious survival value. Only a small part of behaviour is immediately reinforced by food, water, sexual contact or other reinforcers of evident biological significance. Such reinforcers are the primary or unconditioned ones.

Most behaviour is emitted in response to reinforcers which have become associated with or conditioned to primary reinforcers. For instance, if each time food is given to a hungry pigeon a light is turned on, the light eventually becomes a conditioned reinforcer. The light may then be used to condition an operant in the same way as food. A conditioned reinforcer is generalized when it is paired with more than one primary reinforcer. The importance of this is that a generalized conditioned reinforcer, such as money, is useful because it is not attached to just one state of deprivation, such as hunger, but to many. Therefore, under this kind of reinforcement, a response is more likely to occur. Other generalized conditioned reinforcers are attention, approval and affection.

Schedules of reinforcement

Ferster and Skinner (1957) observed that many significant features of the shaping and maintenance of behaviour can be explained only by reference to the properties of schedules of reinforcement, and also that intermittent reinforcement can be a very important source of reinforcement in its own right and not just the poor relation of inevitable or continuous reinforcement. Box 10.3 depicts non-intermittent and intermittent reinforcement schedules.

BOX 10.3
Schedules of reinforcement

Non-intermittent schedules of reinforcement
- *Continuous reinforcement*, where every response emitted is reinforced.
- *Extinction*, where no responses are reinforced.

Intermittent schedules of reinforcement
- *Fixed interval*, in which the first response occurring after a given period of time (for example, five minutes) is reinforced, with another period beginning immediately after the reinforcement.
- *Fixed ratio*, in which every *n*th response is reinforced. (The word 'ratio' refers to the ratio between responses and reinforcements.)
- *Variable interval*, in which reinforcements are scheduled according to a random series of intervals having a given mean and lying between arbitrary values.
- *Variable ratio*, in which reinforcements are scheduled according to a random series of ratios having a given mean and lying between arbitrary values.
- *Multiple*, in which one schedule of reinforcement is in force in the presence of one stimulus and a different schedule in the presence of another stimulus. For instance, there is a fixed interval when the key in the pigeon's experimental box is red, and a variable interval when the key is green.
- *Differential reinforcement of rate of response*, in which a response is reinforced only if it follows the preceding response after a specified interval of time (e.g. three minutes) or before the end of a given interval (e.g. half a second).

Maintenance and extinction

Skinner did not consider the term 'learning' to be equivalent to 'operant conditioning'. Learning emphasizes acquisition of behaviour, whereas operant conditioning focuses on both acquisition and maintenance of behaviour. Thus behaviour continues to have consequences, and if these consequences or reinforcements are not forthcoming then extinction occurs. For instance, when a pigeon's behaviour, such as the lifting of its head, which has been reinforced by the consequence of food, no longer continues to receive this reinforcement, the head-lifting tends to occur with a reduced frequency. Similarly, when people engage in behaviour which no longer has rewarding consequences, they find themselves less inclined to behave that way.

Schedules of reinforcement are relevant to extinction. For example, the resistance to extinction generated by intermittent reinforcement may be much greater than that under continuous reinforcement. The task of a science of behaviour is to account for the probability of a response in terms of its history of reinforcement and extinction. Skinner used the term 'operant strength' to indicate the probability of a given response and observes that with humans the condition of low operant strength resulting from extinction often requires treatment. For instance, psychotherapy might sometimes be viewed as a system of reinforcement designed to reinstate extinguished behaviour.

Shaping and successive approximation

Behaviour may be shaped by reinforcing successive approximations to the desired response. Skinner gives the example of teaching a pigeon to bowl by swiping, with a sharp sideward movement of its beak, a wooden ball down a miniature alley towards a set of toy pins. When he and his colleagues waited for the complete response, which was to be reinforced by food, nothing happened. Then they decided to reinforce any response which had the slightest resemblance to a swipe and, afterwards, to select responses which more closely approximated the final form. This was a highly successful procedure and within minutes the pigeon was striking the ball as if it had been a champion squash player. In another experiment, by reinforcing successive approximations, a rat was conditioned to pull a string to get a marble from a rack, pick up the marble with its forepaws, carry it across the cage to a vertical tube rising two inches above the floor, lift the marble, and drop it into the tube.

Stimulus discrimination and control

Operant behaviour is emitted through important connections with the environment. For instance, in a pigeon experiment, neck-stretching is reinforced when a signal light is on and allowed to extinguish when a signal light is off. The contingencies of reinforcement are that a stimulus (the light) is the occasion, the response is stretching the neck, and the reinforcement is food. The process through which the response is eventually more likely to occur when the light is on is called discrimination. Another way of viewing discrimination is to say that a response has come under the control of a discriminative stimulus or, more briefly, under stimulus control. Once an operant discrimination has been conditioned, the probability of the response occurring may be increased or decreased by presenting or removing the discriminative stimulus. An example of the effect of stimulus control on humans is the increased probability of purchasing behaviour through the effective display of merchandise in a shop.

Stimulus generalization

When the reinforcing effect of one stimulus spreads to other stimuli, the effect is that of generalization or induction. For instance, if a response to a round, red spot one square inch in area is reinforced, a yellow spot of the same size and shape may also be reinforcing through the common properties of size and shape. However, by reinforcing only responses to the red spot with the above dimensions, and by extinguishing the response to the yellow spot, the red spot may be given exclusive discriminative control. An example of stimulus generalization in everyday life is reacting to people in a similar way because they resemble someone we know.

The self

Skinner regarded a self as a repertoire of behaviours appropriate to a given set of rein-forcement contingencies. The traditional view of the causation of behaviour regards people as autonomous agents responsible for their own lives. The scientific view is that people are members of a species shaped by evolutionary contingencies of survival whose behaviour is under the control of the environment in which they live. Although Skinner acknowledged the nomad on horseback in Outer Mongolia and the astronaut in outer space as being different people, he considered that if they had been exchanged at birth they would have taken each other's place (though this might be interfered with by genetic factors which set limits on learning). The ways in which people perceive and know are determined by environmental contingencies. Also, consciousness or awareness is a social product shaped by the environment. Furthermore, the complex activity called thinking is explicable in terms of contingencies of reinforcement. Thus the self is a repertoire of behaviours acquired through an environmental history of reinforcement and maintained or extinguished through current contingencies of reinforcement.

Self-control

A functional analysis of behaviour implies discovering the independent variables which, once they are controlled, in turn control behaviour. In self-control, people manipulate events in their environments to control their behaviour. Self-control involves two inter-related responses. First, there is the controlling response which acts on the environment to alter the probability of the second or the controlled response. For instance, an adult may engage in the controlling response of walking away so that he is able to control his response of anger. Similarly, removal of discriminative stimuli, such as food, may help to avoid over-eating. On the other hand, the presence of certain discriminative stimuli may make desirable behaviours more probable. For instance, a certain desk may act as a stimulus to study behaviour and a knot in a handkerchief may reinforce acting at a later date.

Environmental design

A technology of behaviour which will help humans to design better environments is available. Although such environments will exercise control over behaviour, their task is to release people for more reinforcing activities, consequently also reducing the need for corrective psychotherapy. The basic premise for the design of a culture is that behaviour can be changed by changing the conditions of which it is a function. Humans are the products of both biological and cultural evolution. Though humans are controlled by a culture, it is largely of their own making. The task of evolving a more effective culture may be seen as a gigantic exercise in self-control. Skinner affirmed his belief in operant behaviourism by concluding *Beyond Freedom and Dignity* with the following statement: 'A scientific view of man offers exciting possibilities. We have not yet seen what man can make of man' (Skinner, 1971, p. 210).

WOLPE'S RECIPROCAL INHIBITION

Wolpe acknowledged his debt to other learning theorists, especially Pavlov and Hull, in developing his approach to the learning and unlearning of neurotic behaviour. Wolpe considered that Pavlov's major legacy to behaviour therapy was his discovery of 'experimental neuroses', which his students Erofeeva and Shenger-Krestovnikova demonstrated could be produced and eliminated through conditioning and counterconditioning (Wolpe and Plaud, 1997).

Reciprocal inhibition

Wolpe, in a discussion of the extinctive or unlearning processes, observed that a partial recovery of the response, known as spontaneous recovery, takes place if the stimulus is not applied for some time. The partial nature of spontaneous recovery indicates that two elements are involved in the inhibition of a response during extinction: reactive inhibition, which describes an inhibitory state dissipating with time; and negative conditioning, which leads to a permanent decrease in response probability. The Miller–Mowrer explanation of the extinctive process posits that every time an organism makes a response to a stimulus, there follows a fatigue effect which has an inhibitory effect on a closely following repeat of the same response. Stimuli present at the time are in closest contiguity with the drive reduction associated with cessation of the activity and, in some measure, become conditioned to an inhibition of a response to which previously they were positively joined. The result of this is that, at the next presentation of these stimuli, the strength of the response decreases, even after a time interval long enough to eliminate all reactive inhibition effects. However, when the response is a reinforced one, the positive effects override the development of conditioned inhibition. In other words, in this explanation of conditioned inhibition, the inhibition is built up during extinction through traces of the conditioned stimuli being simultaneous with reactive inhibition of the conditioned response.

Wolpe offered a further explanation of conditioned inhibition. He noted that old habits are often eliminated by allowing new habits to develop in the same situation. The term 'reciprocal inhibition' encompasses all situations in which the elicitation of one response appears to bring about a decrement in the strength of evocation of a simultaneous response. He hypothesized that if an incompatible response were to inhibit the conditioned response and lead to much drive reduction, then a significant degree of conditioned inhibition of the original response would be developed. Eventually, his work led to his framing the following general reciprocal inhibition principle:

> *If a response antagonistic to anxiety can be made to occur in the presence of anxiety-evoking stimuli so that it is accompanied by a complete or partial suppression of the anxiety responses, the bond between these stimuli and the anxiety responses will be weakened.* (Wolpe, 1958, p. 71)

In a later work, Wolpe suggests that the term 'mutual inhibition' might be more comprehensible than reciprocal inhibition (Wolpe and Wolpe, 1988).

The learning and unlearning of neurotic fears and habits in cats

Wolpe conducted fundamental laboratory research on the learning and unlearning of neurotic fears (Wolpe, 1958). The subjects were twelve domestic cats between the ages of 6 months and 3 years. Lasting neurotic effects were induced in all the cats by the administration of several electric shocks in a small experimental cage. Six of the cats were subject to a procedure by which, after control observations, the cat was given five to ten grid shocks preceded by a 'hoot' lasting two to three seconds. The other six cats were subject to a different procedure in which they were first conditioned to perform food-approach responses to a buzzer. This response was strongly reinforced over eight to sixteen experimental sessions. The next stage of the procedure involved sounding the buzzer and shocking the cat when it made its food-approach response until it ceased to do so. The mean number of shocks required was four.

The immediate responses of the cats to the shocks included combinations of the following: rushing hither and thither, clawing at the cage, getting up on hind legs, crouching, trembling, howling, pilo-erection, and rapid respiration. Persistent responses displayed by all animals were:

1. resistance to being put into the experimental cage;
2. signs of anxiety when inside the cage; and
3. refusal to eat meat pellets anywhere in the cage even after one, two or three days' starvation.

The above symptoms were invariably intensified by presentation of the original auditory stimuli. Furthermore, all cats showed some of these symptoms outside the experimental cage.

The learned neurotic reactions of six of the cats were associated with inhibition of feeding. This suggested to Wolpe that under different conditions feeding might inhibit the neurotic reactions. The neurotic anxiety reactions were subsequently removed, or unlearned, in all cats by getting them to eat in the presence of successively larger doses of anxiety-evoking stimuli. The cats were subject to a number of procedures. One procedure was to place the cat in the experimental cage and move pellets of meat towards its mouth on the flat end of a four-inch rod held in the experimenter's hand, in the hope that the human hand would act as a stimulus to overcome the inhibition to eating. After some persistence, four out of the nine cats undergoing this procedure were induced to eat. However, only one of the three cats whose food-approach responses had been shocked was induced to eat in this way. The three cats not subject to the human-hand procedure were induced to eat by Masserman's 'forced solution' procedure. This involved repetitions of a procedure, in the experimental cage, of gradually pushing a hungry, neurotic cat by means of a movable barrier towards an open food box containing appetizing food.

The five cats which remained unaffected by the human-hand method were eventually induced to eat in the experimental cage by a procedure which involved a hierarchy of anxiety-evoking rooms ranging from the most anxiety-evoking, the experimental room or Room A, to the least anxiety-evoking, which turned out to be the passage outside Room D. The five cats initially ate at different points in the hierarchy, but by a method of gradual ascent all cats were eventually induced to eat in Room A and then in the experimental cage. By similar methods the cats' neurotic responses to the conditioned auditory stimuli were inhibited.

Wolpe explained the success of his experiments by stating that, when stimuli to incompatible responses are present simultaneously, the occurrence of the response that is dominant in the circumstances involves the reciprocal inhibition of the other. Thus, as the number of feedings increased, the anxiety responses gradually became weaker, so that to stimuli to which there was initially an anxiety response there was ultimately a feeding response with inhibition of anxiety.

Reciprocal inhibition in therapy

Wolpe states that: 'The behavior therapist deliberately uses competing responses to overcome useless fears' (Wolpe and Wolpe, 1988, p. 27). In overcoming the neurotic reactions of clients or patients, Wolpe considers it vital to conduct a thorough behaviour analysis to determine which stimuli actually or potentially evoke them currently. Suffice it for now to say that Wolpe's method involves deciding which of a number of incompatible or competing responses can most appropriately be used to obtain reciprocal inhibition of neurotic anxiety responses. Wolpe (1958) listed eight incompatible responses at the disposal of therapists through which deliberate intervention for change may be made. These are: assertive responses; sexual responses; relaxation responses; respiratory responses; 'anxiety-relief' responses; competitively conditioned motor responses; 'pleasant' responses in the life situation (with drug enhancement); and (a) interview-induced emotional responses and (b) abreaction.

Relaxation, as part of systematic desensitization, is probably the main incompatible response used in Wolpe's approach to behaviour therapy. Desensitization means that clients become less and less sensitive to whatever has been triggering their fears. Systematic means that only after therapists have accomplished the desensitization at one level of anxiety do they move on to deal with the next level. The purpose of relaxation, achieved through the tensing and relaxing of various muscles, is to bring about a state of emotional calmness. Systematic desensitization is discussed in much more detail in the next chapter.

BANDURA'S SOCIAL COGNITIVE THEORY

All the theorists presented so far in this chapter focused mainly on conditioning. Though Bandura is often listed among the major behavioural theorists (for instance, Wilson, 2000) he differs from the other theorists reviewed here in attributing much more influence to human agency, observational learning, and perceived self-efficacy. Bandura's labelling of his theoretical position as 'social cognitive' acknowledges both the social contribution to how people think and act and the importance of cognitive processes to motivation, emotions and actions. For many academics and practitioners Bandura's theoretical and research input has helped broaden behaviour therapy into cognitive–behaviour therapy. Bandura's writing is voluminous and is treated very selectively here.

Human nature and personal agency

Except for elementary reflexes, people are not equipped with inborn repertoires of behaviour and hence must learn them. Biological factors, however, set limits to the learning process. For instance, genes and hormones affect physical development which, in turn, influences behavioural potentialities. Nevertheless, within biological limits, human nature possesses a vast potential to be fashioned by direct and vicarious experience into a variety of forms.

Thoughts are psychoneural processes. However, it is important to distinguish between psychological laws and biological laws. A simplistic reductionism is to be avoided in which psychology is reduced to biology, which is reduced to chemistry, which is reduced to physics and then to atomic particles. Focusing on psychological knowledge can address questions like how best to create belief systems and personal competences. Such understanding cannot be derived just by studying the neurophysical mechanisms that subserve such activities. An interesting question is how people activate the cerebral processes which go beyond existing cognitive structures to generate new cognitive events and which characterize the exercise of personal agency.

Human agency is the capacity to exercise self-direction through control over one's own thought processes, motivation and action. Human agency has been conceptualized in three main ways: autonomous agency, in which people are totally independent agents of their actions; mechanical agency, where agency rests in environmental determinants; and emergent interactive agency, which is the model of social cognitive theory.

Emergent interactive agency is based on a model of triadic reciprocality. Reciprocal refers to mutual causation between the three factors. Behaviour (B), cognitive and personal factors (P), and environmental influences (E) each operate independently as determinants on one another. Box 10.4 depicts this reciprocal determinism position. The 'influences vary in their selective strength and they do not occur simultaneously' (A. Bandura, personal communication, 1 February 1994).

Although environmental control has been minutely researched, personal control tends to have been neglected. Nevertheless, the fact remains that environments have causes as well as consequences. Environmental determinists, such as Skinner, are inconsistent when they assert that people are controlled by external events and, at the same time, advocate that they apply a technology of behaviour to obtain intentional control over their environments. Furthermore, psychological perspectives on determinism influence behaviour. For instance, personal determinists may be more likely to develop self-directed personalities. In the final analysis, human behaviour is the result of reciprocal interaction of external events and personal determinants such as genetic endowment, acquired competences, reflective thought and self-initiative. People are free to the extent that they are able to exercise self-influence and determine their actions.

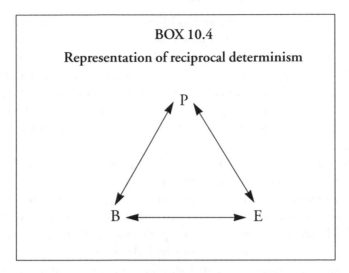

BOX 10.4

Representation of reciprocal determinism

Observational learning

Functions

The two main modes of learning are observational learning (learning by watching), and enactive learning (learning by doing). Most human behaviour and cognitive skills are learned from observing models. Functions that observational learning can perform include the following. Modelling can instruct observers in the skills and rules of behaviour. Also, modelling can inhibit and disinhibit behaviour already in people's repertoires. Yet another function is that of response facilitation. Modelled behaviour can serve as prompts and cues for people to perform behaviour already in their repertoires, yet which is not exhibited. A further function of modelling is that of eliciting emotional arousal. People can perceive and behave differently in states of heightened arousal. In addition, symbolic modelling shapes people's images of social realities by the way in which it portrays human relations and the activities they pursue.

Processes

Learning involves processing information. The power of modelling is derived from its ability to influence this. Observational learning entails four main processes:

1. *Attentional processes.* If people are to learn from modelling it is important that they pay attention to and accurately perceive the modelled behaviour. One set of attentional variables concerns characteristics of the modelling stimuli, such as availability, distinctiveness, personal attractiveness, and the functional value of the modelled behaviour. Another set of attentional variables revolves around observer characteristics, such as sensory capacities, arousal level, perceptual habits, and past reinforcements.

2. *Retention processes.* To be effective modelling must be remembered. This involves either imaginal storing of information or, more frequently, coding of modelled events into readily usable verbal symbols. Material that is meaningful to observers and builds on their prior experience is more likely to be remembered. Further aids to retention include either imaginal rehearsal of the modelled behaviour or actually carrying it out. Observers' cognitive skills and structures can enhance retention. Motivation to learn also plays a part in retention, though incentives are facilitative rather than necessary.

3. *Production processes.* At some stage, symbolic representations of modelled behaviour will probably need to be translated into effective action. Observers require accurate cognitive representations of modelled behaviours against which to compare sensory feedback from their enactments. Corrective modelling is an effective way of providing feedback when observers exhibit performance deficits. Observer variables influencing reproduction of behaviour include their physical capacities, whether their response repertoire already includes the necessary component responses, and their ability to make corrective adjustments when trying out the new behaviour.

4. *Motivational processes.* The distinction between learning and performance is highlighted by the fact that people are not motivated to enact everything they learn. The observer is more likely to adopt the modelled behaviour, if it: (a) brings external rewards; (b) is internally positively valued; and (c) has been observed to bring rewards to the model. Anticipation of positive and negative outcomes affects which aspects of modelled behaviour are observed or ignored.

Modelling thought processes

People can learn thinking skills from observing models. However, often, covert thought processes are inadequately conveyed by modelled actions. For instance, a model may solve a problem cognitively, but the observer only sees the resulting actions without gaining insight into the thought processes leading up to them. An approach to learning cognitive skills is to have models verbalize aloud how they think as they engage in problem-solving activities. Advantages of combining non-verbal with verbal modelling include the ability of non-verbal modelling to gain and hold attention and the chance of overt behaviour conferring added meaning to cognitive processes. Observers' cognitive skills are likely to improve more with models who demonstrate actions and thought processes rather than demonstrate actions alone.

Role of reinforcement

The social cognitive view is that observational learning does not necessarily require extrinsic reward. Such learning occurs through cognitive processing during modelling and before observers perform any responses. With Skinner's operant conditioning model, seemingly observational learning gets achieved when responses corresponding to the model's actions are reinforced, divergent responses are either unrewarded or punished, and others' behaviour becomes a stimulus for matching responses. However, this explanation of observational learning has shortcomings. Observers may not perform modelled behaviour in the same setting in which it was modelled. Neither the model nor the observer may be reinforced. The modelled behaviour may take place days or weeks later. Thus the operant model fails to explain how new response structures are acquired through observation.

The main role of incentives in observational learning is before rather than after modelling. For instance, observers' attention can be increased by anticipation of rewards from using modelled behaviours. Furthermore, anticipated rewards can motivate them to symbolize and rehearse modelled activities. Incentives are facilitative rather than necessary.

Self-efficacy and goals

Defining self-efficacy

Conceptions of personal efficacy are central to human agency. It is not simply a matter of knowing what to do. To enact skilled performance people need to possess both the requisite skills and the self-beliefs of efficacy to use them. Judgements of personal efficacy are different from response outcome expectations. Bandura observes: 'Perceived self-efficacy refers to beliefs in one's capabilities to organize and execute the courses of action required to manage prospective situations' (Bandura, 1995, p. 2). Outcome expectations are judgements about the likely consequences such behaviour will produce. The judgement that one can jump six feet is an efficacy judgement. However, the anticipated social recognition from jumping six feet is an outcome expectation. Outcomes are consequences of acts not the acts themselves.

Magnitude, generality and strength are three important dimensions of efficacy expectations (Bandura, 1977). Efficacy expectations can vary according to the magnitude or level of difficulty of tasks: for instance, being confident about performing well in easy rather than in difficult tasks. Generality refers to the degree of generalization of mastery expectations beyond the specific treatment situation. Strength refers to the persistence of personal mastery expectations despite disconfirming experiences.

Function and effects of self-efficacy

Efficacy beliefs contribute to how people operate in diverse ways. Conceptions of personal efficacy affect choice behaviour: for instance what to do. Perceived efficacy can foster engagement in activities, whereas perceived inefficacy can lead people to avoid potentially enriching experiences. Extreme misjudgements of efficacy are dysfunctional. However, the efficacy judgements that possibly are most functional are those that slightly exceed what one can do at any given moment.

Efficacy beliefs also influence judgements of how much effort to expend and how long to persist in face of setbacks and difficulties. Unlike self-doubt, strong self-efficacy beliefs strengthen people's resilience when engaging in difficult tasks. In addition, efficacy beliefs influence how people think and feel. Those judging themselves inefficacious in dealing with environmental demands tend to exaggerate their personal deficiencies, become disheartened more easily and give up in face of difficulties. Those with a strong sense of efficacy, though they may be temporarily demoralized by setbacks, are more likely to stay task-oriented and to intensify their efforts when their performances fall short of their goals. In endeavours where staying power is needed, it is resiliency of perceived self-efficacy that counts. Traditional behaviourist theory has to answer the question of how organisms capable of forecasting the future have no capacity for self-influence. People can produce their own futures rather than simply foretell them.

Perceived efficacy can influence the development of subskills necessary for complex tasks, whereas perceived inefficacy may retard their development. Perceived efficacy is subject to disincentives and performance constraints. People may possess the requisite subskills and self-efficacy, but have no incentives to use them. Also, efficacious people may lack adequate material and financial resources. Possessing accurate efficacy beliefs can be particularly difficult for cognitive skills, since frequently what is required is not readily apparent from what is easily observable. Sometimes people's efficacy beliefs are inaccurate because of faulty cognitive activities: for instance deficits in perceiving feedback and in memory.

Sources of self-efficacy information

Four important sources self-efficacy information are described below. Any method of treatment may work with one or more of these sources.

1. *Enactive attainment.* Personal experiences of success provide the most fundamental source of efficacy expectations. Success raises efficacy expectations, whereas repeated failure lowers them. Once established, enhanced efficacy beliefs tend to generalize, especially to situations similar to those in which the beliefs were enhanced.
2. *Vicarious experience.* Efficacy expectations may be altered by observing others and noting the positive and negative consequences of behaviour for them. Efficacy expectations induced by modelling are generally weaker than those induced by successful task performance. Modelling affects efficacy beliefs in two ways (A. Bandura, personal communication, 1 February 1994). First, observers make inferences from modelled successes and failures. Seeing people similar to themselves succeed by sustained effort raises observers' beliefs in their capabilities. However, seeing others fail despite high effort lowers observers' judgements of their own efficacy and undermines their motivation. Second, competent models transmit knowledge and teach observers effective skills and strategies for managing environmental demands. Acquisition of better skills raises perceived self-efficacy.
3. *Verbal persuasion.* Verbal persuasion, such as suggestion and exhortation, may also influence self-efficacy. Persuasion may be most useful where it persuades people to try hard enough to succeed which in turn enhances their efficacy beliefs. However, the raising of unrealistic efficacy beliefs that are not corroborated by successful enactment may do more harm than good.
4. *Physiological state.* Physiological and affective states affect efficacy beliefs in three ways. First, when people are tense and anxious, their physiological state or level of emotional arousal can negatively influence their efficacy expectations. High arousal usually debilitates performance and thus lowered expectations of efficacy then become, in part, based on lowered performance. Approaches that lessen debilitating

emotional arousal to subjective threats can enhance both efficacy beliefs and performance. Perceived self-efficacy to control thoughts beneficially influences cognitively generated arousal. When the extent of aversive cognitions is controlled, perceived efficacy or inefficacy to control one's thoughts is strongly related to anxiety level. Second, mood states affect people's judgement of their personal efficacy: positive mood enhances perceived efficacy, depressed mood diminishes it. Third, in activities involving strength and stamina, people judge their fatigue, aches and pain as signs of weak physical efficacy.

Efficacy information from enactive, vicarious, persuasive and physiological sources is cognitively processed. Regarding vicarious efficacy information, observers may consider that models similar or slightly higher in ability provide the most valid comparative information. Regarding persuasive efficacy information, its effect is related to how confident recipients are in the judgement of their persuaders. Physiological efficacy information is also cognitively processed. Salient considerations here include the sources and level of arousal, and past experiences of how arousal affects performance.

Functions of goals

Personal agency or intentional regulation of behaviour operates through two cognitively based sources of motivation: first, forethought, and second, goal-setting with self-evaluative reactions to one's behaviour. Bandura (1989) observes: 'Human motivation relies on *discrepancy production* as well as *discrepancy reduction*. It requires both *proactive control* and *reactive or feedback control*' (pp. 1,179–80). Initially people motivate themselves through setting standards or levels of performance that create a state of disequilibrium and then they strive to attain them. Feedback control involves subsequent adjustments of effort to achieve the desired results. Goals act as motivators by specifying the conditions for self-satisfaction with performance.

In addition, goals are important for the development of self-efficacy; they provide people with standards by which to judge their capabilities. Particularly useful are progressively difficult short-term sub-goals. Such sub-goals provide both incentives for action and, when attained, produce efficacy information and confidence to persist. Perceived inefficacy can cause people to lower their goals and thus decrease their dissatisfaction with substandard performances.

SUMMARY

- *Pavlov conducted extensive researches into the functioning of the cerebral hemispheres of dogs. He discovered the conditioned reflex, otherwise known as classical or respondent conditioning. For example, by pairing a conditioned stimulus (metronome) with an unconditioned stimulus (food), a dog comes to acquire a salivary response in the presence of the conditioned stimulus alone.*

- *Watson viewed behaviourist psychology, termed 'behaviourism', as an objective experimental branch of natural science focused on the behaviour of human beings. He* distinguished between unlearned and learned responses. Most stimuli to which humans respond are learned.

- Some experiments on an 11-month-old boy called Albert illustrated the conditioning of an emotional fear response to a white rat, its transfer to other furry animals, and its persistence. A further experiment on another child unconditioned his fear of furry animals. The cure for personality problems is unconditioning and conditioning.

- Skinner's operant conditioning emphasizes that behaviour operates on the environment to generate consequences. Reinforcers are events which strengthen the probability of a response.

- Contingencies of reinforcement, which describe the interaction between the organism and its environment, are: (a) the occasion on which a response occurs; (b) the response itself; and (c) the reinforcing consequences.

- Other operant conditioning concepts are: positive and negative reinforcement, primary and conditioned reinforcers, schedules of reinforcement, maintenance and extinction of behaviour, shaping and successive approximation, stimulus discrimination and control, and stimulus generalization.

- Wolpe offers a reciprocal inhibition explanation for some conditioned inhibition. Reciprocal inhibition involves eliciting a competing response in order to bring about a decrease in the strength of a simultaneous response.

- A number of responses incompatible with anxiety may be used in therapy. These include relaxation, assertive and sexual responses.

- Bandura asserts that both social and cognitive processes are central to understanding motivation, emotions and action.

- Most human behaviour is learned from observing models. Observational learning involves four main processes: attention, retention, production, and motivation.

- Conceptions of personal efficacy are central to human agency. Perceived self-efficacy is a judgement about one's capability to accomplish a certain level of performance.

- Sources of efficacy information are enactive attainment, vicarious experience, verbal persuasion, and physiological states. Efficacy information is cognitively processed with varying degrees of accuracy.

- People set goals that create states of disequilibrium which act as motivators for action. Goals are also important to developing self-efficacy.

REVIEW AND PERSONAL QUESTIONS

REVIEW QUESTIONS

1. What does Pavlov mean by inborn reflex?
2. What is the function of the cerebral hemispheres in the organism's survival?
3. What is meant by classical conditioning?
4. How does Watson view the connection between stimulus and response?
5. How did Watson and his associates condition and uncondition emotional responses?
6. What does Skinner mean by each of the following terms:

(a) operant conditioning;
(b) contingencies of reinforcement;
(c) positive reinforcement;
(d) negative reinforcement;
(e) primary reinforcers;
(f) conditioned reinforcers;
(g) non-intermittent schedules of reinforcement;
(h) intermittent schedules of reinforcement;
(i) extinction;
(j) shaping and successive approximation;
(k) stimulus discrimination and stimulus control;
(l) stimulus generalization; and
(m) self-control.

7. Express in simple English what Wolpe means by the term 'reciprocal inhibition'.
8. Why does Bandura use the term 'social cognitive theory' to designate his theoretical framework?
9. Describe each of the processes of observational learning.
10. What does the term 'perceived self-efficacy' mean, and why is it important?
11. How does goal-setting influence behaviour and self-efficacy?

PERSONAL QUESTIONS

1. Do you think you have acquired any of your behaviours through classical conditioning? If so, illustrate.
2. Give some examples from your own life of:
   (a) behaviours acquired and maintained through operant conditioning;
   (b) behaviours extinguished by lack of reinforcement.
3. If possible, give examples from your own life of engaging in a competing response to inhibit the anxiety you experienced with an existing response.
4. Identify a significant activity or cognitive skill that you have learned by observing one or more models. Describe the processes by which observational learning became an effective way of acquiring it.
5. Provide one or more examples from your own life of the distinction between an efficacy expectation and an outcome expectation.
6. For a significant area in your life, describe what have been the effects and consequences of your efficacy beliefs.
7. What is the relevance of behavioural theory for understanding your own life?
8. What is the relevance of behavioural theory for how you conduct therapy?

ANNOTATED BIBLIOGRAPHY

Pavlov, I. P. (1927). *Conditioned Reflexes: An Investigation of the Physiological Activity of the Cerebral Cortex* (Anrep translation). Oxford: Oxford University Press.

In this book Pavlov defines terms such as 'reflex', describes his experimental laboratory, and gives details of some of his pathfinding experiments into the functioning of the cerebral hemispheres of dogs.

Watson, J. B. (1931). *Behaviorism.* London: Kegan Paul, Trench and Traubner.
This book presents Watson's answer to the question 'What is behaviorism?' and includes his views on conditioning, instincts, thinking, memory, personality and ethics.

Skinner, B. F. (1938). *The Behaviour of Organisms.* New York: Appleton-Century-Crofts.
In this book Skinner describes his seminal experiments in conditioning rats using a 'box' containing a food- or water-dispenser operated by a lever which could be depressed by a rat. His independent variables included deprivation and satiation, various categories of reinforcement, and aversive consequences.

Skinner, B. F. (1953). *Science and Human Behavior.* New York: Macmillan.
This book presents Skinner's ideas on applying the science of behaviour to individuals and groups. In addition, Skinner examines controlling agencies such as government and law, religion, psychotherapy, economic control, and education.

Skinner, B. F. (1957). *Verbal Behavior.* New York: Appleton-Century-Crofts.
This book presents Skinner's interpretation of language and the uses of language. Verbal behaviour results from the same principles of operant learning as found in other species. Skinner analyses the various controlling relationships in verbal behaviour.

Wolpe, J. (1958). *Psychotherapy by Reciprocal Inhibition.* Stanford, CA: Stanford University Press.
This is Wolpe's seminal book in which he describes his fundamental animal research and its therapeutic applications. The book is a classic in the behaviour therapy literature.

Bandura, A. (1986). *Social Foundations of Thought and Action: A Social Cognitive Theory.* Englewood Cliffs, NJ: Prentice-Hall.
This huge volume is the definitive statement of Bandura's position. In it he presents a theoretical framework for analysing human motivation, thought, and action from a social cognitive perspective.

REFERENCES AND FURTHER READING

Bandura, A. (1969). *Principles of Behavior Modification.* New York: Holt, Rinehart and Winston.
Bandura, A. (1973). *Aggression: A Social Learning Analysis.* Englewood Cliffs, NJ: Prentice-Hall.
Bandura, A. (1977). *Social Learning Theory.* Englewood Cliffs, NJ: Prentice-Hall.
Bandura, A. (1986). *Social Foundations of Thought and Action: A Social Cognitive Theory.* Englewood Cliffs, NJ: Prentice-Hall.
Bandura, A. (1989). Human agency in social cognitive theory. *American Psychologist, 44,* 1,175–84.
Bandura, A. (ed.) (1995). *Self-Efficacy in Changing Societies.* New York: Cambridge University Press.
Bandura, A. (1997). *Self-Efficacy: The Exercise of Control.* New York: Freeman.
Bandura, A. and Walters, R. (1963). *Social Learning and Personality Development.* New York: Holt, Rinehart and Winston.

Cohen, D. (1979). *J. B. Watson, The Founder of Behaviourism.* London: Routledge and Kegan Paul.

Ferster, C. B. and Skinner, B. F. (1957). *Schedules of Reinforcement.* New York: Appleton-Century-Crofts.

Holland, J. G. (1992). B. F. Skinner (1904–90). *American Psychologist, 47,* 665–7.

Holland, J. G. and Skinner, B. F. (1961). *The Analysis of Behavior.* New York: McGraw-Hill.

Jones, M. C. (1924). A laboratory study of fear: The case of Peter. *Pedagogical Seminary, 31,* 308–15.

Pavlov, I. P. (1902). *The Work of the Digestive Glands* (W. H. Thompson trans.). London: Griffin. Original edition published in 1897.

Pavlov, I. P. (1927). *Conditioned Reflexes: An Investigation of the Physiological Activity of the Cerebral Cortex* (Anrep translation). Oxford: Oxford University Press.

Skinner, B. F. (1938). *The Behaviour of Organisms.* New York: Appleton-Century-Crofts.

Skinner, B. F. (1948). *Walden Two.* New York: Macmillan.

Skinner, B. F. (1953). *Science and Human Behavior.* New York: Macmillan.

Skinner, B. F. (1957). *Verbal Behavior.* New York: Appleton-Century-Crofts.

Skinner, B. F. (1958). Reinforcement today. *American Psychologist, 13,* 94–9.

Skinner, B. F. (1969). *Contingencies of Reinforcement.* New York: Appleton-Century-Crofts.

Skinner, B. F. (1971). *Beyond Freedom and Dignity.* Harmondsworth: Penguin Books.

Skinner, B. F. (1974). *About Behaviorism.* New York: Alfred A. Knopf.

Skinner, B. F. (1976). *Particulars of My Life.* London: Jonathan Cape.

Watson, J. B. (1903). *Animal Education.* Chicago: University of Chicago Press.

Watson, J. B. (1913). Psychology as the behaviorist views it. *Psychological Review, 20,* 158–77.

Watson, J. B. (1914). *Behavior.* New York: Holt.

Watson, J. B. (1919). *Psychology from the Standpoint of a Behaviorist.* Philadelphia. Lippincott. 2nd edition 1924, 3rd edition 1929.

Watson, J. B. (1928). *The Psychological Care of the Infant and Child.* New York: W. W. Norton

Watson, J. B. (1931). *Behaviorism.* London: Kegan Paul, Trench and Traubner.

Watson, J. B. and Raynor, R. R. (1920). Conditioned emotional reactions. *Journal of Experimental Psychology, 3,* 1–14.

Wilson, G. T. (2000). Behavior therapy. In R. J. Corsini, and D. Wedding (eds). *Current Psychotherapies* (6th edition, 205–40). Itasca, IL: Peacock.

Windholz, G. (1997). Ivan P. Pavlov: An overview of his life and psychological work. *American Psychologist, 52,* 941–6.

Wolpe, J. (1958). *Psychotherapy by Reciprocal Inhibition.* Stanford, CA: Stanford University Press.

Wolpe, J. (1976) *Theme and Variations: A Behaviour Therapy Casebook.* Oxford: Pergamon Press.

Wolpe, J. (1990). *The Practice of Behavior Therapy* (4th edition). Oxford: Pergamon Press.

Wolpe, J. and Plaud, J. J. (1997). Pavlov's contribution to behavior therapy. *American Psychologist, 52,* 966–72.

Wolpe, J. and Wolpe, D. (1988). *Life Without Fear: Anxiety and Its Cure.* Oakland, CA: New Harbinger Publications.

11

Behaviour Therapy: Practice

The importance of a science of behaviour derives largely from the possibility of an eventual extension to human affairs.

B. F. Skinner

INTRODUCTION

This chapter provides an introduction to some basic methods of behaviour therapy. The term 'behaviour therapy' was originally used to describe a series of therapeutic interventions based mainly on the principles of learning described in Chapter 10. However, Wolpe (1973) observes that the behaviour therapist need not be confined to methods derived from principles, but may also employ methods that have been empirically shown to be effective.

Nowadays definitions of behaviour therapy differ according to whether the therapist mainly emphasizes learning principles based on classical and operant conditioning, or emphasizes personal agency and cognitive intervening variables as well. For instance, Wolpe (1973) defined behaviour therapy as a conditioning therapy involving 'the use of experimentally established principles of learning for the purpose of changing maladaptive behaviour. Unadaptive habits are weakened and eliminated; adaptive habits are initiated and strengthened' (p. xi). Wolpe's approach to behaviour therapy is based largely on classical conditioning (Wolpe, 1958, 1990; Wolpe and Wolpe, 1988). However, traditional behaviour therapy also incorporates operant conditioning assumptions and practices.

Wolpe and Skinner stressed that behaviourism takes into account thinking and feelings. Skinner especially viewed thinking as having the dimensions of behaviour and not as a process involving personal agency. For Skinner, mind was a myth, with all the power of myths (Bjork, 1993). Radical or traditional behaviourists stress the relation between the behaviour, including thinking behaviour, and the context in which it occurs. Reitman and Drabman (1997) observe: 'radical behaviorists study thinking and other private events from within a contextual scientific framework that places, *a priori*, all causal events outside the organism itself' (p. 421). In cognitive behaviourism it is the individual's inner cognitions that cause much of their behaviour. Because of this fundamental difference between radical and cognitive behaviourists in explaining the causes of behaviour, the designation cognitive–behavioural is something of a contradiction in terms.

This chapter focuses predominantly on conditioning methods for altering observable behaviour, traditional behaviour therapy, rather than on approaches to altering behaviour by means of altering cognitions, cognitive–behaviour therapy. Practitioners of traditional behaviour therapy are a declining breed. Galassi and Perot (1992) observe that: 'Undoubtedly, the single most important change is the cognitive revolution that has swept through behaviour therapy in the last dozen years or so' (p. 627). The cognitive revolution gained its momentum in the early 1970s. By 1990, 69 per cent and 27 per cent of American Association of Behavior Therapy members identified themselves as cognitive–behavioural and behavioural, respectively (Craighead, 1990). Now most therapists using the methods described in this chapter, especially the younger ones, are more likely to view themselves as cognitive–behaviour therapists rather than behavior therapists.

Both Skinner and Wolpe were concerned about how cognitive behaviourism deviated from the basic scientific research base on which behaviour therapy rests. Wolpe regarded much of the current practice of behaviour therapy as a retreat from principles. Towards the end of his life Wolpe wrote: '*behavior therapy* was a poor choice of label; *conditioning therapy* would have been both more distinctive and more informative' (Wolpe, 1990, p. 4).

Nevertheless, both traditional behaviour therapy and cognitive–behaviour therapy share a commitment to empirically supported treatment interventions. In addition, both of these approaches to therapy focus on the necessity of changing observable behaviours. Furthermore, debates exist over the exact mechanisms of change in both traditional behaviour therapy and in cognitive–behaviour therapy and over the extent to which the approaches overlap, are suitable for different problems, and might be used to enhance one another.

THERAPY

Behavior therapy is the use of experimentally derived principles and paradigms of learning to overcome maladaptive habits.

Joseph Wolpe

THERAPEUTIC GOALS

At the risk of introducing a level of generality which behaviour therapists, with their emphasis on specific goals for individual clients, might find uncongenial, following is a list of behaviour therapy goals derived from the writings of the five theorists reviewed in the preceding chapter:

- overcoming deficits in behavioural repertoires;
- strengthening adaptive behaviours;
- weakening or eliminating maladaptive behaviours;
- absence of debilitating anxiety reactions;
- the capacity to relax;
- the ability to assert oneself;

- effective social skills;
- adequacy at sexual functioning; and
- capacity for self-control.

The above goals are for individuals. Of the behavioural theorists, Skinner in particular focused on the need for groups to design environments in which humans can behave in more reinforcing ways. Thus, further behavioural goals might focus on groups and include the capacity for group self-control, both by shaping environmental consequences and also by cognitive self-regulation.

Specifying goals in therapy

In behaviour therapy, therapists need to conduct and formulate a behavioural assessment so that treatment goals can be selected and specified. Such an assessment entails descriptions of what the problems are, how they appear to have arisen, and what maintains them. These descriptions are in the form of hypotheses to be tested in therapy. The end product of the behavioural assessment is an exact specification of what variables are in need of modification, be they situational antecedents, components of the problem behaviour itself, and/or consequent reinforcers. Frequently, the main goal or goals of treatment are called target behaviours (Kazdin, 1994). However, many behaviour therapists go beyond stating goals in terms of observable behaviours to specifying anxiety-reduction goals as well.

Selecting goals in turn leads to decisions about how to define them so that therapists and clients can assess whether or not clients change. Clearly defined goals assist therapists to select appropriate interventions to attain them. It is fundamental that behaviour therapists allow clients a major say in establishing treatment goals (Wilson, 2000). Clients tend to have more than one area of concern and, though it may be possible to deal with those simultaneously, sometimes an ordering of priorities is necessary. Here a prime consideration is the extent to which the problem behaviours interfere with clients' abilities to lead satisfactory lives. In most instances, client and therapist will agree on goals and treatment interventions. Where disagreement exists, further discussion may be all that is necessary to resolve the issue. Referral to another therapist may be indicated if disagreement persists.

PROCESS OF THERAPY

Assessment

Early on the behaviour therapist invariably conducts behavioural assessment, sometimes known as a functional analysis, to identify and understand clients' problem areas (Cormier and Cormier, 1998; Wolpe, 1990). Adequate behavioural assessments allow therapists to identify the context, antecedents and consequences of the responses they wish to treat, while inadequate behavioural assessments may lead to the wrong methods being applied to the wrong problems. After initial sessions, behavioural assessment aims to assist both in evaluating treatment effectiveness and in deciding whether to continue, discontinue or alter treatment.

When clients make statements like 'I seem to be very depressed these days', 'I don't seem to have many friends' or 'I get very tense at work', behaviour therapists attempt an analysis based on an *SRC* assessment, where *S* refers to the *stimulus* or *situational antecedents*, *R* to the *response variables* and *C* to the *consequences* or *consequent variables*. The purpose of the *SRC* analysis is to search for the key variables which control clients' behaviour. Sometimes these may be masked: for instance, aggression at work may reflect a poor marital relationship. Behavioural assessment aims for a high degree of specificity. For instance, in analysing a response, information on duration, frequency, generality, and strength of the response should be collected. Therapists seldom ask 'Why?' questions, since those starting with 'How', 'When', 'Where' and 'What' are more useful (Wilson, 2000).

Behaviour therpists differ in the extent to which they gather historical material concerning how the presenting concerns were learned, though this may be important in obtaining an accurate picture. Wolpe (1990), for instance, gathers historical material on his clients' presenting concerns, family life, educational and occupational development, and sexual development. Wolpe also explores his clients' current social relationships.

Other possible elements of initial assessments include observations about clients' verbal and non-verbal behaviour. Socially awkward people may demonstrate at least part of their problems during the interview. Therapists note clients' personal assets and ways of either coping with or avoiding coping with problems. In addition, they assess clients' motivation for change, any influences in their environments which are likely to hinder or help change, and their expectancies regarding the possibility of change. Therapists also notice the kinds of things which clients find reinforcing, such as personal attention or praise, since these may be useful for eliciting behaviour change.

There are a number of additional sources of assessment data, one or more of which therapists may find useful both for generating more-accurate hypotheses about treatment goals and for collecting baseline information against which to assess therapeutic progress and outcomes.

Behavioural observation

Sometimes therapists collect behavioural information by asking clients to role-play situations in which they experience difficulty, with the therapists playing the other person. On other occasions therapists go with clients into real-life settings to observe how they behave. An example of this might be going into pubs or restaurants with clients who experience difficulty drinking or eating in public, then observing and discussing their behaviour and emotions as they happen or shortly afterwards. However, when therapists are present, clients may behave differently from usual.

Another form of observation in real-life settings is to collect information from significant people who interact with clients in their everyday lives, such as teachers or parents in the case of children, or spouses in the case of married people. Therapists need to bear in mind both the degree to which the reported behaviours may be representative of their clients' behaviours in particular situations and also potential contamination by observer bias. Again, if clients know they are being observed they may behave differently. However, there are ethical problems in observing and reporting on clients without their knowledge or consent. Sometimes valid indirect observations in natural settings may be made by making frequency counts of various carefully defined categories of behaviour.

Self-monitoring

Clients may be asked to collect baseline data by monitoring their current behaviour. One way to go about this is to ask clients to fill in three-column daily diary sheets investigating the *SRC* elements of a specific behaviour being monitored – one column heading each for situation, response, and consequences. Such a behavioural monitoring diary might be kept for a week or however long it takes to obtain the relevant information.

Questionnaires

Therapists may ask clients to complete self-report questionnaires. Such measures may focus on overt *behaviour*, or how the client acts, on *emotions*, or how the client feels, and on clients' *perceptions of their environments*. Perhaps the most commonly used type of questionnaire is the sort which asks clients to indicate the kinds of situations which cause them anxiety. One such questionnaire is Wolpe and Lang's *Fear Survey Schedule* in which clients are provided with five categories, ranging from 'not at all' to 'very much', for rating how disturbed they currently feel in 87 situations, such as 'People in authority', 'Angry people', 'Darkness' and 'Airplanes' (Wolpe, 1990; Wolpe and Lang, 1969). A questionnaire focused on self-report of behaviour is Alberti and Emmons' (1995) *Assertiveness Inventory*, with such items as 'Do you speak out or protest when someone takes your place in line?' Another kind of questionnaire, which focuses on activities, events and experiences which clients find rewarding, is MacPhillamy and Lewinsohn's *Pleasant Events Schedule* (Lewinsohn, Munoz, Youngren and Zeiss, 1986). Such a questionnaire is useful in identifying actual and potential reinforcers which may be used in conjunction with treatment.

Additional sources of assessment data include: medical information, including obtaining a medical assessment if there is any suspicion of a physiologically based problem or one with medical implications; and records of previous psychological or psychiatric treatment. An insight into how behaviour therapists assess in practice is Kazdin's conclusion, based on studying the research evidence, that 'the accumulating verdict regarding judgmental biases in decision making in general and, more specifically, within the context of clinical work has not been kind . . . The collection of systematic information in the context of treatment does not eliminate bias' (Kazdin, 1993, p. 13). However, Kazdin also argues that systematic information improves client care more than impressionistic evaluation of treatment progress.

Treatment

Depending on the specification of goals at the end of the behavioural assessment, behaviour therapy offers a range of treatment interventions, including reinforcement procedures, systematic desensitization and assertive training. Homework assignments are a regular part of behaviour therapy.

Behavioural assessment and monitoring take place throughout a course of behaviour therapy and not just at the beginning. One function of such monitoring is to see whether treatment goals are being achieved. Another function is to see whether therapists or clients think it advisable to alter or revise their goals. Perhaps some new situation, such as getting married or acquiring a more responsible position at work, may precipitate changing goals. If goals are altered, treatment interventions have to be amended accordingly.

Often behaviour therapy treatment is short term. For instance, a therapist might contract with a client to pursue a treatment plan for two to three months (approximately eight to twelve sessions) and re-evaluate progress at the end of this period (Wilson, 2000). Therapy lasting from 25 to 50 sessions is also fairly common, though any contact over 100 sessions is rare. Behaviour therapy sessions vary in length, from the traditional therapeutic hour to 30 minutes or even fifteen minutes when specific interventions are in use.

Since therapeutic goals have often been stated clearly at the start of therapy, therapist and client can monitor progress in attaining goals and make termination-of-therapy decisions accordingly. Many behaviour therapists avoid ending abruptly by lengthening the time between successive therapy sessions, from weekly to fortnightly to monthly and so on. Follow-up telephone contact can also help therapists and clients monitor progress and deal with any issues connected with maintaining gains.

THE THERAPEUTIC RELATIONSHIP

Behaviour therapists realize that the quality of the therapeutic relationship can significantly influence the success of therapy. Behaviour therapy is not a mechanistic procedure, rather therapists attempt to form good working relationships with clients in the interests of accurate behavioural assessment and effective treatment. Wolpe (1990) observes that: 'Objectivity, empathy, and sensitivity to suffering are intrinsic to the behavior therapist's approach to his patients' (p. 59). Behaviour therapists are highly accepting of clients since they view their behaviour as a combination of physical endowment and the effects of experience and of current environmental contexts. Clients are not judged as good or bad; instead therapists work with them to discover and modify the controlling variables that interfere with attaining specific goals.

Frequently, early on in initial sessions, therapists offer clients a rationale for their problems in learning terms along these lines: since psychological distress results from learning faulty habits, it makes sense to treat it by using scientific knowledge of how habits are made and broken (Wolpe, 1990). Then therapists invite clients to help them to identify and understand the stimuli that trigger maladaptive thoughts, feelings and behaviour.

Behaviour therapy is basically an educational process. To a large extent, therapists are teachers, and clients are learners. However, unless therapists can use good relationship skills with clients, they will inadequately discover what they need to teach and then teach it with more difficulty than necessary. Some characteristics of skilled behaviour therapists are that they are concerned, sensitive, warm, sincere, task-oriented, thorough, systematic, flexible and appropriately directive.

THERAPEUTIC INTERVENTIONS

Behaviour therapists have a repertoire of interventions which they tailor to assist clients to attain their goals. Where possible, behaviour therapists rely heavily on research findings concerning the effectiveness of an intervention when applied to a particular problem. In those cases where the empirical evidence is insufficiently clear or non-existent, therapists use clinical acumen and judgement within the framework of behavioural principles.

Systematic desensitization

Where behavioural assessments indicate that clients have certain specific anxiety or phobic areas, rather than just general tension, systematic desensitization may be the preferred intervention. However, adequate behavioural assessments are essential. For instance, anxiety about tests or about occupational decisions may be the consequence of inadequate revision or poor decision-making skills. In such instances the anxiety is likely to be more effectively diminished by skills training than by systematic desensitization. There are numerous different theoretical explanations of the efficacy of systematic desensitization, some of which also have procedural implications (Thoresen and Coates, 1978).

Wolpe (1958, 1990; Wolpe and Wolpe, 1988) was the originator of systematic desensitization, a treatment he considered to be based on the reciprocal inhibition principle described in Chapter 10. He acknowledges that systematic desensitization may be conducted concurrently with other behavioural interventions. Systematic desensitization involves three elements:

1. training in deep muscular relaxation;
2. the construction of hierarchies of anxiety-evoking stimuli; and
3. asking the client, when relaxed, to imagine items from the anxiety-evoking hierarchies.

Training in relaxation
The acknowledged pioneer of relaxation training is Edmund Jacobson, the first and second editions of whose major work, *Progressive Relaxation*, appeared in 1929 and 1938 respectively. There are many variants to Jacobson's progressive muscular relaxation procedures, including those described by Wolpe (Wolpe, 1990; Wolpe and Wolpe, 1988), Goldfried and Davison (1976) and Bernstein and Borkovec (1973). Although Bernstein and Borkovec's manual, *Progressive Relaxation Training*, provides a particularly clear introduction to the subject, the following description is drawn from a number of sources.

The physical setting of therapists' offices should be conducive to relaxation. This involves absence of disruptive noise, interior decoration that is restful, and lighting which may be dimmed. Clients may be taught to relax in recliner chairs, or on mattresses, or, at the very least, in comfortable upright chairs with headrests.

From the start therapists can endeavour to see that clients view relaxation training as learning a coping skill which can be used in daily life rather than just treating them as passive persons. Furthermore, clients should understand that success at learning relaxation, just like success at learning any other skill, requires practice and that relaxation homework will be required. Before starting relaxation, therapists can suggest that clients wear loose-fitting, comfortable clothing both during interviews and when doing relaxation homework; furthermore, that it is helpful to remove items such as glasses and shoes.

Bernstein and Borkovec observe that in teaching muscular relaxation there is a succession of events which must be observed with each muscle group. This tension–relax cycle has five elements:

1. *focus*, focusing attention on a specific muscle group;
2. *tense*, tensing the muscle group;
3. *hold*, maintaining the tension for five to seven seconds;
4. *release*, releasing the tension in the muscle group; and
5. *relax*, focusing attention on the letting go of tension and further relaxation of the muscle group.

Clients need to learn this *focus–tense–hold–release–relax* cycle so that they may apply it in their homework.

Having explained the basic tension–relax cycle, therapists may then demonstrate it by going through the cycle in relation to their own right hand and forearm and at each stage asking their clients to do the same. Thus, 'I'm focusing all my attention on my right hand and forearm and I'd like you to do the same' progresses to 'I'm clenching my right fist and tensing the muscles in my lower arm . . .', then on to 'I'm holding my right fist clenched and keeping the muscles in my lower arm tensed . . .', followed by 'I'm now releasing as quickly as I can the tension from my right fist and lower arm . . .', ending with 'I'm relaxing my right hand and forearm, letting the tension go further and further and letting these muscles become more and more relaxed . . .' The final relaxation phase tends to last from 30 to 60 seconds, frequently accompanied by therapist relaxation 'patter' about letting the tension go and acknowledging and experiencing feelings of deeper and deeper relaxation as they occur. Having been through the tension–relax cycle once, especially in the initial sessions the client may be instructed to go through it again, thus tensing and relaxing each muscle grouping twice.

Therapists are then likely to take clients through the muscle groups, demonstrating them as necessary. Box 11.1 shows sixteen muscle groups and suggested tensing instructions. The arms tend to come at the beginning, since they are easy to demonstrate. For most clients, relaxing parts of the face is particularly important because the most marked anxiety-inhibiting effects are usually obtained there.

Once clients have learned how to tense the various muscle groups, they are instructed to keep their eyes closed during relaxation training and practice. Towards the end of

BOX 11.1

Relaxation training muscle groups and tensing instructions

Muscle group	Tensing instructions*
Right hand and forearm	Clench your right fist and tense the muscles in your lower arm.
Right biceps	Bend your right arm at the elbow and flex your biceps by tensing the muscles of your upper right arm.
Left hand and forearm	Clench your left fist and tense the muscles in your lower arm.
Left biceps	Bend your left arm at the elbow and flex your biceps by tensing the muscles of your upper left arm.
Forehead	Lift your eyebrows as high as possible.
Eyes, nose and upper cheeks	Squeeze your eyes tightly shut and wrinkle your nose.
Jaw and lower cheeks	Clench your teeth and pull the corners of your mouth firmly back.
Neck and throat	Pull your chin down hard towards your chest yet resist having it touch your chest.
Chest and shoulders	Pull your shoulder blades together and take a deep breath.
Stomach	Tighten the muscles in your stomach as though someone was about to hit you there.
Right thigh	Tense the muscles of the right upper leg by pressing the upper muscle down and the lower muscles up.
Right calf	Stretch your right leg and pull your toes towards your head.
Right foot	Point and curl the toes of your right foot and turn it inwards.
Left thigh	Tense the muscles of the left upper leg by pressing the upper muscle down and the lower muscles up.
Left calf	Stretch your left leg and pull your toes towards your head.
Left foot	Point and curl the toes of your left foot and turn it inwards.

*With left-handed people, tensing instructions for the left side of the body should come before those for the right.

relaxation sessions, therapists may ask clients for a summary of their relaxation, along the lines of 'Well, how was your relaxation today?' and discuss any issues that arise. Terminating relaxation sessions may be achieved by therapists counting from five to one and when they get to one asking their clients to wake up pleasantly relaxed as though from a peaceful sleep. Bernstein and Borkovec advocate relaxation sessions ending with an 'enjoyment period' of a minute or two in which therapists suggest that clients focus on the very pleasant state of relaxation prior to the counting procedure for terminating relaxation.

The importance of practising muscular relaxation may be further stressed at the end of the initial relaxation session. Clients are likely to be given the homework assignment of practising muscular relaxation for one or two fifteen-minute periods a day. Therapists should ask clients whether they anticipate any obstacles to practising, such as finding a quiet place, and help them to devise strategies for ensuring good homework. There is some evidence that clients who monitor their relaxation practice are much more likely to continue doing it (Tasto and Hinkle, 1973). Consequently, it may be helpful for therapists to give clients logs for monitoring their relaxation homework.

Following are some additional forms of inducing relaxation beyond the sixteen muscle group progressive muscular relaxation procedure.

Brief muscular relaxation procedures   When the full muscular relaxation procedures have been learned and clients are able to attain deep relaxation, briefer muscular relaxation procedures may be introduced. The idea here is to learn to attain deep relaxation with less time and effort. This skill may be useful both within and outside therapy sessions. Brief muscular relaxation procedures may involve sequential or simultaneous application of the tension–relax cycle to various muscle groups, albeit interrelated.

Bernstein and Borkovec (1973) provide examples of sequential brief muscular relaxation procedures. One variation is to tense seven muscle groups: the right arm muscles, the left arm muscles and the facial muscles are each tensed as single groups; the neck and throat muscles are tensed as previously; and the chest, shoulder and stomach muscles, the right leg and foot muscles and the left leg and foot muscles are each tensed as single groups. A four muscle group variation, which, even more than the seven muscle group variation, involves simultaneous as well as sequential relaxation, groups: arm muscles; face, neck and throat muscles; chest, shoulder and stomach muscles; and leg and foot muscles.

Simultaneous muscular relaxation involves tensing virtually all muscles at once. An introductory therapist statement might be 'When I give the signal, I would like you to close your eyes tightly, take a deep breath and simultaneously clench your fists and flex your biceps, frown very deeply, pull your shoulder blades together and tense your legs and feet. Now take a deep breath and tense everything . . . hold for five seconds . . . now release and relax as quickly and deeply as you can.' When using systematic desensitization procedures, simultaneous muscular relaxation may provide therapists with useful economies in interview time. When ready, brief muscular relaxation procedures should be incorporated into clients' relaxation homework.

Mental relaxation   Often as part of systematic desensitization, clients are encouraged to engage in mental relaxation. Such relaxation usually involves imagining a peaceful scene, such as 'lying in a meadow on a nice warm summer's day, feeling a gentle breeze, watching the clouds'. Therapists can discover which particular scenes clients find most conducive to relaxation. Frequently, mental relaxation is used after going through a muscular relaxation procedure.

Relaxation training considerations

Behaviour therapists differ in the number of sessions they take for relaxation training. Furthermore, clients differ in the speed with which they attain a capacity to relax. Wolpe (1990) teaches progressive muscular relaxation in about six lessons and asks his patients to practise at home for two fifteen-minute sessions per day. Wolpe and Wolpe (1988) write: 'It is crucial to realize that the aim of relaxation training is not muscle control *per se*, but emotional calmness' (p. 42). Bernstein and Borkovec (1973) suggest a ten-session relaxation training timetable, with the first three sessions devoted to training in relaxing all muscle groups, the next four sessions to brief muscular relaxation, and the final three sessions to verbal relaxation procedures. Again, daily homework practice is assigned. Therapists may vary their relaxation training timetable according to their clients' needs and their own workload. Nevertheless, it is important that subjects have sufficient sessions to learn relaxation adequately.

Borkovec and Sides (1979) reviewed 25 controlled studies using progressive muscular relaxation and found that fifteen studies reported its superiority over and ten studies its equivalence to control group outcomes. However, of the seven studies characterized by three or more training sessions, live rather than taped training, and clinical as contrasted with normal subjects, only one failed to prove progressive relaxation superior to control group conditions.

Constructing hierarchies

Wolpe (1990) writes: 'An anxiety hierarchy is a thematically related list of anxiety-evoking stimuli, ranked according to the amount of anxiety they evoke' (p. 160). There are a number of considerations in constructing desensitization hierarchies. First, suitable themes have to be identified around which anxiety-evoking stimuli can be clustered. Needless to say, themes or areas which most debilitate clients' functioning receive precedence. Such themes are likely to emerge from behavioural assessments and may concern any one of a number of stimulus situations, for example public speaking, examinations, eating in public, being with a member of the opposite sex, and sexual intercourse.

Second, clients can be introduced to the notion of a subjective scale of anxiety or fear. A common way of checking on the anxiety-evoking potential of hierarchy items is to say that zero is a feeling of no anxiety at all, and 100 is the maximum anxiety possible in relation to a particular theme. Thus individual items can be rated according to their positions on this subjective units of disturbance scale (SUDS).

Third, appropriate hierarchy items need to be generated around each theme. Since clients are going to be asked to imagine the items, the situations require being specifically and graphically described. Therapists indicate the appropriate way for items to be formulated. Sources of hierarchy items may include data gathered in behavioural assessments, self-monitoring homework assignments, suggestions from therapists or clients, and questionnaire responses.

Fourth, the items generated around a particular theme need to be ordered into a hierarchy (see Box 11.2). This involves rating the items on a subjective units of disturbance scale and ordering them accordingly. Some of this work may be done as homework assignments, but therapists will need to check any hierarchy before starting treatment. Also, during treatment, hierarchy items may need to be re-ordered or reworded, or additional items introduced. Some therapists write, or ask their clients to write, items on index cards to facilitate ordering. In general, gaps of over ten units on the subjective anxiety scale are to be avoided. Where such gaps occur, therapists and clients can generate one or more intervening items.

BOX 11.2

Hierarchy for a client with fear of examinations

1. (Rated 5)   Thinking about exams while revising at my desk three months before the exams.

2. (Rated 10)   Thinking about exams while revising at my desk two months before the exams.

3. (Rated 15)   Thinking about exams while revising at my desk one month before the exams.

4. (Rated 20)   Thinking about exams while revising at my desk one week before the exams.

5. (Rated 25)   Thinking about exams while revising at my desk on the night before the exams.

6. (Rated 30)   Being driven in a car on the way to the examinations.

7. (Rated 35)   Waking up on the morning of an examination.

8. (Rated 40)   Going up to the notice board to have a look at the exam results.

9. (Rated 50)   Waiting outside the exam room.

10. (Rated 60)   Going into the exam room.

11. (Rated 70)   Looking at the exam paper for the first time.

12. (Rated 80)   Sitting down in the exam room.

13. (Rated 90)   Sitting in the exam room thinking of the inescapability of three hours in a hall full of people.

14. (Rated 95)   Experiencing a panic attack during the exam and wanting to leave.

15. (Rated. 100) Having to leave the exam room due to panic.

Presenting hierarchy items

During desensitization sessions therapists ask clients to imagine various scenes when relaxed. A basic assumption is that clients are capable of imagining scenes in such a way that they represent real-life situations. Goldfried and Davison (1976) observe: 'It is therefore essential that one check whether a client can become anxious from an image even before considering this procedure' (p. 122). They suggest that clients' imaginal capacities should be tested by asking them, when not relaxed, to imagine a situation which, on the basis of their assessment data, causes them anxiety in real life. Sometimes clients can be helped to imagine scenes by being asked to verbalize what they can see in the situations. Also, therapists may provide fuller verbal descriptions of scenes.

A desensitization session may start with therapists verbally relaxing clients. After therapists are assured that clients have attained states of deep relaxation, they may start presenting scenes along the lines of 'Now I want you to imagine that you are thinking about exams while revising at your desk three months before exams . . .' Therapists start with the least anxiety-evoking scene on hierarchies. Wolpe (1990) used to ask clients to raise their index finger when the scene was clear. Then he would let the scene remain for five to seven seconds and terminate by saying 'Stop the scene.' Next clients would report their subjective units of disturbance (SUDS) level. After 20 to 30 seconds, clients could be asked to imagine the same scene again. If this caused no anxiety, the therapist could withdraw the scene, possibly spend time further relaxing the client, and move on to the next hierarchy item.

In instances where the anxiety created by the presentation is no more than moderate, the therapists can repeat the presentation of the scene, possibly encouraging clients to relax more deeply before further presentations. If a scene repeatedly causes anxiety, therapists can consult with clients about presenting less anxiety-evoking hierarchy items. An important assumption underlying systematic desensitization is that once a low anxiety-evoking item, for example ten units, has ceased to cause anxiety, all the other items in the hierarchy become less anxiety-evoking by ten units. Thus the 100-unit item becomes a 90-unit item, and so on. In general, only weak anxiety-evoking stimuli are presented to clients during desensitization sessions.

Therapists may work from more than one hierarchy during desensitization sessions. Indeed, time spent on desensitization may form only part of longer interviews in which counsellors focus on other problems using other methods. A record is kept of all scene presentations and their outcomes. Wolpe's desensitization sessions last 15–30 minutes and he observes that 'whereas at an early stage eight or ten presentations may be the total at a session, at an advanced stage the number may be 30 or even 50' (Wolpe, 1990).

In vivo *desensitization*
Two kinds of considerations may make *in vivo* or real-life rather than imaginal desensitization the method of choice. First, clients may have difficulty in imagining scenes; and second, the stimuli in clients' hierarchies may lend themselves to real-life presentation. Even using imaginal desensitization, it may be helpful, if not essential, to encourage clients to try out in reality the situations to which they have been desensitized in imagination.

Relaxation may be used as part of *in vivo* desensitization. For instance, a client with a fear of public speaking could be relaxed at the start of each session, then over a number of sessions be asked to give a short talk in front of increasingly large numbers of people, who may also ask increasingly demanding questions. The procedure differs from imaginal desensitization mainly in that the hierarchies are constructed out of real-life situations. Otherwise, many of the imaginal desensitization considerations, such as the level of anxiety within which to present items, apply.

Systematically graduated real-life exposure can form a central part of the behaviour therapy treatment of agoraphobia (Wilson, 2000). Therapists can accompany clients during the exposure sessions and supply support, encouragement and positive reinforcement. Furthermore, therapists ensure that clients understand the importance of staying in the feared situations until their anxiety decreases. Afterwards, therapists debrief clients about what happened.

Assertive training

Often behavioural assessments highlight client deficits in the area of assertion. Wolpe (1990) writes: 'Assertive behavior is the socially appropriate verbal and motor expression of any emotion other than anxiety' (p. 135). An early trend in assertive training was that of standing up for one's rights or what might be termed *oppositional* behaviour. For some time now, assertive training has been extended to include the expression and accurate communication of *affectionate* behaviour, where appropriate. Thus assertive behaviour now encompasses the expression of positive as well as of negative thoughts and feelings (Alberti and Emmons, 1995).

Wolpe regards virtually all clients as inhibited from normal behaviours because of their neurotic fears. Assertive training deconditions unadaptive habits of responding with anxiety to other people's behaviour in two ways: by weakening clients' fears and by changing how they speak and act. Clients require encouragement to express legitimate emotions that are already present in problem situations. Legitimate expression of emotions 'can then successfully compete with the fear that has been inhibiting just this expression, and each time it does so, it weakens to some extent the fear habit' (Wolpe and Wolpe, 1988, p. 54).

Therapists and clients work together to define what may be appropriate behaviours in specific situations: for instance, asking a boss for a pay rise or a girl for a date. This stage involves the generation and consideration of alternative responses. Additionally, clients may be encouraged to observe effective models. Assertiveness must take into account the styles of individual clients and appropriate assertive behaviour should be as 'natural' for them as possible. Responses that might seem appropriate for therapists may not be appropriate for particular clients. Timing is also important, in that clients should not be encouraged to engage in assertiveness tasks for which they are not ready. Consequently, it may be necessary to construct a hierarchy of progressively more difficult assertion tasks.

Once appropriate responses have been formulated, therapists train clients in assertiveness by means of behaviour rehearsal. Alberti and Emmons (1995) stress that assertive training should not focus only on verbal behaviour, but also on other components such as eye contact, body posture, gestures, facial expression, voice tone, inflection and volume, and fluency and timing of assertion. Therapists need to rehearse and coach their clients in these non-verbal and para-verbal aspects of assertiveness. Also, behaviour rehearsals can include rehearsing clients in handling the negative and positive consequences of their assertion as well as in how to handle a variety of situations.

Cassette- and video-recorders are used by some therapists to provide feedback to clients about their assertive behaviours.

Enactment in real life follows behaviour rehearsal. Clients should be set appropriately difficult assertiveness homework assignments. Monitoring their between-session assertive behaviour attempts is likely to help them. Feedback from real-life attempts at assertive behaviour indicates the adequacy of the behaviour and where, if necessary, it might be improved. Furthermore, therapists can draw clients' attention to any positively reinforcing consequences of their assertive behaviour. If the consequences were negative, therapists and clients can review the appropriateness of the targeted behaviours. Even if properly enacted, assertiveness may lead to conflict, and so therapists and clients may need to focus on managing conflict as well as on assertion.

Reinforcement interventions

Reinforcement interventions aim to modify behaviour by altering its consequences and, as such, reflect operant rather than classical conditioning principles. To recapitulate, both positive and negative reinforcement strengthen the probability of a response. Positive reinforcers involve presenting and negative reinforcers removing something in a situation. Punishment, or the presentation of a negative state of affairs, aims to weaken the probability of a response without necessarily increasing the frequency of other behaviours. Extinction also aims to weaken the probability of a response by withdrawal of customary reinforcers. Readers are referred to the section on Skinner in Chapter 10 for further discussion of reinforcement concepts, such as schedules of reinforcement.

Identifying reinforcers

Many reinforcers, such as praise, affection and attention, are given out relatively unthinkingly during the course of everyday life. Reinforcement interventions, however, involve the systematic application of reinforcement to initiate and strengthen adaptive behaviours and to weaken and eliminate maladaptive behaviours. In order to use reinforcement systematically, it is necessary to discover what is reinforcing for individual clients. Ways in which therapists can find out what their clients consider reinforcing include asking them, asking others about them, observing what they say and do in the interview setting, and getting them to observe and monitor themselves outside interviews.

Some self-report questionnaires exist for assessing reinforcers. Cautela (1967a) has devised a *Reinforcement Survey Schedule* to identify possible reinforcing stimuli together with their relative reinforcing values. Another self-report questionnaire is MacPhillamy and Lewinsohn's *Pleasant Events Schedule* (Lewinsohn *et al.*, 1986; MacPhillamy and Lewinsohn, 1971). This instrument consists of 320 events and activities generated after an extensive search of possible 'pleasant events'. Subjects rate each item in the schedule on a five-point scale of pleasantness. A shortened version of the *Pleasant Events Schedule* can be derived from those items associated with improved mood for a substantial proportion of people. Lewinsohn and Graf (1973) list 49 such items and suggest that they fall into three categories: social interactional, effects incompatible with depression, and ego supportive, or activities leading to feelings such as adequacy and competence.

When working with children, pictures may be used instead of words to portray reinforcers. An example of this is the 'reinforcement menu' devised by Daley (1969) for finding effective reinforcers for 8-year-old to 11-year-old mentally retarded children. Twenty-two high-probability activities, such as talking, writing and colouring, were drawn in colour by an artist and enclosed in a single book or 'menu' with one activity per page. Children were encouraged to identify the activities in which they wanted to engage.

Reinforcement programmes and token economies

Positive reinforcement is the major method for changing behaviour in applied settings. Positive reinforcement programmes can be used both to increase desirable behaviours and to decrease undesirable behaviours. The second goal can be accomplished by positively reinforcing alternative or incompatible behaviours (Kazdin, 1994).

In designing reinforcement programmes it is particularly important that, when a behaviour is initiated, the reinforcement contingent upon that behaviour is immediate, otherwise its differential effect may be lost. Acquisition of desired behaviours may initially involve reinforcement of either component behaviours or related behaviours and build up to the desired behaviours by successive approximation. Therapists can use continuous reinforcement to establish behaviours initially. Afterwards, they can use intermittent reinforcement, since resistance to extinction is greater if fewer responses are reinforced.

Reinforcement may either be administered directly, by provision of actual reinforcers, or indirectly, by means of tokens which may later be exchanged for reinforcers. Furthermore, clients may be reinforced vicariously by observing models obtain rewards for desired behaviours (Bandura, 1986). An example of direct reinforcement is Sanborn and Schuster's (1969) use of sweets to reinforce desired behaviours in a remedial reading class. For instance, the first boy to sit down was rewarded with a sweet and the contingency for the reward was verbally transmitted: 'This is for taking your seat.' As the class progressed pupils were rewarded for other specific behaviours.

Sometimes positive reinforcement can reward the wrong behaviours. For instance, institutionalized elderly people can receive the social reward of attention for dependency and helplessness behaviours whereas independence behaviours go unrewarded (Baltes, 1988). For such institutionalized elderly people, a positive reinforcement programme should target increasing the likelihood of appropriate independence responses.

Tokens are tangible conditioned reinforcers which may be exchanged for back-up reinforcers such as prizes, opportunities to engage in special activities, food or other purchases. Token reinforcement programmes need to establish clearly the rules of exchange that specify the number of tokens required to obtain back-up reinforcers (Wilson, 2000). Token economies or token reinforcement programmes have been used with schoolchildren, delinquents and hospital patients. Applications of token economies in elementary and secondary school settings have improved students' classroom performance in reading, writing and arithmetic (Kazdin, 1994). In one American programme, first-grade students received points at various intervals (depending on how well they were working) that they could exchange for prizes ranging in value from $0.05 to $1.50 at a 'good study store' in class (Breyer and Allen, 1975, p. 385).

Kazdin and Bootzin (1972) suggest that extinction of the desired behaviours generally follows removal of token reinforcement. They state that generalization should be planned rather than depended on as an inadvertent consequence of the token economy. One way of enhancing resistance to extinction is to focus on teaching those behaviours which will continue to be reinforced after training. Another way involves gradually removing or fading the token reinforcement, possibly offering substitute kinds of reinforcement such as praise as the fading takes place. Yet another way of maintaining the behavioural gains is to encourage clients to use self-reinforcement by giving themselves reinforcers contingent upon the performance of desired behaviours.

Reinforcement programmes and token economies may involve the co-operation and training of significant others in the clients' environments. For instance, therapists may need to work with teachers or parents in devising reinforcement procedures for individuals or groups of children. Furthermore, both teachers and parents may need to become aware of how they may inadvertently be reinforcing some of the behaviours they say they are trying to stop. Teaching the skills of effective reinforcement involves both theoretical learning and relevant practice. Furthermore, therapists may need to support and guide teachers and parents as they apply their new skills in real-life settings.

Time out and response costs

Time out is a procedure frequently recommended by behaviour therapists for use with disruptive children. It involves removal of clients from situations in which they might otherwise be receiving reinforcement. For instance, a child's attention-seeking behaviour in a classroom may be being reinforced by teacher attention and peer approval, neither of which is available when the child is made to leave the classroom for a set period of time. Time-out procedures involve a clear instruction, adequate warning that the time-out procedure is contingent upon the undesired behaviour and, if this goes unheeded, application of time out in a systematic and unemotional way. Nemeroff and Karoly (1991) observe: 'Most successful programmes with children employ TO durations of between 5 and 20 minutes, and for very young children, periods as short as 1 to 5 minutes may be effective' (p. 150).

Response costs involve deductions of certain amounts from clients' collections of reinforcers if they perform undesired behaviours. For instance, participants in a token economy may lose some of their tokens. Where possible, response costs should be used in conjunction with positive reinforcement of desirable or alternative behaviours.

Helping clients to obtain reinforcement

A very important aspect of behavioural treatment may be that of helping clients to increase the number and scope of reinforcers available to them (Cormier and Cormier, 1998). Another way of saying this is that, instead of passively relying on others, clients can be helped to identify and actively seek out people, activities and situations that provide the desired reinforcements. Lewinsohn and Libet (1972) assert that a low rate of positive reinforcement is a critical antecedent of depressive behaviours and that improvement is likely to be accompanied by an increase of positive reinforcement. They report the findings of a study in which the 160 items from the *Pleasant Events Schedule* which a subject judged to be most pleasant were made into an activity schedule for that subject, who, for 30 consecutive days, was asked to indicate at the end of each day the activities in which he or she engaged. They found a significant association between mood and pleasant activities over their 30 subjects, though there were large individual differences. They see the clinical utility of activity schedules as including: (a) assessing which activities are potentially reinforcing; (b) illustrating to clients their low rates of emitting behaviours which bring positive reinforcement; (c) goal setting; and (d) monitoring behaviour change.

Another study, by Turner and his colleagues, in which the subjects were moderately depressed college students, confirmed the effectiveness of using activity schedules and also instructing the subjects to increase their pleasant activities over their usual level (Turner, Ward and Turner, 1979). A further study, by Zeiss, Lewinsohn and Munoz (1979), indicated that, with depressed outpatients, treatments focusing on interpersonal skills, or cognitions, or activity schedules (with increasing frequency of target activities) all significantly alleviated depression.

Training clients to use self-reinforcement

Training clients to use self-reinforcement is often termed a self-control or self-management strategy. It can involve assisting clients to observe their behaviour, set goals for themselves, identify suitable reinforcers, plan graded steps to attain their goals, and specify when to administer consequences (Cormier and Cormier, 1998; Watson and Tharp, 1997). In helping clients to design self-reinforcement programmes, it is important both that they perceive that they have chosen their goals or target behaviours and also that they have the confidence to complete tasks that will bring desired outcomes. Consequently, frequently therapists design self-reinforcement programmes with graded steps to ensure that clients build up their confidence with success experiences. This enhances motivation both initially and later. Some clients may have to build up component skills prior to initiating self-management programmes.

Self-reinforcers can be external or internal. External reinforcers include: self-administration of new reinforcers that are outside clients' everyday lives, such as a new item of clothing or a special event; and initial denial of some pleasant everyday experience and later administration of it contingent upon some desired action. Internal reinforcers include self-talk statements like 'That's great', or 'Well done', or 'I'm glad I made it' that clearly indicate the client's satisfaction with achieving target actions.

When collaborating with clients to design self-reinforcement programmes, behaviour therapists are mindful of external resources that clients can use. For instance, participating in activities of a social, educational, recreational or religious nature may provide opportunities for gaining confidence and skills. In addition, reading appropriate self-help books and manuals can be incorporated into a programme. Such material should be easily comprehensible to clients, but this is often not the case.

Stimulus control

Thoresen and Mahoney (1974) indicate that there are two general self-control strategies that clients can use to influence their actions. First they can try modifying their environments to control target actions *prior to* their execution. Second, they can self-administer a reward *following* or *contingent upon* an action or series of actions that achieves either a goal or a sub-goal.

Behaviour therapists assist clients to use stimulus control as one form of environmental modification. Stimulus control entails modifying in advance the stimuli or cues associated with maladaptive responses and/or establishing cues associated with adaptive responses. For example, ways in which behaviour therapists might suggest that people on weight reduction programmes modify their environments to control their food intake include: ensuring that food is placed out of sight and of easy reach; equipping their refrigerators with time locks; only keeping as much food in the house as can be consumed in a short period of time; and, where appropriate, avoiding contact with people associated with excessive eating.

Stimulus control can also be used to enhance adaptive behaviours. For example, students can learn to associate their desks with work if they use them only for that purpose. Some behaviour therapists use stimulus control in treating sleep disorders by having insomniac clients only associate their beds with sleep (Morawetz, 1989).

Self-punishment

Above I have mainly emphasized positive self-reinforcement and stimulus control. However, though less frequently used, behaviour therapists can encourage clients to self-administer aversive consequences. For example, weight loss programme clients can give to charity a specified sum of money for every 100 calories in excess of a daily intake limit or they can present themselves with a noxious odour after each extra snack (Thoresen and Mahoney, 1974). Furthermore, clients can imagine themselves experiencing aversive consequences if they perform undesirable actions: for instance throwing up if they eat a piece of chocolate cake. This process is known as covert sensitization (Cautela, 1967b).

Participant modelling

Perhaps Bandura's most direct contribution to behaviour therapy has been his participant modelling approach (Bandura, Jeffery and Wright, 1974; Bandura, Jeffery and Gadjos, 1975; Cormier and Cormier, 1998). This approach emphasizes *in vivo* performance of feared tasks, with the consequences generated by successful performance being viewed as the primary vehicle for psychological change. Participant modelling involves a number of stages. First, therapists repeatedly model feared activities, for instance handling snakes or dogs, to show clients both how they can be successfully performed and that the feared consequences do not occur. Second, joint performance with their therapists may enable clients to start engaging in activities which would be too threatening to engage in on their own. Therapists, who function as guides and anxiety inhibitors, use hierarchies of increasingly difficult sub-tasks.

Third, therapists may introduce response induction aids or protective conditions to reduce expectations of feared consequences and thus help clients to perform the desired tasks. For instance, when treating snake phobias, response induction aids might include the model holding the snake securely by the head and tail, use of protective gloves, and presenting a smaller snake. Fourth, therapists gradually withdraw performance supports to ensure that clients can function effectively without assistance. Fifth, clients may have a period of self-directed performance in which they spend time interacting with the feared object on their own. During the initial period of self-directed performance, therapists may stay in the room with clients, but later withdraw, possibly to observe clients from behind one-way mirrors. The idea is that clients' confidence is best strengthened by independent achievements in which it is clear that successful consequences are due to their ability to master feared situations on their own.

Aversive and flooding methods

This chapter has focused on basic behaviour therapy interventions. Other, less common and more controversial interventions exist, for example aversion therapy and flooding. Both these interventions deliberately heighten clients' levels of distress. Aversion therapy, which entails the presentation of an aversive event such as an electric shock contingent upon some undesired behaviour, might be viewed as a punishment technique. In current flooding techniques, therapists arrange for clients to be exposed to relatively strong fear stimuli which, either real or imagined, are presented continuously. Presentations last until anxiety wanes, which frequently takes from ten minutes to an hour. Sometimes clients are so distressed that they discontinue treatment. Nevertheless, flooding has been used with considerable success for a variety of phobias. However, Wolpe claims that, with few exceptions, desensitization has proved superior to flooding with the added advantage of being less stressful for clients (Wolpe and Wolpe, 1988).

CASE MATERIAL

With the rise of cognitive–behaviourism, it is increasingly difficult to find case material based solely on conditioning assumptions. Case illustrations liberally illustrate Wolpe's (1990) *The Practice of Behavior Therapy*. Wolpe presents vignettes, interview transcripts and also discusses four instructive complex cases: social anxiety, multidimensional automobile phobia, washing compulsion, and reversal of sexual preference.

In *Life Without Fear: Anxiety and its Cure*, Wolpe writes: 'Complex cases are not at all exceptional; rather, they are the rule' (Wolpe and Wolpe, p. 95). In this book Wolpe presents some complex cases, including: a case of anxiety and depression; fear of marriage; a multifaceted case of depression; fear of being alone based on fear of losing control; an unusual case of male sexual failure; and a many-sided phobia.

FURTHER DEVELOPMENTS

Traditional or radical behaviour therapy, based on conditioning principles, possibly had its heyday in the 1960s and 1970s. For some thirty years or more, it has been increasingly challenged by cognitive–behaviour therapy with its internal cognitive rather than external contextual view of the causation of behaviour. Reitman and Drabman (1997) argue for the value of behaviour therapists valuing the differences between the contextual and the cognitive traditions within their fold. They assert that radical behaviour therapy interventions may turn out to be the treatment of choice for some problems.

Behaviour therapy is well represented by associations. In the United States there is the Association for the Advancement of Behavior Therapy (AABT); in Europe, the European Association of Behaviour Therapy; in Britain, the British Association for Behavioural and Cognitive Psychotherapies (BABCP); and in Australia, the Australian Association for Cognitive and Behaviour Therapy (AACBT). In addition, there are active behaviour therapy organizations in many countries of Latin America. Though training in behaviour therapy is widely available, frequently it is more cognitive–behavioural rather than behavioural in orientation.

Numerous journals are devoted to behaviour therapy, with two of the most prominent being *Behavior Therapy*, published by the AABT, and *Behaviour Research and Therapy*. Nowadays, many if not most of the articles in these journals are cognitive–behavioural rather than behavioural.

SUMMARY

- *Traditional behaviour therapy is based on conditioning principles. Increasingly this approach is being challenged by cognitive behaviourists who explain the causes of behaviour more by inner cognitive events than by external contingencies of reinforcement.*
- *Goals for behaviour therapy include: initiating and strengthening adaptive behaviours, weakening and eliminating maladaptive behaviours, and reducing unwanted fears and anxieties.*
- *The process of behaviour therapy starts with a behavioural assessment to specify the factors controlling maladaptive behaviours. The assessment may include data collected both during interviews and from other sources, for instance client self-monitoring.*
- *The end point of a behavioural assessment is a specification of goals in behavioural terms followed by a treatment plan for attaining these goals.*
- *Behaviour therapy is an educational process and the therapeutic relationship takes place within this parameter. Behaviour therapists stress developing good relationships with clients to enhance accuracy of assessment and treatment effectiveness.*
- *Systematic desensitization involves three elements: (a) training in deep muscular relaxation; (b) the construction of thematic hierarchies of anxiety-evoking stimuli; and (c) presentation of hierarchy items to the imagination of deeply relaxed clients. An in vivo variation of systematic desensitization involves graduated exposure to items on real-life hierarchies.*
- *Assertive training, or training in the accurate communication of positive and negative feelings without inhibition or aggression, is mainly approached by shaping and rehearsing targeted verbal and non-verbal behaviours for various situations.*
- *Reinforcement interventions aim to modify behaviour by altering its consequences. Ways of identifying what clients find reinforcing are reviewed.*

- *Reinforcement programmes and token economies aim to change the behaviour of both individuals and groups, for example a classroom of children. Tokens are tangible conditioned reinforcers which may be exchanged for back-up reinforcers such as prizes and food. All reinforcement programmes should plan to overcome extinction of the target behaviours after removal of the reinforcers.*
- *Time out involves removing clients from situations in which they receive reinforcement. Response costs involve deductions of certain amounts from clients' collections of reinforcers if they perform undesired behaviours. Such interventions should always be used in conjunction with positive reinforcement of desirable or alternative behaviours.*
- *Clients may be helped to increase the number and scope of reinforcers available to them, an approach which shows promise in treating depressed people.*
- *Therapists can train clients in how to control the stimuli associated with adaptive and maladaptive responses and in how to use positive and negative self-reinforcement.*
- *Participant modelling involves clients in observing and then enacting the behaviour of therapists who model how to behave in successively more fear-evoking situations.*
- *Aversive and flooding methods deliberately heighten clients' distress and should be used sparingly.*
- *Further research is still being conducted into behaviour therapy interventions based on conditioning principles. However, behaviour therapy is increasingly dominated by cognitive–behaviourists rather than by traditional behaviourists.*

REVIEW AND PERSONAL QUESTIONS

REVIEW QUESTIONS

1. How do traditional behaviour therapists and cognitive–behaviour therapists differ in how they explain the causes of behaviour?
2. What might behaviour therapists view as appropriate goals for clients?
3. What are the functions of behavioural assessment and how do behaviour therapists collect assessment information?
4. Describe the goals and methods of systematic desensitization.
5. Describe the goals and methods of assertive training.
6. How can behaviour therapists assist clients to identify what they find reinforcing?
7. Describe and illustrate what behaviour therapists mean by the terms 'reinforcement programmes' and 'token economies'.
8. How can behaviour therapists assist clients in obtaining reinforcement in their daily lives?
9. What are the goals of stimulus control? Provide an example of stimulus control.
10. Describe and illustrate what is meant by participant modelling.
11. What are some goals of and considerations in using aversion and flooding interventions in behaviour therapy?

PERSONAL QUESTIONS

1. Identify an area of your own behaviour that you wish to change. Formulate your goal(s) in behavioural terms.
2. For the behaviour that you wished to change above, for one week keep a behaviour monitoring diary, collecting material in an *SRC* format.
3. Practise relaxing yourself for fifteen to twenty minutes a day over a period of at least a week. Keep a monitoring log of your relaxation homework. During your relaxation homework cover:
   - progressive muscular relaxation (Box 11.1);
   - brief muscular relaxation; and
   - mental relaxation.
4. Identify themes in your own life which are appropriate for anxiety-hierarchy construction and then, along the lines of Box 11.2, construct one or more hierarchies around them.
5. For one or more of the above hierarchies, apply systematic desensitization to yourself.
6. Pick a specific situation in your life where you consider you could be more assertive. Set yourself verbal and non-verbal behavioural goals for change and self-administer assertiveness training, including rehearsing targeted behaviours, to attain your goals.
7. Make a list of at least 25 items which you personally find reinforcing. Rate each item using the following scale: 1, slightly reinforcing; 2, moderately reinforcing; 3, strongly reinforcing; 4, very strongly reinforcing.
8. Design a positive self-reinforcement programme. Specify:
   (a) your goal in behavioural terms;
   (b) how you intend to observe your behaviour, establish a baseline and monitor progress;
   (c) the positive reinforcer(s) you intend using;
   (d) the precise conditions for self-administering the positive reinforcer(s);
   (e) whether and how you intend using graded steps and sub-goals to attain your goal; and
   (f) a time schedule for your programme.
9. What is the relevance of the practice of behaviour therapy to how you conduct therapy?
10. What is the relevance of the practice of behaviour therapy to how you lead your life?

ANNOTATED BIBLIOGRAPHY

Wolpe, J. (1990). *The Practice of Behavior Therapy* (4th edition). Oxford: Pergamon Press.
   This book describes in detail the author's views on the causes of neurosis, behaviour analysis, and a range of treatment methods including assertiveness training, systematic desensitization and its variations, and operant conditioning. In addition, Wolpe presents some complex cases and provides an evaluation of behaviour therapy.

Kazdin, A. E. (1994). *Behavior Modification in Applied Settings* (5th edition). Pacific Grove, CA.: Brooks/Cole.

> This book takes a scholarly, yet practical, approach to behavioural assessment and the design and evaluation of behaviour modification programmes. Chapters are included on positive and negative reinforcement, punishment, extinction, self-control techniques, and response maintenance and transfer of training.

Wolpe, J. and Wolpe, D. (1988). *Life Without Fear: Anxiety and its Cure*. Oakland, CA: New Harbinger Publications.

> This short book is designed to provide an authoritative account of the essential features of behaviour therapy for professionals in the mental health field and for the educated public. It explores the processes of generating, maintaining and changing useless fears. Then the authors describe the practice of behaviour analysis and therapy. The book contains many case examples.

Wilson, G. T. (2000). Behavior therapy. In R. J. Corsini and D. Wedding (eds). *Current Psychotherapies* (6th edition, 205–40). Itasca, IL: Peacock.

> A chapter by a prominent cognitive–behaviour therapist that overviews the theory, practice, development and current status of behaviour therapy.

Cormier, S. and Cormier, W. H. (1998). *Intervention Strategies for Helpers: Fundamental Skills and Cognitive Behavioral Interventions*. Pacific Grove, CA: Brooks/Cole.

> This huge and extremely detailed book presents skills and strategies for four major stages of the helping process: relationship, assessment and goal setting, strategy selection and implementation, and evaluation and termination.

Reitman, D. and Drabman, R. S. (1997). The value of recognizing our differences and promoting healthy competition: The cognitive behavioral debate. *Behavior Therapy*, *28*, 419–29.

> This article intelligently explores differences between the radical behaviourist and cognitive–behaviour therapists regarding the causal state of cognitions. They assert that the cause of developing empirically supported treatments for clients' problems is best served by encouraging variation to ensure that better therapies emerge.

REFERENCES AND FURTHER READING

Alberti, R. E. and Emmons, M. L. (1995). *Your Perfect Right: A Guide to Assertive Living* (7th edition). San Luis Obispo, CA: Impact Publishers.

Baltes, M. M. (1988). The etiology and maintenance of dependency in the elderly: Three phases of operant research. *Behavior Therapy*, *19*, 301–19.

Bandura, A. (1986). *Social Foundations of Thought and Action: A Social Cognitive Theory*. Englewood Cliffs, NJ: Prentice-Hall.

Bandura, A., Jeffery, R. W. and Gadjos, E. (1975). Generalizing change through participant modeling with self-directed mastery. *Behaviour Research and Therapy*, *13*, 141–52.

Bandura, A., Jeffery, R. W. and Wright, C. L. (1974). Efficacy of participant modeling as a function of response induction aids. *Journal of Abnormal Psychology*, *83*, 56–64.

Bernstein, D. A. and Borkovec, T. D. (1973). *Progressive Relaxation Training: A Manual for the Helping Professions*. Champaign, IL: Research Press.

Bjork, D. W. (1993). *B. F. Skinner: A Life.* New York: Basic Books.

Borkovec, T. D. and Sides, J. K. (1979). Critical procedural variables related to the physiological effects of progressive relaxation: a review. *Behaviour Research and Therapy, 17,* 119–25.

Breyer, N. L. and Allen, G. L. (1975). Effects of implementing a token economy on teacher attending behavior. *Journal of Applied Behavior Analysis, 8,* 373–80.

Cautela, J. (1967a). A reinforcement survey schedule for use in therapy, training and research. *Psychological Reports, 20,* 1115–30.

Cautela, J. (1967b). Covert sensitization. *Psychological Reports, 20,* 459–68.

Cormier, S. and Cormier, W. H. (1998). *Intervention Strategies for Helpers: Fundamental Skills and Cognitive Behavioral Interventions.* Pacific Grove, CA: Brooks/Cole.

Craighead, W. E. (1990). 'There's a place for us: all of us'. *Behavior Therapy, 21,* 3–23.

Daley, M. F. (1969). The 'reinforcement menu': Finding effective reinforcers. In J. D. Krumboltz and C. E. Thoresen (eds). *Behavioral Counseling: Cases and Techniques* (42–5). New York: Holt, Rinehart and Winston.

Galassi, J. P. and Perot, A. R. (1992). What you should know about behavioral assessment. *Journal of Counseling and Development, 70,* 624–31.

Goldfried, M. R. and Davison, G. C. (1976). *Clinical Behavior Therapy.* New York: Holt, Rinehart and Winston.

Jacobson, E. (1929). *Progressive Relaxation.* Chicago, IL: University of Chicago Press.

Jacobson, E. (1938). *Progressive Relaxation* (2nd edition). Chicago, IL: University of Chicago Press.

Kazdin, A. E. (1993). Evaluation in clinical practice: Clinically sensitive and systematic methods of treatment delivery. *Behavior Therapy, 24,* 11–45.

Kazdin, A. E. (1994). *Behavior Modification in Applied Settings* (5th edition). Pacific Grove, CA: Brooks/Cole.

Kazdin, A. E. and Bootzin, R. E. (1972). The token economy: An evaluative review. *Journal of Applied Behavior Analysis, 5,* 343–72.

Lewinsohn, P. M. and Graf, M. (1973). Pleasant activities and depression. *Journal of Consulting and Clinical Psychology, 41,* 261–8.

Lewinsohn, P. M. and Libet, J. (1972). Pleasant events, activity schedules and depression. *Journal of Abnormal Psychology, 79,* 291–5.

Lewinsohn, P. M., Munoz, R. F., Youngren, M. A. and Zeiss, A. M. (1986). *Control Your Depression* (revised edition). New York: Prentice Hall Press.

MacPhillamy, D. J. and Lewinsohn, P. M. (1971). *Pleasant Events Schedule.* University of Oregon: Mimeograph.

Morawetz, D. (1989). Behavioral self-help treatment for insomnia: A controlled evaluation. *Behavior Therapy, 20,* 365–79.

Nemeroff, C. J. and Karoly, P. (1991). Operant methods. In F. H. Kanfer and A. P. Goldstein (eds). *Helping People Change: A Textbook of Methods* (4th edition, 122–60). New York: Pergamon Press.

Reitman, D. and Drabman, R. S. (1997). The value of recognizing our differences and promoting healthy competition: The cognitive behavioral debate. *Behavior Therapy, 28,* 419–29.

Sanborn, B. and Schuster, W. (1969). Establishing reinforcement techniques in the classroom. In J. D. Krumboltz and C. E. Thoresen (eds). *Behavioral Counseling: Cases and Techniques* (131–52). New York: Holt, Rinehart and Winston.

Tasto, D. L. and Hinkle, J. E. (1973). Muscle relaxation treatment for tension headaches. *Behaviour Research and Therapy, 11,* 347–9.

Thoresen, C. E. and Coates, T. J. (1978). What does it mean to be a behavior therapist? *The*

Counseling Psychologist, 7, 3–21.

Thoresen, C. E. and Mahoney, M. J. (1974). *Behavioral Self-Control.* New York: Holt, Rinehart and Winston.

Turner, R. W., Ward, M. F. and Turner, J. (1979). Behavioral treatment for depression: an evaluation of therapeutic components. *Journal of Clinical Psychology*, 35, 166–75.

Watson, D. and Tharp, R. (1997). *Self-Directed Behavior: Self-Modification for Personal Adjustment.* Pacific Grove, CA: Brooks/Cole.

Wilson, G. T. (2000). Behavior therapy. In R. J. Corsini and D. Wedding (eds). *Current Psychotherapies* (6th edition, 205–40). Itasca, IL: Peacock.

Wolpe, J. (1958). *Psychotherapy by Reciprocal Inhibition.* Stanford: Stanford University Press.

Wolpe, J. (1973). *The Practice of Behavior Therapy* (2nd edition). Oxford: Pergamon Press.

Wolpe, J. (1990). *The Practice of Behavior Therapy* (4th edition). Oxford: Pergamon Press.

Wolpe, J. and Lang, P. J. (1969). *Fear Survey Schedule.* San Diego, California: Educational and Industrial Testing Service.

Wolpe, J. and Wolpe, D. (1988). *Life Without Fear: Anxiety and its Cure.* Oakland, CA: New Harbinger Publications.

Zeiss, A. M., Lewinsohn, P. M. and Munoz, R. F. (1979). Nonspecific improvement effects in depression using interpersonal skills training, pleasant activity schedules, or cognitive training. *Journal of Consulting and Clinical Psychology*, 47, 427–39.

12

Rational Emotive Behaviour Therapy

The basic tenet of REBT is that emotional upsets, as distinguished from feelings of sorrow, regret, annoyance, and frustration, largely stem from irrational beliefs.

Albert Ellis

INTRODUCTION

When first developed in 1955, Ellis termed his approach rational therapy (RT). In 1961, he changed its name to rational-emotive therapy (RET). In 1993, Ellis (1993a) further changed its name to rational emotive behaviour therapy (REBT). What Ellis means by 'rational' is cognition that is effective in self-helping rather than cognition merely empirically and logically valid. He wishes that he had used the word 'cognitive' from the start since many people narrowly restrict the word 'rational' to mean intellectual or logico-empirical. People's rationality rests on judging soundly which of their desires or preferences to follow and, therefore, is based on thoughts, emotions and feelings (Ellis, 1990).

Ellis introduced 'behaviour' into his approach's name for the sake of accuracy. From its start, the approach has strongly emphasized behaviour along with cognition and emotion. Ellis writes: 'So, to correct my previous errors and to set the record straight, I shall from now on call it what it has really always been – rational emotive behavior therapy (REBT)' (Ellis, 1993a, p. 258).

Ellis (2000) distinguishes between general REBT and preferential REBT. General REBT is virtually the same as cognitive–behaviour therapy and aims to teach clients rational or appropriate behaviours. Preferential REBT emphasizes a profound philosophic change. At the same time as including general REBT, it also teaches clients how to dispute irrational ideas and self-defeating behaviours and how to use powerful cognitive-emotive-behavioural methods as self-helping skills. This chapter focuses on preferential REBT, which from now on will be referred to as rational emotive behaviour therapy (REBT).

ALBERT ELLIS (1913–)

In 1913, Albert Ellis was born in Pittsburgh, Pennsylvania, and grew up in New York City. He had a brother and sister who were nineteen months and four years younger than him, respectively. His father was absent much of the time. His Jewish mother was benignly neglectful and 'was much more immersed in her own pleasures and ego-aggrandising activities than she was in understanding and taking care of her children' (Ellis, 1991a, p. 3). Aged 12, he discovered that his parents had divorced.

Another childhood misfortune was that, aged 4½, Ellis almost died of tonsillitis and nephritis and for the next few years was frequently hospitalized. When young, Ellis had psychological as well as physical problems. He writes: 'It took me almost two decades to talk myself out of that crap of being ingratiating. I was born and reared to be shy and scared. Throughout my childhood and teens I had a real social phobia. I viewed public speaking as a fate worse than public masturbation' (Ellis, 1997a, p. 69). However, Ellis did very well at school and developed problem-solving skills to make the most of his difficult childhood. For instance, when 19, he overcame his terror of public speaking by persisting in giving political talks over a period of three months. Furthermore, to overcome his shyness with women, he forced himself to talk to a hundred girls in a row in the Bronx Botanical Gardens (Ellis, 1997a). As with public speaking, he was able to make a 180-degree change in how he performed. These experiences were important precursors to REBT because Ellis discovered the great value of reasoning and self-persuasion in changing his dysfunctional feelings and actions.

Beginning his writing career at the age of 12, Ellis turned out scores of stories, essays and comic poems and received scores of rejection slips too. In 1934, despite his early ambition to become the Great American Novelist, Ellis received a bachelor's degree in business administration from the City University of New York. Early occupations included a business matching trousers to still suitable jackets and being personnel manager of a gift and novelty firm. Ellis devoted much of his spare time to writing fiction. Partly because of difficulties getting his fiction published, Ellis turned exclusively to writing non-fiction, especially focusing on the 'sex-family revolution'.

Discovering that he liked therapy as well as writing, in 1942 Ellis entered the clinical psychology programme at Columbia University, receiving a master's degree in 1943. Soon after obtaining his Masters, Ellis began a small private practice in psychotherapy and marital and sex therapy. In 1947, Ellis received his doctorate from Columbia University with a thesis on personality questionnaires, an earlier thesis on love having been censored before it got off the ground. After his doctorate, Ellis's ambition was to become an outstanding psychoanalyst and so he completed a training analysis with an analyst from the Karen Horney group and began to practise psychoanalysis under his teacher's direction. From 1948 to 1952, Ellis worked for the New Jersey Department of Institutions and Agencies, mainly as chief psychologist of the New Jersey State Diagnostic Center and then as chief psychologist of the entire state of New Jersey. He also continued his private practice in New York.

For some time, Ellis had employed active-directive methods in his psychotherapy, marital and sex therapy. Also, before undergoing analysis, Ellis had worked through many of his own problems by reading and practising the philosophies of Epictetus, Marcus Aurelius, Spinoza and Bertrand Russell, and so he started teaching clients the philosophic principles that had helped him. Between 1953 and 1955, Ellis increasingly rebelled against psychoanalysis and began calling himself a 'psychotherapist' rather than a 'psychoanalyst'. He writes: 'I finally wound up, at the beginning of 1955, with RET' (Ellis, 1991a, p. 15). He gave his first paper on it at the American Psychological Association's annual meeting in Chicago on 31 August 1956.

In 1959, Ellis founded the Institute for Rational Living, Inc., now called the Albert Ellis Institute for Rational Emotive Behaviour Therapy, as a non-profit-making scientific and educational organization to teach the principles of rational living. Since then, Ellis has donated all his royalties and income from clients and workshops to the Institute. In 1964, the Institute bought a large New York townhouse, where it is still headquartered.

Ellis is a man of boundless energy, probably a genetic inheritance from his 'two highly energetic parents who both lived reasonably long lives and were active until the last day of their lives' (Dryden, 1989, p. 545). He spends most of his time working. Aged over 83, in a week where he was mainly in New York 'I usually see individual and group clients from 9:30am to 11pm – with a couple of half hour breaks for meals, and mostly for half hour sessions with individual clients. So during each week I may see over 80 individual clients and over 40 more group clients' (Ellis, 1997b, p. 17). In addition, Ellis holds his 8.30–10 p.m. Friday night workshop where he interviews people in public. On Saturday night and Sunday he works on books, writing, research, letters, and various other things (Palmer, 1993). Ellis also gives numerous workshops and seminars in America and overseas and uses the travel time to write and read.

Ellis's work is his main priority. However, he has been married and divorced twice, as well as having relationships with a number of other women. Since 1964, when she was 42, he has been in a stable relationship with Janet Wolfe and comments that his life 'would be greatly bereft of laughter, warmth, and intimacy without her' (Dryden, 1989, p. 541). Ellis and Janet have no children, since they regard it as unfair that, due to his work, he would not have much time to spend with them.

Ellis has had to work around physical disabilities to attain and maintain his phenomenal productivity level (Ellis, 1997b). From age 19, he has been hampered by chronically fatigable eyes. The upshot of this is that he rarely reads for more than twenty minutes and often keeps his eyes shut during therapy sessions. Aged 40, Ellis was diagnosed as having full-blown diabetes and has had to find ways of minimizing the inconvenience attached to this condition. In his late 60s Ellis's hearing began to deteriorate and by his mid-70s he had two hearing aids which, even when in good working order, had their limitations.

Ellis's work has been controversial. His REBT ideas challenged psychoanalytic and Rogerian orthodoxies. His ideas on sex challenged conventional morality. In addition, Ellis has not been afraid to speak his mind. However, over the past thirty years or so, cognitive–behavioural ideas have become increasingly fashionable and Ellis now regards himself as the father of REBT and the grandfather of cognitive–behaviour therapy. Ellis has received numerous honours and awards, including the American Psychological Association's major award for Distinguished Professional Contributions to Knowledge, the American Counselling Association's major Professional Development Award, and the American Humanist Association's Humanist of the Year Award.

Ellis has always been a prolific writer, even before publishing in the area of psychology. He has published over 700 papers in psychological, psychiatric and sociological journals and anthologies. In addition, Ellis has authored or edited over 65 books and monographs including: *Sex Without Guilt*, *Reason and Emotion in Psychotherapy*, *A Guide to Rational Living* (with Robert Harper), *Overcoming Resistance: Rational-Emotive Therapy with Difficult Clients*, *Better, Deeper and More Enduring Brief Therapy: The Rational Emotive*

Behaviour Approach, *The Practice of Rational Emotive Behaviour Therapy* (with Windy Dryden), *Rational Emotive Behaviour Therapy: A Therapist's Guide* (with Catherine MacLaren), *How to Stubbornly Refuse to Make Yourself Miserable About Anything – Yes, Anything!*, *The Albert Ellis Reader* and *How to Make Yourself Happy and Remarkably Less Disturbable*. Ellis is also well known for his rational-humorous songs: for example, 'Beautiful Hangup' to the tune of Stephen Foster's 'Beautiful Dreamer', the first two lines of which are:

Beautiful hangup, why should we part
When we have shared our whole lives from the start?

Apart from humour, the guiding principles of Ellis's work have been 'Science, efficiency, honesty, revolutionism, and passionate skepticism' (Ellis, 1991a, p. 30).

THEORY

People are born, as well as reared, with greater or lesser degrees of demandingness, and therefore they can change from demanding to desiring only with great difficulty.

Albert Ellis

BASIC CONCEPTS

Fundamental and primary goals

Virtually all humans have three fundamental goals (FG): to survive, be relatively free from pain, and to be reasonably satisfied or content. As sub-goals or primary goals (PG), humans want to be happy: when by themselves; gregariously with other humans; intimately, with a few selected others; informationally and educationally; vocationally and economically; and recreationally (Ellis, 1991b). Furthermore, people live in a social world and self-interest requires putting others a close second (Ellis and Dryden, 1997).

REBT sees humans' basic goals as preferences or desires rather than needs or necessities. Rational living consists of thinking, feeling and behaving in ways which contribute to the attainment of the chosen goals, whereas irrational living consists of thinking, feeling and behaving in ways which block or interfere with their attainment. Living rationally consists of striking a sensible balance between short-range and long-range hedonism, or between the pleasures of the here-and-now and the longer-range pleasures gained through present discipline. Thus rationality may be defined as the use of reason in pursuit of chosen short-range and long-range hedonism.

Emotion, cognition and behaviour

In an early paper on 'Rational psychotherapy' Ellis (1958b) proposed three fundamental hypotheses. First, thinking and emoting are closely related. Second, thinking and emoting are so closely related that they usually accompany each other, act in a circular cause-and-effect relationship, and in certain (though hardly all) respects are essentially the same thing, so that one's thinking becomes one's emotion and emoting becomes one's thought. Third, both thinking and emoting tend to take the form of self-talk or internalized sentences and, for all practical purposes, the sentences that people keep saying to themselves are or become their thoughts and emotions. Thus people's internal self-statements are capable of both generating and modifying their emotions. In addition, Ellis (1991b) stresses that thinking and emotion interact with behaviour. For instance, people usually act on the basis of thoughts and emotions and their actions influence how they think and feel.

Healthy and unhealthy emotions

REBT is not an approach of no emotions; rather it emphasizes healthy or appropriate emotions. Negative emotions may be either healthy, unhealthy or mixed (Ellis and MacLaren, 1998). Unhealthy emotions are those which interfere with achieving a sensible balance between short-range and long-range hedonism. For instance, it may be appropriate for people in an alien and difficult world to be fearful, cautious or vigilant so that they may take any necessary steps for realistic protection. However, anxiety and overconcern are unhealthy emotions, since they are based on irrational thinking or unsane beliefs and, in fact, may interfere with or block attaining goals. Similarly, hostility may have a healthy and an unhealthy part. The healthy part of hostility involves acknowledging discomfort or annoyance as a basis for action designed to overcome or minimize the irritation. The unhealthy part of hostility may involve blaming others and the world in such a way as to block effective action and possibly generate even more unhappiness for oneself and further hostility from others.

Pleasurable and enjoyable emotions can also be healthy or unhealthy. For example, people may feel excessive pride when praised by others because they possess an unsane belief about the necessity of others' approval. A sensible balance between achieving short-range and long-range hedonistic goals involves a balance between achieving short-range and long-range appropriate pleasurable emotions.

Two biological tendencies

In all people a tension exists between two opposing biological creative tendencies (Ellis, 1993b, 2000). On the one hand, people have innate tendencies to create, develop and actualize themselves as healthy, goal-attaining human beings. They have a great potential to be rational and pleasure-producing. On the other hand, they have innate tendencies to create, develop and implement irrational cognitions, unhealthy emotions and dysfunctional behaviours. REBT theorizes that often people are 'biologically predisposed to strongly, passionately, and rigidly construct and hold on to their disturbance-creating musts and other irrational beliefs' (Ellis, 1993b, p. 199). Thus, they possess a huge potential to be destructive of themselves and of others, to be illogical and continually to repeat the same mistakes.

Ellis believes that all the major human irrationalities exist in virtually all humans regardless of culture and educational level. Human fallibility has an inherent source. The facts that people seem so easily conditioned into dysfunctional thinking and behaviour and that it is so hard to modify are both viewed as evidence for an innate tendency to irrationality (Ellis, 1980). People's failure to accept reality almost always causes them to manifest the characteristics of emotional disturbance. However, differences exist in genetic predisposition to irrationality.

People are not only born and raised to be irrational, they also have some degree of free choice in how much they make themselves emotionally disturbed. For example, when growing up, Ellis's younger sister chose to make the worst of her childhood conditions (Ellis, 1991a). However, people can use their biological tendency to have some degree of free choice to help as well as to damage themselves. First, they can choose to think differently and more effectively about what is going on. Second, because they possess the capacity to think about how they think, they can choose to acquire and maintain the cognitive skills for containing and counteracting their tendencies to irrationality.

ABC theory of personality

Ellis has an ABC theory of personality to which he has added D and E to cover change and the desirable result of change. In addition, the letter G can be placed first to provide a context for people's ABCs:

G   Goals, both fundamental and primary.
A   Adversities or activating events in a person's life.
B   Beliefs, both rational and irrational.
C   Consequences, both emotional and behavioural.
D   Disputing irrational beliefs.
E   Effective new philosophy of life.

Just as cognitions, emotions and behaviours interact with each other and are virtually never entirely pure, so do the ABCs of REBT. Goals (G), activating events (A), beliefs (B) and consequences (C) 'all seem to be part of a collaboration with one another' (Ellis, 1991b, p. 145).

Rational and irrational beliefs

Ellis (Ellis, 2000; Ellis and MacLaren, 1998) divides belief systems into two basic categories: rational beliefs and irrational beliefs.

1. *Rational beliefs (rBs)* are healthy, productive, adaptive, consistent with social reality, and generally consist of preferences, desires and wants. When thinking rationally about adversities (As) that either block or sabotage their goals (Gs), people engage in preferential thinking. Preferential as contrasted with demanding thinking involves explicitly and/or tacitly reacting with their belief systems (Bs) in realistic ways and experiencing appropriate emotional and enacting goal-oriented behavioural consequences (Cs).

2. *Irrational beliefs (iBs)* are rigid, dogmatic, unhealthy, maladaptive, mostly get in the way of people's efforts to achieve their goals, and are comprised of demands, musts and shoulds. When thinking irrationally about adversities (As) that either block or sabotage their goals (Gs), people engage in demanding thinking.

In reality, people's responses to adversities (As) mainly result from a combination of rational and irrational beliefs, though often one becomes in the 'winning' mode. Ellis (2000) observes that a person's self-defeating behaviour usually follows from the interaction of A (Adversity) and B (Belief about A) and that C (disturbed Consequences) generally follow the formula A × B = C. Box 12.1 contrasts ABCs for preferential and demanding thinking.

BOX 12.1

ABCs for preferential and demanding thinking

Preferential thinking
A   Adversity or activating event perceived as blocking or sabotaging goals.
B   Belief system involving preferential thinking: 'I prefer to have my important Goals unblocked and fulfilled!'
C   Consequences: emotional – frustration and unhappiness; behavioural – avoiding or trying to eliminate the adversity.

Demanding thinking
A   Adversity or activating event perceived as blocking or sabotaging goals
B   Belief system involving demanding thinking: 'I absolutely must have my important Goals unblocked and fulfilled!'
C   Consequences: emotional – anxiety and/or excessive hostility; behavioural – self-defeating overreaction or underreaction to the adversity.

Demanding beliefs and their derivatives
Often irrational belief systems operate on at least four levels: primary demanding belief(s), derivatives of the primary demanding belief(s), secondary demanding belief(s), and derivatives of the secondary demanding belief(s).

Primary demanding belief(s)
The primary demanding belief or beliefs involve people's main demands and commands in relation to the adversity. Ellis has coined the term 'musturbation' to indicate that these beliefs are usually expressed as musts, shoulds, ought to's, have-to's and got-to's. He has identified three major clusters of irrational beliefs that create inappropriate emotional and behavioural consequences (1980):

1. I *must* do well and win approval for all my performances.
2. Others *must* treat me considerately and kindly.
3. Conditions under which I live *must* be arranged so that I get practically everything I want comfortably, quickly and easily.

Derivatives of the primary demanding belief(s)

People usually create highly unrealistic and overgeneralized inferences and attributions as derivatives of their musturbatory and absolutistic demands. Three common irrational derivatives often accompany their musturbatory beliefs (Ellis, 1991b; Ellis and MacLaren, 1998):

1. *Awfulizing.* 'If I don't have my important Goals unblocked and fulfilled as I must, it's awful!' In this context, 'awful' means totally bad or more than bad.
2. *I-can't-stand-it-itis.* 'If I don't have my important Goals unblocked and fulfilled as I must, I can't stand it!'
3. *Damning oneself and others.* 'If I don't have my important Goals unblocked and fulfilled as I must, I'm a stupid, worthless person.' 'Others are bad people for blocking my important goals.'

Secondary demanding belief(s)

Once people make themselves miserable at C, they tend to exacerbate their misery by making themselves miserable about being miserable. In other words, they transform the negative consequence (C) of the primary demanding belief ABC into an adversity or activating event (A) for a secondary level demanding belief ABC. Box 12.2 provides an example of such chaining. Frequently, people make themselves anxious about being anxious, depressed about being depressed, guilty about feeling guilty and so on.

Derivatives of secondary demanding belief(s)

People can now choose to create and derive awfulizing, I-can't-stand-it-itis, and damning oneself and others from their secondary as well as their primary musturbatory beliefs.

BOX 12.2

ABCs for primary and secondary demanding beliefs

Primary ABC
A1   'I did poorly on my job today.'
B1   'Since I must do well, isn't that horrible!'
C1   'I feel anxious, depressed and worthless.'

Secondary ABC
A2(C1) 'I feel anxious, depressed and worthless.'
B2   'Since I must not feel anxious, depressed and worthless, isn't that horrible!'
C2   'I feel even more anxious, depressed and worthless.'

They now have two negative consequences and their derivatives for the price of one. Also, in an ever-spiralling cycle, they can intensify the unhappiness they create with their beautiful hang-ups.

Ego disturbance and low frustration tolerance

Ellis (1988) proposes that neurotic problems can be grouped under two main headings according to the three main musturbatory beliefs and their derivatives: ego disturbance (self-damning) and low frustration tolerance (LFT) or discomfort disturbance. Ego disturbance arises from the belief 'I *must* do well and win approval for all my performances' because it leads to people thinking and feeling that they are inadequate and undeserving persons when they do not do as well as they must. He regards this as godlike grandiosity since people demand that they be special, perfect, outstanding, superhuman.

Low frustration tolerance arises from the grandiose belief that people think they are so special that conditions must be easy and satisfying for them. They then progress to holding either or both of the irrational beliefs: 'Others *must* treat me considerately and kindly' and 'Conditions under which I live *must* be arranged so that I get practically everything I want comfortably, quickly and easily.' Awfulizing and I-can't-stand-it-itis are derivatives of such beliefs. Basically in ego disturbance and low frustration tolerance what people are insisting is that 'I must have an easy life, I must be perfect, and people and conditions should always cater to *me, me, me, me*!' (Ellis, 1988, p. 119).

ACQUISITION

How do people acquire rational and irrational beliefs? Ellis's emphasis is much more on how people sustain their irrationality than on how they initially acquire it. The past cannot be undone and it is counterproductive to excessively focus on how people feel about the past. Ellis advises people to 'Forget your "Godawful" past' (Ellis, 1988, p. 69). He considers that psychology has focused on how people originally become illogical and that this by no means indicates how people maintain or perpetuate their illogical behaviour, or what they should do to change it. Consequently, Ellis's treatment of the development of irrational cognitions and musturbatory beliefs is cursory. However, three main strands may be identified: biology, social learning and choosing irrational cognitions. Since biological or innate tendencies to irrationality have been previously discussed, the main focus here is on social learning and choosing.

Social learning

Given that human beings are born with a distinct proneness to irrationality, this tendency is frequently exacerbated by their environment, especially early in life, when people are most vulnerable to outside influences. Ellis sees humans as basically highly suggestible, but acknowledges innate differences (Ellis, 1977b). Irrational ideas, which once might have been appropriate in view of the helpless state of the child, are acquired for a number of reasons (Ellis, 1991b, 2000; Ellis and Harper, 1997). First, young children are unable to think clearly, in particular insisting on immediate rather than on future gratification and being unable accurately to distinguish real from imagined fears. However, as they grow older, normal children become less insistent on having their desires and demands immediately gratified. Second, frequently, childish demands can be assuaged by magic, for instance parents saying that a fairy godmother will satisfy them. Third, children are dependent on the planning and thinking of others, and their suggestibility or conditionability is greatest when they are very young. Fourth, parents and members of the family group themselves have irrational tendencies, prejudices and superstitions which they inculcate into their children. Fifth, this process is exacerbated by the indoctrinations of the mass media. Lastly, cultures and religions can impart irrational, self-defeating and society-defeating views.

Choosing irrational cognitions

The process of acquiring irrationality is not simply a matter of reacting to how others behave. Humans largely create their own emotional disturbances through not developing and exercising their capacity for rational choice. Negative social learning experiences do not in themselves lead to people acquiring irrational cognitions. Many people who have had negative upbringings choose not to disturb themselves unduly. Still others, with or without support, work through their problems. The reverse is also true. Favourable social learning experiences do not in themselves lead to rational cognitions. Many people who have had favourable upbringings develop significant irrational beliefs. While social learning experiences influence people for good or ill, they still have the capacity to choose how they react to them. Ellis and Dryden (1997) conclude: 'Thus, the REBT theory of acquisition can be summed up by the view that as humans we are not disturbed simply by our experiences; rather we bring our ability to disturb ourselves to our experiences' (p. 21).

MAINTENANCE

Why do people persist in holding their irrational beliefs and their derivatives? People not only become irrational, they stay irrational. In fact, often they become even more irrational. Staying rational in an irrational world is a struggle. Once acquired, people tend to repeat their irrational beliefs again and again and again. Ellis continually stresses that people have strong tendencies to reindoctrinate themselves with their self-defeating ideas. People's irrational beliefs do not continue because they were once 'conditioned' and so now hold them 'automatically'. Instead, people still, here and now, actively reinforce them, and their present active self-propagandizations and constructions keep these beliefs alive (Ellis, 2000).

Reasons contributing to humans staying irrational

Following are some reasons that contribute to humans staying irrational, often at great personal cost to themselves, to others and to society.

Biological tendencies

Humans' biological tendencies to irrationality do not go away with maturation, but are part of their life-long genetic inheritance. Ellis stresses that humans: 'are powerfully predisposed to unconsciously and habitually prolong their mental dysfunctioning and to fight like hell to give it up' (Ellis, 1987, p. 365). Rather than strike a realistic balance between short-range and long-range hedonism, humans mostly embrace short-range hedonism. This preference for the pleasures of the moment is the main source of resistance to change.

Emotional contributions

Absolutistic musts are often 'hot' cognitions that have a strong evaluative-feeling component in them. Such cognitions are held strongly and powerfully and, as such, can be difficult to change. In addition, people then not only develop derivatives of their primary irrational beliefs, but also secondary irrational beliefs and their derivatives. As a result they raise the level of their emotionality and then may think even more irrationally. They may fail to see how upset they are. Furthermore, they are now so upset that they fail to reality-test and dispute their irrational beliefs in ways that they might otherwise do. Instead of the consequences of irrational beliefs making people better, they make them worse.

Insufficient scientific thinking

People continue to disturb themselves because they fail to think scientifically about what is going on in the world (WIGO). To think scientifically people need constantly to observe and check the 'facts' to see the extent to which they are 'true' and whether or not they have changed. Scientific thinking is flexible and requires evidence to uphold or negate viewpoints. Also, the scientific method is sceptical that the universe has any absolute standards of 'good' and 'bad'. Science does not have absolute rules in regard to human behaviour.

Reinforcing consequences

People can emotionally, cognitively and behaviourally reinforce their irrational beliefs. Emotionally, absolutistic musturbatory beliefs lead to strong negative feelings – such as severe anger and depression – that make them seem true. Cognitively and behaviourally, people reinforce their beliefs in different ways according to the belief. For instance, people who must be socially approved avoid taking social risks, and by doing so, convince themselves that it is too difficult and dangerous to do otherwise. Furthermore, when avoiding social situations, they may feel a sense of emotional relief. The combination of their emotional, cognitive and behavioural reactions makes them more rather than less socially anxious.

Emphasizing one's 'Godawful' past

Ellis states as an REBT insight: 'Your early childhood experiences and your past conditioning did not originally make you disturbed. You did' (Ellis, 1988, p. 70). People maintain their emotional disturbance by looking for causes in their pasts. Focusing on the past interferes with people focusing on the present in which they still may be upsetting themselves with the same irrational beliefs with which they upset themselves in their pasts. People cannot undo their pasts, but they can change their presents and futures. Furthermore, often focusing on the past leads to an overemphasis not only on the past relative to the present, but also to an overemphasis on other people's behaviour relative to one's own.

Unrealistic beliefs about change

People's low frustration tolerance can be both cause and consequence of unrealistic beliefs about working to change, with or without professional assistance, their thoughts, feelings and actions. Irrational beliefs about change include (Ellis, 1987, 1993b):

* 'I must be able to change with little discomfort, work and practice on my part.'
* 'Changing how I think, feel and behave shouldn't be so hard.'
* 'I must change quickly and profoundly.'
* 'When changing, I must not have any setbacks.'
* 'Since I tried to change and failed to do so, therefore I will settle for how I function now.'

Other cognitive factors

Following are some other factors and processes whereby people maintain and worsen their irrational beliefs and emotional disturbances (Ellis, 1987; Ellis and Dryden, 1997).

* *Naïvety.* People can have and hang on to hugely naïve personal theories about the nature of their psychological problems and how they are maintained.
* *Ignorance.* People, including therapists, can consider that it is statistically normal and healthy for them to be unnecessarily upset. They fail to distinguish between healthy and unhealthy thoughts, feelings and behaviours.
* *Stupidity.* Many people are too unintelligent to work effectively on their emotional problems. They fail to gain sufficient insight into the fact that they create their own disturbances.
* *Unperceptiveness.* Without therapy, many disturbed people rarely look at their irrational beliefs and ideas and how these create and drive their upsetness. Even when pointed out to them in therapy, many disturbed people are still incapable of grasping how they upset themselves.
* *Rigidity.* Even when they acknowledge their self-defeating irrational beliefs, many people rigidly stick to their musturbatory beliefs and their derivatives, for instance awfulizing and I-can't-stand-it-itis. Some such people may be psychotic or have borderline personality disorders, whereas others are plain rigid thinkers.
* *Defensiveness.* Humans are prone to avoid facing and dealing directly with their problems. They use various methods of distorting and denying problems, for instance rationalization and avoidance.
* *Pollyannaism and indifference.* Some people who are prone to extreme anxiety and suffer from a serious illness, such as heart disease or cancer, may deal with it by denying its seriousness. Sometimes, such defensive manoeuvres may help people to cope. However, on many occasions, such thinking may block efforts to attain physical health and psychological change.

• *Changing the situation.* For many, the easy way out is to change the situation, for instance obtain a divorce, rather than try to change themselves and then consider whether or not to change the situation. For every neurotic who really tries to have a fundamental shift in the way they think, there are probably ten times as many trying to *feel* better by changing the situations in which they behave self-defeatingly rather than *get* better. This ratio holds true whether or not people come for therapy.

• *Other palliative means.* People and their would-be helpers resort to many palliative means for dealing with emotional disturbances rather than get to the root of them. Many clients and potential clients use distraction techniques such as progressive relaxation, biofeedback, meditation and yoga. Some try superficial positive thinking. Many people lose themselves in political, religious and mystical cults. Short-term feel-good remedies like alcohol and drugs are very common. In brief, many disturbed people seek low-level and palliative remedies rather than more rigorous and long-lasting solutions.

Insufficiently challenging beliefs through action

People may reinforce their beliefs through unwillingness to change their actions. Their 'tried and true' self-defeating ways may bring short-term relief at the expense of long-term gain. An Ellis insight is: 'You can change irrational beliefs (iBs) by acting against them: by performing behaviours that contradict them' (Ellis, 1988, p. 109). Why then don't people change their actions to challenge their beliefs? One reason is that they may not have insight into their irrational beliefs, their derivatives, and their emotional and behavioural consequences. Another reason is that people resist the risk and effort involved in taking action. Some people may not be clear what to do. Still others may know what to do, but lack the skills, confidence and support to do it. Another category is people who change their actions, but lack the staying power to maintain them, especially when faced with difficulties and setbacks. Such people suffer from low frustration tolerance.

THERAPY

*The most elegant solution to the problems resulting from irrational demandingness
is to help individuals to become less demanding.*

Albert Ellis

THERAPEUTIC GOALS

Earlier in this chapter, I presented Ellis's GABCDE outline. There are two meanings to E depending on whether the change goals of REBT are inelegant or elegant.

Inelegant change goals

Ellis (1980) writes: 'Inelegant change largely consists of some kind of symptom removal' (p. 13). Here, at D, REBT targets the cognitions, emotions and behaviours that accompany self-defeating feelings, like anxiety and depression, and dysfunctional behaviours, like avoiding social and public speaking situations. The goal of focused or inelegant REBT is that of focused or inelegant change. Here the letter E stands for an effective new philosophy focused on one or more specific symptoms or problems. Effectiveness in relation to these symptoms can be cognitive (similar to rational beliefs), emotional (healthy feelings), and behavioural (desirable behaviours).

Elegant change goals

In contrast to inelegant change, Ellis states: 'Elegant change in RET goes much beyond this kind of symptom removal, and aims at a significant lessening (rather than a complete removal) of clients' *disturbability*' (Ellis, 1980, p. 13). In elegant change, E goes further than an effective new philosophy that supports removal of specific symptoms to assisting clients to develop and implement an effective philosophy of life. Ellis (1997c) writes: 'To do this, clients need to acknowledge how often and how strongly they escalate their healthy goals, desires, and preferences into arrogant and grandiose *must*-urbation – and apply themselves to anti-*mus*turbatory thinking' (p. 337). Thus E stands for the goal of effective new philosophies for specific symptoms in inelegant REBT and for the goal of an effective philosophy of life (which includes effective new philosophies for specific symptoms) in elegant REBT.

As part of teaching anti-*mus*turbatory thinking, Ellis (1999a) actively encourages practically all his clients to achieve three highly important cognitive-emotional-behavioural states or goals:

1. *Unconditional self-acceptance (USA).* Clients can always choose to accept themselves just because they are alive and human, whether or not they perform well or are approved of by others.
2. *Unconditional other acceptance (UOA).* Whatever other people do and however abominably they act, clients can choose to accept the sinner, though not their sins, to try to help them behave better, and to refuse to damn them as persons.
3. *High frustration tolerance (HFT).* Clients can choose to acknowledge that their desires are not needs, adversities are not awful but can be highly inconvenient, they can stand what they do not like, and 'long-range hedonism, or striving for today's pleasures, without neglecting tomorrow's, will often get them more of what they want and less of what they dislike' (Ellis, 1999a, p. 39).

PROCESS OF THERAPY

Right from the start, therapists show clients that REBT is an active-directive structured therapy focusing on helping clients not only to feel better, but, by changing their thinking and behaviour, to get better. Orientation or induction can be by way of pre-therapy demonstrations, brief explanatory lectures at the start of therapy, and using client problem material to illustrate the application of REBT (Ellis and Dryden, 1997).

Before commencing therapy some REBT therapists like clients to fill out a basic biographical information form that also elicits information about clients' presenting problems (see Ellis and Dryden, 1997, pp. 88–95). In addition, therapists may ask clients to fill out a personality data form which asks clients questions about their feelings in the following areas: acceptance, frustration, injustice, achievement, worth, control, certainty and catastrophizing (Ellis and Dryden, 1997, pp. 36–9).

Clients are encouraged to focus on specific problems right from the start. Early in therapy Ellis frequently reads out the client's answer to item 23 in the biographical information questionnaire which asks: 'Briefly list (PRINT) your present main complaints, symptoms and problems.' Then clients are asked to discuss what problem is most bothersome. Probably the main form of assessment in REBT is that which comes from having a number of sessions with clients and working with the material that they share. Towards the end of the initial phase of REBT, both therapist and client should have an understanding of the client's main emotional and behavioural problems and have started to prioritize these to provide a structure for their future work together.

The middle phase of REBT is focused on therapists adopting an educational approach to teaching clients how to strengthen their rational beliefs and weaken their irrational beliefs. This phase of REBT has two main agendas: helping clients solve their particular emotional and behavioural problems, and teaching them the skills of identifying and solving problems. In general, in addition to focusing on what clients have been most bothered about during the previous week, therapists encourage them to work through a consistent problem before moving on to the next. Homework tasks are assigned and particular attention is paid to what the client has learned or failed to learn between sessions so that blocks to the learning process can be addressed. Frequently, clients are asked to fill out REBT self-help forms as part of homework assignments. Hard and persistent challenging of irrational beliefs tends to be a prominent feature of the middle phase.

The main purpose of the end phase of REBT is to help clients become their own therapists. Termination may take place, not when clients have worked through all their problems using REBT skills, but when they feel confident they can use these skills to address the remaining problems on their own. Therapists work toward termination either by decreasing the frequency of sessions or by negotiating a specific termination date. During the end phase, therapists can work with clients to anticipate problems and difficulties and articulate how they might use their REBT skills to deal with these problems. Most REBT therapists schedule follow-up sessions to monitor client progress.

REBT is committed to assisting clients to maintain their changes. However, Ellis (1988) acknowledges the likelihood of backsliding. Right from the start, clients are taught that they can only change and maintain change with work and practice. Throughout therapy, homework assignments are used to help clients build skills for both outside and after therapy. When clients find themselves backsliding, they are told to go back to the ABCs and see what they did to fall back into their old patterns, Then they are encouraged to forcefully dispute (D) these irrational beliefs. They are advised to try and try again until they genuinely replace their irrational beliefs with their effective new philosophies (E).

Most clients are seen by therapists for weekly individual sessions. Ellis's own therapy sessions often last for 30 minutes. Clients normally have five to 50 sessions. Brief therapy of one to ten sessions is used for clients who have specific problems or for those only prepared to stay in therapy for a short time (Ellis, 1996). Individuals who are not too generally disturbed can usually attain the inelegant change of symptom removal in brief therapy. Preferably, individuals with severe problems come for individual and/or group therapy for at least six months so that they can practise what they learn.

REBT can be used with most kinds of clients, ranging from those who are mildly disturbed to juvenile delinquents, borderline personality disorders, psychotics when they have some contact with reality, and individuals with higher grade mental deficiency. Normally, Ellis does not consider REBT suitable for clients who are out of contact with reality, in a highly manic state, seriously autistic or brain injured, and in the lower ranges of mental deficiency. Seriously disturbed clients are often referred for medication in addition to REBT.

REBT is significantly more effective with mildly disturbed clients and with those who have a single major symptom, say sexual inadequacy, than with strongly disturbed clients. Therapists find it much more difficult to assist the latter to change since REBT theory hypothesizes that the causes of musturbatory thinking and emotional disturbance are largely innate.

THE THERAPEUTIC RELATIONSHIP

In REBT, the main role of the therapist is that of an authoritative, but not authoritarian, teacher who strives to impart to clients self-helping skills conducive to thinking rationally, feeling appropriately and behaving effectively so that they can attain their goals. REBT practitioners often employ a fairly rapid-fire active-directive-persuasive-philosophic methodology. In most instances, they quickly pin clients down to a few basic dysfunctional beliefs (Ellis, 2000).

What kind of a therapeutic relationship best supports this active-directive teaching role? Therapists try to build rapport with clients by using empathic listening, including reflecting feelings. Ellis and Dryden (1997) distinguish between *affective* empathy, understanding how clients feel, and *philosophic* empathy, understanding the philosophies or thinking underlying these feelings. Therapists attempt to offer both kinds of empathy. In addition, therapists offer clients unconditional other acceptance (UOA), accepting them as fallible human beings and not judging the goodness or badness of their personhood against predetermined moral standards. However, frequently (if appropriate) therapists will share their reactions to clients' negative behaviours.

REBT therapists do not show undue warmth to most of their clients. They are wary of colluding in clients' dire needs for approval. Also, they try to encourage clients to confront their own problems and assume responsibility for finding their own warmth and happiness rather than seeking it from therapists. Often clients perceive REBT therapists as warm and caring because of their commitment to their welfare and tolerance for all individuals.

Particularly during early sessions, therapists do most of the talking. They do not hesitate to confront clients with how they contribute to their own distress. They forcefully dispute and debate their clients' illogical thinking as well as helping clients to do this for themselves. They freely share their opinions and self-disclose, so long as this is not detrimental to clients. Furthermore they use humour, but never at their clients' expense, since they consider that many of them take themselves and their problems far too seriously. Also, therapists use humour to attack disturbance-producing ideas.

A distinction exists between REBT content and the therapist's style of working with clients. Ellis's therapeutic style, like that of many of his followers, is hard-hitting and forceful. However, Ellis may well go more slowly and gently before doing any vigorous disputing when working with clients who have suffered from extreme traumas, such as rape or child abuse. Other REBT practitioners, either with specific clients or with all of their clients, choose varying degrees of passive and gentle styles.

THERAPEUTIC INTERVENTIONS

Detecting irrational beliefs and their derivatives

Therapists as teachers detect clients' irrational beliefs, their musturbations, and their derivatives – for instance awfulizing. Furthermore, they teach clients how to do this for themselves. In order to relinquish their demandingness, it helps if clients can acknowledge that they may possess this characteristic. Ellis teaches them his ABC system. Within the ABC system, irrational beliefs can be traced cognitively, emotionally and behaviourally. Cognitively, irrational beliefs can be detected through overt or implicit signs of demandingness. In particular, Ellis looks for 'musts', 'shoulds', 'oughts', 'have tos' and 'got tos' that signal clients' musturbatory, absolutistic beliefs. In addition, he looks for explicit and implicit phrases such as 'That is horrible!' and 'I can't stand it' that indicate derivatives of possessing primary and secondary irrational beliefs.

Emotionally, irrational beliefs are signalled by unhealthy feelings, such as panic and depression. Behaviourally, self-defeating actions offer clues to irrational beliefs. Sometimes the cognitive, emotional and behavioural clues are obvious to both therapists and clients. On other occasions, though obvious to therapists, clients may resist acknowledging the evidence. In still other instances clients may hold irrational beliefs in subtle and tricky ways that make them seem natural (Ellis, 1987). Such beliefs can challenge therapists' powers of detection.

Disputing irrational beliefs and their derivatives

It is insufficient for musts and their derivatives to disappear just to acknowledge them. Instead, therapists and clients combine to fight them by disputing them. The technique of disputing is the most typical and perhaps the most often used method of REBT. Disputing involves challenging and questioning unsubstantiated hypotheses that clients hold about themselves, others and the world. In most instances, REBT therapists quickly pin clients down to a few central irrational ideas and their derivatives that they then challenge and dispute. In addition, they teach clients how to dispute their own beliefs. Cognitions, feelings and behaviours interact in how people create and maintain irrational beliefs. Therefore, when disputing irrational beliefs and their derivatives, therapists are likely to be more effective if they work in all three of the cognitive, emotional/experiential and behavioural modalities rather than in one or two. However, no modality is entirely pure or free from the others.

Cognitive interventions

Scientific questioning

Disputing may be approached using either a didactic or a Socratic style. In a didactic or lecturing style, therapists can provide explanations and illustrations. In a Socratic or scientific questioning appproach, through a series of leading questions therapists attempt to pinpoint where clients' thinking, feeling and behaving is becoming problematic. Such questions are not only for therapists to ask clients, but for clients to learn to ask themselves. When practising disputing, it is very important that clients do so outside of stressful situations to give them the chance to build up and fine-tune their skills for the actual situations.

Box 12.3 illustrates four areas of cognitive disputing (Ellis and MacLaren, 1998).

BOX 12.3

Four areas of cognitive disputing

Functional disputes

Functional disputing aims to point out to clients that their beliefs may be interfering with their attaining their goals. Typical questions are:

- 'Is it helping you?'
- 'How is continuing to think this way (or behave, or feel this way) affecting your life?'

Empirical disputes

Empirical disputing aims to help clients evaluate the factual components of their beliefs. Typical questions are:

- 'Where is the evidence that you must succeed at all important tasks you prefer?'
- 'Where is the proof that it is accurate?'
- 'Where is it written?'

Logical disputes

Logical disputing aims to highlight illogical leaps that clients make from desires and preferences to demands when thinking irrationally. Typical questions are:

- 'How does it follow that just because you'd like this thing to be true and it would be very convenient, it *should* be?'
- 'Where is the logic that because you sometimes *act* badly that makes you a *bad person*?'

Philosophical disputes

Philosophical disputing aims to address meaning of and satisfaction in life issues. Often clients get so focused on identified problems that they lose perspective on other areas of life. A typical question might be:

- 'Despite the fact that things will probably not go the way you want some/most of the time in this area, can you still derive some satisfaction from your life?'

The desired cognitive outcome of disputing specific irrational beliefs and their derivatives is a sound set of preferential beliefs or effective new philosophies (E) related to each
belief. Desirable emotional and behavioural effects should stem from and interact with
the effective new philosophies. For clients seeking elegant change, the desirable effect of
learning how to dispute irrational beliefs is an Effective New Philosophy that can be
applied both now and in the future. Box 12.4 provides an ABCDE example, which
includes disputing and its effects (Ellis, 1988).

BOX 12.4

An ABCDE example of cognitive disputing

A   I go for an interview and fail to get the job.

B   'I must never get rejected.'
    'How awful to get rejected!'
    'I can't stand the rejection!
    'This rejection makes me a rotten person.'
    'I'll always do poorly in job interviews.'

C   Undesirable emotional consequences: depression, worthlessness, anxiety, anger.
    Undesirable behavioural consequences: refusing to go for other job interviews;
    functioning poorly on job interviews through anxiety.

D   'Why must I never get rejected?'
    'Why is it awful to get rejected for a job?'
    'Why can't I stand this rejection?'
    'How does this rejection make me a rotten person?'
    'Why must I always do poorly on job interviews?'

E   'I'd prefer to have got this job, but there is no evidence that I absolutely must have
       it.'
    'Nothing makes it awful to get rejected, though I find it highly inconvenient.'
    'I can stand rejection, though I'll never like it.'
    'Rejection never makes me a rotten person, but a person with some unfortunate
       traits.'
    'I don't always have to do poorly on job interviews, especially if I try to learn from
       my errors.'
    Illustrative emotional effect: feeling sorrowful, but not depressed.
    Illustrative behavioural effect: I went for some more job interviews.

Rational coping statements

Therapist and client can formulate rational coping statements. This step is usually taken
after forceful disputing of irrational beliefs, but sometimes it can accompany such

disputing. Some coping statements can be simple encouragements, for instance: 'I can accomplish this task' or 'I don't have to get upset in these situations.' Rational coping statements can also address areas of irrational thinking, for example, statements such as 'I'd prefer to have got this job, but there is no evidence that I absolutely must have it' and 'Nothing makes it awful to get rejected, though I find it highly inconvenient', illustrated in area E of Box 12.4.

Discussion

Therapists can discuss with clients various aspects of their irrational thinking. For instance, with Roger, a 24-year-old computer programmer afraid of public speaking, Ellis discussed the harm of self-rating and how he could choose to unconditionally accept himself whether or not he failed at speaking and whether or not he was anxious about failing and showed his anxiety to others (Ellis, 1991e).

Cognitive homework

Clients need repeatedly to challenge their irrational beliefs and to practise their disputing skills, both to learn them and also to reinforce their new rational philosophies. REBT uses various homework techniques to develop disputing skills.

- *Cassettes of sessions.* Therapists encourage clients to record sessions and listen to each one several times.
- *Self-help forms.* Clients are encouraged to fill out self-help forms. Therapists check the forms to see how accurately clients dispute their irrational beliefs. For instance, in Sichel and Ellis's (1984) form, clients identify an activating event (A) and the con- sequences or conditions (C) they would like to change. Then the form consists of three columns. In the first column, clients circle which of thirteen irrational beliefs (B), for instance 'I MUST do well or very well!' and 'People MUST live up to my expectations or it is TERRIBLE!', lead to their consequences (C). In addition, they can add other relevant irrational beliefs. In the second column, there is space for them to dispute (D) each circled irrational belief. In the third column, they write in effective rational beliefs (E) to replace their irrational beliefs. After the columns there is a space (F) where they can write in feelings and behaviours experienced after arriving at their effective rational beliefs. The form ends with the following self- statement about the necessity of work and practice: 'I WILL WORK HARD TO REPEAT MY EFFECTIVE RATIONAL BELIEFS FORCEFULLY TO MYSELF ON MANY OCCASIONS SO THAT I CAN MAKE MYSELF LESS DIS- TURBED NOW AND ACT LESS SELF-DEFEATINGLY IN THE FUTURE' (Sichel and Ellis, 1984, p. 2).

  Another self-help form is known as DIBS (Disputing Irrational Beliefs). DIBS consists of six questions concerning:

  1. the belief I want to dispute;
  2. whether the belief can be rationally supported;
  3. existing evidence for the belief;

4.   existing evidence against the belief;

5.   the worst that could happen to me if I never achieved what I wanted in respect to the belief; and

6.   good things that might happen if I never achieved what I wanted. (Dryden and Ellis, 1986).

A further self-help form is Dryden and Walker's written self-help form which takes clients through the ABCDE sequence (Dryden and Walker, 1992; Ellis and Dryden, 1997).

- *Reminder cards.* Clients can write out rational coping statements on 3-inch × 5-inch cards and repeat them at various times between sessions.
- *Referenting.* Referenting is a term for asking clients to do a cost-benefit analysis in which they list the real advantages and disadvantages of changing their irrational thoughts and behaviours.
- *Practising REBT on others.* Encouraging clients to practise talking their friends and relatives out of their disturbances.
- *Visualizing.* Clients can be shown how to visualize themselves competently performing situations that they currently fear.
- *Bibliotherapy.* Assigning clients self-help books to read, for instance Ellis (1977a, 1988, 1999b), Ellis and Becker (1982), and Ellis and Harper (1997). Ellis (1993d) is keenly aware of the advantages and disadvantages of self-help materials.
- *Self-help cassettes.* Ellis has made innumerable audio cassettes, including *Solving Emotional Problems* (Ellis, 1982b), *How to be Happy Though Human* (1984) and *How to Stop Worrying and Start Living* (1987b). In addition, clients can watch videotapes of therapists working with clients in areas such as coping with anger and overcoming low frustration tolerance. Many clients find listening to cassettes and observing videotapes to be helpful.

Problem-solving

Clients bring their goals (G) to the activating events and adversities (A) in their lives. These goals present many practical or reality problems for them to try to solve: for instance, obtaining a good education, finding a mate, getting a job, succeeding at work. Clients have a choice about whether they solve these reality problems or choose to upset themselves about them. If clients upset themselves, then they have an emotional problem about their reality problem. In such cases, therapists can assist them to detect and actively dispute the relevant irrational beliefs. Sometimes it is better that clients do not address practical difficulties until they have worked through related emotional difficulties. For instance, an individual or couple might defer a decision to divorce until they have given themselves sufficient chance to see whether or not, with a lessening of their irrational beliefs, they might happily live together.

Therapists willingly assist clients to solve reality problems. However, where necessary, they also insist on vigorously detecting and disputing accompanying irrational beliefs. In assisting problem-solving, therapists help clients to state problems and goals clearly, generate and evaluate alternative strategies, outline the steps to attain goals, identify resources and supports, and develop the requisite practical skills for success.

Emotive/experiential interventions

REBT therapists use emotional/experiential interventions to supplement and reinforce cognitive interventions (Ellis and MacLaren, 1998). Such interventions include the following.

Rational-emotive imagery

In rational-emotive imagery (REI), clients are encouraged to imagine one of the worst activating events or adversities (A) that could happen to them, for instance, rejection by someone whose approval they really want (Ellis, 1993f; Ellis and MacLaren, 1998). They vividly imagine this adversity occurring and bringing a host of problems into their life.

Then they are encouraged to get in touch with the undesirable negative emotional consequence triggered by this adversity (A) – for instance, anxiety, depression, rage, self-hatred or self-pity – and really, really feel it (C1). They should spontaneously feel what they feel and not what they are supposed to feel. Once they feel unhealthily upset at C1, they should hold on to this feeling for a minute or two. Then, keeping the same adversity (A) in their imagination, they should work on changing their disturbed negative feeling to a prescribed healthy negative feeling consequence (C2), such as sorrow, disappointment, regret, frustration, irritation or displeasure. The way to do this is by telling themselves strongly and repetitively sensible rational beliefs or coping statements: for example, 'Yes, they really did treat me shabbily and unfairly, which I wish they wouldn't have done. But there is no reason why they must treat me fairly, however preferable that would be . . .' (Ellis, 1993f, p. ii–9). Clients should persist with their imagery and rational statements until they change their unhealthy feeling (C1) to a healthy negative feeling (C2) – it usually takes only a few minutes. They should have the homework assignment of carrying out this imagery procedure daily for about 30 days for each disturbed feeling they are trying to change.

Forceful disputing

Forceful disputing may be performed both by therapists on clients and by clients on themselves (Ellis, 1993e). Since many irrational beliefs involve hot cognitions that possess a large emotional component, they require forceful and vigorous disputing. Often therapists need to strongly argue, persuade and point out the shaky logic of their clients' beliefs. Weak or moderately strong disputing may be insufficient. Ellis showed Roger, a computer programmer, how to create strong anti-worrying statements about public speaking and say them to himself forcefully: for example 'I NEVER, NEVER, NEVER have to speak well or unnervously in public, though it would be nice if I did!' (Ellis, 1991e, p. 454). In addition, Ellis worked out with Roger a dialogue with himself in which he cassette-recorded some of his potent irrational beliefs, e.g. 'I'm a nervous slob who deserves to be mute rather than risk making a fool of myself in public!' and in which he vigorously, forcefully and heatedly disputed them. Clients can make, and remake more powerfully, such cassettes for themselves as homework. Then they can play them back to themselves, their therapists and, if in therapy groups, to the other group members.

Role-playing

Ellis uses role-playing as a way of showing clients what their false ideas are and how they affect relating to others. In role-playing, therapists place clients in simulated situations and offer assistance in thinking more effectively in them. For instance, Roger role-played giving a difficult talk in front of Ellis and the therapy group he had joined as an adjunct to individual sessions. When Roger appeared anxious during the role-play, Ellis stopped the performance to let Roger ask himself 'What am I telling myself right now to *make* myself anxious? And what can I do right now to think and feel away this anxiety?' (Ellis, 1991e, p. 454).

Reverse role-playing

Reverse role-playing is another REBT forceful disputing technique. Client and therapist switch roles, so clients are now in a position to dispute actively their own irrational beliefs, which the therapist holds on to as strongly as the client did in earlier sessions. For example, Ellis role-played Roger tenaciously holding on to some of his irrational beliefs so that Roger could practise forcefully attacking them (Ellis, 1993e).

Unconditional acceptance

The therapist's basic acceptance of them as persons helps clients feel and think that they are acceptable, despite any negative characteristics.

Humour

The judicious use of humour can help reduce clients' irrational beliefs and self-defeating behaviours to absurdity. Therapists frequently exaggerate clients' nutty ideas and use 'various kinds of puns, witticisms, irony, whimsy, evocative language, slang, and deliberate use of sprightly obscenity . . .' (Ellis, 1980, p. 26). For example, Ellis said to Roger, his public-speaking phobia client: 'You really should feel ashamed of avoiding making speeches. Every other person your age speaks fluently and has no anxiety. What a unique jerk you are!' (Ellis, 1991e, p. 454). Encouraging clients to sing to themselves rational-humorous songs (Ellis, 1977d) and telling amusing anecdotes are further methods to counteract clients' tendencies to take themselves, others and the world too seriously.

Behavioural interventions

As with emotional/experiential interventions, REBT therapists use behavioural interventions to supplement and reinforce cognitive interventions. Ellis doubts whether people ever truly change their irrational beliefs until they act many times against them. When young, Ellis suffered from severe fears of public speaking and meeting new women. He forced himself to repetitively engage in activities, giving political talks and talking to women on a park bench in the Bronx Botanical Gardens, that challenged his fears. In both instances his actions helped rid him of his irrational fears (Ellis, 1997a). Following are some REBT behavioural interventions.

Assignments that challenge demandingness

Clients who have musturbatory beliefs about approval and derivatives of these beliefs about the awfulness of rejection may be encouraged to ask someone for a date or force themselves to socialize. Simultaneously they convince themselves that it is not awful, but only inconvenient to get rejected. Clients who have perfectionist beliefs may have the assignment of deliberately making a real attempt to speak badly in public.

Clients are encouraged to do their assignments *repetitively*. For instance, Roger, the speech-anxious client, was asked to speak in public as often as he could, once or twice a week (Ellis, 1991e). Often clients are asked to do their assignments *floodingly*, staying in situations they perceive as highly dangerous until they see that their 'danger' is largely imagined. For instance, clients afraid of riding on buses or underground trains are urged to do this immediately, many times a day in rush hours, if that is what they most fear. Concurrently, in all instances where clients dispute their musturbatory beliefs behaviourally, they can dispute them cognitively too.

Shame-attacking exercises

Ellis hypothesizes that ego anxiety is highly related to feelings of shame, guilt, embarrassment and humiliation. Consequently, the more people confront the irrational beliefs behind these feelings, the less they are likely to disturb themselves. Clients are encouraged to do things in public that they regard as particularly shameful or embarrassing. Examples are yelling out the stops on elevators, buses or underground trains or asking for sex-related items in loud voices in chemist shops.

After explaining the principle of shame-attacking exercises, REBT therapists can negotiate exercises with clients. The purpose of these exercises is to prove that these behaviours in themselves are really not shameful and that they can be done with relative comfort and self-acceptance. In addition, clients are urged to disclose more about what they perceive, or what they perceive others perceive, as shameful. Box 12.5 provides an example of a shame-attacking exercise (Ellis, 1996, pp. 91–4).

Skill training

The distinction between behavioural skills and cognitive skills is imprecise. Always, when therapists assist clients with behavioural skills – for instance assertion and communication skills – they train clients cognitively in disputing the accompanying irrational beliefs and derivative self-statements. Sometimes, clients are asked to seek additional training experiences to acquire relevant skills. For instance, Ellis thought that speech-anxious Roger showed insufficient assertion skills at work, for instance not refusing to do presentations when genuinely unprepared. Ellis encouraged Roger to attend a six-week assertion course at his Institute as well as take a five-month public-speaking course at a local college (Ellis, 1991e).

Box 12.5
Example of a shame-attacking exercise

The therapist
Albert Ellis.

The client
Chana, who was anxious about test-taking, kept procrastinating on her studies, and refused to take some important subjects at school because she knew that taking them would entail several tests during the term. Chana was afraid of people finding out how poorly she did on tests.

The shame-attacking exercise
Chana chose the exercise of asking strangers for a dollar bill. Ellis instructed Chana, when asking strangers for dollar bills, to work on possible feelings of humiliation and embarrassment and then choose to make herself feel unashamed and unembarrassed.

During the exercise
At first Chana felt very nervous and tongue-tied about going up to a stranger. However, she reminded herself that she did not need the stranger's approval and, by the third time she tried it, she really began to feel shameless and, by the fifth time, started enjoying the exercise.

After the exercise
As a result of the exercise Chana saw that she could do shame-attacking exercises with people who knew her in which she talked about her test-taking problems. As part of this process, Chana developed the Effective New Philosophy: 'I don't need their goddamned approval. Let them think what they think!'

Use of rewards and penalties

REBT therapists use rewards and penalties to encourage clients to do homework and implement self-change programmes (Ellis, 1980; Ellis and Dryden, 1997). For instance, every time Roger filled out an RET Self-Help Report or gave a public speech, he would reward himself by listening to one of his favourite CDs. Whenever he failed to carry out an assignment he would talk to his boring aunt for 30 minutes. Two doses of this excruciating penalty cured Roger of not doing assignments! (Ellis, 1991e).

Overcoming resistance

When clients resist following therapy procedures and doing homework assignments, they mainly do so because of the following irrational beliefs (Ellis, 1986a):

1. 'I *must* do well at changing myself';
2. 'You (the therapist and others) *must* help me change'; and
3. 'Changing myself *must* occur quickly and easily.'

Stemming from such beliefs (B), resisters have negative feelings consequences, for instance depression, self-pity; and behavioural consequences, for instance, procrastination and withdrawal. In addition, they employ derivatives of irrational beliefs, such as awfulizing. The main REBT approach to resistant clients is to teach them to find and forcefully dispute the main irrational beliefs contributing to their resistance.

Therapists can encourage resistant clients to use rational coping statements, for instance 'Therapy doesn't have to be easy. I can, in fact, enjoy its difficulty and its challenge' (Ellis, 1986a, p. 262). In addition, therapists can ask clients to list the disadvantages of resisting and the advantages of working at therapy and then regularly review and think about these lists. Furthermore, some resistant clients can be helped by proselytizing REBT and using it on friends and relatives.

CASE MATERIAL

Ellis has been conscientious about providing case demonstrations of REBT in action, only some of which are mentioned here. Ellis presents a case example containing verbatim transcripts of the first, second and fourth sessions with a woman who comes to therapy because she is self-punishing, impulsive and compulsive, afraid of males, has no goals in life, and is guilty about her relationship with her parents (Ellis, 1971; Wedding and Corsini, 2001).

Ellis provides verbatim transcript, plus commentary, of his conducting a first session of REBT brief therapy with Ted, a 38-year-old African-American, married twenty years, with two children who became panicked whenever he took the train to work or back to his office and whenever he thought about having intercourse with his wife (Ellis, 1996). Another verbatim transcript case example is that of the first fifteen minutes of an initial interview Ellis conducted with a 25-year-old single woman, Sara, who worked as the head of a computer programming section in her firm and who, without any traumatic or violent history, was very insecure and self-denigrating (Ellis, 2000). Ellis also discusses Sara's overall treatment of a further six sessions of individual work, followed by 24 weeks of REBT group therapy and one weekend of a rational encounter marathon group.

A further verbatim transcript case example is that of Ellis working with a woman therapist who volunteers to bring up problems of feeling inadequate as a therapist and as a person. Ellis and Dryden then review the transcript and analyse its REBT aspects (Ellis and Dryden, 1997). In yet another case example of REBT, though this time without transcripts, Ellis illustrates the cognitive, emotive and behavioural methods he used during therapy with Jane, a 27-year-old woman afflicted with severe social and work anxiety (Ellis and Dryden, 1997).

Ellis may also be seen conducting therapy. An early example is his work with Gloria in the *Three Approaches to Psychotherapy* film series (Ellis, 1965). In addition, videos of Ellis and other prominent REBT therapists conducting sessions are available from the Albert

Ellis Institute (address and website at end of chapter). For example, Ellis has made a videotape in which he conducts therapy with a woman dealing with guilt over her husband's suicide. In another videotape, entitled *Dealing with Addictions*, Ellis interviews a 32-year-old man with low frustration tolerance, short-term hedonism and polyabuse.

FURTHER DEVELOPMENTS

Other applications of REBT include group therapy and marathons either along with individual counselling or instead of it (Ellis, 1992; Ellis and Dryden, 1997). In group REBT, members are taught to apply detecting and disputing irrational beliefs to one another (Ellis, 2000). They also get practice at attacking their ego disturbance irrational beliefs through disclosing material that they perceive as risky. In addition clients in groups, while working on assertion and other communication skills, can partake in role-plays.

Ellis has a major interest in the application of REBT to marital, couples and family relationship problems (Ellis, 1986b, 1991c, 1991d, 1993c, 2000; Ellis and Dryden, 1997). Therapists usually see marital or love partners together, listen to their complaints, and then teach them that even though their complaints may accurately describe behaviour at A, their upsetness at C is not justified. In particular, work focuses on musturbatory beliefs generating hostility. Also, frequently, therapists teach partners compromising and relationship skills. In family REBT, tolerance for oneself and others, independent of how obnoxious specific behaviours may be, is repeatedly taught to both parents and children.

Possibly Ellis is the most influential English-speaking psychological educator of the twentieth century in terms of helping ordinary people learn how to overcome their emotional disturbances and become more self-actualizing. Through his books and cassettes, he has made a major contribution to educating the public in America and elsewhere on how to live more effectively. Also, he has influenced numerous other writers of self-help books. A recent public education application of REBT has been the development of nine-hour intensive workshops (Ellis and Dryden, 1997).

REBT is practised widely throughout the world, with institutes or centres established in Britain, Australia, the United States, France, Germany, Holland, Italy, India, Israel and Mexico. Ellis concludes that REBT is what its name implies: rational and emotive, realistic and visionary, empirical and humanistic. Such an approach befits humans in all their complexity (Ellis, 2000).

SUMMARY

- *Rational emotive behaviour therapy (REBT) is not a purely intellectual approach, but strongly emphasizes the interplay of feeling, behaviour and cognition.*
- *Humans' fundamental goals are survival, freedom from pain, and happiness. Their feelings can be healthy and appropriate or unhealthy and inappropriate.*
- *People have biological tendencies both to actualizing themselves as healthy goal-attaining human beings and to being irrational and disturbing themselves.*

- *Ellis has expanded his ABC theory of personality to a GABCDE theory with: G, goals; A, adversities or activating events; B, beliefs, both rational and irrational; C, consequences, both emotional and behavioural; D, disputing irrational beliefs; and E, effective new philosophy.*
- *In pursuit of their goals (G), people create unhealthy emotions and self-defeating behaviours at C because they have demanding, as contrasted with preferential, beliefs at B in relation to adversities and activating events at A. In addition, they have derivatives of their demanding beliefs, for instance, awfulizing, I-can't-stand-it-itis, and damning themselves and others. These beliefs and their derivatives can be grouped into two main headings: ego disturbance and low frustration tolerance.*
- *As well as their innate tendencies to irrationality, humans acquire irrational beliefs partly by social learning, but also because they do not develop and exercise their capacity for rational choice.*
- *Reasons why people persist in maintaining irrational beliefs include: biological tendencies to irrationality, the emotional strength of their beliefs, insufficient scientific thinking, reinforcing consequences, emphasizing their 'Godawful' pasts, unrealistic beliefs about change, and insufficiently challenging their beliefs through action.*
- *REBT has inelegant goals, symptom removal, and elegant goals, helping clients become less disturbable through possessing an effective new philosophy. It aims to help clients not only feel better, but get better by changing from rigid and demanding to preferential thinking. As part of this process clients are helped to develop unconditional self-acceptance (USA), unconditional other acceptance (UOA) and high frustration tolerance (HFT).*
- *REBT is an active-directive structured therapy in which clients are encouraged to focus on specific problems right from the start.*
- *The REBT therapist is a teacher who uses a variety of cognitive, emotive/experiential and behavioural interventions to assist clients to dispute (D) their irrational beliefs and their derivatives so that they can develop an effective new philosophy (E).*
- *Disputing by means of scientific questioning is the main cognitive intervention. Four areas of cognitive disputing are: functional, empirical, logical, and philosophical. In addition, therapists help clients to solve genuine problems in their lives.*
- *Emotive/experiential interventions include rational-emotive imagery, forceful disputing, role-playing and reverse role-playing, unconditional acceptance and humour.*
- *Behavioural interventions include assignments that challenge demandingness, shame-attacking exercises, skill training and use of rewards and penalties.*
- *REBT aims to assist clients to maintain their changes through stressing work and practice, assigning homework, and teaching clients, if they backslide, to go back to their ABCs and then dispute irrational beliefs that cause them to revert to previous behaviours.*
- *Other applications of REBT include group therapy, marital and family therapy, and psychological education. REBT institutes and centres exist in North and South America, Europe, the Middle East and Australia.*

REVIEW AND PERSONAL QUESTIONS

REVIEW QUESTIONS

1. Why does Ellis now call his approach rational emotive behaviour therapy?
2. Describe the differences between healthy or appropriate and unhealthy or inappropriate emotions.
3. What does Ellis consider to be the biological basis of personality?
4. Give an example of Ellis's ABC theory, where B represents:
   (a) demanding musturbatory thinking; and
   (b) preferential thinking.
5. Critically discuss Ellis's ideas about the derivatives of irrational beliefs.
6. Discuss the roles of social learning and free choice in acquiring irrational beliefs.
7. Describe the contribution of each of the following factors to maintaining, and possibly strengthening, irrational beliefs:
   (a) biological tendencies;
   (b) emotional contributions;
   (c) insufficient scientific thinking;
   (d) reinforcing consequences;
   (e) emphasizing one's 'Godawful' past;
   (f) unrealistic beliefs about change; and
   (g) insufficiently challenging beliefs through action.
8. What are the differences between inelegant and elegant therapy goals?
9. Outline the process of REBT individual therapy.
10. What is the nature of the therapist–client relationship in REBT?
11. Give at least one example of each of the following ways of disputing irrational beliefs: functional, empirical, logical, and philosophical. Apart from scientific questioning, what other cognitive interventions do REBT therapists use?
12. Describe emotional/experiential interventions used in REBT.
13. Describe behavioural interventions used in REBT.
14. Critically discuss the issue of overcoming resistance in REBT.

PERSONAL QUESTIONS

1. Identify at least two irrational beliefs based on absolutistic demanding thinking in relation to each of the following:
   (a) yourself;
   (b) others; and
   (c) the conditions under which you live.
2. For one of the irrational beliefs you identified above, state:
   (a) how you acquired it; and
   (b) how you maintain it.
3. From your own life, give an example of each of the following:
   (a) the ABCs of rational thinking;

(b) the ABCs of irrational thinking.
4. Choose one of your irrational beliefs (B) that you wish to change. How could you dispute (D) it by:
    (a) cognitive methods;
    (b) emotive/experiential methods; and
    (c) behavioural methods.
    What new effective philosophy (E) would you arrive at?
5. What relevance, if any, has the theory and practice of rational emotive behaviour therapy for how you conduct therapy?
6. What relevance, if any, has the theory and practice of rational emotive behaviour therapy for how you live?

ANNOTATED BIBLIOGRAPHY

Ellis, A. and Dryden. W. (1997). *The Practice of Rational Emotive Behaviour Therapy.* London: Free Association Books and New York: Springer.

> This book presents the general theory and basic practice of rational emotive behaviour therapy (REBT), with special chapters on how it is used in individual, couples, family, group, marathon, and sex therapy. It brings the original seminal book on REBT, *Reason and Emotion in Psychotherapy* (Ellis, 1962), up to date, and gives details of many REBT procedures.

Ellis, A. and MacLaren, C. (1998). *Rational Emotive Behavior Therapy: A Therapist's Guide.* San Luis Obispo, CA: Impact Publishers.

> Practical and accessible, this REBT therapist guide includes chapters on the philosophical and personality theory foundations of REBT, its theory of personality disturbance and change, assessment, cognitive techniques, emotive/experiential techniques, behavioural techniques and the integration of REBT with other systems of therapy.

Ellis, A. (2000). Rational emotive behavior therapy. In R. J. Corsini and D. Wedding (eds). *Current Psychotherapies* (6th edition). Itasca, IL: Peacock, 168–204.

> An authoritative overview of the theory and practice of rational emotive behaviour therapy written by its originator.

Ellis, A. (1991b). The revised ABC's of Rational-emotive therapy (RET). *Journal of Rational-Emotive and Cognitive Behavior Therapy, 9,* 139–72.

> An important paper in which Ellis discusses: basic human goals and values; the ABCs of emotional disturbance; interactions of As, Bs and Cs; the ABCs of interpersonal relationships; and using the ABCs in therapy.

Ellis, A. and Harper, R. A. (1997) *A Guide to Rational Living.* North Hollywood, CA: Wilshire Books.

> This is a completely revised and rewritten version of the REBT self-help classic which is often recommended by cognitive–behaviour therapists to clients. The book is a succinct, straightforward approach to REBT based on self-questioning and homework and shows how readers can help themselves with various emotional problems.

Ellis, A. (1999b). *How to Make Yourself Happy and Remarkably Less Disturbable.* Atascadero, CA: Impact Publishers.

> Every therapist is at risk of crooked thinking. An excellent way to learn about REBT is to apply it to yourself. This entertaining self-help book presents Ellis's views on emotional disturbance and on the importance of scientific thinking. Readers are then presented with a series of chapters showing them in simple language 'how to' take and maintain more control of their thoughts, feelings and actions.

Dryden, W. (1999). *Rational Emotive Behaviour Counselling in Action* (2nd edition). London: Sage.

> This introductory book succinctly and systematically presents the theory and practice of REBT. The book's three parts are: (1) the basic principles of rational emotive behaviour counselling; (2) the rational emotive behaviour counselling sequence; and (3) the rational emotive behaviour counselling process.

REFERENCES AND FURTHER READING

Dryden, W. (1989). Albert Ellis: An efficient and passionate life. *Journal of Counseling and Development, 67,* 539–46. (Interview with Albert Ellis.)

Dryden, W. (1999). *Rational Emotive Behaviour Counselling in Action* (2nd edition). London: Sage.

Dryden, W. and Ellis, A. (1986). Rational-emotive therapy (RET). In W. Dryden and W. Golden (eds). *Cognitive-Behavioural Approaches to Psychotherapy* (129–68). London: Harper and Row.

Dryden, W. and Walker, J. (1992). ABC of emotional and behavioural problems (self-help form). New York: Albert Ellis Institute for Rational Emotive Behaviour Therapy.

Ellis, A. (1958a). *Sex Without Guilt.* New York: Lyle Stuart.

Ellis, A. (1958b). Rational psychotherapy. *Journal of General Psychology, 59,* 35–49.

Ellis, A. (1962). *Reason and Emotion in Psychotherapy.* Secaucus, NJ: Citadel.

Ellis, A. (1971) A twenty-three-year-old woman, guilty about not following her parents' rules. In A. Ellis. *Growth Through Reason: Verbatim Cases in Rational-Emotive Therapy.* Hollywood: Wilshire Books, 223–86. (Reprinted in D. Wedding and R. Corsini (eds) (2001). *Case Studies in Psychotherapy.* Itasca, IL: Peacock.)

Ellis, A. (1977a). *Anger: How to Live With and Without It.* Sydney: MacMillan Sun Books.

Ellis, A. (1977b) The basic clinical theory of rational-emotive therapy. In A. Ellis and R. Grieger (eds). *Handbook of Rational-Emotive Therapy* (3–34) . New York: Springer Publishing Co.

Ellis, A. (1980). Overview of the clinical theory of rational-emotive therapy. In R. Grieger and J. Boyd (eds). *Rational-Emotive Therapy: A Skills-based Approach* (1–31). New York: Van Nostrand Reinhold.

Ellis, A. (1985). *Overcoming Resistance: Rational-Emotive Therapy with Difficult Clients.* New York: Springer.

Ellis, A. (1986a). Rational-emotive therapy approaches to overcoming resistance. In A. Ellis and R. Grieger (eds). *Handbook of Rational-Emotive Therapy,* Vol. 2 (246–74). New York: Springer.

Ellis, A. (1986b). Application of rational-emotive therapy to love problems. In A. Ellis and R. Grieger (eds). *Handbook of Rational-Emotive Therapy,* Vol. 2 (162–82). New York: Springer.

Ellis, A. (1987). The impossibility of achieving consistently good mental health. *American*

Psychologist, 42, 364–75.

Ellis, A. (1988). *How to Stubbornly Refuse to Make Yourself Miserable about Anything – Yes Anything!* Sydney: Pan MacMillan.

Ellis, A. (1990). Is Rational-Emotive Therapy (RET) 'Rationalist' or 'Constructivist'? In A. Ellis and W. Dryden. *The Essential Albert Ellis* (114–41). New York: Springer.

Ellis, A. (1991a). My life in clinical psychology. In C. E. Walker (ed.). *The History of Clinical Psychology in Autobiography*, Vol. 1 (1–37). Pacific Grove, CA: Brooks/Cole.

Ellis, A. (1991b). The revised ABC's of Rational-emotive therapy (RET). *Journal of Rational-Emotive and Cognitive Behavior Therapy*, 9, 139–72.

Ellis, A. (1991c). Using RET effectively: Reflections and interview. In M. E. Bernard (ed.). *Using Rational-Emotive Therapy Effectively* (1–33). New York: Plenum.

Ellis, A. (1991d). Rational-emotive behavior marriage and family therapy. In A. M. Horne (ed.). *Family Counseling and Therapy* (3rd edition, 489–513). Itasca, IL: Peacock.

Ellis, A. (1991e). Rational-emotive treatment of simple phobias. *Psychotherapy*, 28, 452–6.

Ellis, A. (1991f). Achieving self-actualization: The rational-emotive approach. In A. Jones and R. Crandall (eds). Handbook of self-actualization (Special Issue.) *Journal of Social Behavior and Personality*, 6 (5), 1–18.

Ellis, A. (1992). Group rational-emotive and cognitive–behavioral therapy. *International Journal of Group Psychotherapy*, 42, 63–80.

Ellis, A. (1993a). Changing Rational-Emotive Therapy (RET) to Rational Emotive Behavior Therapy (REBT). *The Behavior Therapist*, 16, 257–8.

Ellis, A. (1993b). Reflections on rational-emotive therapy. *Journal of Consulting and Clinical Psychology*, 61, 199–201.

Ellis, A. (1993c). The rational-emotive therapy (RET) approach to marital and family therapy. *The Family Journal: Counselling and Therapy for Couples and Families*, 1, 292–307.

Ellis, A. (1993d). The advantages and disadvantages of self-help therapy materials. *Professional Psychology: Research and Practice*, 24, 335–9.

Ellis, A. (1993e). Vigorous RET disputing. In M. E. Bernard and J. L. Wolfe (eds). *The RET Resource Book for Practitioners* (117). New York: Institute for Rational-Emotive Therapy.

Ellis, A. (1993f). Rational-emotive imagery: RET version. In M. E. Bernard and J. L. Wolfe (eds). *The RET Resource Book for Practitioners* (ii–8–10). New York: Institute for Rational-Emotive Therapy.

Ellis, A. (1994). *Reason and Emotion in Psychotherapy* (revised edition). Secaucus, NJ: Citadel.

Ellis, A. (1996). *Better, Deeper and More Enduring Brief Therapy: The Rational Emotive Behavior Approach*. New York: Brunner/Mazel.

Ellis, A. (1997a). The evolution of Albert Ellis and rational emotive behavior therapy. In J. K. Zeig (ed.). *The Evolution of Psychotherapy: The Third Conference* (69–82). New York: Brunner/Mazel.

Ellis, A. (1997b). Using rational emotive behavior therapy techniques to cope with disability. *Professional Psychology Research and Practice*, 28, 17–22.

Ellis, A. (1997c). Extending the goals of behavior therapy and of cognitive behavior therapy. *Behavior Therapy*, 28, 333–9.

Ellis, A. (1999a). Three methods of rational emotive behavior therapy that make my psychotherapy effective. *Psychotherapy Bulletin*, 34, 38–9.

Ellis, A. (1999b). *How to Make Yourself Happy and Remarkably Less Disturbable*. Atascadero, CA: Impact Publishers.

Ellis, A. (2000). Rational emotive behavior therapy. In R. J. Corsini and D. Wedding (eds). *Current Psychotherapies* (6th edition). Itasca, IL: Peacock, 168–204.

Ellis, A. and Becker, I. M. (1982). *A Guide to Personal Happiness.* Hollywood, CA: Wilshire Book Co.

Ellis, A. and Blau, S. (eds) (1998). *The Albert Ellis Reader.* Secaucus, NJ: Carol Publishing Group.

Ellis, A. and Dryden. W. (1997). *The Practice of Rational Emotive Behaviour Therapy.* London: Free Association Books and New York: Springer.

Ellis, A. and Harper, R. A. (1997) *A Guide to Rational Living.* North Hollywood, CA: Wilshire Books.

Ellis, A. and MacLaren, C. (1998). *Rational Emotive Behavior Therapy: A Therapist's Guide.* San Luis Obispo, CA: Impact Publishers.

Palmer, S. (1993). In the counsellor's chair: Stephen Palmer interviews Dr. Albert Ellis. *Counselling, 4,* 171–4.

Sichel, J. and Ellis, A. (1984). RET self-help form. New York: Institute for Rational-Emotive Therapy.

Wedding, D. and Corsini, R. (eds) (2001). *Case Studies in Psychotherapy.* (3rd edition). Itasca, IL: Peacock.

Ellis on cassette (illustrative)

Ellis, A. (1977d). *A Garland of Rational Songs* (with songbook). New York: Institute for Rational Emotive Behavior Therapy.

Ellis, A. (1982b). *Solving Emotional Problems.* New York: Institute for Rational Emotive Behavior Therapy.

Ellis, A. (1984). *How to Be Happy Though Human.* New York: Institute for Rational Emotive Behavior Therapy.

Ellis, A. (1987b). *How to Stop Worrying and Start Living.* Washington, DC: Psychology Today Tapes.

Ellis on videotape (illustrative)

Coping with the Suicide of a Loved One (49 mins).
Dealing with Addictions (55 mins).

For further details of REBT publications, cassettes and videotapes, contact:

Albert Ellis Institute for Rational Emotive Behavior Therapy, 45 East 65th Street, New York, NY 10021-6593, USA. Tel: (212) 535-0822. Fax: (212) 249-3582. Website: www.rebt.org e-mail: info@rebt.org

Ellis on film

Ellis, A. (1965). Rational-emotive therapy. In E. Shostrom (ed.). *Three Approaches to Psychotherapy.* Santa Ana, CA: Psychological Films.

13

Cognitive Therapy

Cognitive therapy aims to adjust information-processing and initiate positive change in all systems by acting through the cognitive system.

Aaron Beck

INTRODUCTION

Cognitive therapy was initially developed in the early 1960s by Dr Aaron Beck of the University of Pennsylvania. The theory postulates that during clients' cognitive development they learn incorrect habits of processing and interpreting information. Cognitive therapists attempt to unravel clients' distortions and help them to learn different and more realistic ways of processing and reality-testing information.

Cognitive therapy's theoretical underpinnings come from three main sources (Beck and Weishaar, 2000). First, the phenomenological approach to psychology, which posits that the individual's view of self and personal world are central to how they behave. Second, structural theory and depth psychology; in particular Freud's theory contributed to Beck's structuring cognition into primary and secondary processes. Third, the work of more modern cognitive psychologists like George Kelly influenced Beck. For example, Kelly's concept of personal constructs is similar to Beck's idea of schemas (Beck, Freeman *et al.*, 1990).

Influences on the practice of cognitive therapy include Rogers, Ellis and the behaviour therapists. The gentle style of questioning and emphasis on unconditional acceptance owes much to person-centred therapy. The emphasis on finding solutions to conscious problems resembles rational emotive behaviour therapy. Setting goals and session agendas, testing hypotheses, using specific behaviour change procedures, and assigning homework are among the contributions from behaviour therapy.

AARON BECK (1921–)

Aaron Temkin 'Tim' Beck was born on 18 July 1921, in Providence, Rhode Island, the fourth, but third surviving, son of Russian Jewish immigrant parents. In 1919, Beck's parents lost their only daughter in an influenza epidemic, an event that precipitated a deep depression in his mother which lasted off and on the rest of her life. Aged 7, Beck had a near-fatal illness which reinforced his mother's over-protectiveness. While his father was tranquil, Beck did not like his mother's moody, inconsistent and excitable behaviour. Beck's father, who ran a printing business, encouraged his interest in science and nature. At high school, Beck edited the school paper and graduated first in his class. When growing up, Beck developed many anxieties and phobias, including fears of abandonment, surgery, suffocation, public speaking and heights (Weishaar, 1993).

In 1942, Beck graduated from Brown University, having majored in English and political science. He took pre-medical courses both before and after graduating and, in 1946, received his MD from Yale University School of Medicine. From 1946 to 1948 Beck served a rotating internship and a residency in pathology at the Rhode Island Hospital. From 1950 he started a neurology residency at the Cushing Veterans Administration Hospital in Framingham, Massachusetts. Due to a shortage of psychiatry residents, against his wishes Beck was forced to complete a six-month rotation in psychiatry. Deciding to remain in psychiatry, from 1950 to 1952, he was a Fellow in psychiatry at the Austen Riggs Center in Stockbridge, Massachusetts. In 1953, the American Board of Psychiatry and Neurology certified Beck in psychiatry and, in 1958, Beck graduated from the Philadelphia Psychoanalytic Institute. Since 1954, Beck has been a faculty member in the University of Pennsylvania's Department of Psychiatry. Currently he is University Professor Emeritus of Psychiatry and President of the independent Beck Institute for Cognitive Therapy and Research, where staff are affiliated with the University Psychiatry Department.

The period from 1960 to 1963 saw the development of cognitive therapy. Beck was researching and re-examining psychoanalytic theory and ended by discarding it. He observes: 'There's nothing that I've been associated with since 1963 the seeds of which were not in the 1962 and 1964 articles. That was the critical period: changing from psychoanalysis to developing a new theory of therapy' (Weishaar, 1993, p. 21). Beck's process of developing theory is that he first observes patients, then develops ways of measuring these observations, then formulates a theory if the observations are validated by a number of cases, then designs interventions congruent with the theory, then over time and through further experimentation continues to assess whether the theory is confirmed or negated. When developing theory Beck also uses self-observation.

Beck has authored or co-authored over 375 articles in professional and scientific journals. His fourteen books include *Cognitive Therapy and the Emotional Disorders*; *Cognitive Therapy of Depression*, co-authored with Rush, Shaw and Emery; *Anxiety Disorders and Phobias*, co-authored with Emery and assisted by Greenberg; *Love is Never Enough*; *Cognitive Therapy of Personality Disorders*, co-authored with Freeman and associates; *The Integrative Power of Cognitive Therapy*, co-authored with Alford; *Scientific Foundations of Cognitive Theory and Therapy of Depression*, co-authored with Clark and Alford; and *Prisoners of Hate: The Cognitive Basis of Anger, Hostility and Violence*. Tests and measures that Beck has developed with colleagues include the *Beck Depression Inventory*, the *Beck Hopelessness Scale*, the *Suicide Intent Scale*, the *Suicide Ideation Scale*, and the *Beck Self-Concept Test*.

Beck's awards and honours include being awarded: in 1979, the American Psychiatric Association's Foundation Fund Prize for Research in Psychiatry for his research in depression and the development of cognitive therapy; in 1989, the American Psychological Association's Distinguished Scientific Award for Applications of Psychology; in 1997, the Cummings PSYCHE Award for Lifetime Achievement; and, in 1998, the Lifetime Achievement Award of the Association for the Advancement of Behavior Therapy. In addition, in 1987 Beck was elected a Fellow of Britain's Royal College of Psychiatrists.

Beck continues to be highly active in writing, research and training. In 1950, Beck married his wife Phyllis, a continuing source of strength and support, who developed her own career by becoming a Pennsylvania Superior Court Judge. The Becks have four adult children and many grandchildren

THEORY

In the theory of cognitive therapy, the nature and function of information processing (i.e., the assignment of meaning) constitute the key to understanding maladaptive behavior and positive therapeutic processes.

Aaron Beck

BASIC CONCEPTS

Cognition is the key to understanding and treating psychological disorders. Alford and Beck write: '"Cognition" is defined as that function that involves inferences about one's experiences and about the occurrence and control of future events' (1997, p. 14). Humans need to adapt to changing environmental circumstances. Cognition includes the processes involved in identifying and predicting complex relations among events for the purposes of adaptation. Humans have the capacity both for primal/primitive and for higher level cognitive processing.

Schemas

Schemas are structures that consist of people's fundamental beliefs and assumptions. Schemas are meaning-making cognitive structures. There are two categories of meaning: first, the objective or public meaning of an event, which may have few significant implications for the individual; and second, its personal or private meaning. Meaning assignment controls the psychological systems, such as behavioural, emotional, attentional and memory, so that the individual can activate strategies for adaptation.

Schemas are relatively stable cognitive patterns that influence, through their beliefs, how people select and synthesize incoming information. They are developed early in life from personal experiences and identifications with significant others and reinforced by further learning experiences. Schemas are not pathological by definition – they may be adaptive or maladaptive. They are analogous to George Kelly's (1955) formulation of personal constructs. People categorize and evaluate their experiences through a matrix of schemas.

Schemas possess structural qualities such as degree of breadth, flexibility, and their relative prominence in a person's cognitive organization. In addition, according to the degree of energy invested in them at any time, schemas can range from latent to predominant. When schemas are hypervalent, they are prepotent and easily triggered.

Psychopathology is characterized not only by the activation of inappropriate schemas but, in all probability, by their crowding out or inhibiting more-adaptive schemas.

Modes

Contemporary cognitive theory stresses the concept of modes. Modes are networks of cognitive, affective, motivational and behavioural schemas. Modes are fundamental to personality since they interpret and adapt to emerging and ongoing situations (Beck and Weishaar, 2000). In earlier writings, cognitions were viewed as the mediating variable that triggered people's affective, motivational and behavioural systems. Now, instead of a linear relationship, all aspects of human functioning are viewed as acting together as a mode. Alford and Beck observe: 'The operation of a mode (e.g, anger, attack) across diverse psychological systems (emotion, motivation) is determined by the idiosyncratic schematic processing derived from an individual's genetic programming and internalised cultural/social beliefs' (1997, p. 10).

Modes can be primal, which means that they are universal and linked to survival. Anxiety is an example of a primal mode. Examples of modes under conscious control include conversing and studying. Primal modes include primary process thinking that is primitive and that conceptualizes situations in global, rigid, biased and relatively crude ways. Primal modes of thinking may originally have been adaptive in an evolutionary sense, yet they can become maladaptive in everyday life when triggered by systematically biased thinking and misinterpretations.

In addition, humans are capable of higher levels of cognitive processing that tests reality and corrects primal, global conceptualizations. However, in psychopathology, these corrective functions become impaired and primary responses can escalate into full-blown psychiatric disorders. Nevertheless, conscious or higher level thinking can override primal thinking and make it more flexible and realistic. Cognitive therapy approaches dysfunctional modes by deactivating them, modifying their content and structure, and by constructing adaptive modes to neutralize them.

Cognitive vulnerability

The term 'cognitive vulnerability' refers to humans' cognitive frailty. Because of their schemas, each person has a set of unique vulnerabilities and sensitivities that predispose them to psychological distress. People's schemas and beliefs influence the way they process data about themselves. When they exhibit psychological problems, their dysfunctional schemas and beliefs lead them systematically to bias information in unhelpful ways.

Beck (Beck, Freeman *et al.*, 1990) gives the example of Sue, who heard noises coming from the next room where her boyfriend Tom was working on some chores. Sue's first thought was that 'Tom is making a lot of noise.' However, Sue's information processing continued and she made the following interpretation of her experience: 'Tom is making a lot of noise *because he's angry at me.*' Her attribution of causality was produced by a conditional schema or belief that 'If an intimate of mine is noisy, it means he is angry at me.' Further down her hierarchy were the beliefs that 'If people reject me, I will be all alone' and 'Being alone will be devastating.' At the most basic level Sue had the belief or schema that 'I am unlovable.' When activated, Sue's basic belief (or schema) 'I am unlovable' acted as a 'feed-forward' mechanism moulding the information about Tom's behaviour in a way to fit the schema. Beck provides an alternative explanation that might have better fitted the information available to Sue, namely that 'Loud hammering is a sound of exuberance.'

Automatic thoughts

Automatic thoughts are less accessible to awareness than voluntary thoughts, but not so deeply buried as beliefs and schemas. These thoughts are similar to what Freud termed 'preconscious' thinking and what Ellis terms 'self-statements'. People's self-evaluations and self-instructions appear to be derived from deeper structures – their self-schemas. Automatic thoughts reflect schema content – deeper beliefs and assumptions. In normal functioning self-appraisals and self-evaluations operate more or less automatically to help people stay on-course. However, in psychopathology certain automatic thoughts operate to help people stay off-course. Most psychological disorders are characterized by specific systematic biases in processing information. For example, depressive disorders are characterized by a negative view of self, experience and the future, and anxiety disorders by fear of physical or psychological danger.

Following are some salient characteristics of automatic thoughts. Automatic thoughts:

- are part of people's internal monologue – what and how they talk to themselves;
- can take the form of words, images, or both;
- occur very rapidly and usually at the fringe of awareness;
- can precede and accompany emotions, including feelings and inhibitions – for instance, people's emotional responses to each other's actions follow from their interpretations rather than from the actions themselves;
- are generally plausible to people who assume that they are accurate;
- have a recurring quality, despite people trying to block them out;
- affect tone of voice, facial expression and gestures, even though they may not be expressed verbally;
- can be linked together with more subtle thoughts underlying more obvious thoughts – for instance, when a husband boasts about his wife's cooking, his wife's secondary obvious automatic thought is 'He's fishing for a compliment', while her primary subtle automatic thought is 'They'll think that's all I'm good for' (Beck, 1988); and
- though often hard to identify, therapists can train clients to pinpoint these thoughts with great accuracy.

Cognitive distortions

Dysfunctional beliefs embedded in cognitive schemas contribute to systematic cognitive distortions, more accessible in automatic thoughts, that both characterize and maintain psychological distress. Box 13.1 includes some of the main cognitive distortions (Beck and Weishaar, 2000).

BOX 13.1

Cognitive distortions

Arbitrary inference
The process of drawing specific conclusions without supporting evidence and sometimes in the face of contradictory evidence. An example of arbitrary inference is that of the working mother who, after a busy day, concludes, 'I am a terrible mother.'

Selective abstraction
Selectively attending to a detail taken out of context at the same time as ignoring other more salient information. An example of selective abstraction is that of the boyfriend who becomes jealous at seeing his girlfriend tilt her head toward a man at a noisy party in order to hear him better.

Overgeneralization
Drawing a general rule or conclusion from one or a few isolated incidents and then applying the rule too broadly to unrelated situations. An example of overgeneralization is the woman who concludes, after a disappointing date, 'All men are alike. I'll always be rejected.'

Magnification and minimization
Evaluating particular events as far more or far less important than they really are. An example of magnification is the student who catastrophizes 'If I appear the least bit nervous in class it will mean disaster.' An example of minimization is that of a man describing his terminally ill mother as having a 'cold'.

Personalization
Having a tendency without adequate evidence to relate external events to oneself. For instance concluding, when an acquaintance walking down the opposite side of a busy street does not acknowledge a wave of greeting, 'I must have done something to offend him/her.'

Dichotomous thinking
Black-and-white, either/or, and polarized thinking are other terms for dichotomous thinking. Thinking in extreme terms, for instance 'Unless I do extremely well on this exam, I am a total failure.'

Evolutionary and genetic factors

The cognitive structures and schemas relevant to depression, anxiety disorders and personality disorders reflect our evolutionary history (Beck, 1991; Beck, Freeman *et al.*, 1990). Beck writes: 'It is reasonable to consider that the notion of long-standing cognitive-affective motivational processes influences our automatic processes: the way we construe events, what we feel, and how we are disposed to act' (Beck, Freeman *et al.*,

1990, p. 24). Much animal behaviour is regarded as programmed, with underlying processes reflected in overt behaviour. Though there are risks in extrapolating from animal to human ethology, similar developmental processes may be operative in humans. Animal analogies may clarify many aspects of normal and abnormal human behaviour. For instance, observations of primate behaviour seem highly relevant to depressed behaviour in humans.

'Strategies' are forms of programmed behaviour designed to serve biological goals. Regarding anxiety and anger, Beck (Beck and Emery, 1985) suggests four 'primal' survival strategies – fight, flight, freeze, and faint – to perceptions of threat. Also, he proposes that strategies associated with traditional personality disorders may have possible antecedents in our evolutionary past (Beck, Freeman *et al.*, 1990). The dramatic strategy of the histrionic personality may have roots in the display rituals of non-human animals. The attack strategy of the antisocial personality may have roots in predatory behaviour.

Human strategies may be adaptive or maladaptive depending on their circumstances. The strategies adopted by people with personality disorders are maladaptive exaggerations of normal strategies. For instance, with the dependent personality disorder the cognitive substrate or basic belief is 'I am helpless' which leads to a strategy of attachment based on fear of abandonment. With the avoidant personality disorder, the basic belief is 'I may get hurt' which leads to a strategy of avoidance.

Genetic factors

Mention was made above of the role of evolution in laying the foundation for cognitive schemas and behavioural strategies. In addition, biological factors such as variation in the gene pool differentiate individuals in terms of their vulnerability to different kinds of distress. For instance, predisposing factors in depression are hereditary susceptibility and diseases that cause persistent neurochemical abnormalities.

Beck (Beck, Freeman *et al.*, 1990) regards the evidence as strong for relatively stable temperamental and behavioural differences being present at birth. These innate 'tendencies' can be strengthened or weakened by experience. For instance, because of the quality of their interpersonal interactions and learning experiences, not all shy children become shy adults. Furthermore, mutually reinforcing cycles can be established between people's innate tendencies and others' reactions to them. For instance, individuals with innate care-eliciting tendencies can elicit care-producing behaviour in others, even beyond the age when such behaviour is adaptive.

ACQUISITION

This section on acquisition seeks to answer two main, yet interrelated, questions. First, how are cognitive schemas, automatic thoughts and cognitive distortions initially acquired? Second, how are symptoms of psychiatric and other disorders activated? Here my focus is on dysfunctional cognitions and behaviour, though much that follows is relevant to acquiring adaptive cognitions and behaviour.

Acquisition of vulnerability

Cognitive therapy views the acquisition of the potential for psychological distress as the result of many interacting factors: evolutionary, biological, developmental, and environmental. Though many of the factors are common across individuals, each individual has his or her unique variations and way of attaching personal meaning to events. Below are some ways in which people acquire vulnerabilities.

Childhood traumas

Specific affect-laden incidents in childhood may create the potential for later distress by generating dysfunctional underlying beliefs (Beck and Emery, 1985). One example is the client who suffered a sense of doom and dread every Christmas season. His earliest memory of this feeling was when, aged 7, he saw his mother taken away to a tuberculosis sanatorium. His underlying belief became 'Something bad is going to happen over the Christmas holidays.' Another example is the 5-year-old who went away on a trip and returned to find the family dog dead, developing the belief 'When I'm not physically close to others, something bad will happen to them.' A further example is that of the 7-year-old whose father left the family permanently after a marital fight, developing the underlying belief 'If I make others angry they will leave me.'

Negative treatment in childhood

Children can be subject to ongoing negative treatment which affects their self-esteem and later makes them vulnerable to psychological distress. Furthermore, parents and significant others can model abusive behaviour which their children later use against others. Box 13.2 provides examples of acquiring cognitive vulnerability in childhood (Beck, 1988; Beck, Freeman *et al.*, 1990).

Social learning

Beck endorses social learning theory. However, he also stresses that individuals have unique learning histories and idiosyncratic ways of attaching meanings to earlier events. Many reasons exist for personality disorders – for example, obsessive-compulsive and paranoid behaviour may develop either as a compensation or from fear. However, the reinforcement of relevant strategies by parents and significant others is among the reasons for specific personality disorders. For instance, the dependent personality's help-seeking and clinging strategies may have been rewarded and attempts at self-sufficiency and mobility discouraged. Identification with other family members can be important in what personality disorder strategies get developed. In addition, negative life experiences may worsen an initial predisposition so that, for instance, the shy child turns into an avoidant personality.

Modelling is a key process in social learning theory. For example, marital partners have memories about how their parents behaved. Parental modelling provides a basis for rules, shoulds and should-nots, that they bring into their own marriages. Beck (1988) provides the example of Wendy and Hal who married very young and had trouble freeing themselves from parental modelling and reinforcement. Wendy had absorbed her mother's

---

BOX 13.2
Childhood abuse and later cognitive vulnerability

Example 1: Dysfunctional belief: 'I am a wimp'
Gary had periodic violent outbursts against Beverley, whom he perceived as needling him all the time for not doing chores. Gary had suffered from being brought up in a household where people controlled each other through power and might. His father and older brother intimidated him and Gary developed a core schema 'I am a wimp.' To compensate for this belief, Gary adopted an interpersonal strategy of intimidation to control other people's inclination to dominate him like his family had earlier done.

Example 2: Dysfunctional belief: 'I am a bad kid'
In her childhood, a 28-year-old single woman who now suffered from panic disorder had come home from school early one day and her mother screamed at her for waking her up, saying 'How dare you interrupt my sleep!' Despite the fact that her mother drank a lot and was irritable and unpredictable, the woman developed the beliefs 'I am a bad kid' and 'I am wrong because I upset my mother.'

Example 3: Dysfunctional tendency to self-criticism
A female client kept criticizing herself unnecessarily. She lessened her self-criticism when she re-experienced childhood scenes of criticism and obtained the insight 'I criticize myself now not because it's right to do so, but because my mother always criticized me and I took this over from her.'

---

traditional rule that 'The role of a wife is to take care of her husband.' When Wendy failed to live up to the rule, she disparaged herself. Hal's father had stressed and rewarded perfectionism so much that Hal had developed the belief 'I can never do anything right.' His mother reinforced his self-doubts because she had a negative attitude towards men: 'Men can't do anything – they're weak and helpless.' Hal's rules and beliefs made him vulnerable both to creating and dealing with difficulties in his marriage.

Inadequate experiences for the learning of coping skills
People may have been inadequately provided with personal experiences to learn coping skills. For example, an element in the anxious person's assessment of a threat is their ability to cope with the threat. A boy who has developed the coping skills of dealing with a bully is likely to feel less anxious about the bully because of this. People who fail to develop adequate assertion skills may be more prone to depression, first since they may lose self-esteem through others' actions, and second, since they may then disparage themselves for lack of assertion. Most couples have learned insufficient skills in marital communication 'and so unwittingly produce continual abrasions, misunderstandings, and frustrations' (Beck, 1988, p. 275).

Activation of vulnerability

The term *cognitive shift* describes the shift of energy away from normal or higher level cognitive processing to a predominance of processing by pathological primal schemas. According to the disorder, energy is used to activate and inhibit unconscious patterns. For instance, in depression, generalized anxiety disorders and panic attacks, the depressive, danger and panic modes are energized, respectively. The concept of mode reflects the manner in which a schema is expressed. For example, a schema such as 'I'm inadequate' may lead to a predominance of catastrophizing cognitions when the anxiety mode is activated and to a predominance of self-blame and hopelessness cognitions when the depressed mode is activated.

Thinking and behaving in ways that indicate vulnerability is a matter of degree. The *continuity hypothesis* suggests that anxiety disorders, depression and personality disorders are exaggerated mechanisms of normal functioning. People can acquire dysfunctional schemas, rules, automatic thoughts and behaviours and not have them activated so that they become full-blown disorders or highly damaging factors in marital relationships.

The cognitive shift gets triggered when people perceive their vital interests are at stake or have been affected. Often, initially, the shift into psychopathology is activated in response to major life stressors. Later the shift may be activated by less severe stressors (A. Butler, personal communication, 8 April 1994). With repeated activations over the life span, people become increasingly sensitive to triggers so that it takes objectively less severe or salient stressors to precipitate a shift.

In nonendogenous unipolar depression, people have a cognitive vulnerability that is triggered by stressful life events or a series of traumatic experiences. An example of the development of vulnerability to activation of the cognitive shift is that of a person with recurrent depression whose first episode may have been precipitated by a severe life stressor (e.g., losing a job). Later episodes may be precipitated by relatively minor and less directly relevant stressors (e.g., hearing of a friend in another area of work being fired) that take on inordinate meaning due to prior experiences.

Three activating or precipitating factors are proposed for generalized anxiety disorders (Beck and Emery, 1985). First, people may face increased demands, for instance after the birth of a child or a job promotion. Second, there may be increased threat in an area of a person's life, for example, a new mother having a baby susceptible to infections, or an employee getting a hostile new boss. Third, stressful events and reversals may undermine confidence. An example is that of a young lawyer who failed his bar examination and, about the same time, was told by his girlfriend that she did not love him. Fearing for his future as a lawyer and family man, he became chronically anxious.

MAINTENANCE

When people's cognitive vulnerabilities get activated and their cognitive processes go awry, why do they stay that way? Many people cope with the activation of their cognitive vulnerabilities by instigating adaptive cognitive and behavioural strategies. However, those with psychopathological disorders and those with deeply distressed marriages may remain stuck in faulty patterns of information processing and behaviour, to their own and other people's great disadvantage. There is no single cause why people continue to process information inefficiently. The evolutionary history of the species and genetic influences play a part. Also, the extent and depth of people's experiences of childhood traumas, negative treatment in childhood, faulty social learning and inadequate experiences of learning coping skills play their parts too.

Failure to turn off predominant modes

The type of schema that is evoked may be determined by the mode that is active at any given time. Normally there is a balance between modes so that when one predominates or is hypervalent for a long time, an opposing mode is activated. For instance, during a period of elation a person may become aware of negative feedback, or hostility may be counterbalanced by anxiety. In psychopathological disorders there seems to be an interference in the turn-off of the dominant mode. This results in systematically biased interpretations of negative events in depression, of positive events in mania and of dangerous events in anxiety disorders. Beck considers the reasons are obscure why the opponent mode remains relatively inactive, thus failing to contribute to a more balanced view of reality. One possibility is that neurochemical disturbances either stimulate a prolonged overactivity of the dominant mode or fail to stimulate sufficient activity in the opposing mode.

Inability to reality-test dysfunctional interpretations

Since clients accept their dysfunctional beliefs so readily during anxiety and depression, Beck believes that they have temporarily lost their ability to reality-test their interpretations. Their information processing, based on dysfunctional schemas and beliefs, is permeated with automatic thoughts containing cognitive distortions. Cognitive distortions are not only manifestations of psychopathology, they serve to maintain it by interfering with clients' ability to test the reality of their thinking. Clients think in rigid, stereotypical terms. They fail to distinguish adequately between fact and inference. Instead of viewing the content of their thoughts as testable hypotheses, they jump to conclusions on inadequate evidence and then view their conclusions as facts. They insufficiently take into account any feedback that might modify or negate their thoughts and perceptions. Thus information processing systems become closed, instead of remaining open to assessing new data as they become available.

Resistances to change

Many reasons exist for why clients resist changing. For instance, clients may be fearful of the negative effects of their changing on others. Marta was a 42-year-old woman living with her mother and diagnosed as having a dependent personality disorder. Whenever she thought of moving she feared that this would kill her mother – and her mother reinforced this thinking (Beck, Freeman *et al.*, 1990). Many highly anxious, depressed and suicidal clients fear change as an unknown. Sometimes clients fear the positive as well as the negative consequences of change, for instance having to deal with the added responsibility of a promotion or marriage.

Beck (1988) considers that partners in distressed relationships may need to confront many beliefs, possibly expressed in the form of automatic thoughts, that weaken their motivation for change. Such thoughts include: 'My partner is incapable of change' and 'He/she hurt me. He/she deserves to be hurt.'

Cognitive models

A systematic bias in information processing characterizes most psychological disorders. Overviews of Beck's cognitive models of depression, anxiety disorders, distressed couple relationships, and personality disorders are now presented.

Cognitive model of depression

Beck views depression not just as a mood state, but a cognitive state as well (Beck, 1991; Beck, Rush, Shaw and Emery, 1979). Depression entails clients activating three major cognitive patterns known as *the cognitive triad*, involving negative views of:

- *themselves* as unlovable, worthless, helpless and lacking in ability to attain happiness;
- *their past and present experiencing of the world* – their personal world is extremely demanding and presents huge obstacles to achieving goals;
- *the future,* which is viewed as hopeless and unlikely to improve – this hopelessness may bring about ideas of suicide.

These cognitive patterns lead to the motivational, behavioural and physical symptoms of depression. An illustrative motivational symptom is *paralysis of will* created by the belief that one lacks the ability to cope with or control an event's outcome. Inertia and fatigue are illustrative behavioural and physical symptoms, respectively.

Depressive schemas are formed early in life. Situations of loss similar to those originally embedding the schema may trigger a depression. Series of traumatic events may also activate depressions. As the depression worsens, depressive schemas become hypervalent to the point where clients may become unable to view their negative thoughts objectively and find themselves completely preoccupied with repetitive negative thoughts. As dysfunctional schemas become more activated, so does the incidence of systematic cognitive distortions.

Cognitive model of anxiety disorders

The main cognitive theme in anxiety disorders is danger. Anxiety is a strategy in response to threat. In anxiety disorders the normal evolutionary survival mechanism of anxiety becomes exaggerated and malfunctioning. Beck (Beck and Emery, 1985) adopts Lazarus' (1966) distinction between primary and secondary appraisal. Primary appraisal is the first impression of a situation that suggests the situation is noxious. Then successive re-appraisals are made concerning the nature and relevance of the threat to a person's vital interests, including physical and psychological injury. Secondary appraisal involves the person assessing his or her resources for dealing with the threat. This process takes place at the same time as evaluating the nature of the threat. As with depression a person's underlying dysfunctional schemas and beliefs may predispose them to anxiety. Their dysfunctional beliefs may be activated by increased demands, threats and stresses which may interact with previous problems. Cognitive distortions reflecting dysfunctional schemas include overestimating the probability and severity of the threat, magnification of the negative consequences (catastrophizing), underestimating one's resources for dealing with the threat, and insufficiently taking into account support factors, for instance the presence of others who might help. In brief, anxious individuals maximize the likelihood of harm and minimize their ability to cope.

Cognitive model of distressed couple relationships

Beck observes: 'what attracts partners to each other is rarely enough to sustain a relationship' (Beck, 1988, p. 46). Poor communication skills are one reason for marital difficulties. In addition, partners bring much personal baggage into the relationship in terms of hidden expectations of each other and the relationship. The expectations in marriage are less flexible than in uncommitted relationships. Furthermore, much behaviour in marriage has idiosyncratic symbolic meanings attached to it revolving around symbols of love or rejection, security or insecurity.

When disappointment in a relationship sets in and emotions run high, partners lose some or virtually all of their ability to reality-test their interpretations of their own and each other's thoughts, feelings and actions. Instead they react to their 'invisible reality' which is likely to be based more on their internal states, fears and expectations than on what actually happens. Dysfunctional schemas and beliefs can be triggered, leading to a negative cognitive set about the other person. A distressed couple's voluntary and automatic thinking contains numerous cognitive distortions. Partners tend to fixate on what is wrong in their relationship rather than on what is right. They misperceive and misinterpret what the other says or does, engage in mind-reading and attribute undesirable and malicious motives to each other, and fail to check out the accuracy of their negative explanations and illogical conclusions.

In addition, partners send each other barbed messages that trigger hurt and anger. They perceive they have been wronged, get angry, feel impelled to attack, and attack. Hostility is part of a primitive fight–flight survival mechanism. However, acting on the primitive urge to attack is often destructive to the relationship. It increases the level of threat in the relationship and hence partners' tendencies to think in rigid and erroneous ways. Furthermore, hostility can increase partners' resistances to working on their relationship.

Cognitive model of personality disorders

Personality disorders, along with other kinds of psychopathology, partly represent evolutionary strategies that have been insufficiently adapted to today's individualized and technological society (Beck, Freeman *et al.*, 1990). Also, genetic predisposition and differing learning experiences influence which disorders different individuals develop. Each personality disorder is characterized by a basic belief and a corresponding overt behavioural strategy. Different overt responses represent important structural differences in basic beliefs (or schemas). The dependent personality disorder has the basic belief 'I am helpless' and the overt strategy of attachment. The corresponding beliefs and strategies in the other personality disorders are:

- avoidant disorder, 'I may get hurt', avoidance;
- passive–aggressive disorder, 'I could be stepped on', resistance;
- paranoid disorder, 'People are potential adversaries', wariness;
- narcissistic disorder, 'I am special', self-aggrandizement;
- the histrionic disorder, 'I need to impress', dramatics;
- obsessive–compulsive disorder, 'Errors are bad, I must not err', perfectionism;
- antisocial disorder, 'People are there to be taken', attack; and
- schizoid disorder, 'I need plenty of space', isolation.

Another way of looking at strategies is that each personality disorder reflects both overdeveloped and underdeveloped strategies: for example, in the paranoid disorder 'mistrust' is overdeveloped and 'trust' is underdeveloped. A fuller cognitive profile may be drawn for each personality disorder.

When particular modes are hypervalent, their constituent schemas are readily triggered. In personality disorders a cognitive shift occurs in which there is a redirection of energy away from normal cognitive processing into the different schemas that constitute the disorders. As part of this process more adaptive schemas may get inhibited. Because of the tenacity of their dysfunctional schemas, cognitive therapy with clients with personality disorders is generally longer term and involves a fuller exploration of the origin of schemas than for clients with depression or anxiety disorders.

THERAPY

Cognitive therapy initially addresses symptom relief, but its ultimate goals are to remove systematic biases in thinking and modify the core beliefs that predispose the person to future distress.

Aaron Beck

THERAPEUTIC GOALS

Cognitive therapy 'aims explicitly to "reenergize" the reality-testing system' (Beck, Freeman *et al.*, 1990, p. 37). In varying degrees, clients with psychopathological disorders and couples in distressed relationships have lost the ability to reality-test dysfunctional interpretations. Cognitive therapy teaches clients adaptive metacognition – how to think about their thinking – so that they can correct faulty cognitive processing and develop assumptions that allow them to cope. While cognitive therapy may initially address symptom relief, its ultimate goal is to remove systematic biases in how clients think. In addition, cognitive therapy aims to impart behavioural skills relevant to clients' problems, for instance, listening and communication skills for distressed couples or assertion skills for shy people.

Clients are told that a goal of cognitive therapy is for them to learn to become their own therapists (Beck and Weishaar, 2000). When working with clients' cognitions, goals include teaching them to:

1. monitor their negative automatic thoughts;
2. recognize the connections between cognition, affect and behaviour;
3. examine and reality-test the evidence for and against distorted automatic thoughts;
4. substitute more realistic interpretations for biased cognitions; and
5. learn to identify and alter the beliefs that predispose them to distort their experiences. (Beck, Rush, Shaw and Emery, 1979)

Clients need not be highly intelligent to gain from cognitive therapy – in fact Beck's researches show no relationship between intelligence and cognitive therapy outcomes.

Cognitive therapy works best with clients who can focus on their automatic thoughts and take some responsibility for self-help. It is not recommended for clients with impaired reality-testing, such as hallucinations and delusions, or for clients with impaired memory and reasoning abilities, such as with organic brain syndromes. For some disorders, such as recurrent major depressive episodes, a combination of cognitive therapy and medication is recommended.

PROCESS OF THERAPY

At the Beck Institute for Cognitive Therapy and Research in suburban Philadelphia, clients undergo a three-hour intake protocol consisting of a clinical interview and psychological tests. The clinical interview provides a thorough history of the background factors contributing to the client's distress. The interview also assesses the current level of functioning, prominent symptoms and expectations for therapy. The *Beck Depression Inventory* (Beck *et al.*, 1961), the *Anxiety Checklist* (Beck, 1978), and the *Dysfunctional Attitudes Scale* (Weissman, 1979) are prominent among psychological tests used during the intake protocol.

The initial interview has many purposes: initiating a relationship, providing a rationale for cognitive therapy, producing symptom relief, and eliciting important information. Right from the start, therapists impart to clients the expectation that cognitive therapy will be time-limited. During the initial interview, therapists start to define problems. Definitions of problems entail both functional and cognitive analyses.

The *functional analysis* seeks to answer questions such as: 'What are the component parts of the problem?', 'How is it manifested?', 'In what situations does it occur?', 'What is its frequency, intensity and duration?', and 'What are its consequences?'

The *cognitive analysis* identifies the client's thoughts and images when emotion is triggered, the extent to which the client feels in control of thoughts and images, and predictions about the likelihood of the problem occurring and what will happen. From the beginning, therapists train clients to monitor their feelings, thoughts and behaviour and to recognize the connections between them. Homework is a feature throughout cognitive therapy. An example of an early homework assignment might be asking clients to record their automatic thoughts when distressed.

During initial sessions, therapists and clients draw up problem lists. Problem lists can consist of specific symptoms, behaviours or pervasive problems. Their function is to assign treatment priorities. Considerations in prioritizing treatment include magnitude of distress, symptom severity, and pervasiveness of theme. Therapists approach each problem by choosing the appropriate cognitive and behavioural techniques to apply. Therapists always offer a rationale for each technique. In addition, both when suggesting and implementing techniques, therapists elicit feedback from clients.

While the early stages of therapy may focus on symptom removal, middle and later stages are more likely to emphasize changing clients' patterns of thinking. Clients are helped to understand the interrelationships between their thoughts, feelings and behaviours. Once they can challenge automatic thoughts that interfere with effective functioning, then they can identify and examine the underlying assumptions or beliefs generating such thoughts. Assumptions may be revealed as themes in automatic thoughts across time and across situations. Once assumptions and core beliefs have been identified and their disruptive power understood, then cognitive therapy aims to assist clients to examine their validity and current usefulness and then discard or amend them, as appropriate.

As cognitive therapy progresses, clients develop their skills of being their own therapists. Clients assume more responsibility for identifying problems, analysing their thinking and creating suitable homework assignments. The role of the therapist shifts from being fairly didactic to facilitating clients as they develop their cognitive self-helping skills. The frequency of sessions decreases as clients become more proficient.

Being mainly a short-term structured approach, cognitive therapy tends to have its ending built into its beginning. Therapy ends when goals are reached and clients feel confident about implementing their new skills. From the outset therapists discuss with clients criteria and expectations for termination. There are a number of ways of assessing progress, including relief from symptoms, changes in reported and observed behaviour, and changes in thinking both inside and outside therapy. Performance in homework assignments, such as filling in the *Daily Record of Automatic Thoughts* log and carrying out specific tasks and experiments, also assists in assessing progress. In particular, therapists look out for clients' ability to reality-test and, if necessary, modify or discard distorted interpretations. Often termination is gradual, say from weekly to biweekly sessions, followed by booster sessions one and two months after termination. The purpose of such sessions is to consolidate gains and assist clients to keep employing their new skills (Beck and Weishaar, 2000).

Cognitive therapy sessions generally last for 45 minutes. The standard treatment length for unipolar depression is eight to sixteen sessions at weekly intervals. Moderately to severely depressed clients may be seen twice a week for the first two or three weeks. Clients with anxiety disorders generally receive from five to fifteen sessions (Clark and Beck, 1988). The treatment of personality disorders generally takes longer and may last for a year or more.

THE THERAPEUTIC RELATIONSHIP

Cognitive therapy is an educational process in which therapists are active in developing relationships with clients and using their expertise in helping clients examine and modify beliefs and behaviour. The quality of the therapist–client relationship is an important medium for improvement. Cognitive therapy is not an impersonal approach, but one in which therapists seek to understand their clients as individuals. Beck regards his therapeutic style as somewhat Rogerian. Therapists strive to create an emotional climate of genuine warmth and non-judgemental acceptance. Furthermore, cognitive therapists give clients their phone numbers in case of emergency.

Cognitive therapists attempt to demystify counselling by using language that clients can understand. They treat clients with respect by offering rationales both for their overall approach and for each technique that they propose. In addition, they share responsibility for what happens in therapy by discussing case conceptualizations and involving clients in setting goals and session agendas. Also, cognitive therapists elicit feedback from clients about both their suggestions and their behaviour. Therapists are sensitive to signs of transference and allow clients' reactions to them to be aired. Therapists can use these transference reactions to identify and work with clients' automatic thoughts and interpersonal distortions.

With most personality-disordered clients, cognitive therapists offer a closer and warmer relationship than in acute disorders, such as anxiety and depression. Therapists can face problems of non-collaboration from clients, especially those with personality disorders (Beck, Freeman *et al.*, 1990).

Serving as co-investigator – collaborative empiricism

In addition to offering accepting and warm relationships, cognitive therapists play an active role in the therapy process. Therapists encourage clients to play an active role too. All of the client's cognitions are viewed as testable hypotheses. Therapists and clients collaborate together in the scientific endeavour of examining the evidence to confirm or negate the client's cognitions. Based on what clients say and how they say it, therapists develop hypotheses that can identify cognitive errors as well as underlying assumptions and beliefs. Therapists then ask clients to comment on whether their hypotheses fit the facts. By this means, clients are encouraged both to view their thoughts as personal views of reality and to build their skills of evaluating their validity. Throughout the process of identifying and exploring the evidence for biased thinking, as appropriate either the therapist or the client takes the more active role.

Serving as a guide – guided discovery

There are a number of different facets to guided discovery. Therapists can operate as guides to assist clients to discover the themes that run through their present automatic thoughts and beliefs. This can be taken one stage further where therapists and clients link the beliefs to analogous experiences in the past and collaboratively piece together the developmental history of the beliefs. Another use of guided discovery is that therapists act as guides in assisting clients to reality-test their possible errors in logic by designing new experiences that involve the client experimenting with different behaviour. Therapists do not use cajoling, disputation and indoctrination to assist clients to reality-test their thinking and adopt new beliefs. Rather, they encourage clients to develop their own skills of using and assessing information, facts and probabilities in order to obtain more realistic perspectives than sometimes offered by their initial thoughts.

THERAPEUTIC INTERVENTIONS

Both cognitive and behavioural interventions are used in cognitive therapy. The interventions selected depend on such factors as the nature of the client's problems, the therapeutic goals, and how well they are functioning.

Cognitive interventions

Following are some of the main cognitive interventions used by cognitive therapists to assist clients to replace their distorted automatic thoughts and beliefs with more realistic ways of processing information.

Eliciting and identifying automatic thoughts

In order to change their thinking, clients need first to become aware of their thought processes. Included below are some specific interventions for eliciting and identifying automatic thoughts.

Providing reasons

Therapists can provide reasons for the importance of examining the connections between how clients think, feel and act. Furthermore, they can introduce the concept of automatic thoughts and provide an example of how underlying perceptions influence feelings. In addition, therapists can communicate that a major assumption of cognitive therapy is that clients are experiencing difficulties in reality-testing the validity of their interpretations. Box 13.3 provides an example of a cognitive therapist showing the relationship between cognition, affect and behaviour (Beck *et al.*, 1979, pp. 147–8).

Questioning

Clients may be questioned about automatic thoughts that occur during upsetting situations. Where clients experience difficulty in recalling thoughts, imagery or role-playing may be used. When questioning, therapists observe clients carefully for signs of affect that may offer leads for further questioning.

Using a whiteboard

When clients see their initial thoughts written up on the board, this may trigger them to reveal less obvious and more frightening thoughts.

BOX 13.3

Example of showing the influence of cognitions on affect and behaviour

The client
A 43-year-old depressed male patient.

The scene
The therapist instructed the client to imagine a person was home alone one night and heard a crash in another room.

Interpretation 1
This person thinks 'There's a burglar in the room.'

Possible consequences of interpretation 1
The therapist then asked the client:
- 'How do you think this person would feel?', to which the client answered 'Very anxious, terrified.'
- 'And how might he behave?', to which the client replied he might hide or phone the police.

Interpretation 2
The therapist then instructed the client to imagine that the person heard the same noise and thought: 'The windows have been left open and the wind has caused something to fall over.'

Possible consequences of interpretation 2
The therapist then asked the client:
- 'How would he feel?', to which the client replied the person wouldn't be afraid, though he might be sad if he thought something valuable had been broken.
- 'And would his behaviour be different following this thought?', to which the client replied it would be different in that he would probably go and see what the problem was and certainly wouldn't phone the police.

Main teaching points
The therapist emphasized that this example showed:
- that usually there were a number of ways the client could interpret a situation, and
- the way he interpreted a situation would affect how he felt and behaved.

Encouraging clients to engage in feared activities
Frequently, during sessions, clients are encouraged to engage in anxiety-evoking activities: for instance, making phone calls or writing letters they had been putting off. As they perform the activity, therapists can ask the question 'What is going through your mind right now?' Therapists can also go with clients into real-life situations where they experience difficulty, for instance crowded places, and get them to verbalize what they think.

Focusing on imagery
Gathering information about imagery can be an important way of accessing automatic thoughts. Though individual differences exist, clinical observations suggest that many people visualizing scenes react to them as though they were real.

Self-monitoring of thoughts
Clients may be set homework in which they record their thoughts. They may complete a Daily Record of Automatic Thoughts log in which they record in their respective columns:

- *date*;
- *situation* leading to negative emotion(s);
- *emotion(s)* felt and their degree on a 0–100% scale;
- *automatic thought(s)* and a rating of how strongly they believed the automatic thought(s) on a 0–100% scale.

Therapists may encourage some clients to use wrist counters to help them learn to recognize automatic thoughts as they occur.

Reality-testing and correcting automatic thoughts
Interventions for assisting clients to treat their thoughts as hypotheses that require testing against reality and, if necessary, discarding, modifying or replacing include the following.

Conducting Socratic dialogues
Questions compose the largest category of verbal statements in cognitive therapy. Questions reflect the basic empirical orientation of the approach and have the immediate goal of converting clients' closed belief systems into open systems. More specifically, questions seek to help clients: become aware of what their thoughts are; examine them for cognitive distortions; substitute more balanced thoughts; and make plans to develop new thought patterns. A basic raising-awareness question is to ask clients 'What is going through your mind right now?'

   Therapists use questioning rather than indoctrination and disputation. Conducted in an emotional climate of warmth and acceptance, the Socratic style of questioning assists clients to expand and evaluate how they think. Typical questions are:

- 'Where is the evidence?'
- 'Where is the logic?'
- 'Are there other ways of perceiving the situation?'
- 'What do I have to lose?'
- 'What do I have to gain?'
- 'What would be the worst thing that could happen?'
- 'What can I learn from this experience?' (Beck and Emery, 1985)

Clients learn to ask themselves the same questions that their therapists have asked. For instance, however plausible their automatic thoughts may 'feel', clients in distressed relationships can question their validity by asking themselves the following series of questions:

- 'What is the evidence in *favour* of my interpretation?'
- 'What evidence is *contrary* to my interpretation?'
- 'Does it *logically follow* from my spouse's actions that my spouse has the motive that I assign to him or her?'
- 'Is there an *alternative* explanation for his or her behaviour?' (Beck, 1988)

Box 13.4 provides an example of some of Beck's questions to challenge a client's thinking (Beck, 1976, pp. 249–52).

BOX 13.4

Case example: Challenging the thought that 'Failure is a catastrophe'

The client
A medical student inhibited in numerous situations where assertion was essential. Here the therapist focuses on the client's fears of giving a talk in front of his class tomorrow.

The therapist's questions
'What are you afraid of?'
'Suppose you do make a fool of yourself, why is that so bad?'
'Now look here, suppose they ridicule you, can you die from it?'
'Suppose they decide that you are the worst public speaker that ever lived, will this ruin your career?'
'But if you flubbed it would your wife or parents disown you?'
'Well, what would be so awful about it?'
When the client answers that he would feel pretty bad, the therapist asks:
'For how long?' and the client replies 'For about a day or two' and the therapist then says:
'And then what?', to which the client replies 'Then I'd be OK.'

The therapist's summary
The therapist pointed out to the client that, somewhere along the line, his thinking got fouled up, and that he tended to regard failure as a catastrophe. The client needed to start challenging his wrong premises and get failures labelled accurately as failures to attain goals and not as disasters.

Subsequent therapy sessions
As therapy proceeded the therapist coached the client in changing his notion that failure was a catastrophe as well as challenged maladaptive attitudes producing psychological distress in other social situations.

Identifying cognitive distortions

Therapists can teach clients what the common cognitive distortions are, for instance arbitrary inference and magnification. Both during therapy and as homework clients can be challenged to identify the distortions in how they think. Clients may use the three-column technique for this:

- column one – describe a situation that elicits negative emotions;
- column two – identify their automatic thoughts in the situation;
- column three – list the types of distortions in these thoughts.

Decatastrophizing

In decatastrophizing, the basic question is 'So what if it happens?' Areas covered in this technique include: the event's probability and severity, the client's coping capacity and support factors, and the client's ability to accept and deal with the worst possible outcomes.

Reattribution

Reattribution techniques test automatic thoughts and underlying beliefs by considering alternative ways of assigning responsibility and cause. Clients can be encouraged to rate on a 0–100 scale the degree of responsibility they feel for negative events and feared outcomes. By means of questioning, the therapist attempts to loosen them up by generating and evaluating alternative explanations.

Redefining

Redefining problems entails making them more concrete and stating them in terms of what the client might do. For example, a lonely person who feels uncared for may redefine his or her problem as 'I need to reach out to other people and be caring.'

Decentring

Decentring involves assisting clients to challenge their belief that everyone is focusing on them. Clients can be encouraged to evaluate more closely what others are doing: for instance, other students may be daydreaming, looking at their lecturer, or taking notes. In addition, clients can be asked to closely observe how frequently they attend to others. This may help them realize how limited their observations are, and thus infer that other people's observations are the same.

Forming rational responses

Cognitive therapists train clients in how to form more rational responses to their automatic thoughts. Again, questioning is an important way to assist clients in learning to use their inner monologue *for* rather than *against* themselves. Box 13.5 provides an example of a client providing a counteracting rational response to herself (Beck, 1988, p. 264). Finding a rational response can help clients see their automatic thoughts as an interpretation rather than as 'the truth'.

BOX 13.5

Example of forming a rational response

The situation

Wendy, who was phoned by her husband Hal to say he was tied up at the office.

- *Emotional reaction*   Anger.
- *Automatic thought*   'It's not fair – I have to work too. If he wanted to, he could be home on time.'
- *Rational response*   'His job is different. Many of his customers come in after work.'

Daily recording of rational responses

When ready, clients can be encouraged to fill out the rational response and outcome columns on their *Daily Record of Automatic Thoughts* log. In the outcome column, clients:

- re-rate their beliefs in their automatic thought(s) on a 0–100% scale, and
- specify what their subsequent emotions are and rate them on a 0–100% scale.

Imagery techniques

Numerous imagery techniques are discussed by Beck and Emery (1985). Among these techniques are assisting clients to gain more realistic perspectives through repeated visualizations of fantasies, through projecting themselves into the future and looking back on their present situations, and by getting them to exaggerate images, for instance of harming others.

Identifying and modifying underlying beliefs

Underlying beliefs may be harder for therapists and clients to access than automatic thoughts. Often they fall into one of three main belief clusters centring on issues of:

- acceptance – for instance, 'I'm flawed and therefore unacceptable';
- competence – for instance, 'I'm inferior'; and
- control – for instance, 'I have no control.'

Underlying beliefs are signposted by the themes in clients' automatic thoughts. Clients' behaviour, coping strategies and personal histories are additional sources for therapists to form belief hypotheses. Most clients find it difficult to articulate their beliefs without assistance. Generally, therapists present hypotheses to clients for verification. Where clients disagree, therapists can work with them to form more accurate statements of their beliefs.

Following are some cognitive interventions for modifying beliefs.

Socratic questioning
Therapists can use questions that encourage clients to examine their beliefs: for instance 'Does the belief seem reasonable?', 'Can you review the evidence for it?', and 'What are the advantages and disadvantages of maintaining the belief?'

Hypothesis testing
Together therapists and clients can set up experiments that encourage clients to test the reality of their beliefs. Box 13.6 provides an example of such an experiment (Beck, 1988, p. 224)

BOX 13.6

Example of hypothesis testing concerning a belief

The client
Marjorie, who was afraid to make a mental commitment to her spouse, Ken, because she was afraid she might find out that she could not trust him.

Marjorie's underlying belief
'I must never allow myself to be vulnerable.'

Consequence of Marjorie's distorted thinking
Her aloof behaviour and fault-finding created distance in their relationship.

The experiment
Beck and Marjorie set up a three-month experiment for her to test the hypothesis: 'If I totally commit myself to the relationship, look for the positive instead of the negative, I will feel more secure.' During the experiment, Marjorie was to change how she thought and acted.

Result of the experiment
Marjorie discovered that she was more secure and had fewer thoughts about leaving Ken.

Using imagery
Imagery can be used to assist clients to 'relive' past traumatic events and so restructure their experiences and the beliefs derived from them.

Reliving childhood memories
Beck (Beck *et al.*, 1990) considers that with chronic personality disorders it is crucial to use childhood material to assist clients in reviewing and loosening their underlying beliefs. By re-creating 'pathogenic' developmental situations through role-playing and role reversal, clients have an opportunity to restructure or modify beliefs formed during this period.

Refashioning beliefs

Therapists can assist clients to refashion their beliefs. Beck gives the example of M.K., a director of a research institute at a major university, who suffered from a major depressive disorder and generalized anxiety disorder. The client had strong beliefs of inadequacy and rejection which he crystallized as 'I must be *the best* at everything I do.' One of M.K.'s beliefs was refashioned thus: 'It is rewarding to succeed highly, but lesser success is rewarding also and has no bearing on my adequacy or inadequacy. I am adequate no matter what' (Beck and Rush, in press, p. 48).

Behavioural interventions

Behavioural interventions have many purposes in cognitive therapy. First, behavioural interventions can lay the foundation for later cognitive work. An issue arises whether to focus on behaviour first, cognition first, or both concurrently. Behavioural interventions may sometimes be used before cognitive interventions to promote symptom relief and enhance motivation. For instance, severely depressed clients may be encouraged to perform small tasks to counteract their withdrawal, get them involved in constructive activities, and open their minds to the possibility of gaining satisfaction from previously pleasurable activities. However, in contrast to normal people, depressed clients can change their behaviour markedly, but do not necessarily change their negative hyper-valent cognitions (Beck *et al.*, 1979). In working with couples, Beck (1988) concentrates on changing behaviour first since he regards it as easier to change actions than thinking patterns. Also, spouses may immediately reward each other's changes in behaviour.

Second, behavioural interventions can be used to assist clients in reality-testing their automatic thoughts and beliefs. A third use of behavioural interventions is, along with cognitive interventions, to assist clients to engage in feared activities. A fourth use is to train clients in specific behavioural skills. Since the uses of behavioural interventions overlap, below they are not categorized according to purpose.

Following are some of the main behavioural interventions used by cognitive therapists.

Activity scheduling

Activity scheduling is a form of timetabling. Planning specific activities with clients can be important in helping clients to realize that they can control their time. A principle of activity scheduling is to state what activity the client agrees to engage in rather than how much they will accomplish. Clients can set aside time each evening to plan their activities for the next day.

Rating mastery and pleasure

Using 0–10 scales, clients can rate the degree of mastery and the degree of pleasure they experienced in each activity during the day. Mastery and pleasure ratings can give depressed clients an insight into the activities that reduce their dysphoria.

Hypothesis testing

Hypothesis testing has both behavioural and cognitive components (Beck and Weishaar, 2000). Especially later in therapy, behavioural experiments may be designed to provide information that may contradict existing automatic thoughts, faulty predictions and underlying beliefs. A young man about to cancel a date because of the fear 'I won't know what to say' was encouraged to go on the date and treat not knowing what to say as an experimental hypothesis. The findings of this particular experiment disproved his hypothesis (Beck and Emery, 1985). In the earlier example Marjorie was engaging in a behavioural as well as a cognitive experiment to test her underlying belief 'I must never allow myself to be vulnerable.'

Rehearsing behaviour and role-playing

Behaviour rehearsal can be used to develop clients' skills for specific social and stressful situations. Demonstration and video feedback can be used as part of skills training. Behaviour rehearsals should have a number of trials and rehearse clients in a variety of responses. Also, clients can rehearse situations by using their imaginations.

Assigning graded tasks

Often clients fail at tasks because they try to do too much too soon. Therapists and clients can develop hierarchies of feared or difficult situations. Then clients can perform less threatening before moving on to more threatening activities.

Using diversion techniques

Clients may be encouraged to engage in activities that divert them from their strong negative emotions and thinking. Such activities include work, play, socializing and doing something physical.

Assigning homework

Homework forms an important part of cognitive therapy. Its purpose is both to shorten the time spent in therapy as well as facilitate the development of cognitive and behavioural skills for use after counselling. Homework assignments include self-monitoring, activities designed to reality-test automatic thoughts and underlying beliefs, implementing procedures for dealing with specific situations, and activities for developing cognitive skills such as identifying cognitive distortions, rational responding and refashioning beliefs.

CASE MATERIAL

Beck, collaborating with Rush and other colleagues (1979, pp. 225–43), presents an initial interview with a depressed 40-year-old female clinical psychologist client who had recently been left by her boyfriend. The interview transcript is broken down into five parts: questioning to elicit vital information, broadening the client's perspective, 'alternative therapy', obtaining more-accurate data, and closure. Beck and Young (1985, pp. 206–44) illustrate in the case example of a depressed young female client how cognitive therapists elicit and challenge maladaptive thoughts and assumptions throughout treatment. Beck and Weishaar (2000) illustrate in the case example of a 21-year-old highly anxious male college student both behavioural and cognitive interventions for attaining therapeutic goals. Throughout his book *Love is Never Enough*, Beck (1988) provides numerous vignettes of the use of cognitive interventions in relationship therapy.

Other sources of case material include: Scott, Williams and Beck's edited *Cognitive Therapy in Clinical Practice: An Illustrative Casebook* (1989); Freeman and Dattillio's edited *Comprehensive Casebook of Cognitive Therapy* (1992); Greenberger and Padesky's *Mind Over Mood* (1995); and Judith Beck's *Cognitive Therapy: Basics and Beyond* (1995), which uses a single case throughout to illustrate how to employ various cognitive therapy interventions.

FURTHER DEVELOPMENTS

Cognitive therapy has been used with all ages, from children to the elderly. Beck reports that several controlled studies have shown it to be at least as effective as antidepressant medication in treating elderly depressed clients. Cognitive therapy has been used for group work with families. Some newer applications of cognitive therapy include working with clients with schizophrenia, post-traumatic stress disorders, substance abuse problems, hypertension and dissociative disorders as well as with clients who have committed sexual offences, such as exhibitionism and incest. Schema-focused approaches to personality disorders have been an important development in cognitive therapy.

There are over ten training centres for cognitive therapy in the United States, including the Beck Institute for Cognitive Therapy and Research, directed by Beck's daughter, Dr Judith Beck. In addition, training in cognitive therapy is widely available elsewhere, including Britain and Australia. With the current emphasis on containing costs through managed care, cognitive therapy's short-term approach will be increasingly popular with both third-party payers and clients (Beck and Weishaar, 2000).

SUMMARY

- *Beck's cognitive therapy views clients as faulty processors of information. Humans have the capacity for primal and higher level cognitive processes. As well as voluntary thoughts, thinking consists of schemas and automatic thoughts.*
- *Schemas are relatively stable cognitive patterns that influence through people's beliefs how they select and synthesize incoming information. When activated, dysfunctional schemas and beliefs can lead people to systematically bias information. Modes are networks of cognitive, affective, motivational and behavioural schemas.*
- *Automatic thoughts, which occur very rapidly and at the fringe of awareness, are not so deeply buried as schemas and reflect schema content. Dysfunctional beliefs can lead to systematic cognitive distortions.*
- *Evolutionary and genetic causes contribute to how people think and behave. Humans acquire cognitive vulnerability through childhood traumas, negative treatment in childhood, social learning, and inadequate experiences for learning coping skills. Cognitive vulnerability can be activated by perceived losses, increased demands and stress.*

- *Factors maintaining psychological distress include failure to turn off hypervalent modes, inability to reality-test dysfunctional interpretations, and resistances to change. Beck's cognitive models of depression, anxiety disorders, distressed couple relationships, and personality disorders are overviewed.*
- *The main goal of cognitive therapy is to re-energize the client's reality-testing system. Cognitive therapy teaches clients how to evaluate and modify their thinking. In addition, therapy focuses on symptom relief and on helping clients to develop adaptive behaviours.*
- *Cognitive therapy tends to be highly structured and short-term. The process of therapy starts with defining problems and case conceptualization. While the early stages of therapy may focus on symptom relief, middle and later stages of therapy focus on using cognitive and behavioural interventions to change clients' patterns of thinking.*
- *Therapists provide clients with good human relationships. In addition, they collaborate with clients to investigate problems and act as guides in helping them to reality-test possible errors in logic.*
- *Cognitive interventions focus on eliciting and identifying automatic thoughts, reality-testing and correcting automatic thoughts, identifying underlying beliefs, and modifying underlying beliefs. Socratic questioning is a central activity of the cognitive therapist.*
- *Behavioural interventions may be used to support both cognitive and behavioural change. Behavioural interventions include activity scheduling, conducting experiments to test thinking, and rehearsing behaviour and role-playing.*
- *Training in cognitive therapy is available in many countries. Especially in an era emphasizing short-term managed care, cognitive therapy has wide applicability.*

REVIEW AND PERSONAL QUESTIONS

REVIEW QUESTIONS

1. What are schemas and modes, and why are they important?
2. What are automatic thoughts, and why are they important?
3. What are cognitive distortions, and why are they important?
4. What are Beck's views on the following causes of cognitions and behaviour:
   - evolutionary causes; and
   - genetic causes?
5. What is the nature and role of each of the following factors in helping people acquire cognitive vulnerability: childhood traumas, negative treatment in childhood, social learning, and inadequate experiences for learning coping skills?
6. What are some factors relevant to activating cognitive vulnerability?
7. What is the nature and role of each of the following factors in helping people maintain cognitive vulnerability: failure to turn off hypervalent modes, inability to reality-test dysfunctional interpretations, and resistances to change?
8. Critically discuss the goals of cognitive therapy.
9. Describe the nature of the therapist–client relationship in cognitive therapy.
10. Describe the process of cognitive therapy.

11. What are some of the main cognitive interventions used in cognitive therapy for:
    * eliciting and identifying automatic thoughts;
    * reality-testing and correcting automatic thoughts; and
    * identifying and modifying underlying beliefs?
12. What are some of the main behavioural interventions used in cognitive therapy?

PERSONAL QUESTIONS

1. List any significant factors when you were growing up that may have contributed to your acquiring faulty ways of processing information.
2. Think of a specific problem in your life. Elicit and identify some of your automatic thoughts regarding it.
3. Identify characteristic cognitive distortions, if any, in the way you process information.
4. Identify an automatic thought in a problem area and challenge it by means of Socratic questioning.
5. In a problem area, identify a thought that lends itself to being reality-tested through changing your behaviour. Design and implement a behavioural experiment to reality-test your thought.
6. What relevance, if any, has the theory and practice of cognitive therapy for how you conduct therapy?
7. What relevance, if any, has the theory and practice of cognitive therapy for how your live?

ANNOTATED BIBLIOGRAPHY

Beck, A. T., Rush, A. J., Shaw, B. F. and Emery, G. (1979). *Cognitive Therapy of Depression*. New York: John Wiley.
    This book presents Beck's cognitive model of depression. The bulk of the book is a clinical handbook devoted to practical aspects of treating depressed clients, for instance the therapeutic relationship, the application of both cognitive and behavioural interventions, and problems related to termination and relapse.

Beck, A. T. and Emery, G. (1985). *Anxiety Disorders and Phobias: A Cognitive Perspective*. New York: Basic Books.
    Part 1 of the book, written by Beck, is entitled 'Theoretical and clinical aspects' and presents his cognitive model of anxiety. Part 2 of the book, written by Emery, is entitled 'Cognitive therapy: Techniques and applications' and has chapters on the principles of cognitive therapy, techniques for cognitive restructuring, modifying imagery, affect, and behaviour, and on restructuring assumptions.

Beck, A. T. (1988). *Love is Never Enough: How Couples Can Overcome Misunderstandings, Resolve Conflicts, and Solve Relationship Problems Through Cognitive Therapy*. New York: Harper and Row.
    This book describes the power of negative and biased thinking in couple relationships. Beck shows how partners can improve their relationship by identifying and modifying their maladaptive automatic thoughts and underlying beliefs.

Beck, A. T., Freeman, A. and Associates (1990). *Cognitive Therapy of Personality Disorders*. New York: The Guilford Press.

> Part 1 of this book, written by Beck and Freeman, presents Beck's cognitive model of personality disorders as well as the history of and research on cognitive therapy for personality disorders. Part 2 of the book, written by a series of associates, focuses on clinical applications of cognitive therapy for each of the personality disorders.

Beck, A. T. and Weishaar, M. E. (2000). Cognitive therapy. In R. J. Corsini and D. Wedding (eds). *Current Psychotherapies* (6th edition). Itasca, IL: Peacock, 241–72.

> An authoritative chapter reviewing the theory and practice of contemporary cognitive therapy.

Beck, J. S. (1995). *Cognitive Therapy: Basics and Beyond*. New York: Guilford Press.

> Beck's daughter Judith wrote this manual for cognitive therapy. Starting with case conceptualization, she shows the reader how to identify and work with deeper level cognitions, prepare for termination, and anticipate problems.

Padesky, C. A. and Greenberger, D. (1995). *Clinician's Guide to Mind Over Mood*; and Greenberger, D. and Padesky, C. A. (1995) *Mind Over Mood: Change How You Feel by Changing The Way You Think*. New York: Guilford Press.

> These companion volumes are designed as step-by-step guides to the techniques and strategies of cognitive therapy. The manual is designed as a self-help workbook, and the clinician's guide provides therapists with instructions on how to incorporate the workbook into individual and group psychotherapy.

Weishaar, M. E. (1993). *Aaron T. Beck*. London: Sage Publications.

> Weishaar has been both a student and collaborator of Beck's, so she writes with authority. The five chapters in the book cover: Beck's life, his theoretical contributions, his practical contributions, some criticisms and rebuttals, and Beck's overall influence.

REFERENCES AND FURTHER READING

Alford, B. A. and Beck, A. T. (1997). *The Integrative Power of Cognitive Therapy*. New York: Guildford Press.

Beck, A. T. (1963). Thinking and depression. 1. Idiosyncratic content and cognitive distortions. *Archives of General Psychiatry, 9*, 324–33.

Beck, A. T. (1964). Thinking and depression. 2. Theory and therapy. *Archives of General Psychiatry, 10*, 561–71.

Beck, A. T. (1976). *Cognitive Therapy and the Emotional Disorders*. New York: New American Library.

Beck, A. T. (1978). *Anxiety Checklist*. Philadelphia, PA: Center for Cognitive Therapy.

Beck, A. T. (1988). *Love is Never Enough: How Couples Can Overcome Misunderstandings, Resolve Conflicts, and Solve Relationship Problems Through Cognitive Therapy*. New York: Harper and Row.

Beck, A. T. (1991). Cognitive therapy: A 30-year retrospective. *American Psychologist, 46*, 368–75.

Beck. A. T. (1999). *Prisoners of Hate: The Cognitive Basis of Anger, Hostility and Violence*. New

York: HarperCollins.

Beck, A. T. and Emery, G. (1985). *Anxiety Disorders and Phobias: A Cognitive Perspective.* New York: Basic Books.

Beck, A. T. and Rush, A. J. (in press). Cognitive therapy. In H. I. Kaplan and B. J. Sadock (eds). *Comprehensive Textbook of Psychiatry*, Vol VI. Baltimore, MD: Williams and Williams.

Beck, A. T. and Weishaar, M. E. (2000). Cognitive therapy. In R. J. Corsini and D. Wedding (eds). *Current Psychotherapies* (6th edition). Itasca, IL: Peacock, 241–72.

Beck. A. T. and Young, J. E. (1985). Cognitive therapy of depression. In D. Barlow (ed.). *Clinical Handbook of Psychological Disorders: A Step-by-Step Treatment Manual* (206–44). New York: Guildford Press.

Beck, A. T., Freeman, A. and Associates (1990). *Cognitive Therapy of Personality Disorders.* New York: The Guilford Press.

Beck, A. T., Kovacs, M. and Weissman, A. (1979). Assessment of suicide intention: The scale for suicide ideation. *Journal of Consulting and Clinical Psychology, 47,* 343–52.

Beck, A. T., Rush, A. J., Shaw, B. F. and Emery, G. (1979). *Cognitive Therapy of Depression.* New York: John Wiley.

Beck, A. T., Ward, C. H., Mendelson, M., Mock, J. E. and Erbaugh, J. K. (1961). An inventory for measuring depression. *Archives of General Psychiatry, 4,* 561–71.

Beck, J. S. (1995). *Cognitive Therapy: Basics and Beyond.* New York: Guilford Press.

Clark, D. M. and Beck, A. T. (1988). Cognitive approaches. In C. G. Last and M. Hersen (eds). *Handbook of Anxiety Disorders* (362–85). New York: Pergamon.

Clark, D. M., Beck, A. T. and Alford, B. A. (1999). *Scientific Foundations of Cognitive Theory and Therapy of Depression.* Philadelphia: John Wiley.

Freeman, A. and Dattillio, F. M. (eds). (1992). *Comprehensive Casebook of Cognitive Therapy.* New York: Plenum Press.

Greenberger, D. and Padesky, C. A. (1995). *Mind Over Mood: Change How You Feel by Changing The Way You Think.* New York: Guilford Press.

Kelly, G. (1955). *The Psychology of Personal Constructs.* New York: Norton.

Kendall, P. C., Hollon, S. T., Beck, A. T., Hammen, C. L. and Ingram, R. E. (1987). Issues and recommendations regarding use of the Beck Depression Inventory. *Cognitive Therapy and Research, 11,* 289–99.

Lazarus, R. S. (1966). *Psychological Stress and the Coping Process.* New York: McGraw-Hill.

Padesky, C. A. and Greenberger, D. (1995). *Clinician's Guide to Mind Over Mood.* New York: Guilford Press.

Scott, J., Williams, J. M. G. and Beck, A. T. (eds) (1989). *Cognitive Therapy in Clinical Practice: An Illustrative Casebook.* London: Routledge.

Weishaar, M. E. (1993). *Aaron T. Beck.* London: Sage Publications.

Weissman, A. (1979). *The Dysfunctional Attitudes Scale.* Philadelphia, PA: Center for Cognitive Therapy.

Beck on audio-cassette and videotape

Beck, A. T. (1977). *Demonstration of the Cognitive Therapy of Depression: Interview#1 (Patient with a Family Problem).* Audio and video available.

Beck, A. T. (1979). *Cognitive Therapy of Depression: Interview#1 (Patient with a Hopelessness Problem).* Audio and video available.

Beck, A. T. (1985). *Cognitive Therapy of Anxiety and Panic Disorders: First Interview Techniques.* Audio and video available.

Beck, A. T. (1990). *Cognitive Therapy of an Avoidant Personality.* Two audio-cassette set.

All the above are available from:

The Beck Institute, GSB Building, City Line and Belmont Avenues, Suite 700, Bala Cynwyd, PA 19004-1610, USA. Phone: 610.664.3020. Fax: 610.664.4437. e-mail: beckinst@gim.net Website: www.beckinstitute.org

14

Multimodal Therapy

Multimodal therapy is a comprehensive, systematic, and holistic approach to psychotherapy that seeks to effect durable change in an efficient and humane way.
Arnold A. Lazarus

INTRODUCTION

Multimodal therapy is an approach developed by Arnold A. Lazarus, a clinical psychologist, in response to the constraints of traditional behaviour therapy. Lazarus's first book on multimodal therapy was entitled *Multimodal Behavior Therapy* (Lazarus, 1976). However, he considered including the word 'behavior' in the title to be misleading, since it did not take into account working with other modalities, such as cognition and imagery. Consequently, he shortened the name to multimodal therapy.

Lazarus (2000) observes that the multimodal orientation transcends the behavioural tradition by adding unique assessment procedures and by dealing in great depth and detail with sensory, imagery, cognitive, and interpersonal factors and their interactive effects. Clients' needs are often better served if therapists work in multimodal rather than unimodal or bimodal fashions. Multimodal therapy rests heavily on multimodal assessment to choose the most appropriate techniques for particular clients with their unique psychological profiles and circumstances. Lazarus observes about the term 'multimodal therapy', 'It might have been better to call it "multimodal assessment and comprehensive psychotherapy" or something like that' (Dryden, 1991, p. 107).

ARNOLD A. LAZARUS (1932–)

On 27 January 1932, Arnold Lazarus was born in Johannesburg, South Africa, the youngest of four children. His father ran a small retail business. At the time of his birth, his two sisters were 14 and 17 and his bother was 8. Lazarus grew up feeling that as the youngest family member 'I was typically ignored and my opinion was considered unimportant' (Dryden, 1991, p. 101). This contributed to his feeling shy, inadequate and hypersensitive. Lazarus was a 'skinny kid who was bullied a lot' (Dryden, 1991, p. 1) and, consequently, spent much time on body-building activities. He exhibited an early interest in writing and, in his teens, had some stories published in local newspapers. Another youthful writing assignment was that of associate editor of a South African body-building magazine. When Lazarus was growing up, broadening experiences included attending several high schools, spending time on a farm, working in a department store, and selling houses.

Lazarus started university with a view to becoming a journalist and writer. However, on discovering that he could be a psychotherapist without going through a formal medical education, he became seriously interested in psychology and psychotherapy. In 1955 Lazarus received a BA with psychology and sociology majors, in 1956 a BA honours in psychology, in 1957 an MA in experimental psychology, and in 1960 a PhD in clinical psychology, all degrees conferred by the University of the Witwatersrand in Johannesburg. His PhD research on 'New group techniques in the treatment of phobic conditions' used group systematic desensitization. Joseph Wolpe was chairman of his dissertation committee.

Lazarus's occupational history started with a part-time psychologist position in 1958–59 with the Mental Health Society in Johannesburg. From 1959 to 1963 and then from 1964 to 1966 he was in private practice as well as being a part-time lecturer at Witwatersrand Medical School. Albert Bandura, on the basis of seeing a write-up of Lazarus' PhD findings in the *Journal of Abnormal and Social Psychology* (Lazarus, 1961), invited him to Stanford University where, from 1963 to 1964, he was a Visiting Assistant Professor in the Psychology Department. Uneasy with apartheid and the South African political situation, in 1966 Lazarus and his family returned to the United States, where in 1976 he became a naturalized American citizen.

From 1966 to 1967, Lazarus directed the Behavior Therapy Institute in Sausalito, California. From 1967 to 1970 he was a Professor of Psychology in the Department of Behavioral Science in Temple University Medical School, Philadelphia. Joseph Wolpe, his former supervisor, was also at Temple University, but he and Lazarus had an acrimonious falling out when Wolpe perceived Lazarus's views on the broadening of behaviour therapy to include cognition and 'technical eclecticism' as heretical and threatening to what he was propounding. From 1970 to 1972, Lazarus was Visiting Professor and Director of Clinical Training in Yale University's Department of Psychology. In 1972 he moved to Rutgers University in New Jersey, being from 1972 to 1974 a Professor in and Chairman of the Psychology Department, and from 1974 onwards a Distinguished Professor in the Graduate School of Applied and Professional Psychology.

Lazarus has held numerous consultant positions and editorial board appointments. His professional awards include: in 1982, the American Board of Professional Psychology's Distinguished Service to the Profession of Psychology Award; in 1992, the American Psychological Association's Division of Psychotherapy's Distinguished Psychologist Award; in 1996, he was the first recipient of the prestigious Annual Cummings PSYCHE Award for his innovative contributions to time-effective psychotherapy; and in 1999 he received two lifetime achievement awards, one from the California Psychological Association and the other from the Association for Advancement of Behavior Therapy.

Lazarus's early interest in writing has continued unabated. He has published numerous journal articles and book chapters. His books include *Behavior Therapy Techniques* (with Joseph Wolpe), *Behavior Therapy and Beyond*, *Clinical Behavior Therapy* (as editor and contributor), *Multimodal Behavior Therapy* (with eleven contributors), *In the*

Mind's Eye: The Power of Imagery for Personal Enrichment, Marital Myths, Don't Believe It For a Minute! (with Clifford Lazarus and Allen Fay), *The 60-Second Shrink: 101 Strategies for Staying Sane in a Crazy World* (with Clifford Lazarus), *The Practice of Multimodal Therapy* and *Brief but Comprehensive Psychotherapy: The Multimodal Way.*

Lazarus values his humanity and works in order to live. In 1956, he married Daphne, and in 1959 their daughter Linda was born, followed in 1961 by their son Clifford. His priorities are: first, wife and family; second, meaningful friendships and the pursuit of fun (plays, music, tennis, etc.); and third, work. By work, he means intellectual stimulation, making a social contribution and surviving economically. Given another life he has a fantasy that he would like to direct and create movies like Steven Spielberg. The question Lazarus always asks when someone dies is, 'Did this person have enough fun on this earth?' (Dryden, 1991, p. 14). If not, he feels they may have had wasted lives.

Regarding his professional work, Lazarus mentions three contributions: first, showing that behaviour therapy can be more humanistic; second, in Ellis's footsteps, broadening behaviour therapy's horizons to include cognitions; and third, developing 'an even broader and more systematic framework in my writings on multimodal methods' (Dryden, 1991, p. 112). Lazarus's son Clifford is a clinical psychologist and his proud father derives 'infinitely more pleasure from helping his ideas grow than from reiterating my own' (Dryden, 1991, p. 113).

THEORY

The importance of breadth without sacrificing depth became a primary focus and culminated in the multimodal orientation.

Arnold A. Lazarus

BASIC CONCEPTS

Technical eclecticism

Eclecticism is not a unitary construct (Lazarus, 1989a). Instead there are many different kinds of eclecticism. Lazarus distinguishes unsystematic eclecticism, where therapists require neither a coherent rationale nor empirical validation for the techniques they use, and systematic (technical) eclecticism, where therapists are guided by a preferred theory but also draw techniques from other orientations.

Lazarus also distinguishes theoretical eclecticism from technical eclecticism. Unlike their theoretically eclectic counterparts, technically eclectic therapists use procedures from different sources without necessarily subscribing to the theories or disciplines that spawned them (Lazarus, 2000). Systematic technical eclectics neither choose techniques that 'feel right' nor hop from theory to theory. Lazarus writes: 'The hallmark of technical eclecticism is the use of prescriptive treatments based on empirical evidence and client need, rather than theoretical and personal predisposition' (Lazarus, 1989a, p. 252). Technical eclectics mainly use cognitive–behavioural ideas and techniques. In addition, they may draw from Adlerian, Rogerian, Eriksonian, psychodrama, gestalt, reality and trans-actional analysis schools, but without embracing any of these diverse theories. They regard as excess baggage the needless addition or multiplication of explanatory princi-ples.

An important distinction exists between observations and theories. Theories are essen-tially speculations trying to account for various phenomena. Observations reflect clinical data without trying to offer explanations. Lazarus gives the example of 'Adolescents tend to imitate the behavior of peers whom they respect' as a statement based on observation and 'They do so unconsciously due to inadequate parental introjects' as a statement based on theory (Lazarus and Messer, 1991). Though acknowledging that clinical practice cannot be totally atheoretical, his technically eclectic therapy is governed by many observations (not theories) from different sources.

Unlike technical eclecticism, theoretical integration attempts to synthesize different therapy techniques as well as the theories underlying change from different orientations. Lazarus sees technical eclecticism as a step towards eventual integrationism. However, he urges caution in proceeding with integrationism. There is the danger of superficially merging theoretical tenets that are intrinsically incompatible (Lazarus, Beutler and Norcross, 1992; Lazarus, 1997). Furthermore, therapists can become more intent on attaching theoretical labels to what they do than on precisely stating both what they do with each client and how they select what they do.

Thresholds

Physiologically, people react to a variety of arousing stimuli with differing and distinctive patterns of autonomic nervous system activity. Lazarus (1997, 2000) uses the term 'threshold' to describe people's differing capacities to tolerate negative stimuli such as pain, frustration, stress, cold, noise and pollution. People whose autonomic nervous systems are stable, which usually indicates high thresholds to many events, have a differ-ent personality pattern and are likely to be less anxiety-prone than those whose autonomic reactions are labile, which usually correlates with low thresholds.

Thresholds, with their large innate component, can limit the effectiveness of psycho-logical interventions. Lazarus gives the example of the limitations of hypnosis and other psychological techniques on a person with extremely low pain tolerance. While their pain tolerance may be raised, their innate threshold to overreact to pain stimuli neverthe-less remains.

The seven modalities: BASIC I.D.

The concept of modalities is the bedrock of comprehensive multimodal assessment and treatment. Human personality can be divided into seven discrete, yet interacting, modal-ities or dimensions. Lazarus writes: 'These modalities exist in a state of reciprocal transaction and flux, connected by complex chains of behavior and other psychophysio-logical processes' (Lazarus, 1992, p. 236). Box 14.1 presents the seven modalities, each illustrated by its description in the Structural Profile, a multimodal self-assessment ques-tionnaire (Lazarus, 1997, p. 141). The acronym BASIC I.D. is formed by using the first letter of each modality. This provides a useful shorthand descriptor of the seven modalities. In addition, the acronym serves as a memory aid.

BOX 14.1

The seven BASIC I.D. modalities

1. *Behaviour.* 'Some people may be described as "doers" – they are action-oriented, they like to busy themselves, get things done, take on various projects. How much of a doer are you?'

2. *Affect.* 'Some people are very emotional and may or may not express it. How emotional are you? How deeply do you feel things? How passionate are you?'

3. *Sensation.* 'Some people attach a lot of value to sensory experiences, such as sex, food, music, art and other "sensory delights". Others are very much aware of minor aches, pains, and discomforts. How "tuned in to" your sensations are you?'

4. *Imagery.* 'How much fantasy or daydreaming do you engage in? This is separate from thinking or planning. This is "thinking in pictures", visualizing real or imagined experiences, letting your mind roam. How much are you into imagery?'

5. *Cognition.* 'Some people are very analytical and like to plan things. They like to reason things through. How much of a "thinker" and "planner" are you?'

6. *Interpersonal.* 'How important are other people to you? This is your self-rating as a social being. How important are close friendships to you, the tendency to gravitate toward people, the desire for intimacy? The opposite of this is being a "loner".'

7. *Drugs/biology.* 'Are you healthy and health-conscious? Do you avoid bad habits like smoking, too much alcohol, drinking a lot of coffee, overeating etc.? Do you exercise regularly, get enough sleep, avoid junk foods, and generally take care of your body?'

Lazarus acknowledges that people's behaviour is specific to situations, other people, and when it occurs. Nevertheless, people have tendencies, usually evident in the first decade of their lives, to favour some BASIC I.D. modalities over others. People's BASIC I.D. tendencies determine the tone and quality of how they function. For instance, to call someone an 'imagery reactor' means that their most highly valued and predominant modality is visual. Though they may not do so all the time, they are inclined to respond to and organize the world in terms of mental images. On the other hand, 'cognitive reactors' respond to the world from their intellects. In terms of brain research, the right hemisphere is probably dominant for imagery reactors and the left hemisphere for cognitive reactors. Sensory reactors may be subdivided according to the predominance of each of the five basic senses. Lazarus observes: 'To "know" or to "understand" another person is to have full access to his or her BASIC I.D. Self-knowledge implies an awareness of the content of one's own BASIC I.D. as well as insight into the interactive effects therein' (Lazarus, 1989b, pp. 16–17).

Thresholds and preferred modalities interact. For example, the person with low pain tolerance, high frustration tolerance, high activity, and vivid imagery is very different from a person with low frustration tolerance, moderate activity, highly analytical (cognition), and capable of only forming fleeting images (Lazarus, 2000).

ACQUISITION

Lazarus has never developed a full theoretical statement of his own regarding how people acquire and maintain their BASIC I.D. modalities and their personality strengths and weaknesses. Instead he prefers to be more of an empiricist and leave the theorizing to others. Nevertheless, he endeavours to understand other theorists' frameworks and principles to see which are the best scientifically proven ideas upon which he can draw. Lazarus has studiously avoided theoretical integration and stresses that multimodal therapy is not a conglomeration of psychoanalysis, behaviour therapy and many other systems (Lazarus, 2000).

People's personalities stem from their genetic endowment, physical environment and social learning history. Multimodal therapy is not atheoretical: instead its technically eclectic stance operates within a consistent *social cognitive learning theory* (Bandura, 1986). However, when dealing with dyadic and family, and other complex interactions, Lazarus adds explanatory concepts from communication and systems theory (Kwee and Lazarus, 1986).

Seven key constructs shape and maintain human personality:

1. associations and relations among events;
2. modelling and imitation;
3. non-conscious processes;
4. defensive reactions;
5. private events;
6. metacommunication; and
7. thresholds. (Lazarus 1992, 1997)

1. Associations and relations among events

Association, in the form of events occurring simultaneously or in close succession, is important in all learning processes. Much human behaviour is the result of classical and operant conditioning. For instance, many aversions appear to originate from *classical conditioning*. Lazarus (2000) provides the example of the client who had experienced post-operative nausea a few years previously and been in a hospital bed next to a man who kept playing a cassette of Beethoven's *Moonlight Sonata*. Later the client became sick to his stomach any time he heard that music.

Operant conditioning, where the probability of behaviour recurring is mediated by its consequences, is another major social learning process. For instance, a depressed woman can reinforce her depression by locking herself up in her bedroom and avoiding rewarding social contacts (Kwee and Lazarus, 1986). Another example is that of a woman who states 'I now realize that my headaches were in large part due to the fact that the only time my husband showed me any real caring was when I was in pain' (Lazarus, 2000).

2. Modelling and imitation

Modelling and vicarious processes are also important in learning. People learn from observing and imitating what others do. Furthermore, they learn from perceiving the positive and negative consequences of others' behaviour.

3. Non-conscious processes

Much learning is neither conscious nor deliberate. Non-conscious processes are not to be confused with the Freudian notion of the unconscious. What Lazarus means by non-conscious processes is that 'people have different levels and degrees of awareness, and that unrecognized – subliminal – stimuli can influence one's thoughts, feelings, and behaviors . . .' (Lazarus, 1992, p. 235). Frequent demonstrations have illustrated that, during altered states of consciousness, people have access to memories and skills that are unavailable to conscious recall.

4. Defensive reactions

Through their social learning experiences people may acquire a variety of unnecessary defensive reactions. Defensive reactions are avoidance responses attenuating pain, discomfort, anxiety depression and guilt (Lazarus, 1997). Such reactions entail people lessening their awareness, denying or distorting their perceptions and mislabelling their feelings. Included among defensive reactions are: denial; overintellectualization and rationalization; projection, wrongly attributing one's feelings to others; and displacement, for instance of aggression on to other people, animals or things.

5. Private events

People filter and can override their conditioning and modelling because of their intervening thoughts about these stimuli. They do not respond to the real environment, but to their *perceived* environment. Factors influencing their perceptions include: idiosyncratic use of language, selective attention, problem-solving competences, goals, performance standards, attributions, self-efficacy, expectancies, and values, attitudes and beliefs. Such thoughts determine which stimuli are noticed, how they are perceived and valued, and how long they are remembered.

Misinformation and missing information are two of the major means through which people's private thoughts lead to emotional problems and disorders (Dryden, 1991). With *misinformation*, people have learned incorrect assumptions and beliefs about life and living. One area of misinformation encompasses the perfectionist beliefs held in Western society, for instance that lifelong happiness results from fame and fortune. Other areas of misinformation include: the inability of people to realize that their lives are mainly controlled by their own thoughts and perceptions rather than by external events; the belief that it is good to ventilate anger; the belief in the importance of pleasing others; and the idea that it is better to play safe by leading a life where there are no risks. Marital misinformation includes the myths that 'Romantic love makes a good marriage' and 'If you feel guilty, confess' (Lazarus, 1985a).

With misinformation, people have acquired erroneous ideas. With *missing information*, people do not possess the information to enact basic skills required for successful living. Social skills provide an important area of missing information about such matters as eye contact and how to converse. In addition, many people lack information on how to handle job interviews and present themselves favourably.

Lazarus regards as terrifying the amount of ignorance pervading the world. Even events such as international terrorism and drug smuggling can be 'tied into extreme misinformation and missing information that people have about the sort of values and skills that could make for a happier world' (Dryden, 1991, p. 15).

6. Metacommunication

Humans can both communicate and communicate about their communications, otherwise known as metacommunication. People can step back and examine the content and processes of their own relationships and patterns of communication. For example in couples therapy partners can either skilfully or unskilfully explore and discuss the processes of their relationship, including identifying unhelpful communication patterns. The ability to metacommunicate characterizes all high quality relationships between friends, relatives and lovers.

7. Thresholds

For a review of Lazarus's ideas on thresholds, the reader is referred back to the relevant section on page 364.

MAINTENANCE

People's personalities are not only acquired but also maintained through the interaction of genetic endowment, social learning and environmental influences. For example, people's genetic endowment persists in the form of different thresholds and favoured BASIC I.D. modalities. Social learning influences the maintenance of personality in a number of ways. People learn maladaptive habits or conditioned emotional reactions 'through various associations and unfortunate connections of events' (Dryden, 1991, p. 9). Such habits may be simple or complex and persist in interfering with their happiness. In addition, through conditioning and modelling, they learn not only behaviours, but perceptions of self-efficacy, performance standards and goals that they maintain for good or ill. In addition, people's environments can continue to offer reinforcements and models that contribute to maintaining their thoughts, feelings and behaviours.

Non-conscious processes influence maintenance of personality. People may remain unaware of what they have learned and keep learning from others. Consequently, such thoughts, feelings and behaviours are less easy to change. Once learned, defensive reactions act as habits that block people from full awareness of how they and others behave. Defensive reactions make it harder for people to work on their problems since they lack insight both into their defensive reactions and into their negative consequences. Consequently, defensive reactions are both part of and serve to maintain unhelpful aspects of people's BASIC I.D.s.

Lazarus assigns a pivotal role to misinformation and missing information in maintaining behaviour and in causing people to become therapy clients. Gaps in people's repertoires, because they were never given necessary information and essential coping processes, render them ill-equipped to deal with societal demands (Lazarus, 2000). In addition, people can communicate about their communication in ways that maintain rather than solve problems, for instance by blaming one another.

Following are other factors, interacting with those already mentioned, that can contribute to people maintaining dysfunctional thoughts, feelings and behaviours (Dryden, 1991).

Conflicting or ambivalent feelings or reactions

People can possess approach-approach or avoidance-avoidance conflicts resulting in extreme indecisiveness. Their prior learning experiences have contributed to their indecision and inertia. Their indecisiveness may be both self-maintaining and also contribute to their inability to change aspects of how they function.

Interpersonal inquietude

Many people remain upset because of undue dependencies, excessive hates and misplaced loves. Lazarus sees such interpersonal inquietude stemming from skills deficits and from unrealistic demands that people impose upon each other.

Poor self-acceptance

People maintain negative feelings about themselves because they do not understand the difference between accepting their totality as human beings and functionally evaluating specific shortcomings and personal limitations. Self-acceptance means 'Don't put your ego on the line, accept yourself, your totality, even though there might be lots of little "i's" as part of the big "I", that are less than exemplary' (Dryden, 1991, p. 13). For instance, people can make mistakes and possess skills deficits without feeling totally crushed as persons.

THERAPY

In essence, effective therapy calls for appropriate techniques, correctly administered, within the context of a trusting and caring relationship.

Arnold A. Lazarus

The practice of multimodal therapy possesses six distinctive features:

1. The specific and comprehensive attention given to the entire BASIC I.D.
2. The use of second-order BASIC I.D. assessments.
3. The use of Modality Profiles.
4. The use of Structural Profiles.
5. Tracking the modality firing order.
6. Deliberate bridging procedures. (Lazarus, 1992, p. 250)

Though not in the order listed above, this section reviews how each of these distinctive features forms part of multimodal therapy.

THERAPEUTIC GOALS

Long-range hedonism is a guiding philosophy (Dryden, 1991). Though Lazarus does not define fun, a major goal for most humans is to have fun while alive. However, people need to attain a good balance between long-range and short-range hedonism.

Though individuals differ in their predominant modalities, the BASIC I.D. suggests illustrative sub-goals for effective functioning:

*   *Behaviour.* Taking effective actions in pursuit of realistic goals.
*   *Affect.* Acknowledging, clarifying and recognizing feelings; coping with negative feelings and enhancing positive feelings.
*   *Sensation.* Being in touch with and enjoying one's senses.
*   *Imagery.* Being in touch with one's imagination; using coping images.
*   *Cognition.* Possessing sufficiently accurate and complete information; thinking realistically.
*   *Interpersonal.* Possessing good relating skills, for instance assertion and conversational skills; capacity for healthy interdependency.
*   *Drugs/biology.* Taking good care of one's body and physical health; eating and drinking in moderation.

People can have deficits in one or more of the above modalities and still be happy. Humans are fallible, with a biological penchant sometimes to be self-defeating. However, people can feel self-acceptance, accept their fallibility, at the same time as attempting to be less fallible.

Multimodal therapy goals are tailored to particular clients and take into account their 'goals, coping behaviors, situational contexts, affective reactions, "resistances", and basic beliefs' (Lazarus, 1992, p. 237). Rigidity is to be avoided in all aspects of therapy, including assessment and goal-setting. In some instances, clients' main problems are obvious and a thorough assessment of all seven BASIC I.D. modalities is unnecessary.

In most cases, multimodal therapy rests on a thorough assessment of the BASIC I.D. which leads to constructing a Modality Profile listing salient problems and recommended treatments within each modality. Outcome goals, namely overcoming or coping with the problem, are implicit for each problem listed by modality in the profile. For instance, depression is one of the problems listed in the Affect section of a client's

Modality Profile. An outcome goal for this problem relates to a lessening of the client's depressed feelings, preferably in some measurable way. Inasmuch as Modality Profiles also list recommended interventions, decision and process goals are implicit in them. A therapist decision-making goal is to select the most effective treatments of choice for each problem. Could the therapist have selected better treatments of choice for the client's depression problem than the recommended interventions of coping imagery and increasing rewarding activities? Once chosen, to what extent does each intervention, on its own or in combination, contribute to the problem or outcome goal of lessening the client's depression?

PROCESS OF THERAPY

Multimodal therapy may be conducted in either complete or brief forms. The average duration of a complete course of multimodal therapy is approximately 50 hour-long sessions (weekly sessions for about a year). Lazarus (2000) observes that fewer than 30 per cent of the clients seen at the various Multimodal Therapy Institutes seem to require or are willing to participate in 50 hours of therapy. The majority favour brief therapy consisting of about one to fifteen hour-long sessions, which may take place either over a short period of time or extend over many months (Lazarus, 1997). Lazarus contends that by using the multimodal framework, therapy can be both brief and comprehensive.

Initial sessions

Initial sessions follow no rigid format. Therapists may meet with individuals, couples or families. They may begin with small talk and collecting basic information, for instance address and phone number, before embarking on a more detailed inquiry. Two main questions relating to clients' presenting complaints are: 'What has led to the current situation?' and 'Who or what is maintaining it?' (Lazarus, 2000, 1992). In addition, therapists look for signs of psychosis, organic problems and depression. From the start, therapists are attuned to noting information about which modalities of the BASIC I.D. their clients' complaints apply to. In addition, they try to assess clients' expectations about therapy and the most appropriate kind of relationship style to adopt. Furthermore, they look for clients' strengths and positive attributes. Quite often in initial interviews therapists use specific interventions, for instance cognitive disputation. At the end of the initial interview, therapists give most adult clients the fifteen-page *Multimodal Life History Inventory* (Lazarus and Lazarus, 1991; Lazarus, 1997). This inventory asks numerous questions about antecedent events and maintaining factors with the answers being divided into BASIC I.D. categories.

An important multimodal therapy principle is 'Know your own limitations and other clinicians' strengths' (Dryden, 1991, p. 30). Referrals should be made where other therapists have skills that the therapist does not possess or more appropriate personal styles for particular clients. Lazarus does not consider himself particularly good at working with seriously disturbed people – for instance schizophrenics, substance abusers, and antisocial personality disorders. He seeks out more expert or gifted people for such clients. Often referrals to other therapists are best made before bonding with the original therapist occurs. Lazarus also refers clients to self-help groups, such as Alcoholics Anonymous, Self Management and Recovery Training (SMART), Overeaters Anonymous and Parents without Partners.

The Modality Profile

Lazarus (1992) writes: 'the mainstay of multimodal assessment centers on Modality Profiles and Structural Profiles' (p. 246). A Modality Profile is a BASIC I.D. chart listing problems and interventions within each modality. Lazarus only draws up such profiles when therapy is not going quickly enough and unforeseen problems arise. Around the start of the third session, therapists have usually gleaned enough information from interviews and the life history inventory to spend fifteen to twenty minutes drafting a preliminary Modality Profile for the client. Sometimes clients are asked to draft their own Modality Profiles separately from their therapists and then the two compare notes. Multimodal therapists treat their clients' Modality Profiles as sets of hypotheses. Modality Profiles are shared and discussed with clients.

Box 14.2 provides an example of a Modality Profile for a 37-year-old man in therapy for generalized anxiety (Lazarus, 1992, p. 242).

The Structural Profile

The Structural Profile comes toward the end of the *Multimodal Life History Inventory*. Here clients are asked to rate themselves across each of the BASIC I.D. modalities on a seven-point scale with 1 being the lowest and 7 being the highest. The descriptions for each modality were provided earlier in this chapter when introducing the seven BASIC I.D. modalities. The Structural Profile provides useful additional information to both therapist and client about how the client interacts with the world. It can be easily depicted on a bar graph.

In addition to the seven questions that form part of the *Multimodal Life History Inventory*, Lazarus has developed a 35-item standardized instrument called the *Structural Profile Inventory* (SPI) (1989b, 1997). In 1995, an *Expanded Structural Profile* was developed by Lazarus's son Clifford (Lazarus, 1997, pp. 145–8).

The SPI has proved very useful in couples therapy. The profiles pinpoint reasons for misunderstanding and can lead to fruitful discussions of what to do about them. Sometimes the profiles may indicate that divorce therapy is a more realistic prospect than marital therapy: for instance, where one partner values affective expression and interpersonal intimacy and is low on behaviour and cognition, and the other partner has the opposite profile.

Tracking

Clients have fairly reliable patterns or orderings of modalities in how they generate negative affect, though on occasion these patterns may vary. Tracking refers to the careful assessment of the 'firing order', the ordering of the chain reaction of the different modalities. For instance, one client may generate negative emotions through dwelling first on sensations (S) (e.g. heart palpitations) which 'fire' cognitions (C) (e.g. 'I may get very ill

BOX 14.2

Example of a Modality Profile

Modality	Problem	Intervention
Behaviour	Procrastination Tends to pout or withdraw when frustrated Volatile and explosive	Contingency contracting Modelling and role-playing of assertiveness skills Relaxation and communication training
Affect	Anxiety Depression	Breathing and deep muscle relaxation; stress inoculation training Coping imagery; increase rewarding activities
Sensation	Tension (esp. in jaws and neck) Lower-back pain	Relaxation training Orthopaedic exercises
Imagery	Lonely images Images of failure	Picturing various coping responses
Cognition	Perfectionism Negative scanning Dichotomous thinking Self-downing	Cognitive restructuring
Interpersonal relationships	Passive–aggressive Unassertive Has few friends	Social skills and assertiveness training
Drugs/biology	Insufficient exercise Overweight	Healthy lifestyle programme

or die') which 'fire' aversive images (I) (e.g. pictures of catastrophic disease) which 'fire' maladaptive behaviour (B) (e.g. extreme withdrawal) (Lazarus, 2000). Another client, instead of the SCIB firing order outlined above, may display a CISB pattern (cognitive–imagery–sensation–behaviour).

One purpose of tracking is to provide clients with insight into the precise processes by which they generate negative affect so that they can intervene appropriately. Another purpose is to assist therapists in selecting and prioritizing treatment interventions. Box 14.3 provides an example of a female client tracking her firing order and then the therapist planning treatment accordingly (Lazarus, 2000). Had the client a different firing order, the therapist would have trained her in a different sequence and encouraged her to use this different sequence in real life.

Second-order BASIC I.D. assessments

When impasses occur in treating clients, therapists may perform second-order BASIC I.D. assessments. Such assessments allow a more detailed review of behaviours, affective responses, sensory reactions, images, cognitions, interpersonal factions, and drugs and biological factors in relation to the area in which change is proving difficult. For instance, unassertive behaviours may persist, despite role-playing, behaviour rehearsal, modelling and other relevant training. When, as part of her second-order assessment, one client was asked for her BASIC I.D. associations to the concept of assertiveness, her answers were as follows: behaviour, attacking; affect, angry; sensation, tension; imagery, bombs bursting; cognition, get even; interpersonal, hurting; and drugs/biologicals, high blood pressure (Lazarus, 2000). Although the therapist had attempted to convey to her the difference between assertion and aggression, the second-order BASIC I.D. showed that she still

---

BOX 14.3

Example of tracking

Tracking the firing order
An agoraphobic woman tracked in herself a CISA firing order:
- an illustrative cognition (C) was 'What if I pass out?'
- followed by mental images (I) of herself hyperventilating and fainting
- which fired sensations (S) of light-headedness and sweaty palms
- which fired feelings (A) of panic and anxiety.

Treatment based on the client's firing order
Following the client's firing order, her therapist:
- first provided her with self-instructional training (Meichenbaum, 1977) to counteract her self-defeating cognitions;
- next, she was taught coping imagery in which she vividly imagined herself remaining calm and controlled in feared situations (such as shopping in a supermarket); and
- in the sensory modality, her therapist taught her slow abdominal breathing and differential muscle relaxation.

The client was instructed to practise her training in real life. When shopping in a supermarket, she was to follow the sequence of:
- using positive self-instructions (C)
- then adding coping imagery (I)
- and then using abdominal breathing while deliberately relaxing muscles not in use at the time (S).

---

regarded assertive responses as tantamount to vicious attacks. Box 14.4 provides another example of a second-order BASIC I.D. profile (Lazarus, 1997, pp. 58–9).

BOX 14.4

Example of a second-order BASIC I.D. profile

The client
The client had an established alcohol addiction, and one of the items on his Modality Profile was 'Urges to Use Alcohol or Cravings'.

His second-order BASIC I.D. profile
When asked about the impact of these urges or cravings across the BASIC I.D., the following profile emerged

• Behaviour	Clenches jaw.
	Starts pacing or wringing hands.
• Affect	Anxiety.
	Depression.
• Sensation	Muscle tension.
	Dry mouth.
• Imagery	Visualizes drinking alcohol.
	Imagines smell and taste of drink.
	Pictures sense of intoxication.
• Cognition	Thoughts of unfairness.
	Belief that craving will never subside.
	Idea that intake can be controlled.
	Various other rationalizations.
• Interpersonal	Withdraws from social interaction or lashes out irritably at others.
• Drugs/biology	Smokes a cigarette or has a cup of coffee.

Possible strategies
The most obvious strategies based on this profile include:
1. more attention to deep muscle relaxation;
2. success images of turning away from alcohol; and
3. cognitive disputation.

Selection of interventions

A fundamental premise of the multimodal approach is that clients are usually troubled by a multitude of specific problems that should be dealt with by a multitude of specific treatments (Lazarus, 2000). How do multimodal therapists select treatment interventions? Box 14.2 provides, as part of a Modality Profile, the techniques selected for a man in therapy for generalized anxiety. Multimodal therapists need to be aware of and skilled in a wide repertoire of techniques or interventions. If unaware of or unskilled in certain interventions they are unlikely to help clients with certain conditions. The first or main requirement for selecting interventions is the extent to which there are research data to support them. Empirical data exist for documenting treatments of choice across a variety of conditions including 'bulimia nervosa, compulsive rituals, social skill deficits, bipolar depression, schizophrenic delusions, focal phobias, tics and habit disorders, pain management, hyperventilation, panic disorders, autism, enuresis, vaginisimus and other sexual dysfunctions, and a variety of stress-related disorders . . .' (Lazarus, Beutler and Norcross, 1992). However, probably some 'grey areas' will always exist. Practising therapists should familiarize themselves with the research outcome literature.

Multimodal therapists take a number of other factors into account in selecting and prioritizing interventions. Such factors include clients' priorities, firing orders, and the desirability of early success experiences. Careful consideration is given to answers to the following three items on page 4 of the *Multimodal Life History Inventory*: 'In a few words, what do you think therapy is about?', 'How long do you think your therapy should last?', and 'What personal qualities do you think the ideal therapist should possess?' (Lazarus, 1992, pp. 242–3). For instance, clients thinking the ideal therapist is an active listener may take unkindly to active-directive, task-oriented therapists.

Multimodal therapists start 'with the most obvious and logical procedures' (Kwee and Lazarus, 1986, p. 335). Once selected, therapists still need to accommodate their chosen interventions to the unique characteristics of each client in order to promote adherence and compliance. While the initial selection of interventions may be relatively straightforward, their implementation 'requires clinical experience, acumen, and artistry' (Kwee and Lazarus, 1986, p. 337). If the initially selected interventions do not work, Lazarus may draw on other well-researched interventions. Sometimes he goes beyond well-researched interventions to try other interventions that may help specific clients: for example the technique from neurolinguistic programming (NLP) of shrinking the feared object down to size or using the conceptualization of Parent, Adult and Child from transactional analysis (Dryden, 1991). In addition, second-order BASIC I.D. assessments may be conducted to look for significant factors that may have been overlooked in initial assessment procedures.

Progress evaluations

Ongoing evaluations of progress are integral to multimodal therapy. Since Modality Profiles are commonly drawn up, therapists can evaluate progress for each problem within each of the seven BASIC I.D. dimensions. Such information is relevant both during therapy and for making termination of therapy decisions. Lazarus provides the following example of how a multimodal therapist specified a client's gains and achievements (Lazarus, 2000):

Behaviour:	Less withdrawn; less compulsive; more outspoken.
Affect:	More warm, less hostile; less depressed.
Sensation:	Enjoys more pleasures; less tense, more relaxed.

Imagery:	Fewer nightmares; better self-image.
Cognition:	Less self-downing; more positive self-statements.
Interpersonal:	Goes out on dates; expresses wishes and desires.
Drugs/biologicals:	Stopped smoking; eats well; exercises regularly.

THE THERAPEUTIC RELATIONSHIP

The therapeutic relationship can be divided into relationship behaviours that are universal and those that differ for specific clients. One universal relationship behaviour is the attempt to develop a collaborative alliance whenever possible. Multimodal therapists endeavour to work together with clients. A second relationship universal is never to attack a client's sense of dignity as a person, though their maladaptive behaviours may be assailed.

'"Relationships of choice" are no less important than "techniques of choice" for effective psychotherapy' (Lazarus, 1993, p. 404). For most clients the purpose of the therapeutic relationship is to provide 'the soil that enables the techniques to take root' (Dryden, 1991, p. 17). Unlike Rogers who would offer the same kind of 'carefully cultivated warmth, genuineness and empathy to all his clients' (Dryden, 1991, p. 18), Lazarus tries to match the nature of the relationship not only to the client, but also to the client's observed needs at different times in therapy. For some clients, good listening is sufficient. However, many clients require therapists to select and use specific techniques to help them develop coping skills for problems identified in their Modality Profiles. Thus, therapists need to offer relationships that go beyond good listening.

Lazarus emphasizes flexibility and versatility and uses the metaphor of the 'authentic chameleon' (Lazarus, 1993, 1997) to indicate that multimodal therapists vary their relationship styles to provide a goodness-of-fit with clients' expectancies, personalities, problems and goals. He describes four different yet overlapping ways of varying relationships with clients.

1. *The relationship continuum.* Multimodal therapists view helping relationships on a continuum from 'a very close-knit, dependent bonding at the one end, to a rather formal, businesslike involvement at the other' (Kwee and Lazarus, 1986, p. 333). Throughout therapy, the relationship is used flexibly to fit each client's expectancies and preferred modalities. For instance, some people do not respond well to therapist warmth and empathy and like a more businesslike approach.

2. *Matching therapist styles.* Therapist styles that Lazarus seeks to match to individual clients include: 'whether and when to be cold, warm, or tepid; when and when not to be confrontational; when and whether to be earthy, chummy, casual and informal rather than "professional"; when to self-disclose or remain enigmatic; when to be soft-nosed, gentle and tender, and when to come on like a tough army sergeant; and how to adjust my levels of supportiveness and directiveness' (Lazarus, 1993, p. 405).

3. *Supportivness and directiveness dimensions.* During therapy, multimodal therapists continually ask themselves how supportive and how directive they need be with their clients. Four possibilities are: high direction–high support, low direction–low support, low direction–high support and high direction–low support. Effective

therapists switch among and between all four modes 'in the chameleon sense' (Dryden, 1991, p. 19). Lazarus works mostly in the high direction–high support mode, since he sees therapy as an educational process in which the therapist's main role is that of a clinical teacher. Furthermore, clients change most rapidly when ready for high direction and high support.

4. *Relationships differing with selected techniques.* Lazarus uses techniques that draw upon the work of Freud, Rogers, Perls, Ellis, Adler, Haley, and the behaviourists among others. As part of tailoring his interventions to the needs of each client, he also flexibly utilizes the kind of relationship implicit in these techniques (Lazarus, 1989b). For instance, he may use Rogerian reflection, gestalt psychodrama and imagery techniques, or behavioural assertiveness training, and accordingly adjust the kind of relationship he offers.

The two *client* variables that most influence Lazarus's relationship style are his perceptions of their readiness for change and of their reactance level. Ongoing therapy interactions play a dominant part in selecting relationship of choice. For instance, Lazarus adopted an extremely gentle stance in which he was almost whispering to a very timid and shy young woman who expressed strong reactions about her dealings with 'loud, pushy, or obnoxious people' (Lazarus, 1993, p. 406). The outcome was that the client, who had poor relationships with her two previous therapists, co-operated well with him.

Bridging

Bridging is a rapport enhancement technique that illustrates the flexibility of the multimodal therapy relationship. When bridging, therapists deliberately tune in to the clients' preferred modalities before gently helping them cross bridges into other modalities that may prove more productive (Lazarus, 1992, 1997, 2000). Clients are more likely to feel understood by therapists who first respond within their preferred representational

---

BOX 14.5

Example of bridging

The multimodal therapist is interested in understanding an initial emotional reaction.

Original interaction
Therapist: 'How did you feel about your father's decision to leave home?'
Client: 'My father tended to put his needs first, and neither my mother nor I were factored into the equation.'

Staying in the cognitive modality
Rather than pressure the client into the affective modality, the therapist might first join with the client in the cognitive modality.

Bridging into the sensory modality
Then, after about five minutes, the therapist could bridge into a modality that was less threatening than the affective modality, for instance the sensory modality with a question like:

Therapist: 'By the way, can you tune in to some sensations anywhere in your body?'

Bridging into the affective modality
Then, after discussing sensations, the therapist could bridge into the affective modality with a question such as:

Therapist: 'I really wonder how you feel about the things your father has done?'

By now the client should be much less defensive about revealing feelings.

system. Other ways of describing bridging are that therapists first 'talk their clients' language' or 'start from where they are' before moving into less preferred modalities. An advantage of doing this is that clients then become less resistant to working in these other modalities. Box 14.5 provides an example of bridging (Lazarus, 1992, pp. 247–9).

THERAPEUTIC INTERVENTIONS

Following are principal multimodal interventions or techniques for each BASIC I.D. dimension (Kwee and Lazarus, 1986; Lazarus, 1989b). Frequently, these interventions are used in combination. Interventions should be used sparingly according to the assessed needs of individual clients.

Behaviour

- *Behaviour rehearsal.* Therapists, who start by playing the other person, repeatedly rehearse clients in how to behave in specific situations. Dialogues are either cassette- or video-recorded and played back. When ready, clients enact their skills in the actual situations.
- *Modelling.* Therapists provide role models for specific behaviours which clients are encouraged to imitate. Therapists may model behaviours in real-life settings: for instance assertively returning faulty goods to a shop.
- *Non-reinforcement.* By not attending to specific client behaviours, therapists and others in clients' social environments can facilitate their extinction.
- *Positive reinforcement.* To strengthen specific client behaviours, therapists can dispense social reinforcers such as praise, recognition and encouragement. With children and adolescents, therapists may use tangible reinforcers, such as food and money. Therapists may also use tokens that may be exchanged for tangible rewards.
- *Recording and self-monitoring.* Therapists encourage clients to engage in the systematic recording, charting and/or counting of targeted behaviours.
- *Stimulus control.* The absence or presence of certain stimuli is related to the frequency of behaviours. For example, people trying to lose weight can keep snacks and

desserts out of their homes. Students trying to increase study behaviours can arrange their desks without distracting stimuli and only sit at them when studying.

- *Systematic exposure.* Therapists encourage clients to expose themselves step-by-step to their feared situations. Many additional techniques, for instance *goal rehearsal* or *coping imagery*, may be used to overcome avoidances in conjunction with systematic exposure.

Affect

- *Anger expression.* Anger expression means assisting clients to own and express their anger. It is not an end in itself and clients may require *behaviour rehearsal* in how to express anger assertively. Techniques to get clients in touch with angry feelings include coaxing them to say louder and louder 'I am angry' and getting them to pummel and kick foam-rubber cushions, pillows and inflatable objects.
- *Anxiety management training.* First therapists teach clients general *relaxation training* and *goal-rehearsal or coping imagery.* Then they teach clients to generate anxiety-evoking cognitions and imagery and immediately after to relax and dwell on calm sensations, picture serene images, dispute irrational ideas, and concentrate on optimistic and relaxing thoughts.
- *Feeling-identification.* Labelling feelings accurately is one area of feeling-identification: for instance, clients may say they are 'depressed' when their symptoms are more those of 'anxiety'. The main area of feeling-identification is exploring the client's affective domain to help them identify significant feelings that might be unclear or misdirected.
- *The empty chair.* The client faces an empty chair and imagines it occupied by a significant other. The client starts a dialogue with this other person and then switches chairs back and forth to conduct both parts of the dialogue. Therapists may offer prompts about what to say, for instance, 'Ask her to tell you exactly how she would have wanted you to respond.' As well as assisting clients to own and express feelings, the empty chair helps them appreciate others' viewpoints.

Sensation

- *Biofeedback.* There are biofeedback devices that can help clients to monitor and modify physiological functions like muscular tension, heart rate, brain wave activity, galvanic skin response and skin temperature. For example, for a client suffering from painful tension in the jaw, the therapist can attach electrodes to the jaw muscles that are wired to a machine that provides tonal feedback (the more tension the louder the sound) according to the degree of muscular tension. Clients can learn to maintain a low decibel level or eliminate the tone altogether.
- *Focusing.* Therapists encourage clients in contemplative and relaxed states to tune in to their spontaneous thoughts and feelings until one major felt bodily expression emerges. After several minutes of intense focusing, clients are asked to extract something new from their sensations, images and emotions.
- *Hypnosis.* Therapists can usefully learn several methods for inducing trances to

maximize their chances of success with individual clients. Hypnotic-induction techniques mostly involve sensory fixation (e.g. focusing on a spot on the ceiling) and monotonous repetitions, such as 'calm and relaxed'.

- *Meditation.* Therapists can teach clients meditation, for instance sitting down, gradually closing their eyes, and inwardly repeating a 'mantra' such as the word 'in' on inhaling and the word 'out' on exhaling. As thoughts float in and out of awareness, the meditator continues to think the words 'in' and 'out'. Often two daily twenty-minute sessions are advocated. However, some clients gain most from mini-meditations of two- or three-minute sessions several times daily.

- *Relaxation training.* Clients can learn total relaxation and/or differential relaxation. Total relaxation is another term for progressive muscular relaxation involving alternate tensing and letting go of each major muscle area. Differential relaxation entails learning to relax those muscles not in use when performing various tasks. For instance, a person tensing their jaw, shoulders and neck and holding their breath when sitting and writing can deliberately relax the tense muscles and breathe abdominally in a slow and rhythmic fashion.

- *Sensate focus training.* Usually prescribed for sexually dysfunctional couples, sensate focus refers to sensual rather than to sexual pleasuring. The pleasuring partner is forbidden to touch the genitals or female breasts and no pressures for sexual performance are permitted. Instead the pleasuring partner massages, touches and stimulates any part of the body that the recipient enjoys having stimulated. Afterwards, partners can reverse roles.

- *Threshold training.* Threshold training is a common technique for the treatment of premature or rapid ejaculation. The female manually stimulates the man's penis. When he feels a preorgasmic sensation he says 'stop' and/or removes her hand until the sensation abates. This procedure is repeated. Later more advanced variations can be added: for instance, manual stimulation using a lubricant, and effecting vaginal entry and withdrawing on feeling a preorgasmic urge. Within a few weeks, many men can delay ejaculation for long periods.

Imagery

- *Anti-future shock imagery.* This intervention helps prepare clients for changes likely to happen in the coming months or years: for instance, becoming a parent, being promoted, or moving to a new location. Clients are encouraged to visualize themselves coping with these changes.

- *Associated imagery.* When clients experience unwanted emotions for which they are unable to account, therapists can ask them to focus immediately on any image that comes to mind and see it as vividly as possible. New images that emerge are to be visualized as clearly as possible. If no new images emerge, the original image is to be examined as if through a zoom lens, with this process often eliciting other images for tracking. Frequently clients report significant insights from using this technique.

- *Aversive imagery.* Clients can learn to associate unpleasant images with behaviour that is unwanted, yet self-reinforcing (e.g. alcoholism, sexual deviations, overeating).

For instance, clients on diets can be trained to imagine that someone has vomited over the rich food they wish to eat.

- *Goal rehearsal or coping imagery.* Clients are trained to break down the steps involved in difficult upcoming events. For each step, they visualize themselves faltering, but coping. For instance, a woman with an aversion to hospitals had the goal of visiting and supporting a sick friend. She imagined herself coping with the difficulties involved in the hospital visit and her sense of achievement for helping her friend.
- *Positive imagery.* Positive imagery entails visualizing a pleasant scene, real or imagined, past, present or future. Beneficial effects of positive imagery include: reducing tension, inhibiting anxiety and enhancing enjoyment.
- *The step-up technique.* Clients unduly anxious about upcoming events, for instance a public speech, are asked to picture the worst thing imaginable and then imagine themselves coping with the situation and surviving the most negative outcomes. Some clients require self-instructional training along with the step-up technique.
- *Time projection (forward or backward).* Time projection or 'time tripping' can be used to help clients relive and work through past events. In addition, clients can imagine both what might happen in the future, for instance depressed clients picturing themselves engaging in more and more rewarding activities, and how the present might look from the vantage point of the future, for instance picturing an event after a few months and realizing the temporary nature of some current problem.

Cognition

- *Bibliotherapy.* A well-chosen self-help book 'can be worth more than a dozen sessions' (Lazarus, 1989b, p. 243). Books should be thoroughly read, even summarized in notebooks, and readings discussed during sessions.
- *Correcting misconceptions.* Therapists can provide clients with factual information to correct misconceptions about society, other people and themselves. Sexual misconceptions are common. Therapists should learn the relevant facts and realities. *Bibliotherapy* can form an important component of correcting misconceptions.
- *Ellis's A-B-C-D-E paradigm.* Therapists can teach clients Ellis's A (activating event), B (beliefs), C (consequences), D (disputing) and E (effects) paradigm. Clients can learn to identify their irrational beliefs (B) about activating events (A) which lead to negative consequences (C). Disputing these irrational beliefs (D) can result in the effect (E) of the diminution or elimination of negative consequences.
- *Problem-solving.* Clients can learn to apply the rudiments of scientific methodology to problems. Problem-solving involves generating plausible hypotheses that can be strengthened or weakened by gathering relevant information. Decisions are made on the basis of facts and probability rather than by mysticism or chance.
- *Self-instructional training.* Therapists can train clients to replace negative self-statements with positive, task-oriented statements that facilitate coping. For instance, clients anxious about a forthcoming event could instruct themselves to: develop a plan; handle the situation one step at a time; if anxious, to pause and take a few deep breaths; remind themselves that they only have to keep fear manageable rather than

eliminate it; focus on what they need to do; acknowledge the link between controlling self-talk and controlling fear; and recognize that it gets easier each time they use their self-instructions.

- *Thought-blocking.* Thought-blocking is a technique to combat obsessive and intrusive thoughts. Clients can be taught to sub-vocally scream 'STOP!' over and over again. A variation of thought-blocking is for clients to flick their wrists with a rubber band when they scream 'STOP!' Some clients find it helps to picture huge neon signs flashing the letters 'S T O P' on and off.

Interpersonal

- *Communication training.* Therapists can train clients in how to send and receive communications. Sending skills include eye contact, body posture, voice projection and the use of simple concrete terms. Receiving skills include active listening and rewarding senders for communicating. Role-playing and behaviour rehearsal are especially useful in communication training.
- *Contingency contracting.* Clients agree to make rewards or negative consequences (usually self-imposed) contingent upon increasing, decreasing or maintaining a specific behaviour.
- *Friendship training.* In friendship training, therapists identify and train clients in how to interact in pro-social and affectionate ways. Skills that therapists emphasize include empathy, showing caring and concern, self-disclosing, positive reinforcement and give-and-take. Clients are taught to avoid competitiveness and self-aggrandizement.
- *Graded sexual approaches.* Partners are advised to engage in sensual and sexual activities only so long as pleasurable feelings predominate. They terminate such activities when anxious feelings erupt. With each encounter anxieties can recede, and greater sexual arousal and intimacy become possible.
- *Paradoxical strategies.* Symptom prescription, for instance therapists telling compulsive clients to increase their checking and ritualistic behaviours, is a common paradoxical strategy. Clients may decrease their unwanted behaviours if their therapists prescribe that they exaggerate symptoms. Another common paradoxical strategy is that of forbidding a desired response. An example is that of therapists forbidding men with erectile difficulties to have intercourse until they get specific permission. Clients whose desired responses are forbidden may be more likely to enact them, for instance by engaging in sexual intercourse.
- *Social skills and assertiveness training.* Four specific assertive response patterns or abilities that therapists can train clients in are: saying 'No'; asking for favours and making requests; expressing positive and negative feelings; and initiating, continuing and terminating conversations. Behaviour rehearsal and modelling are two major techniques employed in social skills and assertiveness training.

Drugs/biology

Multimodal therapists encourage clients take responsibility for their health and to develop good habits of eating nutritiously, exercising and engaging in recreational activities. Therapists refer clients to physicians where they suspect organic problems or consider biological interventions, such as anti-depressant medication, indicated.

Strategies for saving time

In therapy, especially brief therapy, it is important that therapists do not waste their clients' and their own time. In brief therapy it is most important to select clearly defined goals quickly and to move into specific problem-solving interventions as soon as possible. Sometimes the application of an intervention may come well before assessment has been completed.

Clients can be educated as to the benefits of brief therapy. Furthermore, therapists can use time between sessions to good effect by thinking about clients' progress and, where necessary, revising their game plans. In addition, therapists can use phones, faxes, letters and e-mail to amend homework assignments or make sympathetic enquiries.

Brief therapy requires an educational stance and should avoid conversational therapy. Lazarus (1997) observes: 'Passive and reflective therapists are anathema to the process of brief and effective psychotherapy' (p. 67). He disabuses clients of the widespread over-valuation of insight and the need to focus heavily on the past. Multimodal therapists as educators may use bibliotherapy and prime clients as to the importance of practising homework assignments. Furthermore, Lazarus is not afraid to prompt clients with ideas, strategies and solutions rather than wait for these to emerge from clients themselves.

CASE MATERIAL

Case studies presented by Lazarus include his work with George, a 32-year-old agoraphobic patient who had previously been treated without success by a number of therapists (Lazarus, 1989b; Lazarus, 2001). Another example of Lazarus's work is that with Al and Lisa, the former presenting with inhibited sexual desire (Lazarus, 1997). Lazarus spent two initial conjoint sessions, eight individual sessions with Al, six individual sessions with Lisa, and then three final conjoint sessions in improving this couple's emotional and sexual relationship. A further case study is Lazarus's work over eight months with a 33-year-old woman, married to a successful company president, who was afraid of becoming pregnant, and was insecure and unassertive (Lazarus, 2000). Additional case material is contained in a chapter providing an example of the multimodal assessment and treatment of a case of panic, anxiety and social phobia, and a marital therapy case compounded by depression (Lazarus, Hasson and Glat, 1991). In 1985, *A Casebook of Multimodal Therapy*, edited by Lazarus, was published (Lazarus, 1985b). This book describes fourteen different case studies in a variety of settings and situations.

FURTHER DEVELOPMENTS

Multimodal therapy, with its BASIC I.D. assessment and interventions, has been applied in many areas in addition to individual personal therapy. Multimodal therapy has been used in marital work and in group work. In addition, multimodal therapy has provided a framework for career counselling and for Employee Assistance Program (EAP) counselling. Other areas of application of multimodal principles include: working with children in classroom settings; developing gifted adolescents; parent training; working with in-patients in mental hospitals; and counselling and therapy education. Thus multimodal therapy, at the same time as espousing breadth in how therapists assess and treat clients, has broad applicability to a wide range of areas.

Since 1972, training in multimodal therapy has been a formal aspect of the clinical psychology doctoral programme at Rutgers University in the United States. There are a few major multimodal therapy institutes in the United States as well as some smaller centres. In Britain, training in multimodal therapy is available at the Centre for Stress Management in London. Multimodal therapy is also taught and practised in other countries in Europe: for instance, in The Netherlands under the auspices of Dr M. G. T. Kwee, several therapists are using the approach. Multimodal therapy is also taught in South America. In Argentina, Dr Roberto Kertesz and his colleagues have practised multimodal therapy, offered training seminars, and translated many of Lazarus's books into Spanish (Lazarus, 1997). Thus, the influence of multimodal tharapy spreads well beyond the United States.

SUMMARY

- *Multimodal therapy is a technically eclectic approach which uses a range of techniques selected on the basis of empirical evidence and client need rather than theoretical predisposition.*
- *Physiologically, people have different thresholds for tolerating negative symptoms such as pain, frustration and stress. Human personality can be divided into seven discrete, yet interacting, dimensions that form the acronym BASIC I.D.: behaviour, affect, sensation, imagery, cognition, interpersonal, and drugs/biology. People tend to respond to situations according to their favoured modalities.*
- *Multimodal therapy is not atheoretical and is broadly based on social cognitive learning theory, without being shackled to it. People's personalities are acquired and maintained through the interaction of genetic endowment, social learning and environmental influences.*
- *Seven key constructs explain how human personality is shaped and maintained: (1) associations and relations among events; (2) modelling and imitation; (3) non-conscious processes; (4) defensive reactions; (5) private events; (6) metacommunication; and (7) thresholds.*
- *Multimodal therapy goals are tailored to the BASIC I.D. needs of individual clients, though sometimes a thorough assessment of all seven modalities is unnecessary.*
- *Frequently, on the basis of initial interviews and the client's responses to the Multimodal*

Life History Inventory, multimodal therapists draw up Modality Profiles. Modality Profiles are BASIC I.D. charts listing problems and interventions within each modality.

- *Structural Profiles illustrate how clients see themselves on each of the BASIC I.D. dimensions.*
- *Tracking refers to how clients order modalities when they generate particular negative affects, for instance sensations may 'fire' cognitions.*
- *When impasses occur in treatment, therapists can perform second-order BASIC I.D. assessments that allow a more detailed review of each dimension in the problem area proving difficult.*
- *The therapist is an 'authentic chameleon' who varies the style of the therapy relationship to provide goodness-of-fit with individual clients. When bridging, therapists deliberately tune in to clients' preferred modalities before moving into other modalities.*
- *When selecting techniques, multimodal therapists pay great attention to empirical evidence. Therapists start with the most logical and obvious techniques. They attempt to implement techniques taking into account clients' unique characteristics. Principal multimodal techniques for each of the seven modalities are reviewed.*
- *The BASIC I.D. provides a framework for evaluating client progress and making termination of therapy decisions.*
- *Beyond individual therapy, other applications of multimodal therapy include couples work, group work, and parent training.*
- *Training in multimodal therapy is available in the United States, Europe and South America.*

REVIEW AND PERSONAL QUESTIONS

REVIEW QUESTIONS

1. Why does Lazarus call his approach 'multimodal'?
2. What does the term 'technical eclecticism' mean?
3. What seven key constructs does Lazarus use to explain how human personality is shaped and maintained?
4. To what extent does multimodal therapy have a theoretical base? Why is Lazarus afraid of his approach being too closely tied to any theory?
5. What are the goals of multimodal therapy?
6. What is the role of assessment in multimodal therapy and how do therapists go about it?
7. Critically discuss the role of the therapist–client relationship in multimodal therapy.
8. What does Lazarus mean by bridging and tracking? Provide examples.
9. How do multimodal therapists select interventions?
10. What are some principal multimodal interventions for changing:
    - behaviour;
    - affect;
    - sensation;
    - imagery;

- cognition;
- the interpersonal modality;
- the drugs/biology modality?
11. How do multimodal therapists evaluate clients' progress?

PERSONAL QUESTIONS

1. Identify a specific problem area in your life. To what extent do each of Lazarus's seven key factors for explaining how human personality is shaped and maintained contribute to your acquiring and maintaining your problem?
2. Develop your Structural Profile by rating yourself, using a seven-point scale (1, 2, 3, 4, 5, 6, 7), on each of the BASIC I.D. modalities.
3. Develop a Modality Profile for yourself.
4. Select and implement interventions to help you with one of your problems.
5. What relevance, if any, has the theory and practice of multimodal therapy for how you conduct therapy?
6. What relevance, if any, has the theory and practice of multimodal therapy for how you live?

ANNOTATED BIBLIOGRAPHY

Lazarus, A. A. (1997). *Brief but Comprehensive Psychotherapy: The Multimodal Way.* New York: Springer.

Based on the central message 'Don't waste time', this book succinctly sets out the main rationale and distinctive assessment and therapy techniques employed in brief but comprehensive multimodal therapy. Elements of effective brevity are identified and case examples are provided from individual and couples therapy.

Lazarus, A. A. (1989b). *The Practice of Multimodal Therapy: Systematic, Comprehensive and Effective Psychotherapy* (revised edition). Baltimore, MA: The Johns Hopkins University Press.

This book is exactly the same as the 1981 version apart from a 1989 epilogue and the addition of the 35-item Structural Profile Inventory as Appendix 4. The book includes chapters on multimodal therapy's basic rationale, its basic concepts for practice, the initial interview, multimodal assessment–therapy connections, relationship factors and the selection of techniques. In addition, there are chapters on multimodal marriage therapy, multimodal sex therapy, and multimodal therapy in special situations, for instance working with children. In addition to the Structural Profile Inventory appendix, the book has appendices containing a glossary of 37 principal techniques, the Multimodal Life History Inventory, and the Marital Satisfaction Questionnaire.

Lazarus, A. A. (2000). Multimodal therapy. In R. J. Corsini and D. Wedding (eds). *Current Psychotherapies* (6th edition, 340–74). Itasca, IL: Peacock.

This chapter includes material on multimodal therapy's basic concepts, history and current status, theory of personality, theory of psychotherapy, process and mechanisms of therapy, applications and evaluation. A case example is provided.

Lazarus, A. A. (1992). Multimodal therapy: Technical eclecticism with minimal integration. In J. C. Norcross and M. R. Goldfried (eds). *Handbook of Psychotherapy Integration* (231–63). New York: Basic Books.

> This chapter presents Lazarus ideas on systematic (technical) eclecticism and the risks of integration. Lazarus describes the distinctive features of the multimodal approach and how it differs from other eclectic approaches. Research findings are reviewed and suggestions made for clinical training and desirable future directions for psychotherapy.

Lazarus, A. A. (1984). *In the Mind's Eye: The Power of Imagery for Personal Enrichment*. New York: The Guilford Press.

> This is a well-written book of imagery techniques that therapists can use with clients and people can use for self-help. The book is divided into four parts: the power of imagery; using imagery to build confidence and skill; using imagery to overcome problems; and some additional imagery exercises.

REFERENCES AND FURTHER READING

Bandura, A. (1986). *Social Foundations of Thought and Action: A Social Cognitive Theory*. Englewood Cliffs, NJ: Prentice-Hall.

Dryden, W. (1991). *A Dialogue with Arnold Lazarus: 'It Depends'*. Milton Keynes: Open University Press.

Kwee, M. G. T. and Lazarus, A. A. (1986). Multimodal therapy: The cognitive–behavioural tradition and beyond. In W. Dryden and W. Golden (eds). *Cognitive-Behavioural Approaches to Psychotherapy* (320–55). London: Harper and Row.

Lazarus, A. A. (1961). Group therapy for phobic disorders by systematic desensitization. *Journal of Abnormal and Social Psychology*, *63*, 505–10.

Lazarus, A. A. (1971). *Behavior Therapy and Beyond*. New York: McGraw-Hill.

Lazarus, A. A. (ed.) (1972). *Clinical Behavior Therapy*. New York: Brunner/Mazel.

Lazarus, A. A. (1976). *Multimodal Behavior Therapy*. New York: Springer.

Lazarus, A. A. (1981). *The Practice of Multimodal Therapy*. New York: McGraw-Hill.

Lazarus, A. A. (1984). *In the Mind's Eye: The Power of Imagery for Personal Enrichment*. New York: The Guilford Press.

Lazarus, A. A. (1985a). *Marital Myths*. San Luis Obispo, CA: Impact Publishers.

Lazarus, A. A. (ed.) (1985b). *A Casebook of Multimodal Therapy*. New York: Guilford.

Lazarus, A. A. (1989a). Why I am an eclectic (not an integrationist). *British Journal of Guidance and Counselling*, *17*, 248–58.

Lazarus, A. A. (1989b). *The Practice of Multimodal Therapy: Systematic, Comprehensive and Effective Psychotherapy* (revised edition). Baltimore, MA: The Johns Hopkins University Press.

Lazarus, A. A. (1992). Multimodal therapy: Technical eclecticism with minimal integration. In J. C. Norcross and M. R. Goldfried (eds). *Handbook of Psychotherapy Integration* (231–63). New York: Basic Books.

Lazarus, A. A. (1993). Tailoring the therapeutic relationship, or being an authentic chameleon. *Psychotherapy*, *30*, 404–7.

Lazarus, A. A. (1997). *Brief but Comprehensive Psychotherapy: The Multimodal Way*. New York: Springer.

Lazarus, A. A. (2000). Multimodal therapy. In R. J. Corsini and D. Wedding (eds). *Current Psychotherapies* (6th edition, 340–74). Itasca, IL: Peacock.

Lazarus, A. A. (2001). The case of George. In D. Wedding and R. Corsini (eds). *Case Studies in Psychotherapy* (3rd edition). Itasca, IL: Peacock, 183–93.

Lazarus, A. A., Beutler, L. E. and Norcross, J. C. (1992). The future of technical eclecticism. *Psychotherapy*, *29*, 11–20.

Lazarus, A. A., Hasson, C. and Glat, M. (1991). Multimodal therapy. In K. N. Anchor (ed.). *Handbook of Medical Psychotherapy* (123–40). Toronto: Hogrefe and Huber.

Lazarus, A. A. and Lazarus, C. N. (1991). *Multimodal Life History Inventory.* Champaign, IL: Research Press.

Lazarus, A. A. and Lazarus, C. N. (1997). *The 60-Second Shrink: 101 Strategies for Staying Sane in a Crazy World.* San Luis Obispo, CA: Impact Publishers.

Lazarus, A. A., Lazarus, C. N. and Fay, A. (1993). *Don't Believe it for a Minute!* San Luis Obispo, CA: Impact Publishers.

Lazarus, A. A. and Messer, S. B. (1991). Does chaos prevail? An exchange on technical eclecticism and assimilative integration. *Journal of Psychotherapy Integration*, *1*, 143–58.

Meichenbaum, D. H. (1977). *Cognitive-Behavior Modification.* New York: Plenum.

Wolpe, J. and Lazarus, A. A. (1966). *Behaviour Therapy Techniques.* Oxford: Pergamon Press.

Lazarus on cassette and videotape

Lazarus, A. A. (1976b). *Learning to Relax.* New York: Institute for Rational Living.

Lazarus, A. A. (1982). *Personal Enrichment through Imagery* (3 cassettes plus workbook). New York: BMA Audio Cassette Publications.

Lazarus, A. A. (1984a). *Mental Imagery: Your Hidden Potential.* Washington, DC: American Psychological Association (Psychology Today).

Lazarus, A. A. (1984b). *Mental Imagery: Techniques and Exercises.* Washington, DC: American Psychological Association (Psychology Today).

Videotapes of Lazarus doing multimodal therapy have been published by the American Psychological Association and by Allyn and Bacon.

15

Cognitive–Humanistic Therapy

Cognitive–humanistic therapy aims to combine the technical efficiency of the West with the humane wisdom of the East.

Richard Nelson-Jones

INTRODUCTION

Cognitive–humanistic therapy (CHT) takes as its starting point the challenges, problems and existential concerns of ordinary people. Historically counselling and therapy have been too grounded in the problems of seriously distressed clients and those clients whose level of functioning falls below conventional normality. However, there are two further clienteles for therapy: first, normal people, many of whom are the 'walking wounded', suffering without fully realizing it or being prepared to admit it; and, second, those people functioning well, but who would like to function even better.

To address the needs of different kinds of clients, cognitive–humanistic therapy consists of two, somewhat overlapping, components: lifeskills therapy and mental discipline therapy. Lifeskills therapy is basically therapy for conventional adaptation. Such therapy aims to assist clients to attain the mind, communication and action skills whereby they can function at a 'normal' level in the societies of which they are a part.

Mental discipline therapy aims to assist clients attain higher level functioning or supra-normalcy. Paradoxically, mental discipline therapy develops the mind to awaken and strengthen the heart. Such therapy trains the mind to access, activate and implement in action the positive inner core of one's being. Important goals include achieving genuine human sympathy and developing skills for cultivating happiness and eliminating suffering for others as well as for oneself.

I cannot stress too strongly that the development of cognitive–humanistic therapy, especially the mental discipline therapy component, is therapy in the making rather than a finished product.

RICHARD NELSON-JONES (1936–)

On 2 December 1936, I was born in London, having been conceived in Hong Kong where my father was a doctor. Fearing Japanese aggression, my parents settled back in Britain, though they were soon to separate. From 1940 to 1945, with my mother and older brother, I was a war refugee in the San Francisco Bay area, going to a boarding school at around age 5. After the Second World War, my parents reunited, but were never able to attain lasting happiness. After the relative freedom and prosperity of California, I found returning to post-war Britain to be a traumatic experience.

To cut a long story short, I then had a mainly unhappy childhood. One reason for this is that my basically decent parents had a deeply distressed marriage. Unfortunately, my stay-at-home pre-feminism middle-class mother had a huge psychological toothache and would ruthlessly burden me with her marital unhappiness. My father, who had broken off contact with and never mentioned his own authoritarian father, had strict ideas of right and wrong. Home was not a psychologically safe place for a growing boy. In addition, the boarding schools to which I was sent emphasized turning out conventional private school products rather than emotionally literate persons. Outwardly I pretended to cope, but inwardly I was increasingly scared and anxious.

I spent two reluctant years as a national service officer in Malaysia and Germany, completed a three-year economics degree at Cambridge University, and then worked for two years in the finance industry in London and San Francisco. In the autumn of 1962, I commenced the two-year MBA programme at the Stanford University Business School where, in my first term, I did extremely well in organizational psychology and poorly in economics. At the end of the first term, I switched to the School of Education, enrolling in a Masters in Counselling and Guidance programme. Later I went on to complete a PhD at Stanford with a double major in counselling and guidance and in higher education.

Along with my new studies I started a series of 50 or so individual counselling sessions with the then Counseling Center director, Dr John Black, a skilled client-centred counsellor. In addition, I attended a series of three different psychotherapy groups at the Stanford Medical Center, one of which was co-led by Dr Irvin Yalom. In particular, the work I did with John Black provided a very solid foundation for turning my life around. In 1966 I left Stanford and was to continue my personal therapy for a year or so afterwards.

Brief details of my career include eighteen months as Associate Director and Acting Director of the New England Board of Higher Education; eighteen months as a full-time Research Associate for the Association of Canadian Medical Colleges; twelve years as a counsellor trainer at the University of Aston in Birmingham, coupled with being a sessional counselling psychologist in the university's Health Service; just over a year running my own business called the London Centre for Counselling Psychology; and thirteen years as a counsellor and later counselling psychologist trainer at the Royal Melbourne Institute of Technology, during which period I also saw clients privately and in an organizational setting. In 1997 I took early retirement from RMIT and moved to Chiang Mai in northern Thailand. On 1 January 2000, I opened the Cognitive-Humanistic Institute in Chiang Mai, whose main purpose is to develop psychological theory and practice blending Western and Eastern influences.

Regarding the origins of cognitive–humanistic therapy, in 1976 I had written a long unpublished paper on 'Personal responsibility therapy' that I wanted to develop into a book. During 1983–4, I wrote *Personal Responsibility Counselling and Therapy*, the first published step in my journey to developing cognitive–humanistic therapy. The approach advocated in this book represented an integration of existential-humanistic and cognitive–behavioural perspectives. From 1984 to 1997, throughout my time in Australia, I developed the practical application of the approach in what came to be called lifeskills counselling (Nelson-Jones, 1993, 1997).

Though an earlier article signalled my move towards cognitive–humanistic therapy (Nelson-Jones, 1999a), the current chapter is the first statement of this approach. Since the approach's underlying intellectual and therapeutic influences become apparent in the chapter, to avoid repetition I omit to chronicle them here. However, I owe a big debt of gratitude to the numerous people whose work is mentioned here. Lastly, since cognitive–humanistic therapy touches on some important areas addressed by religions, I mention that I am an agnostic.

THEORY

We create our minds and, to a large extent, how we feel, physically react, act and communicate emanates from how skilfully or unskilfully we think.

Richard Nelson-Jones

BASIC CONCEPTS

Hard and soft humanism

In the early 1960s, humanistic psychology developed in the West as an identity for those interested in human capacities and potentials without wishing to subscribe to behaviourist or psychodynamic viewpoints. However, arguably, much of Western humanistic psychology, with its emphasis on experiencing feelings and personal growth, has insufficiently lived up to the ideals of humanism. Important features of humanism are a concern with human rather than supernatural or divine matters, an intent to foster the interests, welfare and ideals of humankind, a commitment to solely rational ways of solving problems, a wish to develop humans as progressive and responsible beings, and an emphasis on optimal functioning rather than psychopathology.

Cognitive–humanistic therapy is based on hard rather than soft humanism. Hard humanism is unselfish rather than self-centred psychology and is focused on developing the better and higher qualities of human beings. It is a disciplined way of thinking that synergistically fosters the interests and ideals of self, others and humankind. It can be contrasted with soft humanism where individuals tend to mainly focus on their own feelings, need gratification and self-expression.

Innate goodness

Every person has a biologically based inner nature comprised of elements that are common to the species and those that are unique to the individual. Much of Western thinking sees this inner nature as egotistic, selfish and destructive, summed up in one of Freud's favourite quotes, which came from the Roman writer Plautus: 'Man is a wolf to man.' This 'bad animal' view of humans tends to be based on those who are not functioning at a high level rather than on the psychologically healthiest human beings (Maslow, 1971). Furthermore, it ignores the ample evidence that humans can be cooperative and caring as well as hostile and uncaring (Argyle, 1991; Beck, 1999).

Buddhism views our inner nature more positively than much of Western psychology. To Buddhists the natural state of the mind is one of radiance and purity. It is because of defilements, such as craving, anger and delusion that individuals suffer and become aggressive. The matter of instincts and instinct remnants is complex. Human instincts overlap, can be of varying degrees of strength, and those with positive and negative outcomes can be mixed together. The position taken here regarding the basic 'goodness' or 'badness' of human nature is neutral in that, at its deepest levels, human nature is both sublime and savage. Consequently humans have the potential to act constructively and destructively in their daily lives. How people act is largely a matter of training and of how much their animal nature is frustrated.

It is important to acknowledge humans' innate goodness and not just to focus on aggressive and destructive tendencies. Allport (1964) observed that debasing theoretical assumptions degrade human beings and generous assumptions exalt them. Innate goodness refers to the positive core of one's being, which encompasses biological tendencies towards affirming life, affiliation, co-operation, compassion, nurturing, caring, and altruism. At its most highly developed level, innate goodness is unselfish concern for and striving to cultivate the happiness and eliminate the suffering of oneself, others and the human species.

Human sympathy

Charles Darwin referred to humans possessing an 'instinct of sympathy' and this appears to be an important survival instinct for the species (Dalai Lama and Cutler, 1998). An important goal of cognitive—humanistic therapy, especially of mental discipline therapy, is to foster human sympathy. Human sympathy can be defined as identifying and feeling a sense of fellowship with others who are made of the same human clay, go through the same cycle of birth, life and death, and who want to be happy and to avoid suffering just like oneself. Human sympathy entails the capacity for compassion and for enhancing oneself and others through giving.

Adler's concept of social interest comes close to describing what I mean by human sympathy (Adler, 1998). Individuals move beyond manipulation, or using others as objects, and beyond being nice, or needing to be liked by others, to being genuinely involved in synergistically promoting others' welfare along with their own. Beck (1999) has also noted the human capacity for sympathy. He contrasts the altruistic mode, favouring others, with the narcissistic mode, favouring the self. In the altruistic mode people get gratification from subordinating their needs to others and are vigilant about protecting the rights of underdogs, the underprivileged and the disadvantaged. People can alternate between narcissistic and altruistic modes depending on circumstances.

Happiness and suffering

To some extent happiness and suffering are two sides of the same coin. To the extent that we are happy, we are not suffering and vice versa. The following are some ways in which the terms 'happiness' and 'suffering' are used in CHT.

Psychological suffering

Psychological suffering refers to the non-physical component of suffering, the latter best being described as physical pain. Psychological suffering consists of any form of mental discomfort, unhappiness or distress, however large or small. Such suffering is of two main types: existential and self-created. Existential psychological suffering connected with sickness, ageing, death, tragic events and external misfortunes is a natural part of being human. Self-created psychological suffering, or alienation from the positive core of one's being, mainly results from an insufficiently skilful and disciplined mind. Existential suffering can be compounded by self-created suffering. For instance, sometimes it seems as though the Western pursuit of happiness ignores the basic fact of existential suffering and, in doing so, can create even more suffering when false expectations go unfulfilled.

Happiness

On a physical level, happiness is freedom from pain and access to the basic necessities of life, such as food, water, shelter and reasonable health. On a more psychological level, the prime source of happiness consists of feelings of contentment, self-worth and well-being arising from connecting with the positive core of your own or another's being. As such, happiness exists in being the generator, giver or recipient of thoughts and actions reflecting innate goodness. There is a large mental component in happiness. One mental consideration is that happiness tends to be more a matter of how people perceive their situations rather than of the absolute conditions in their life, such as being rich or poor. Consequently, happiness can be increased and suffering decreased by learning to use one's mind skilfully.

Mind

To alter one's own or another's behaviour without recourse to drugs or surgery, it is useful to have the concept of mind. While a person's mind is a central integrating concept in Buddhist psychology, it is curiously absent in Western cognitive and cognitive–behavioural psychology.

A person's mind is a complex entity ultimately based on physical processes. It is the seat of awareness, thought, imagery, volition, feeling and of personal identity and agency. The mind can be thought of in terms of layers of consciousness: for example, consciousness, preconsciousness and/or automatic thoughts, and unconsciousness. Biological influences on the mind include: instincts and instinct remnants, including a cluster of instincts related to innate goodness; individual differences, for instance in personality types such as introversion and extroversion; and the innate component of sexual and affectionate orientation.

People's minds are subject to a flow of experiencing and, as such, the mind has the function of a thought, imagery, sensation and feeling generator of its own accord. However, people also have the capacity to influence and to create their minds. The mind possesses a super-cognitive capacity that enables individuals to think about their thinking. To a large extent, individuals can choose the content of their minds – what they think about. In addition, they can exert control over their mental processes. Furthermore, individuals can consciously train their minds to develop and engage in mental processes that cultivate happiness and lessen or eliminate self-created suffering.

Self

The Western construct of self can be viewed within the framework of mind. There are three main components. First, there is the natural self or a person's underlying animal nature, biological tendencies and unique propensities. Second, there is the learned self, which is the product of cultural, social, parental and other learning influences as well as of what the individual has made of them. This learned self consists of mental self-conceptions, what the person refers to as 'I' or 'me'. The learned self also consists of mind skills and communication and action skills, which are often not clearly acknowledged as part of the self since most people do not think of themselves in skills terms. Third, there is the choosing self or executive self, which represents people's capacities to make their lives through their present and future choices. Thus people not only have existing mental concepts of themselves, they can use their minds to create different self-concepts and to think and act more skilfully.

Lifeskills

Apart from such obviously biological functions as breathing, virtually all of human behaviour can be viewed in terms of lifeskills. One meaning of the word 'skills' pertains to *areas* of skill. For instance, albeit overlapping, broad areas of skills include: relating skills, study skills, leisure skills, health skills and work skills. A second meaning of the word 'skills' refers to *level of competence* or expertise. For instance, in a specific area of skill you can be skilled, unskilled or a mixture of the two. The third meaning of the word 'skills' is less common. This meaning relates to the knowledge and *sequence of choices* entailed in implementing a skill. The concept of skills is best viewed not in either/or terms in which you either possess or do not possess a skill; rather, in any area of skill, it is preferable to think of yourself as possessing either good skills or poor skills, or a mixture of the two. If you make good choices, this is a strength. If you make poor choices, this is a deficiency. In all areas of skill, in varying degrees you are likely to possess elements of both good skills and poor skills.

The term 'lifeskills' in itself is a neutral concept. Lifeskills may be positive or negative depending on the extent to which they help people survive and to maintain and develop potentials. Another way of viewing lifeskills is in terms of whether they are being used for sub-normal, normal or supra-normal functioning. Basically *lifeskills are sequences of choices that people make in specific areas of skill*. There are two main categories of lifeskills: mind skills and communication/action skills.

Mind skills

Mind skills are mental processes in which people can be trained and train themselves. Box 15.1 provides brief descriptions of seven central mind skills derived from the work of leading cognitive therapists, such as Aaron Beck and Albert Ellis.

BOX 15.1

Seven central mind skills

- *Creating awareness.* You develop your capacity to become aware of your feelings, physical sensations and thoughts. You can observe and listen to the flow of your inner and outer experiencing and allow it to unfold without feeling the need to direct it in any way. Unlike the other mind skills, which are more active, creating awareness is a receptive or passive mind skill.

- *Creating self-talk.* Instead of talking to your self negatively before, during and after specific situations, you can acknowledge you have choices and make coping self-statements that assist you to stay calm and cool, establish your goals, coach you in what to do, and affirm the strengths, skills and support factors you possess.

- *Creating visual images.* You can use visual images in ways that calm you down, assist you in acting competently to attain your goals, and help you to resist giving in to bad habits.

- *Creating rules.* Your unrealistic rules make irrational demands on yourself, others, and the environment: for instance, 'I must always be happy', 'Others must look after me', and 'My environment should not contain any suffering.' Instead you can develop realistic rules: for instance, 'I prefer to be happy much of the time, but it is unrealistic to expect this all the time.'

- *Creating perceptions.* You can avoid perceiving yourself and others either too negatively or too positively. You can create compassionate rather than competitive or negative perceptions of the human race. You distinguish between fact and inference and make your inferences as accurate as possible.

- *Creating explanations.* You can explain the causes of events accurately. You avoid assuming too much responsibility by internalizing, 'It's all my fault', or externalizing, 'It's all other people's fault.'

- *Creating expectations.* You are realistic about the risks and rewards of future actions. You assess threats and dangers accurately. You avoid distorting relevant evidence with unwarranted optimism or pessimism. Your expectations about how well you will communicate and act are accurate.

In reality, some of the mind skills overlap. For instance, all of the skills, even visualizing, involve self-talk. However, here self-talk refers to self-statements relevant to coping with specific situations. Interrelationships between skills can also be viewed on the dimension of depth. Arguably, people who believe in the rule 'I must always be happy' are more prone to perceiving events as negative than those who do not share this belief.

Communication/action skills

Communication and action skills involve observable behaviours. They are what you do and how you do it rather than what and how you feel and think. For instance, it is one thing to feel human sympathy, and another to act on this feeling. How do you communicate to others and act to show your sympathy and compassion for them? Communication and action skills vary by area of application: for instance, relating, study, work, leisure, health and social participation. Box 15.2 presents the five main ways in which people can send communication/action skills messages.

BOX 15.2

Five main ways of sending communication/action skills messages

1. *Verbal messages.* Messages that you send with words.
2. *Vocal messages.* Messages that you send through your voice: for example, through volume, articulation, pitch, emphasis and speech rate.
3. *Bodily messages.* Messages that you send with your body: for instance, through your gaze, eye contact, facial expression, posture, gestures, physical proximity and clothes and grooming.
4. *Touch messages.* A special category of bodily messages. Messages that you send with your touch through the part of body that you use, what part of another's body you touch, how gentle or firm you are, and whether or not you have permission.
5. *Action-taking messages.* Messages that you send when you are not face-to-face with others, for example sending flowers or a legal writ.

How people communicate and act can never be divorced from how they think. For example, relationship skills such as becoming more outgoing, listening better, showing caring, sharing intimacy, enjoying sex together, managing anger and communicating assertively, and managing relationship problems each contain two elements: creating skilful communications and creating skilful thinking to support and guide the skilful communications (Nelson-Jones, 1999b).

Mind, heart and animal nature

People are human animals. Cognitive–humanistic therapy does not ignore feelings and physical reactions. Quite the reverse, it actively encourages people to feel happy and avoid suffering. In addition, the approach encourages people to get in touch with their innate tendencies towards goodness and human sympathy. A major goal of CHT is to help people to experience themselves and others compassionately and deeply and to communicate and act appropriately. Nevertheless feelings and physical reactions, however low or lofty, are not in themselves skills, but rather part of our animal nature. The way people can influence how they experience, express and manage their feelings is through altering their minds and by changing how they communicate and act.

Focusing on developing the mind enhances people's abilities to feel a range of feelings that illustrate their underlying animal nature. It can liberate rather than stifle people's capacity to feel fully human. Generally people feel better and enjoy enhanced health when they feel genuine affection for others rather than anger and alienation. The way people can increase their chances of feeling more affection and less anger is through cultivating their minds and altering their behaviour. Another example of the connection between mind and feelings and physical reactions comes from sexual behaviour. How people think about sex strongly influences how well they perform. Noted sex therapists and sexual behaviour researchers Masters and Johnson stated that inhibitions and guilt, performance anxiety, erotic boredom, and blind acceptance of sexual misinformation accounted for about 80 per cent of sexual dissatisfaction in American society (Masters, Johnson and Kolodny, 1986).

Personal responsibility

Cognitive–humanistic therapy adopts the existential notion of people as responsible for the authorship of their lives (Nelson-Jones, 1984). Another metaphor is that people are responsible for inventing their lives. Authorship or invention requires a continuous process of choosing. Personal responsibility entails assuming responsibility for creating and disciplining one's mind, getting in touch with innate goodness, restraining destructive tendencies, and communicating and acting in ways that lead to the creation of happiness and lessening of suffering for oneself, others and the human species.

Another way of looking at personal responsibility is in terms of the five Rs possessed by skilled or good persons. Such human beings are in touch with and able to show their humanity to a high degree. These five Rs, which overlap and interact, are responsiveness, realism, relating, rewarding activity and right-and-wrong (see Box 15.3).

ACQUISITION

How do people learn to develop the skills to assume personal responsibility for cultivating their own and others' happiness and to lessen their own and others' suffering? Occasionally people attain what Maslow has called 'full humanness'. More often, people seem to function at the level of normalcy or 'the kind of sickness or crippling or stunting that we share with everybody else and therefore don't notice' (Maslow, 1971, p. 27). All too frequently in Western societies, people seem to undergo experiences that can lead them too much in the direction of personal insecurity, selfishness, short-term hedonism, craving external affirmation and outer success, and appearing rather than being good.

BOX 15.3

The five Rs of skilled or good persons

1. *Responsiveness* includes existential awareness, awareness of feelings, physical reactions and sensuality, ability to listen to 'inner voices', human sympathy and sensitivity to anxiety and guilt.
2. *Realism* refers to developing and using the mind skills listed earlier – creating awareness, self-talk, visual images, rules, perceptions, explanations and expectations.
3. *Relating* refers to developing and using person-to-person communication skills including: initiating, conversing, disclosing, listening, showing caring, sharing intimacy, co-operating, asserting oneself, and managing anger and conflict.
4. *Rewarding activity* skills include identifying interests, work skills, study skills, leisure skills, and looking after physical health skills.
5. *Right-and-wrong* skills include those demonstrating human sympathy, showing compassion and living ethically within one's immediate environment and in the larger community.

Along with these tendencies, there is insufficient encouragement and training for human sympathy and acknowledging and actualizing higher human potentials. In addition, with the decline in religious beliefs, people pay less attention to the Christian ideals of agape, selfless love, and caring for others.

Becoming good or skilled persons in Western societies is also hampered by a paucity of systematic psychological frameworks or visions of what constitutes high-level human functioning. Psychology and psychiatry have focused more on remedying sub-normal functioning rather than on attaining full humanness. Allied to this, the concepts of mind and mental development have been insufficiently stressed. Furthermore, there is resistance to the notion of people needing to acquire skills to assert their full humanity. Having expressed the above general reservations, I now provide a brief overview of some processes whereby people learn to function well or poorly.

Supportive relationships are crucial to humans of all ages. Children seem to require at least one primary supportive relationship in which they are loved, celebrated as beautiful and receive much human warmth just for being alive. Bowlby (1979) emphasized the concept of a secure base, otherwise referred to as an attachment figure. He noted accumulating evidence that humans of all ages are happiest and most effective when they feel that standing behind them is a trusted person who will come to their aid should difficulties arise. Rogers (1959) also stressed the importance of parental empathy, unconditional positive regard and respect. Secondary and, sometimes, primary supportive relationships can be provided by many people other than parents: for instance, relatives and teachers.

Learning from example or from observing is a major way in which people acquire poor or good lifeskills (Bandura, 1986). How to think, feel and act can be learned from others' examples. Frequently people remain unaware of behaviours they demonstrate to children. If either or both parents are emotionally inexpressive, children miss opportunities for observing how to express emotions. If parents and others use ineffective mind skills, for example unfair blaming and overgeneralizing, children may be quick to do likewise. In addition, children may acquire from parents' examples poor communication and action skills for relationships, work, leisure, health care and showing human sympathy in the wider community. The converse is also true in that good skills in how to feel, think, communicate and act may be acquired from the role-modelling of parents and significant others, including examples from the media. Just as teaching by example is often unintentional, so is learning by example. People may absorb from example deficient skills for thinking, feeling, communicating and acting and then possess the added barrier of remaining unaware this has happened.

Learning from observing role models is frequently intermingled with *learning from rewarding or unrewarding consequences*. For example, parents poor at showing emotions may also be poor at receiving children's emotions. Rewarding consequences can be either primary or secondary. Primary rewarding consequences are rewarding independent of learning histories: for instance, food, shelter, sex and human warmth. However, only a small part of behaviour is immediately reinforced by rewards of evident biological significance. Most behaviour is emitted in response to secondary rewards, such as approval or money, that have become associated or conditioned to primary rewards. In addition, people do not just receive rewarding or unrewarding consequences, they think about past consequences they have received, present consequences they are receiving, and make rules and predictions to guide their future behaviour (Bandura, 1986).

Poor skills can be developed and self-esteem undermined by people receiving unrewarding messages that their whole personality is bad rather than that specific behaviours are insufficiently skilled. Last but not least, many people find it more difficult to become truly skilled due to negative consequences because of their biological sex, race, social class or culture.

Psychologists researching animal behaviour stress the importance of learning from example and consequences. However, humans are unique in possessing the capacity for symbolic thought and communication. Hence, they can *learn from instruction and from self-instruction*. However, poor as well as good skills can be imparted. Furthermore, for various reasons, including differences in preferred teaching and learning styles, those instructed may resist instructors. Sometimes instructors are poor at drawing out learners rather than just telling them what to do. Lifeskills need to be communicated clearly enough for learners to instruct themselves afterwards. Much instruction falls far short of this self-instructional objective.

The degree to which people learn good or poor lifeskills is also influenced by their *access to information and opportunity*. For example, keeping children ignorant about basic facts of sexuality and death impedes self-awareness and emotional responsiveness. Intentionally or unintentionally, adults often relate to their children on the basis of lies, omissions of truth and partial truths (Steiner, 1974). Furthermore, necessary information may not be readily available outside the home. For instance, schools differ greatly in the adequacy of the career information they provide.

Children, adolescents and adults alike need available opportunities to test out and develop lifeskills. Ideally, such opportunities are in line with their maturation and state of readiness. People may have different opportunities on account of their sex, race, culture, social class, financial position and schooling, to mention but some barriers. Furthermore, people can be fortunate or unfortunate in having parents who open up rather than restrict learning opportunities. Children and adults also have a role in seeking out information and opportunities. Some are better at this than others.

Lastly, *anxiety and confidence* are important factors influencing how lifeskills are learned. Children grow up having both helpful and harmful experiences for developing self-esteem. Those who are fortunate acquire a level of anxiety that both protects against actual dangers and also motivates them toward realistic achievements. Those less fortunate may acquire debilitating anxieties through role modelling, instruction and provision of faulty consequences. Even parents who communicate carefully can bruise children's fragile self-esteem. Far worse are parents who communicate aggressively and then become defensive. Deficient behaviours resulting from as well as manifesting anxiety include unwillingness to take realistic risks, tense and nervous rather than relaxed learning, and a heightened tendency to say and do the wrong things. Performing different skills poorly may heighten anxiety still further and make future lifeskills learning even more difficult. However, people who are helped or who help themselves to acquire anxiety management skills may learn lifeskills more easily than those without such skills.

Dehumanizing factors

I do not wish to encourage a victim mentality in which people go around saying 'Ain't life awful.' The Western way of life has much to recommend it and prosperous Western countries are the envy of many in the former Soviet empire and in the Third World. Nevertheless, people exist in social contexts and there are many powerful factors making it hard for people to think skilfully and experience themselves as fully human. Below I briefly mention a few of these potentially dehumanizing factors.

Already, I have emphasized the *inadequacy of existing psychological frameworks*. At risk of repetition, in Western societies there has tended to be a 'bad animal' rather than a neutral or cautiously positive view of human nature, insufficient attention paid to developing secular frameworks or models of supra-normal functioning, and insufficient acknowledgement of the need for mental development for everyone.

The success of capitalism has helped to humanize most people in the West by freeing them from subsistence existences and providing them with a reasonable level of basic economic security. In the nineteenth century, the alienation of labour from their work stimulated the rise of Marxism (Fromm, 1961). Today, many people still feel *dehumanized by the processes of production*: for example, blue-collar workers doing repetitive tasks on car assembly lines. In addition, the pressures on chief executive officers and managers to create shareholder value increasingly lead to people being viewed as units of production to be hired, fired, downsized or relocated as perceived economic realities dictate. Business is 'war without bullets' and the psychological suffering caused by the ruthless competition of the marketplace can be staggering.

Now people can be even more *alienated from their humanity* because not only are they cogs in the processes of production, but in *the processes of consumption as well*.

Consumerism, which is rampant in Western societies, is a major dehumanizing factor in contemporary life. Furthermore, the situation is probably getting worse. Instead of people being freed to enjoy the fruits of greater wealth, under an illusion of freedom they are encouraged to enslave themselves to a never-ending process of creating and consuming wealth. Because businesses need to sell the goods they produce, from a tender age people are urged by clever advertising to buy, buy, buy. For example, Greer (1999) observes that magazines encouraged by the beauty industry target young girls to start building up early their habits of consuming beauty products.

Consumers are encouraged to live up to and beyond their incomes in a compulsive search for artificially induced happiness. Perceived needs for new purchases expand to fill the income and credit available for them. Thus free market economies have helped many step out of unhappiness through not having basic necessities of life and step into psychological suffering connected with the effects of possessing false values that emphasize selfishness, short-range hedonism, and thinking one never has enough material possessions or wealth. Many add to their suffering by getting badly into debt. Further avoidable suffering is caused by people valuing themselves and others on economic rather than human criteria. Even rich people can suffer by comparing themselves to even richer people, acquisitively feeling that they need to accumulate more, and being insecure about not making money quickly enough or about losing it.

The staggering *rate of technological change* is another potentially dehumanizing factor. The gap caused by scientific advances outstripping current levels of human wisdom grows. In addition, if people are not careful, they can easily feel inadequate because of failure to keep up with change. Furthermore, often young people show less respect to their elders than previously, partly because older people are no longer perceived as sources of knowledge and wisdom in an ever-changing world. This disparagement dehumanizes both generations who need to live in mutual respect to experience themselves and one another as fully human.

Another dehumanizing factor is the *mechanistic approach to education* adopted in many Western educational institutions. The scientific approach to knowledge and education is absolutely vital to advancing the human race. Nevertheless, it needs to be smart science that realizes its limitations, fosters creativity, encourages wisdom, and does not cut all knowledge up into small research study units. Pressures to think small and to avoid exploring relationships between head and heart can get in the way of both staff and students studying about and developing their full humanity.

Numerous other dehumanizing factors contribute to people learning to live less skilfully than desirable. These factors include the effects of nationalism, religious intolerance, poverty, and discrimination – for instance, cultural, racial, social class, gender and homophobic.

MAINTENANCE

How do people keep functioning at sub-normal, normal and supra-normal levels? In relation to mind skills and communication/action skills, all people have two pasts. The first past refers to how they acquired good and poor skills initially, with the second past being how they have maintained or altered their skills once acquired. Since many skills were acquired when people were relatively powerless as children, the first past is more 'What others have done to me.' However, the second past, when people were older, is more a matter of 'What I kept doing to myself.' This section focuses on why many people choose to stay stuck at lower levels of functioning than desirable.

Inadequate mind skills

A contributing factor to maintaining poor mind and communication/action skills is that many people do not possess a clear concept of mind and insufficiently think about how they think and act in skills terms. Furthermore, people may settle for less than they are capable of because they do not have adequate visions of what their true nature is and of what being fully human entails

Continuing to create poor mind skills in each of the areas depicted in Box 15.1, 'Seven central mind skills', maintains living at a lower level of humanness than possible. For example, people remaining insufficiently aware of their feelings and sensations continue having a poor base for guiding and improving their lives. Much thinking takes place in the form of self-talk. If people keep repeating anxiety- and anger-engendering thoughts to themselves, this habit sustains negative feelings and increases the probability of self-defeating communications and actions. In addition, negative visual images may be repetitively rehearsed. Regarding rules, people may continue to place perfectionist demands upon themselves, others and their environment rather than think in preferential terms.

People's perceptions of themselves tend to be that they are mainly rational human beings. The more insecure they are, the more they are likely to have rigid perceptions about the sort of persons they are. Instead of having what Rogers termed openness to experiencing, both inner and outer, they are likely to react defensively by denying and distorting information that differs from their self-pictures (Raskin and Rogers, 2000).

Regarding creating explanations, people may possess insufficient awareness of their personal responsibility for making the most of their own and others' lives by cultivating happiness and lessening suffering. Furthermore, tendencies to blame others for misfortunes are widespread (Beck, 1999). People who do not acknowledge their contributions to creating their suffering are in poor positions to do anything about it. People can also create unrealistically negative expectations about the possibility of change interfering with making a real effort to change. Such expectations include: 'I've tried before' and 'My partner will never change.'

Fear of goodness

I do not wish to set up a simplistic 'good guy/bad guy' distinction, since virtually all humans show some warmth and compassion. Nevertheless, assuming that all people possess an inner core of goodness or a cluster of instincts of varying levels of strength towards affirming their own and others' human life, the questions then become: 'What gets in the way for so many people of expressing this inner core more fully?' and 'Why do so many people fear actually being as contrasted with seeming to be good?' For most, the inward journey towards true human sympathy involves the conflict between heeding quiet inner voices and overcoming fears. The journey is one of renunciations of less essential ideas to come closer to more essential values of being fully human. The following discussion illustrates just some of the fears blocking people from awakening their hearts.

One of the main fears stems from shattering the illusion of being nice. When people glimpse their potential for genuine goodness, if they are honest with themselves, they also glimpse how far short they fall of fulfilling this potential. To put this in Jungian terms, they are confronted with the darker side of their shadow. Another illusion that people may need to give up is that of being special. Compassion entails seeing other human beings as essentially the same as oneself. Buddhist psychology goes even further to suggest that the idea of having a separate self is an illusion.

Becoming more sensitive to the plight of others can provide further psychological challenges. In Western culture, especially for males, becoming more in touch with tender feelings towards other humans is sometimes associated with being soft and vulnerable. Such fears may generate further fears such as those concerned with being feminine, being taken advantage of, and being different. In addition, people may fear being overwhelmed by acknowledging the true extent of misery in the world. This fear can be somewhat mitigated by acknowledging the extent of happiness and of the overcoming of suffering too.

If the suffering of other humans is more clearly acknowledged and experienced, the next question is 'What are you going to do about it?' Fears connected with answering this question include fears about having sufficient inner strength and detachment to make a contribution in others' lives without getting drowned in their suffering and fears connected with giving time, concern and money for cultivating others' rather than one's own happiness. In addition, people can worry about not being appreciated by others.

Negative external influences

The negative factors that originally contributed to people learning to function poorly may continue. For instance, people may still suffer from absence of the kind of supportive relationships that will help them become better and more skilled persons. They may continue to be exposed to significant others demonstrating poor mind and communication/action skills and limited human sympathy. Role-models for supra-normal functioning are still rare in our culture. In addition, people may fail to be rewarded for constructive thoughts and actions and succeed in being rewarded for the wrong reasons.

People may still suffer from receiving inadequate or no instruction in mind skills and communication/action skills. In addition, they may continue being exposed to insufficient or mis-information about how to live effectively and lack suitable opportunities in their personal and work environments to develop their skills and potential. Furthermore, the dehumanizing factors mentioned earlier such as inadequate psychological frameworks, consumerism, rapid technological change, and a mechanistic approach to education, are each likely to persist into the foreseeable future.

The persistence of negative external influences may make it more difficult to change for the better and easier to change for the worse. However, the most important factor in resisting and surmounting these influences is how skilful people are at creating and using their minds.

THERAPY

Many people possess more inner beauty than they dare to reveal both to themselves and to others and require loving and skilled assistance in showing it.

Richard Nelson-Jones

THERAPEUTIC GOALS

Cognitive–humanistic therapy consists of both lifeskills therapy and mental discipline therapy components, the latter being in the early stages of development. A unifying link is that clients need to be helped to use their minds better for assuming responsibility for creating happiness and lessening suffering. Already, I have presented the five Rs of skilled or good persons – responsiveness, realism, relating, rewarding activity, and right-and-wrong.

In lifeskills therapy goals are decided in conjunction with clients. Such goals can range from helping them handle a specific problem or problem situation to more fundamental work on developing mind and communication/action skills. A basic assumption of lifeskills therapy is that problems tend to repeat themselves. Consequently, just having goals that address managing current problems and problem situations is insufficiently thorough. Lifeskills therapy aims to educate clients in self-helping skills so that they can manage their lives better once they leave therapy. If anything, what happens after therapy is more important than what happens during it.

Invariably an important part of lifeskills therapy is developing mind skills. Mental discipline therapy aims to takes this process further. Some reasonably well-functioning clients want to develop their minds so that they can be even more successful in the conventional terms of status, promotions and money. The goal here is greater mental efficiency for personal gain rather than any inner transformation focused on the wider good.

However, the main purpose of mental discipline therapy is to help those clients who want to take the inner journey towards getting more in touch with their innate goodness and, thus, becoming more fully human. Drawing on Eastern and Western traditions, qualities of the good person include equanimity, autonomy, mental purification, human sympathy, honesty both with self and others, inner strength, heightened concentration, wisdom, generosity and compassionate service (Batchelor, 1997; Salzberg, 1997; Walsh, 2000).

Mentally developed people are able to maintain a balanced or middle way between asserting positive and restraining negative aspects of themselves, between attachment and detachment. This is not an ego-less state of being, but rather one in which the individual's ego or self remains strong and intact, yet capable of a compassionate identification with the human species. Mental discipline therapy seeks inner transformation by reshaping, deepening and humanizing the self and its ego processes rather than doing away with them altogether.

PROCESS OF THERAPY

Lifeskills therapy

Lifeskills therapy is structured around DASIE, a systematic five-stage therapy process model. The model provides a framework or set of guidelines for therapist choices. DASIE is a five-stage model not only for managing or solving problems but also for addressing underlying problematic skills. Therapists, in the best interests of clients, need to apply the DASIE model flexibly. Therapy rarely proceeds according to neatly ordered stages. The stages tend to overlap. Furthermore, therapy may revert to earlier stages as more information and new problems emerge. Following are DASIE's five stages.

Stage 1	D	DEVELOP the relationship and clarify problems.
Stage 2	A	ASSESS and restate problems in skills terms.
Stage 3	S	SET goals and plan interventions.
Stage 4	I	INTERVENE to develop lifeskills.
Stage 5	E	EMPHASIZE take-away and end.

Stage 1: Develop the relationship and clarify problems

Stage 1 starts with pre-helping contact with clients and either ends some time in the initial interview or may take longer. It has two main overlapping functions: developing the therapeutic relationship, and working with clients to identify and obtain fuller descriptions of problems. Many of the therapist skills used in Stage 1 are the same as those used in other approaches: for example, empathic responding and summarizing. Therapists begin by giving clients the space to tell their stories. Then therapists collaborate with clients to explore, clarify and understand problems and problem situations. Together they act as detectives to 'sniff out' and discover what are clients' real problems and agendas. Once a problem or problem situation has been selected for working on, therapists ask further questions to clarify feelings, physical reactions, thoughts, images, communications, actions, relevant background information, and any medical considerations. Medical checks are absolutely vital if there is any chance of a physical problem being involved.

When structuring initial sessions therapists can introduce the concept of skills. One possibility is that, once clients have had a chance to tell their stories, a therapist might make the following kind of statement to structure the remainder of the session.

You've given me some idea of why you've come. Now I'd like to ask some more questions to help us to clarify your problem(s) (specify). Then, depending on what we find, I should be in a position to suggest some skills to help you cope better. Once we agree on what skills might help you, then we can look at ways to develop them. Does this way of proceeding sound all right?

Stage 2: Assess and restate problems in skills terms

The object of this stage is to build a bridge between *describing* and *actively working* on problems and their underlying poor skills. In Stage 1, problems were described, amplified and clarified largely in everyday language. In Stage 2, therapists build upon information collected in Stage 1 to generate and investigate propositions or hypotheses about how clients think, communicate and act that contributes to maintaining their difficulties. Stage 2 ends with a restatement of at least either the main or the most pressing problem in skills terms.

The emphasis in therapists' questions differs in Stage 2 from that in Stage 1. In Stage 1, therapists ask questions to clarify clients' existing frames of reference. In Stage 2 therapists are likely to question as much from their own as from their clients' frames of reference. While the major focus is on pin-pointing skills deficits, attention is also paid to identifying skills strengths and resources.

Therapists need to develop good skills at restating problems in skills terms and communicating and negotiating these working definitions with clients. Restatements of problems in skills terms are essentially hypotheses, based on careful analysis of available information, about clients' mind skills and communication/action skills deficiencies. As hypotheses they are open to modification in light of further or better information. I write restatements in skills terms on whiteboards. Visual presentation makes it easier for clients to retain what you say, if necessary suggest alterations and make changes in language, and make written records. I use a simple diagram to present mind and communication/action skills hypotheses for sustaining each problem.

Box 15.4 provides an example of a restatement in skills terms for George, a highly

---

BOX 15.4

Restatement of George's depression problem in skills terms

Mind skills to improve

Unrealistic rules
- 'I must have approval.'
- 'I must not get depressed.'
- 'I must feel guilty.'
- 'I must keep looking for work and not take a break/enjoy myself.'

Perceiving inaccurately
- 'I'm a failure, worthless, inadequate.'
- 'Others are more powerful than they are.'
- 'Jill is more vulnerable than is really the case.'

Explaining cause inaccurately
- 'I'm totally responsible for Jill's well-being and for her feelings.'

Unrealistic expectations
- 'The future is hopeless.'
- 'I'm powerless to influence my future.'

Communication/action skills to improve

Job-seeking skills
Assertion skills (verbal, voice, body)
- especially when Jill disparages me

Friendship skills
- spending time on own with friends
- disclosing my feelings more

Pleasant activities skills
- taking a vacation
- playing sports with friends

Managing sleep skills
- sleeping too much in day and then not sleeping well at night.

depressed former CEO who, after getting fired, had been out of work for some months. George's depression was not being helped by a worsening relationship with his wife, Jill, who gave him a daily dose of disparagement over his job-seeking efforts at the same time as not countenancing returning to work herself.

Stage 3: Set goals and plan interventions

Stage 3 consists of two phases: stating poor skills as goals and planning interventions. Assuming therapists succeed in restating problems in skills terms, setting goals becomes a relatively simple matter. Working goals are the flip-side of restatements: positive statements of good skills to replace existing poor skills. Therapists can easily change on the whiteboard statements of poor skills into statements of goals. For instance, 'Unrealistic rules' can become 'Develop realistic rules'. Therapists should ensure that clients understand and agree with the statement of goals. Then client and therapist each write down this statement on a form provided by the therapist as a basis for their future work.

Stating poor skills so that they become goals for change provides the bridge for choosing interventions. Therapists not only hypothesize about goals, but also about ways to attain them. Plans are statements of how to combine and sequence interventions to attain goals. Plans may be of varying degrees of structure. Most often I work with open plans that allow clients and myself flexibility to choose which interventions, to attain which goals, when. Clients may be more motivated to work on skills and material relevant at any given time than run through predetermined programmes independent of current considerations.

Stage 4: Intervene to develop lifeskills

Lifeskills therapists are user-friendly coaches. To intervene effectively they require good relationship skills and good training skills. Skilled therapists strike appropriate balances between relationship and task orientations; less skilled helpers err in either direction.

Therapists work much of the time with the three training methods of 'tell', 'show' and 'do'. 'Tell' entails giving clients clear instructions concerning the skills they wish to develop. 'Show' means providing demonstrations of how to implement skills. 'Do' means arranging for clients to perform structured activities and homework tasks.

Within a supportive relationship, therapists deliver specific mind skills and communication/action skills interventions designed to help clients manage problems and develop lifeskills strengths. Whenever appropriate, therapists assist clients to acknowledge that they are learning and using skills. Frequently clients are asked to fill out 'take-away' sheets on which they record skills-focused work done on the whiteboard during sessions. In addition, between-session activities form a regular part of lifeskills therapy. Instructions for between-session activities are also recorded on take-away sheets so that clients are clear what they have agreed to do.

Stage 5: Emphasize take-away and end

Most often either therapist or clients bring up the topic of ending before the final session. This allows both parties to work through the various task and relationship issues connected with ending the contact. A useful option with some clients is to fade contact by spacing out the final few sessions. Certain clients may appreciate the opportunity for booster sessions, say one, two, three or even six months later.

Lifeskills therapy seeks to avoid the 'train and hope' approach. Transfer and maintenance of skills is encouraged by such means as developing clients' self-instructional abilities, working with real-life situations during therapy, and using between-session time productively to listen to session cassettes and to rehearse and practise skills. Often therapists make up short, take-away cassettes focused on the use of specific skills in specific situations: for instance, the use of coping self-talk to handle anxiety when waiting to deliver a public speech. In addition, therapists work with clients to anticipate difficulties and setbacks to taking away and maintaining lifeskills. Then together they develop and rehearse coping strategies for preventing and managing lapses and relapses. Sometimes clients require help in identifying people to support their efforts to maintain skills. Therapists can also provide information about further skills-building opportunities.

Mental discipline therapy

Clients vary in realizing the extent to which it is necessary to discipline their minds if they want to function at above normal levels. For some clients, longer-term lifeskills therapy may become more like mental discipline therapy as they increasingly recognize that they can create their minds in ways that make them more effective workers, spouses, parents, friends, etc. Therapists can assist clients to discipline their minds when facing new problems and problem situations. With some modifications to take into account the absence of their therapists, clients can be taught to use the DASIE model as a self-helping tool. They can become proficient at confronting their problems, assessing their poor skills, stating poor skills as goals, intervening for change, and evaluating what they have done. In addition, therapists can help clients identify specific mind skills in which they are vulnerable – for instance, creating demanding rules – and train them to identify, dispute and change their rules so that it becomes more a way of life, what Ellis would call elegant change.

The process of mental development therapy for those interested in getting more in touch with their innate goodness, developing human sympathy, and being more actively compassionate in how they relate to the world can lead out of lifeskills therapy or be more of a therapeutic approach on its own. Clients need to be reasonably strong and skilled people to start with – if not, they may be better off starting with lifeskills therapy to help them to a conventional level of functioning before trying to attain supranormalcy. The process of mental discipline therapy for those already functioning well can consist of the following elements:

- providing a safe atmosphere in which clients can acknowledge and experience their yearnings to be better human beings;
- helping them experience both good and bad aspects of themselves;
- teaching them about the concept of mind and of mind skills;
- helping them use their minds to disencumber their inner blocks to getting in touch

with the positive core of their being and also helping them to curb negative emotions;
* training them in specific mind skills; and
* using mind training activities and human sympathy activities to help them to build up their capacity to demonstrate and not just feel human sympathy.

THE THERAPEUTIC RELATIONSHIP

The nature of the therapeutic relationship in cognitive–humanistic therapy differs according to such factors as the level of vulnerability of the client, whether the therapist is working more within a lifeskills therapy framework or a mental discipline framework, and according to the stage of the therapeutic process.

In lifeskills therapy, therapists attempt to work at a pace that is congenial for the client. For example, recently-bereaved clients may require space to share feelings and not want to get too focused on detail too soon. Clients badly emotionally undernourished when growing up may require a more gentle and nurturing relationship and spend more time in Stage 1 than more robust clients who may want to focus on specific problems. In Stage 1, therapists support clients as they tell and elaborate on their stories in the safety of a humane and caring relationship. In Stages 2 and 3, therapists are more active in helping clients to make sense of their stories, so both end up knowing which skills they want to work on. In Stages 4 and 5, therapists create safe environments in which clients can both learn and try out new skills.

Overall, the role of the therapist is that of client-centred coach. Therapists try to draw on clients' resources as much as possible to help them become self-reliant. Clients are encouraged to be active participants in the learning process by jointly establishing session agendas, tailor-making their new skills to their personal styles and preferred use of language, setting up within session skills trials and 'take-away' activities, anticipating difficulties and setbacks, and monitoring and evaluating themselves. The idea is for clients to learn to relate to themselves so that, after helping ends, they can provide self-therapy in their targeted skills.

Whereas in the lifeskills therapy component of CHT the therapist might be termed a client-centred coach, in the mental discipline therapy component a better analogy might be that of the therapist as a wise guide or mentor assisting clients in the inner journey of accessing and implementing their innate goodness. The assumption is that clients are better and wiser than they know, but require empathic and knowledgeable help so that they listen to their biological nature more deeply and clear away negative and cultivate positive aspects of their minds. Since therapists and clients are on the same inner journey, it is important that therapists model the human sympathy and compassionate actions that clients seek to make contact with and elicit from themselves. The ultimate emphasis is on self-therapy, with clients learning to relate to themselves so that they become their own wise guides or mentors.

THERAPEUTIC INTERVENTIONS

Lifeskills therapy

Interventions in lifeskills therapy can focus on mind skills, communication/action skills, and on feelings (Nelson-Jones, 1997, 2000a). Such interventions are the same or similar to those used by many cognitive–behavioural therapists. However, cognitive–humanistic therapists are more likely than CBT therapists to educate clients in the notion that they have minds that they can use for good or ill, and to help them to think in skills terms about their mental processes and communications and actions. Communication and action skills are rarely, if ever, addressed without also addressing the mind skills element in enacting them skilfully.

Mind skills interventions

These vary according to which skills are targeted. A common sequence within a mind-skills area is that of increasing awareness of weaknesses in the targeted skill, challenging faulty thinking, and training in effective thinking. For example, a therapist working with a client, one of whose goals is to create a more realistic rule about approval, can intervene in the following sequence:

1. Introduce and raise awareness of the skill of creating realistic rules.
2. Identify the current unrealistic rule and its consequences.
3. Dispute the unrealistic rule.
4. Restate the unrealistic rule as a more realistic rule, for instance, 'Though I would prefer to be liked by my colleagues, what is more important is that I respect myself and do my job as well as I can.'
5. Encourage the client to change his or her actions to accord with the changed rule, for instance, by being more assertive.
6. Emphasize practice and self-helping.

Communication/action skills interventions

These include developing clients' self-monitoring skills, sequencing graded tasks, conducting role-plays and rehearsals, scheduling activities, using exercises and games, using therapists' aids, and assisting clients to identify supports in their home environments for their changed communications and actions. Since poor relationships skills are so widespread, the most frequently used intervention is that of conducting role-plays and rehearsals focusing on verbal, voice and body communication. Sometimes therapists work with clients to set up experiments in which clients use their new skills in real-life settings on a try-out basis. Clients develop 'If . . . then . . .' statements. In the 'If' part of the statement they stipulate a specific situation and the targeted skills they will use in it. In the 'then' part of the statement they predict the consequences of using their changed communications. After a period of rehearsal and practice, clients try out their changed skills in real life. Then, together with their therapists, they evaluate the consequences.

Interventions for feelings

These emphasize developing clients' mind skills and communication/action skills relevant to influencing how they feel. In redefining problems and stating goals, therapists need to distinguish between experiencing feelings, expressing feelings, and managing unwanted feelings. Interventions for assisting clients to *experience* their feelings include legitimizing the importance of feelings, rewarding listening, using feelings questions, role-play methods, confronting inauthenticity, training in inner listening, and developing appropriate mind skills. Interventions for *expressing* feelings are the same as the interventions for developing communication skills described above. Interventions for *managing* feelings vary according to the feeling to be managed. For instance, as in the earlier case of George (see Box 15.4) mind skills interventions for managing depression can target unrealistic rules, inaccurate perceptions of self and others, inaccurate explanations and negative expectations. Communication/action skills interventions for managing depression can target relationship skills and engaging in pleasant activities skills.

Mental discipline therapy

Mental discipline therapy intertwines with lifeskills therapy rather than being separate from it. Many people, including aspiring counsellors and therapists, seek to help others out of deficiency rather than growth motivation (Maslow, 1962). As a general rule, the more people possess effective lifeskills for dealing with their own problems and problem situations, the more energy and interest they can spare for cultivating the happiness and alleviating the suffering of others.

Mind-training activities

These can be conducted inside and outside of therapy sessions. I deliberately do not use the word 'meditation' for mind-training activities because of the diversity of meditation approaches and the word's religious connotations. Clients can be taught to become more aware that what they call their 'self' or 'I' is a mental construction that, to a large extent, they can create for good or ill. Therapists can assist clients to train their minds to restrain negative qualities as well as to cultivate positive qualities (Chodron, 1990; Dalai Lama and Cutler, 1998; Kornfield, 1993; Salzberg, 1997; Thitavanno, 1995; Walsh, 1999, 2000). For example, therapists can work with clients to conduct thorough self-assessments of poor mind skills that contribute to excessive pride, greed and anger. Here, the idea is not to do away with ego or self, but to make it more focused, tough and humane by divesting it of self-defeating thoughts and mental processes. Elsewhere, I have outlined more specifically how to address poor skills in creating self-talk, visual images, rules, perceptions, explanations and expectations (Nelson-Jones, 1997, 1999b), deficiencies in each of which may contribute to a false sense of self and others.

Therapists can also help clients identify the effects of dehumanizing features in their environments, for instance consumerism, and develop strategies to manage these environments as effectively as possible. In addition, where appropriate, therapists can train clients to become more aware of their own mortality and of the challenge to make the most of their lives (Batchelor, 1997; Thera, 1962; Yalom, 1980).

Addressing negative qualities can sometimes best be conducted by cultivating positive qualities as well. Clients can be helped to possess a realistically more positive view of human nature that, in turn, makes feeling and showing human sympathy easier than if they possess a 'bad animal' view of human nature. Therapists can encourage clients to access, nurture and prize their own and one another's potential to demonstrate innate goodness. Training clients to have a compassionate identification with other humans is both positive in itself and helps them to overcome problems of false pride and of anger. Furthermore, therapists can train clients to develop greater equanimity by learning both unconditional self-acceptance and unconditional acceptance of others (Ellis, 1999).

Mind-training activities can also be used as a direct stimulus for demonstrating human sympathy. For example, with their therapists' assistance, clients can train their minds to become more aware of positive impulses towards others. Clients can be helped to create skilful self-talk and visual images for showing compassion, expressing gratitude, and expressing sympathetic joy in others' good fortune. Clients can be helped to challenge and restate rules that can inhibit generosity: for example, 'I must always accumulate wealth.' Clients may also train their minds to challenge rules that interfere with persisting with showing compassion: for instance, 'People must always show gratitude for what I do.' Selfless service can require a high degree of detachment from the need for others' approval.

Therapists can assist clients to develop the mind skill of perceiving more clearly the benefits to themselves and others of demonstrating human sympathy, including that they are fulfilling part of their fundamental human nature. Furthermore, therapists can help clients to train their minds so that they keep giving personally responsible explanations for engaging in or failing to engage in generous communications and actions. In addition, clients can train their minds to create realistic expectations concerning the consequences of specific compassionate actions.

A disciplined state of mind takes time to develop and must be nourished by daily practice. Learning is a first step, to be followed by other steps such as developing conviction of the need to change, increasing one's commitment, developing determination to change, and making a sustained effort to implement the actual changes (Dalai Lama and Cutler, 1998).

Human sympathy activities
A disciplined state of mind is insufficient if not translated into daily actions. Batchelor (1997) observes that, when faced with the complexities of the moment, 'the question is not "What is the right thing to do", but "What is the compassionate thing to do?"' (p. 48). Therapists can assist clients, through appropriate in-session and out-of-session activities, to build up their ability to communicate and act in ways that are beneficial to others and do not harm them. Actions that flow from mental discipline and human sympathy include:

- patience and tolerance;
- living simply without showing off or competing;
- showing gratitude and appreciation;

- actively making others happy;
- acting compassionately to those who are suffering;
- showing sympathetic joy in others' happiness and good fortune.

As appropriate, therapists can work with clients to develop verbal, voice, body, touch and action-taking communications in each area. As a guideline, therapists and clients should take a step-by-step approach in changing communications and actions so that the changes genuinely become integrated as wholesome habits in clients' ways of relating to others. One approach is for therapists and clients to collaborate to set up human sympathy experiments in which clients agree to change their actions, monitor how they think, feel and act, and then evaluate the consequences for themselves and others of behaving differently.

As with a disciplined state of mind, developing disciplined ways of acting skilfully in showing human sympathy takes not only learning and training, but conviction, commitment, determination, and making a sustained effort as clients gradually liberate themselves to be more loving persons. Mind skills connected with showing and persisting in showing human sympathy should be addressed and integrated at all stages of the process.

In addition, clients can be encouraged to identify like-minded people, be they secular or religious, with whom they may have ongoing contact as friends and mentors. In these relationships clients may be challenged, nourished, supported and, sometimes, humbled and inspired by their friends' and mentors' examples. Furthermore, as time goes by, clients in turn may increasingly be able to provide challenge, nourishment and support for these people.

CASE MATERIAL

Sources of case material for the lifeskills therapy component of CHT include the use of the approach with Louise Donovan, a redundant executive who needed to address her very poor interview skills, which were the tip of an iceberg of poor professional relationship skills (Nelson-Jones, 2000b). The fourth edition of my textbook *Practical Counselling and Helping Skills* contains numerous vignettes of good use of skills at each stage of the DASIE therapy process model (Nelson-Jones, 1997). In addition, my book *Creating Happy Relationships: A Guide to Partner Skills* presents vignettes that show the application of good mind skills and communication skills in various relationship skills areas (Nelson-Jones, 1999b). To date, there are no published case studies of the mental discipline component of CHT, a situation I intend to rectify by the next edition of this book.

FURTHER DEVELOPMENTS

Occidental and oriental cultures have much to learn from one another, as well as much in common in terms of universal values, such as benevolence. Cognitive–humanistic therapy is still work in progress. In particular I want to develop the mental discipline therapy component. Recently, I established the Cognitive-Humanistic Institute in Chiang Mai to provide a setting for spending time and resources doing this.

Some problems that have already existed in the second millennium will become much more pressing in the third. As technological advances continue to outstrip human development, the issue of creating not just richer but better human beings becomes increasingly important. Indeed, the survival of the human race may depend on the humans' success in synergistically creating better people and better societies. In addition, as issues of economic sufficiency become less worrisome for many humans, they are faced with how to create happiness and alleviate suffering more starkly than when struggling for economic survival. Experience in prosperous Western countries indicates that humans have a long way to go in learning how to be happy in the midst of plenty. This problem may become even more acute as material wealth increases and unhappiness stemming from mental poverty persists, if not worsens.

Attaining supra-normal compassionate functioning has been insufficiently addressed in the counselling and therapy literature. This state of affairs needs to change. The development of cognitive–humanistic therapy is but a small step in what needs to be a much larger attempt within the helping professions to create therapy and training approaches that raise the bar for normalcy at the same time as encouraging higher levels of supra-normal psychological functioning.

SUMMARY

- *Cognitive–humanistic therapy consists of two, somewhat overlapping, components: lifeskills therapy, aimed mainly at conventional adaptation; and mental discipline therapy, whose goal is supra-normal functioning.*
- *Hard humanism involves disciplining the mind to synergistically foster the interests and ideals of self, others and humankind.*
- *Innate goodness refers to the positive core of a person's being, which encompasses biological tendencies towards affirming life, co-operation, and human sympathy. It is important to acknowledge innate goodness and not just to focus on destructive tendencies.*
- *Psychological suffering consists of two parts: existential suffering, which is the lot of all humans, and self-created suffering, through using one's mind insufficiently skilfully. Happiness reflects a person's ability to make contact with and demonstrate innate goodness.*
- *A person's mind is the seat of awareness, thought, imagery, feeling and of personal identity and agency. People can exert control over their mental processes. Furthermore, they can use their minds to create and alter their self-concepts, what they refer to as 'I' or 'me'.*
- *Lifeskills are sequences of choices that people make in specific areas of skill. There are two main categories of lifeskills: mind skills and communication/action skills.*
- *Seven central mind skills are creating awareness, self-talk, visual images, rules, perceptions, explanations and expectations.*
- *Communication/action skills vary by area of application. Five main ways of sending communication/action skills messages are: verbal, voice, body, touch, and action-taking.*
- *People are personally responsible for developing and using good skills in each of the five Rs of good or skilled persons: responsiveness, realism, relating, rewarding activity, and right-and-wrong.*
- *Processes by means of which people learn to function well or poorly include: supportive*

relationships, learning from example and consequences, instruction and self-instruction, information and opportunity, and anxiety and confidence.

- Dehumanizing factors, such as being a link in the chain of production, consumerism, and a mechanical approach to education, contribute to people failing to attain their full humanness.
- Processes by which people maintain low levels of functioning include inadequate mind skills and negative external influences.
- Goals for lifeskills therapy focus on the skills required for addressing specific problems and problem situations both now and in future. Goals for mental discipline therapy focus on developing one's mind to feel and show more human sympathy.
- Lifeskills therapy is structured around DASIE, a systematic five-stage model of the therapy process. DASIE's five stages are: (1) Develop the relationship and clarify problems; (2) Assess and restate problems in skills terms; (3) Set goals and plan interventions; (4) Intervene to develop lifeskills; (5) Emphasize take-away and end.
- The process of mental discipline therapy includes facilitating self-assessment, teaching people the concepts of mind and mind skills, and engaging in mind training and in human sympathy activities.
- The lifeskills therapist provides a relationship like that of a client-centred coach, whereas the mental discipline therapist is more like a wise guide or mentor.
- Interventions in lifeskills therapy can focus on mind skills, communication/action skills and on influencing feelings. Therapists help clients to think in skills terms about their mental processes and communications.
- Interventions in mental discipline therapy include mind-training activities and human sympathy activities.
- Cognitive–humanistic therapy addresses some problems that are likely to grow in the third millennium, such as the gap between technological advances and developments in human goodness and the fact that economic prosperity is insufficient to alleviate mental poverty.

REVIEW AND PERSONAL QUESTIONS

REVIEW QUESTIONS

1. Critically discuss the idea of innate goodness.
2. Critically discuss the concepts of: psychological suffering; and happiness.
3. Why does cognitive–humanistic therapy stress the concept of mind?
4. What are lifeskills? What do you think of the distinction between mind skills and communication/action skills?
5. Critically discuss the ideas presented in the chapter on how people learn to function well or poorly.
6. What do you consider to be some of the main dehumanizing factors in your culture?
7. Critically discuss how people maintain their level of functioning, sometimes at great personal cost.
8. What do you think of the goals of cognitive–humanistic therapy? Do you think it a

good idea to distinguish between lifeskills therapy goals and mental discipline therapy goals?

9. Describe the process of lifeskills therapy and mental discipline therapy.
10. What is the nature of the therapeutic relationship in lifeskills therapy and mental discipline therapy?
11. How, if at all, do you consider interventions for mental discipline therapy differ from those for lifeskills therapy?

PERSONAL QUESTIONS

1. How do you see your own basic human nature? What evidence, if any, is there of innate goodness?
2. To what extent do you see yourself as either suffering or happy, or a mixture of the two? Please give reasons.
3. In relation to one of your poor mind skills and/or poor communication/action skills:
   (a) how did you acquire it in the first place; and
   (b) how have you maintained it in the past and how are you currently maintaining it?
4. How skilled a person are you? Answer with respect to each of the five Rs: responsiveness, realism, relating, rewarding activity, and right-and-wrong.
5. Confront a problem situation in your life and restate it in skills terms by identifying at least one poor mind skill and one poor communication/action skill.
6. Do you think you need develop into someone capable of feeling and showing more human sympathy? If so, how might you go about changing?
7. What relevance, if any, has the theory and practice of cognitive–humanistic therapy for how you conduct therapy?
8. What relevance, if any, has the theory and practice of cognitive–humanistic therapy for how you live?

ANNOTATED BIBLIOGRAPHY

Nelson-Jones, R. (1999b). *Creating Happy Relationships: A Guide to Partner Skills*. London: Cassell.

This book is divided into three parts. Part 1, 'Introduction', discusses creating your mind, communication and feelings and the influences of your past. Part 2, 'Empowering your Mind', has chapters on creating self-talk, visual images, rules, perceptions, explanations and expectations. Part 3, 'Developing your communication', reviews communication and mind skills in seven relationship areas: becoming more outgoing, listening better, showing you care, sharing intimacy, enjoying sex together, managing anger and communicating assertively, and managing relationship problems.

Nelson-Jones, R. (1997). *Practical Counselling and Helping Skills: Text and Exercises for the Lifeskills Counselling Model* (4th edition). London: Cassell.

This book is aimed at people training either to be professional counsellors or for roles with a large counselling content. Part 1 provides a theoretical framework, overviews the lifeskills counselling model, and looks at counsellors as persons. Parts 2 to 6 present the component skills for each of the five stages of the DASIE counselling process model. Part 7 focuses on developing your counselling skills still further.

Nelson-Jones, R. (2000a). *Introduction to Counselling Skills: Text and Activities.* London: Sage.
Intended as a general counselling skills text, this book provides an introduction to the component skills of cognitive–humanistic therapy. The book heavily emphasizes building effective counselling relationships involving heart and head and introduces readers to how to develop clients' mind skills and communication/action skills.

Nelson-Jones, R. (1984). *Personal Responsibility Counselling and Therapy: An Integrative Approach.*
Milton Keynes: Open University Press.
The first part of this book reviews the concept of personal responsibility in the theory and practice of different counselling approaches. The second part develops the theory and practice of a counselling approach with personal responsibility as a central integrating concept. The book represents a developmental stage in what was to become cognitive–humanistic therapy.

Dalai Lama, His Holiness the, and Cutler, H. C. (1998). *The Art of Happiness: A Handbook for Living.* Sydney: Hodder.
This easily readable book beautifully illustrates the humane wisdom of the East. Howard Cutler, a psychiatrist, presents and comments upon extensive conversations with the Dalai Lama. The book's five parts are called the purpose of life, human warmth and compassion, transforming suffering, overcoming obstacles, and closing reflections on living a spiritual life.

REFERENCES AND FURTHER READING

Adler, A. (1998) *Social Interest: Adler's Key to the Meaning of Life.* Oxford: Oneworld. First published in 1933.

Allport, G. W. (1964). The fruits of eclecticism: Bitter or sweet? *Acta Psychologica, 23,* 27–44.

Argyle, M. (1991). *Cooperation: The Basis of Sociability.* London: Routledge.

Bandura, A. (1986). *Social Foundations of Thought and Action: A Social Cognitive Theory.* Englewood Cliffs, NJ: Prentice-Hall.

Batchelor, S. (1997). *Buddhism Without Beliefs: A Contemporary Guide to Awakening.* London: Bloomsbury Publishing.

Beck, A. T. (1999). *Prisoners of Hate: The Cognitive Basis of Anger, Hostility, and Violence.* New York: HarperCollins.

Bowlby, J. (1979). *The Making and Breaking of Affectional Bonds.* London: Tavistock.

Chodron, T. (1990). *Taming the Monkey Mind.* Lutterworth: Tynron Press.

Dalai Lama, His Holiness the, and Cutler, H. C. (1998). *The Art of Happiness: A Handbook for Living.* Sydney: Hodder.

Ellis, A. (1999). Three methods of rational emotive behavior therapy that make my psychotherapy effective. *Psychotherapy Bulletin, 34,* 38–9.

Fromm, E. (1961). *Marx's Concept of Man.* New York: Frederick Ungar Publishing.

Greer, G. (1999). *The Whole Woman.* London: Anchor.

Kornfield, J. (1993). *A Path with Heart: A Guide Through the Perils and Promises of Spiritual Life.* New York: Bantam.

Maslow, A. H. (1962). *Toward a Psychology of Being.* New York: Van Nostrand.

Maslow, A. H. (1971). *The Farther Reaches of Human Nature.* Harmondsworth: Pelican.

Masters, W. H., Johnson, V. E. and Kolodny, R. C. (1986). *Masters and Johnson on Sex and Human Loving.* London: Pan MacMillan.

Nelson-Jones, R. (1984). *Personal Responsibility Counselling and Therapy: An Integrative Approach.* Milton Keynes: Open University Press.

Nelson-Jones, R. (1993). *Practical Counselling and Helping Skills: How to Use the Lifeskills Helping Model* (3rd edition). London: Cassell.

Nelson-Jones, R. (1997). *Practical Counselling and Helping Skills: Text and Exercises for the Lifeskills Counselling Model* (4th edition). London: Cassell.

Nelson-Jones, R. (1999a). Towards cognitive–humanistic counselling. *Counselling, 10,* 49–54.

Nelson-Jones, R. (1999b). *Creating Happy Relationships: A Guide to Partner Skills.* London: Cassell.

Nelson-Jones, R. (2000a). *Introduction to Counselling Skills: Text and Activities.* London: Sage.

Nelson-Jones, R. (2000b). Lifeskills counselling. In S. Palmer (ed.). *Introduction to Counselling and Psychotherapy: The Essential Guide* (126–39). London: Sage.

Raskin, N. J. and Rogers, C. R. (2000). Person-centered therapy. In R. J. Corsini and D. Wedding (eds). *Current Psychotherapies* (6th edition, 133–67). Itasca, IL: Peacock.

Rogers, C. R. (1959). A theory of therapy, personality, and interpersonal relationships, as developed in the client-centered framework. In S. Koch (ed.). *Psychology: A Study of Science* (Study 1, Volume 3, 184–256). New York: McGraw-Hill.

Salzberg, S. (1997). *Lovingkindness: The Revolutionary Art of Happiness.* London: Shambhala.

Steiner, C. (1974). *Scripts People Live: Transactional Analysis of Life Scripts.* New York: Bantam.

Thera, N. (1962). *The Heart of Buddhist Meditation: A Handbook of Mental Training Based on the Buddha's Way of Mindfulness.* London: Rider and Company.

Thitavanno, Ven. Pra, (1995). *Mind Development.* Bangkok, Mahamakut Buddhist University.

Walsh, R. (1999). *Essential Spirituality: Exercises from the World's Religions to Cultivate Kindness, Love, Joy, Peace, Vision, Wisdom and Generosity.* New York: John Wiley.

Walsh, R. (2000). Asian psychotherapies. In R. Corsini and D. Wedding (eds). *Current Psychotherapies* (6th edition, 407–44). Itasca, IL: Peacock.

Yalom, I. D. (1980). *Existential Psychotherapy.* New York: Basic Books.

16

Cultural Issues

See how cruel the whites look. Their lips are thin, their noses sharp, their faces furrowed and distorted by folds. Their eyes have a staring expression; they are always seeking something. What are they seeking? The whites always want something; they are always uneasy and restless. We do not know what they want. We do not understand them. We think they are mad.

Ochwiay Biano (Mountain Lake), a Pueblo Indian, to C. G. Jung

INTRODUCTION

Over the past twenty to thirty years, there has been growing interest in diversity-sensitive counselling and therapy. The differences on which this burgeoning literature focuses include culture, race, gender, sexual and affectionate orientation, disability, religion, socioeconomic status, and mixtures of these, among others (Weinrach and Thomas, 1998). In the following two chapters, I provide introductory reviews of two dimensions of diversity that affect all therapists and clients: namely, culture and gender.

Critics of existing counselling and therapy theories assert that their Euro-American cultural bias means that Western-oriented therapists may be failing their actual and potential cultural minority group client populations in a number of significant ways (Sue, Ivey, and Pedersen, 1996; Sue and Sue, 1999). Counselling and therapy services are under-utilized by minority groups because of issues like mistrust, perceived irrelevance and cultural insensitivity. Assessment may insufficiently take into account differences in how behaviours are perceived in different cultures. In addition, therapists may fail to understand and address the chronic stresses attached to being in a cultural minority group and the emotional disruption of migration to a different culture. Once therapy begins, apart from obvious language difficulties, therapists may experience difficulty in comprehending the communication patterns and personal and social contexts of their clients' problems. If clients have not discontinued already, therapists may establish goals and intervene on the basis of mainstream cultural assumptions that run counter to the cultural norms and personal meanings of their clients. Furthermore, therapists may focus too much on dealing with individuals rather than dealing with individuals in the context of their families and their social networks. In addition, the helping professions insufficiently attend to the need for institutional and social change to counteract the oppression of minority groups.

The terminology of culture

Many of the terms associated with culture possess different shadings of meaning according to who does the defining. The following discussion of some key terms and concepts relevant to cultural issues in therapy is illustrative rather than prescriptive. Some of these terms and concepts will be elaborated as the chapter progresses.

Culture

Following are various definitions of culture that illustrate some of the concept's different meanings. Herskovits (1948) views culture as that part of the environment that is shaped or created by humans. Spindler, who taught the author a course in educational anthropology at Stanford University, defines culture as 'a patterned system of tradition-derived norms influencing behavior' (Spindler, 1963, p. 7). He goes on to observe that cultural norms are in a constant state of flux. Another definition of culture is that it refers to 'an integrated pattern of human behavior that includes thoughts, communications, actions, customs, beliefs, values, and institutions of a racial, ethnic, religious or social group' (Cross *et al.*, 1989, p. iv). A colloquial definition of culture is 'the way we do things here.'

Enculturation

Enculturation refers to the transmission of cultural norms within a given culture. Another way of viewing enculturation is as the socialization process in which younger members learn cultural rules from their elders. Nowadays, there are many different avenues for cultural transmission, for instance the media and the Internet.

Acculturation

Acculturation refers to the behavioural and psychological changes that occur in individuals as a result of their interaction with a different culture. For example, all migrants to Britain and Australia undergo acculturation. However, in both countries, migrants acculturate at varying rates and attain different levels of assimilation to the mainstream culture.

Culture shock

Culture shock, of varying levels of severity, is a fairly common reaction to stresses of adapting to a new culture. Its symptoms can include anxiety, a sense of loss, confusion of roles, feelings of helplessness and a desire for a more familiar and predictable environment. If marked, culture shock can engender pathological symptoms, such as depression and psychological and physical withdrawal.

Cultural change

Cultures are not static. Change can come from within and without, or a mixture of the two. For instance, in Britain and Australia there are traditional mainstream cultures adhered to mainly by the older generation, as well as emergent cultures being created predominantly by the younger generation. Intermarrying between different ethnic groups is another stimulus for cultural change coming from within a country.

In addition, cultural change can come from without: for example, in Britain the influence of other European cultures has increased with entry into the Common Market and more business, educational and holiday travel to and from other European countries. Similarly, Australian culture changed with the post-Second World War influx of southern European migrants and the post-Vietnam War influx of Southeast Asian migrants. Furthermore the world is increasingly a 'global village' with cultural changes mediated by technological advances such as cable TV and the Internet. Hermans and Kempen observe: 'In an increasingly interconnected world society, the conception of independent, coherent and stable cultures becomes increasingly irrelevant' (1998, p. 1,111). Some changes due to globalization may lead to a blurring of cultural distinctions and some lessening of distinctive cultural identities.

Multiculturalism

The central value of multiculturalism is that of cultural pluralism and acknowledging that nations like Britain, Australia and America are cultural mosaics rather than cultural melting-pots (Sue *et al.*, 1998). Multiculturalism can be contrasted with monoculturalism where high value is attached only to the patterns of behaviour of the dominant or mainstream culture.

Cultural cohesion

Cultural cohesion or social cohesiveness refers to the extent to which the norms of a culture or nation help it to stick together. In Britain, Australia and the United States many of the problems of cultural minorities are those of equality of access to opportunities within the mainstream culture rather than the fact that a mainstream culture exists. In such culturally diverse countries, a balance needs to be struck between multiculturalism and cultural cohesion. If taken to extremes, in a highly culturally diverse country like Australia, multiculturalism could lead to each ethnic group following its own agenda and so coming into conflict with other ethnic groups. Northern Ireland provides a good example inadequate cohesion, with its two main cultural groups insufficiently finding common ground.

Race

Race refers to human sub-groups possessing distinctive physical characteristics that distinguish them from other human sub-groups. Such physical characteristics include skin colour, head form, facial features, and amount, colour and texture of body hair. Racial groups include Caucasian, Aboriginal, African, Asian, Polynesian or various combinations of mixed race.

Ethnic minority

A neutral definition of ethnic minorities is that they are groups differentiated from the main population of a country by racial origin and/or cultural background. A more telling definition of a minority, be it ethnic or otherwise, is that it is 'a group of people who, because of physical or cultural characteristics, are singled out from others in the society in which they live for differential and unequal treatment, and who therefore regard them-selves as objects of collective discrimination' (Wirth, 1945, p. 347).

Culture and demography

Some indication of the importance of culture can be found in the demographic statistics of various countries. Demography is the study of population sizes, movements and trends, including those concerning ethnic minorities. In Britain, in 1995/96, Caucasians formed 94.2 per cent of the total population of 56.2 million people. The overall ethnic minority population, comprising both those born abroad and those born in the UK, was estimated to have been 5.8 per cent or about 1 in 18 of the total population. The four largest ethnic minority groups were: Indian, 1.5 per cent; Pakistani, 1.0 per cent; Black-Caribbean, 0.9 per cent, and Black African, 0.5 per cent (Haskey, 1997). The above figures disguise the full extent of cultural differences in Britain, for instance between the Welsh, Irish, Scots and English as well as between the more racially distinguished ethnic groupings.

Australia is one of the most multicultural and, increasingly, multiracial countries in the world. In 1995, 22.8 per cent or nearly a quarter of the population of 18.2 million was born overseas: with the two largest overseas-born groupings being European, 13.1 per cent, and Asian, 4.8 per cent. Of the Asian born, 2.6 per cent came from Southeast Asia, 1.4 per cent from Northeast Asia, and 0.8 per cent from Southern Asia. In 1995–96, nearly 40 per cent of settler arrivals were Asian born: 18.8 per cent from Northeast Asia; 13.3 per cent from Southeast Asia; and 7.8 per cent from Southern Asia (Department of Immigration and Multicultural Affairs, 1997). The rates of migration from Asia point to an increasingly Eurasian future for Australia. In addition, Australia has over a quarter of a million people of Aboriginal and Torres Strait Islander descent.

Like Australia, the United States is undergoing a marked change in its racial/ethnic population distribution. Currently, approximately one-third of the total population and about 45 per cent of the public school population are from ethnic minorities. From 1980 to 1990 the growth of the white population was just 6.0 per cent, whereas the growth rates for the minorities were: African American 13.2 per cent; Native American 38 per cent; Hispanic/Latino American 53 per cent; and Asian American/Pacific Islander, 107.7 per cent. Demographic projections indicate that non-white will outnumber white persons sometime between the years 2030 and 2050 (Sue and Sue, 1999). The US popu-lation is scheduled to jump from 255 million to 383 million by the year 2050 (US Census Bureau, 1992).

THEORY

Current theories of counseling and psychotherapy inadequately describe, predict and deal with the richness and complexity of a culturally diverse population.

Derald Sue, Allen Ivey and Paul Pedersen

Culture and full humanness

An important issue in thinking about cultures is the extent to which they are conducive to developing the full humanness of their individual members (Maslow, 1971). The idea that all cultures are equally benign in promoting the human potential of their members is both false and naïve: for example, think of the demeaning position of women in Taliban-ruled Afghanistan. Maslow was cautiously optimistic about the biological nature of human beings. However, he thought that positive aspects of human nature, such as altruistic concern for others, were frequently weak, needed a benign culture for their appearance, and could be inhibited or shattered by bad cultural conditions.

The noted anthropologist Ruth Benedict used the notion of *synergy* to describe the healthy interaction between individual and society (Benedict, 1942). There is a reciprocal interaction between the development or lack of development of individuals and the cultures or societies to which they belong. Maslow considered that 'Individual and social interests under healthy social conditions are synergic and not antagonistic' (1970, p. 85). A criticism of the multicultural literature is that it has been insufficiently rigorous in addressing how cultures differ in being encouraging, benign, inhibiting or antagonistic to developing both the basic lifeskills and the higher potentials of their members. All cultures are not equally worthy of respect in all of their aspects.

Culture and values

One of the main dimensions of a culture is that of values or the underlying principles that guide how people live their lives. However, there is no exact relationship between how people think they ought to behave, their values, and their actual behaviour

Universal values

Schwartz is a prominent researcher in the area of values (Schwartz, 1992; Schwartz and Bilsky, 1990). Schwartz classified values into ten types: power, achievement, hedonism, stimulation, self-direction, universalism, benevolence, tradition, conformity, and security. Based on information from twenty countries in six continents, Schwartz (1992) confirmed that each of the ten values was found in at least 90 per cent of the countries he surveyed, suggesting that his value types are near universal.

Cultural dimensions

One of the major cross-cultural research endeavours in recent years was the collection of data on work-related attitudes in 50 countries and three regions by the Dutch psychologist Hofstede (1980, 1983). Hofstede identified four cultural dimensions or factors in those countries and regions (see Box 16.1).

BOX 16.1

Hofstede's four cultural dimensions

Power distance   Refers to social inequality and the amount of power one person has over others.

Uncertainty avoidance   Relates to how a culture deals with conflict, especially the creation of beliefs and institutions to deal with disagreements and aggression.

Individualism versus collectivism   Individualistic cultures are those in which people only care for themselves and their close relations. In collectivistic cultures, people belong to ingroups or collectives which care for them in return for loyalty.

Masculinity–femininity   Refers to two opposite sets of cultural values. In masculine cultures, the dominant values are success and money. In feminine cultures, the dominant values evolve around caring for others and quality of life.

Australia was one of the countries Hofstede studied. Of the four dimensions, Australia, relative to other countries, scored very high on individualism, mid-range on uncertainty avoidance and masculinity–femininity, and relatively low on power distance. Southeast Asian countries like Hong Kong, Malaysia and Singapore scored high to very high on power distance, high on uncertainty avoidance and collectivism, and mid-range on masculinity–femininity.

Asian values

In Britain, the two main ethnic minorities stem from Southern Asia: namely, Indians and Pakistanis. In Australia, the two main migrant groups are Northeast Asian and Southeast Asian. Though here I present two overlapping versions of Asian values, in reality there are numerous differences between Asian countries and within the populations of each country.

Laungani (1999a) suggests that there are four interrelated core values of factors that distinguish Western from Eastern cultures. In particular, he focuses on differences between British and Indian cultures. Laungani stresses that the two concepts underlying each of the factors summarized in Box 16.2 should be regarded as extending along a continuum rather than as dichotomous. Note that the one factor which overlaps with Hofstede's four dimensions is that of Individualism–Communalism (Collectivism),

---

BOX 16.2

Laungani's four core values or factors distinguishing Western (British) from Eastern (Indian) cultures

Individualism–Communalism (Collectivism)
Individualism   Emphasizes self-control, personal responsibility, self-achievement, individuals achieving an identity, and nuclear families.
Communalism (Collectivism)   Emphasizes dependence on elders and other family members, collective responsibility, collective achievement, family and caste-related identity ascribed at birth, and extended families.

Cognitivism–Emotionalism
Cognitivism   Emphasizes rationality and logic, keeping feelings and emotions in check, work and activity, and relationships based on shared interests.
Emotionalism   Emphasiszs feelings and intuition, expressing emotions openly, relationships as extremely important, and relationships being caste- and family-based.

Free will–Determinism
Free will   Emphasizes freedom of choice, being proactive, success or failure largely due to effort, self-blame or guilt as a residual consequence of failure, and the possibility of failure leading to blaming the victim.
Determinism   Emphasizes limited freedom of choice, being reactive, despite success being important it is related to one's karma, no guilt is attached to failure, and no blame is attached to the victim.

Materialism–Spiritualism
Materialism   Emphasizes the world as 'real' and physical, rejection of contradictory explanations of phenomena, reality is external to the individual, and reality is perceived through the scientific enterprise.
Spiritualism   Emphasizes the world as illusory, the co-existence of contradictory phenomena, reality being internal to the individual, and reality being perceived through contemplation and inner reflection.

---

which is perhaps the most frequently cited value differentiating Western from Eastern cultures.

Ho (1992) lists seven values held in common by Asian cultures that may be operating among Asian Americans, who are predominantly from Southeast and Northeast Asia. These values, which overlap with Laungani's Eastern (Indian) values, are also likely to be held by Southeast Asian and Northeast Asian migrants to Australia. Following is a summary of Ho's seven Asian values.

1. *Filial piety*, or a high degree of respect for parents.
2. *Shame*, or loss of face used as a method of reinforcing proper behaviour.
3. *Self-control*, requiring modesty in behaviour, humbleness in expectations, and hesitation, even when individuals highly desire an object.
4. *Assumption of the middle position*, or the Asian emphasis on consensus as a process that fosters the individual's sense of belong and togetherness.
5. *Awareness of the social milieu*, involving an awareness and sensitivity to others' opinions and feelings and being prepared to subordinate one's feelings in the interests of solidarity.
6. *Fatalism*, a belief system that accepts events as predetermined.
7. *Inconspicuousness*, based on the fear of attracting attention.

One of the issues of any migrant group is the extent to which the values of the parents who originally migrated are held by their children and grandchildren. Laungani provides some research evidence indicating that maintenance of parental values is the case among British-born Indian schoolchildren. However, a greater degree of assimilation into mainstream British culture is likely as the generations become further removed from their original migrant ancestors.

Often, conflicts arise *between* migrants, who value their cultures of origin, and their children, who are under considerable pressure to adapt to their host cultures. These conflicts are heightened because the children of migrants often perceive young people in Western cultures as being more independent and free than those in Eastern cultures. Conflicts inevitably also take place *within* the hearts and souls of migrants and their children, all of whom, in varying degrees and in differing ways, experience the pulls and pushes of being caught between two cultures.

Theoretical assumptions of Asian therapies

In the above discussion on values, it is apparent that assumptions underlying Asian approaches to therapy will differ from those underlying Western approaches. It is possible to divide people's developmental status into pre-conventional, conventional and post-conventional stages of growth. Walsh (2000) considers that, while capable of addressing lower levels, Asian psychotherapies aim primarily at post-conventional growth and the transpersonal domains, which are the special interest of Asia.

The concepts of mind and of mental development are central to understanding Asian therapies, whose starting point is that people's usual state of mind is underdeveloped. Because this state of affairs is so widespread, it often goes unnoticed. People suffer from a case of mistaken identity in that their true nature is something far more remarkable than the self-concept of 'ego' that they mistakenly assume to be their true selves. Psychological suffering is a function of insufficient mental development. It is possible to train and develop the mind both to reduce conventional self-created suffering and to develop supra-normal capacities such as heightened concentration and compassion. Meditation and yoga are included among effective ways of training the mind to function at higher levels and to access a vastly greater unconscious system than that offered by Freudian psychology (Walsh, 2000).

CULTURAL IDENTITY DEVELOPMENT

Cultural identity development theory is based on the assumption that individuals in cultural, racial and other minority groups possess varying levels of consciousness or awareness about their membership both of their minority group and of the wider society. In addition, cultural identity development theory is relevant to mainstream or majority groups in relation to themselves, minority groups and the wider culture.

Helms (1995) presents two racial identity models for the United States, one for members of the white majority culture and another for people of colour. She assumes that whites and coloured people have to work through issues of racism in different ways: for example, many, though not all, whites may start by assuming entitlement to the privileges society offers, and many non-whites may perceive their position as one of being oppressed and excluded from equal opportunity. For Helms, the most highly developed white people attain an 'autonomy status', involving an informed and positive commitment to racial equality and the capacity to give up the privileges of racism. The most highly developed coloured people attain the 'integrative awareness status' involving a capacity to value their own collective identities, as well as the ability to empathize and collaborate with members of other oppressed groups.

A five-stage model of cultural identity development focused on minority rather than majority groups is presented by Cheatham and his colleagues (Cheatham *et al.*, 1997). In this model people start by being 'asleep' in that they have little awareness of themselves as cultural beings and progress to attaining a level of consciousness in which they both possess a knowledgeable pride about their culture and recognize positive dimensions of the mainstream culture. Cheatham and his colleagues' model is summarized in Box 16.3. The model can be extended to deal with the consciousness raising of other minority groups such as women, and gays and lesbians.

Therapists and trainees can assess their own level of cultural identity development and, where necessary, take steps to improve their level of awareness of themselves as cultural beings. Therapists need also be aware of their client's level of cultural identity and, where appropriate, use this knowledge to assist their clients in attaining higher levels of cultural consciousness. However, therapists need to be careful not to impose cultural agendas on clients whose concerns lie elsewhere, for instance passing an upcoming test.

A theory of multicultural counselling and therapy

Sue, Ivey and Pedersen (1996) consider current theories of counselling and therapy are too ethnocentric and monocultural and lack conceptual frameworks that incorporate culture as a core concept in the therapeutic relationship. They propose a metatheory or theory about theories that they call Multicultural Counselling and Therapy (MCT). This metatheory is intended to offer a framework for understanding the numerous helping approaches that have been developed in both Western and non-Western cultures.

MCT consists of six propositions, each of which has corollaries. The first proposition is that MCT is a metatheory. The second proposition stresses that therapist and client

---

BOX 16.3

A model of cultural identity development

Stage 1: Naïvety
Individuals have little awareness of themselves as cultural beings: for example, children do not distinguish skin colour as an important feature.

Stage 2: Encounter
Individuals encounter experiences in their environments that clearly demonstrate that their earlier naïve views were inadequate.

Stage 3: Naming
Naming involves identifying one's cultural or minority group and the nature of oppression against it, for instance, Afro-Caribbean-British, Indian-British or Vietnamese-Australian and racism; gays and lesbians and homophobia; women and sexism.

Stage 4: Reflection on self as a cultural being
Individuals develop a keener awareness of themselves as Afro-Caribbean-British, Indian-British or Vietnamese-Australian. Individuals may turn inwards towards their own cultures and away from the majority culture. The developmental task is establishing a definite cultural consciousness.

Stage 5: Multiperspective internalization
Individuals develop pride in their cultures, yet accept worthwhile dimensions of the predominant culture. They can use important dimensions of all stages of development.

---

identities are embedded in many levels of experience and contexts, for example, individual, family and culture, and that the totality of these experiences must be the focus of treatment. The third proposition emphasizes the importance of the development of therapist and client cultural identity, including attitudes about dominant–subordinate relationships among culturally different groups.

The fourth proposition is that MCT theory is likely to be enhanced when therapists define goals and use modalities consistent with the life experiences and cultural values of their clients. The fifth proposition stresses the importance of multiple helping roles, often involving larger social units, developed by culturally different groups. The final proposition emphasizes that the liberation of consciousness is a basic MCT goal. For example, to develop in clients a critical consciousness, therapists, who draw on both Western and non-Western systems of helping, may often teach clients about the underlying cultural dimensions of their present concerns.

THERAPY

Counsellors of all races and backgrounds will increasingly be called upon to assist clients who possess markedly different worldviews.

Ingrid Grieger and Joseph Ponterotto

THERAPEUTIC GOALS

There are many different client groups for whom cultural considerations are important: for example, indigenous people, such as Australian Aborigines and Torres Strait Islanders; first-generation migrants, with many different reasons for seeking out a life in a new country; descendants of migrants at varying levels of assimilation to the mainstream culture; and members of the mainstream culture, among others. Following are some goals, which may overlap, for working with clients in whose problems issues of culture play a significant role.

Support

Migrants require culture-sensitive support when they first arrive in their new home countries. Think of the cumulative stresses involved in moving to a new culture, including change of home, parting from loved ones and previous support networks, language difficulties, climate change, change in physical environment (for instance the countryside and buildings look different), homesickness, loneliness, financial worries, concerns about children's education, and, for many migrants, racist incidents.

Dealing with post-traumatic stress

Many migrants are refugees and some suffer from post-traumatic stress disorders. Reasons for their traumatization include being war victims, witnessing violence, and living through missile attacks, torture, starvation, imprisonment, internment, and rape. Such migrants may suffer persistent re-experiencing of traumatic events, hyper-arousal, numbing of affect, or oscillate between hyper-arousal and numbing of affect. Traumatized migrants, with their families and support networks, require special culture-sensitive post-traumatic stress disorder therapy.

Assisting acculturation and assimilation

The multicultural literature is often overly negative about the virtues of mainstream cultures such as those in Britain, Australia and America. In addition, much of the literature seems to insufficiently address the need for cultural cohesion as well as for cultural diversity. Most migrants move because the perceived benefits of their new countries far outweigh those of their former ones. Migration can be a time of great opportunity. However, it is also a time of considerable challenges. Migrants require practical help with such matters as housing, health, education, and employment. Furthermore, all migrants bring psychological strengths and deficiencies to their transitions to a new culture. Some may require culturally-sensitive psychological assistance so as not to activate self-defeating patterns for dealing with change and stress, for instance withdrawal, being unwilling to alter old ways of behaving, and aggressively disparaging their new countries.

Assisting clients to handle cross-cultural relationships

Difficulties in cross-cultural relationships can take many forms. Therapists can assist existing members of host countries and first-generation migrants to develop skills of accepting difference, reaching out to one another, and of building bridges rather than barriers between cultures. Therapists may also need skills in assisting migrants and their children to deal with issues of intergenerational conflict, for instance choice of boyfriends/girlfriends. In a country like Australia, where cross-cultural relationships are common, therapeutic goals can also include helping partners in intimate relationships to understand and accommodate to one another's cultural differences.

Consciousness raising and liberation

For those clients who suffer from discrimination and oppression on account of culture and race, therapeutic goals can and should address issues of cultural identity development. Some readers may wish to review Box 16.3, 'A model of cultural identity development'. Ethnic minority clients can be assisted to take pride in their cultures, liberate themselves from internalized negative stereotypes, and join the broader struggle against external oppression on account of culture and race. Consciousness raising and liberation can also be important therapeutic goals for mainstream culture clients, who require assistance in relinquishing negative aspects of their enculturation, such as a false sense of cultural and racial superiority. Some mainstream culture clients may then also participate in the fight for cultural and racial equality.

Avoiding further marginalization

Therapists need to be aware that, if they pursue cultural agendas clumsily, they can do more harm than good. Where appropriate, therapists can and should help ethnic minority group clients be assertive about attaining their human rights. However, there is a danger that therapists collude when some minority clients further marginalize themselves by unfairly 'demonizing' their host cultures, making their lives out to be worse than they are, and playing the psychological game of 'Ain't it awful', at the same time as doing little positive to change their situations. When dealing with issues of acculturation and change, people of all cultures and races can be inflexible and self-defeating.

Attaining higher levels of development

The goals of some culturally different clients may be more oriented towards growth rather than adaptation to a mainstream culture. What constitutes higher levels of development can vary according to culture and to the therapeutic approach employed. For instance, Eastern cultures stress heightened concentration, mental purification, kindness, compassion, sympathetic joy in one another's accomplishments, equanimity, wisdom and selfless service (Walsh, 2000).

The good society

A broader goal of multicultural counselling and therapy is to develop formal and informal norms within societies that are synergistic rather than antagonistic to developing the full human potential of all members. This goal requires therapists to play social engineering and change agent roles, especially in regard to combating institutions and organizations that are instruments of cultural and racial oppression.

THERAPEUTIC APPROACHES

As may be seen from the above list of goals, there are many different considerations in selecting therapeutic approaches for problems that contain a significant cultural component. The issue of culturally relevant counselling and therapy can be addressed in at least three different ways: first, by making existing Euro-American therapies more culture-sensitive; second, by therapists developing multicultural counselling and therapy competences; and third, by engaging in non-Western approaches to counselling and therapy.

Making existing Euro-American therapies more culture-sensitive

To what extent can cultural issues be addressed by modifying the theory and practice of existing Western counselling and therapy approaches so that they become more culture-sensitive? The following discussion addresses some issues in applying person-centred therapy and the cognitive–behavioural therapies to minority group and mainstream culture clients.

With mainstream culture clients, person-centred therapists can use Rogerian empathy to assist them to experience and explore their cultural and racial concerns. However, this will only happen in those instances where clients have sufficient awareness and interest to work on such issues. The person-centred concept of empathy can be expanded to include cultural empathy (Ridley and Lingle, 1996). Person-centred therapists who see themselves and their clients as cultural beings can encourage non-Western clients to share their experiences by such methods as listening carefully for and responding to culturally relevant cues rather than not attending to them, and also by openly acknowledging that they are from a different culture and then asking their client's assistance in understanding the cultural context of their concerns. When clients reveal experiences, therapists can consciously try to understand the cultural implications of clients' communications. Furthermore, when therapists respond they can be tentative in checking out the extent of their cultural understanding.

There are barriers to Western therapists being perceived as empathic by ethnic minority clients (Laungani, 1999b; Sue and Sue, 1999). For example, Asian clients want to perceive their therapists as expert and expect more direction from them. Furthermore, Asian clients may be reluctant to talk about their problems outside of their families. Communication may be made even more difficult because clients and therapists may not understand the meanings and nuances of one another's spoken and non-verbal communication. In addition, there is a distinct possibility that the Western therapist does not understand the Asian client's cultural worldview, including the importance attached to family relationships, and may project parts of her/his own worldview on to the client. These difficulties can be addressed to some extent, if person-centred therapists, or any other therapists for that matter, are trained to understand the cultures and communication styles of one or more specific cultural groups from whom many of their clients come. However, really getting to grips with the mind-set of any foreign culture is much easier said than done. Ideally, learning about another culture in depth requires learning the relevant language and spending much time immersed in that culture.

The cognitive–behavioural therapies provide another example of how it is possible to extend existing Euro-American therapeutic approaches to become more culture-sensitive. Such therapies can be used to help both mainstream clients and minority group clients think more rationally and realistically regarding culture and race. However, there is a paucity of literature regarding how to do this and where the cross-cultural difficulties lie.

Regarding rational emotive behaviour therapy, Ellis (Ellis, 1998) includes racial prejudice in his list of prejudice-related irrationalities. In REBT, clients' cultural and racial irrational beliefs and prejudices can be detected, disputed and, where appropriate, restated in preferential and rational terms. Similarly, in cognitive therapy, questioning by skilled therapists can assist clients to identify their underlying cultural and racial automatic thoughts, explore how realistic they are, and formulate more realistic thoughts and perceptions for the future. Regarding multimodal therapy, Palmer (2000) claims it is sufficiently flexible to use with most ethnic minority clients suffering from stress.

Multicultural counselling and therapy competences

An American approach to issues of culture and race in counselling and therapy has been to develop a statement of multicultural counselling competences for culturally skilled counsellors and therapists (Sue *et al.*, 1998). This statement is the work of a committee of the American Psychological Association's Division of Counseling Psychology. The committee saw multicultural counselling competences as having three main dimensions: awareness of own assumptions, values and biases; understanding the worldview of the culturally different client; and developing appropriate strategies and techniques. Each dimension is divided into beliefs and attitudes, knowledge and skills. The United States has a long history of serious, and often brutal, racial oppression which provided one of the main contexts in which this statement was compiled. One of the statement's major assumptions was that of widespread and systematic cultural and racial oppression.

Awareness of own assumptions, values and biases
The beliefs held by culturally skilled counsellors and therapists include being sensitive to their own cultural heritage, being comfortable with the differences of clients from other

cultures and races, and recognizing the limitations of their competence and expertise. Counsellors and therapists should know about their cultural and racial heritage and how this affects the therapeutic process, understand how oppression, racism and discrimination may affect them personally and in their work, and know about the impact of how they communicate on culturally different clients. Skills include seeking out relevant educational and training experiences, actively understanding oneself as a cultural and racial being, and seeking a non-racial identity.

Understanding the worldview of the culturally different client

Beliefs and attitudes for culturally skilled counsellors and therapists include being aware of their negative emotional reactions and of the stereotypes and preconceived notions that they may hold towards culturally and racially different groups. Therapists should know about the cultural experiences, cultural heritage and historical backgrounds of any particular group with whom they work, acknowledge how culture and race can affect help-seeking behaviour, know how culture and race can influence assessment and the selection and implementation of therapeutic interventions, and know about the oppressive political and environmental influences impinging on the lives of ethnic and racial minorities. Skills include keeping up-to-date on research findings relevant to the psychological well-being of various ethnic and racial groups, as well as being actively involved with minorities outside work settings to gain deeper insight into their perspectives.

Developing appropriate intervention strategies and techniques

Culturally skilled counsellors' and therapists' attitudes and beliefs include respecting clients' religious and spiritual beliefs about physical and mental functioning, respecting indigenous helping practices, and valuing bilingualism. Their knowledge base includes understanding how the culture-bound, class-bound and monolingual characteristics of counselling clash with the cultural values of various minority groups, being aware of institutional barriers to minority groups using helping services, knowing about the potential for bias in assessment instruments, and understanding minority group family structures, hierarchies, and community characteristics and resources. Skills include the ability to send and receive verbal and non-verbal communication accurately, interacting in the language requested by clients or making appropriate referrals, tailoring the therapeutic relationship and interventions to the clients' stage of cultural and racial identity development, and engaging in a variety of helping roles, beyond being a therapist. Box 16.4 identifies some of these additional helping roles (Atkinson, Thompson and Grant, 1993; Sue, Ivey and Pedersen, 1996).

The statement of multicultural competences is ambitious and has much to recommend it. However, possible reservations include the following. The statement assumes a high degree of cultural and racial oppression by the white mainstream culture, which may not be true in all instances. For example, some of the strongest supporters of minority group rights are white people. Furthermore, many white people are tolerant of and some are very positive about cultural differences, as witnessed by the growing number of cultural and racial intermarriages in countries like Australia and America (Kerwin and Pon-

---

BOX 16.4

Additional roles for multicultural counsellors and therapists

1. *Adviser*   Advising clients how to solve or prevent problems and providing relevant information.
2. *Advocate*   Representing and speaking up for clients' best interests to other individuals, groups or organizations.
3. *Facilitator of indigenous support systems*   Knowing about and appropriately involving support systems, such as the client's extended family and community elders.
4. *Facilitator of indigenous healing systems*   Either referring clients to healers or, if sufficiently knowledgeable and skilled, actually using the indigenous healing methods.
5. *Consultant*   Working collegially with clients to impact or change a third party, including organizational change.
6. *Change agent*   Initiating and implementing action-oriented approaches to changing social environments that may be oppressing clients.

---

terotto, 1995). In addition, cultural and racial biases are not the sole preserve of white people, and this fact should be more openly acknowledged and addressed. Another reservation is that the potential for modifying existing Euro-American counselling and therapy may be underestimated. Last, as migrants become more assimilated into their host cultures and as globalization increases the common ground among cultures, the need for a multicultural approach may become less pressing.

Despite these reservations, in countries like Britain, Australia and America, both obvious and more subtle oppression of cultural and racial minorities definitely exists. All therapists, regardless of their culture and race, need to address their own level of cultural identity development and their ability to offer culturally sensitive services to all clients, be they from minority groups or from the mainstream culture.

Non-Western approaches to counselling and therapy

Non-Western therapies come from many cultures – for instance, Asian and African. Such therapies may be the treatment of choice not only for some ethnic minority group clients, but also for some mainstream culture clients. In Asia, there is a long tradition of training the mind to foster interdependence, minimize suffering and create happiness. The main teaching of Buddhism, which is a system of psychology as well as a religion, can be summarized in the Buddha's statement: 'Refrain from evil, do good and purify the mind.' Here I use meditation and Naikan therapy to illustrate some Asian approaches to therapy.

Meditation

Meditation tends to be central to Asian therapeutic approaches. It falls into two main categories: mindfulness of breathing or breath meditation, and awareness or insight meditation. All meditation approaches require practice, with perseverance increasing the likelihood of better results. Meditation can be significantly enhanced by attending retreats in which clients engage in continuous meditation practice for days or weeks.

Breathing meditation consists of relaxed concentration on the flow of your breathing, on the in-breaths and on the out-breaths. Breathing meditation may be performed sitting, standing, walking or reclining. Buddhist insight meditations include calmly becoming aware of the impermanence of whatever experiences and sensations arise, and meditations that cultivate the four divine abodes of mind – loving kindness, compassion, sympathy and equanimity (Thitavanno, 1995).

Walsh (2000) observes that meditation can lead to a wide variety of insights and experiences over time. For instance, many clients gain insight into their customary lack of mental control or 'monkey minds'. Meditators come to recognize that everything in their mind is in a state of constant change and that the notion of an unchanging self, or even a self for that matter, is an illusory construction. With this insight egocentricity may be lessened and compassionate identification with others may increase. In advanced states of meditation, supra-normal capacities emerge, such as heightened concentration, perceptual sensitivity, and profound peace.

Naikan therapy

Naikan therapy is a Japanese approach adapted from a more intensive Buddhist meditation practice (Reynolds, 1990). It is aimed at assisting clients to find meaning in their lives, recognize human interdependence, feel and show gratitude, and repair relationships. Naikan therapy assumes that narrowly focusing on oneself creates suffering both for oneself and others.

Clients are encouraged to establish a calm meditative state and then to reflect specifically on three things:

1. what another person or other people have done for them;
2. how much gratitude is due to those others; and
3. the difficulties they have caused others and how little they have demonstrated gratitude.

Naikan therapy can elicit various thoughts and feelings, for instance guilt and unworthiness. However, many clients also get in touch with kinder and more generous feelings towards their care-givers. Clients may realize that, despite their weaknesses and failings, they were looked after and helped. Furthermore, they may start feeling very grateful to people in their pasts and want to make amends for their own inadequacies towards them.

CONCLUDING COMMENTS

At present, the mainstream cultures of Britain, Australia and America are insufficiently conducive to developing the full human potential of their members, and this is especially true for those in cultural, racial and other minority groups. Maslow (1970) raises the issue of whether it is possible to be a psychologically healthy person in an unhealthy culture. He cites resistance to enculturation as one of the distinguishing characteristics of his sample of self-actualizing people. Because of the deficiencies in American culture, such people were unable to attain mental wellness. However, they managed 'to get along by a complex combination of inner autonomy and outer acceptance . . . a kind of detached withholding from complete cultural identification' (p. 174).

The development of culture-sensitive counselling and therapy should not be restricted to any one of the three broad approaches mentioned above. Existing Euro-American therapies require further development to deal with the cultural issues pertaining to both minority and mainstream groups. All counsellors and therapists need to develop a set of core multicultural competences as well as competences specific to the main ethnic minority and racial groups with which they interact. Much more work is needed in defining, researching and providing good training materials that illustrate these core and culture-specific therapeutic competences. In addition, greater attention needs to be paid to raising Western therapists' awareness of non-Western therapies. Furthermore, more research needs to be conducted into the effectiveness of these therapies, either on their own or in combination with Western therapies, with clients from a range of cultures. East, West, North and South can learn therapeutic insights and skills from one another, to the benefit of all.

SUMMARY

- *Critics of existing counselling and therapy theories say their Euro-American cultural bias means that Western-oriented therapists may be failing their actual and potential minority group clients in significant ways.*
- *Key terms in understanding the influence of culture on therapy include: culture, enculturation, acculturation, culture shock, cultural change, multiculturalism, cultural cohesion, race, and ethnic minority.*
- *Demographic statistics show that Britain's ethnic minorities account for about 6 per cent of the total population. Australia and the United States have large ethnic minority populations and are rapidly becoming increasingly multicultural and multiracial societies.*
- *Cultures and societies can promote or inhibit the development towards full humanness of their members.*
- *Some cultural values appear to be universal, whereas others are more culture-specific. Hofstede identified four cultural work-related value dimensions: power distance, uncertainty avoidance, individualism versus collectivism, and masculinity–femininity.*
- *Laungani identified four interrelated core values distinguishing Western (British) and Eastern (Indian) cultures: individualism–communalism, cognitivism–emotionalism, free will–determinism, and materialism–spiritualism.*
- *Asian psychotherapies assume that people's usual state of mind is underdeveloped. It is possible to train and develop the mind to reduce conventional self-created suffering and to develop supra-normal capacities such as heightened concentration and compassion.*
- *Cultural identity development theory assumes that individuals are at varying levels of awareness and sophistication in relation to their cultural identity. Cheatham* et al.'s *cultural identity development model lists five stages: naïvety, encounter, naming, reflection on self as a cultural being, and multiperspective internalization.*

- *Sue, Ivey and Pedersen have presented a metatheory of multicultural counselling and therapy (MCT) consisting of six propositions, each with corollaries. The six propositions cover both theory and practice.*
- *Goals for culturally sensitive counselling and therapy include: support, dealing with post-traumatic stress, assisting acculturation and assimilation, assisting clients to handle cross-cultural relationships, consciousness raising and liberation, avoiding further marginalization, attaining higher levels of development, and the good society.*
- *Euro-American therapies can be made more culture-sensitive. The concept of empathy can be extended to cultural empathy. Rational emotive behaviour therapists can dispute cultural and racial irrational beliefs, and cognitive therapists can assist clients to identify their cultural and racial automatic thoughts and explore how realistic they are.*
- *Because of the deep-seated and pervasive nature of culture, there are limitations to how far the process of making Western therapies more culture-sensitive can go.*
- *Another approach to culture-sensitive therapy is that all therapists should possess multicultural counselling and therapy competences in three dimensions: awareness of own assumptions, values and biases, understanding the worldview of culturally different clients, and developing appropriate strategies and techniques.*
- *Additional roles for multicultural counsellors and therapists include: adviser, advocate, facilitator of indigenous support systems, facilitator of indigenous healing systems, consultant and change agent.*
- *Non-Western therapies come from many cultures. Asian therapeutic approaches include meditation and Naikan therapy. Meditation falls into two categories: mindfulness of breathing or breath meditation, and awareness or insight meditation. In advanced states of meditation supra-normal capacities emerge.*
- *Naikan therapy focuses on getting clients to realize their interdependence on others by recognizing what others have done for them, how much gratitude is due to others, and the difficulties clients have caused others and how little they have demonstrated gratitude.*
- *Culture-sensitive counselling and therapy can best be fostered by enhancing existing Euro-American therapies, developing multicultural competences, and developing and learning from non-Western therapies.*

REVIEW AND PERSONAL QUESTIONS

REVIEW QUESTIONS

1. What is the meaning of each of the following terms:
   - culture;
   - enculturation;
   - acculturation;
   - culture shock;
   - cultural change;
   - multiculturalism;
   - cultural cohesion;

- race; and
- ethnic minority?
2. Describe and evaluate each of the following:
   - Schwartz's universal value types;
   - Hofstede's four cultural dimensions; and
   - Laungani's and Ho's views of Asian values.
3. Critically discuss Cheatham *et al.*'s views of cultural identity development.
4. Critically discuss the goals for culture-sensitive therapy presented in the chapter.
5. What are some ways of making existing Euro-American therapies more culture sensitive?
6. What are multicultural counselling and therapy competences? What is your reaction to Sue *et al.*'s statement of competences?
7. What are some non-Western approaches to counselling and therapy?

PERSONAL QUESTIONS

1. How would you describe:
   - your ancestral background;
   - if an ethnic minority group member, the distinguishing features of your culture;
   - for all readers, the distinctive features of the mainstream culture in which you live?
2. To what extent do you consider the values you hold are universal and to what extent do you consider they are specific to your culture? Give reasons for your answer.
3. Describe instances, if any, in which you have been:
   - the recipient of cultural and/or racial oppression;
   - the purveyor of cultural and/or racial oppression.
4. What is your level of cultural identity development? Provide reasons for your answer.
5. To what extent and how can the main counselling and therapy approach you use be adapted for culturally different clients?
6. How can make yourself a more culturally sensitive counsellor or therapist, both now and in future?

ANNOTATED BIBLIOGRAPHY

Palmer, S. and Laungani, P. (eds) (1999). *Counselling in a Multicultural Society*. London: Sage.
This many-authored British book contains eight chapters on such topics as the challenges of counselling in a multiracial society, culture and identity, racial issues, models of counselling and therapy for a multiethnic society, counselling needs of ethnic minorities, client-centred or culture-centred counselling, and the search for effective counselling across cultures.

D'Ardenne, P. and Mahtani, A. (1999). *Transcultural Counselling in Action* (2nd edition). London: Sage.
This book is written by two clinical psychologists, one with a white English and the other with an Indian background, working in London's East End. The book introduces the concept of transcultural counselling and then reviews practical issues concerned with clients, counsel-

lors, starting the counselling process, sharing a common language, the therapeutic relationship, change and growth, and ending counselling. The book is illustrated by four case studies with clients with Bangladeshi, English, French and Nigerian cultural backgrounds.

Sue, D. W. and Sue, D. (1999). *Counseling the Culturally Different: Theory and Practice* (3rd edition). New York: John Wiley.
This book is focused on the United States and consists of five parts: (1) the political dimensions of mental health practice; (2) the practice of multicultural counselling and therapy; (3) worldviews in multicultural counselling and therapy; (4) multicultural counselling and therapy competence; and (5) counselling and therapy with specific populations (mainly American minority groups).

Sue, D. W., Carter, R. T., Casas, J. M., Fouad, N. A., Ivey, A. E., Jensen, M., LaFromboise, T., Manese, J. E., Ponterotto, J. G. and Vazquez-Nutall, E. (1998). *Multicultural Counseling Competencies: Individual and Organizational Development.* London: Sage.
This American book introduces the concepts of multiculturalism and ethnocentric monoculturalism and then presents the multicultural counselling competences. Chapters follow on understanding the Euro-American worldview and on understanding racial/ethnic minority worldviews. Much of the remainder of the book focuses on multicultural organizational development, with the final chapter looking at issues of personal, professional and organizational multicultural competence.

Walsh, R. (2000). Asian psychotherapies. In R. Corsini and D. Wedding (eds). *Current Psychotherapies* (6th edition, 407–44). Itasca, IL: Peacock.
This chapter examines the assumptions underlying Asian therapies, compares Asian with Western therapies, provides a theory of personality from an Asian perspective, reviews Asian views of psychopathology and psychological health, and then describes different therapeutic approaches. The chapter includes a case example.

REFERENCES AND FURTHER READING

Atkinson, D. R., Thompson, C. E. and Grant, S. K. (1993). A three dimensional model for counseling racial/ethnic minorities. *The Counseling Psychologist, 21,* 257–77.

Benedict, R. (1942). Unpublished lectures on Synergy in Society, Bryn Mawr, USA.

Cheatham, H., Ivey, A. E., Ivey, M. B., Pedersen, P., Rigazio-DiGillio, S., Simek-Morgan, L. and Sue, D. W. (1997). Multicultural counselling and therapy: 1 Metatheory – Taking theory into practice; 2 Integrative practice. In A. E. Ivey, M. B. Ivey and L. Simek-Morgan. *Counseling and Psychotherapy: A Multicultural Perspective* (4th edition, 133–205). Boston, MA: Allyn and Bacon.

Cross, T. L., Bazron, B. J., Dennis, K. W. and Isaacs, M. R. (1989). *Towards a Culturally Competent System of Care.* Washington, DC: Child and Adolescent Service System Technical Assistance Center.

D'Ardenne, P. and Mahtani, A. (1999). *Transcultural Counselling in Action* (2nd edition). London: Sage.

Department of Immigration and Multicultural Affairs (1997). *Australia's Population Trends and Prospects 1996.* Canberra: Author.

Ellis, A. (1998). The biological basis of human irrationality. In A. Ellis and S. Blau (eds). *The*

Albert Ellis Reader (271–91). Secaucus, NJ: Citadel.

Haskey, J. (1997). Population review: (8) The ethnic minority and overseas-born populations of Great Britain. *Population Trends*, *88*, 13–30.

Helms, J. E. (1995). An update of Helms's white and people of color racial identity models. In J. G. Ponterotto, J. M. Casas, L. A. Sizuki and C. M. Alexander (eds). *Handbook of Multicultural Counseling* (181–98). Thousand Oaks, CA: Sage.

Hermans, H. J. M. and Kempen, H. J. G. (1998). Moving cultures: The perilous problems of cultural dichotomies in a globalizing society. *American Psychologist*, *53*, 1,111–20.

Herskovits, M. J. (1948). *Man and his Works*. New York: Knopf.

Ho, M. K. (1992). *Minority Children and Adolescents in Therapy*. Newbury Park, CA: Sage.

Hofstede, G. (1980). *Culture's Consequences: International Differences in Work-Related Values*. London: Sage.

Hofstede, G. (1983). Dimensions of national culture in fifty cultures and three regions. In J. B. Deregowski, S. Dziurawiec and R. C. Annis (eds). *Expiscations in Cross-Cultural Psychology* (335–55). Lisse, The Netherlands: Swets and Zeitlinger: Sage.

Kerwin, C. and Ponterotto, J. G. (1995). Biracial identity development: Theory and research. In J. G. Ponterotto, J. M. Casas, L. A. Sizuki and C. M. Alexander (eds). *Handbook of Multicultural Counseling* (199–217)). Thousand Oaks, CA: Sage.

Laungani, P. (1999a). Culture and identity: Implications for counselling. In S. Palmer and P. Laungani (eds). *Counselling in a Multicultural Society* (35–70). London: Sage.

Laungani, P. (1999b). Client centred or culture centred counselling. In S. Palmer and P. Laungani (eds). *Counselling in a Multicultural Society* (133–52). London: Sage.

Maslow, A. H. (1970). *Motivation and Personality* (2nd edition). New York: Harper and Row.

Maslow, A. H. (1971). *The Farther Reaches of Human Nature*. Harmondsworth: Penguin Books.

Palmer, S. (2000). Developing an individual therapeutic programme suitable for use by counselling psychologists in a multicultural society: A multimodal perspective. *Counselling Psychology Review*, *15*, 32–50.

Palmer, S. and Laungani, P. (eds) (1999). *Counselling in a Multicultural Society*. London: Sage.

Reynolds, D. (1990). Morita and Naikan therapies – Similarities. *Journal of Morita Therapy*, *1*, 159–63.

Ridley, C. R. and Lingle, D. W. (1996). Cultural empathy in multicultural counseling: A multidimensional process. In P. B. Pedersen, J. G. Draguns, W. J. Lonner and J. E. Trimble (eds). *Counseling Across Cultures* (4th edition). Thousand Oaks, CA: Sage, 21–46.

Schwartz, S. H. (1992). Universals in the content and structure of values: Theoretical advances and empirical tests in 20 countries. In M. Zanna (ed.). *Advances in Experimental Social Psychology*, *25*, 1–65, New York: Academic Press.

Schwartz, S. H. and Bilsky, W. (1990). Toward a theory of the universal content and structure of human values: Extensions and cross-cultural replications. *Journal of Personality and Social Psychology*, *53*, 550–62.

Spindler, G. D. (1963). *Education and Culture: Anthropological Approaches*. New York: Holt, Rinehart and Winston.

Sue, D. W., Carter, R. T., Casas, J. M., Fouad, N. A., Ivey, A. E., Jensen, M., LaFromboise, T., Manese, J. E., Ponterotto, J. G. and Vazquez-Nutall, E. (1998). *Multicultural Counseling Competencies: Individual and Organizational Development*. London: Sage.

Sue, D. W., Ivey, A. E. and Pedersen, P. B. (1996). *A Theory of Multicultural Counseling and Therapy*. Pacific Grove, CA: Brooks/Cole.

Sue, D. W. and Sue, D. (1999). *Counseling the Culturally Different: Theory and Practice* (3rd edition). New York: John Wiley.

Thitavanno, P. (1995). *Mind Development.* Bangkok: Mahamakut Buddhist University.

U.S. Census Bureau (1992) *Statistical Abstract of the United States: The National Data Book* (112th edition). Washington, DC: Author

Walsh, R. (2000) Asian psychotherapies. In R. Corsini and D. Wedding (eds). *Current Psychotherapies* (6th edition, 407–44). Itasca, IL: Peacock.

Weinrach, S. G. and Thomas, K. R. (1998). Diversity-sensitive counseling today: A postmodern clash of values. *Journal of Counseling and Development, 76,* 115–22.

Wirth, L. (1945). The problem of minority groups. In R. Linton (ed.). *The Science of Man in the World Crisis* (347–72). New York: Columbia University Press.

17

Gender Issues

Because of our social circumstances, male and female are really two different cultures and their life experiences are utterly different.

Kate Millet

INTRODUCTION

Many therapeutic approaches seem based on the assumption of unisex therapists and clients. This chapter aims to provide a brief and basic introduction to some gender issues connected to the theory and practice of counselling and therapy. Of necessity, it is a tour of some of the main points rather than a detailed analysis of any of them.

Gender issues have been around since time immemorial. However, in the last third of the twentieth century the rise of feminism and the growth of the men's movement have accelerated the debate over male and female roles. Gender issues permeate therapy: for example, in the gender-related assumptions that therapists and clients bring to their personal lives and to therapy. Nevertheless, the fact remains that all the theorists whose work is presented in this book are men and all were educated before the last third of the twentieth century.

This chapter is closely related to the previous one, since cultural issues and gender issues overlap. The quotation that starts this chapter suggests that the life experiences of Western women and men form utterly different cultures. One of the main functions of enculturation is to transmit gender roles from one generation to another. However, to some extent, peer groups may be taking over from parents in performing this central aspect of enculturation (Maccoby, 1990).

Cultures have both similarities and differences in the roles they assign to men and women. Furthermore, as Hofstede's (1980, 1983) work shows, cultures vary in subscribing to masculine and feminine values. In addition, the acculturation of migrants can be much more difficult if there are large gender role differences between previous and new cultures. For instance, in their cultures of origin men may have mediated between the home and the outside world, whereas in their new cultures women may work outside the home and also be the main breadwinners (Eleftheriadou, 1999).

Gender can also be an important aspect of cultural change and conflict, with the changes in women's roles affecting men and *vice versa*. Many British, Australian and American women strongly feel that they, like ethnic and racial minorities, are oppressed by white, male-dominated mainstream cultures. Cultural change can also influence how people learn gender roles: for example, with the movement from agrarian economies stemming from the industrial revolution, many men have spent less time with their families and local communities, to the possible psychological impoverishment of all concerned. Consequently, boys in Western cultures may have less opportunity than previously to learn from their fathers and other mentors how to be confident and at ease in being male (Biddulph, 1995).

The terminology of gender

Like the terms associated with culture, many of the terms associated with gender possess different shadings of meaning according to who is doing the defining. Below is an introduction to some key terms.

Sex
In this context, sex refers to biological differences between males and females, such as differences in genitals, reproductive functioning, bone structure, and size.

Gender
Gender refers to the cultural and social classification of characteristics, attitudes, values and behaviours as appropriate for either females or males.

Gender role
The role that a person adopts or that is ascribed to her/him on the dimensions of 'masculinity' and 'femininity'. The concept of gender role incorporates the power relations between men and women.

Gender role identity
This relates to how a person views herself or himself on the dimensions of 'masculinity' and 'femininity'.

Gender role socialization
The processes of enculturation whereby children and adults acquire, internalize and maintain the characteristics, attitudes, values and behaviours associated with femininity, masculinity or a mixture of both.

Gender role conflict
Gender role conflict can be both within a person, in relation to others, or a mixture of both. The most common form of gender role conflict within a person is where the gender role the individual either adopts or wishes to adopt is at variance with the gender role prescribed by their culture or reference group. Gender role conflicts between people relate to differences in perceptions regarding appropriate gender roles: for example, different ideas between partners in dual career couples.

Sexism

Sexism refers to external oppression on account of a person's biological sex. In turn, sexism can become internalized self-oppression. *Individual sexism* relates to any thoughts, feelings and actions that assume the superiority of one sex over the other. *Institutional or organizational sexism* relates to political, institutional and organizational structures that discriminate against, oppress and devalue a person on the grounds of sex. *Heterosexism* extends sexism to focus on individuals and organizations that assume the superiority of heterosexual thoughts, feelings and actions over homosexual or bisexual thoughts, feelings and actions.

THEORY

In the animal kingdom, the rule is, eat or be eaten; in the human kingdom, define or be defined.

Thomas Szasz

Biology and gender

Do gender role differences reflect nature rather than nurture? Underlying the issue of gender roles is the extent to which the sexes are biologically similar. From the viewpoint of evolutionary psychology, men and women should share the same characteristics in those situations where they have faced the same or similar adaptive problems. However, men and women would evolve different characteristics in situations where their adaptive demands substantially diverge (Darwin, 1871; Buss, 1995). For example, from the viewpoint of the male, sexual selection involves successfully out-competing members of one's own sex to gain access to more numerous or more desirable mates. From a female viewpoint, sexual selection might involve identifying males willing and able to supply resources and protection through pregnancy and lactation.

Evolutionary psychology emphasizes the interaction between the biological and the social rather than assumes that biological characteristics between the sexes are immutable. For example, the primary difference in the trend towards small changes in cognitive abilities between the sexes is in the area of spatial ability, which is important to being a skilled hunter. However, as men evolve in societies which do not require hunting as a survival skill, this sex difference could gradually diminish.

Moir and Jessell review research indicating that from birth males and females are different. The main behavioural difference is the natural, innate aggression of men. These authors present evidence that the sexes are different because their brains are different and observe: 'To maintain that they are the same in aptitude, skill or behaviour is to build a society based on a biological and scientific lie' (Moir and Jessell, 1989, p. 5). Moir and Jessell report men as being better than women in skills requiring spatial ability. Both aggression and spatial ability skills are characteristics which may originate in male roles at earlier stages of evolution.

There are three possibilities for how the nature–nurture controversy can be positively resolved. One possibility is that 'masculinity' and 'femininity' become outmoded concepts because further research indicates that the two sexes are biologically highly similar. Another possibility is that additional research supports Moir and Jessell's assertion that there are important biological sex differences and that men and women then manage to use one another's strengths for everyone's benefit. Still a third possibility is that, over time, men and women evolve, possibly hastened by appropriate nurturing, so that biological sex differences no longer figure so prominently.

Masculinity, femininity, androgyny and gender schemas

In Western societies, certain psychological characteristics have traditionally been viewed as being either feminine, masculine or neutral. The American researcher Sandra Bem (1974) developed the Bem Sex-Role Inventory (BSRI) with the purpose of being able to characterize a person as masculine, feminine or androgynous. Final items were on the basis of being more socially desirable in American society for one sex than for the other. Illustrative Masculine items were: aggressive, ambitious, analytical, assertive, competitive, dominant, independent, individualistic, self-reliant, and willing to take risks. Illustrative Feminine items were: affectionate, compassionate, eager to soothe hurt feelings, gentle, loves children, sensitive to the needs of others, sympathetic, understanding and warm. Illustrative neutral items were: adaptable, conscientious, conventional, reliable, and truthful. In addition to Masculinity and Femininity scores, the BSRI provides an Androgyny score.

The androgynous sex role represented an equal endorsement of both masculine and feminine attributes. Other ways to define androgyny include either striking a balance between masculine and feminine characteristics or the ability to choose from among the most desirable masculine and feminine characteristics. In her summary of the research on androgyny and sex types, Cook (1987) observed: 'The evidence delineating the types is not as compelling as many proponents of the typology would like . . . Most differences between the categories are simply of degree, usually with modest differences in absolute size' (p. 483). Another consideration relating to sex types, including androgyny, is that they are heavily influenced by cultural norms regarding what constitutes masculinity, femininity and androgyny (Ravinder, 1987).

Traditional gender role or sex role typing can cause considerable problems for both men and women. In Western societies this may be particularly the case for women. Cook (1987) refers to 'the masculine supremacy effect' in American society, with masculine characteristics being more highly valued than feminine ones. However, a higher valuation of certain feminine characteristics, for instance understanding and compassion, is likely to be a feature of genuinely healthy cultures.

Bem (1981) extended her discussion of sex types to develop gender schema theory. Perception is a process in which individuals make constructions of incoming information. A gender schema is a cognitive structure consisting of a network of associations that organize and guide individuals' sex-linked perceptions. Sex typing derives, in part, from 'a generalized readiness to process information on the basis of sex-linked information that constitute the gender schema' (p. 354). Society should become a-schematic and stop projecting gender into situations irrelevant to genuine biological differences. If this were to happen, human behaviours and personality attributes would cease to have gender.

WOMEN AND GENDER ROLES

But the time is at hand when the voices of the feminine mystique can no longer drown out the inner voice that is driving women on to become complete.

Betty Frieden

Feminism

Feminism has a long history as the advocacy of women's rights on the grounds of equality between the sexes. In 1963 Betty Frieden provided an impetus to the modern women's movement with her seminal book *The Feminine Mystique* chronicling the apathy and frustration of many post-Second World War American wives trapped in comfortable domestic concentration camps (Frieden, 1963). Frieden advocated a new life plan for women that would allow them to use their intelligence, enjoy adult company, and undertake serious careers.

Greer asserts that liberation rather than equality is the goal for feminists. She writes: 'If we accept that men are not free, and that masculinity is as partial an account of maleness as femininity is of femaleness, then equality must be seen as a poor substitute for liberation' (Greer, 1999, p. 395). Liberation entails women defining their own values and proudly asserting genuine life-affirming female, as contrasted with feminine, differences from males. Though not heavily stressed by Greer, women's liberation also entails challenging men to assert life-affirming male differences from females.

The unequal distribution of power is a central issue in feminist thinking. Whereas Freud thought females envied males because they possessed penises, the neo-Freudian analyst Karen Horney considered their envy was about men's greater power and status in society (Chaplin, 1999). Watkins, Rueda and Rodriguez (1999) note that by the 1970s, the women's movement contained three discernible groups: radical feminists, socialist feminists and liberal feminists. Radical feminists saw the main problem as patriarchy. Patriarchy is a form of social organization in which the men rule and descent is reckoned through the male line. As well as men's superior position in the political, bureaucratic, business, church and military establishments, men also had power over women and children in their homes. Socialist feminists saw the problem as a combination of patriarchy and of class exploitation. These women emphasized making alliances with other oppressed groups and classes. Liberal feminists thought both radical and socialist feminists were going too far. They focused on correcting rather than overturning the system by lobbying governments for pro-women reform and trying to influence decision-makers. A common theme running throughout all three groups is that of women having less power than men and this situation needing to be redressed. In addition to those mentioned above, other feminist groupings include lesbian feminists and feminists in particular ethnic and racial minority groups. By the end of the 1970s, the radical feminists had grown more influential than the socialist feminists (Watkins *et al.*, 1999). Nowadays, many feminists see the women's movement as an ally to all human rights movements.

A large number of women who actively favour women's equality and liberation may not apply the label 'feminist' to themselves. Some of these women even go so far as to hate the word 'feminism' because to them it connotes anger, militancy and lesbianism (Tavris, 1989).

Oppression of women

Central to the thinking of many feminists is the idea that men have used their positions of power and influence to oppress women both inside and outside the home. Taylor (1996) provides a modified version of this position when she states: 'So while there is a recognition that men have been the victims of a sexist culture and its rigid patterns of socialization, it is still men who hold the balance of power and receive a disproportionate share of social rewards and privileges . . .' (p. 208). Men are on the inside and women on the outside.

Sue and Sue (1999) see mainstream white male culture as inherently biased against racial ethnic minorities, women, gays/lesbians and other culturally different groups. They delineate five components of oppression against such minority groups, which I have adapted to focus on the oppression of women.

1. *Belief in the superiority of men.* Men may possess conscious and unconscious feelings of superiority and consequently of entitlement to better treatment.
2. *Belief in the inferiority of women.* Women can be devalued because their capacities, including their sexuality, are viewed as inferior to those of men.
3. *Power to impose standards.* Men have the power to impose their standards on women. Early examples of this oppression involved excluding women from property and voting rights. Because of their generally having more control over financial resources, men are in a powerful position to impose their standards in the home. Threatened or actual use of greater physical strength can also be used as an instrument of control and subjugation of women at home.
4. *Manifestation in institutions.* Chains of command in organizations and institutions favour men over women. Educational and training opportunities favour boys and men over girls and women.
5. *The invisible veil.* Since all people are the products of their cultural conditioning, including their gender role conditioning, their values and beliefs can operate as an invisible veil outside of conscious awareness. Thus, even well-intentioned individuals may experience difficulty in acknowledging that some of their thoughts, feelings and actions are sexist. Unconsciously and unintentionally, they may collude in perpetuating sexist biases and discrimination. Furthermore, the victims of oppression may fail to see that they have internalized the standards of the mainstream culture and so become the agents of their own oppression.

A final point is that at the heart of feminism are two different, and possibly contradictory, explanations for the past and current oppression of women. One explanation is that oppression results from men's greater power – 'Men did and are doing it to us.' Yet feminists also explain that the best way to gain more equality is through women banding together and being more assertive and socially active – 'We women have the power to bring about change.' One way to reconcile these explanations is to accept that not only men's greater power but also women's prior and possibly present insufficient social action to combat that power maintained, and may still be maintaining, women's oppression.

Women's experience and issues

A major criticism of existing counselling and therapy approaches is that they insufficiently address women's experience and issues. The women's movement stresses the importance of women understanding and valuing their own experience. It also stresses the importance of men understanding the extent and ways in which women's experiencing of life is different from theirs. A common theme in the literature on women and gender roles is that women's self-esteem tends to be lower than that of men.

One way of looking at women's experience is in terms of the interaction of the social, the political and the personal. Here concepts like patriarchy, oppression and social action are important. Another way to look at women's experience is in terms of the particular challenges throughout the life span inherent in being a woman: for example, premenstrual tension, infertility and miscarriage, giving birth, post-natal depression, mothering, menopause, and frequently outliving a spouse. Still a further way to look at women's experience is in terms of problems that beset women in varying degrees: for example, domestic violence, sexual harassment, sexual abuse, relentless pressure to be beautiful, anorexia, bulimia, rape, abortion, single parenting, attitudes that constrain career choice, workplace discrimination, and depression and exhaustion resulting from carrying a disproportionate share of work/family responsibilities (Greer, 1999).

Women's identity development

Some models of women's identity development exist that are comparable to models of cultural identity development discussed in the previous chapter. Such models take into account and are stimulated by the oppression and subjugation that many women experience and feel. These models trace the development of women's consciousness or awareness from going along with the prevailing gender-role norms to becoming autonomous and socially active. Box 17.1 presents a summary of the five-stage model of McNamara and Rickard (1998).

Cheatham and his colleagues (1997) have also presented a five-stage model of women's identity development using the same five stages that they used in their model of cultural identity development: naïvety, encounter, naming, reflection on self as a cultural (in this case gender) being, and multiperspective internalization. Stage models of feminist and of women's identity development are hypotheses that reflect the cultural, historical and political situations at the time of their development. Such models are open to question, for instance radical feminists are uncomfortable with the notion of synthesis in the McNamara and Rickard model.

BOX 17.1
A model of feminist identity development

Stage 1: Passive acceptance
Passive acceptance of traditional gender roles, men considered superior to women, and prejudice and discrimination denied.

Stage 2: Revelation
Sexist events occur that cannot be ignored, an awakening to prejudice and discrimination, anger, dichotomous thinking in that all men are seen as oppressive and all women as positive.

Stage 3: Embeddedness-emanation
Close emotional and supportive relations formed with other women, sharing of emotions, solidifying of feminist identity, less absolutistic thinking regarding men.

Stage 4: Synthesis
A positive feminist identity is fully developed, less absolutistic thinking about sexism as the cause of all problems, ability to take an independent feminist stance.

Stage 5: Active commitment
Interest in turning attention to making societal changes.

MEN AND GENDER ROLES

The Men's Movement of the Nineties isn't a reaction to the Women's Movement. It's the Women's Movement's missing half.

Steve Biddulph

The men's movement

For relationships between the sexes to take place on the basis of genuine equality, both women and men need to change. Partly in response to feminism, there has been a growing men's movement in Western countries. For example, several hundred men's groups exist in Australia (Biddulph, 1995). In important respects, the men's movement is complementary to rather than in opposition to the women's movement. Both seek equality between the sexes and liberation for persons, whatever their sex, to develop their full humanity without the limitations of rigid gender role prescriptions.

The men's movement has been slower in gaining strength than the women's movement and appears more fragmented. Men's issues have not had prominent advocates as articulate as Betty Frieden and Germaine Greer. Furthermore, the men's movement lags behind the women's movement in publishing books and research articles.

Increasingly the men's movement's emphasis is less about feminizing men to create Sensitive New Age Guys (SNAGS) and more about developing a positive image of maleness and of men's inner life and experiences. Men who are confident and in touch with their feelings are able to be more flexible in how they deal with others at home and at work rather than live out phoney stereotypes of how men should be that fail to meet others' and their own needs.

The overall trend in Western societies is still to bring men up for the traditional male roles of providers and protectors and, as such, to encourage aggression, competitiveness, self-reliance and not showing vulnerability. Often men are brought up that it is 'sissy' to show weakness, cry, be artistic, and want close relationships with other males. Biddulph (1995) considers that men are a mess, with their three main enemies being isolation, compulsive competition, and lifelong emotional timidity.

Another factor in the rise of the men's movement has been anger at the extent to which some feminist writers have successfully portrayed women as victims and men as perse-cutors. Furthermore, some such advocates appear insensitive to the damage this overgeneralized negativity causes to boys' and men's self-esteem and to achieving mutually respectful men–women relationships. In addition, those feminist writers who sweepingly portray men as oppressors insufficiently acknowledge the responsibility of women in their own oppression and women's contribution to socializing both boys and girls into oppressive sex-role stereotypes.

Often there is scant recognition in the feminist literature of the pressures and sacrifices many men undergo to provide for their families. Most men are not in positions of great power at work and have to get along as subordinates, sometimes with considerable humiliation and long dull hours, to do as best as they can to support their families. In addition, in areas like domestic violence, men as well as women can be the victims (for example, Tavris, 1989). However, the outcomes of male violence can be more severe due to their relatively greater strength and, especially in America, their tendencies to use guns and knives. Furthermore, in Australia, Britain and America the criminal statistics are heavily weighted towards male violence.

Men can also be angry or cynical about feminists who seem to 'want it both ways': retaining women's existing privileges at the same time as gaining access to those of men. In addition, men are angered by the phenomenon of men-bashing that occurs in many areas in ways that would probably be considered unacceptable if applied to women (Biddulph, 1995; Tavris, 1989). For instance, in advertising men are often portrayed as jerks in men–women relationships. In addition, in television, for example *The Golden Girls*, and movies, for example *The First Wives Club*, much of the humour is at the expense of men. Anti-male greeting cards are popular and, in Australia, calendars and diaries of the 'All Men Are Bastards' variety have sold well. Another example of men-bashing is that of 'Post-it' notes, with captions such as 'There are only two things wrong with men. Everything they say and everything they do.'

Men's gender role conflict

Given the limitations of men's enculturation, many men find that they do not fit the mould. O'Neill and his colleagues (1986) have developed a Gender Role Conflict Scale (GRCS) that identifies four gender role conflict patterns or factors for American men. Box 17.2 briefly describes each of the GRCS's four factors.

BOX 17.2

Factors measured by the Gender Role Conflict Scale (GRCS)

Success, power and competition
This factor represents an emphasis on over-achievement, control, strength, needing to move up the career ladder and being perceived as a 'winner'.

Restrictive emotionality
Here men are frightened of the feminine part of themselves and by feelings that seem womanly. They experience difficulty with their own emotional self-disclosure as well as discomfort with the emotional expressiveness of others.

Restrictive affectionate behaviour between men
This is an index of the degree to which men keep other men at a distance by restricting expressions of caring, being wary of friendly male overtures, and protecting themselves from feelings of anxiety or shame about feelings of attraction towards other men that might be interpreted by themselves or others as a gay orientation.

Conflict between work and family relations
This factor measures the level of distress experienced by men due to the impinging of work or study on personal and family life.

The underlying idea behind the GRCS is that the process of male socialization creates conflict, stress and anxiety for men when they deviate from masculine ideals. For example Good and his colleagues (1996) used the GRCS to examine the relation between masculine role conflict and psychological stress in a sample of university counselling centre clients. Their findings supported earlier studies conducted with non-clinical samples of gender role conflict being associated with higher levels of depression and interpersonal sensitivity. In addition, high scores on masculine role conflict significantly predicted paranoia, psychoticism and obsessive-compulsivity. In another study that compared non-clinical samples of college-aged and middle-aged men, middle-aged men were less conflicted about success, power and competition, but were more conflicted between work and family responsibilities (Cournoyer and Mahalik, 1995). Such studies could be extended to take into account differences in culture and occupation, such as differences between business executives and blue-collar workers.

The work on men's gender role conflict highlights the fact that males as well as females can feel trapped by their gender role socialization. Furthermore, these studies illustrate that wanting to deviate from traditional masculine roles often comes at a psychological price. The gender role conflict research suggests there is a place for models of men's as well of women's identity development in regard to gender roles. Currently numerous men remain at low levels of awareness about the effects of gender conditioning on their psychological well-being.

Men's experience and issues

Though formulated by men, perhaps existing counselling and therapy approaches are insufficiently sensitive to men's as well as women's experience and issues. A case can also be made for the institutional oppression of men as well as of women. For example, in times of war, men rather than women are called up to the horrors of combat and the possibility of serious injury, if not death. Another example is that some men consider that women are favoured when it comes to taking paid leave for child care and in divorce court decisions about child custody. Regarding life-span problems, men do not have the kind of problems that women do, for instance going through the menopause. However, men's life expectancy is five or six years lower than women's and this important life-span issue could be highlighted and addressed more by both sexes. In addition, there is a high incidence of prostate cancer in men. Furthermore, boys and men commit suicide four times more frequently than girls and women (Biddulph, 1995).

There are psychological problems that beset boys and men: for example, behavioural problems in school, hurt stemming from absent or neglectful fathers (sometimes called 'father hunger'), work-related stress, alcoholism, being physically violent, pressure to initiate relationships with the opposite sex, pressure to perform sexually (men cannot fake erections), difficulty showing tender feelings and vulnerability, insufficient preparation for fatherhood, insufficient intimacy with same-sex friends, pressure to be financially successful, loss of identity through unemployment, and loss of daily contact with children after a relationship break-up.

Furthermore, many men are challenged to adjust to the changes brought about in their partners by the women's movement. Women easily outnumber men as clients in therapy (Good, Dell and Mintz, 1989). This imbalance indicates that another problem for men may be their greater unwillingness to admit and seek psychological assistance when experiencing difficulties themselves and creating difficulties for others.

THERAPY

Mental health professionals recognize today that strong adherence to traditional sex-role standards can have negative consequences for men's and women's psychological functioning.

Ellen Piel Cook

THERAPEUTIC GOALS

Where gender role issues are involved, it is possible to state therapeutic goals for both sexes and for each sex. Gender role counselling and therapy for both sexes 'involves general goals common in therapeutic practice, with an explicit awareness of how these are uniquely colored by issues of sex roles . . .' (Cook, 1985, p. 3). These general goals include helping individual clients use their strengths and potential, make appropriate choices, remedy poor skills, and develop positive and flexible self-concepts. In addition, therapeutic goals relating to gender roles can often involve both male and female partners: for example, learning to deal with demand/withdraw interaction patterns in marital conflict (Christensen and Heavy, 1993) and handling the numerous issues confronting dual career couples in a time of rapid technological and economic change (Fallon, 1997; Serlin, 1989).

Therapeutic goals for women

Chaplin (1999) observes that women and others at the bottom of hierarchies usually have considerable experience of being put down and losing self-esteem. She continues: 'Feminist counselling aims instead to empower people and develop more self-confidence and control over their lives' (p. 8). Two studies of feminist therapy throw some light on the goals of feminist therapy in practice. Maracek and Kravetz (1999) studied 25 experienced feminist therapists in the American state of Wisconsin. They report that most feminist therapists, when asked 'What does it mean to you to say that your therapy is feminist?', did not mention re-socialization, raised consciousness or political and social change. Instead respondents focused on the processes of feminist therapy and, in particular, on how the therapist enacts the therapeutic relationship.

Chester (1994) surveyed 140 Australians who considered themselves to be both feminists and counsellors, though just over 14 per cent did not consider themselves feminist counsellors as such. Participants were asked to choose, from a list of 26 characteristics, which ones they considered essential for feminist counsellors. Box 17.3 presents characteristics that the participants chose as essential. Underneath I have translated these characteristics into goals for feminist counselling, the most essential goals being women valuing themselves on their own terms and becoming free of sex-role stereotypes.

BOX 17.3

Characteristics of Australian feminist counsellors translated into goals for feminist counselling

Essential feminist counsellor characteristics	% of Respondents
Encourages women to value themselves on their own terms	92
Encourages clients to free themselves from sex-role stereotypes	83
Encourages female clients to increase their sense of commonality with other women	68
Encourages female clients to work for social change	44
Encourages androgyny	17

Goals for feminist counselling
Valuing herself on her own terms
Freeing herself from sex-role stereotypes
Increased sense of commonality with other women
Working for social change
Androgynous functioning

Statements of therapeutic goals that take women's sex and gender issues into account can focus both on women's life-span issues and on problems that are much more commonly faced by women than by men. For example, gender-aware and feminist therapists can counsel mid-life women to cope with the menopause constructively (Huffman and Myers, 1999). In addition, suitably trained and qualified therapists can help women address issues such as insufficient assertion, eating disorders, domestic violence and sexual harassment.

Therapeutic goals for men

Since considerably fewer men than women come for therapy, one broader goal may be to increase the number of men prepared to address their gender-role and other problems in therapy. Men, like women, need to free themselves from limiting gender-role stereotypes and develop more of their unique potential. Consequently, another therapeutic goal is, where appropriate, to make men aware of the extent to which their thoughts, feelings and behaviours have been and continue to be heavily determined by their past and current gender role socialization.

Therapeutic goals for men can include addressing at least three of the issues identified in the Gender Role Conflict Scale: excessive need for success, power and competition; restrictive emotionality; and restrictive affectionate behaviour between men. Though coping with the fourth GRCS factor, conflict between work and family relationships, is a legitimate therapeutic goal, this problem is shared by both sexes – there has been a long-term trend towards women's increased participation in the paid workforce, often accompanied by longer hours. Other therapeutic goals for men clients include stopping being physically violent both inside and outside of the home, dealing with work-related stress, overcoming tendencies to treat women as sexual objects, and developing better health-care skills.

Since women are redefining their gender roles faster than men, many men are then put in positions of exploring, understanding and altering their own gender roles. Positive maleness, combining tenderness and toughness, and treating women with respect and as equals, is a desirable outcome from this change process. Men as well as women can take pride as they struggle to achieve inner strength and beauty. Boys and men are likely to be more constructive and caring if assisted to become confident in their manhood rather than seeking to prove themselves all the time by pretending to be what they are not.

THERAPEUTIC APPROACHES

The above discussion indicates that there are many goals for gender-aware counselling and therapy. Here I present four overlapping approaches to women's and men's gender issues and problems: making existing therapies more gender sensitive, developing gender-relevant counselling and therapy competences, feminist therapy, and men's therapy.

Making existing therapies more gender sensitive

Undoubtedly the rise of feminism and of the men's movement has already had an effect in influencing many therapists of both sexes to perform therapy with a greater focus on healing psychological distress stemming from restrictive gender role socialization and sexism. Of the two psychodynamic approaches presented in this book, Jung's analytical therapy emphasizes the importance of the feminine much more than Freud's psycho-analysis. Jung acknowledged the importance of the mother archetype, which appears in numerous aspects (Jung, 1982). Furthermore, Jung saw people as psychologically bisexual, with men possessing an anima (the personification of the feminine nature in their unconscious) and women possessing an animus (the personification of the mascu-line nature in their unconscious). Thus Jungian psychology provides a base on which to explore gender role issues at varying levels of consciousness (Schaverin, 1999).

Humanistic counselling and therapy approaches can also be used and adapted to deal with gender-role issues. Clients in person-centred therapy can experience and explore issues connected with prior gender role socialization, and current gender-role issues and conflicts, in an emotional climate of safety and trust. Gestalt therapists can use interven-tions like awareness experiments, the use of the empty chair, and dream analysis to focus on clients' gender-role learnings and behaviours that block excitement and authentic living. Furthermore, in transactional analysis, therapists can assist clients to explore script directives about gender-role behaviours and to gain freedom of choice in regard to abandoning damaging ones.

The cognitive–behavioural approaches too lend themselves to focusing on gender-role issues. For instance, in rational emotive behaviour therapy, gender-related irrational beliefs can be detected, disputed and either discarded or restated more rationally. In cognitive therapy, therapists and clients can identify and question the reality of gender-related automatic thoughts that confuse fact with inference. Afterwards, where necessary, therapists can work with clients to replace previous sexist and self-oppressing automatic thoughts with conscious and realistic ones.

Gender-relevant counselling and therapy competences

In the previous chapter, I presented a statement of multicultural counselling and therapy competences (Sue *et al.*, 1998). This statement can be adapted for gender-relevant coun-selling and therapy competences which consist of three main dimensions: awareness of own assumptions, values and biases; understanding the worldview of the sex-different client; and developing appropriate strategies and techniques. Each dimension is divided into beliefs and attitudes, knowledge, and skills. The basic presumption in stating these competences is that all therapists need to address their own levels of gender identity development and their ability to offer gender-sensitive services.

Awareness of own assumptions, values and biases
The beliefs held by gender-skilled therapists include being sensitive to their own gender heritage, being comfortable with differences that exist between them and clients of the other sex, and recognizing the limitations of their competence and expertise. Therapists should know about their gender heritage and how this affects the therapeutic process, understand how sexist oppression and discrimination may affect them personally and in their work, and know about the impact of how they communicate on clients of the other

sex. Skills include seeking out relevant educational and training experiences on gender-related factors in psychological wellness, actively understanding oneself as a gender being, and seeking an autonomous and appropriately flexible gender identity.

Understanding the worldview of the sex-different client

Beliefs and attitudes for gender-skilled therapists include being aware of their negative emotional reactions and of the stereotypes and preconceived notions that they may hold towards clients of the other sex. Therapists should know about the gender-related experiences, heritage and historical backgrounds of any particular group of men or women with whom they work, acknowledge how gender can affect help-seeking behaviour, know how gender can influence assessment and the selection and implementation of therapeutic interventions, and know about the oppressive political and environmental influences impinging on the lives of women and men. Skills include keeping up-to-date on research findings relevant to the psychological well-being of women and men, as well as being actively involved with minority and other relevant groups outside work settings to gain deeper insight into their gender perspectives.

Developing appropriate intervention strategies and techniques

Therapists' skills include the ability to send and receive verbal and non-verbal communication accurately, making appropriate referrals to either the same sex or the other sex therapists, tailoring the therapeutic relationship and interventions to take into account the gender-related dimensions of clients' problems, and engaging in a variety of helping roles, beyond being a therapist, for example, adviser, advocate, consultant and change agent.

Feminist therapy

Feminist therapists can subscribe to many different theoretical orientations (Chaplin, 1999; Chester, 1994). Feminist therapy is perhaps best described by the values or principles that have emerged from the joining of feminism with therapy. Box 17.4 describes five such central principles underlying feminist therapy (Ballou, 1996; Cheatham *et al.*, 1997).

What are some specific interventions in dealing with women clients? Often assertiveness training, gender-role analysis and consciousness raising are particularly appropriate for the needs of women. Chester (1994) asked her feminist counsellor sample whether they used any techniques or interventions related to their feminism. Ninety-one per cent of the respondents replied in the affirmative. The most commonly cited interventions were challenging sex-role stereotypes and challenging patriarchal norms (each around 15 per cent), assertiveness training, strategies to encourage a sense of empowerment, and self-disclosure (each around 12 per cent). Needless to say, many women clients bring to therapy specific issues, such as procrastination, for which gender-related interventions can be, but are not always, irrelevant.

An issue in feminist therapy is whether and how to confront clients with issues of sexism. It may be important for therapists to assess and take into account the level of

BOX 17.4

Five central principles of feminist therapy

1. *Egalitarian relationships*   Feminist therapists are extremely sensitive to issues of power and its distribution. They emphasize sharing power with clients and believe that hierarchical forms of power distribution are inappropriate. Self-disclosure of one's own experiences as a woman can be an important part of the therapeutic process.

2. *Pluralism*   Feminist theory acknowledges and values difference, including complex and multiple-level diversities. Respect for others, including their differences, is a basic tenet of feminist therapy.

3. *Working against oppression*   Feminist therapists work against all forms of oppression: for instance, on the basis of sex, affectional/sexual orientation, race, culture, religious belief, lifestyle choice, and physical disability.

4. *External emphasis*   External factors, such as social/political/economic structures, are crucial to shaping the views of women, how they see themselves and how others see them. Women as individuals are shaped by and interact with political, environmental, institutional and cultural factors.

5. *Valuing women's experiences*   Relying on the actual experiences of women for descriptions of 'reality'. Grounding knowledge claimed about women on the actual women's experience. Valuing highly the experience of women rather than ignoring or discounting it and assuming men's experience to be normative.

gender identity development of clients. In addition, therapists need to help women clients anticipate and deal with the consequences of changing their gender roles. One danger of bringing up issues of sexism too soon is that clients resist the explanation and do not see its relevance. The opposite is also possible in that clients simplistically latch on to a sexist oppression analysis of their situations, get extremely angry with their partners, and prematurely leave them rather than attempt to work through their relationship issues.

Many feminist therapists develop their own approaches to working with clients. For example, the British therapist Jocelyn Chaplin (1999) has developed a 'cognitive feminism' approach. Chaplin distinguishes between the masculine control model, in which opposites, such as mind–'masculine'–strong and body–'feminine'–vulnerable, are split hierarchically into superior and inferior constructs, and the feminine rhythm model. In the rhythm model there is flow and balancing between extremes, for instance alternating between joy and sorrow throughout a day. Each client needs to find her own unique rhythms and balance between her 'active' and 'resting' sides, her 'private' and 'public' sides, and her 'self-expression' and 'caring for others' sides.

Therapy starts with a trust-building mothering stage. Depending on the client, in varying degrees the therapist acts as a container, non-judgemental presence, and provides a space for emotionally letting go. The second stage involves focusing on specific issues, identifying themes and separating out the opposites: for instance the head must rule the heart. The third stage explores the past to understand where the opposites and inner hier-archies came from. The next stage involves dissolving the inner hierarchies, facing ambivalence and accepting opposites. Then therapy progresses to the last stage where clients make decisions and behave differently in the world. During this stage, assertive-ness training helps many women express themselves more effectively, for instance by asking clearly for a change.

Men's therapy

I include a section on men's therapy to highlight the need for more work on therapeutic approaches to men's problems and issues. Many boys and men are suffering psychologi-cally and need assistance to become confident and positive males. Virtually all of negative behaviours towards women chronicled by Greer (1999) are symptomatic of men's psy-chological wounds and insufficient personal development rather than of their innate badness. Unfortunately, the behaviours of some wounded men, for instance aggression and violence, do little to generate sympathy for their underlying suffering and low self-esteem.

There needs to be a greater development of men's therapy to complement – and definitely not to compete against – responsible feminist therapy. In many books on counselling and therapy (for example, Woolfe and Dryden, 1996; Sue, Ivey and Pedersen, 1996; Sue and Sue, 1999), there is more attention paid to women's issues than to men's issues. Much of the existing literature on men's issues focuses on changing negative aspects of men's behaviour, such as curbing domestic violence and sexual abuse. There is a dearth of counselling and therapy books and articles advocating positive maleness and how to achieve it (for example, Biddulph, 1995). However, the American Psychological Association's recently inaugurated journal *Psychology of Men and Masculin-ity* may go some way to redressing this deficiency.

Just as the men's movement can be seen as the missing half of the women's movement, men's therapy can be seen as the missing half of feminist therapy. Men's therapy can be conducted both on an individual basis, in men's groups and as part of working with couples and families. In addition, sometimes both men's and women's issues are addressed in mixed-sex groups. The goals for men's therapy are like those of feminist therapy – valuing himself on his own terms, gaining freedom from sex-role stereotypes, an increased sense of commonality with other men, and working for social change. With some adaptation, the five central principles of feminist therapy – egalitarian relation-ships, pluralism, working against oppression, external emphasis, and valuing the experience of one's own sex (see Box 17.4) – are highly relevant for men's therapy too. Many therapists need to become more skilled at working with the specific issues facing boys and men. Then they can help these clients to celebrate, liberate and develop the better parts of their male humanity.

CONCLUDING COMMENT

No one can be perfectly free until all are free;
No one can be perfectly moral until all are moral;
No one can be perfectly happy until all are happy.
Herbert Spencer

Though a promising start has been made in developing a counselling and therapy literature that takes gender-role issues and their treatment into account, much still remains to
be done. There are risks as well as benefits in focusing on gender-role issues. The benefits
include a lessening of sexist oppression, a greater chance for people to develop their full
human potential rather than lead lives constricted by gender-role stereotypes, and greater
attention paid to developing interventions for the specific problems that beset each sex.

There are also risks in changing the current balance of gender roles. For example, 'the
masculine supremacy effect' in which masculine values are more honoured in market-
driven Western cultures, may lead women to feel under pressure to relinquish some of
their feminine virtues, for instance compassion, as they compete in a workforce dominated by masculine values. In addition, gender-role liberation can play into people's
selfishness in already highly individualistic Western cultures. Both men and women may
sacrifice communal values, and possibly the welfare of children too, in the interests of
their own individual development.

For the most part, existing counselling and therapy approaches have insufficiently
addressed gender role socialization and the therapeutic problems and issues arising from
it. Feminist therapy is the main example of an attempt to redress this neglect. There is
still considerable scope for originating new counselling and therapy approaches, as well
as for modifying existing ones, to promote equality between the sexes and to liberate
girls, women, boys and men to become more fully human.

SUMMARY

- *Despite gender issues permeating therapy, many therapeutic approaches seem based on the
  assumption of unisex therapists and clients.*
- *Gender role refers to the cultural and social classification of characteristics, attitudes,
  values and behaviours as appropriate for either females or males. Sexism refers to external
  oppression on account of one's biological sex.*
- *Underlying the issue of gender roles is the extent to which the sexes differ biologically
  because of evolutionary differences in their brains: for instance, men have better spatial
  ability.*
- *People can be sex or gender-role typed as masculine, feminine and androgynous.
  Sex/gender-role typed individuals process information on the basis of sex-linked associations that constitute gender schemas.*
- *Different ways of defining androgyny include equally endorsing masculine and feminine
  characteristics, striking a balance between them, and the ability to choose from among the
  most desirable masculine and feminine characteristics.*

- *Feminists advocate equality between the sexes and the liberation of women from restrictive gender-role stereotypes.*
- *Five characteristics of oppression against women are: belief in the superiority of men, belief in the inferiority of women, greater male power to impose standards, manifestation in institutions, and the invisible veil.*
- *The women's movement stresses the importance of women understanding and valuing their own experience. Women have distinctive life-span problems, for instance those connected with the menopause, as well as other problems, such as contending with serious domestic violence.*
- *Stage models of women's identity development describe a movement from lack of awareness to gender-role autonomy and commitment to social change.*
- *Partly in response to feminism, a men's movement has developed to address men's gender-role issues and to promote a positive vision of maleness.*
- *Four areas in which men, in varying degrees, experience gender role conflict are success, power and competition, restrictive emotionality, restrictive same-sex affectionate behaviour, and conflict between work and family relations.*
- *Boys' and men's problems include father hunger, school behaviour problems, work-related stress, alcoholism, being physically violent, and work and unemployment pressures. In addition, men use helping services much less than women.*
- *Therapeutic goals for both sexes include liberating themselves from gender-role stereotypes and developing appropriate skills to enact their changed roles. In addition, goals can focus on ameliorating the specific problems of both women and men. Broader therapeutic goals involve challenging and changing organizational and institutional sexism.*
- *Therapists using existing therapeutic approaches can work in ways that are sensitive to and, where appropriate, emphasize clients' gender-role issues.*
- *Therapists can develop gender-relevant competences in three main dimensions: awareness of own assumptions, values and biases, understanding the worldview of the sex-different client, and developing appropriate intervention strategies and techniques.*
- *Feminist therapists subscribe to many different theoretical orientations. Five central principles of feminist therapy are: egalitarian relationships, pluralism, working against oppression, acknowledging the importance of external factors in shaping women's views, and valuing women's experience.*
- *Men's therapy is the missing half of feminist therapy. To date, approaches to men's problems have focused more on curbing the negative aspects of masculinity than on accentuating the positive aspects of maleness.*
- *Considerable scope still exists for originating new counselling and therapy approaches, as well as for modifying existing ones, to promote equality between the sexes and liberation from oppressive gender-role stereotypes.*

REVIEW AND PERSONAL QUESTIONS

REVIEW QUESTIONS

1. What are some of the areas of overlap between cultural and gender-role issues:
   * in theorizing about counselling and therapy; and
   * in practising counselling and therapy?
2. What do each of the following terms mean:
   * gender role;
   * gender role identity;
   * gender role socialization;
   * gender role conflict; and
   * sexism?
3. What is feminism and what are some of the ways in which women are oppressed?
4. What is the men's movement and why is it important?
5. Describe some therapeutic goals that apply:
   * to both sexes;
   * to women more than men; and
   * to men more than women.
6. What are some ways of making existing counselling and therapy approaches more applicable to gender-role issues?
7. Describe and critically discuss the idea of gender-relevant counselling and therapy competences.
8. Describe and critically discuss feminist therapy.
9. What role, if any, do you see for men's therapy?

PERSONAL QUESTIONS

1. How would you describe:
   * the process of your gender role socialization; and
   * the influence of your culture on your gender role socialization?
2. To what extent do you consider that your attitudes, values and behaviours are masculine, feminine or androgynous?
3. Describe instances, if any, in which you have been:
   * the victim of sexism; and
   * the purveyor of sexism.
4. To what extent and in what ways do you possess psychological problems involving gender-role issues?
5. Assuming that you possess some psychological problems involving gender-role issues, either what are you doing or what do you intend doing about them?
6. How can you make yourself a more gender-sensitive counsellor or therapist both now and in future?

ANNOTATED BIBLIOGRAPHY

Chaplin, J. (1999). *Feminist Counselling in Action* (2nd edition). London: Sage.
     This book presents a multi-stage rhythm model of feminist therapy already briefly described in this chapter. Chaplin illustrates each stage of the process with three case studies.

Biddulph, S. (1995). *Manhood: An Action Plan for Changing Men's Lives* (2nd edition). Sydney: Finch Publishing.
     This book emphasizes having a positive view of maleness, the desirability of fathers and sons understanding one another's experience, and the importance of caring and involved fathers and male mentors in the raising of boys. The book also addresses topics such as sex, relating to women, friendship between men, spirituality and men's groups. The book ends with a contact list of men's groups and organizations in Australia.

Seu, I. B. and Heenan, M. C. (eds) (1999). *Feminism and Psychotherapy: Reflections on Contemporary Theories and Practices*. London: Sage.
     This book discusses the theory and practice of contemporary feminist therapies. Chapters include those on feminism and narrative therapy, object relations therapy, Jungian therapy, Chaplin's rhythm model, and systemic therapy. Other chapters discuss psychotherapy in relation to sexually abused clients, eating-disordered clients, and working-class women. The book concludes with a chapter on questions, answers and absences in feminist therapy.

Greer, G. (1999). *The Whole Woman*. London: Anchor.
     Greer eloquently argues that women throughout the world are still at risk and that, despite gains made by feminism, their lives are becoming more difficult. She provides a comprehensive, irreverent, amusing, earthy and thoroughly one-sided tour of contemporary women's issues in 35 self-contained 'chapterkins' divided into four main areas: body, mind, love and power. Feminist therapy is not one of the topics Greer covers.

Moir, A. and Jessel, D. (1989). *Brain Sex: The Real Difference Between Men and Women*. London: Mandarin Paperbacks.
     Based on the research of many scientists around the world, this book claims that men and women are different because their brains are different. The twelve chapter headings are: the differences, the birth of difference, sex in the brain, childhood differences, the brains come of age, the ability gap, hearts and minds, like minds, the marriage of two minds, why mothers are not fathers, minds at work, and bias at work.

REFERENCES AND FURTHER READING

Ballou, M. (1996). MCT theory and women. In D. W. Sue, A. E. Ivey and P. B. Pedersen (eds). *A Theory of Multicultural Counseling and Therapy* (236–46). Pacific Grove, CA: Brooks/Cole.
Bem, S. L. (1974). The measurement of psychological androgyny. *Journal of Consulting and Clinical Psychology*, *42*, 155–62.
Bem, S. L. (1981). Gender schema theory: A cognitive account of sex typing. *Psychological Review*, *88*, 354–64.
Biddulph, S. (1995). *Manhood: An Action Plan for Changing Men's Lives* (2nd edition). Sydney: Finch Publishing.

Buss, D. M. (1995). Psychological sex differences: Origins through sexual selection. *American Psychologist, 50,* 164–8.

Chaplin, J. (1999). *Feminist Counselling in Action* (2nd edition). London: Sage.

Cheatham, H., Ivey, A. E., Ivey, M. B., Pedersen, P., Rigazio-DiGillio, S., Simek-Morgan, L. and Sue, D. W. (1997). Multicultural counselling and therapy: 1 Metatheory – Taking theory into practice; 2 Integrative practice. In A. E. Ivey, M. B. Ivey and L. Simek-Morgan. *Counseling and Psychotherapy: A Multicultural Perspective* (4th edition, 133–205). Boston, MA: Allyn and Bacon.

Chester, A. (1994). *Feminist Counselling in Australia.* Unpublished MA (Women's Studies) thesis, University of Melbourne.

Christensen, A. and Heavy, C. L. (1993). Gender differences in marital conflict: The demand/withdraw interaction pattern. In S. Oskamp and M. Constanzo (eds). *Gender Issues in Contemporary Society* (113–41). Newbury Park, CA: Sage.

Cook, E. P. (1985). A framework for sex role counseling. *Journal of Counseling and Development, 64,* 253–8.

Cook, E. P. (1987). Psychological androgyny: A review of the research. *The Counseling Psychologist, 15,* 471–513.

Cournoyer, R. J. and Mahalik, J. R. (1995). Cross-sectional study of gender role conflict examining college-aged and middle-aged men. *Journal of Counseling Psychology, 42,* 11–19.

Darwin, C. (1871). *The Descent of Man and Selection in Relation to Sex.* London: Murray.

Eleftheriadou, Z. (1999). Assessing the counselling needs of ethnic minorities in Britain. In S. Palmer and P. Laungani (eds). *Counselling in a Multicultural Society* (113–32). London: Sage.

Fallon, B. (1997). The balance between paid work and home responsibilities: Personal problem or corporate concern? *Australian Psychologist, 32,* 1–9.

Frieden, B. (1963). *The Feminine Mystique.* London: Penguin Books.

Good, G. E., Dell, D. M. and Mintz, L. B. (1989). Male role and gender role conflict: Relations to help seeking in men. *Journal of Counseling Psychology, 36,* 295–300.

Good, G. E., Robertson, J. M., Fitzgerald, L. F., Stevens, M. and Bartels, K. (1996). The relation between masculine role conflict and psychological distress in male university counseling center clients. *Journal of Counseling and Development, 75,* 44–9.

Greer, G. (1999). *The Whole Woman.* London: Anchor.

Hofstede, G. (1980). *Culture's Consequences: International Differences in Work-Related Values.* London: Sage.

Hofstede, G. (1983). Dimensions of national culture in fifty cultures and three regions. In J. B. Deregowski, S. Dziurawiec and R. C. Annis (eds). *Expiscations in Cross-Cultural Psychology* (335–55). Lisse, The Netherlands: Swets and Zeitlinger: Sage.

Huffman, S. B. and Myers, J. E. (1999). Counseling women in midlife: An integrative approach to menopause. *Journal of Counseling and Development, 77,* 258–66.

Jung, C. G. (1982). *Aspects of the Feminine.* London: Routledge.

Maccoby, E. (1990). Gender and relationships: A developmental account. *American Psychologist, 45,* 513–20.

Maracek, J. and Kravetz, D. (1999). Power and agency in feminist therapy. In I. B. Seu and M. C. Heenan (eds) (1999). *Feminism and Psychotherapy: Reflections on Contemporary Theories and Practices* (13–29). London: Sage.

McNamara, K. and Rickard, K. M. (1998). Feminist identity development: Implications for feminist therapy with women. In D. R. Atkinson and G. Hackett (eds). *Counseling Diverse Populations* (271–82). Boston: McGraw-Hill.

Moir, A. and Jessel, D. (1989). *Brain Sex: The Real Difference Between Men and Women*. London: Mandarin.

O'Neill, J. M., Helms, B. J., Gable, R. K., David, L. and Wrightsman, L. S. (1986). Gender role conflict scale: College men's fear of femininity. *Sex Roles*, *14*, 335–50.

Ravinder, S. (1987). Androgyny: Is it really a product of educated, middle class Western societies? *Journal of Cross-Cultural Psychology*, *18*, 208–20.

Schaverin, J. (1999). Jung, the transference and the psychological feminine. In I. B. Seu and M. C. Heenan (eds) (1999). *Feminism and Psychotherapy: Reflections on Contemporary Theories and Practices* (172–88). London: Sage.

Serlin, B. (1989). Counseling dual-career couples. *Journal of Career Planning and Employment*, *50*, 80–6.

Seu, I. B. and Heenan, M. C. (eds) (1999). *Feminism and Psychotherapy: Reflections on Contemporary Theories and Practices*. London: Sage.

Sue, D. W., Carter, R. T., Casas, J. M., Fouad, N. A., Ivey, A. E., Jensen, M., LaFromboise, T., Manese, J. E., Ponterotto, J. G. and Vazquez-Nutall, E. (1998). *Multicultural Counseling Competencies: Individual and Organizational Development*. London: Sage.

Sue, D. W., Ivey, A. E. and Pedersen, P. B. (eds) (1996). *A Theory of Multicultural Counseling and Therapy*. Pacific Grove, CA: Brooks/Cole.

Sue, D. W. and Sue, D. (1999). *Counseling the Culturally Different: Theory and Practice* (3rd edition). New York: John Wiley.

Tavris, C. (1989). *Anger: The Misunderstood Emotion* (revised edition). New York: Simon and Schuster.

Taylor, M. (1996). The feminist paradigm. In R. Wolfe and W. Dryden (eds). *Handbook of Counselling Psychology* (201–39). London: Sage.

Watkins, S. A., Rueda, M. and Rodriguez, M. (1999). *Introducing Feminism*. Duxford: Icon Books.

Woolfe, R. and Dryden, W. (eds). (1996). *Handbook of Counselling Psychology*. London: Sage.

18

Evaluating Counselling and Therapy Approaches

Life is the art of drawing sufficient conclusions from insufficient premises.
Samuel Butler

Evaluating counselling and therapy approaches can be viewed in terms of two overlapping factors: their quality and their quantity. The quality factor is that of how good and effective are the therapeutic approaches, be they new or old. The quantity factor is that of whether currently there are sufficient high quality therapeutic approaches and, if not, what can be done to address this situation.

You have now had a chance to read about the many counselling and therapy approaches presented in this book. Undoubtedly, you have already started drawing your own conclusions about the usefulness of the different approaches and how comfortable you would be implementing each of them. In this final chapter I want to broaden your perspectives about evaluating the quality of counselling and therapy approaches by reviewing eight key issues. Some of these issues are also pertinent to the whole enterprise of originating counselling and therapy approaches.

The quantity factor as well as quality factor is important in any genuinely comprehensive evaluation of counselling and therapy approaches. I conclude both this chapter and the book by addressing the quantity issue. I assert that both academic institutions and the helping professions need to rise to the challenge of originating and developing therapeutic approaches and examine the prospects for doing this.

EIGHT QUALITY ISSUES

Issue 1
What is the relationship between theorists' personal histories and their therapeutic approaches?

In Chapter 1 I mentioned that, without exception, all the theorists whose work is described in this book encountered periods of significant psychological suffering in their lives. Furthermore, theorists' suffering motivated them to create therapeutic approaches that would help themselves as well as others. Being highly motivated to develop therapeutic approaches that they could use themselves has both advantages and disadvantages. In evaluating the theory and practice of the different originators, relevant questions are:

'How much of their own problems were or are the theorists projecting onto clients at large?' and 'Is the approach that worked or works for any particular theorist necessarily that which is best for all clients?' The same sorts of questions can be asked of those studying counselling and therapy approaches. For example, when evaluating the different theoretical approaches, 'How much are your own needs and problems restricting your ability to be objective?'

Issue 2
What is the influence of the theorists' historical and cultural contexts on their therapeutic approaches?

Undoubtedly theorists are influenced by the historical and cultural contexts in which they live. When evaluating therapeutic approaches, relevant questions include how much the problems affecting clients change over time and across cultures. For instance, the current breakdown of respect for authority may mean that many young people, unlike Rogers, are facing problems of too little rather than too much structure. In addition, the materialism and rampant consumerism of Western societies may be exacerbating people's tendencies to greed and consequent feelings of depression and alienation when their attempts to buy happiness fail. In the twenty-first century, the increasing pace of technological change may also create new sets of problems, which current therapeutic approaches may be insufficiently equipped to address, stemming from changes in how people work and communicate.

As illustrated in the chapter on cultural perspectives, culture influences the creation of theory. To what extent and how are each of the therapeutic approaches presented in this book limited because their Euro-American originators either were or still are wearing cultural blinkers?

Issue 3
What is the influence of all the major theorists being men?

In *The Female Eunuch*, Germaine Greer observed that Freud was the father of psychoanalysis and that it had no mother (Greer, 1971). Though many women have also been prominent in developing therapeutic approaches, all of the major theorists presented in this book are men. In addition, none of the theoretical approaches presented in *Current Psychotherapies* (Corsini and Wedding, 2000), probably the most authoritative American therapy textbook, were developed by women.

A number of interesting questions are raised by the predominance of men in developing major therapeutic approaches, such as 'Do some theories contain male bias?' As mentioned in the previous chapter, Freud's notion of penis envy is uncongenial to many women who envy men their power rather than their penises. Furthermore, if women had been more prominent in theorizing, 'Might we have seen the emergence of different and more humane therapeutic approaches?' In addition, given equal mental ability between the sexes and women's greater interest than men in relationships, 'Why have women not made more of a contribution to originating major counselling and therapy approaches?'

Issue 4
What is the nature of human nature?

In the chapter on cognitive–humanistic therapy, I drew attention to Maslow (1971) raising the issue of whether psychology has been based too much on a 'bad animal' rather than a 'good animal' underlying view of human nature. Both Freud and Jung were mainly pessimistic about human nature and emphasized the darker individual and collective unconscious forces lying beneath the veneer of civilization. If anything, the psychodynamic theories stress curbing negative instincts and impulses rather than culti-vating positive ones.

The traditional behaviourists view people's behaviour as the result of evolutionary drives, for instance for sex, food and shelter, and conditioning. Their mechanistic view of human nature is scarcely flattering to humans. The cognitive–behaviourists allow for personal agency. Nevertheless, if anything, theorists like Ellis, with his focus on biologi-cal tendencies to irrationality, and Beck, with his underlying maladaptive schemas, have focused more on the negative than on the positive aspects of human nature. Of the theo-rists in this book, Rogers is perhaps the only one to take predominantly a good animal view of human nature. For Rogers, the actualizing tendency in humans is positive and it only becomes negative to the extent that it is blocked and frustrated by environmental forces.

A fundamental question in evaluating theories is the extent to which they are realistic about humanity's underlying animal nature. Neither neutrality nor cautious optimism involves the need to deny humanity's huge potential for destructive and aggressive behav-iours, but just balances it by noting humans' huge potential to think, feel, act and communicate constructively. Thus, therapy can become a matter of releasing and culti-vating higher human potentials as well as of containing and overcoming destructive tendencies.

Issue 5
To what extent does the approach address sub-normal, normal and supra-normal functioning?

When evaluating the different therapeutic approaches, consider the populations for which their originators intended them. You may remember that Jung thought his analyt-ical therapy more suitable for patients searching for meaning in the afternoon of their lives than those requiring help with conventional adaptation in the morning of their lives.

It is possible to look at human functioning in three broad categories – sub-normal, normal and supra-normal – with, at any given moment, individuals being placed some-where along this continuum. Sub-normal functioning is that where individuals are psychologically distressed and have problems that are more severe than the normal run of the population. Such clients might suffer from the mental disorders that are listed in the American Psychiatric Association's *Diagnostic and Statistical Manual of Mental Disorders* (APA, 1994). Normal functioning is that where people are capable of conventional adap-tation to the societies in which they live. Such individuals may still experience problems for which counselling and therapy are appropriate: for instance, relationship problems, stress problems, and study problems.

Some clients who are functioning well may want to function even better. Supranormal functioning refers to going above, beyond or transcending normal human functioning. Psychotherapy has its origins more in dealing with the problems of the subnormal and normal than in trying to assist well-functioning people to develop their full human potential. There has yet to be a major therapeutic approach developed by professionals, such as counselling psychologists or counsellors, who predominantly deal with normal client populations, let alone superior functioning ones.

Some theorists in this book, for instance Rogers and Ellis, have paid attention to defining full human functioning. Nevertheless, none of the approaches presented sufficiently addresses helping clients to be compassionate, engage in selfless service and synergistically foster the interests and ideals both of themselves and of humankind. A possible criticism of Western psychotherapy is that it errs too much in the direction of being self-centred therapy. The Austrian psychiatrist Alfred Adler, with his emphasis on social interest and community feeling, stands out as an advocate of the need to show more concern for others and for the human species (Adler, 1998).

Issue 6
To what extent does the therapeutic approach foster self-therapy for afterwards?

Sooner or later all clients are going to part from their therapists. Though a full course of psychoanalysis or of analytical therapy may last for years, that option is for the few. Nowadays there is great pressure from those paying for therapeutic services, for example governments and insurance companies, to encourage short-term managed care. Furthermore, most private clients have limited resources, which makes paying for long-term therapy either difficult or impossible. Even though some clients genuinely require longer-term contact, increasingly most counselling and therapy is short-term, say from one to ten sessions, or medium-term, say from eleven to twenty-five sessions. Important questions then become: 'What are the ingredients of effective time-limited therapy?', 'How can therapeutic gains best be maintained afterwards?', and 'To what extent is the therapy a training in self-therapy?'

In Chapter 1 I mentioned that one of the functions of theories was to provide languages both for the therapeutic conversation and so that clients can converse with themselves. Choosing from among the theories presented here, Freud's psychoanalysis, Jung's analytical therapy, Rogerian person-centred therapy and Perlsian gestalt therapy appear not to give high priority to sharing the language in which the therapy is conceptualized with clients. For instance, Rogerian therapists do not share concepts like actualizing tendency, conditions of worth, and organismic valuing process with their clients. Though clients in each of these four approaches may end therapy able to lead their lives more skilfully, the skills of so doing tend not to be clearly articulated during therapy. Clients may learn self-therapy skills, but this is more a by-product of the therapy rather than an integral part of it. For example, person-centred therapists assist clients to listen to their feelings and 'inner voices' and in doing so clients can learn to do this better on their own. However, person-centred therapists do not teach these skills directly to clients.

In the cognitive–behavioural school the therapist's role is more that of an educator than in either the psychodynamic or the humanistic schools. As part of the therapeutic process the language of the approach gets shared with clients. For instance, in rational emotive behaviour therapy, clients learn to detect, analyse in ABC terms, dispute and restate irrational beliefs both during therapy sessions and when completing homework assignments. In inelegant REBT, this sharing of language may be only in relation to specific symptoms, but in elegant REBT, this sharing can lead to disputing irrational beliefs becoming a way of life.

In cognitive therapy, clients learn that they need to test the reality of their thinking and are taught how to do this. By sharing a common language with clients and educating them in cognitive and, sometimes, in behavioural skills as well, these cognitive–behavioural approaches may be more clearly helping clients to become better at self-therapy than those approaches leaving relevant skills to be indirectly acquired and maintained. Perhaps adherents of other than cognitive–behavioural approaches might further develop their theory and practice, without losing the essence, so that clients can learn more about how to conduct self-therapy for afterwards.

Issue 7
What is the role of research in evaluating therapeutic approaches?

Though counselling and therapy approaches may have different goals, nevertheless a pertinent question in evaluating any approach is always going to be 'Where is the research evidence for its effectiveness?' Dictionary definitions of research tend to use adjectives like 'careful' and 'systematic' and nouns like 'study', 'inquiry' and 'investigation'. In Chapter 1 I stated that a function of counselling and therapy theories was to provide research hypotheses. Good theory provides good research hypotheses, poor theory provides poor ones.

Research can have a role in laying the scientific base for a therapeutic approach. However, here my emphasis is on the role of research in evaluating the practice of therapeutic approaches. A pertinent question is 'What therapy, conducted by which therapists, is appropriate for which clients, with which problems, under what circumstances?' Conducting research into therapeutic approaches can be difficult since there are so many considerations to take into account.

Research variables

Below are suggestions of variables, albeit sometimes interrelated, that can be explored when researching therapeutic approaches.

- *Therapist variables.* Therapist variables include age, sex, race, culture, professional training, relevant background and experience, and emotional well-being.
- *Client variables.* Client variables include age, sex, race, culture, nature of problem or

problems, prior history of therapy, severity of disturbance, degree of family and environmental support, and whether any and what medication is involved.

- *Process variables.* Process variables consist of specific details concerning the content and management of therapy. Such variables include frequency and duration of sessions, what interventions were used and how, and how between-session time was used.

- *Outcome variables.* Outcome variables are criteria for measuring what changes occurred at the end of therapy and the degree to which they were maintained. Sources of outcome information include tests and measures, and therapist, client and third-party observations.

Research methods

Methods for evaluating counselling and therapy approaches fall into two main categories: qualitative and quantitative. *Qualitative* approaches to researching therapeutic approaches include detailed case descriptions and open-ended interviews. *Quantitative* approaches emphasize the systematic collection and analysis of quantitative information. Both quantitative and qualitative research methods can be used in evaluating therapeutic approaches – they are not mutually exclusive.

In quantitative research, client change can be estimated by comparing information obtained at different times: for example, at the start of therapy, when it ends, and after one or more stipulated follow-up periods. Often quantitative information is in the form of answers to standardized questionnaires measuring variables such as anxiety or depression. Another important source of quantitative information can be recording the frequency and duration of specific thoughts and behaviours.

Quantitative research designs fall into two main categories: comparison group designs and single case designs. In a simple comparison group design, those receiving treatment would form a treatment group and those not receiving treatment would form a control group. Comparison group designs can be more elaborate: for example, as well as a control group, there could be two or three experimental groups, each being varied in some clearly defined way.

Increasingly single case designs are being used in counselling and therapy research. Kazdin writes: 'Single case experiments permit inferences to be drawn about intervention effects by using the patient as his or her own control. The impact of treatment is examined in relation to the patient's dysfunction over time' (Kazdin, 1986, p. 39). He states that there are four main characteristics of single case designs: clear specification of goals, use of repeated observations, the delineation of time periods in which different conditions (baseline, treatment) apply, and relatively stable data – the more variable the data, the more difficult it is to draw conclusions about intervention effects (Kazdin, 1986).

Empirically supported treatments

Especially in the United States, research into therapeutic approaches is being used to establish empirically supported treatments (ESTs). In 1993, the Society of Clinical Psychology (Division 12) of the American Psychological Association established a Task

Force to identify treatments with scientifically proven effectiveness for particular mental disorders. This Task Force has identified a number of effective, or probably effective, psychological treatments for disorders including: depression, eating disorders, marital discord, panic disorder with and without agoraphobia, post-traumatic stress disorder, social phobia, and smoking cessation (Barlow, Levitt and Bufka, 1999).

A number of observations are relevant about empirically supported treatments. Where such treatments exist, there is a professional and ethical obligation on the part of therapists to find out about them. Furthermore, unless they have good reason for not doing so in terms of particular clients' circumstances, therapists must seriously consider either implementing the treatments themselves or referring clients to those competent to do so. Currently, there is a research–practice gap in which therapists under-utilize evidence-based treatments emanating from the findings of their research-oriented colleagues (McLeod, 2000). One reason for this gap is that some therapists require further training before they can properly implement the protocols for specific empirically supported treatments. Another reason is that the presentation of therapy research findings tends not to be user-friendly to practitioners. Relatively few empirically supported or evidence-based treatments come from outside the area of cognitive–behaviour therapy (Lazarus, 1997).

Limitations of research

Clearly research studies have an important role to play in evaluating therapeutic approaches. Furthermore, all therapists should be reflective practitioners willing to honestly evaluate their own therapeutic processes and outcomes. However, good researchers, like good practitioners, should acknowledge the limitations as well as the strengths of their endeavours. Even in those areas where empirically supported treatments exist, there may be still better ways of treating clients. Skilled researchers not only find out what they know, they often obtain a sharper insight into what remains to be discovered. The concerns of many clients do not fall into circumscribed problem areas, and the unavoidable messiness of much of therapeutic practice does not easily lend itself to narrow research studies. In addition, currently some important issues, such as how to encourage supra-normal functioning, obtain scant research attention.

Issue 8
How adequately is the theory of each therapeutic approach stated?

In Chapter 1, I mentioned that counselling and therapy theories may be viewed as possessing four main dimensions if they are to be stated adequately:

1. a statement of the *basic concepts* or assumptions underlying the theory;
2. an explanation of the *acquisition* of helpful and unhelpful behaviour;
3. an explanation of the *maintenance* of helpful and unhelpful behaviour; and
4. an explanation of how to help clients *change* their behaviour and *consolidate* their gains when therapy ends.

Box 18.1 provides the reader with a basic checklist of questions to ask when assessing how adequately a therapeutic approach's theory is stated.

BOX 18.1

A checklist for assessing a therapeutic approach's theoretical statement

Model of human development
  1. What are the basic concepts of the theory and how adequate are they?
  2. How well does the theory say how helpful and unhelpful thoughts, feelings, physical reactions, and communications/actions are acquired?
  3. How well does the theory say how helpful and unhelpful thoughts, feelings, physical reactions, and communications/actions are maintained?

Model of therapy
  4. How clear and adequate are the approach's therapeutic goals?
  5. How clearly articulated and adequate is the approach's process of therapy?
  6. What is the nature of the therapeutic relationship and what are its strengths and weaknesses?
  7. What interventions are used in the approach and what are their strengths and limitations?
  8. To what extent are cultural and gender considerations adequately taken into account in the approach's theory and practice?
  9. How consistent is the approach's model of human development with its model of therapeutic practice?
 10. What is the research evidence for the effectiveness of the approach with different kinds of clients?

Readers can use the checklist in Box 18.1 to identify gaps in how thoroughly theories are stated. For example, a theoretical statement may be more thorough in assessing how behaviour is maintained than how it was acquired in the first place, or *vice versa*.

Another way to use the checklist is to evaluate how well the theoretical statement answers each question. For example, one way to answer the question about the basic concepts of the theoretical statement is in terms of how adequately they lay the building blocks for the therapeutic approach. Freud's concepts of levels of consciousness and the tripartite structure of the mental apparatus provide a good foundation for the remainder of his theory and practice.

Another way of reviewing an approach's basic concepts involves assessing its assumptions about human nature. As you probably gathered from the cognitive–humanistic therapy chapter, I find some theoretical statements contain an overly negative view of human nature. Furthermore, I would like to see a clearer statement about the concept of mind and a clearer acknowledgement of the importance of mental development and discipline throughout life in the basic concepts of all theoretical approaches, even rational emotive behaviour therapy and cognitive therapy. Above, I have provided you with a few ideas on how to answer the first question on the checklist. When answering all questions on the checklist, remember to have the courage to think for yourself and to think critically.

CREATING NEW THERAPEUTIC APPROACHES

The second factor in evaluating counselling and therapy approaches is the quantity factor. Frequently this factor gets overlooked in the research and professional literature assessing the status of therapy. When evaluating therapeutic approaches, we need to look at the size of the forest as well as at the quality of the individual trees.

In Chapter 1, I mentioned that one of the most worrying aspects when analysing the creation of counselling and therapy approaches is that so little original work of high quality appears to be of recent origin. The creation of therapeutic approaches needs to be a vital and ongoing process. We know a lot, but we can discover a lot more. Generating new therapeutic approaches and insights is a challenge to both academic and professional members of the helping professions. Much more time, money and attention are required for this fundamentally creative endeavour.

Possibly we are not asking some of the right questions, and being too restrictive in where and how we are looking. Past theory creation should not only illuminate the present and future, but be a stepping-stone for new ideas and directions. In addition, while some human problems remain the same over time, others develop in relation to changing circumstances. For example, a whole new set of problems and opportunities may face the .com generation.

Counselling and therapy approaches can be created and refined in at least five main ways, albeit somewhat overlapping. First, existing approaches can be developed and improved. For example, Mearns' focus on relational depth (Mearns, 1997) and Rennie's focus on reflexivity, process identification and process direction (Rennie, 1998) are attempts to develop person-centred theory and practice. Second, attempts can be made to develop new theoretical positions by integrating existing theories and philosophical positions. For example, cognitive–humanistic therapy is an attempt to integrate cognitive, humanistic and existential theory.

Third, there can be collective attempts to address issues inadequately covered in existing therapeutic approaches. Feminist therapy and multicultural counselling and therapy are two prime examples of the continuing development of therapeutic approaches focused on important issues. Fourth, therapeutic approaches can be developed and refined from both experimental research studies and from the conduct of therapy process and outcome research. However, such research studies may be more useful for evaluating and improving what exists than for creating what is new.

Last, one or more outstandingly talented and creative minds may break through the existing conventional wisdom and practices of counselling and therapy. Such theorists may present exciting new visions, conceptual frameworks, therapeutic languages and research hypotheses for validation.

Some barriers

Unfortunately, many barriers exist that can impede and possibly stifle genuinely creative contributions to originating and developing counselling and therapy approaches. An interplay exists between internal and external factors that can make it extremely hard for creativity to come to fruition.

Internally, to break through to something that is truly their own, counselling and therapy theorists have constructively to deal with and move beyond the residues of both their personal and professional pasts. Furthermore, it takes courage for budding theorists to listen to their inner voices, trust their judgement, be different, and face the many external barriers to acceptance of new ideas. It is easy to get discouraged, squashed and crushed rather than to have the courage of one's convictions and the persistence to publish them.

Many external factors can impede creating new therapeutic approaches. At the front of his book *Freedom to Learn*, Rogers quotes Einstein's observation: '. . . It is in short nothing short of a miracle that the modern methods of instruction have not yet entirely strangled the holy curiosity of inquiry; for this delicate little plant, aside from stimulation, stands mainly in need of freedom; without this it goes to wrack and ruin without fail' (Rogers, 1969). Modern methods of instruction reflect modern academic values such as excessively breaking down knowledge into small parts, the tyranny of the narrow research study, undervaluing the subjective and theoretical, undervaluing applied as contrasted with 'pure' approaches to generating knowledge, and emphasizing quantity rather than quality and originality of output.

It is not just students whose potential to create new therapeutic approaches is put at risk by current academic values, but professors and lecturers as well. Arguably, there are two main components to research: creating ideas and evaluating them. In academic institutions the evaluative component may be stifling the theoretical or creative component and what Einstein calls the 'holy curiosity of inquiry'. To some extent, academic research has turned against itself by undervaluing and undermining its creative base.

Furthermore, besides theory building and therapy skills, an originator of a therapeutic approach currently working in an academic institution requires a range of other professional skills, such as statistical, computing, teaching and administrative skills. It is not surprising that most originators of major therapeutic approaches have spent the bulk of their careers outside of academic institutions.

Other barriers to creating original theories stem from the weight of existing knowledge. It may have been easier to create therapeutic approaches when the field was young than now it is maturing. Accreditation and certification requirements are such that now it takes an increasingly long time to qualify as counsellors and psychotherapists. Aspiring theorists spend more time learning what is already known at some risk of getting out of touch with their creative inner voices. Furthermore, it may seem arrogant to promulgate new theories in the shadow of major present and past figures. However, all the major theorists in this book had to struggle for more widespread acceptance of their ideas.

Still a further factor with potential to restrict the development of creative theoretical visions is the trend toward short-term managed care. Counselling and therapy academics and practitioners are under increasing pressure to train and deliver services focusing on 'accurate de-individualising (symptom-based) diagnosis and uniform, protocol driven, brief therapy for all' (Yalom, 2000, p. 1). If anything, what is economically valued is the creation of therapeutic approaches that address identifiable problems rather than whole persons.

Future directions

Looking into the future, the barriers to creating fresh counselling and therapy approaches are such that, overall, the area is likely to continue to under-perform its potential. Nevertheless, progress will be made. Existing theoretical positions will continue to be developed and improved. Serious attempts to merge existing therapeutic approaches in such a way that the integrated whole is more valuable than its various parts may have greater success than heretofore. Collective development of counselling theory and practice to improve service provision in such areas as gender, culture, sexual orientation and physical disability may well gain momentum. In addition, researchers will continue to generate knowledge about what practical applications of which theories work best for whom.

Probably it is in the area of originating major new visions or theoretical positions that the under-performing in creating therapeutic approaches will be most serious. Addressing the issue of insufficient theoretical creativity in the helping professions starts with genuine acknowledgement of the problem. Further steps might be to allocate some positions in academic institutions for staff good at conceptualizing and developing counselling theory and practice. As with theoretical physics – Einstein being the prime example – theoretical psychology is important to developing the field. Such staff could team up with colleagues strong in research design and methods to validate theoretical and practical hypotheses. In addition, journals might be more solicitous of and sympathetic to theoretical as well as research contributions. Furthermore, helping service professors and lecturers can make an even greater effort to nourish in themselves and in their students that delicate little plant, the holy curiosity of inquiry. More attention also can be paid to developing articulate, clear and cogent written communication skills.

However, if the past is a guide to the future, many important advances in creating major counselling and therapy approaches are likely to originate outside of academic settings. Counselling and psychotherapy practitioners have vital roles to play in creating new theories.

CONCLUDING COMMENT

You have now been introduced to many counselling and therapy approaches. I hope that you have enjoyed studying these approaches and want to learn more about this fascinating field. All people are personality theorists, with ideas about what makes themselves and others 'tick'. The systematic study of counselling and therapy approaches should assist you in developing a good working model of human development and of therapy to guide your practical work with clients. Reading an introductory counselling and therapy textbook like this one is an early step along the path of what should be a very stimulating and rewarding journey. I hope that the results of this journey are of great benefit to you and those whom you help both now and in future.

The next generation of counselling and therapy theorists will be drawn from the current generation of helping service students, young academics and practitioners. I would be delighted if future counselling and therapy textbooks contained original work by one or more readers of this book.

SUMMARY

- *Evaluating counselling and therapy approaches can be viewed in terms of two overlapping factors: their quality and their quantity.*
- *Counselling and therapy approaches may be influenced for good or ill by the personal histories of their originators. All approaches in this book were developed by 'wounded theorists' whose psychological suffering may have skewed their perspectives.*
- *Approaches to therapy also reflect the historical and cultural contexts of their originators. The new century is likely to throw up new problems that existing therapeutic approaches may inadequately address.*
- *All the really first-rank counselling and therapy theorists are men. Though many women have also been prominent in developing therapeutic approaches, it is interesting to speculate why they have not made an even greater contribution.*
- *The nature of human nature is a complex area. Possibly most therapeutic approaches are based on an overly negative or 'bad animal' view of human nature that leads to insufficient emphasis on acknowledging and cultivating humanity's higher potentials.*
- *Human functioning may be viewed on sub-normal, normal and supra-normal dimensions. A possible criticism of Western psychotherapy is that it errs too much in the direction of being self-centred therapy.*
- *In particular it is the cognitive–behavioural approaches, with their educational emphasis, that share their languages with clients so that clients can perform a degree of self-therapy once formal therapy ends.*
- *Research plays an important role in evaluating therapeutic approaches. Research can focus on therapist, client, process and outcome variables. Therapy research can be qualitative, quantitative or a mixture of both. Attempts are being made to identify empirically supported treatments (ESTs).*
- *Limitations of research include the complexity of the subject matter, insufficient attention to supra-normal functioning, and an undervaluing of the creative as contrasted with the evaluative aspects of research.*
- *A ten-item checklist for assessing the adequacy of a therapeutic approach's model of human development and of therapy is presented.*
- *Helping service academics and practitioners need to make a concerted effort to originate and develop high quality counselling and therapy approaches. To do so requires surmounting both internal and external barriers.*
- *The systematic study of counselling and therapy approaches should assist readers in developing a good working model of human development and of therapy to guide their practical work with clients.*

REVIEW AND PERSONAL QUESTIONS

REVIEW QUESTIONS

1. What do you consider the influence of each of the following factors on the development of the counselling and therapy approaches presented in this book:
   - the theorists' personal histories;
   - the theorists' historical and cultural contexts; and
   - the fact that all the theorists were or are men?
2. Taken as a group, do you consider the theorists are too negative or positive in their views about human nature? Provide reasons for your answer.
3. Critically discuss the role of research in evaluating therapeutic approaches.
4. Apply the checklist for assessing the adequacy of a therapeutic approach's theoretical statement (see Box 18.1) to at least one of the counselling and therapy approaches presented in this book.
5. Critically discuss the proposition that helping service academics and professionals need to rise to the challenge of originating and developing high quality counselling and therapy approaches.

PERSONAL QUESTIONS

1. What do you consider the influence of each of the following factors on how you might develop your own approach to counselling and therapy:
   - your personal history;
   - your historical and cultural context; and
   - your sex?
2. In light of reading this book, what are your present preferences regarding counselling and therapy approaches, and why?
3. If and when you develop a theoretical statement for your own therapeutic approach, use the checklist provided in Box 18.1 to assess its adequacy and guide you in strengthening your statement.

REFERENCES AND FURTHER READING

Adler, A. (1998) *Social Interest: Adler's Key to the Meaning of Life.* Oxford: Oneworld. Original edition 1933.

American Psychiatric Association (1994). *Diagnostic and Statistical Manual of Mental Disorders* (4th edition). Washington, DC: Author.

Barlow, D. H., Levitt, J. and Bufka, L. F. (1999). The dissemination of empirically supported treatments: A view to the future. *Behaviour Research and Therapy, 37*, 147–62.

Corsini, R. J., and Wedding, D. (eds.) (2000). *Current Psychotherapies* (6th edition). Itasca, IL: Peacock.

Greer, G. (1971). *The Female Eunuch*. London: Paladin.

Kazdin, A. E. (1986). Research designs and methodology. In S. L. Garfield and A. E. Bergin (eds).

Handbook of Psychotherapy and Behavior Change (3rd edition, 23–68). New York: Wiley.

Lazarus, A. A. (1997). *Brief but Comprehensive Psychotherapy: The Multimodal Way.* New York: Springer.

Maslow, A. H. (1971). *The Farther Reaches of Human Nature.* Harmondsworth: Pelican.

McLeod, J. (2000). Research issues in counselling and psychotherapy. In S. Palmer (ed.). *Introduction to Counselling and Psychotherapy: The Essential Guide* (331–40). London: Sage.

Mearns, D. (1997). *Person-Centred Counselling Training.* London: Sage.

Rennie, D. (1998). *Person-Centred Counselling: An Experiential Approach.* London: Sage.

Rogers, C. R. (1969). *Freedom to Learn.* Columbus, Ohio: Charles E. Merrill.

Yalom, I. D. (2000). Biographical Information. www.yalom.com

Glossary

Abbreviations:
AT, Jung's analytical therapy; BT, behaviour therapy; CHT, cognitive–humanistic therapy; CT, cognitive therapy; ET, existential therapy; GT, gestalt therapy; LT, logotherapy; MMT, multimodal therapy; PA, Freud's psychoanalysis; PCT, person-centred therapy; REBT, rational emotive behaviour therapy; RT, reality therapy; TA, transactional analysis.

ABCDE theory (REBT) A theoretical model for understanding psychological distress and change in which A = Adversities or activating events in a person's life, B = Beliefs, both rational and irrational, C = Consequences, both emotional and behavioural, D = Disputing irrational beliefs, and E = Effects and/or effective philosophy of life.

Active imagination (AT) is a technique devised by Jung to help people get in touch with unconscious material. Clients begin by concentrating on a starting point. Then they allow their unconscious to produce a series of images, which may make a complete story.

Activity scheduling (CT) Activity scheduling involves planning and timetabling specific activities with clients. A principle of activity scheduling is to state what activity the client agrees to engage in rather than how much they will accomplish.

Actualizing tendency (PCT) is an active process representing the inherent tendency of the organism to develop its capacities in the direction of maintaining, enhancing and reproducing itself.

Adult (TA) An ego state oriented towards objective, autonomous data-processing and probability estimating.

Anima and the animus (AT) The anima is the personification of the feminine nature in a man's unconscious, whereas the animus is the personification of the masculine nature in a woman's unconscious.

Archetypes (AT) are 'primordial images' and 'primordial thoughts' rather than the representations of the images or thoughts themselves. Archetypes provide instinctive patterns for mental activity.

Assertive training (BT) involves training clients in the appropriate verbal and non-verbal behaviours for expressing both negative and positive thoughts and feelings. Contemporary assertive training often focuses on thinking assertively as well as on behaviour.

Automatic thoughts (CT) are less accessible to awareness than voluntary thoughts, but not so deeply buried as beliefs and schemas. Automatic thoughts are part of people's internal monologue – what and how they talk to themselves – can take the form of words, images, or both, occur very rapidly, and are usually at the fringe of awareness.

Autonomy (TA) refers to the capacity for non-script behaviour which is reversible, with no particular time schedule, developed later in life, and not under parental influence.

Awareness technique (GT) is a concentration technique in which clients are asked to become aware of their body language, their breathing, their voice quality and their emotions as much as of any pressing thoughts.

BASIC I.D. (MMT) Human personality can be divided into seven discrete, yet interacting, modalities or dimensions: behaviour, affect, sensation, imagery, cognition, interpersonal, and drugs/biology.

Basic needs (RT) Choice theory sees humans as driven by five basic needs that are genetic in origin: survival, love and belonging, power, freedom, and fun.

Behavioural assessment (BT) sometimes known as functional analysis, allows therapists to identify the context, antecedents and consequences of the responses they wish to treat. When conducted after initial sessions, behavioural assessment aims to assist both in evaluating treatment effectiveness and in deciding whether to continue, discontinue or alter treatment.

Being (ET) 'Being' as a participle of a verb implies that someone is in the process of becoming something. When used as a noun 'being' can mean potential.

Bridging (MMT) A rapport enhancement technique in which therapists deliberately tune into the clients' preferred modalities before gently helping them cross bridges into other modalities that may prove more productive.

Child (TA) The Child or archaeopsychic ego state is a set of feelings, thoughts, attitudes and behaviour patterns which are archaic relics of an individual's childhood. The Child ego state is exhibited in two major forms: the adapted Child, which follows parental directives, and the natural Child, which is autonomous.

Choice theory (RT) or internal control psychology explains that, for all practical purposes, humans choose everything they do, including the misery they feel.

Choice theory language (RT) Language which assumes personal responsibility for one's total behaviour, for instance using active verbs like depressing, and allows others' freedom of choice to assume responsibility for their total behaviour.

Classical conditioning (BT), also known as respondent conditioning, is a form of learning whereby existing responses are attached to new stimuli by pairing these stimuli with those that naturally elicit the response.

Cognitive–behaviour therapy A term describing therapies that extend behaviour therapy to have a major focus on changing covert thoughts as well as overt behaviours: examples include cognitive therapy, rational emotive behaviour therapy, and multimodal therapy.

Cognitive distortions (CT) are information processing errors that both characterize and maintain psychological distress: for instance, arbitrary inference, selective abstraction, overgeneralization and dichotomous thinking.

Cognitive vulnerability (CT) refers to humans' cognitive frailty. Because of their schemas, each person has a set of unique vulnerabilities and sensitivities that predispose them to psychological distress.

Collaborative empiricism (CT) Therapists and clients collaborate together in the scientific endeavour of examining the evidence to confirm or negate the client's cognitions, all of which are viewed as testable hypotheses.

Collective unconscious (AT) At its deepest levels the unconscious is a vast collective and universal historical storehouse whose contents belong to mankind in general. The contents of the collective unconscious have never been in consciousness, but owe their existence to heredity.

Complexes (AT), which are an important feature of the personal unconscious, are accumulations of associations, sometimes of a traumatic nature, that possess strong emotional content – for example, the mother complex.

Conditions of worth (PCT) The internalization or introjection of others' evaluations, which do not truly reflect the person's actualizing tendency but may serve to impede it.

Congruence (PCT) Consistency between the thoughts and feelings the therapist experiences and her or his professional demeanour. Not putting on a professional façade.

Contact boundary (GT) is the boundary between organism and environment where all feelings, thoughts and actions take place. Contacting the environment represents forming a gestalt, whereas withdrawal is either closing a gestalt completely or mobilizing resources to make closure possible.

Counselling A relationship in which counsellors assist clients to understand themselves and their problems better. Then, where appropriate, counsellors use various interventions to assist clients to feel, think, communicate and act more effectively. The term 'counselling' is often used interchangeably with psychotherapy. Since there are many different theoretical orientations, it may be more accurate to speak of counselling approaches than counselling.

Death anxiety (ET), the fear of ceasing to be, can be both conscious and unconscious. It is the fundamental source of anxiety, whether it be neurotic, normal or existential. Strong death anxiety is likely to be repressed.

Decision (TA) A childhood commitment to a certain form of behaviour, which later forms the basis of character.

Defence mechanisms (PA) are infantilisms which operate unconsciously to protect the ego and may impede realistic behaviour long after they have outlived their usefulness. Examples include repression, reaction formation, projection, fixation and regression.

Dehumanizing pressures (CHT) External pressures which can have, but do not necessarily have, negative consequences in helping people think skilfully so as to experience and express their full humanity: for example, consumerism, rapid technological change, and a mechanical approach to education.

Dereflection (LT) Dereflection aims to counteract hyper-reflection, or excessive attention, by assisting clients to ignore their symptoms: for example, a woman dereflects excessive self-observation regarding sexual performance by becoming more focused on her partner.

Disputing (REBT) involves challenging and questioning unsubstantiated hypotheses that clients hold about themselves, others and the world.

Dream analysis (AT) Dreams are utterances or statements from the unconscious and are comparable to texts that appear unintelligible, but the therapist has to discover how to read them. An understanding of myths and symbols is fundamental for analysing dreams.

Dreamwork (GT) Dreams are existential messages, not just unfinished situations, current problems or symptoms. There are four stages to dreamwork: sharing the dream, retelling the dream in the present tense, talking to the different actors in the dream, and conducting a dialogue between different elements in the dream.

Eclecticism (MMT) The practice of drawing from different counselling and therapy approaches in formulating client problems and implementing treatment interventions. A distinction can be made between theoretical eclecticism and practical or technical eclecticism.

Ego (PA) The ego or 'I' acts as an intermediary between the id and the external world and strives to bring the reality principle to bear upon the id in substitution for the pleasure principle.

Ego disturbance (REBT) arises from the demanding and irrational belief 'I *must* do well and win approval for all my performances' because it leads to people thinking and feeling that they are inadequate and undeserving persons when they do not do as well as they must.

Ego state (TA) A consistent pattern of feeling and experience directly related to a corresponding consistent pattern of behaviour.

Empathy (PCT) The therapist's capacity to comprehend accurately the client's inner world or internal frame of reference and to sensitively communicate back this understanding.

Excitement (GT) The energy people create, which coincides with the physiological function of excitation.

Existential (ET) The word 'existence' is derived from the Latin word *existere*, literally meaning 'to stand out, to emerge'. Existential approaches to therapy are concerned with the science and processes of being.

Existential defence mechanisms (ET) In addition to conventional defence mechanisms, there are specific defences for each of the four ultimate concerns – death, freedom, isolation and meaninglessness – to defend people against these fundamental fears.

Existential frustration (LT) results when the will to meaning is frustrated. Apathy and boredom are the main characteristics of existential frustration.

Existential guilt (ET) Three forms of existential guilt are failure to live up to one's potential; distorting the reality of one's fellow humans; and 'separation guilt' in relation to nature as a whole.

Existential psychodynamics (ET) Existential conflicts and existential anxiety flow from people's inescapable confrontations with the givens of existence – death, freedom, isolation and meaninglessness.

Existential ultimate concerns (ET) Four existential ultimate concerns are death, freedom, isolation, and meaninglessness. Each concern begets a different existential conflict.

Existential vacuum (LT) describes a state in which people complain of an inner void. They suffer from a sense of meaninglessness, emptiness and futility.

Experiments (CT) Beliefs are treated as testable hypotheses. Together therapists and clients set up cognitive and behavioural experiments that encourage clients to test the reality of their beliefs.

Experiments (GT) Therapists and clients develop experiments in which clients try out different ways of thinking and acting. Repeatedly clients are encouraged to 'Try this and see what you experience.'

External control psychology (RT) involves choosing to control and allow oneself to be controlled by others. Choosing to coerce, force, compel, punish, reward, boss, manipulate, motivate, criticize, blame, complain, nag, badger, rank, rate, and withdraw.

Fear of goodness (CHT) A cluster of overt and underlying fearful feelings and unskilful thoughts concerning getting in touch with the positive core of one's being and showing human sympathy.

Feminist therapy Approaches to counselling and therapy that address women's problems and issues in the context of constricting gender role socialization and power imbalances in society. Feminist therapy emphasizes egalitarian therapist–client relationships, valuing women's experiences, liberating women from sex-role stereotypes, and working against oppression.

Flooding (BT) In contemporary flooding techniques, therapists arrange for clients to be exposed to relatively strong fear stimuli which, either real or imagined, are presented continuously.

Free association (PA) Clients must tell their analysts everything that occurs to them, even if it is disagreeable and even if it seems meaningless. The object of free association is to help lift repressions by making unconscious material conscious.

Frustration (GT) Providing situations in which clients experience being stuck in frustration and then frustrating their avoidances still further until they are willing to mobilize their own resources.

Game (TA) An ongoing series of complementary ulterior transactions progressing to a well-defined predictable outcome or payoff.

Gestalt (GT) means form or shape and among the meanings of the German verb *gestalten* are to shape, to form, to fashion, to organize and to structure. Other terms for gestalt are pattern, configuration or organized whole.

Happiness (CHT) On one level happiness is freedom from want and having the basic necessities of life. On another level, happiness consists of feelings of contentment, self-worth and well-being arising from connecting with the positive core of one's own or another's being. Being the generator, giver or recipient of thoughts and actions reflecting innate goodness.

Homeostasis (GT) Homeostasis or organismic self-regulation is the process by which the organism satisfies its needs by restoring balance when faced with a demand or need which upsets its equilibrium.

Human sympathy (CHT) Identifying and feeling a sense of fellowship with others as being of the same human clay as oneself in going through the cycle of birth, life and death and wanting to be happy and to avoid suffering. The capacity to view oneself and others compassionately.

Id (PA) The id or 'it' contains everything that is inherited and fixed in the constitution. Filled with energy from the instincts, the id strives to bring about the satisfaction of instinctual needs on the basis of the pleasure principle.

Incongruence (PCT) A discrepancy between the self as perceived and the actual experience of the organism.

Individuation (AT) is the process by which the person becomes differentiated as a separate psychological individual, a separate whole as distinct from the collective psychology.

Inelegant and elegant change (REBT) Inelegant change largely consists of some kind of symptom removal. Elegant change goes further than developing an effective new philosophy that supports removal of specific symptoms to assisting clients to develop and implement an effective philosophy of life.

Innate goodness (CHT) The positive core of one's being and an important survival instinct for the human species. Biological tendencies towards affirming life, affiliation, compassion, nurturing, caring, and altruism.

Instincts (PA) represent somatic or biological demands upon the mind, which are grouped into two basic instincts, *Eros* and the *destructive instinct*.

Integration (MMT) Attempting to blend together theoretical concepts and/or practical interventions drawn from different therapeutic approaches into coherent and integrated wholes.

Interpretation (PA) involves offering constructions or explanations. Interpreting dreams represents an important – sometimes the most important – part of the analyst's work.

Introjections (GT) are experiences which are swallowed as a whole rather than being properly digested and assimilated. The outcome of introjection is that undesirable as well as desirable thoughts, feelings and behaviours get retained.

Irrational beliefs (REBT) are rigid, dogmatic, unhealthy, maladaptive beliefs that mostly get in the way of people's efforts to achieve their goals. Such beliefs are characterized by demands, musts and shoulds.

Lifeskills (CHT) Sequences of choices affirming or negating psychological life that people make in specific skills areas. The main categories of lifeskills are mind skills and communication/action skills.

Lifeskills therapy (CHT) Therapy for conventional adaptation. Assisting clients to attain the mind, communication and action skills required for functioning effectively in the societies of which they are a part.

Logotherapy (LT) is an education for responsibility that seeks to unblock clients' will to meaning. It is the treatment of choice for persons suffering from noogenic or existential neurosis.

Low frustration tolerance (REBT) or discomfort disturbance arises from the grandiose belief that people think they are so special that conditions must be easy and satisfying for them.

Medical ministry (LT) A term for how logotherapists work with somatogenic cases where the somatic cause cannot be removed. Where possible, logotherapists assist the non-diseased part of clients in finding meaning in the attitude that they take towards their suffering.

Men's therapy An underdeveloped area of counselling and therapy focusing on men's problems and issues. Many feminist therapy goals and principles are applicable to men's therapy, which is sometimes considered feminist therapy's missing half.

Mental discipline therapy (CHT) Therapy for higher level functioning or for supra-normalcy. Training the mind to access, activate and implement the positive inner core of one's being. Therapy that goes beyond imparting lifeskills for everyday adaptation to train and discipline the mind for achieving genuine human sympathy and skills for helping others as well as oneself.

Mind (CHT) A complex entity based ultimately on physical processes. The seat of awareness, thought, imagery, volition, feeling and personal agency. Ways of viewing the mind include individual differences in mental capacities, levels of consciousness, the mind's contents, and the mental processes by which people create and influence their thoughts, images, feelings, physical reactions, communications and actions.

Mind skills (CHT) The mental processes through which people can create and influence how they think: for example, by creating self-talk, visual images, rules, perceptions, explanations of cause and expectations.

Modality Profile (MMT) A BASIC I.D. chart listing problems and interventions within each modality.

Modes (CT) are networks of cognitive, affective, motivational and behavioural schemas. Modes are fundamental to personality since they interpret and adapt to emerging and ongoing situations.

Multicultural therapy Approaches to counselling and therapy that take into account the cultures and worldviews of clients and therapists. Such approaches include making existing Euro-American therapies more culture-sensitive, developing multicultural counselling and therapy competences, and using non-Western therapeutic approaches.

Multimodal Life History Inventory (MMT) A fifteen-page inventory that asks numerous questions about antecedent events and maintaining factors, with the answers being divided into BASIC I.D. categories.

Observational learning (BT) Learning behavioural and cognitive skills by observing models, including observing how the models' behaviours get reinforced.

Operant conditioning (BT) A form of learning in which the person or animal has to operate on the environment to produce a response. Responses are maintained, modified or extinguished by the likelihood of eliciting reinforcing consequences.

Non-being (ET) The opposite of being is nonbeing or nothingness. Death is the most obvious form of non-being. However, there are numerous other threats to being in the form of loss of potentiality through anxiety and conformity and through lack of clear self-awareness.

Noogenic neurosis (LT) refers to those cases where the existential vacuum leads to clinical symptomatology. Existential frustration plays a large part in noogenic neuroses.

Openness to experience (PCT) Allowing all significant sensory and visceral experiences to be perceived, the capacity for realistic perception without defensiveness.

Organismic valuing process (PCT) refers to a person's continuous weighing of experience and the placing of values on that experience in terms of its ability to satisfy the actualizing tendency.

Quality world (RT) A personal picture album consisting of detailed pictures of what an individual wants to satisfy her or his needs. The pictures in people's quality worlds fall into three categories: (1) the people they most want to be with; (2) the things they most want to own or experience; and (3) the ideas or systems of belief that govern much of their behaviour.

Paradoxical intention (LT) In paradoxical intention, clients are invited to intend precisely that

which they fear. Their excessive fear or hyperintention is replaced by a paradoxical wish: for instance, fear of perspiring is replaced by trying as hard as possible to perspire.

Parent (TA) The Parent or exteropsychic ego state is a set of feelings, thoughts, attitudes, and behaviours which resemble those of parental figures. The Parent ego state may be seen in one of two forms: the controlling Parent and the nurturing Parent.

Participant modelling (BT) involves therapists repeatedly modelling feared activities, for instance handling snakes or dogs. Then joint performance with therapists may enable clients to start engaging in activities which would be too threatening to engage in on their own. Ultimately clients perform the feared activities on their own.

Persona (AT) A concept derived from the mask worn by actors in antiquity. At one level, the persona is the individual's system of adaptation or way of coping with the world. At a different level, the persona is not just an individual mask, but a mask of the collective psyche.

Personal unconscious (AT) The contents, which are definitely personal, fall into two main categories: material that lost its intensity either because it was forgotten or repressed; and material which never possessed sufficient intensity to reach consciousness but has somehow entered the psyche – for instance, some sense-impressions.

Preconscious (PA) The preconscious is latent and capable of becoming conscious, while the unconscious is repressed and is unlikely to become conscious without great difficulty.

Psychodynamics (PA) The concept of psychical or mental energy and its distribution among the id, ego and super-ego is central to psychoanalysis.

Psychological suffering (CHT) Any form of mental discomfort, unhappiness or distress, however large or small. Existential psychological suffering connected with sickness, ageing, tragic events, external misfortunes and death is a natural part of being human. Self-created psychological suffering, or alienation from the positive core of one's being, mainly results from an insufficiently skilful and disciplined mind.

Psychotherapy Literally 'mind healing'. More accurate to speak of 'the psychotherapies' since there are many different theoretical and practical approaches to psychotherapy.

Rational beliefs (REBT) Healthy, productive and adaptive beliefs that are consistent with social reality, and are stated as preferences, desires and wants.

Rational coping statements (REBT) range from articulating simple words of encouragement to generating longer statements containing preferential thinking. This step often, but not necessarily, follows vigorous disputing.

Rational-emotive imagery (REBT) In rational-emotive imagery (REI) clients: (1) vividly imagine an adversity; (2) once feeling unhealthily upset, hold on to the image for a minute or two; and (3) then tell themselves strongly and repetitively sensible rational beliefs or coping statements.

Reattribution techniques (CT) test automatic thoughts and underlying beliefs by considering alternative ways of assigning responsibility and cause.

Reciprocal inhibition (BT) encompasses all situations in which the elicitation of one response appears to bring about a decrement in the strength of evocation of a simultaneous response.

Reinforcement (BT) The presentation of a reward or the removal of an aversive stimulus following a response. Reinforcement always increases the future probability of the reinforced response. Schedules of reinforcement can be either intermittent or non-intermittent.

Relationships of choice (MMT) Not only matching the nature of therapeutic relationship to the client, but also matching it to the client's observed needs at different times in therapy.

Schemas (CT) are structures that consist of people's fundamental beliefs and assumptions. They are relatively stable cognitive patterns that influence, through their beliefs, how people select and synthesize incoming information.

Script (TA) A life plan based on a decision made in childhood, reinforced by the parents, justified by subsequent events, and culminating in a chosen alternative. The purpose of script analysis is to get clients out of their script and thus to behave autonomously.

Search for meaning (LT) The basic human need is a search for meaning rather than a search for the self. Identity is only achievable through being responsible for the fulfilment of meaning. Work, love, suffering, the past and the supra-meaning are each sources of meaning.

Second-order BASIC I.D. assessments (MMT) When impasses occur in treating clients, second-order BASIC I.D. assessments allow a more detailed review of behaviours, affective responses, sensory reactions, images, cognitions, interpersonal factions, and drugs/biological factors in relation to the area in which change is proving difficult.

Self (AT) The self is the central archetype, the archetype of order. The self, which expresses the unity of personality as a whole, encompasses both conscious and unconscious components.

Self-actualizing (GT) is a process involving an effective balance of contact and withdrawal at the contact boundary and the ability to use energy or excitement to meet real rather than phoney needs.

Self-actualizing (PCT) A process of living and of personal development, based on the individual's organismic valuing process, that genuinely reflects their unique actualizing tendency.

Self-concept (PCT) is the self as perceived and the values attached to these perceptions, or what a person refers to as 'I' or 'me'.

Self-transcendence (LT) The human capacity to reach out beyond the boundaries of oneself by either fulfilling a meaning or encountering another person lovingly.

Shadow (AT) The shadow archetype reflects the realm of humans' animal ancestors and, as such, comprises the whole historical aspect of the unconscious. For the most part, the shadow consists of inferior traits of personality that individuals refuse to acknowledge.

Socratic dialogue (CT) A Socratic style of questioning assists clients to expand and evaluate how they think. Typical questions are: 'Where is the evidence?'; 'Where is the logic?'; 'Are there other ways of perceiving the situation?'; and 'What would be the worst thing that could happen?'

Stimulus control (BT) entails modifying in advance the stimuli or cues associated with maladaptive responses and/or establishing cues associated with adaptive responses.

Structural analysis (TA) consists of diagnosing and separating one feeling-thinking-and-behaviour pattern or ego state from another.

Structural Profile (MMT) Clients rate themselves across each of the BASIC I.D. modalities on a seven-point scale, with 1 being the lowest and 7 being the highest.

Super-ego (PA) The super-ego is a residue formed within the ego in which parental influence is prolonged. Parental influence may be defined broadly to include cultural, racial and family influences.

Supra-normalcy (CHT) Above, beyond and transcending contemporary normal human functioning. The processes and outcomes of higher levels of mental training and discipline. Attaining a high degree of human sympathy, awareness, equanimity, autonomy and wisdom.

Systematic desensitization (BT) involves three elements: (a) training in deep muscular relaxation; (b) the construction of hierarchies of anxiety-evoking stimuli; and (c) asking the client, when relaxed, to imagine items from the anxiety-evoking hierarchies.

Technical eclecticism (MMT) Technically eclectic therapists use procedures from different sources without necessarily subscribing to the theories or disciplines that spawned them.

Thresholds (MMT) People's differing capacities to tolerate negative stimuli such as pain, frustration, stress, cold, noise and pollution. Physiologically, people react to a variety of arousing stimuli with differing and distinctive patterns of autonomic nervous system activity.

Token economies (BT) Reinforcement programmes that use tokens as tangible conditioned reinforcers which may be exchanged for back-up reinforcers such as prizes, opportunities to engage in special activities, food or other purchases. An example is that of points for good classroom behaviour being exchangeable for prizes of differing value.

Total behaviour (RT) is always the sum of the following four components: acting, thinking, feeling and physiology. Acting and thinking are under voluntary control; feeling and physiology can only be changed by altering acting and thinking.

Tracking (MMT) refers to the careful assessment of the 'firing order', the ordering of the chain reaction of the different modalities, to assist therapists in selecting and prioritizing treatment interventions.

Transaction (TA) In transactional analysis a stroke or unit of recognition is viewed as the fundamental unit of social interaction. An exchange of strokes constitutes a transaction. Transactions take place between ego states. Transactions between ego states may be complementary, crossed and/or ulterior.

Transference (PA) Clients perceive their analysts as reincarnations of important figures from their childhoods and transfer onto them moderate to intense feelings and emotions appropriate to these earlier models.

Unconditional positive regard (PCT) consists of two dimensions: first, prizing and feeling positively towards clients and, second, non-judgemental acceptance of clients' experiencing and disclosures as their subjective reality.

Unconditional self-acceptance (REBT) Clients can always choose to accept themselves just because they are alive and human, whether or not they perform well or are approved of by others.

Unconscious (PA) The unconscious, or unconscious proper, consists of material that is inadmissible to consciousness through repression. The censorship on unconscious material coming into awareness is very strong indeed.

WDEP system (RT) Each letter represents a cluster of skills and techniques for assisting clients to make better choices in their lives: W, asking clients what they want; D, asking clients what they are doing and their overall direction; E, asking clients to conduct a searching self-evaluation; and P, asking clients to make plans to fulfil their needs more effectively.

Will to meaning (LT) The fundamental motivating drive since people are confronted with the need to detect and find meaning literally until their last breaths.

Appendix 1:
Training Information

Following is a selective listing of sources of training information in Britain and Australia.

Freud's psychoanalysis

Britain

The Chair, Psychoanalytic and Psychodynamic Psychotherapy Section, United Kingdom Council for Psychotherapy, 167–169 Great Portland Street, London W1N 5FB.

Australia

Centres for the training of psychoanalysts exist in Adelaide, Melbourne and Sydney. Information may be obtained from:
The Australian Psychoanalytic Society, c/o Francis Thomson-Salo, Secretary, PO Box 2226, Caulfield Junction, Melbourne, Victoria 3161.

Jung's analytical therapy

Britain

Association of Jungian Analysts, 7 Eton Avenue, London NW3 7EL.

British Association for Psychotherapists, 37 Mapesbury Road, London NW2 4HJ.

Independent Group of Analytical Psychologists, PO Box 1175, London W3 6DS.

Society of Analytical Psychology, 1 Daleham Gardens, London NW3 5BY.

Australia

Regional centres for the training of Jungian analysts exist in Melbourne, Perth and Sydney. Information may be obtained from:
Australian and New Zealand Society of Jungian Analysts – ANZSJA, c/o Anne Brown, Secretary, 11 Eckersley Court, Blackburn South, Melbourne, Victoria 3130.
e-mail: anne@preston.starway.net.au

Person-centred therapy

Britain

Centre for Counselling Studies, School of Education and Professional Development, University of East Anglia, Norwich NR4 7TJ.

Counselling Unit, Faculty of Education, University of Strathclyde, 76 Southbrae Drive, Glasgow, Scotland G13 1PP.

Australia

Masters in Counselling, School of Education, La Trobe University, Bundoora, Melbourne, Victoria 3083.

Gestalt therapy

Britain

The Gestalt Psychotherapy Training Institute in the UK, 2 Bedford Street, London Road, Bath BA1 6AF.

Professor Petruska Clarkson, PHYSIS, 12 North Common Road, London W5 2QB.
Tel/Fax: 020-8567-3531.

Australia

Gestalt Institute, Suite 40, 45 Riversdale Road, Hawthorn, Melbourne, Victoria 3122.
Tel: 03-9815-0050.

Gestalt Institute, 81 Frederick Street, Toowong, Queensland 4066.
Tel: 07-3371-8163.

Transactional analysis

Britain

Dr Ian Stewart, The Berne Institute, Berne House, 29 Derby Road, Kegworth DE74 2EN.
Tel/Fax 01509-673649.

Australia

Robin Maslen, MAASW, 37 Downing Street, Hove, South Australia 5048.
Tel: 089-296-2768.

Reality therapy
Britain
John Brickell, Centre for Reality Therapy (UK),
Green House, 43 George Street, Leighton Buzzard,
Bedfordshire LU7 8JX.
Tel: 01525-851-588. Fax: 01525-851-800.
e-mail: john.brickell@dtn.ntl.com

Australia
Ms Kerry Panitz and Associates, 7 Teak Street,
Shailer Park, Queensland 4128.
Tel: 07-3209-9912. Fax: 07-3209-9912.

Behaviour therapy
Britain
Information about behavioural and cognitive thera-
pies training is available from:
British Association for Behavioural and Cognitive
Psychotherapies (BABCP), PO Box 9, Accrington
BB5 2DG. Executive Officer: Howard Lomas.
Tel/Fax: 01254-875277.
e-mail: membership@babcp.org.uk

Australia
Information about Australian behavioural and cog-
nitive therapies training is available from:
Dr Ray Wilks, Victorian Branch of the Australian
Association for Cognitive and Behaviour Therapy
(AACBT), PO Box 1170D, Bundoora, Mel-
bourne, Victoria 3083.
Tel: 03-9925-7722. Fax: 03-9925-7303.
e-mail: wilks@rmit.edu.au

Rational emotive behaviour therapy
Britain
MSc., Rational Emotive Behaviour Therapy,
PACE, Goldsmiths College, New Cross, London
SE14 6NW. Tel: 020-7919-7872.
Contact person: Professor Windy Dryden.

Centre for Rational Emotive Behaviour Therapy, 156
Westcombe Hill, Blackheath, London SE3 7DH.
Tel: 020-8293-4114 (Course details).
Website: http://www.managingstress.com

Australia
Australian Institute for REBT, 118 Balcombe Road,
Mentone, Victoria 3802. Tel: 03-9585-1881.
Contact person: Monica O'Kelly.

Cognitive therapy
Britain
Information about behavioural and cognitive thera-
pies training is available from:
British Association for Behavioural and Cognitive

Psychotherapies (BABCP).
For contact details, see Behaviour therapy information above.

Australia
Information about Australian behavioural and cog-
nitive therapies training is available from:
Dr Ray Wilks, Victorian Branch of the Australian
Association for Cognitive and Behaviour Therapy
(AACBT).
For contact details, see Behaviour therapy informa-
tion above.

Multimodal therapy
Britain
The Centre for Multimodal Therapy, 156 West-
combe Hill, Blackheath, London SE3 7DH.
Tel: 020-8293-4114 (Course details).
Website: http://www.managingstress.com

PROFESSIONAL ASSOCIATIONS

Training information may also be obtained from
the following professional associations.

Britain
British Association for Counselling, 1 Regent Place,
Rugby CV21 2PJ.
Tel: 01788-57832. Fax: 01788-562189.
e-mail: bac@bac.co.uk
Website: http//www.counselling.co.uk

British Psychological Society, St Andrews House,
48 Princess Road East, Leicester LE1 7DR.
Tel: 0116-254-9568. Fax: 0116-247-1787.
e-mail: enquiry@bps.org.uk
Website: www.bps.org.uk

United Kingdom Council for Psychotherapy,
167–169 Great Portland Street, London W1N 5FB.
Tel: 020-7436-3002. Fax: 020-7436-3013.
e-mail: ukcp@psychotherapy.org.uk
Website: www.psychotherapy.org.uk

Australia
Australian Psychological Society, PO Box 126,
Carlton South, Melbourne, Victoria 3053.
Tel: 03-9663-6166. Fax: 03-9663-6177.
e-mail: naltoff@psychsociety.com.au
Website: http//www.aps.psychsociety.com.au

Psychotherapy and Counselling Federation of Aus-
tralia, PO Box 481, Carlton South, Melbourne,
Victoria 3053.
Tel: 03-9639-8330. Fax: 03-9639-8340.
e-mail: PACFA@bigpond.com
Website: www.pacfa.org.au

Appendix 2:
Journal Information

Following is a selective listing of counselling and therapy journals.

Psychoanalysis

International Journal of Psycho-Analysis
British Psychoanalytic Society, Byron House, 112 Shirland Road, London W9 2EQ, England.

Journal of the American Psychoanalytic Association
American Psychoanalytic Association, 309 East 49th Street, New York, NY 10017, USA.

Psychoanalytic Quarterly
175 Fifth Avenue, Room 810, New York, NY 10010, USA.

Psychodynamic Counselling
Routledge, Taylor & Francis Ltd, Customer Services Department, Rankine Road, Basingstoke, Hants RG24 8PR, England.
Tel: 01256-813002. Fax: 01256-330245
(This journal covers different psychodynamic approaches)

Analytical therapy

The Journal of Analytical Psychology
1 Daleham Gardens, London NW3 5BY, England.

Quadrant
28 East 39th Street, New York, NY 10016, USA.

The San Franscisco Jung Institute Library Journal
2040 Gough Street, San Franscisco, CA 94109, USA.

Harvest
194 Castellain Mansions, Castellain Road, London W9 1HD, England.

Person-centred therapy

The Person-Centered Journal
ADPCA, PO Box 6881, San Carlos, CA 94090, USA.
Tel: (415) 493-5000; ext: 4334.

Person-Centred Practice
PCCS Books, Llangarron, Ross-on-Wye, HR9 6PT, England.
Fax: (01989) 770 700.
e-mail: books@pccs.telme.com

Gestalt therapy

The Gestalt Journal
The Gestalt Journal Press, PO Box 990, Highland, NY 12528-0990, USA.
Tel: (914) 691-7192. Fax: 1-209-671-3843
e-mail: tgjournal@gestalt.org
Website: www.gestalt.org

The Gestalt Review
PO Box 1807, Lawrence, KS 66044-8897, USA.
Tel: 1-785-843-1236. Fax: 1-785-843-1274
e-mail: TAPJournal@analyticpress.com

British Gestalt Journal
PO Box 2994, London N5 1UG, England.
Tel/Fax: 0117-907-7539.

Transactional analysis

The Transactional Analysis Journal
International Transactional Analysis Association,
436 14th Street, Suite 1301, Oakland, CA 94612-
2710, USA.
Telephone: (510) 625-7725.

Reality therapy

The International Journal of Reality Therapy
Dr Lawrence Litwack, Editor, 203 Lake Hall,
Boston Bouve College, Northeastern University,
360 Huntington Avenue, Boston, MA 02115,
USA.

Behaviour therapy

Behavior Therapy
Association for Advancement of Behavior Therapy,
15 West 36th Street, New York, NY 10018, USA.

Behaviour Research and Therapy (incorporating
Behavioural Assessment)
Elsevier Science Ltd, The Boulevard, Langford
Lane, Kidlington, Oxford OX5 1GB, England.

Behavioural and Cognitive Psychotherapy (Journal of
the British Association for Behavioural & Cogni-
tive Psychotherapies (BABCP))
Cambridge University Press, The Edinburgh
Building, Shaftesbury Road, Cambridge CB2 4RU,
England.

Behaviour Change (Journal of the Australian Associ-
ation for Cognitive and Behaviour Therapy)
Australian Academic Press, 32 Jeays Street, Bowen
Hills, Queensland 4006, Australia.

All the above journals contain considerable cognitive–behavioural content.

Rational emotive behaviour therapy

*The Journal of Rational-Emotive & Cognitive-
Behavior Therapy*
Human Sciences Press, Inc., 72 Fifth Avenue, New
York, NY 10011-8004, USA.

The Rational Emotive Behaviour Therapist
Centre for Rational Emotive Behaviour Therapy,
156 Westcombe Hill, Blackheath, London SE3
7DH, England.

Cognitive Therapy and Research
Plenum Press, 233 Spring Street, New York, NY
10013, USA.
(This journal focuses on the cognitive therapies.)

Cognitive therapy

Cognitive Therapy Today Newsletter
The Beck Institute, GSB Building, City Line and
Belmont Avenues, Suite 700, Bala Cynwyd, PA
19004-1610, USA.
Phone: 610.664.3020. Fax 610.664.4437
e-mail: beckinst@gim.net
website: www.beckinstitute.org

*Journal of Cognitive Psychotherapy: An International
Quarterly*
International Association for Cognitive Psychother-
apy, Department of Psychology, University of
Southern Mississippi, Hattiesberg, MS 39406,
USA.

Cognitive Therapy and Research
Details above.

Behavioural and Cognitive Psychotherapy (Journal of
the British Association for Behavioural & Cognitive Psychotherapies (BABCP))
Details above.

Behaviour Change (Journal of the Australian Association for Cognitive and Behaviour Therapy)
Details above.

Name Index

Subject Index